FUNDAMENTALS
of EDUCATIONAL
RESEARCH

FUNDAMENTALS *of* EDUCATIONAL RESEARCH

Second Edition

Thomas K. Crowl

*The College of Staten Island,
City University of New York*

Brown & Benchmark
PUBLISHERS

Madison, WI Dubuque Guilford, CT   Chicago Toronto London
Mexico City Caracas Buenos Aires Madrid Bogotá Sydney

Book Team

Executive Publisher *Edgar J. Laube*
Managing Editor *Sue Pulvermacher-Alt*
Developmental Editor *Suzanne M. Guinn*
Production Editor *Ann Fuerste*
Proofreading Coordinator *Carrie Barker*
Designer *Anna Manhart*
Art Processor *Rita Hingtgen*
Photo Editor *Leslie Dague*
Production Manager *Beth Kundert*
Production/Imaging and Media Development
    Manager *Linda Meehan Avenarius*
Marketing Manager *Amy Halloran*
Copywriter *Jennifer Smith*

Basal Text *10/12 Times Roman*
Display Type *Garamond and
    Helvetica*
Typesetting System *Penta
    DeskTopPro*™
Paper Stock *50# Mirror Matte*

Vice President of Production and New Media Development *Vickie Putman*
Vice President of Sales and Marketing *Bob McLaughlin*
Vice President of Business Development *Russ Domeyer*
Director of Marketing *John Finn*

A Times Mirror Company

Chapter opener photos: **1** M-G-M (Courtesy Kobal); **2** © Kevin Syms/David Frazier
Photolibrary; **3** © Brown and Benchmark Publishers/Photo by Sharon Dague; **4** © 1990
Arni Katz/Unicorn Stock Photos; **5** M-G-M (Courtesy Kobal); **6** © Melanie Carr/
Picturesque Stock Photo; **7** The Bettmann Archive; **8** © F. Tetefolle/Photo Researchers;
9 © Archive Photos; **10** M-G-M (Courtesy Kobal); **11** United Artists (Courtesy Kobal);
12 © James L. Shaffer; **13** © Kevin Syms/David Frazier Photolibrary; **14** Digital Stock
Professional; **15** Courtesy NASA; **16** Motion Picture and Television Photo Archive;
17 Courtesy NASA

Cover image from Digital Stock Professional Photo CD

Copyedited by Anne E. Scroggin

Printed in the United States of America by Times Mirror Higher Education Group, Inc.,
2460 Kerper Boulevard, Dubuque, IA 52001

10   9   8   7   6   5   4   3   2   1

*I dedicate this book to the memory of **BILL AMMON**, who helped in countless ways to enhance its quality.*

Brief Contents

Detailed Table of Contents

Section III

Preliminary Considerations in Designing Research 74

Preface

My goal in writing the first edition of *Fundamentals of Educational Research* was to produce a book that approached research from the student's point of view and addressed student needs in a way that made sense to beginners. The enthusiastic endorsements from students who used the first edition have convinced me that I am on the right track. It is gratifying when my students recommend the book to friends who are taking research courses at other institutions, particularly when these friends write to tell me how helpful they have found the book.

In writing the second edition my goal has not changed, except that I hope to be even more successful in achieving it with this edition. To do so, I have deleted some things; added some things; changed some things; and kept a lot of things just as they were, including my writing style, which students and faculty consistently find ''user friendly.''

To the Student

There are a couple of things you can do to increase the likelihood that you will learn a lot about research and have a good time doing so. If your research course is like most others around the country, you will be expected to choose a topic and prepare a research proposal describing how you would carry out a study on a research question related to your topic. You may also be expected to carry out your proposed study.

Think carefully about the research question you choose. It is best to select a research question on which you could actually carry out a study—even if you are only required to submit a research proposal. Why? Because by focusing on questions you really could investigate, you will increase the chances of selecting one that is both meaningful and interesting to you. As educators, we know that interest and meaningfulness make all the difference in whether students become bored or excited about learning.

The more actively you engage in learning about research, the more you will learn. Why not at least plan to carry out a pilot study with a small number of subjects? Most students find it fascinating to discover if their predictions were correct. Perhaps you would consider carrying out a study on a larger scale, with the idea of presenting it at a professional conference or submitting it for possible publication in a professional journal. Students of mine who have published their studies have found the experience exhilarating.

My twenty or so years of teaching research have led me to the firm conviction that the key to enjoying the course and to learning a lot is to pick a research question that you find personally meaningful and interesting.

To the Instructor

In addition to suggested activities and test items you will find in the Instructor's Manual that accompanies this text, you will find a set of review exercises at the end of each chapter in the text itself. The review exercises serve the same function as chapter summaries, but they require the student to actively participate in summarizing the chapter's content. The exercises may be used as assignments to be submitted or as the basis for class discussion. A computer disk containing the test items appearing in the Instructor's Manual is available at no charge to adopters of the text. You may also wish to have your students use the Student Study Guide, which contains supplemental exercises and review materials for each chapter in the text.

As I have urged students in the preceding section, if your course requires students only to submit a research proposal, why not consider having them carry out a pilot study as well? Students in my own research course are required to carry out a study and submit a final report, and for many it is while carrying out the study that the disparate parts of the research process really begin to "click." Furthermore, most students are astonished by how enjoyable and gratifying it is to carry out their own study.

Structure of the Book

The book's chapters are organized in seven sections. Section I, Fundamental Information About Research, contains a single chapter. Section II, Developing a Research Idea, contains three chapters describing how to select a research topic, how to review the literature, and how to formulate hypotheses. Section III, Preliminary Considerations in Designing Research, contains three chapters describing ethical and legal aspects of conducting research, various sampling techniques, and how to locate and construct measuring instruments. Section IV, Understanding Statistics, contains one chapter about descriptive statistics and the normal curve and another chapter about inferential statistics.

Section V, Research Methods, contains six chapters, each of which discusses a particular kind of research. This section also contains reprints of nine journal articles in order to demonstrate to students the variety of research strategies actually used by educational researchers conducting historical research, ethnograhic research, survey research, correlational research, regression analysis, group comparison research (including ex post facto, experimental, and quasi-experimental designs) and single-subject research. Each article is accompanied by a critical review. Section VI, Guidelines for Writing and Evaluating Research and section VII, Technology and Educational Research, each contain a single chapter.

There are nine appendixes that include a copy of the Ethical Standards of the American Educational Research Association (appendix A), sample consent forms (appendix B), a flowchart for determining when to use which statistical procedure for analyzing data (appendix C), tables of significant values (appendices D through G), and two annotated copies of research proposals and final reports written by former students of mine that other students may use as models (appendices H and I). There is also a glossary of terms commonly used in educational research.

Changes in the Second Edition
- Each of the nine reprinted research articles is accompanied by a critical review and evaluation. Portions of an article about which critical comments have been made are printed in a different color, and each portion is identified by a letter in the margin. The same letter is used to identify the corresponding comment, each of which is listed alphabetically at the end of the article. The use of different colored print makes it easy to determine exactly which portion of an article a particular comment refers to.
- Information on ethnographic research has been expanded and included as a separate chapter.
- Information on technology and educational research has been expanded and included as a separate chapter.
- Each chapter begins with a list of chapter objectives to orient students to the chapter contents.
- Each chapter ends with a list of chapter highlights to provide students with an overview of the chapter contents.
- Chapters on statistics and preliminary considerations in designing research appear prior to chapters describing various research methods.
- Step-by-step procedures are presented for manually computing the mean and standard deviation, r, X^2, t for independent means, t for nonindependent means, and a two-way analysis of variance with a Scheffe test.
- Step-by-step procedures are presented for using SPSSPC to compute r, t for independent means, t for nonindependent means, and a two-way analysis of variance with a Scheffe test.
- Guidelines are presented for eliminating or controlling potential sources of race and gender bias.
- The Ethical Standards of the American Educational Research Association are reprinted in full.
- Sample copies of informed consent forms for subjects and guardians of subjects are included.

Acknowledgments

I thank Denise Aubrey, Margaret Hamilton, Meg Lukawski, and Gail Rossi for granting me permission to publish the research proposals and final reports they completed while students in my research course. I am grateful to the Literary Executor of the late Sir Ronald A. Fisher, F.R.S.; to Dr. Frank Yates, F.G.S.; and to Longman Group Ltd., London, for permission to reprint adapted versions of Tables III, V, and VII from their book *Statistical Tables for Biological, Agricultural and Medical Research* (6th ed., 1974). I am also grateful to the University of Adelaide; the Institute of Mathematical Statistics; the American Psychological Association; the ERIC Processing and Reference Facility; and Oryx Press for their permission to reprint previously published materials.

For their support and suggestions, I thank Professors Reneé Blumstein, Barry Friedman, Sally Kaminsky, Irwin Kaufman, Jed Luchow, Andrea Malek, Len Mendola, Christine Nucci, David Podell, Ionas Sapountzis, Richard Schere, and Vivian Shulman, all of whom are members of the faculty at the College of Staten Island and used the first edition of this book in their research courses. I also thank the librarians at the College of Staten Island for their help: Professors Walter Dornfest, Wilma Dornfest, Raja Jayatilleke, Wilma Jones, Jerome Mardison, Allen Natowitz, Michael O'Donnell, and Karen Svenningsen. I thank Sue Alt, Suzanne Guinn, Chris Cornish, Leslie Dague, Ann Fuerste, Anna Manhart, Rita Hingten, and Anne Scroggin of Brown & Benchmark Publishers for their cooperation and support during the publication of the text. Finally, I thank my students for their eager help in providing thoughtful comments and ideas for the final version of this text.

Special thanks to reviewers: Jerry B. Ayers, Tennessee Technical University; John R. Bing, Salisbury State University; Barbara L. Boe, Carthage College; George F. Bohrer, Jr., Fitchburg State College; Dr. Ronald Bradberry, Tarleton State University; William H. Castine, Florida A & M University; Joan K. Gallini, University of South Carolina; David A. Gilman, Indiana State University; Gail Hackett, Arizona State University; R. Burke Johnson, University of South Alabama; Edythe P. Leupp, D.Ed., Southern Nazarene University; Kenny O. McDougle, Pittsburg State University; Jack McKay, University of Nebraska at Omaha, and Michael A. Sherman, University of Pittsburgh.

Thomas K. Crowl

Section I

Fundamental Information About Research

The purpose of this section is to give you a sense of what the forest of educational research looks like before we begin to examine in later chapters the individual trees. You will be given an overview of how researchers go about conceptualizing and carrying out their work. You will also be introduced to some basic terms, so that you can begin to think about educational issues the way educational researchers do.

As you read the introductory chapter, try to focus on the overall structure of the research process. Don't worry about each and every detail. Everything in this chapter is covered in more depth in subsequent chapters that are presented in a sequential order designed to enhance your learning. As you progress through this book, you will gradually acquire more and more contextual information that will enable you to understand concepts that may initially seem confusing.

Chapter 1

The Nature of Research: An Overview

Empirical research involves conducting a firsthand investigation in which researchers see for themselves what has taken place.

Chapter Objectives

After completing this chapter, you should be able to:

- explain why educators should know about research
- define the following terms: *reviewing the literature, the scientific method, theory, research,* and *empirical research*

- list at least four reasons for carrying out research
- explain how *basic, applied,* and *action research* differ
- describe the purposes of *evaluation research* and *policy research*
- describe the relationship between *values* and *variables*
- describe the relationship between *populations* and *samples*
- give at least one example of a research question that is best investigated by *qualitative methods* and one that is best investigated by *quantitative methods*
- identify examples of historical, ethnographic, survey, correlational, ex post facto, experimental, and quasi-experimental research

This book is designed for students who have had no previous formal instruction in research principles or methods. It is assumed throughout the book that, in terms of research, you are a beginner. None of the material requires that you have already studied any specific courses, such as statistics, measurement, psychology, anthropology, or sociology. If you have studied such courses, so much the better. Such a background is not necessary, however, in order for you to grasp thoroughly the contents of this text.

Most textbooks dealing with research assume that the only purpose of carrying out research is to generate new knowledge. It is probably for this reason that authors of these textbooks feel compelled to include so much detailed information. This book deals with research in a different way by assuming that another important function of *carrying out* research is to provide students an opportunity to *learn about* research. The primary goal of this book is to enable you to understand enough about the research process to be able to make informed judgments about the reasonableness and validity of the various kinds of research you will come across in your professional career. To bring the overall picture of the research process into sharper focus, technical details have been held to a minimum. For students wishing to explore research in more detail, there are numerous educational research texts available, one of the most comprehensive of which is by Borg and Gall (1989).

Why Should Educators Have to Know About Research?

Education is a research-based discipline. The evolution of educational practices affecting students in classrooms stems from countless research findings. Numerous government agencies and private foundations spend millions of dollars every year to support educational research projects. Examples of educational research findings may be found in *What Works* (U.S. Department of Education, 1987).

Knowledge of the research process will help you to understand better and evaluate more critically published research articles in professional journals. It will help you decide whether to accept the conclusions authors reach on the basis of their research findings.

Teachers as Researchers

Along with the many reforms in teacher training and certification practices occurring throughout the United States, a reconceptualization of the teacher's role is gradually emerging. Many school boards and school administrators are beginning to increase teachers' power to make educational decisions. In an ever-growing number of schools, teachers no longer merely implement educational policies handed down by the administration. Instead, teachers are becoming active participants in the decision-making process.

To gather information on which to base decisions, more teachers are carrying out research in their own classrooms (Goswami & Stillman, 1987). Many decisions affecting classroom practices may be made on the basis of research carried out by a classroom teacher. For example, to determine whether one method is superior to another in teaching a particular subject, a teacher may carry out an experiment with the students in his or her own classroom. A teacher might carry out a study to determine what kind of seating arrangement leads to improved student performance.

An elementary school teacher, who was a former student of mine, was concerned about the apparent lack of interest many of the parents of children in her class showed in their children's educational progress. She decided to carry out a research project to find out if students in her class would perform better academically if their parents became more involved with the school. She invited parents of one half of the pupils to visit her classroom and assist with various tutoring and clerical chores. She did not invite parents of the other half. At the end of one semester, she found that the children of parents who helped out in the classroom did in fact perform better academically than the children whose parents had not been contacted.

That is not all she found out, however. As is often the case in research, there were other, unanticipated findings. The teacher taught in a neighborhood comprised primarily of families who had recently immigrated to the United States. Many of the parents spoke little or no English. Many also had little formal education and came from cultures in which teachers enjoy high esteem. From her interactions with parents, it became clear to the teacher that many of them displayed enormous concern about their children's progress.

She learned that before she invited parents to visit her classroom, many parents had been avoiding contact with her because they were frightened of approaching a person with so much formal education, or they were embarrassed by their limited command of English. One unexpected result occurred during the study: parents who had *not* been invited began to ask the teacher if they too could help in the classroom. The teacher resolved the dilemma by assuring these parents that they could assist in the future. Word of the study's success spread, and as a result, the principal implemented a parental involvement program throughout the entire school the next year.

Project START (Student Teachers as Researching Teachers), initiated by the Graduate School of Education of the University of Pennsylvania, reflects the increasing emphasis on having teachers acquire competency as researchers. Student teachers in Project START not only engage in traditional student teaching, but also collaborate with their cooperating teachers in carrying out a classroom research project ("A New Assignment," 1988).

Teachers as Decision Makers

It is tempting to answer the question of why teachers should be required to know about research with a long exhortation about the teacher's professional responsibility and the serious implications of research findings for teachers. The answer need not, however, be put in lofty terms that lack practical meaning. Your professional responsibility, put in the simplest terms, is to help the students in your class develop to their fullest potential in every way possible. In carrying out your teaching responsibilities you make dozens of decisions daily that affect these students. To what extent are your decisions good or bad for them? A general knowledge of the principles of research can help you make wiser decisions because you will have learned how to examine behavioral outcomes more objectively and analytically.

Perhaps most importantly, you will have learned what constitutes legitimate evidence on which to make educational decisions. Armed with a knowledge of research, you will be able to distinguish more easily between traditional practices that have merit and those that don't, and you are less likely to be duped into following blindly whatever the latest educational fad happens to be.

The Scope of Educational Research

Although the role of teachers as producers of research is a relatively new idea, the idea of teachers as consumers of research is not. Regular classroom teachers, however, are not the only educators who are expected to make educational decisions on the basis of educational research findings. Educators in other roles, such as special education teachers, vocational education teachers, counselors, supervisors, administrators, school psychologists, and educational policy makers are also expected to take educational research findings into account when making decisions.

Fortunately, the principles of educational research described in this book apply to virtually every facet of education. Differences in the kinds of research useful to educators carrying out different roles lie mainly in the nature of the researched topic. School administrators, for example, might be interested in research dealing with school climate or staffing arrangements, while counselors might be interested in the latest research dealing with small-group therapy.

Regardless of topic, the methods of conducting research typically remain constant or require relatively minor adjustments. For example, a special educator may realize the need to use some means other than paper-and-pencil tests to collect research data from students with severe behavioral problems. In general, however, differences in research methods carried out on the various facets of education are trivial. More important is the question of what the term *research* means.

The first thing many students think of when they encounter the word *research* is library work. Most students have written so-called research papers. Usually such papers require the student to locate materials in the library, read the materials, and write a paper that presents a summary as well as an analysis and interpretation of what has been read. The process of locating and analyzing materials in the library that pertain to a particular topic is not what is meant by the term *research* in this book. Locating and analyzing materials in the library is an important part of the research process, but it is only a part. This part of the research process is called reviewing the literature. More will be presented later about this topic.

Although different people would no doubt define research in somewhat different ways, virtually any definition would include the notion that research refers to a particular way of knowing. Other ways of knowing include relying on tradition, appealing to authority, or using our own experiences (Eichelberger, 1989). The distinguishing feature of research as a way of knowing is its emphasis on systematic investigation.

Some kinds of research involve applying the scientific method. Briefly, the scientific method involves the systematic sequence of defining a problem, formulating one or more hypotheses to solve the problem, collecting data to test the hypotheses empirically, and determining if the hypothesis is or is not supported.

We often use the scientific method in informal ways to solve problems that occur in our daily lives. For example, I encountered a problem with my personal computer. Suddenly, I was unable to retrieve a document I had saved on drive B. Several hypotheses immediately came to mind: (a) drive B had become defective; (b) drive B was all right, but the disk on which the document had been saved was defective; (c) the disk was all right except for the part containing the document; (d) something was wrong with the word processing program's "retrieve" command; or (e) something was wrong with the word processing program's "save" command. I tested each hypothesis and eventually rejected all of them except hypothesis (a), for when a new B drive was installed, I was able to retrieve the document I wanted.

Not all problems that interest researchers, however, are amenable to investigation by the scientific method. For example, historians usually do not follow the scientific method in carrying out their research. Whereas the scientific method entails first formulating hypotheses and then collecting data to test the hypotheses empirically, historians usually do the reverse: they first collect data and then formulate hypotheses. Furthermore, because historical events have already occurred, it is not possible to test historical hypotheses empirically. Similarly, researchers who are interested in describing a situation, such as what takes place in a third grade classroom, do not use the scientific method. Only after spending considerable time observing what takes place in a situation can researchers begin to identify variables and formulate hypotheses that account for what occurs.

One common goal of educational research is to develop theories that explain and predict how educational phenomena are related. Theories are general statements about how phenomena are related. For example, one educational theory states that students learn more if they engage in active rather than passive learning. From this theory one could generate a number of hypotheses predicting that students who are learning a variety of things will learn more if they engage in active rather than passive learning. For example, students who produce a play portraying the Boston Tea Party will learn more about the Boston Tea Party than students who have the play read to them; students who conduct a laboratory experiment involving pendulums will learn more about the properties of pendulums than students who view a film strip about the properties of pendulums.

In this book the term **research** is used to denote the systematic process of: (a) identifying a problem; (b) reviewing the literature dealing with the problem; (c) developing one or more research hypotheses or questions related to the problem; (d) collecting data by means of empirical investigation; (e) analyzing the data; and (f) interpreting the results of the investigation. Each of these processes is discussed in detail in later chapters. The type of research discussed in this book is empirical research. This is not the only type of research that is carried out (see, for example, Scriven, 1988), nor is it the only worthwhile kind of research that can be done. However, in education, the overwhelming majority of research is empirical.

Empirical research involves conducting a firsthand investigation in which researchers see for themselves what has taken place. An example of a piece of empirical research is a study Orpha Duell (1994) conducted to find out if students' academic performance varied as a function of wait time (i.e., the amount of time a teacher waits after asking a question before calling on a student to answer). Duell had the same teacher present a scripted lecture with predetermined questions to two groups of students. For one group the teacher waited three seconds after asking a question before calling on a student; for the other group the teacher waited six seconds. After the lecture was completed, students in both groups took a test on the material covered in the lecture, and Duell was able to see for herself if students' performance on the test differed as a function of the amount of wait time to which they had been exposed.

As another example of empirical research, consider the work of Reitzug (1994) on teacher empowerment. *A Nation Prepared: Teachers for the 21st Century,* published in 1986 by the Carnegie Forum on Education and the Economy, recommended, among other things, that teachers be empowered by giving them "a greater voice in decisions that affect school" (p. 24). Six years later, however, Short (1992) noted that although in the meantime much had been written about teacher empowerment, there had been little systematic inquiry about how teacher empowerment in fact takes place.

To help remedy this situation Reitzug (1994) carried out a case study to gather empirical evidence about how one school principal went about giving teachers in his school a greater voice in school-related decisions. For a period of three months, Reitzug regularly visited a single elementary school to conduct interviews with the school's principal; observe the principal at work; and examine a number of school documents and records, including logs that 10 teachers kept of their interactions with the principal. These activities permitted Reitzug to see for himself how the process of teacher empowerment was actually carried out.

Purposes of Research

Although the intent of all researchers is to obtain knowledge, their reasons for seeking knowledge cover a wide range. A brief description of a few of the common reasons why researchers conduct empirical studies follows.

Researchers who engage in what is often called "basic research" typically carry out studies for the purpose of addressing some theoretical question. Piaget's well-known investigations of children's performance on various kinds of cognitive tasks are examples of research undertaken to gather empirical evidence to test his theory of cognitive development.

Researchers who engage in what is often called "applied research" carry out studies for the purpose of obtaining knowledge that will lead to the solution of a real life problem. For example, an applied researcher might carry out a study to determine if the installation of metal detectors in schools with a history of violent incidents reduces the number of such incidents. The intent of both basic and applied research is to generalize the findings of the study to settings and persons similar to those in the study. Consequently, such studies are conducted with samples chosen to represent the populations to which the findings are to be generalized.

Another purpose of research is to find out what works in a particular situation with a particular group of people. This type of research, often called "action research," does *not* concern itself with generalizing findings to other settings and persons. The goal of action research is to obtain knowledge that pertains only to the setting and persons under investigation. Teachers often carry out action research with students in their classes. The previously mentioned project my former student carried out on the effects of parental involvement is an example of action research whose aim was to provide knowledge that would help her solve the problem of improving her students' academic performance.

Researchers also carry out evaluation research to determine the effectiveness of existing programs (Patton, 1987) or policy research to obtain information to help determine what kinds of new programs should be developed (Majchrzak, 1984). Still others conduct research for the purpose of exploring, describing, explaining, or predicting various phenomena.

Variables in Empirical Research

Empirical research always systematically examines one or more variables. It is important that you understand what a variable is at the very outset of your study of research. (For a comprehensive discussion of variables, see Kerlinger, 1979.) Variables are the building blocks of empirical research. A variable can be defined as any entity that may take on one of two or more mutually exclusive values. "Gender" is a variable that may take on one of two mutually exclusive values: female or male. "Day of the week" is a variable that may take on any one of seven mutually exclusive values: Sunday, Monday, Tuesday, Wednesday, Thursday, Friday, or Saturday. "Age" is a variable that can take on a large number of mutually exclusive values. A person's age, for example, may be 6 months, 5 years, 12 years, 34 years, and so forth, but any given person has only one specific age at any given time.

Populations and Samples

To examine variables, researchers must select one or more groups of people to study, and each selected group constitutes either a population or a sample. **Populations** are groups consisting of all people to whom researchers wish to apply their findings. Sometimes researchers conduct their studies using entire populations. More often, however, researchers conduct studies using **samples,** which are subsets of people used to represent populations.

Types of Educational Research

Figure 1.1 gives an overview of the major types of educational research. Before discussing these types, however, you should be alerted to the unfortunate fact that the terminology used to describe research can be confusing because it is possible to describe research from a number of different perspectives. For example, one can describe research in terms of methods of gathering data, research designs, techniques of data collection, or methods of data analysis. It is unimportant if at the moment you know nothing about the various perspectives used to describe research because you will learn about them as you progress through this book. It is important, however, to understand that multiple perspectives are used to describe research.

The way in which some of the terms used to describe research have evolved can lead to confusion because they "often refer to wildly different—and noncomparable—logistical aspects of the investigation" (LeCompte & Preissle, 1993, p. 32). As LeCompte and Preissle note, for example, *case study, field study,* and *survey* are terms commonly used to identify particular kinds of research designs, but each refers to a different aspect of a study. *Case study* refers to the number of units under investigation, which is one (although the unit may be a single individual or a single group). *Field study* on the other hand refers to the location in which the study takes place, that is, in the natural environment of the persons participating in the study. *Survey* refers to a method used to collect data. Furthermore, various methods of collecting data may be used with any of these designs.

Figure 1.1   Overview of Major Types of Educational Research

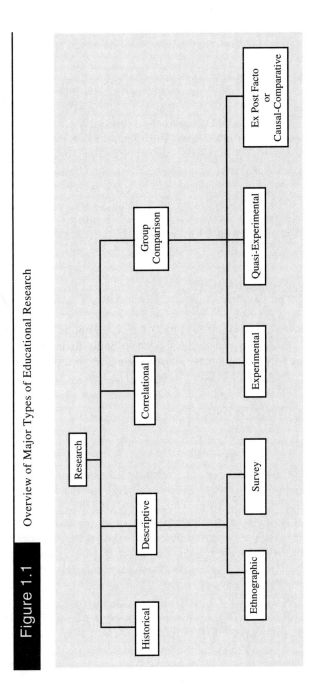

Educational researchers conventionally classify all research methods as either qualitative or quantitative. The distinction is important because the kind of method selected by a researcher offers an important clue to what the researcher is trying to find out. Whether a researcher uses qualitative, quantitative, or a combination of the two depends on the nature of the questions the researcher is addressing.

Qualitative research methods are used to examine questions that can best be answered by verbally describing how participants in a study perceive and interpret various aspects of their environment. The previously mentioned study of how a principal empowered teachers in his school is an example of the use of qualitative research methods. By interviewing the principal, observing the principal at work, and analyzing the contents of teachers' logs describing their interactions with the principal, the researcher was able to describe verbally the process of teacher empowerment from the perspectives of the principal and the teachers who participated in the study.

Quantitative research methods are used to examine questions that can best be answered by collecting and statistically analyzing data that are in numerical form. The previously mentioned study of the effects of wait time on students' academic performance (Duell, 1994) is an example of the use of quantitative methods. The researcher did not attempt to answer the question by providing a verbal description of students' interpretations of their academic performance. She answered the question by carrying out a statistical analysis of the average test scores of two groups of students who had been exposed to different amounts of wait time.

Some researchers tend to use primarily qualitative methods; others tend to use primarily quantitative methods. Nevertheless, it is important to understand that the use of both qualitative and quantitative methods may occur in a single study. For example, although Reitzug (1994) relied primarily on qualitative methods in his study of teacher empowerment, he used quantitative methods to collect and analyze some data, such as the ethnic breakdown of students attending the school.

Historical Research

The ultimate goal of historical research is to determine the nature of causal relationships among variables at some point in the past. It is, of course, not possible for historians to manipulate the variables in which they are interested to determine how one variable affects another. Historians consequently must infer causal relationships among variables by interpreting various written documents or other records of past events. It is critical that historians determine that the records they analyze are authentic and that the information contained in the records is plausible. Historians use authentic, credible information as evidence to support hypotheses they construct about the ways in which phenomena in the past were related.

It is not unusual for historians to describe and explain how influential educators of the past, such as Mary Bethune, John Dewey, Horace Mann, or Maria Montessori changed the nature of various aspects of the field of education. Nor is it unusual for historians to describe how historical forces and events have led to the evolution of some current educational issue, such as the use of school vouchers or the implementation of teacher certification at the national level. Chapter 10 describes historical research in detail and includes a reprint of ''Trends in Elementary Writing Instruction, 1900–1959,'' an actual piece of historical research carried out by Barbara von Bracht Donsky (see pages 202–209).

Ethnographic Research

Ethnographic research is a form of descriptive research that relies heavily on qualitative methods largely developed by anthropologists and sociologists. The purpose of ethnographic research is to provide a rich, detailed verbal description of how members of a culture perceive the culture. Ethnographic researchers carry out their studies in natural settings, using methods originally used by anthropologists to study exotic cultures in remote parts of the world. Today, however, a growing number of educational researchers are conceptualizing classrooms and schools as cultural entities that are amenable to study through the use of ethnographic methods.

Ethnographic researchers carry out their studies in natural settings primarily by means of participant observation and interviewing. As participant observers, the researchers participate in group activities and at the same time observe what is occurring within the group. The researchers may also identify and interview specific members of the group who seem particularly insightful about how the group operates. Chapter 11 describes ethnographic research in detail and includes a reprint of ''The New Dependencies of Women,'' an actual piece of ethnographic research carried out by Lynn Woodhouse (see pages 220–230).

Survey Research

Although all ethnographic research is inherently descriptive, not all descriptive research uses ethnographic methods. Survey research methods are often used to collect descriptive data that are quantitative. For example, polls carried out prior to an election are typical of such descriptive studies. Researchers conducting an election poll are attempting to describe how values associated with the variable ''voter preference'' are distributed among a group of potential voters. If there are two candidates running for office, the values associated with the variable would be: a preference for candidate A, a preference for candidate B, or no preference. The distribution of these values would be described in terms of percentage of persons polled. For example, the results of the poll might reveal that 46% prefer candidate A, 42% prefer candidate B, and 12% have no preference.

A study conducted in a school district to determine the percentage of students who receive a high school diploma within the four-year period following the date they entered high school is an example of survey research in the field of education. The variable in this study is ''high school graduation,'' and the values are graduated and did not graduate. The distribution of the values would be described in terms of the percentage of freshmen who did and did not receive diplomas within the specified time period.

Another example of survey research in education is a study to find out how the variable of years of teaching experience is distributed among a group of teachers in a state. The results of the study might be expressed in terms of the percentage of teachers having taught less than 1 year, the percentage having taught between 1 and 5 years, the percentage having taught between 6 and 10 years, and so forth. Chapter 12 describes survey research in detail and includes a reprint of ''High School Seniors React to the Teachers and their Schools,'' an actual piece of survey research carried out by David L. Clark (see pages 242–251).

Correlational Research

The purpose of correlational research is to determine for a single group of people the extent to which the distribution of a set of values associated with one variable is related to the distribution of a set of values associated with another variable. Determining the relationship between the height and weight of individual members of a group of people is an example of a correlational study. In carrying out such a study, a researcher would obtain the height and weight of each member of the group and rank order the members first in terms of height and then again in terms of weight.

If the results of the study showed perfect correlation between height and weight, the rank order of members of the group on both variables would be identical. In other words, the person who is the tallest would be the same person who is the heaviest. The second tallest person would also be the second heaviest person, and so forth. A person's ranking on one variable would be exactly the same as his or her ranking on the other variable. As a result, knowledge of the person's ranking on one variable would predict with perfect accuracy the person's ranking on the other variable. If one knew that a person ranked ninth in terms of height, one would also know that that person ranked ninth in terms of weight. Conversely, if one knew that a person ranked sixth in terms of weight, one would also know that that person ranked sixth in terms of height.

Correlational research has wide application in education. For example, college admissions officers often rely on correlational studies of students' performance on tests, such as the Scholastic Assessment Test, and grade point average to make decisions about which applicants to admit to the freshman class. Similarly, research examining the correlation between students' academic performance and performance on various diagnostic tests has provided a basis for identifying students with learning disabilities. Chapter 13 describes correlational research in detail and includes a reprint of "Relationship of Computer Science Aptitude with Selected Achievement Measures among Junior High Students," an actual piece of correlational research carried out by Linda Coates and Larry Stephens (see pages 258–262).

Group Comparison Research

While correlational research examines the relationship among *two or more variables* within a *single group* of people, group comparison research examines how the values associated with a *single variable* may be distributed differently among *two or more groups* of people. For example, a researcher might want to determine how the self-concepts of special education students who have been mainstreamed may differ from the self-concepts of special education students in self-contained classrooms. In such a study, the variable under consideration is "self-concept," and the two groups are special education students who have been mainstreamed and special education students who have not been mainstreamed.

In order to determine the self-concepts of students in the two groups, the researcher would probably administer a self-concept scale, which would be scored in such a way that the higher the student's score, the more positive the student's self-concept. The values associated with the variable "self-concept" would consequently be the scores students received on the self-concept scale. Typically in a group comparison study, the researcher calculates the average score (i.e., the average value) for each group. After calculating the average self-concept score for the two groups, the researcher then reports whether one group, on the average, exhibits a more positive self-concept than the other, or whether there is no difference between the groups' average self-concept scores.

Another example of a group comparison study is to determine if the average score on a reading comprehension test achieved by a group of children who have attended nursery school differs from the average score achieved by children who have had no nursery school experience. In this case, the variable is "reading comprehension," and the two groups are children who have and children who have not attended nursery school. Children's scores on the reading test represent the values associated with the variable "reading comprehension."

Group comparison research may be classified into three distinct types: (a) ex post facto or causal-comparative, (b) experimental, and (c) quasi-experimental. The way in which the groups have been formed determines which type of group comparison research the study represents.

Ex Post Facto or Causal-Comparative Studies. The group comparison study described above, in which the reading comprehension scores of children with and without nursery school experience were compared, is an example of an ex post facto, or causal-comparative, study. The characteristic that distinguishes an ex post facto study from the other types of group comparisons is the fact that the groups under investigation have already been formed according to values associated with a variable of interest *before* the researcher has begun the study. In an ex post facto study, the researcher is investigating preexisting groups. The study is carried out after the fact—hence, the use of the Latin term *ex post facto.*

The terms *ex post facto* and *causal-comparative* mean exactly the same thing. Some researchers prefer to use the term *causal-comparative* to indicate that the researcher is examining *possible* causal relationships. Others, including the author of this text, prefer the term *ex post facto* because it makes it clear that the researcher is studying groups that already exhibit different values of a variable of interest. To reduce confusion, the term *ex post facto* is used throughout this book.

The other group comparison study described previously, which compared the self-concepts of mainstreamed and nonmainstreamed special education students, is another example of an ex post facto study. Prior to the start of the study, students had already been grouped according to one of two mutually exclusive values of class placement: mainstreamed or nonmainstreamed.

Experiments. The major characteristic that distinguishes an experiment from an ex post facto study is that the researcher does not investigate existing intact groups, but rather establishes the groups to be investigated by a process called *individual random assignment.* The researcher first identifies the people who are going to participate in the experiment and then forms two or more groups by randomly assigning each person to one group or another until everyone has been assigned.

The ex post facto study that compared the self-concepts of mainstreamed and nonmainstreamed students could be changed into an experiment if the researcher were able to use the process of individual random assignment. For example, suppose that before the study began, no special education students had been mainstreamed. It would then be possible for the researcher to obtain a list of all the special education students attending a school and randomly assign some of them to be mainstreamed and some of them not to be mainstreamed. After a specified amount of time had elapsed, the researcher would administer a self-concept scale. The groups under investigation would still consist of a mainstreamed group and a nonmainstreamed group. But the study would be classified as an experiment because it was the researcher who determined which students belonged to which group.

| Figure 1.2 | Formation of Groups in Group Comparison Studies |

Kind of Study	Method of Forming Groups
Ex Post Facto	Groups Already Formed
Experiment	Random Assignment of Individuals
Quasi-Experiment	Random Assignment of Intact Groups

Quasi-Experiments. Quasi-experiments differ from experiments in that the researcher forms the groups to be studied by randomly assigning intact groups rather than individual persons. For example, suppose a researcher wishes to determine whether seventh graders who are taught science by a "hands-on" approach will score higher on a science test than will seventh graders taught by the lecture method. To carry out such a study, the researcher might select two different seventh-grade classes and use the "hands-on" approach to teach one class and the lecture method to teach the other. The researcher might decide which class is to receive which method of instruction by flipping a coin. In other words, an entire group of students would be randomly assigned to one method of instruction and another entire group to the other method.

In contrast to experiments, quasi-experiments involve the random assignment of intact groups rather than the random assignment of individual people. In contrast to ex post facto studies, quasi-experiments use the process of random assignment. In ex post facto studies, no random assignment takes place.

Although both ex post facto studies and quasi-experiments use existing groups, in ex post facto studies the groups are already grouped according to values associated with some variable of interest to the researcher. In quasi-experiments, however, the researcher must assign the groups to values of the variable of interest. Figure 1.2 shows how group comparison studies differ in terms of how groups are formed.

In educational settings, it is often more convenient to carry out research using intact groups because students are already grouped into different classrooms. Consequently, many group comparison studies in the field of education are quasi-experimental in nature.

Chapter 14 describes group comparison research in detail and includes reprints of "Summer Birth Date Children: Kindergarten Entrance Age and Academic Achievement," an actual ex post facto study carried out by Sandra L. Crosser (see pages 276–288); "Effects of Computer-Assisted Telecommunications on School Attendance," an actual experiment carried out by Carroll M. Helm and Charles W. Burkett (see pages 301–307); and "The Effects of Peer Evaluation on Attitude Toward Writing and Writing Fluency of Ninth Grade Students," an actual quasi-experiment carried out by Joyce Katstra, Nona Tollefson, and Edwyna Gilbert (see pages 311–320).

Chapter Highlights

- Educators should know about research because education is a research-based discipline.
- Research is a way of knowing that emphasizes systematic investigation.

- *Reviewing the literature* is that part of the research process that involves locating and analyzing materials in the library that pertain to a particular topic.
- Some kinds of research use the scientific method, which involves defining a problem, formulating one or more hypotheses to solve the problem, collecting data to test each hypothesis empirically, and determining if each hypothesis is or is not supported.
- The scientific method is not used in historical or descriptive research.
- Theories are general statements about how phenomena are related.
- Hypotheses based on theories are predictions about how specific instances of the theoretical phenomena are related.
- The term *research* denotes the systematic process of:
  1. identifying a problem
  2. reviewing the literature dealing with the problem
  3. developing one or more research hypotheses or questions related to the problem
  4. collecting data by means of empirical investigation
  5. analyzing the data
  6. interpreting the results of the investigation
- Empirical research involves carrying out a firsthand investigation.
- Common reasons for conducting educational research are to: test theoretical concepts, solve practical problems, evaluate existing programs, and develop new programs.
- *Basic research* is carried out to address some theoretical question.
- *Applied research* is carried out to solve a real life problem.
- *Action research* is carried out to find out what works in a particular situation with a particular group of people.
- *Evaluation research* is carried out to determine the effectiveness of existing programs.
- *Policy research* is carried out to obtain information to determine what kinds of new programs should be developed.
- Research is also carried out to explore, describe, explain, or predict various phenomena.
- A *variable* is any entity that may take on two or more mutually exclusive *values.*
- *Populations* are groups consisting of all people to whom a researcher wishes to apply the findings of a study.
- *Samples* are subsets of people used to represent populations.
- The terminology used to describe research can be confusing because it is possible to describe research from multiple perspectives.
- The major kinds of educational research are: historical, descriptive, correlational, and group comparison.
- Descriptive research may be ethnographic or survey.
- Group comparison research may be experimental, quasi-experimental, or ex post facto (causal-comparative).

- *Qualitative research methods* are used to examine questions that can best be answered by verbally describing how participants in a study perceive and interpret various aspects of their environment.

- *Quantitative research methods* are used to examine questions that can best be answered by collecting and statistically analyzing data that are in numerical form.

- A single piece of research may use qualitative methods, quantitative methods, or both.

- *Historical research* attempts to determine the nature of causal relationships among variables at some point in the past.

- *Ethnographic research* attempts to provide a rich, detailed verbal description of how members of a culture perceive the culture.

- *Participant observation* is a data collection technique used by ethnographic researchers that entails simultaneously participating in group activities and observing what is occurring in the group.

- *Survey research* describes how values of variables are distributed among various groups of people.

- *Correlational research* examines the relationship between two or more variables for a single group of people.

- *Group comparison research* examines possible differences in the distribution of values of a single variable among two or more groups of people.

- The manner in which groups are formed determines the type of group comparison being made.

- In *ex post facto* designs, the groups being studied have already been formed according to values of a variable before the researcher has begun the study.

- In *experiments,* the researcher randomly assigns people on an individual basis to the groups to be investigated.

- In *quasi-experiments,* the researcher randomly assigns intact groups of people to form the groups to be investigated.

Review Exercises

1. Why should educators know about educational research?
2. Explain how research differs from other ways of knowing.
3. Describe the scientific method.
4. Explain how theories and hypotheses differ.
5. Name the six steps involved in the research process.
6. Describe the fundamental characteristic of empirical research.
7. Give an example of a research question that could be addressed by:
   a. basic research   c. action research   e. policy research
   b. applied research   d. evaluation research

8. Name the variable to which each of the following sets of values belong:

   a. algebra
   history
   biology

   b. algebra
   geometry
   calculus

   c. learning disabled
   physically handicapped
   emotionally disturbed

   d. varsity
   basketball
   glee club
   school paper

9. Name two values for each of the following variables: type of school, academic major, reading performance.

10. Describe how one could determine empirically if girls in a particular third-grade classroom are better readers than boys. Is the third-grade classroom a population or a sample? Why?

11. Give an example of a research question that could best be addressed by using qualitative methods.

12. Describe ways in which historical researchers might use quantitative as well as qualitative methods in carrying out a study.

13. A teachers union wishes to carry out an investigation to determine:

    a. what percentage of union members have filed at least one grievance during the past three years

    b. whether there are more elementary or secondary school teachers serving as union officers

    c. the relationship between the number of union meetings teachers attend yearly and how long they have been members of the union

    d. how teachers interact with their students' parents

    Which kind of study does each of these investigations exemplify? Give reasons for your choices.

14. Name two primary methods ethnographic researchers use to collect data.

15. Describe how group comparison and correlational research differ.

16. Which type of group comparison research do the following represent? Give reasons for your answers.

    a. In order to determine if public and parochial school students have different attitudes toward school, a researcher had students from both types of school complete a questionnaire that measures attitudes toward school.

    b. A high school physics teacher had one class of students carry out a series of experiments in the laboratory and another class carry out the same series of experiments as simulation exercises on a computer in order to find out if students' comprehension of the material differed as a function of the method used to conduct the experiments.

    c. A teacher randomly assigned individual students to complete an arithmetic worksheet under one of two conditions: (a) where computational problems preceded word problems and (b) where word problems preceded computational problems. Half of the students completed the worksheet under each condition. The teacher wanted to find out if the order in which arithmetic problems are presented affects students' performance.

Section II

Developing a Research Idea

*T*his section provides information that will help you select a research topic and develop one or more questions related to it. Library resources and the procedures for using them are described in detail. You will not only learn how to use library materials to help you generate your own research idea, but also how to locate published and unpublished literature dealing with your topic. The relationship among topics, hypotheses, and variables is clarified. Also, the various kinds of hypotheses in the research literature are explored, and the important issue of defining variables operationally is discussed.

*C*hapter 2

Selecting a Research Topic

One of the most useful ways to select a researchable topic is to shift your focus momentarily from what topics interest you to the kinds of people to whom you have relatively easy access and who could serve as participants in your study.

Chapter Objectives

After completing this chapter, you should be able to:

- define the term *topic* and give an example of a topic conceptualized at two levels of specificity
- name two practical criteria in selecting your own research topic
- list at least three different kinds of sources of research ideas
- explain how to locate information about a topic by using the *Current Index to Journals in Education*
- describe the process of narrowing a topic to a research question or hypothesis
- describe two ways of turning a published study into a researchable topic

The previous chapter introduced you to some of the basic terminology and concepts characterizing research in education. In addition, the process of conducting research was described briefly to help you develop a global understanding of what empirical research is about. Beginning with this chapter, various aspects of the research process will be explained in detail. The first aspect to be considered is the important issue of topic selection.

What Is a Topic?

Intuitively, we all have some idea of what a research topic is. Since the selection of a topic is so fundamental to the research process, we should consider more carefully what constitutes a topic. Unfortunately, there is no simple definition of the term. Perhaps that is because research topics can be conceptualized at varying levels of specificity. A research topic may be conceptualized in extremely broad or narrow terms, and often it is difficult to decide what the appropriate level of conceptualization is.

In general, a **topic** can be defined as an area of interest distinct from other areas of interest. If one selects "gifted children" as a topic, the area of interest concerning them is clearly differentiated from other areas of interest, such as "adults with mental retardation" or "methods of teaching reading." All three of these areas of interest probably constitute different topics. All three are also stated in very broad terms.

Within each of these broad topics there are countless narrower ones. For example, the topic of "methods of teaching reading" includes the narrower topics of "methods of teaching reading to emotionally disturbed students" or "the use of peer group instruction in the teaching of reading." Each of these narrower topics may be broken down into even narrower ones. "Methods of teaching reading to emotionally disturbed students," for example, includes such topics as "teachers' attitudes toward various methods of teaching reading to emotionally disturbed students" or "emotionally disturbed students' reading performance as a function of instructional method." Again, these topics could be conceptualized in even more narrow terms.

Are broad topics better than narrow ones, or vice versa? At the initial stage of selecting a research topic, broader topics are probably more helpful, because the broader the topic is, the more numerous are the kinds of research questions that can be asked.

Note that a topic is not the same as a hypothesis. Hypotheses are related to topics, but they are more specific and are statements that predict the outcome of a study. "The use of peer group instruction in the teaching of reading" is an example of a topic. There are usually a number of possible hypotheses related to a topic. One hypothesis related to this topic might be "Students given peer group instruction in reading will score significantly higher on a reading comprehension test than students not given such instruction." Another hypothesis related to the same topic might be "Students given peer group instruction in reading will have significantly more positive attitudes toward reading than students not given such instruction." More detailed information on hypotheses appears in chapter 4.

Getting Started with a Research Topic

Before discussing some ways to decide on a suitable topic for your own research, there are some practical points that should be noted. Assume for the moment that there are 20 topics that you might wish to investigate. How would you decide which to pursue?

You should use two guiding principles in making your selection. First, and by far the more important criterion, is the degree of interest you have in the topic. If you do not genuinely feel some sense of excitement about the topic, the best policy is to drop it and move on. Whatever topic you ultimately choose, you will be sticking with it for a rather long time and spending considerable effort and energy pursuing it. If the topic is inherently dull to you, the whole research process will be a boring academic exercise and you will fail to learn one of the most fascinating parts of the research process—the excitement that pursuing a genuinely interesting research topic can generate.

One of the best ways to choose an interesting topic is to limit your selection to topics that you could actually investigate. As you go about selecting a topic, keep in mind that you want to design a study that, given your resources, could really be implemented. By restricting your focus to topics that are feasible to investigate, you will increase the likelihood of uncovering an area that is both interesting and personally meaningful. Reading the research literature on a topic that has personal meaning inevitably injects a sense of purpose into what could otherwise be a tedious and meaningless task whose only function is to fulfill a class or degree requirement.

As you read other people's studies to find out what has been discovered about a topic you care about, you will find that the research literature is dynamic. It is fascinating to discover that others have carried out research on a topic that interests you. You are apt to find yourself reading the research literature with a sense of anticipation and suspense similar to that generated by a good mystery. Curiosity is a well-documented source of motivation that you can take advantage of by selecting a topic you are anxious to know about.

Picking a Topic of Interest to You

Follow your own interests. The purpose of your research project is simply to help you learn about the process of research. The topic you pick need interest only you; it doesn't have to spark excitement in anybody else, and it doesn't have to be of earthshaking importance. It need not be so absorbing that you lie awake at night wondering what the outcome will be. It should be important and interesting enough to you that you honestly care about the outcome.

A few examples will help you grasp the role that interest can play in making your research experience more rewarding and enjoyable. In one case, two young teachers in my research class had been employed for a year or so in an elementary school. The principal had enforced a relatively strict dress code for teachers, resulting in a great deal of resentment. One of the most common complaints was that a teacher's attire couldn't possibly have anything to do with the students' learning. It was that complaint that the teachers turned into an interesting research question. Does the way teachers dress affect students' achievement levels? The answer was of interest to these two teachers, and their interest was evident in the zest with which they approached their research topic. Both learned a lot from their research experience and had a good time carrying out the project.

Another example comes from a former student who was not working as a teacher but was employed in the development office of a private school. His principal duty was to raise funds to cover the school's operating costs. He took seriously the suggestion of selecting a topic of personal interest and developed a study that was of interest both to him and the school's Board of Trustees. The parents of children attending the school were a prime source of funds: there were a number who contributed generously to the school beyond the cost of tuition, but others who rarely made monetary gifts to the school. It occurred to the student that there could be numerous differences between the parents who gave and those who did not. For example, the contributors might simply have larger incomes than the noncontributors. Interaction with the parents over several years, however, indicated that there were differences in attitudes toward the school exhibited by various parents. The student wondered if one difference between contributors and noncontributors could be in their attitudes toward various facets of the school's operation.

With the Board of Trustees' permission, the student designed an attitudinal questionnaire and administered it to a group of parents. Two things were accomplished by analyzing the responses: (a) Valuable information was obtained regarding parents' reactions to various facets of the school's program, and (b) the student was able to ascertain to what extent financial contributions were related to parents' views of the school. This case has a particularly happy ending. The Board was so impressed by the merit of the study that it decided to pay the student's tuition for the research course.

Combining Interest with Feasibility

The second practical criterion to consider in deciding on a research topic is the feasibility of completing it. There are a number of reasons why a particular topic might be impracticable. Some research questions simply do not lend themselves very well to empirical investigation. Suppose you have a hunch that children could easily be reading at the third-grade level by the time they enter first grade if, from the time they are 1 year old, their parents would spend one hour a day teaching them to read. Even if you succeeded in convincing a group of parents to follow your plan, you would still have to wait 5 years before your hypothesis could be supported or not.

There are, of course, many reasons other than the nature of the research question itself that might make a study virtually impossible to carry out. However, instead of considering factors that limit the possibility of turning a research idea into an actual study, it is more helpful to focus on factors that can increase the likelihood of translating an idea into a workable empirical investigation.

Focusing on Potential Participants

One of the most useful ways to select a researchable topic is to shift your focus momentarily from what topics might interest you to the kinds of people to whom you have relatively easy access and who could serve as participants in your study. If you are teaching second graders, why not start considering topics that could be carried out with second graders? If you are working with the neurologically impaired, topics pertaining to the neurologically impaired are a good place to start your search. In general, if you are teaching or working in some other capacity with a group of people, the selection of a topic dealing with those people is likely to yield a study that can be carried out with relative ease and that holds a certain amount of interest for you.

The suggestion to think in terms of the people you are teaching may be fine for those of you who happen to be teaching at the moment. For those who are not teaching, the selection of a research topic may be more difficult, but the same suggestion applies. To what groups of people do you have access? Do you have access to parents? Might you be able to gain access to some local youth group, such as a scout troop? Might you get a group of teachers at a local school to participate in a study? Surely graduate and undergraduate students at your college or university comprise one group to which you have easy access. To carry out research, it is not essential that you use a group that you are teaching. There are all kinds of bona fide educational research questions that do not deal directly with the act of teaching. Any of the groups mentioned previously, and many others, provide opportunities to ask interesting research questions that legitimately fall within the domain of education.

Education and Schooling

Do not confuse the term *education* with the term *schooling*. Education is a fairly broad term, and schooling is an important part of the process of education. Not all education takes place in schools. Just think of how much children have learned before they ever set foot in a classroom. Education has more aspects than the formal ones we designate as ''schooling.''

Many students have carried out excellent research projects while they have not been teaching. For example, one former student of mine was performing clerical duties in a large company. Using the people in her office as a point of departure, she developed a study that addressed one of the most basic educational research questions one can ask. She was concerned about whether going to college makes a difference in a person's life. She divided her colleagues at the office into two groups: those who had college degrees and those who did not. She then administered a questionnaire that permitted her to ascertain to what extent college graduates engaged in different kinds of leisure-time activities than noncollege graduates. Leisure time is one of the most important aspects of life, and the extent to which college graduates choose to spend their leisure hours differently from noncollege graduates is a vital educational issue.

If you bear in mind the two practical criteria of interest and feasibility in choosing a research topic, you will have made enormous progress in making sure that your study will turn out to be a richly rewarding and pleasant learning experience. It is rare that one instantly finds a topic that is simultaneously interesting and feasible. Often the search takes time, and often it is necessary to compromise between the two criteria. Nevertheless, it is worth keeping both notions in mind.

Sources of Research Ideas

One of the most fertile sources of research ideas is you. If you are observant as you go about your daily activities, you may hit on an idea that has potential and appeal as a research topic. It is interesting and exciting to find out what the research literature has to say about some of your own informal observations and experiences. All the students described in the earlier examples came across their research ideas by imaginatively looking at their immediate environments.

Your colleagues and friends are another helpful source of ideas. Tell people you are trying to come up with an interesting research topic. Discussions with others about possible topics may be just what you need to spark a research idea that meets the criteria of interest and feasibility. Even the most imaginative and creative among us need to have our thinking stimulated, and talking with others can force us to look at things from different perspectives.

Have you ever had debates or disagreements with any of your colleagues about some educational issue? You might be able to design a study that can help resolve the controversy.

You might want to think back to your own experiences as an elementary or secondary student, particularly in terms of subjects you found interesting. If you always enjoyed studying science, for example, you might speak with a professor of science education to learn what the latest research issues are. Perhaps the professor is actively engaged in some research project and can suggest some related research questions. If you enjoyed math or social studies or art or music or any other subject, try talking to an education professor whose area of specialization coincides with your own interests.

Library Books and Textbooks

One helpful way to approach the process of topic selection is to consult the card catalogue or computerized files in your college library. Many subject headings under which books are classified constitute possible research topics. Books dealing with a particular topic often provide an overview of the topic in relatively broad terms and include a bibliography of other books and articles dealing with the topic. For a comprehensive description of library resources that goes far beyond the use of the card catalogue, see Mann (1987).

Another possible source of research ideas are textbooks that you may have used in education courses you have taken. For example, educational psychology texts typically present a synthesis of empirical research findings dealing with various topics. These texts often also include descriptions of theories that are applicable to education, such as theories of learning (Gagne, 1985), cognitive development, motivation, moral development, language acquisition, and so forth. A research topic that has a theoretical base is particularly useful for at least two reasons. First, if the theory is relatively well known, it should not be difficult to locate professional literature dealing with the theory. Second, theories usually provide the necessary framework within which to formulate a hypothesis.

Useful Reference Books

Perhaps the most useful of all sources of ideas for a research topic is the work carried out by professional educational researchers. There are ways to find out fairly rapidly what kinds of topics researchers have investigated. One way is to consult various reference books that present overviews of the existing research literature. A second way is to look through various professional journals in which individual studies are published.

Encyclopedia of Educational Research. There are several reference books designed specifically to provide summaries and reviews of research on practically every conceivable educational topic. Perhaps the first reference you should consult is the *Encyclopedia of Educational Research* (Alkin, 1992). This four-volume encyclopedia works like every other encyclopedia you have ever used. Educational topics are listed in alphabetical order and summaries of published research findings appear under each topic heading. The main purpose of the *Encyclopedia* is to give you a broad and rapid survey of the countless topics pursued by educational researchers. Use the *Encyclopedia* to stimulate your thinking about topics, not to gather the most recent information on a topic. Just by scanning the topic headings, you may pick up an idea or two. Certainly those of you who have been having trouble coming up with a topic will be astonished to see the many topics that have been investigated. Spending a few minutes with this valuable research tool has frequently been the catalyst for a research idea. One of the assets of the *Encyclopedia* is the ease with which it can be read. One doesn't have to be very sophisticated in terms of research to be able to comprehend its contents.

Handbook of Research on Teaching. More limited in scope, but nevertheless very functional in its own right, is the *Handbook of Research on Teaching* (Wittrock, 1986). As its title implies, the *Handbook* deals only with research on teaching. (The *Encyclopedia* covers research on teaching as well as on a variety of other educational topics.) However, if you think you might be interested in carrying out a research project dealing with some aspect of teaching, the *Handbook* is a vital source of information. The *Handbook* is divided into five major sections: (a) theory and method of research on teaching; (b) research on teaching and teachers; (c) the social and institutional context of teaching; (d) adapting teaching to differences among learners; and (e) research on the teaching of subjects and grade levels.

The *Handbook* covers topics in much more depth than the *Encyclopedia* does. Of particular interest to special educators are chapters in part 4 on teaching gifted learners and on special educational research on mildly disabled learners. Regular educators may find the chapters dealing with specific subjects and grade levels in part 5 helpful in identifying a topic of interest. One of the most useful features of the *Handbook* is its detailed documentation of the material it presents. The *Handbook* contains an extensive bibliography of research articles, so the reader has immediate access to a large number of empirical investigations that may prove helpful in designing one's own study.

Review of Research in Education. Another helpful survey of research topics is the series of books entitled *Review of Research in Education* (1973–present), one volume of which has been published each year since 1973 by the American Educational Research Association, the country's leading professional organization dedicated to educational research. Each chapter is written by an authority in the field and contains a comprehensive listing of pertinent empirical studies, so, as with the *Handbook,* the reader has an instant comprehensive set of studies to refer to. In addition, because the *Review* is published yearly, the information it contains is up-to-date. Consequently, the *Review* can provide the reader with an exhaustive and current overview of a particular topic. The biggest disadvantages of the *Review* are that the number of topics covered in each volume is relatively small and the topics vary from year to year.

Handbooks Dealing with Specific Subjects. If you are interested in carrying out a study in a particular academic field, you might find one of the following handbooks of interest:

Handbook of Reading Research
Handbook of Research on Curriculum
Handbook of Research on Educational Administration
Handbook of Research on Mathematics Teaching and Learning
Handbook of Research on Multicultural Education
Handbook of Research on Music Teaching and Learning
Handbook of Research on Science Teaching and Learning
Handbook of Research on Social Studies Teaching and Learning
Handbook of Research on Sport Psychology
Handbook of Research on Teacher Education
Handbook of Research on Teaching the English Language Arts
Handbook of Research on the Education of Young Children

Journal Articles

The final suggestion for helping you locate a research topic is to look at the numerous journals dealing with educational research. Looking at journals that publish empirical research articles will not only give you ideas about the kind of topic you may wish to select, but it will also give you a good idea of what an empirical study looks like. Furthermore, published research articles often end with a list of suggestions for further research, which may include an idea you can use.

Not all educational journals publish empirical research. To help you get an idea of what empirical studies look like, consult issues of the following journals, all of which publish empirical research dealing with topics in education. The list is not exhaustive, merely suggestive.

Adolescence
American Educational Research Journal
American Journal of Mental Deficiency
Child Development
Cognition and Learning
Contemporary Educational Psychology
Counselor Education and Supervision
Developmental Psychology
Education and Urban Society
Educational Administration Quarterly
Educational Research Quarterly
Health Education
Journal of Agricultural Education
Journal of Counseling Psychology
Journal of Educational Administration
Journal of Educational Psychology
Journal of Educational Research
Journal of Experimental Education
Journal of Learning Disabilities
Journal of Marital and Family Therapy
Journal of Personnel Evaluation in Education
Journal of Research in Childhood Education
Journal of Research in Science Teaching
Journal of Special Education
Journal of Speech and Hearing Disorders
Journal of Teacher Education
Journal of Teaching in Physical Education
Journal of Vocational Behavior
Peabody Journal of Education
Psychology in the Schools
Reading Research Quarterly
Research in Rural Education
Review of Educational Research

Articles appearing in journals constitute what is frequently called the *periodical liter-ature*. The term *periodical* applies to magazines as well as to journals, both of which are published at regular intervals. One distinction between magazines and journals is the audi-ence for whom the publication is intended. Usually, magazines carry articles of interest to the general public. Journals, on the other hand, feature articles of interest to people within a specific profession or discipline. There are various journals published specifically for ed-ucators, and these journals constitute the bulk of the professional literature in the field.

Locating Journal Articles About a Topic. Typically, students know that the easiest way to locate a book in the library on a specific topic is to search the library's card catalogue either manually or by computer. Sometimes, however, students do not know how to locate a journal article on a specific topic. The best way to find an article on a particular topic is to use one of several indexes. Indexes function with respect to journal articles in a way analogous to the way the card catalogue functions with respect to books in a library. One looks up the name of the topic in an index and finds a list of journal articles on that topic. There are several indexes used frequently to locate journal articles (*Current Index to Journals in Education, Education Index,* and *Psychological Abstracts*) and to locate nonjournal arti-cles (*Dissertation Abstracts International* and *Resources in Education*) dealing with edu-cational topics. A detailed discussion of these indexes appears in chapter 3. For information on searching indexes electronically, see chapter 17.

Current Index to Journals in Education. Following is a brief description of one of the most useful indexes to the periodical literature of education, the *Current Index to Journals in Education (CIJE)* (1969–present). *CIJE* is published monthly and lists articles appearing in numerous journals on all kinds of educational topics. You can use *CIJE* to get an overview of topics and locate journal articles on a particular topic.

One section of *CIJE* is called ''Subject Index,'' which consists of an alphabetical listing of all the topics under which journal articles have been classified. By scanning the topic headings in the Subject Index, you may find a topic related to your own interests.

Under each topic heading appears the title of one or more articles pertaining to that topic. Each title has an EJ number assigned to it (EJ stands for Educational Journal). If a particular title sounds interesting and you want to locate the actual article, go to another section of *CIJE,* which is called ''Main Entry Section.'' In the Main Entry Section you will find a numerical listing of EJ numbers. Locate the EJ number of the title you found inter-esting, and beneath the number you will find, among other things, the title of the article, the names of the authors of the article, the journal in which the article has been published (including year of publication, volume number, and pages), and a brief summary of the article.

First read the summary of the article to get a better idea of what the article is about. If the article still seems to be of interest, find out if your library has a copy of the journal in which the article appears. It can be frustrating to find an interesting article, only to learn that the library does not subscribe to the journal in which the article has been published. More will be presented in chapter 3 about how to obtain a copy of an article in a journal that your library does not have.

Research articles appearing in journals will turn out to be the material ... ll rely on most heavily for your own study. At the momer... icles as a source of ideas for a possible research topic. La... to document what is known about a particular topic and ... dures you intend to follow in your own study.

Gradually Narrowing a Topic

The more widely one reads the literature dealing with ... to settle on a specific research question. It is not a good ... question too rapidly, because your knowledge of the kind ... asked about a particular topic is likely to be fairly limited ... studies. It takes time to look through the professional literatu... the more likely it is that different ideas will occur to you, and ... interesting. You will become more knowledgeable about a top... ...y selecting a topic are increased.

Broad topics are most useful at the initial stages of topic se... ...ultimately one must narrow the topic down to a specific research question. It is ... ...ole to narrow down a topic as gradually as possible. The more gradual the narrowing process, the longer one can keep various research options open. Once a specific research question has been chosen, serious constraints are placed on the process of carrying out a study.

For example, one might initially start with a broad topic, such as students' attitudes toward school. As one begins to look through the professional literature dealing with this topic, one is likely to uncover studies addressing a variety of narrower topics, such as studies investigating students' attitudes toward school as a function of students' ages. One may locate studies examining the relationship between students' attitudes toward school and students' academic performance. Other studies may compare the attitudes of students attending different kinds of schools, such as private or public schools.

Each of these narrower topics deals with the relationship between two variables and may be conceptualized as a research question or a research problem. For example, one might state a research problem as determining the nature of the relationship between students' ages and students' attitudes toward school. One could pose the research question of whether younger students have more positive attitudes toward school than do older students. One could ask a research question if students who perform well academically have more positive attitudes toward school than do students who perform poorly. When one has narrowed a topic so that a research question can be asked concerning the nature of the relationship among variables, one has probably identified a researchable topic.

For example, two students in one of my research classes began their search for a research topic with the general topic of students' attitudes toward school. Gradually they narrowed the topic to attitudes toward school as a function of the school's organization. They further narrowed the topic to the question of whether there are differences in attitude toward school between ninth graders attending a junior high school and ninth graders attending a senior high school. They reasoned that there might be differences between the two groups' attitudes toward school because ninth graders in a junior high school are the oldest students in the school, while ninth graders in a senior high school are the youngest students. (A copy of this study appears in appendix I.) Figure 2.1 illustrates one possible way in which these

General Topic: Student attitudes
Possible narrower topics related to "Student attitudes":

a. Students' attitudes toward school
b. Students' attitudes toward an academic subject
c. Students' attitudes toward disabled classmates

Possible narrower topics related to "Student attitudes toward school":

a. Ninth graders' attitudes toward school
b. Community college students' attitudes toward school
c. Graduate students' attitudes toward school

Possible narrower topics related to "Ninth graders' attitudes toward school":

a. Ninth graders' attitudes toward school as a function of type of school
b. Ninth graders' attitudes toward school as a function of gender
c. Ninth graders' attitudes toward school as a function of grade point average

Possible questions related to "Ninth graders' attitudes toward school as a function of type of school":

a. Do ninth graders attending a junior high school have different attitudes toward school than ninth graders attending a senior high school?
b. Do ninth graders attending a vocational high school have different attitudes toward school than ninth graders attending an academic high school?
c. Do ninth graders attending a parochial school have different attitudes toward school than ninth graders attending a public school?

Based on a review of the literature, possible hypotheses related to the question "Do ninth graders attending a junior high school have different attitudes toward school than ninth graders attending a senior high school?":

a. Ninth graders attending a junior high school will have significantly more positive attitudes toward school than ninth graders attending a senior high school.
b. Ninth graders attending a senior high school will have significantly more positive attitudes toward school than ninth graders attending a junior high school.
c. There will be no significant difference in attitudes toward school between ninth graders attending a junior high school and those attending a senior high school.

students' research idea may have evolved from a broad topic of interest. (Note that the last hypothesis in Figure 2.1 is an example of a null hypothesis and would not normally serve as a research hypothesis. See chapter 4 for a discussion of null hypotheses.)

Generating a Researchable Topic from a Published Study

Empirical research articles in the literature sometimes conclude with a statement of related research questions that the authors feel need to be investigated. Typically, such research questions are prompted by the results of the original study and the authors' interpretation of the results. For example, the finding that ninth graders in a junior high school had more positive attitudes toward school than did ninth graders in a senior high school suggests the research question of whether sixth graders in an elementary school setting (i.e., the oldest students in the school) have more positive attitudes toward school than sixth graders in a middle school setting (i.e., the youngest students in the school).

This research question stems from the authors' interpretation of their finding with ninth graders. In other words, the authors concluded that it is likely that ninth graders in a junior high school expressed more favorable attitudes toward school than ninth graders in a senior high school because the ninth graders in the junior high school were the oldest students in the school. Consequently, if the authors' interpretation is correct, it would seem reasonable to anticipate that sixth graders in an elementary school would have more positive attitudes toward school than those in a middle school because the sixth graders in an elementary school are the oldest students in the school.

The reader of an article whose authors suggest possible future studies need only plan to carry out one of the suggestions to have a researchable topic. However, not all studies conclude with recommendations for further research. It also may not be feasible, for a variety of reasons, for the reader of an article to investigate any of the related research questions suggested by the authors.

When reading studies for the purpose of generating a researchable topic, it is useful to try to think of possible studies that are related, but not identical, to the study being read. Developing a research topic related to a study you have read requires a certain amount of creativity. There is no magic formula to follow. There are, however, ways in which you can approach the literature that may help you to develop a research question.

Changing the Population to Be Studied

Notice that the variables in the study concerning ninth graders' attitudes toward school are "attitudes toward school" and "kind of school organization." Notice too that the population in the study consists of ninth graders. It is sometimes possible to generate a new research question simply by changing the population to be investigated. This is exactly what the authors have done when they suggest as a new research question an investigation of the attitudes of sixth graders in elementary and middle schools.

There may be several ways to alter the population. For example, instead of changing the grade level of students whose attitudes are to be compared, you might decide to investigate the attitudes of other kinds of ninth graders. The original study used a population of regular ninth-grade students in two different school settings. You might decide to compare the school attitudes of special education ninth graders in the two school settings, changing the population from regular ninth graders to special education ninth graders. Or you might decide to compare the attitudes of various subgroups within the studied population. For example, you might compare attitudes of ninth-grade boys to those of ninth-grade girls in the two different settings. One way to generate a researchable topic is to replicate an existing study using a different population.

Changing the Variables to Be Studied

Another way to use an existing study to generate a new research topic is to alter one or more of the variables that were originally investigated. For example, instead of comparing the attitudes toward school among ninth graders in two different school settings, you might choose to compare the self-concepts of the two groups. You might decide to compare the kinds of extracurricular activities of ninth graders in the two settings. You might compare the academic achievement of ninth graders in the two settings.

It is sometimes possible to devise a new research question by simultaneously changing the population and the variables used in a published study. For example, you could change the population from ninth-grade students in the two settings to ninth-grade teachers in those settings and instead of comparing attitudes toward school, you could compare teachers' attitudes toward teaching. It may be that ninth-grade teachers teaching in a junior high school have more positive attitudes toward teaching than ninth-grade teachers teaching in a senior high school. Although the variable ''attitudes toward teaching'' is different from ''attitudes toward school,'' the two variables are nevertheless conceptually related. If you decide to change both the population and the variables in a published study to generate a new research idea, make sure that the original and changed variables are related conceptually. If they are not, your new research idea will lack a conceptual link to the study you have read. For example, it makes no sense to take a study that examines students' attitudes toward school and change the population and variable to generate a study that investigates teachers' (not students') attitudes toward swimming (not school). There is no conceptual relationship between attitudes toward school and attitudes toward swimming.

Examples of Student Research Topics

The following is a list of topics that have been successfully investigated by students in my own research courses. The topics are merely suggestive and in no sense adequately reflect the wide range of topics students have researched.

- The relationship of reading achievement and family size among first graders
- The effect of listening skill training on oral reading comprehension among second graders
- Reading achievement among third graders as a function of personality scores on the California Test of Personality
- Fifth graders' mathematics achievement as a function of their teachers' desire to teach mathematics
- Adolescent girls' performance on word problems in mathematics as a function of gender-role- and nongender-role-related wording of problems
- The effects of individualized versus group instruction on time spent on task and science achievement
- The relationship between maternal employment and gender-role stereotyping among kindergarten children
- The relationship between teacher age and degree of burnout
- The effect of prior knowledge on reading comprehension
- Gender differences in mathematics achievement
- The effect of advance imagery training on second-grade children's performance on a memory task
- The relationship between writing apprehension and writing performance among community college students
- Question position and third graders' reading comprehension
- Regular and special educators' attitudes toward emotionally disturbed children
- Occupational stress of teachers of emotionally disturbed and learning disabled students

- The effectiveness of an incremental approach to the teaching of spelling words
- Social status of the learning disabled youngster
- Improving writing skills through proofreading and revision
- Teacher burnout among public and private school teachers
- Pedestrian skills for the severely retarded: Skill acquisition in simulated environments
- Preschool attendance and first graders' reading readiness scores
- Fifth graders' perceptions of reading and reading achievement
- Preservice teachers' attitudes toward mainstreaming students with emotional impairments
- Remediation of letter reversals through stimulus fading
- Word recognition and comprehension among first graders with and without pictorial cues
- The effectiveness of sentence-combining activities on syntax acquisition of ninth graders reading below grade level
- The effect of wide- and narrow-spaced paper on the writing accuracy of kindergarten children
- The relationship between television viewing habits and reading habits among fourth graders
- The use of filmstrips in changing attitudes of the nondisabled toward their disabled peers
- The effectiveness of the cloze procedure in teaching comprehension skills to fifth-grade students

---

Chapter Highlights

- A *topic* is an area of interest that is distinct from other areas of interest.
- There are numerous *questions* related to any given topic.
- A *hypothesis* is an anticipated answer to a question.
- From a practical point of view it is best to select a topic that is both interesting and feasible.
- Possible sources of research ideas include yourself, other people, books, indexes, and journal articles.
- It is best to narrow a topic gradually.
- It is often possible to generate a researchable topic by changing the population and/or variables in a published study.

Review Exercises

1. Name two broad topics that interest you and two narrower ones related to each.
2. Why is it better to start with a broad topic rather than with a narrow topic?
3. Why are topics derived from theories particularly good to investigate?
4. List the names of three reference books that are useful sources of research ideas.
5. Describe the Subject Index and Main Entry Section of *CIJE*.

6. Using *CIJE,* locate a journal article reporting an empirical investigation dealing with "reading achievement." List the article's EJ number, the title of the article, and the name of the journal in which the article appears. Indicate whether your college library subscribes to the journal.

7. Using the article you found in Exercise 6, write a brief summary of the article, describing the kinds of subjects who participated in the study, how the study was carried out, and what the findings were. Design another study related to the one you read by altering the population and/or the variables to be investigated.

8. Pick one of the examples of student research projects listed earlier in this chapter and formulate one question and one hypothesis related to it.

9. List two topics related to the area of education in which you are currently working or plan to be working.

Chapter 3

Reviewing the Literature

Even if discrepancies cannot be resolved, evidence contrary to one's beliefs should not be swept under the carpet.

Chapter Objectives

After completing this chapter, you should be able to:

- describe the process of reviewing the literature and explain its purpose
- describe how the Educational Resources Information Center (ERIC) acquires and disseminates information
- use library reference tools to search the professional literature for journal articles and documents related to any educational topic
- synthesize topical information obtained from multiple sources

The previous chapter presented information to help you find a suitable and interesting research topic. It was suggested that one of the best ways to begin the search for a research topic is to consult one or more of the reference works described in the last chapter. Reference works can help you in at least two ways: (a) by providing you with a means of rapidly scanning a large number of research topics; and (b) by providing you with an overview of research that has been carried out on various topics. You are more likely to develop an interesting and personally meaningful research question if you gradually narrow your search for a topic rather than hastily settling for the first idea that occurs to you.

This chapter describes how to explore in depth the literature on a given topic. The process of locating, analyzing, and synthesizing the published research articles and opinion papers pertaining to a particular topic is called **reviewing the literature.** Reviewing the literature is not, however, a unitary process. How you go about reviewing the literature, at least initially, depends to a large extent on how specifically you have narrowed your research question.

The Purpose of Reviewing the Literature

Before learning about the mechanics of conducting a search of the literature, it is important that you understand the purpose of reviewing the literature. In addition to providing you with information about what other researchers have found out about your topic, reviewing the literature can assist you in deciding how to design your study, what measuring instruments you might use, and how to go about analyzing your data. In a well-written research report, the review of the literature is a major part of the introduction section of the report and serves several functions: (a) It provides the reader with an overview of the background or context within which the research question has emerged; (b) it alerts the reader to the importance of the research question by explaining why it is worth the effort to carry out a study to try to answer the question; (c) most importantly, it constitutes an analysis of the existing literature on a topic that provides a documented, logical rationale for the questions or hypotheses posed in the study. The questions or hypotheses of one's own study should flow naturally from one's analysis of what already is known about a topic. If one is designing a study to test one or more hypotheses, the review of the literature should enable the researcher to write a compelling argument, based on the findings of others, for predicting the outcome of his or her own study.

One must, however, constantly evaluate a research article to decide whether the study has been executed well or poorly and if one should take the study seriously. Pay attention to the findings of various studies and what kind of pattern, if any, emerges. Note also the procedures other researchers have used in carrying out their studies. Often one can model one's own study after someone else's.

It is important to keep an open mind when reviewing the literature. One's initial feelings about how one's own study ought to turn out may be completely revised after evaluating the evidence from other studies. The findings of studies that run contrary to one's own beliefs should not be ignored, but rather examined carefully. The research literature is replete with studies whose findings are contradictory. Try to resolve the discrepancies among the findings of various studies by trying to determine in what ways the studies with different findings may have been carried out differently. Even if discrepancies cannot be resolved, evidence contrary to one's beliefs should not be swept under the carpet. There is no need to pretend contradictory evidence does not exist. The existence of contradictory evidence merely indicates that the outcome of the study is not completely predictable, given the nature of the existing research literature on the topic.

Formulating good research questions and hypotheses involves continual interplay between thinking about a topic and reading about it. The key to developing interesting and sound research questions is to revise your thinking about the topic on the basis of what you read. In other words, you should think about a topic, read about it, revise your thinking in light of what you have read, read some more, revise your thinking again, and read some more. The deliberate effort to revise your thinking about a topic on the basis of what you read will yield enormous dividends. You will gradually narrow your focus and identify variables to incorporate into your study. Such an approach virtually guarantees that you will have no difficulty in writing a documented, logical rationale for your research question or hypothesis.

Students who approach the literature with a specific research question or hypothesis already in mind fail to understand the purpose of reviewing the literature. Furthermore, they frequently are not able to write a logical, documented rationale supporting their idea for one simple reason: There is no literature related to their hypothesis. To take a ludicrous example, suppose for whatever reason a student believes that children who prefer the color red to the color green are better readers than children with the opposite preference. Searching the literature for evidence supporting such a belief is not only frustrating, it is silly.

Your research question or hypothesis should evolve from your interpretation of the literature you read. The object of reviewing the literature is not to find literature that supports some preexisting idea you may have. It's rather to shape your thinking about an idea on the basis of what is currently known about it.

The hypothetical student who believes reading performance and color preference are related should approach the literature initially by searching for studies dealing with reading performance in general or studies dealing with color preference in general. It is doubtful, of course, that the student would find any information linking color preference to reading performance. On the other hand, the student would find information about other variables related to color preference or reading performance and could use this information as the basis for designing a different study. Only by first examining the literature generally can one eventually develop a question or hypothesis related to the existing literature.

Reviewing a Broad Topic of Interest

If you are beginning your literature review with a relatively broad topic of interest, you should read widely about that topic, with the idea of formulating a more narrowly defined research question. For example, if you decide that you are interested in the topic of gifted students, but you do not yet know what research question you wish to ask, you should scan a large number of articles dealing with gifted students to get a general idea of what kinds of questions other researchers have asked. It is possible to ask a wide variety of questions, some of which may hold more interest for you than others. Your initial review of the literature should focus on selecting a research question that interests you.

For example, one could ask questions concerning various characteristics of gifted students: What kinds of interests do such students have? How do they perform in areas other than academic achievement, such as in artistic or creative endeavors? What kinds of social skills do they exhibit or how do they perform in athletics? What kinds of families do they come from? What are their attitudes toward school, toward special class placement? What kinds of occupational aspirations do they have? The list of possible questions goes on and on.

Using gifted students as a population, it is possible to ask a research question about the relationship between two variables among that population. For example, one might ask what is the nature of the relationship between gifted students' performance in mathematics and their performance in music. One could establish subgroups within the population and compare them with respect to some variable. For example, do gifted girls have different occupational aspirations than gifted boys?

Another approach to formulating a research question is to compare the population of gifted students to some other population with respect to some variable. For example, one might ask whether gifted students are more intrinsically motivated than nongifted students, or whether the self-concepts of gifted and nongifted students differ.

Reviewing a Research Question

Once you have a fairly good idea of what research question you want to ask, your search of the literature should focus not on the general topic you have chosen to investigate but rather specifically on your research question. In other words, your search of the literature becomes more restricted. Suppose, for example, that you have decided to ask the question whether gifted junior high school students have different self-concepts from nongifted junior high school students. Your task then becomes to locate studies in the literature that have investigated this question, or at least a closely related question.

If there are numerous studies that have compared the self-concepts of gifted and nongifted junior high school students, you should restrict your search to those studies. Often, however, there may be few or no studies dealing exactly with your research question. Consequently, you may have to broaden your literature search to include studies that have compared the self-concepts of gifted and nongifted students at any grade level. The scope of your literature review is in part determined by what literature exists.

In reviewing the literature to select a research topic, it is best to start broadly and gradually narrow down. However, in searching the literature for material pertaining to a research question, it is best to focus narrowly and then broaden the search only when necessary, that is, if you are unsuccessful in uncovering relevant information.

Primary and Secondary Sources

Primary sources of information are publications written by persons who actually carried out the study. If Professor Smith carries out a study and publishes the findings in the form of a journal article, the article is a primary source of information.

Secondary sources of information are publications written by someone other than the persons who actually carried out the study. If, for example, Professor Brown describes in another article the work that Professor Smith did, Brown's article is a secondary source of information. In other words, the same information may come from a primary or secondary source.

When possible, it is best to use primary rather than secondary sources to ensure accuracy. Secondary sources necessarily reflect someone else's interpretation of the original work, so the risk of error is increased. The author of the secondary source may incorrectly interpret or fail to report all important aspects of the work in the primary source.

Locating Pertinent Information

Just as one uses a library's card catalog to locate books on a particular topic, one uses various indexes to locate journal articles on a topic. There are several indexes useful to educators, each of which is published monthly in a paperback edition. The monthly editions, usually covering a 6- or 12-month period, are combined and published in hardcover cumulative editions. It is best to begin the literature review with the most recent indexes and work backward.

Each index lists the articles published in several hundred journals; all the new articles appearing in all the journals that month are classified by topic. The indexes then publish lists of articles arranged alphabetically by topic heading. By looking in the indexes under your topic of interest, you can locate articles pertaining to the topic published in numerous journals. Some journals are covered by only one index and others are covered by several.

The process of locating journal articles by looking under a topic heading is simple enough, except for one thing. You have to find out what topic headings are used in the indexes to classify articles pertaining to your topic. Perhaps the indexes use a term different from the one you use to designate your topic. Consequently, you may discover that there are no articles on your topic if you look under the term you have in mind, or you may find that the indexes use your term to designate some other topic. For example, if you are interested in a research question dealing with the issue of retaining students in the same grade for more than one year and you look under the topic heading "retention," you will discover a list of research articles on memory.

The major source of information pertaining to a research question will be articles appearing in professional journals. In the previous chapter you were briefly introduced to *CIJE,* one of the indispensable indexes for searching the educational journal literature. In this chapter not only will *CIJE* be described in more detail, but several additional indexes and other important tools for locating journal articles and educational documents will be explained.

Educational Resources Information Center (ERIC)

The problem of lengthy time lags between the completion of a study and the availability of the findings in published form is not unique to research in education. Research in practically all academic disciplines suffers from the same problem. However, it was in the field of education that the first serious attempt was made to overcome the problem. In part to solve the time lag problem, the United States Office of Education established in 1965 the Educational Resources Information Center or ERIC, as it is usually called.

ERIC was established to provide a mechanism by which new educational information, particularly information generated by projects funded by the federal government, could be made available rapidly and relatively inexpensively to the public. The expense and time delays of printing were eliminated by simply photographing the original typed pages of any document and producing microfiche copies.

Microfiche are film negatives about the size and shape of a postcard. Each fiche can contain up to 96 miniature photographic negatives of each page of a document. If a document contains more pages than a single fiche can accommodate, additional fiche are used. It is necessary to use a microfiche reader that magnifies the pages. Libraries subscribing to the

ERIC system generally have microfiche readers as well as microfiche reader-printers, which permit one to print an 8 1/2 × 11 hard copy of each document page.

The use of microfiche permits ERIC to distribute rapidly and relatively inexpensively massive quantities of information to libraries throughout the United States. Most college and university libraries in the United States subscribe to the ERIC system and receive monthly shipments of microfiche.

ERIC Clearinghouses

To facilitate the collection and processing of educational documents, there are 15 to 20 ERIC clearinghouses located throughout the country, each of which is responsible for gathering and processing documents dealing with a particular aspect of education. Current clearinghouses, for example, include one on Urban Education, which is located at Teachers College, Columbia University in New York City; one on Disabled and Gifted Children, located at the Council for Exceptional Children in Reston, Virginia; and one on Reading and Communication Skills located at the National Council of Teachers of English in Urbana, Illinois. The exact number of clearinghouses varies from time to time as some are dropped and others are added.

Educational documents are acquired by the various clearinghouses in two ways. Researchers may send a copy of a completed study directly to the appropriate clearinghouse, or the clearinghouse may request a copy of a report directly from a researcher. For example, it is common for a staff member of a clearinghouse to write to someone who has presented a paper at a professional conference and request that a copy of the paper be sent to the clearinghouse for inclusion in the ERIC system.

The educational documents appearing on ERIC microfiche are not journal articles. They consist mainly of reports of various educational projects that have been funded by the federal government, papers that have been presented at professional conferences, program descriptions and evaluations, curriculum and teaching guides, instructional and resource materials, and papers written by individual educators who have submitted copies of their work to ERIC. If you wish, you can send a copy of your project to ERIC to be considered for inclusion in the system.

Assume that at the same moment an educational document is produced on microfiche, an issue of a journal is published, and a new book is printed. The time lag between when the information was originally generated and when it is available for public consumption is shortest for the educational document, longest for the book, and somewhere in the middle for articles in the journal. The difference in time lags results from the amount of time necessary to produce the three different sources of information. Although it is desirable to use recent information, it is more important to use accurate information, a topic that will be discussed later in this chapter.

Reference Tools Produced by ERIC

In addition to collecting educational documents through its clearinghouses and disseminating microfiche copies to libraries, ERIC is responsible for producing three vitally important reference tools: CIJE (the Current Index to Journals in Education, which was briefly described in chapter 2); Resources in Education; and the Thesaurus of ERIC Descriptors.

CIJE and *Resources in Education (RIE)* are both indexes. *CIJE* is an index to articles appearing in journals. (It is not the only index to journal articles. Other indexes will be described later in this chapter.) *RIE* is the index to educational documents appearing on ERIC microfiche. It is the only index to these documents.

Consider for a moment how an index such as *CIJE* is produced. ERIC subscribes to several hundred educational journals. To produce a copy of *CIJE*, ERIC staff must read all the articles in all the journals that ERIC receives during a given month and decide what topic headings should be used for indexing each article. These workers ask themselves, "What are the terms someone is likely to use to locate a particular article?"

An article is typically indexed under more than one topic heading. For example, an article comparing the reading performance of fifth graders who have been grouped homogeneously with the performance of fifth graders who have been grouped heterogeneously would be indexed under topic headings such as "ability grouping," "homogeneous grouping," "heterogeneous grouping," "reading instruction," "reading achievement," "grade 5," and probably other terms as well.

The task of classifying an article according to various terms or topic headings is exceedingly important. If an article is not indexed under terms that readers are likely to use, it is impossible for the reader to locate that article by using *CIJE*.

The people responsible for producing *RIE* each month face exactly the same task as those who produce *CIJE*, except that instead of reading and classifying journal articles, they read and classify educational documents appearing on ERIC microfiche. The people who read and classify journal articles and educational documents sometimes make errors. Consequently, you should not be surprised if you find that sometimes information in which you are interested has not been correctly classified.

Thesaurus of ERIC Descriptors

The problem of deciding which topic headings to use for indexing an article or a document is so important that ERIC has produced a *Thesaurus of ERIC Descriptors*. The *Thesaurus* contains a list of topic headings (or **descriptors**) used to index articles in *CIJE* and to index educational documents in *RIE*. If you wish to locate information about a topic in *CIJE* or *RIE*, you *must* use one of the descriptors appearing in the *Thesaurus*. No matter what you think is a reasonable term for a topic heading, you will not be able to locate information concerning the topic until you find out what descriptor term ERIC has assigned to the topic.

Suppose, for example, you wish to locate information from the indexes on the topic of reading enjoyment. You will be unsuccessful in your search because reading enjoyment is not a descriptor term appearing in the *Thesaurus*. If you are interested in reading enjoyment, you must use the descriptor "LITERATURE APPRECIATION." The importance of using the *Thesaurus* before using *CIJE* or *RIE* cannot be overemphasized. The *Thesaurus* provides the keys for unlocking the indexes and allowing you to locate the professional literature on a particular topic. When my students report to me that there is no professional literature on some topic, my first question is whether the student has consulted the *Thesaurus*. In 99% of the cases the student has not. Once the student uses the *Thesaurus*, the problem of finding no professional literature usually disappears.

The *Thesaurus* is divided into four main sections: (a) an alphabetical listing of descriptors, (b) a two-way hierarchical display of descriptors, (c) a rotated display of descriptors, and (d) a listing of group codes. Each of these sections is described in detail.

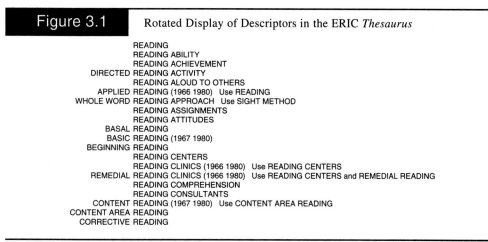

| Figure 3.1 | Rotated Display of Descriptors in the ERIC *Thesaurus* |

```
                        READING
                        READING ABILITY
                        READING ACHIEVEMENT
        DIRECTED READING ACTIVITY
                        READING ALOUD TO OTHERS
        APPLIED READING (1966 1980)   Use READING
WHOLE WORD READING APPROACH   Use SIGHT METHOD
                        READING ASSIGNMENTS
                        READING ATTITUDES
            BASAL READING
            BASIC READING (1967 1980)
     BEGINNING READING
                        READING CENTERS
                        READING CLINICS (1966 1980)   Use READING CENTERS
      REMEDIAL READING CLINICS (1966 1980)   Use READING CENTERS and REMEDIAL READING
                        READING COMPREHENSION
                        READING CONSULTANTS
           CONTENT READING (1967 1980)   Use CONTENT AREA READING
      CONTENT AREA READING
        CORRECTIVE READING
```

Reprinted from the *Thesaurus of ERIC Descriptors*, 11th Edition. Used with permission from The Oryx Press, 4041 N Central Ave, Phoenix, AZ 85012 (800) 279–6799.

Rotated Display of Descriptors. Some descriptors consist of a single word; some consist of several words. In the section of the *Thesaurus* that lists descriptors alphabetically, the first word of a descriptor consisting of several words is used to place the descriptor alphabetically. For example, the descriptor "DIRECTED READING ACTIVITY" is alphabetized using the word "directed." In the section of the *Thesaurus* called the Rotated Display of Descriptors, however, each descriptor is listed alphabetically by each word. "DIRECTED READING ACTIVITY" is listed alphabetically three different times, once for each word comprising the descriptor. One can locate the descriptor by looking up "directed," "reading," or "activity."

It is best to begin your literature search with the Rotated Display of Descriptors. The advantage of starting your search with the Rotated Display is that you may discover terms consisting of more than one word that you would not have located in the alphabetical listing because you may not have thought of the first word. Note that in Figure 3.1 "DIRECTED READING ACTIVITY" has been alphabetized by the word "reading," which is the second word in the descriptor.

Suppose, for example, you were interested in the general topic reading activities. If you looked up the term in the alphabetical listing, you would find no entry, because the first word of the descriptor is "directed." However, by looking up "reading activities" in the Rotated Display, you would discover the descriptor "DIRECTED READING ACTIVITY," which no doubt would be useful in helping you locate literature on your topic.

There are a couple of other things to note about the Rotated Display in Figure 3.1. Look at the term "WHOLE WORD READING APPROACH." "WHOLE WORD READING APPROACH" is *not* a legitimate ERIC descriptor. Instead, you are instructed to use "SIGHT METHOD." Now look at the term "CONTENT READING." Notice that after the term the dates 1967 and 1980 appear in parentheses. This indicates that between the years 1967 and 1980, "CONTENT READING" was used as an ERIC descriptor. However, in 1980 the term was dropped from the list of descriptors. You are also instructed to use the descriptor "CONTENT AREA READING." In other words, if you are searching for material dealing with content reading that was indexed between 1967 and 1980, you should use the descriptor "CONTENT

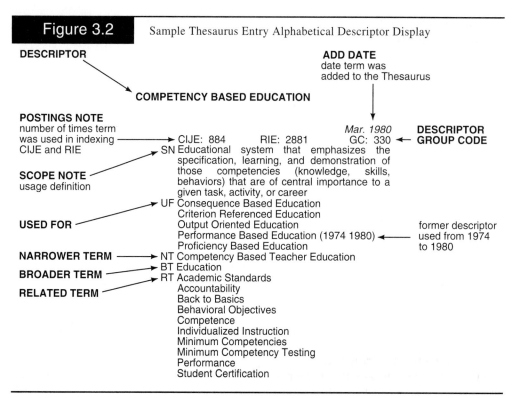

Figure 3.2 Sample Thesaurus Entry Alphabetical Descriptor Display

DESCRIPTOR

ADD DATE
date term was
added to the Thesaurus

COMPETENCY BASED EDUCATION

POSTINGS NOTE
number of times term
was used in indexing
CIJE and RIE

Mar. 1980   **DESCRIPTOR**
GROUP CODE

CIJE: 884   RIE: 2881   GC: 330

SCOPE NOTE
usage definition

SN Educational system that emphasizes the specification, learning, and demonstration of those competencies (knowledge, skills, behaviors) that are of central importance to a given task, activity, or career

USED FOR

UF Consequence Based Education
Criterion Referenced Education
Output Oriented Education
Performance Based Education (1974 1980)
Proficiency Based Education

former descriptor
used from 1974
to 1980

NARROWER TERM

NT Competency Based Teacher Education

BROADER TERM

BT Education

RELATED TERM

RT Academic Standards
Accountability
Back to Basics
Behavioral Objectives
Competence
Individualized Instruction
Minimum Competencies
Minimum Competency Testing
Performance
Student Certification

Reprinted from the *Thesaurus of ERIC Descriptors,* 11th Edition. Used with permission from the Oryx Press, 4041 N Central Ave, Phoenix, AZ 85012 (800) 279–6799.

READING.'' If, on the other hand, you are searching for material dealing with content reading that was indexed *after* 1980, you must use the descriptor ''CONTENT AREA READING.''

Alphabetical Listing of Descriptor Terms. Figure 3.2 shows how the descriptor ''COMPETENCY BASED EDUCATION'' appears in the alphabetical listing of descriptor terms in the *Thesaurus.* This example was taken from the 1987 edition of the *Thesaurus.* ''COMPETENCY BASED EDUCATION'' was first introduced as an ERIC descriptor in March 1980. Prior to 1980 the *Thesaurus* contained no such descriptor. Between 1980, when the term first became a descriptor and 1987, the date in which this edition of the *Thesaurus* was published, there were 884 journal articles indexed under the term in *CIJE* and 2,881 educational documents indexed under the term in *RIE.*

It is, of course, useful to know when a descriptor was first used in ERIC because it would be fruitless to look for the term in indexes published prior to that date. Similarly, it can be helpful to have an idea of how many articles and educational documents have been listed under a particular descriptor. If the number of listings is relatively small, it may signal that one should seek additional descriptors.

In Figure 3.2 the symbol SN stands for ''scope note.'' Not all descriptors have a scope note, but when a scope note is listed, it is important to read it. The scope note defines briefly the meaning the indexers have assigned to the descriptor. Some descriptors can be interpreted

Figure 3.3	Two-Way Hierarchical Term Display

```
: : ABILITY
 : VERBAL ABILITY
READING ABILITY
 . READING SKILLS
 . . READING COMPREHENSION
 . . READING RATE
```

Reprinted from the *Thesaurus of ERIC Descriptors,* 11th Edition. Used by permission of the Oryx Press, 4041 N Central Ave, Phoenix, AZ 85012 (800) 279–6799.

in several different ways, and one must be careful that one's own interpretation of a descriptor coincides with the indexers' interpretation.

UF is the symbol that stands for "used for." Any term following the symbol UF is *not* an ERIC descriptor. If, for example, you were to look up the term "CONSEQUENCE BASED EDUCATION," you would find the statement: "Use COMPETENCY BASED ED-UCATION." The only time a term appearing after UF could be profitably used is when the term is followed by dates in parentheses. For example, "PERFORMANCE BASED EDU-CATION" is followed by the dates 1974 and 1980. This means that if you are searching through indexes published during this period, you will find listings under "PERFORMANCE BASED EDUCATION," because during this period the term was in fact a descriptor. However, prior to 1974 or after 1980 the term was *not* used as a descriptor.

The symbols NT (narrower term), BT (broader term), and RT (related term) can be used productively to help you carry out your literature review. All terms following any of these three symbols are ERIC descriptors. If you have a fairly specific research question in mind, and a narrower term seems appropriate, you should search under the narrower term rather than the original term you selected. On the other hand, if a term you have been using for your search is yielding little useful information, you should switch to a broader term and continue to search.

Related terms can be particularly useful if you are at the initial stages of topic selection. Sometimes students have only a vague idea of what topic they wish to investigate. It may be that one of the related terms listed under the original term you have selected will help you specify what topic you wish to pursue.

Group Code Listing. Note in Figure 3.2 the Descriptor Group Code (GC) number 330. All of the ERIC descriptors have been classified into 1 of 41 conceptually related groups of descriptors. Each descriptor is assigned a GC number. If one looks up the GC number of a descriptor in the group code listing, one will find numerous conceptually related descriptor terms, many of which do *not* appear as broader, narrower, or related terms in the main alphabetical listing. A successful review of the literature depends heavily on the choice of accurate descriptors, and the list of terms classified by GC number may provide you a more precise term than you could otherwise locate.

Two-Way Hierarchical Term Display. Descriptor terms are listed in the Two-Way Hierarchical Display so that conceptually related terms are shown both in increasing levels of generality and in increasing levels of specificity. Look at the descriptor "READING ABILITY" in Figure 3.3. Terms appearing above "READING ABILITY" are preceded by one or more colons and terms appearing below "READING ABILITY" are preceded by one or more periods. Terms preceded by one or more colons are more general terms than

Figure 3.4	Sample Listing in the *CIJE* Subject Index

Individualized Education Programs

Parents' and Educators' Participation in IEP Conferences. *Education and Treatment of Children;* v8 n2
p153-62 Spr 1985   EJ 331 424

Parents as Partners in the I.E.P. Process. *Volta Review;*
v21 n3 p309-19 Jan 1986   EJ 331 476

Curriculum: The Keystone for Special Education Planning.
Teaching Exceptional Children; v18 n3 p220-23 Spr
1986   EJ 331 520

Reprinted from the *Current Index to Journals in Education.* Used with permission from the Oryx Press, 4041 N Central
Ave, Phoenix, AZ 85012 (800) 279–6799.

the original term, and the level of generality is indicated by the number of colons. Similarly, terms preceded by one or more periods are more specific terms than the original term, and the level of specificity is indicated by the number of periods.

''VERBAL ABILITY'' and ''ABILITY'' both appear above ''READING ABILITY,'' indicating that both are more general terms than ''READING ABILITY.'' However, ''ABILITY'' is preceded by two colons but ''VERBAL ABILITY'' is preceded only by a single colon. This indicates that ''ABILITY'' (two colons) is a more general term than ''VERBAL ABILITY'' (one colon).

A similar format is used to indicate terms that are more specific than the original descriptor. ''READING SKILLS,'' ''READING COMPREHENSION,'' and ''READING RATE'' are all more specific descriptors than ''READING ABILITY.'' All are listed below ''READING ABILITY'' and all are preceded by one or two periods. However, ''READING COMPREHENSION'' and ''READING RATE'' (preceded by two periods) are more specific terms than ''READING SKILLS'' (preceded by only one period).

Terms preceded by a single colon are the same as the broader terms (BT) appearing in the alphabetical listing of descriptors, and those preceded by a single period are the same as the narrower terms (NT). The principal difference between the two-way hierarchical display and the alphabetical listing is that the two-way hierarchical display includes terms that are conceptually broader (i.e., terms preceded by more than one colon) and narrower (i.e., terms preceded by more than one period) than the broader and narrower terms appearing in the alphabetical listing.

Current Index to Journals in Education (CIJE)

Each monthly issue of *CIJE* is divided into several sections, the most important of which are the Subject Index and the Main Entry Section. Every 6 months the monthly issues are combined into two hardbound volumes. One volume contains the Subject Indexes for those 6 months and the other volume contains the corresponding Main Entry Sections. If you are using hardbound copies, it is necessary to work with both companion volumes.

The Subject Index consists of an alphabetical listing of topic headings (descriptors) followed by the titles of pertinent articles, each of which is assigned an Educational Journal (EJ) number. (See Figure 3.4.) There are three articles listed under the descriptor INDIVID-UALIZED EDUCATION PROGRAMS. The last article, called ''Curriculum: The Keystone for Special Education Planning,'' appears on pages 220–223 in volume 18, issue number 3 of the journal called *Teaching Exceptional Children,* which was published in Spring 1986. This article has been assigned the number EJ 331 520.

| Figure 3.5 | Sample Listing in the *CIJE* Main Entry Section |

EJ 331 520   **EC 181 937**
Curriculum: The Keystone for Special Education
Planning. Goldstein, Marjorie T. *Teaching Ex-*
ceptional Children; v18 n3 p220-23 Spr 1986
(Reprint: UMI)
Descriptors: *Disabilities; *Curriculum
    Development; *Individualized Education
    Programs; Elementary Secondary Education;
    Program Development
The article highlights the role of curriculum in special
education within the contexts of the Individualized Education Program and a 6-S paradigm of the instructional
program (someone, something, somebody, somehow,
somewhere, and sometime). (CL)

Reprinted from the *Current Index to Journals in Education.* Used with permission from The Oryx Press, 4041 N Central Ave, Phoenix, AZ 85012 (800) 279–6799.

If one wished to find more information about this article, one looks up EJ 331 520 in the Main Entry Section. (See Figure 3.5.) In the Main Entry Section, articles are listed numerically by their EJ numbers. (Each article is also assigned an ERIC Clearinghouse number, which in this case is EC 181 937. It is only the EJ number you need pay attention to.) In addition to the information provided in the Subject Index, one finds that the author of the article is Marjorie T. Goldstein.

Major and Minor Descriptors. Some of the descriptors listed under EJ 331 520 are preceded by an asterisk and some are not. All of the descriptors are terms that appear in the ERIC *Thesaurus.* Descriptors preceded by an asterisk are Major Descriptors, which designate what the primary topics are that the article addresses. (An article may be assigned as many as six Major Descriptors.) Descriptors without an asterisk are Minor Descriptors, which indicate that the article deals with these topics, but they are not central to the article's content.

It is important to understand that any descriptor may be major or minor, depending on whether it reflects a primary or ancillary aspect of the article. A descriptor such as ''PRO-GRAM DEVELOPMENT,'' which is a minor descriptor for EJ 331 520, would be a major descriptor and preceded by an asterisk for any article whose primary focus is program development. Generally, major descriptors are of more importance in carrying out a review of the literature than minor descriptors are.

Descriptors listed for a particular article may serve as additional terms to use in searching the literature. One can use any Major Descriptor listed for an article to locate that article. For example, the term ''INDIVIDUALIZED EDUCATION PROGRAMS'' was used to locate article EJ 331 520. However, one could have also located the article under the terms ''DISABILITIES'' or ''CURRICULUM DEVELOPMENT.'' (Articles are not listed under minor descriptors in *CIJE,* although minor descriptors may be used to locate articles when carrying out a computer search. More will be presented later about using computers to search the literature.)

Summary of Article. No doubt the most important information provided in the Main Entry Section is the summary of the article. The summary usually provides enough detail about the article's content so that one can decide whether the article is worth reading in its entirety or whether it is unimportant to one's own research question and need not be read. Sometimes, titles turn out to be the most interesting part of an article. The content may be quite different from what one had in mind. If an article seems unimportant, one has saved a great deal of time by not first having to locate the journal in which the article is published to find out what the article is about. The effective use of summaries can dramatically reduce the amount of time spent reviewing the literature.

After some summaries there appears a list of terms called "Identifiers." Identifiers are basically unimportant in carrying out a review of the literature. Identifiers are really terms that may eventually become descriptors in their own right and be included in forthcoming editions of the ERIC *Thesaurus*.

Author and Journal Contents Indexes. In addition to the Subject Index and the Main Entry Section, each issue of *CIJE* contains an Author Index and a Journal Contents Index. The Author Index may be useful if you know the name of a particular researcher who has carried out work on your topic of interest. You can simply look the researcher's name up in the Author Index to see if he or she has published other articles related to your research question.

The Journal Contents Index lists alphabetically the names of all journals that have been indexed in that particular issue of *CIJE*. Beneath each journal name is a list of the titles of all articles in that journal that have been indexed. The Journal Contents Index can be particularly useful at the initial stage of topic selection. Suppose, for example, one were generally interested in a topic such as early childhood education. One convenient way to locate information dealing with the topic would be to look up the *Journal of Early Childhood Education* in the Journal Contents Index to find out what articles have been published in the journal.

Locating a Copy of an Article. Suppose that after reading the summary of an article you have located in *CIJE,* you decide the article is pertinent to your interests and wish to read it. The first step is to find out if the library in which you are working has a copy of the journal you need. Generally, libraries have a list of periodicals, which lists alphabetically the names of all journals housed in the library. If the name of the journal you are looking for appears in the list, all you have to do is find the journal in your library.

CIJE indexes several hundred journals, and it is not uncommon for students to discover that their library does not subscribe to a journal that contains a promising article. It can be quite frustrating when one fails to find the name of a journal on the library's list of periodicals. Just because your library may not house a journal you are interested in does not mean it is impossible to obtain a copy of the article you want.

Many libraries have access by computer to the On-line Computer Library Center (OCLC), which provides a listing of books and journals located at more than 4,800 libraries. By having a librarian check through OCLC for a journal (or a book), it may be possible to locate a nearby library that has material not available at your own library. It is also possible to request that a copy of a journal article be sent to your library. Sometimes there is a nominal fee for this service; sometimes the service is free, depending on the library's policy. Similarly, one may ask to have a book sent on loan to your library, a service for which there is normally no charge. The time lapse between requesting an article or a book and actually receiving it generally ranges from two to four weeks.

Writing to Authors. Although *CIJE* provides the names of authors of articles, it unfortunately does not provide information about authors' institutional affiliations. However, many journal articles are written by college and university faculty members. It is sometimes possible to find an author's address by consulting either the *Faculty Directory of Higher Education* or the *National Faculty Directory.*

The *Faculty Directory of Higher Education* is a multivolume work, with each volume consisting of names and addresses of faculty in a particular discipline. Volume 4 contains a list of education faculty. The *National Faculty Directory* also provides an alphabetical listing of names and addresses of faculty, but the list is not divided by academic discipline. However, even if there are several faculty listed with the same name, it is generally not difficult to determine which person is the author of the article you are interested in because the faculty member's department is listed. It is likely that an author of an article on an educational topic is affiliated with a department of education or a department with related interests, such as psychology.

One may write directly to the author and request a reprint of the article. It is not necessary to write an elaborate letter; a simple postcard requesting a reprint of the article will do. Many authors send reprints fairly quickly, and there is no charge for the reprint.

You may wish to write directly to an author for a reprint of an article even if you have access to the journal in which the article was published to save yourself the price of photocopying the article. Many journal articles include the address of the author and sometimes ask interested readers to write to the author for a reprint of the article. However, unless the article has been published fairly recently, you should not write to the author without first checking one of the faculty directories to ascertain that the author has not changed institutions in the meantime.

Resources in Education (RIE)

The format of *RIE* is virtually identical to that of *CIJE*. Monthly issues contain several sections, the most important of which are the Subject Index and Document Resumes. (Document Resumes is analogous to the Main Entry Section of *CIJE*.) Cumulative hardbound editions consist of two companion volumes, one containing the Subject Index and the other containing Document Resumes.

The Subject Index consists of an alphabetical listing of descriptors, each of which is followed by one or more titles of relevant documents. Each document is assigned an Educational Document (ED) number. Figure 3.6 shows an example of two entries in the Subject Index. Notice that there are 11 documents pertaining to "READING INSTRUCTION" but only one document pertaining to "READING MATERIALS."

To use *RIE,* you locate a descriptor in the ERIC *Thesaurus* and look up that descriptor in the Subject Index of *RIE*. For example, suppose you were interested in finding documents on "READING INSTRUCTION." After locating the descriptor term in the Subject Index, you look for titles of documents that appear interesting. If you want to find more information about a particular document, you only need to look up the document's ED number in the Document Resumes section.

If you wanted to find out more about the document titled "Phonics and Comprehension: A New Look," for example, you would look up ED 292 075 in the Document Resumes section. (See Figure 3.7.) The information given in the Document Resumes section is similar

Figure 3.6	Sample Listing in the *RIE* Subject Index

Reading Instruction

Chapter One in Ohio. Education Consolidation and Improvement Act. 22nd Annual Evaluation Report. Fiscal 1987.

ED 292 908

Chapter 1/P.S.E.N. Remedial Reading and Mathematics Program 1985-86 End of the Year Report. OEA Evaluation Report.

ED 292 906

A Classroom Observation Study of Reading Instruction in Kindergarten. Technical Report No. 422.

ED 292 074

The Effect of Reading Games on the Improvement of Fourth Grade Reading Skills Scores.

ED 292 078

Only Connect: How Literature Teaches Children To Read and Write.

ED 292 114

Phonics and Comprehension: A New Look.

ED 292 075

Read. . . for the Fun of It! A Compilation of Reading Incentive Programs.

ED 292 055

Reading Aloud to Children and Its Effect on Their Attention Span.

ED 292 077

Speech Recognition Technology: An Application to Beginning Reading Instruction. Technical Report.

ED 292 059

Success of Children at Risk in a Program That Combines Writing and Reading. Technical Report No. 417.

ED 292 061

Teacher Thinking and Instructional Materials: Some Relationships Between a Case Study and a Literature Review.

ED 292 782

Reading Materials

Summertime Favorites.

ED 292 080

Reading Motivation

Good Book Lookers: A Three-Week Introductory Module in the Language Arts To Foster Independent Reading among Third Graders.

ED 292 056

Only Connect: How Literature Teaches Children To Read and Write.

ED 292 114

Success of Children at Risk in a Program That Combines Writing and Reading. Technical Report No. 417.

ED 292 061

From Resources in Education, August 1988. Courtesy of ERIC Processing and Reference Facility, Rockville, MD. Reprinted by permission.

to that given in the Main Entry section of *CIJE* (see Figure 3.5). One finds the authors' names, the title of the document, the number of pages the document contains, a list of major and minor descriptors, identifiers, and a summary (or resume) of the document.

Obtaining copies of ERIC documents is usually much more convenient than obtaining copies of a journal article if one is using a library that subscribes to the ERIC system. One simply asks the librarian for microfiche number ED 292 075.

| Figure 3.7 | Sample Listing in the *RIE* Document Resumes |

ED 292 075   **CS 009 079**

Sainz, JoAnn   Biggins, Catherine M.
Phonics and Comprehension: A New Look.
Pub Date—Apr 88
Note—20p.; Paper presented at the Annual Read-On Rally of the New Jersey Chapter of Literacy Volunteers of America (10th, Holmdel, New Jersey, April 30, 1988).
Pub Type—Reports-Research (143)—Speeches/-Meeting Papers (150)
EDRS Price - MF01/PC01 Plus Postage.
Descriptors—Case Studies, Content Area Reading, * Decoding (Reading), Grade 8, Junior High Schools, Readability, Reading Achievement, Reading Difficulties, Reading Improvement, * Reading Instruction, Reading Research, * Remedial Reading, Skill Development
Identifiers—Reading Motivation

    For a potential drop-out who had difficulty comprehending what she had read because she could not recognize a word, even though she often knew its meaning, a methodology for teaching word decoding provided an effective technique for achieving systematic early gains. Lessons for the eighth-grade girl followed this methodology: (1) decoding the unfamiliar word, based on syllabication; (2) recognizing syllables in words in print; (3) recognizing syllables in words by counting vowels; (4) practicing blending single consonants with the vowel stem; (5) learning basic pronunciation rules; (6) recognizing the individual consonant in its sound-symbol relationship; (7) listening to consonants and vowel sounds; and (8) exercising higher order skills such as literal interpretation, creative comprehension, and inference concomitantly with the sound-symbol relations. After tutoring, the Stanford Diagnostic Reading Test, Blue Level was administered in two sessions as a power test in which no time constraints were set. Results showed large discrepancies between reading comprehension (7.5) and word meaning (5.2), but the great improvement that she made in five months was significant. The gains in word decoding contributed to improved performance in reading and was a major treatment component for the girl's emotional, attitudinal and behavioral problems that were blocking effective instruction. (Nineteen references are attached.) (JK)

From Resources in Education, August 1988. Courtesy of ERIC Processing and Reference Facility, Rockville, MD. Reprinted by permission.

The Educational Document Reproduction Service. Notice the entry EDRS Price—MF01/PC01 Plus Postage. (This entry is used in *RIE* but not in *CIJE*.) If you are using a library that does not subscribe to the ERIC system, you may purchase a copy of the document from the Educational Document Reproduction Service (EDRS) in microfiche (MF) form or as a printed copy (PC). The cost of the MF or PC is indicated by a code number (in this case, 01). The cost of a document depends on how many pages the document has, and the code number indicates the price of that particular document. If you order a MF copy, you must have access to a microfiche reader to be able to read it. PCs may be read without use of a machine.

Publication Type Index. Another entry appearing in *RIE* but not in *CIJE* is Publication Type (Pub Type). Pub Type indicates the kind of document. For example, documents may be classified as Reports—Descriptive, Reports—Research, Opinion Papers, and so forth. Document ED 292 075 is classified under Reports—Research and Speeches/Meeting Papers. Each Pub Type is followed by a three-digit number in parentheses, for example, (143) and (150). In addition to a Subject Index, a Document Resumes section, and an Author Index, each issue of *RIE* has a Publication Type Index.

The Publication Type Index contains a numerical list of all publication types, under each of which appear all educational documents of that type that have been indexed in that issue of *RIE*. The Publication Type Index can be particularly useful to students who are carrying out research projects. It is not uncommon for students to encounter difficulty in locating a measuring instrument to use in collecting data for their study. Publication Type 160 is assigned to documents containing actual copies of tests, questionnaires, and other measuring instruments. Consequently, by looking up Pub Type 160 in the Publication Type Index, the student will find a list of educational documents containing various measuring instruments.

Relying Solely on Educational Documents. Many college and university libraries subscribe to the ERIC system and receive copies of all ERIC microfiche. It is especially enjoyable to work with the ERIC microfiche at such a library, because one knows that a microfiche one is interested in will be available at the library. Instant access to microfiche contrasts sharply with the frustration of working with journals, where it sometimes happens that one locates an interesting article only to learn that the library does not subscribe to the journal in which the article is published.

Some students become so enthralled with ERIC microfiche that they never want to be bothered with looking through the journal literature. That is a mistake. One of the prices one pays for the rapid dissemination of information provided by ERIC is the relatively lax policy ERIC seems to follow in deciding what to include in the system. Educational documents in the ERIC system are not subjected to the rigorous scrutiny applied to studies appearing in good journals. The quality of studies appearing in ERIC varies drastically, with many studies falling at the low end of the quality continuum.

ERIC documents can be useful, but they should not be used exclusively. One can find good studies among the ERIC documents, and even if one encounters a poor study, the list of references given at the end of the study may provide useful leads to studies of high quality. Just because a study appears as an ERIC document, it does not necessarily mean that the study does not appear as a journal article as well. Most ERIC documents, however, do not appear in the journal literature.

Exceptional Child Educational Resources (ECER)

In addition to *CIJE* and *RIE,* which contain material pertaining to all areas of education, there is another index that contains material solely in the area of special education: *Exceptional Child Education Resources (ECER)*. *ECER,* published four times a year by the Council for Exceptional Children, provides summaries of both educational documents and journal articles. All of the educational documents published in *ECER* also appear in *RIE*. However, although some of the journal articles indexed in *ECER* also appear in *CIJE,* not all of them do. It is necessary to use *ECER* in addition to *CIJE* to cover the special educational journal literature thoroughly.

One of the main attractions of *ECER* is that all entries are indexed under the same descriptor terms appearing in the ERIC *Thesaurus.* One looks up descriptor terms in the Subject Index and finds a list of abstract numbers following each descriptor. One then turns to the Abstract section, where summaries, including bibliographic information, are listed numerically. Summaries of journal articles and educational documents are intermixed. Each year the abstract numbers for that year begin again with the number 1. After you have familiarized yourself with using *CIJE* and *RIE,* using *ECER* should present no problems.

Education Index

The ERIC system no doubt provides the most comprehensive set of tools for accessing the professional literature in education. However, one drawback, particularly for students interested in historical research, is that ERIC dates back only to 1965. Prior to that date, the major index to the educational periodical literature was *Education Index. Education Index* was begun in 1929 and still continues to produce monthly issues. Although the way in which one uses any index is basically the same, there are some notable differences between *Education Index* and either *CIJE* or *RIE.*

Education Index consists of a combined topic and author index. Topic headings and authors' names are intermixed and listed alphabetically. Unfortunately, *Education Index* does not have a thesaurus of topic headings, so one has to discover by trial and error what terms are used for classifying material on a given topic. Many cross-references aid the user.

The names of journals listed in *Education Index* are abbreviated. (No abbreviations are used in journal listings in *CIJE.*) At the beginning of each issue of *Education Index* is a list of the abbreviations for each journal. It is important to check this listing to make sure you have the correct title of a journal. Sometimes the same abbreviation is used for more than one term. For example, *J Educ Psychol* stands for the *Journal of Educational Psychology,* but *J Exp Educ* stands for the *Journal of Experimental Education.* The abbreviation *Educ* has two meanings.

Listings in *Education Index* provide the title of the article, the names of the authors, the abbreviated title of the journal in which the article appears, the journal's volume number followed by a colon, and the page numbers. The month (or season) of the journal is listed as an abbreviation (e.g., *My* stands for May, *Mr* for March, *Spr* for spring, etc.) and is followed by the year of publication, which is shown with an apostrophe followed by the last two digits of the year (e.g., '88 stands for 1988). The term *bibl* indicates that the article has a bibliography, or a list of references, at the end of the article.

Perhaps the biggest disadvantage in working with *Education Index* is that no summary or abstract of the article is given. *Education Index* provides only the necessary bibliographic information for locating an article. To determine what the article is about, one has to obtain a copy of the journal in which the article was published.

The Psychological Research Literature

Sometimes the topics that students in education select for investigation are as much psychological as they are educational, and it may prove useful to look through the psychological research literature. Articles appearing in psychological journals published not only in the United States but in countries around the world are indexed in *Psychological Abstracts. Psychological Abstracts* has been published since 1927 by the American Psychological Association.

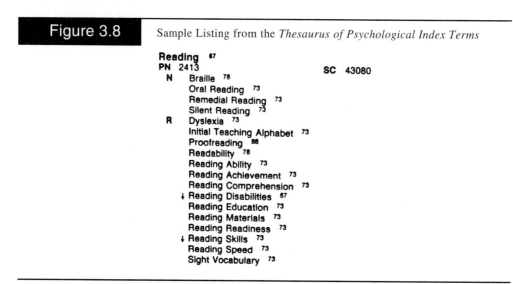

Figure 3.8   Sample Listing from the *Thesaurus of Psychological Index Terms*

Paperback issues are published monthly, and, largely because of the enormous amount of published psychological literature, hardback cumulative editions are published quarterly.

Thesaurus of Psychological Index Terms

The *Thesaurus of Psychological Index Terms* contains a list of terms used to index articles in *Psychological Abstracts*. The *Thesaurus* is divided into three main sections: (a) Relationship Section, (b) Rotated Alphabetical Terms Section, and (c) Alphabetical Term Clusters Section. The *Thesaurus* basically works the way the ERIC *Thesaurus* does. With minor exceptions it uses the same symbols found in the ERIC *Thesaurus*. Figure 3.8 shows the listing of the term ''Reading'' in the Relationship Section. The number ''67,'' appearing as a superscript next to ''Reading,'' indicates that the term was first used in 1967. The symbol PN stands for ''Posting Note,'' and the number next to PN indicates how many times the term has been used since it was first introduced. Each term is assigned its own unique Subject Code (SC) number, which can be used instead of the term when searching by computer. The down arrow symbol is used to indicate a more specific term.

Psychological Abstracts

The monthly paperback issues of *Psychological Abstracts* are divided into two sections: a Brief Subject Index and Abstracts. Cumulative hardback editions consist of two companion volumes, one containing the Brief Subject Index for a 3-month period and the other the corresponding Abstracts for that period.

To locate journal articles, books, and chapters in books on a topic, one first selects an appropriate term from the psychology *Thesaurus* and then looks up the term in the Brief Subject Index. Each term is followed by one or more abstract numbers. Numbers following

Figure 3.9   Sample of the Brief Subject Index in *Psychological Abstracts*

Reading Comprehension—Serials: 12350, 12932, 12935, 13945, 13962, 15419, 15430, 15481, 15483, 15487, 15565
Chapters: 12011, 12375

Figure 3.10   Sample Abstract in *Psychological Abstracts*

12350. **Mills, Carol B.; Diehl, Virginia A.; Birkmire, Deborah P. & Mou, Lien-chong.** (Goucher Coll, Towson, MD) **Procedural text: Predictions of importance ratings and recall by models of reading comprehension.** *Discourse Processes,* 1993(Jul–Sep), Vol 16(3), 279–315. —Two models of text comprehension, a referential model proposed by W. Kintsch and T. A. van Dijk (1978) and a causal model proposed by T. Trabasso and L. J. Sperry (see PA, Vol 74:18270), were tested in 2 experiments with 8 procedural texts. In Exp 1, 24 female college students rated the importance of propositions, idea units, and sentences to the overall procedure described in the texts. In Exp 2, 16 female college students recalled each of the 8 texts. Predictors derived from the models were used to predict the ratings and the recall. For the ratings, the causal model accounted for significantly more variance than the referential model. For the recall, the causal model generally accounted for more variance, but the difference was not significant.

the term ''Serials'' refer to journal articles; those following ''Chapters'' refer to chapters in books. For example, in Figure 3.9 the abstracts of 11 journal articles and two book chapters have been indexed under the term ''Reading Comprehension.'' The abstracts themselves appear in numerical order in the Abstract section. Figure 3.10 shows Abstract 12350, which is the first number listed under ''Serials.''

Notice in Figure 3.10 that in addition to the standard bibliographical information pertaining to the article, the institutional affiliation of the authors is shown in parentheses after the authors' names. This information is quite useful if one wishes to write to the authors to request a reprint of an article.

One has to exercise caution in using abstract numbers appearing in hardbound cumulative issues of *Psychological Abstracts.* Each year the numbers assigned to abstracts begin again with the number one. Consequently, when you want to read an abstract, it is important to make sure you go to the companion Abstract volume covering the same time period as the Brief Subject Index volume in which you found the abstract number. Articles listed in different volumes can have identical abstract numbers. (In *CIJE* and *RIE,* EJ and ED numbers continue from one year to the next, so there is only one article with a given EJ number and only one document with a given ED number.)

Dissertation Abstracts International

It is understandable that many doctoral candidates select a current topic of research interest as the focus of their dissertations. Consequently, the bulk of existing research literature dealing with a current topic of interest may be available only in the form of unpublished doctoral dissertations. Abstracts of all doctoral dissertations are published in a reference work called *Dissertation Abstracts International.* Microfilm copies of all doctoral dissertations are available from an organization called University Microfilms. Information about how to order a copy of a dissertation and how much it costs appears in *Dissertation Abstracts International.*

You were already urged to pick a research topic of interest to you. If a topic interests you, it may interest many other educators and perhaps is being explored by numerous doctoral students. Therefore, as you search the various indexes for research literature on the topic, you may encounter many references to *Dissertation Abstracts International.* This creates the anomalous situation where one reference work lists another reference work rather than the actual study itself.

There are a couple of ways you can use *Dissertation Abstracts International* to your advantage. First, the abstracts appearing in this reference work are often longer and more detailed than the abstracts of articles appearing in the other indexes, so frequently the abstract itself contains sufficient information for your purposes. Generally it is probably not worth the time or money to write for a microfilm copy of the entire dissertation unless it seems virtually identical to your own study.

Second, you now know the names of recent recipients of doctorates who have explored your topic of interest. It is fairly common for persons who have recently received the doctoral degree to try to publish a journal article based on their dissertation. So you might go back to the journal indexes beginning with the year in which the dissertation was completed and look up the name of the author of the dissertation to see if the author has published a journal article subsequent to receiving the doctorate.

Using Cited References

All of the indexes described in the chapter so far may be used to locate articles and educational documents about a given topic. Articles and documents provide you not only with information about a topic but, importantly, they also provide you with a list of references cited in the article that may also be related to your topic. Remember that the author of a published article has gone through the same process of reviewing the literature that you are going through. You can take advantage of the author's review by using some of the references provided by the author without having to locate them yourself through the various indexes. The list of references at the end of an article can yield important information and speed up your own review.

Obviously, references cited in an article had to have been published prior to the date the article was published. For example, if you have an article that was published in 1994, it is impossible for the list of cited references to contain any articles or documents published after 1994. In fact, given the typical time lag in publication, it is unlikely that the most recent reference would have been published later than 1992 or 1993. Consequently, bibliographies or lists of references appearing at the end of an article are helpful in locating additional information published *prior* to the publication of that article, but not in finding information published after.

Social Sciences Citation Index

Sometimes in reviewing the literature on a given topic, one finds references to the same one or two articles in practically every article one reads. Some articles are really seminal works in an area of research and generate considerable interest among other researchers who want to carry out additional studies in the area. These seminal works are cited over and over again in new articles dealing with the topic. For example, George Miller in 1956 published his now well-known work, ''The Magical Number Seven Plus or Minus Two,'' which had profound implications for researchers working in the area of human information processing. Many later studies on information processing refer to Miller's work.

If one were interested in information processing as a possible research topic, one would no doubt be interested in locating articles that refer to Miller because such articles would also likely deal with information processing. It is possible to find such articles by using the *Social Sciences Citation Index*. By looking up Miller's name in the *Index*, one would find a list of journal articles in which Miller's work is cited. All of these articles will have been published *after* Miller's article first appeared. It can be extremely useful to be able to locate later articles based on a seminal study.

Conducting a Manual Literature Search

There are several ways to go about searching the literature on a given topic. Which way you use depends in part on which indexes are being searched and the kinds of searching facilities you have access to. Prior to the widespread use of computers, the only way to search the professional literature was to carry out a manual search. It is, of course, still possible to carry out a manual search using any or all of the indexes described earlier in this chapter. However, in addition it is possible now to carry out searches using some indexes by either on-line computer searching or by the use of compact discs. See chapter 17 for detailed information about computer searches.

A manual search of the literature means that the search will be conducted without using any computer facilities. After you have selected topic headings that seem appropriate, look up one of the headings in various indexes and search the titles of articles or documents listed under that heading in hopes of finding titles that seem relevant to your own research question. For example, suppose you are interested in examining the relationship between second graders' attitudes toward reading and their performance in reading. You might begin the search by selecting a term such as ''READING ATTITUDES'' and look for articles under that heading that also deal with students' reading performance.

On the other hand, you might choose to begin the search by selecting the term ''READING ACHIEVEMENT'' and look for articles under that heading that also deal with students' attitudes toward reading. When you are searching the literature manually, it is possible to enter an index with only a single topic heading. Then you must scan the many titles appearing under that heading for ones that seem related to your research question. It is, of course, extremely likely that most of the titles will not deal with your topic of interest, but scanning titles is the only procedure available to you.

Keeping Track of Your Literature Search

Searching the literature manually is often a rather time-consuming process, and it is likely that you will return to the library time and again to pick up the search where you left off. Unless you keep track of which volumes of which indexes you have consulted, you may forget and waste valuable time checking indexes you have already checked. As you proceed with a literature search, it is often desirable to revise the initial set of descriptor terms used to try to locate pertinent articles. You may discover that some terms you originally thought would be helpful turn out to yield no relevant material and other terms, which you did not think of at the outset of your search, turn out to be quite useful. Consequently, it is wise to develop a system to determine which terms you have checked in which volumes of which indexes.

One simple effective system is to take a sheet of paper for each index you intend to consult. Down the left-hand margin list in reverse chronological order the dates of the index, beginning with the most recent monthly unbound issues and continuing with the bound semiannual or annual volumes. Across the top of the paper list the descriptor terms you intend to use with the index. As you go through the indexes, place a check under the column heading of the terms you have used next to the particular issue or volume you have used. If some original terms are not useful, simply cross them out. If you discover new terms, add them at the top of the page. Remember to go back to indexes you have already consulted to check under your new terms.

Generally it is best to start with the most recent issues of an index and work backward. The more recent the index is, the more updated the bibliographic references will be. Sometimes it is necessary to consult indexes out of chronological sequence, however, because other students may be using an issue you want at the time you need it. An additional benefit of the system described is that it will be apparent from your records if you have skipped any issues of the index.

In addition to keeping track of the indexes and terms you have used, it is helpful to keep a record of which articles or ERIC documents you have consulted. After awhile you will have read so many titles that it is almost impossible to remember which ones you have already looked at and which ones are new. The easiest way to keep track is to list the bibliographic citation for each article or document on an index card and keep the cards arranged alphabetically by the last name of the first author.

Bibliographic Citations

There are numerous styles used to write bibliographic citations. It is best to find out what style your college or institution uses and start using it immediately. Many schools of education use the style endorsed by the American Psychological Association. The 1994 edition of the *Publication Manual of the American Psychological Association* advocates one style for manuscripts and a different style for student papers. (For manuscripts, the first line of reference entries in the list of references is indented 5 to 7 spaces, underlining is used to indicate italics, and the right-hand margin is not justified.) Figures 3.11 through 3.13 contain examples of bibliographic citations and information about how to cite journal articles (Figure 3.11), ERIC documents (Figure 3.12), and books (Figure 3.13) in accordance with the style advocated for student papers and theses (*Publication Manual of the American Psychological Association* 1994, pp. 334–335).

Figure 3.11   How to Cite Journal Articles

Some journals start each volume with page 1 and continue using sequential page numbers from one issue to the next; others start each issue with page 1. If each issue starts with page 1, you must list the issue number; otherwise omit it.

• Example of an article from a journal in which each volume (but not each issue) begins with page 1:

Alexander, P. A., Kulikowich, J. M., & Schulze, S. K. (1994). How subject-matter knowledge affects recall and interest. <u>American Educational Research Journal, 31,</u> 313–337.

• Example of an article from a journal in which each issue begins with page 1:

Cziko, G. A. (1992). Purposeful behavior as the control of perception: Implications for educational research. <u>Educational Researcher, 21</u>(9), 10–18.

Note:

1. The first line of the citation is flush with the left-hand margin, but subsequent lines are indented 2 spaces.
2. List the last name of each author followed by each author's initials. *No first names are used.* The name of the last author is preceded by a comma and an ampersand.
3. Capitalize *only* the first word, any proper nouns, and the first word following a colon in the title of the article. Do *not* put the title in quotation marks.
4. Capitalize all major words and use no abbreviations in the name of the journal. The name of the journal should be underlined or italicized.
5. The journal's volume number should be underlined or italicized and followed by an underlined or italicized comma unless each issue of the journal begins with page 1, in which case, put the issue number inside parentheses directly next to the volume number followed by a comma. The issue number is *not* underlined or italicized.
6. Do *not* use "pp." or "pg." when giving page numbers.

Figure 3.12   How to Cite ERIC Educational Documents

• Example of an ERIC educational document:

Chinn, C. A., & others. (1993). <u>Situated actions during reading lessons: A microanalysis of oral reading error episodes</u> (Technical Report No. 582). Urbana, IL: Center for the Study of Reading. (ERIC Document Reproduction Service No. ED 361 654)

Note:

1. The first line of the citation is flush with the left-hand margin, but subsequent lines are indented 2 spaces.
2. List the last name of each author followed by each author's initials. *No first names are used.* The name of the last author is preceded by a comma and an ampersand. If there are multiple authors, list all of their names if they are given; otherwise use ", & others."
3. Capitalize *only* the first word, any proper nouns, and the first word following a colon in the document's title. The title should be underlined or italicized. Do *not* put the title in quotation marks. If the document is a technical report, list that information in parentheses immediately after the document's title without underlining or italicizing.
4. Give the city and state followed by a colon and the name of the institution where the document was prepared.
5. The ED number consists of two three-digit figures separated by a space. Do *not* put a period at the end.

•Example of an entire book:
Kuhn, T. S. (1970). <u>The structure of scientific revolutions.</u> Chicago: University of Chicago Press.

  Note:

1. The first line of the citation is flush with the left-hand margin, but subsequent lines are indented 2 spaces.
2. List the last name of each author followed by each author's initials. *No first names are used.* The name of the last author is preceded by a comma and an ampersand.
3. Capitalize *only* the first word, any proper nouns, and the first word following a colon in the book's title. The title should be underlined or italicized.
4. Give the place of publication followed by a colon and the name of the publisher.

•Example of a chapter in an edited book:
Soltis, J. F. (1990). The ethics of qualitative research. In E. W. Eisner, & A. Peshkin (Eds.), <u>Qualitative inquiry in education: The continuing debate</u> (pp. 247–257). New York: Teachers College Press.

  Note:

1. The first line of the citation is flush with the left-hand margin, but subsequent lines are indented 2 spaces.
2. List the last name of each author of the chapter followed by each author's initials. *No first names are used.* The name of the last author is preceded by a comma and an ampersand.
3. Capitalize *only* the first word, any proper nouns, and the first word following a colon in the title of the article. Do *not* put the title in quotation marks.
4. The editors' initials precede their last names. The name of the last editor is preceded by a comma and an ampersand. After the editors' names put in parentheses "Ed." if there is one editor or "Eds." if there is more than one editor.
5. Capitalize *only* the first word, any proper nouns, and the first word following a colon. The title should be underlined or italicized.
6. Place the page numbers of the chapter preceded by "pp." in parentheses.
7. Give the place of publication followed by a colon and the name of the publisher.

Notetaking

Notetaking serves two major purposes: (a) to make sure you have all the information you need from every article you have read and (b) to help you organize information that you are obtaining from numerous sources. You can make sure you have all the information you need if for each article you read you carry out the following eight steps.

1. Copy the complete citation of the article.
2. Copy all hypotheses or research questions.
3. List the number and types of subjects.
4. Describe briefly the materials used, including tests or measuring instruments.
5. Describe the research procedures used.
6. Report the results, noting which hypotheses have or have not been supported or how the research questions have been answered.
7. Note important points from the discussion section.
8. Critically evaluate the article.

To organize information from multiple sources it is useful to establish a separate set of notes for various aspects of your topic. You will then have recorded in a single place all information about a particular aspect of your topic regardless of where the information comes from. Suppose, for example, you have located twelve articles dealing with the topic of teacher burnout. Code each article with a number from 1 to 12. Then identify various apsects of teacher burnout that appear in the 12 articles. Such aspects might include: burnout among teachers compared to burnout among other professionals; various ways of measuring burnout; characterisics of the teachers studied, such as gender, age, years of teaching experience, grade level taught, kinds of students taught, and so forth.

You would then record the information you have uncovered for each aspect and indicate by code number the article in which the information appeared. Having all the information about each aspect in one place will help you determine how to design your own study. It will also help you later in writing the introduction to your proposal.

What to Do If You Find No Studies Related to Your Topic

The first thing to do if you are unable to find any published studies dealing with your topic is to make sure that you have consulted the ERIC *Thesaurus* and are looking up the correct topic headings in the various indexes.

Next, ask yourself if you are defining the scope of your literature review too narrowly. Often students approach a review of the literature expecting that the study they intend to do must already have been carried out several times by other people, and the purpose of reviewing the literature is to locate these studies. It almost never happens that someone else has carried out a study identical to the one a student is planning to do.

Suppose you are planning to carry out an experiment in which you will teach a science unit on magnetism to third graders using a discovery approach with one group of students and a demonstration approach with another group. It is highly unlikely that anyone else has already carried out the exact same study, and if you search the literature with the intention of finding such a study, you will probably spend your time in vain.

It is more realistic to search the literature in hopes of finding studies comparing the discovery and demonstration methods of teaching any topic in science to elementary school students at any grade level. A published study comparing the relative effectiveness of the discovery and demonstration methods in teaching fifth graders about the properties of acids and bases would be germane to your own study even though the published study concerns older students and a different topic in science. If the published study finds one method superior to the other, it is reasonable to hypothesize that the same outcome should occur among third graders learning about magnetism.

If you can locate no studies in which the two methods have been used to teach science, you may have to rely on studies in which the two methods have been used to teach other subject areas. For example, if a published study reports that one method has been found superior to the other in teaching fourth graders the mathematical procedures for converting fractions into decimals, you can argue that the same method should prove superior in teaching third graders about magnetism.

Conceptually Related Studies

In short, one tries to find studies that are as similar as possible to the study one is planning to carry out. The studies need only be conceptually related, not identical, to one's own study. Sometimes it is useful to think of one's study as representing one exemplar of some more general phenomenon. For example, suppose you are unable to locate any studies that compare the discovery method with the demonstration method for teaching anything. You might at that point ask yourself why you believe one method should be superior to the other. Let us assume you think the discovery method should turn out to be better than the demonstration method. What is it about the two methods that makes you conclude the discovery method should be superior?

Perhaps you feel that students will learn better by the discovery method because they will be actively manipulating materials, and active learning ought to be superior to passive learning. In other words, you have now conceptualized the study in the more general terms of active versus passive learning, and the discovery and demonstration methods are merely specific instances of the more general phenomenon. Having done this, any studies dealing with active and passive learning are germane to your own study even if the studies do not deal specifically with discovery and demonstration methods of teaching.

One of my former students was interested in carrying out a study comparing the use of computer-assisted instruction with the use of workbooks. She was unable to locate any studies in the literature comparing these two methods. However, when she asked herself why she thought computer-assisted instruction should be superior, she decided it was because computers provide immediate feedback. As soon as she conceptualized her research study as a single instance of the more general phenomenon of immediate and delayed feedback, she had access to countless pertinent studies appearing in the professional literature.

Nonempirical Articles

One final point should be made about reviewing the literature. Because so much emphasis has been placed on empirical studies, students sometimes come to the erroneous conclusion that only empirical studies can be used in a review of the literature. There are many articles in the professional literature that are not empirical, but which nevertheless may be pertinent to your study. A review of the literature may include any information that is germane, including opinion papers written by experts in the field or articles containing theoretical discussions of your topic.

Emphasis has been placed on empirical studies only because students generally are less familiar with articles dealing with empirical studies than with other kinds of articles. However, you should not conclude that unless an article deals with an empirical study it is of no value to you.

It is often helpful to use nonempirical articles to give the reader of your study a conceptual background on your topic and to explain why the topic is worth investigating. Suppose, for example, that you were interested in the topic of higher order thinking skills. You might want to highlight the importance of investigating the topic by referring to articles that claim too many American students graduate from high school ill prepared to cope with the kinds of thinking demanded by jobs in today's marketplace.

You might also want to include nonempirical articles dealing with various ways scholars define higher order thinking. This would lay the groundwork for explaining why you have decided to define higher order thinking in a particular way. You might also include articles containing suggestions about how students' higher order thinking skills could be improved, even though the articles offer no empirical evidence documenting that the suggestions actually work. It is common for various educational claims to be made with little or no empirical evidence to support the claim. The lack of empirical evidence supporting a claim is an important reason justifying why you are carrying out your study.

Chapter Highlights

- The purpose of reviewing the literature is to help researchers design a new study on a topic and develop a logical rationale underlying their hypotheses and questions.

- In searching for a research question it is best to begin reviewing the literature broadly and gradually narrow the search.

- Once a research question has been formulated, the strategy for reviewing the literature changes from one of breadth to one of depth.

- *Primary sources* are reports written by persons who have conducted research; *secondary sources* are reports about research written by persons other than those who conducted the research.

- Major forms of disseminating research findings include books, chapters in books, journal articles, educational documents, and papers presented at professional conferences.

- The Educational Resources Information Center (ERIC) produces the *Thesaurus of ERIC Descriptors,* the *Current Index to Journals in Education* (*CIJE*), and *Resources in Education* (*RIE*).

- *CIJE* is an index to educational journal articles, *RIE* is an index to educational documents, and the ERIC *Thesaurus* lists the descriptor terms under which articles and documents are classified in *CIJE* and *RIE,* respectively.

- There are 15 ERIC clearinghouses, each of which is responsible for gathering and disseminating information about a particular aspect of the field of education.

- Other indexes to education-related journal articles are the *Education Index* and *Psychological Abstracts.*

- There are several styles of citing references, one of the most common of which is that endorsed by the American Psychological Association. Different citation formats are used for books, articles in edited books, journal articles, and educational documents.

- Preparing a separate set of notes for each aspect of a topic permits one to organize information obtained from multiple sources.

- Conceptualizing a research question as one exemplar of a more general phenomenon may overcome the problem of failing to find any literature about the question.

- The review of literature may include nonempirical articles as well as empirical articles.

Review Exercises

1. Describe how searching the literature to select a research topic differs from searching the literature after you have selected a specific research question.

2. How do primary and secondary sources differ?

3. What kinds of documents can be found on ERIC microfiche?

4. What is the basic difference between the materials indexed in *CIJE* and those indexed in *RIE?*

5. Why is it important to use the ERIC *Thesaurus* prior to using *CIJE* or *RIE?*

6. Describe the four sections comprising the ERIC *Thesaurus.*

7. In searching the *Thesaurus* for a topic, which section should you consult first? Why?

8. Using the ERIC *Thesaurus,* look up a topic of interest to you and record the date the descriptor was first used. How many articles and documents have been indexed under the descriptor in *CIJE* and *RIE,* respectively?

9. Tell what the following symbols used in the ERIC *Thesaurus* mean: SN, UF, NT, BT, and RT.

10. Explain the difference between the use of periods and colons in the Two-Way Hierarchical Term Display.

11. Describe the difference between Major and Minor Descriptors.

12. If you wish to write to an author of an article but do not know the author's address, name two reference works in which you can locate the address.

13. What section for *RIE* corresponds to the Main Entry Section of *CIJE?*

14. How would you obtain a copy of a microfiche of an educational document that interests you?

15. What does Pub Type 160 stand for and why is it frequently useful to students who are carrying out a research project?

16. What index in addition to *CIJE* and *RIE* is of particular use for special educators?

17. Describe the similarities and dissimilarities of *CIJE* and the *Education Index.*

18. In many ways *Psychological Abstracts* is similar to *CIJE.* However, one only needs an article's EJ number to locate a summary of the article in *CIJE.* The abstract number of an article listed in *Psychological Abstracts,* however, is not sufficient for locating an abstract of the article. What additional information is needed?

19. What reference work is particularly useful in locating information about a relatively new area of research interest?

20. In what major way does the *Social Sciences Citation Index* differ from other indexes?

21. Why is it advantageous to begin a search of the literature with the most recent indexes and work backward?

22. What steps should you take if you are unable to locate any literature pertaining to your topic?

23. Describe a system of notetaking that permits one to organize and synthesize information obtained from different sources.

*C*hapter 4
Formulating Research Hypotheses

A hypothesis is a prediction about the outcome of a study in terms of the variables being investigated. Such a hypothesis is often called a research hypothesis.

Chapter Objectives

After completing this chapter, you should be able to:

- distinguish between a study's objective and its purpose
- define the term *hypothesis*
- explain the hierarchical relationship between values and variables
- distinguish between labels and operational definitions
- distinguish pseudohypotheses from hypotheses
- describe the role the related literature plays in formulating hypotheses
- explain how directional and nondirectional hypotheses differ
- outline the steps in generating your own hypothesis

It is best to search the professional literature broadly when trying to select a research topic and gradually narrow the topic to a specific research question. Once you have formulated your research question, the nature of reviewing the literature shifts. The new focus of the search becomes depth rather than breadth. It is your analysis of the literature that provides a framework within which to formulate the objectives of your study. It is your objectives that determine the kind of study you should carry out.

Do not confuse a study's objective with its purpose. **Objective** refers to what is to be investigated empirically in a study; **purpose** refers to why and for whom the study is being carried out. For example, the *objective* of a given thesis or dissertation may be to compare the mathematics achievement of fifth graders who are, and who are not, assigned homework. The *purpose* of the study, however, is to complete requirements for a degree.

The objectives of a study often take the form of asking one or more questions or testing one or more hypotheses about the nature of the relationship among variables; either form is acceptable as long as it is clear what the study's objective is. **Questions** ask how the variables under investigation might be related; **hypotheses,** on the other hand, are tentative, testable statements about the way in which the variables are related. Research questions and hypotheses both deal with relationships among variables. Before discussing ways in which researchers may state hypotheses, let us examine more carefully the nature of variables.

Defining Variables as Sets of Values

The way one defines a **variable** frequently determines the particular set of **values** associated with that variable. For example, "kind of school" is a variable that may take on various sets of values, depending on how one conceptualizes the variable. One might define "kind of school" in terms of the source of funding, in which case the variable might take on two values: public school or private school. Any school funded by the government would be classified as public; any school funded by private sources would be classified as private. The two values are mutually exclusive. A school may either be public or private, but not both.

On the other hand, one might define "kind of school" in terms of the grade levels of students attending the school. In this case the variable could assume values such as elementary school, middle school, junior high school, or senior high school. Again, these values are mutually exclusive. A school, for example, cannot be an elementary and a senior high school simultaneously (except, of course, in the special case of a small private or public rural school in which all grades are in one building).

In fact there are numerous ways to define the variable "kind of school," and each definition has its own unique set of values. Suppose one wished to define "kind of school" in terms of geographic location. The values associated with such a definition might be: urban school, suburban school, or rural school. One might decide to define "kind of school" in terms of the discipline studied at a school. Values associated with such a definition might be: school of pharmacy, school of nursing, school of education, or school of business administration. Any given definition of a variable has its own set of values, and values within a set must be mutually exclusive.

Distinguishing Between Variables and Values

Sometimes students who are new to research have difficulty distinguishing between variables and values. There are two major reasons that often account for this difficulty. The first is that students may fail to realize that they are defining a variable in more than one way and,

Figure 4.1   Hierarchical Relationship Between Variables and Values

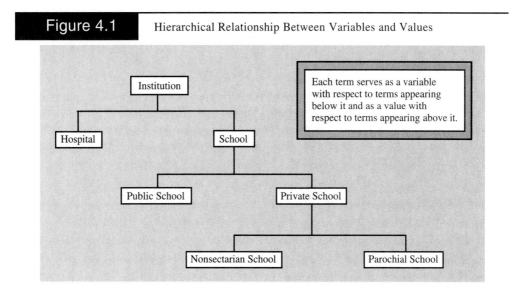

consequently, the values associated with the different definitions are not mutually exclusive. For example, "kind of school" may be incorrectly assigned values, such as private school, elementary school, public school, and senior high school. The difficulty here is that a school may be both private and elementary or both public and elementary, and so forth.

Private and public school belong to the set of values associated with "kind of school" when the variable is defined in terms of source of funding. On the other hand, elementary and senior high school belong to the set of values associated with "kind of school" when the variable is defined in terms of the grade levels of students attending a school. It is incorrect to mix elements of two different sets of values.

A second source of difficulty students sometimes encounter in differentiating between values and variables is that a value associated with one variable may itself be a variable with its own sets of values. For example, private school may be a value associated with the variable "kind of school." However, "private school" could itself be conceptualized as a variable with the values parochial and nonsectarian. The definitions of values and variables are interdependent, with variables always representing a more general or global conceptualization than the values associated with them.

Note the hierarchical relationship among terms connected by vertical lines in Figure 4.1. A term is a value with respect to a term appearing above it, but a variable with respect to terms appearing below it. School is a value associated with the variable "institution." On the other hand, "school" is a variable with the values of public school and private school. Similarly, private school is a value associated with the variable "school," but a variable with the values of parochial school and nonsectarian school.

In quantitative research, the researcher identifies variables of interest before conducting a study. The researcher's objective is to discover various kinds of information about these variables. A researcher, for example, may want to describe the dropout rate of students in particular school districts. The researcher knows in advance that the variables of interest are "dropout rate" and "school district." Similarly, a researcher wishing to determine the relationship between dropout rate and size of school, knows at the beginning of the study that the variables are ''dropout rate'' and ''school size.''

In ethnographic research, however, the researcher's objective is to identify variables of interest as they evolve during the course of investigating a particular phenomenon. An ethnographic researcher interested in the question of dropping out of school does not know in advance what variables may turn out to be of interest. By interviewing and observing students who have dropped out of school, and perhaps comparing that information with information obtained from students who have not dropped out, the researcher attempts to identify important variables and describe the process by which these variables led the particular students under investigation to drop out of school.

Operational Definitions

The matter of defining variables is so important in empirical research that a special term is given to the kind of definition used to define a variable. The term is **operational definition.** An operational definition is quite different from the kind of definition one might find in a dictionary. The important aspect of an operational definition that distinguishes it from other kinds of definitions is the prominent role of measurement. An operational definition of a variable is a definition that gives the variable meaning by describing how the variable is measured. See Ennis (1964) for a comprehensive account of operational definitions.

Operational Definitions and Labels

An operational definition of the variable, ''mathematical ability,'' might be the score a person receives on a standardized mathematics test. Another operational definition of ''mathematical ability'' might be the grade in mathematics appearing on a report card. In both cases the variable is ''mathematical ability,'' but what is meant by the variable is different in one case than in the other. Practically any variable can be defined operationally in a number of different ways. In empirical research, the label assigned to a variable is not nearly as important as how the variable is measured. Without knowing how the researcher has measured the variable, it is difficult to know with very much precision what the researcher means by it. Different researchers using different operational definitions may nevertheless refer to their definitions by the same name. In other words, a variable that has the same name in two different studies may not really be the same variable at all because of the different kinds of measurements used to define it operationally.

Some variables are much easier to define operationally than others. When a variable is defined operationally, one is often attempting to express the variable in some quantifiable form. Variables that are more easily expressed as numbers are easier to define operationally. The variable ''age,'' for example, is quite easy to define operationally because we typically express age in the form of a number. It is easy to express what value of the variable characterizes a particular individual, because that value is simply the person's age. We measure a person's age by subtracting the person's birth date from the date on which the person participates in the study. The term **construct** is often applied to terms we invent to refer to complex phenomena that consist of a constellation of unobservable characteristics. Examples of constructs include self-concept, underachievement, anxiety, and creativity.

Defining Nonquantifiable Variables

One of the most frequently appearing variables in educational research is "method of instruction." This variable is particularly difficult to define operationally because there is virtually no way in which it can be quantified. About the only way in which one can approach defining a method of instruction in operational terms is to provide a detailed list of the kinds of activities that comprise the instructional method. Methods of instruction that are given the same label may mean very different things to different people. It is perhaps for this reason that so many studies comparing Method A with Method B yield conflicting results.

It is not unusual to encounter studies in which a researcher is comparing the effectiveness of some new method with a traditional method. Typically, the researcher describes in some detail what the new method of instruction consists of, but often it is left up to the reader's imagination to figure out what is meant by the term "traditional method of instruction."

At one point numerous studies comparing the outcomes of instruction in "open classrooms" with the outcomes of instruction in "traditional classrooms" began to appear in the research literature. The number of such studies has dropped sharply because of their failure to produce much knowledge that is generalizable. No doubt this failure is attributable to the widely varying array of definitions given the two types of classrooms. Such studies demonstrate the confusion that can arise when different people use the same term to refer to different things.

Eliminating Ambiguity

The kind of language we use in everyday conversation is fraught with ambiguity, and in empirical research it is imperative to eliminate as much ambiguity as possible. Consider the possibility of a group of teachers discussing the topic of creativity. It is likely that all teachers would agree that it is desirable to encourage students to exhibit as much creativity as possible. However, it is also likely that the teachers in the group would have various notions about what constitutes creativity. If one were to ask the teachers to define creativity operationally by specifying how they would measure creativity, one might soon discover that there is little consensus about the meaning of the term.

A discussion about creativity seems silly if there is little agreement about what the term means. Without defining the term operationally, however, the fact that there is disagreement about the meaning of the term might go undetected. The failure to detect differences in meaning is unimportant as long as the discussion is carried out in general terms. Differences in meaning do become important if the discussion shifts from the level of conversation to the level of intellectual debate.

A term that we use in our daily conversations with others, such as *creativity,* may camouflage serious differences in meaning that are not tolerable in research. For example, it may be that two researchers have investigated the same question regarding some aspect of creative behavior and have reached different conclusions. One reason that might account for the difference in the findings of the two studies could be that the researchers have applied different operational definitions to the same variable. If variables or constructs are measured differently, it is reasonable to expect differences in the outcomes of studies dealing with those variables or constructs.

Specificity and Vulnerability

The use of operational definitions serves to open lines of communication. By specifying how a variable is measured, the definition of the variable becomes public. One need not get inside the researcher's head to understand what the researcher means by a particular variable. Operational definitions define variables in observable terms. Anyone can observe how the researcher has measured a variable, and everyone is free to agree or disagree with the definition the researcher has chosen.

The fact that operational definitions force a variable to be expressed in measurable, observable terms has another important consequence. The researcher becomes vulnerable. By defining a variable in observable form, it makes it relatively easy for others to attack the definition as being inaccurate or inadequate. In research, vulnerability and disagreement are highly useful properties, because it is often through the process of disagreement that new knowledge is generated and ideas are clarified.

Even if a variable is defined operationally, it will be up to you to decide if the researcher's definition is reasonable in terms of how the variable is typically conceptualized in the research literature. If the variables in a hypothesis are defined operationally, the hypothesis may or may not be a good one. However, if the variables in a hypothesis are not expressed in operational form, the hypothesis is surely a poor one from the standpoint of providing much useful research information.

Variables and Hypotheses

A hypothesis is a prediction about the outcome of a study in terms of the variables being investigated. Such a hypothesis is often called a **research hypothesis.** A typical research hypothesis might be: "Students taught by Method A will score significantly higher on a reading comprehension test than students taught by Method B." The variables in this hypothesis are "methods of instruction" and "reading comprehension scores." "Methods of instruction" can take on one of two values. The methods of instruction are either Method A or Method B. The nature of the predicted relationship between "methods of instruction" and "reading comprehension scores" is clear. It is predicted that Method A will be associated with higher reading comprehension scores and Method B with lower reading comprehension scores.

Another typical research hypothesis is: "Among high school seniors, there will be a significant positive relationship between students' self-concept scores and their grade point averages." The variables are "self-concept scores" and "grade point averages." "High school seniors" is not a variable. It merely defines the population to which the study's findings may be applied. Given the nature of the predicted relationship between self-concept scores and grade point averages, the researcher anticipates that students with high self-concept scores will have high grade point averages and those with low self-concept scores will have low grade point averages.

It can be confusing to identify variables when the term used to define a population of a study is also a value that a variable can assume. Suppose the hypothesis above had been: "The self-concept scores of high school seniors will be significantly higher than the self-concept scores of high school freshmen." The term *high school seniors* defines a population to which the findings may be applied and is simultaneously a value that the variable, "high school students," can take on.

Generally, students can recognize a hypothesis. Any difficulty associated with hypotheses is more apt to occur in stating a hypothesis in testable form. All the previous examples of hypotheses are stated in testable form. The prediction that high school seniors will have higher self-concept scores than high school freshmen can be tested by administering a self-concept questionnaire to the two groups of students and seeing if their average scores are significantly different. We could similarly test the other two hypotheses.

Pseudohypotheses

Pseudohypotheses tend to come in two forms. The most common form is a pseudohypothesis that fails to include any basis for comparison. Consider the following pseudohypothesis: "Students taught by Method A will be better readers." This pseudohypothesis cannot be tested because we do not know what "better" means. The term *better* implies a comparison, but the pseudohypothesis provides no clue to the comparison intended. Does it mean that students taught by Method A will be better readers than students taught by some other method? Or does it mean that students taught by Method A will do better in reading than they do in mathematics? The research question the pseudohypothesis is addressing is unclear.

Another form of pseudohypothesis is the one that is really a value judgment. Any pseudohypothesis that basically predicts that it would be "good" if something happened is nothing more than an expression of one's personal set of values. One cannot test such values by means of empirical investigation.

Converting Pseudohypotheses into Hypotheses

Often there is a testable hypothesis underlying one's values, but it is necessary for the hypothesis to address a researchable question, not a value. Consider the statement, "All junior high school boys should be required to take a course in home economics." That is a value judgment. If asked why it would be "good" for all junior high school boys to take a course in home economics, the person might reply that such a course would help boys think and behave in less gender-role stereotypic ways.

Whether gender-role stereotypic thinking and behavior should be reduced is itself a value judgment, but it is at least possible to frame a testable hypothesis that underlies the judgment. One cannot conclude on the basis of empirical investigation whether it is "good" for boys to behave in less gender-role stereotypic ways. We can test empirically the question whether a course in home economics will reduce such behavior, by stating the following hypothesis: "Junior high school boys who have taken a course in home economics will exhibit significantly less gender-role stereotyping behavior than junior high school boys who have not taken a course in home economics."

Hypotheses and the Related Literature

Many textbooks on research methodology state that one should not formulate a hypothesis until after one has completed an exhaustive review of the related literature. Although such an approach seems defensible, from a practical point of view, such a procedure is rarely followed by professional researchers. In the real world of research, frequently researchers first come up with a pretty good idea of what hypothesis they wish to test and only then do they turn to the related literature. Sometimes in the course of reviewing the related literature, it becomes necessary to alter the hypothesis. In other words, it is common to work back and forth between reviewing the literature and revising a research hypothesis. Conceptually, one can define reviewing the literature and stating a hypothesis as two neatly separated activities in which the review always precedes the hypothesis. In practice, the two activities are rarely either so neat or so separate.

To clarify how the review of related literature actually determines the final form of a hypothesis, let us look at an example. Suppose an elementary school teacher feels, on the basis of her personal teaching experience, that Method A is the best way to teach students to read. Perhaps some of her colleagues disagree and ardently support Method B. The teacher decides to carry out a study to see if one method is better than the other. The teacher's purpose should be to try to find the best way to teach her students, whatever that way may be. The teacher should try to keep as open a mind as possible. Sometimes that is not easy, but one should try to guard against letting one's feelings interfere with the attempt to carry out an objective piece of research.

The teacher may, of course, initially hypothesize that, after a given amount of instruction, students taught by Method A will score significantly higher on a reading comprehension test than students taught by Method B. To develop a documented rationale for her hypothesis, however, the teacher must conduct a review of the related literature. Now, there are several possible outcomes that can result from reviewing the literature. The teacher may discover that the research evidence shows that: (a) Method A is better than Method B; or (b) Method B is better than Method A; or (c) sometimes Method A has been found to be better and sometimes the opposite; or (d) there is no difference between the two methods.

Let us first consider outcome (d). The evidence suggests that the two methods are equally effective, so the wisest decision the teacher can make is to abandon the idea of comparing the two methods.

Directional Hypotheses

If outcome (a) occurs, the teacher will retain the initial hypothesis that in her study students taught by Method A will perform better than students taught by Method B. Such a hypothesis is called a **directional hypothesis** because it predicts the direction of the outcome of the study; that is, the teacher is predicting which group of students will perform better. The review of the literature has only corroborated what the teacher had suspected in the first place. The study, of course, is not likely to be particularly interesting because the teacher will be exerting effort merely to confirm what is already generally acknowledged.

If the outcome of the literature review shows that Method B is better than Method A, the teacher, regardless of her feelings to the contrary, should reformulate her hypothesis to predict that in her study Method B will turn out to be better than Method A. This hypothesis is also a directional hypothesis. It differs from the directional hypothesis stated in the preceding paragraph only in that now students taught by Method B are expected to perform better than students taught by Method A. Notice that altering the direction of the hypothesis does not in any way alter the research question being investigated. The point is, a hypothesis should be stated in terms of what the existing research evidence supports, not in terms of the researcher's intuitive hunches.

Nondirectional Hypotheses

The most disconcerting outcome of the literature review is outcome (c). The results of previous investigations are not clear-cut, an outcome that occurs much more frequently than you might suspect. How does the teacher go about stating her hypothesis so that it can be supported by the existing evidence, which consists of contradictory findings?

The teacher would probably compare the studies that found Method A superior to Method B with those that found the reverse to try to determine what might account for the discrepancy. For example, she may discover that the students who participated in one set of studies tended to come from families of a lower socioeconomic level living in large metropolitan areas, while the other set of studies was generally done with students from more affluent suburban areas. The difference in the two kinds of populations might account for the different findings. Of course, there are many other differences between the two sets of studies that might account for the discrepant findings. For example, it may be that in one set of studies reading comprehension was measured by some sort of multiple choice test, while in the other set, reading comprehension was measured by the cloze procedure.

If the teacher can uncover one or more factors that differentiate the two sets of studies, she should examine the conditions surrounding the study she is planning to conduct to see which set is more similar to her own situation and state her hypothesis in terms of those outcomes. If, for example, the studies that found Method B superior to Method A were generally done with lower income students from large metropolitan areas, and the teacher intends to carry out her study with the same kind of students, it is clear that she should predict her study will show that Method B is better than Method A.

Suppose, however, after comparing the sets of studies having contradictory findings, the teacher is unable to ascertain what factor accounts for the discrepant results. In that case, she would state her hypothesis in nondirectional form. In other words, she would state that there will be a significant difference in the reading comprehension scores of students taught by Method A and the scores of students taught by Method B, without predicting which group will score higher. The only difference between a directional and a **nondirectional hypothesis** is that the former specifies which group should score higher, but the latter does not. In terms of carrying out a study, it is unimportant whether a hypothesis is directional or nondirectional. Exactly the same procedures are followed in collecting and analyzing the data.

Figure 4.2 shows the general formats for stating hypotheses in directional and nondirectional form for studies using correlational or group comparison designs.

Generating Your Own Hypothesis

It will be helpful to summarize briefly some of the information in this chapter so that you can get an overview of what is involved in generating your own research hypothesis. Approach your study first with the idea of selecting a topic, not a hypothesis. Gradually narrow down your topic until you are focusing on a relatively specific question and have a clear idea of the population or populations from which you are going to select the subjects for your study. A hypothesis is a tentative, testable statement about the relationships among variables. Make sure you have defined the variables in your study operationally and that your hypotheses are testable, not merely value judgments. State your hypotheses in directional or nondirectional form, depending on the findings in the research literature related to your question.

The following are general formats you can use to state hypotheses for correlational and group comparison designs. In each example, substitute the names of the groups and variables to be used in your study.

Correlational Designs

•Directional Form:

It is hypothesized that there will be a significant _____(positive/negative)_____ relationship between ___(Variable 1)___ and ___(Variable 2)___ among _____(Name of Group)___.

•Nondirectional Form:

It is hypothesized that there will be a significant relationship between ___(Variable 1)___ and ___(Variable 2)___ among ___(Name of Group)___.

Group Comparison Designs

•Directional Form:

It is hypothesized that ___(Group 1)___ will score significantly ___(higher/lower)___ than ___(Group 2)___ with respect to ___(Name of Variable)___.

•Nondirectional Form:

It is hypothesized that there will be a significant difference between ___(Group 1)___ and ___(Group 2)___ with respect to ___(Name of Variable)___.

Chapter Highlights

- A study's *objective* refers to what is to be investigated empirically; its *purpose* refers to why and for whom the study is being carried out.

- A *hypothesis* is a tentative, testable statement about relationships among variables.

- Different conceptualizations of the same variable consist of different sets of values.

- Variables and values have a hierarchical relationship in which variables are conceptually broader than values.

- Some concepts may simultaneously be a variable with its own set of values and a value with respect to another variable.

- *Operational definitions* define variables and constructs in terms of how they are measured.

- Terms that we invent to refer to complex phenomena that consist of unobservable characteristics are called *constructs;* examples of constructs are creativity, anxiety, and self-concept.

- Pseudohypotheses either have no basis for comparison or reflect value judgments that are not testable.

- Researchers' interpretations of the literature related to a research question determine the form in which they state their hypotheses.
- In group comparison studies, directional hypotheses state which group should have the higher mean; in correlational studies they state whether the correlation should be positive or negative.

Review Exercises

1. How does a study's purpose differ from its objective?
2. Define the term *hypothesis*.
3. Give one example of a concept that is a value with respect to some variable and simultaneously a variable with its own set of values. (See Figure 4.1.)
4. Explain differences between how variables are identified in ethnographic research and research using quantitative techniques.
5. How does an operational definition differ from the kind of definition one might find in a dictionary?
6. What is the best way to define operationally variables that are nonquantifiable?
7. What major contribution do operational definitions make to research?
8. Give an example of a pseudohypothesis.
9. Explain the relationship between the related literature and the way in which research hypotheses are stated.
10. Which of the following hypotheses are directional? Nondirectional?
    a. There will be a significant negative relationship between the number of hours students watch television and their grade point averages.
    b. There will be a significant relationship between the number of hours students watch television and their grade point averages.
    c. There will be a significant difference in attitudes toward school exhibited by students who do and students who do not participate in extracurricular activities.
    d. Students who participate in extracurricular activities will exhibit significantly more positive attitudes toward school than students who do not participate in extracurricular activities.

Section III

Preliminary Considerations in Designing Research

*T*his section deals with several important issues to consider in designing a study, including ethical concerns and legal responsibilities associated with conducting research. The chapters in this section also describe several techniques for selecting samples of subjects to participate in a study and address how large a sample should be.

Many variables in educational research are defined operationally by scores on tests. The two most important characteristics of tests, reliability and validity, are discussed in detail. Information is provided about where to locate commercially available tests and how to choose one, as well as how to construct your own test or measuring instrument.

Chapter 5

Ethical and Legal Aspects of Conducting Research

The researcher must decide if the scientific and social benefits of carrying out a study outweigh the possible cost or risk to the persons who will participate in it.

Chapter Objectives

After completing this chapter, you should be able to:

- identify circumstances that would make it unethical to carry out a particular research project
- describe the components of *informed consent*
- distinguish between *concealment* and *deception* and describe the controversial issues involved in their use

- describe special ethical concerns educators face when they wish to use their own students in a study
- list the responsibilities researchers have at the conclusion of a study
- list measures researchers can take to increase the chances that the confidentiality of a study will be maintained
- list at least five potential sources of gender and racial bias in conducting research and ways of controlling them
- describe the function of Institutional Review Boards

Most educational research involves using human beings as subjects, and it is the researcher's responsibility to protect the people participating in a study. As educators, we are all aware of numerous ethical and legal consequences of our treatment of students. We know, for example, that it is not only ethically and, in most school districts, legally wrong to administer physical punishment to a student, it is also wrong to risk possible psychological damage on students by severely humiliating or ridiculing them. All the legal and ethical considerations that apply to us as educators also apply in conducting research. Researchers, however, are accountable to additional ethical and legal constraints that go beyond those that apply to educators generally.

Research Ethics

Detailed information concerning ethical issues of concern to educational researchers may be found in Kimmel (1988) as well as in the *Ethical Principles of Psychologists and Code of Conduct* published in 1992 by the American Psychological Association and the *Ethical Standards of the American Educational Research Association,* a copy of which appears in appendix A. Especially helpful information about ethical issues pertaining to conducting research may be found in *Ethical Principles in the Conduct of Research with Human Participants* published in 1982 by the American Psychological Association. These principles are described briefly in the following sections.

Dealing with ethical issues rarely involves applying a set of hard and fast rules. On the contrary, many ethical issues involve the application of careful and considered judgment that takes into account the purpose of the research and the context within which a particular study is to be conducted. Readers who wish more detailed information concerning ethical issues in research with human subjects should consult the references noted.

Weighing the Benefits and Risks of Conducting Research

The researcher must decide if the scientific and social benefits of carrying out a study outweigh the possible cost or risk to the persons who will participate in it. The principal benefit for most students conducting research is that they will learn about the research process. In such cases, it seems defensible only to carry out research that poses no potential risk to the subjects of the study.

In cases where the purpose of conducting research is to generate knowledge rather than to learn about the research process, however, it is frequently necessary to confront the issue of how much possible risk is justifiable given the importance of the knowledge to be gained.

The potential benefit of new drugs that may be effective in treating various kinds of diseases, for example, may justify conducting research even though there is some risk that people participating in the study may suffer unanticipated side effects.

In some instances, such as the study of new drugs, the decision *not* to carry out research may itself be unethical because one is knowingly refusing to gather potentially important information. Once the decision is made to conduct research, however, the researcher is responsible for maintaining ethical standards throughout the entire project and for making sure that subjects receive ethical treatment from anyone who may be assisting in the project.

Research in education sometimes involves providing students in an experimental group with strategies the researcher has reason to believe will help them learn more effectively. If the results of the study support the researcher's belief, the researcher has the ethical responsibility of making sure that students who were in the control group are later provided with the same strategies.

Informed Consent

Subjects who participate in a research project should give their **informed consent** to do so. Except under circumstances to be described later, you should not initiate a study of your own unless you have received the subjects' permission to do so. If you are carrying out a study with mentally competent adults, you should get their permission before you involve them. If your subjects are adults who may not be mentally competent or children, you should get permission from the administrative head of the institution, such as the principal of a school or the director of a hospital or a psychiatric center. If you have any doubts about who has the authority to give consent, get the written consent of potential subjects' parents or legal guardians before proceeding with the study. (Sample consent forms for participants and parents or guardians appear in appendix B.) If you are unable to get the necessary permission, select another research question.

From an ethical perspective it is desirable to inform prospective subjects about the nature of the research, particularly those aspects of the study that may affect their decision to participate or not. Those aspects of a study that prospective subjects should be informed of, however, vary considerably from study to study. Furthermore, the consequences of informing subjects of the nature of the research also vary from study to study.

It is not unusual to find situations in which providing subjects with information about the nature of the research can affect the results of the study. A particularly difficult issue is deciding how much information it is ethical to withhold from subjects in order not to affect the outcome of the study. For example, if the length of time subjects will spend participating in the study is particularly long, should they be told so before they consent to participate?

Similarly, if the research is being sponsored by an organization whose goals some subjects may find offensive (e.g., an organization with a particular view on abortion), should subjects be informed about the sponsor? Such information could drastically alter the nature of the sample of people who will be willing to participate in the study and consequently alter the population to which the results of the study may be generalized. The ethical issue is whether the goal of achieving a more representative sample outweighs the principle of informing subjects about a particular aspect of the study.

The increasing use of qualitative methods in educational research has led to new ethical concerns. Consider, for example, the issue of informed consent as it applies to ethnographic studies (Howe & Dougherty, 1993). Contrary to quantitative researchers, who design a detailed plan of the research procedures to be followed before the study actually gets underway, ethnographic researchers prior to beginning a study have only a general idea of what procedures they will use and frequently alter their procedures as the study proceeds. Consequently, although a quantitative researcher can provide subjects with reasonably accurate information about what participation in a study will entail before they consent to participate, an ethnographic researcher cannot. Because the objectives of ethnographic research usually evolve as the study progresses, often researchers can only inform potential subjects in general terms rather than in precise detail what participation in the study will entail.

Concealment and Deception

Deciding to withhold information from subjects is sometimes referred to as **concealment.** Concealment occurs when a researcher tells subjects the truth, but not the whole truth. More troublesome than concealment is the use of **deception,** in which the researcher purposely provides subjects with false information. Deception may be used for several purposes: to encourage people to participate in a study, to camouflage the true objective of a study, or as a part of the research procedure itself.

People may be more likely to complete and return a mailed questionnaire if they are told that the names of all persons completing the questionnaire will be entered into a raffle in which several people will win prizes of various kinds. If in fact no raffle is held, the number of people completing the questionnaire has been increased by deceiving those who would not have completed and mailed back the questionnaire without the promise of potentially receiving a prize.

In my own doctoral dissertation I used deception to camouflage the true objective of my research (Crowl, 1971). I asked teachers to listen to audiotapes of students giving answers to several questions and to grade each answer in terms of how well it answered the question. I told the teachers that I was developing a set of norms for grading students' oral responses. The real objective of the investigation, however, was to determine the effect of students' voice qualities on the grades teachers assigned. Had I initially told the teachers of the true objective of the study, it is likely that they would have consciously attended to students' voices and assigned grades that they otherwise would not have assigned.

Sometimes deception is used to achieve a desired experimental effect. Suppose one is interested in examining gifted students' reactions to academic failure. Since it is unlikely that gifted students experience much academic failure, a researcher might administer an examination to the students and then tell them they had failed even though they had not. In this way the researcher could investigate how gifted students react when they believe they have failed academically.

Some researchers believe the use of deception so flagrantly violates the basic principle of an open and honest relationship between the researcher and the participant that they would consider any use of deception unethical. Since your primary purpose in carrying out an investigation is to learn about the research process rather than to generate new knowledge, it is best to avoid research questions that involve deception or concealment.

Additional Precautions When Using Deception. Other researchers believe that under certain circumstances the potential benefits of a study may outweigh the use of deception,

particularly if additional conditions are satisfied. For instance, the use of deception may be justified if the researcher (a) explains to the subjects at the conclusion of the study why it was necessary to use deception; and (b) has reason to believe that when told of the deception, the subjects will find its use reasonable. Other conditions that *may* make the use of deception more ethically acceptable are to make it clear to subjects that they may withdraw from the study at any time and that they may refuse to allow their data to be used after being told of the deception.

Dehoaxing and Desensitization. Two other conditions that *may* make the use of deception more ethically acceptable are **dehoaxing** and **desensitization.** Dehoaxing is the process by which the researcher makes sure after the completion of the study that subjects fully understand that they have been deceived, so that no permanent damage can be done to the subjects (Holmes, 1976a). For example, after having informed gifted students that they were falsely told they had failed an examination, one could show the students the actual scores they made.

Desensitization is the process of dealing with behaviors subjects may have displayed during an experiment that might cause them to feel negatively about themselves (Holmes, 1976b). Subjects who have participated in a study investigating conditions under which cheating behavior may occur, for example, may feel guilty for having cheated. The researcher has the obligation to help subjects eliminate their feelings of guilt. The researcher may accomplish this by explaining that it is the nature of the experimental situation that causes honest people to cheat and that most other subjects in the study also cheated.

The Use of Volunteers

Ideally in conducting research one would like all of the prospective subjects to agree to participate in the study voluntarily. What are the consequences, however, if some subjects either refuse to participate or, after having completed part of the study, decide they do not wish to continue participating? To what extent is it ethical to exert pressure on subjects to participate against their will? As noted previously, the refusal of some prospective subjects to participate in a study limits the generalizability of the study's findings to the population of people who would voluntarily agree to participate in the study.

One cannot generalize the findings to the entire population from which the sample was drawn because one has no way of knowing how people who refuse to participate differ systematically from those who volunteer. Several ethical questions arise in such situations. How important is it that the sample used in the study be an accurate representation of the population? How stressful are the research procedures likely to be for subjects? For example, are subjects to be exposed to potentially harmful drugs, or asked to memorize a list of nonsense syllables? What inducements are to be used to encourage subjects to participate and what sanctions may be imposed on subjects for the failure to participate?

Students who are conducting research for the purpose of learning about the research process should carry out studies only with people who volunteer to participate. It is only when research is being conducted to generate new knowledge that the question of generalizing the findings becomes important. The decision whether to exert pressure on subjects to participate or not must take into account the ethical questions listed previously.

Special Concerns for Educators Conducting Research with Students. Of special concern to students carrying out research projects to fulfill a requirement in an educational research course is that many such students are teachers, counselors, or school administrators who wish to carry out studies with their own students. Consequently, the researcher often has a position of authority over the subjects participating in a study.

Extra care must be taken to make sure that students who volunteer to participate in a study are not doing so because they are afraid that if they don't, they may anger the researcher (i.e., the authority figure) who may hold their refusal against them in the future. In such cases the researcher may take extra precautions, such as having somebody who does not know the students collect the data and by keeping students' responses anonymous. It should be made clear to whoever is collecting the data that students are free not to participate in the study from the very outset or at any time after the data collection procedure has started.

It would also be unethical to reward students for participating in a study with special favors that impinge on other aspects of the student's role as student. For example, it would be unethical to reward students who agree to participate in a study by giving them higher grades or excusing them from homework assignments.

Protection from Physical Danger and Mental Stress

The likelihood of exposing subjects to physical danger in educational research is usually minimal, given the kinds of questions educational researchers typically pursue. Nevertheless, such occasions may occur, and researchers need to be aware of the ethical issues involved. Consider the following examples:

1. A researcher wishes to study students' ability to process information as a function of distracting noise level. It is possible for the noise level to be increased to the point where students' hearing may be permanently damaged.
2. An industrial arts teacher wishes to investigate the effectiveness of teaching a unit on metalwork using equipment that is complicated to operate and, if used improperly, can injure students.
3. A physical education teacher wishes to study the effects of increasing the use of calisthenics on the endurance levels of members of a sports team. It is possible to increase the use of calisthenics to the point of physical exhaustion.

It should be obvious that beginning researchers should not undertake studies that involve a level of risk as high as that in the examples. If such studies were to be carried out, the researcher must not only weigh the benefit of the outcome of the study against the risk involved, but also make sure that subjects understand the possible risks and that they may withdraw from the study at any time.

It is more likely that mental stress rather than physical harm may be a risk in educational research. As mentioned earlier in the section dealing with deception, subjects may feel guilty for having displayed some sort of behavior during an experiment. Subtle forms of mental stress may also occur in studies that do not involve deception. Subjects who perform poorly on an academic achievement test given during a study investigating academic performance as a function of various factors may conclude on the basis of their performance that they are truly poor students.

Subjects may feel ashamed or embarrassed when asked to provide certain kinds of information about themselves or their families, such as how they feel about their siblings or parents. The researcher must try to anticipate aspects of the study that may be psychologically stressful for subjects and, if necessary, terminate the study unless there are compelling reasons for continuing.

Studies that investigate the effects of stressful variables such as loss of self-esteem or high levels of anxiety purposely place subjects under stress. If possible, subjects should be told of possible stressful feelings that they may experience as a result of participating in the study. In instances where revealing the potential stressful situation would affect the outcome of the study, subjects should be placed under the minimum level of stress for the least amount of time possible.

Sometimes it is possible to use simulated situations instead of placing subjects in actual situations to study the effects of variables. Instead of creating stressful situations and recording how subjects behave in the situation, one might ask subjects to describe how they *think* they would react in a hypothetical situation. The results of studies using simulated situations, of course, do not guarantee that subjects would behave in real situations the way they claim they would. Such a limitation is relatively unimportant for the purpose of most students' research projects.

It is sometimes also possible to investigate the effects of stressful variables by examining the effects of removing rather than applying stress. For example, ethically it is more desirable to investigate subjects' performance as a function of anxiety by creating a situation that reduces anxiety rather than one that increases it.

Researcher Responsibilities at the Conclusion of a Study

After a study has been completed, the researcher has the obligation to inform subjects as fully as possible about the nature of the research. In addition to telling subjects about any uses of deception, the researcher should explain why the study was carried out and what role the subject played in the study. Every effort should be made to make sure that subjects do not leave the experiment with misconceptions about what took place. Subjects should also be given the opportunity to learn the results of the study after the study has been completed.

Researchers should exercise special care when using children as subjects. Children may interpret even innocuous aspects of the experimental situation in ways that may never occur to an adult. Researchers should encourage children to ask questions about the research to clear up any misconceptions. In studies where children may have experienced failure at some task, researchers often end the study by using tasks that guarantee the child will succeed; this reduces the likelihood that the child will leave the experiment with a feeling of failure.

Anonymity and Confidentiality

Anonymity means that the researcher does not know who the participants in a study are. **Confidentiality,** on the other hand, means that the researcher knows who the participants are but will not divulge their names. Although anonymity is not possible in all studies, confidentiality is, and it is the researcher's responsibility to make sure that confidentiality is maintained. Researchers should not only inform subjects that information obtained during the course of a study will be treated confidentially, but take active measures to make sure that it is. Researchers should not reveal information about the subject to other persons, such as members of the subject's family or the subject's teachers. If others may have access to the information, you should explain this to subjects when you are receiving their informed consent to participate.

Keep subjects anonymous by assigning them a code number. It is sometimes easy for data sheets containing information about subjects to be seen by people who have no right to know the information. Compiling information by code number rather than by the subject's name reduces the likelihood that private information will be inadvertently revealed.

Try to avoid pursuing research questions that involve material that might be regarded as sensitive. The purpose of your study can be met without asking students such questions as how they feel about their parents or their siblings. If you feel your study must involve sensitive information, it is imperative to get written consent from adult subjects or from the parents or legal guardians of subjects who are children.

The issue of confidentiality applies not only to the individuals who participate in a study but also to places, such as institutions where the data were collected. When writing a final report about the study, it is best not to mention institutions by name. It is informative enough to the reader of a report to learn that data were collected from a public elementary school in a particular kind of socioeconomic area.

Eliminating Race and Gender Bias in Research and Evaluation

In 1985 the American Educational Research Association published a set of guidelines for eliminating race and gender bias in educational research and evaluation. The guidelines focus on threats to research that occur as a result of bias against women and minorities, who have historically been underrepresented and discriminated against. Figure 5.1 lists potential sources of such bias and possible ways of eliminating it.

Legal Aspects of Conducting Research

Laws pertaining to carrying out research stem largely from two pieces of legislation enacted in 1974: the National Research Act and the Family Educational Rights and Privacy Act, often referred to as the Buckley Amendment. The major thrust of all government regulations applying to researchers is to protect the rights of individuals who participate in a study. The Buckley Amendment protects the confidentiality of students' educational records, including the stipulation that research data be collected in ways that preclude the possibility of personally identifying students from whom data are collected.

As a result of the National Research Act, most universities and colleges have established Institutional Review Boards, whose function is to review research proposals to make sure that the rights of subjects are not violated. According to the *Code of Federal Regulations*, all research proposals involving human subjects must come before the Board for review, except those falling into one of the following categories. Many educational research projects fall into one of the categories and are exempted from review.

1. Research conducted in established or commonly accepted educational settings, involving normal educational settings, involving normal educational practices, such as:
   a. research on regular and special education instructional strategies or
   b. research on the effectiveness of or the comparison among instructional techniques, curricula, or classroom management methods.

Figure 5.1 Potential Sources of Race and Gender Bias and Possible Ways of Eliminating or Controlling Them

Potential Source of Bias

a. Research Topics

   Possible preventive measure: include women's and minorities' views about the topic.

b. Staffing

   Possible preventive measure: include minority and majority women and men on research and evaluation teams.

c. Research Design

   Possible preventive measure: report information on variables, such as socioeconomic status, that may be highly correlated with group membership and take into account the relationship when interpreting results.

d. Reviewing the Literature

   Possible preventive measure: include reviews of published research specifically focused on women and minorities and address important characteristics of potential participants.

e. Population and Sample Selection

   Possible preventive measure: if results are to be generalized across gender or race groups, make sure these groups are included in the sample; generalizations should be limited to members of gender or race groups represented in the sample.

f. Measuring Instruments

   Possible preventive measure: avoid offensive or inappropriate language or questions; include material relevant to women and minorities; make available relevant validity evidence for women and minorities.

g. Observations

   Possible preventive measure: control for possible effects of observers' stereotypes of appropriate behavior for members of different racial and gender groups.

h. Interviews

   Possible preventive measure: use interviewers who are balanced with respect to the gender and race of participants and, where possible, analyze data in terms of the interaction between interviewers' and participants' gender and race.

i. Documents

   Possible preventive measure: attempt to locate documents that reflect the experiences of women and minority men; if such materials are not available, the limitations of interpretations and generalizations should be described.

j. Interpretations and Conclusions

   Possible preventive measure: conclusions should be referenced directly to the study and alternative explanations not related to gender or cultural background should be explored.

k. Reporting Results

   Possible preventive measure: results should be reported to the public in ways to minimize the formation of unfounded conclusions about race and gender; results should be reported to participants and it should be pointed out if the design of the study precludes the inference of causal relationships.

2. Research involving the use of educational tests (cognitive, diagnostic, aptitude, achievement), if information taken from these sources is recorded in such a manner that subjects cannot be identified, directly or through identifiers linked to the subjects or that confidentiality will be protected by procedures appropriate to the sensitivity of the data.

3. Research involving survey or interview procedures, except where *all* (emphasis added) of the following conditions exist:
    a. responses are recorded in such a manner that the human subjects can be identified, directly or through identifiers linked to the subjects,
    b. the subject's responses, if they became known outside the research, could reasonably place the subject at risk of criminal or civil liability or be damaging to the subject's financial standing or employability, and
    c. the research deals with sensitive aspects of the subject's own behavior, such as illegal conduct, drug use, sexual behavior, or use of alcohol. All research involving survey or interview procedures may be deemed to be exempt when the respondents are elected or appointed public officials or candidates for public office.
4. Research involving the observation (including observation by participants) of public behavior, except where all of the following conditions exist:
    a. observations are recorded in such a manner that the human subjects can be identified, directly or through identifiers linked to the subjects,
    b. the observations recorded about the individual, if they became known outside the research could reasonably place the subject at risk of criminal or civil liability or be damaging to the subject's financial standing or employability, and
    c. the research deals with sensitive aspects of the subject's own behavior such as illegal conduct, drug use, sexual behavior, or use of alcohol.
5. Research involving the collection or study of existing data, documents, records, pathological specimens, or diagnostic specimens, if these sources are publicly available or if the information is obtained by the investigator in such a manner that subjects cannot be identified directly or through identifiers linked to the subjects, or that confidentiality will be protected by procedures appropriate to the sensitivity of the data.

A key provision in exempting a piece of educational research from review is the stipulation that the research involve *normal educational practices.* Howe and Dougherty (1993) point out, however, that the vagueness of this phrase leaves it open to varying interpretations and raises the issue of whose interpretation should be used. They note that interpretations by an Institutional Review Board, whose members generally are university faculty and typically have little idea of what normally takes place in public schools, might be at odds with interpretations by an educational researcher, who has a vested interest in conducting the research. As a solution, they suggest that the review process formally include school people to offer additional perspectives on what constitutes normal educational practices.

Existing regulations, of course, may change and there may be state as well as federal regulations that apply to carrying out research. A good source of information concerning government regulations is the grants officer of your college or university. An example of a request for approval by an Institutional Review Board for a research proposal involving human participants appears in Figure 5.2.

Plagiarism

Plagiarism involves using someone else's ideas or writings and passing them off as one's own. When preparing a written report of a study, the researcher has an ethical and legal responsibility to give credit to others for their ideas by providing appropriate reference citations.

Figure 5.2	Example of a Request for Approval by an Institutional Review Board for a Research Proposal Involving Human Participants

REQUEST FOR APPROVAL OF PROPOSAL INVOLVING HUMAN PARTICIPANTS

Date: _____

To: The College of Staten Island Institutional Review Board

From: _____ , Principal Investigator

Re: _____ , Proposal Title

Attached is a detailed description of my project and how I propose to use subjects.

I hereby certify that I have read the City University of New York policy and procedure statements with respect to the protection of human participants.

It is my belief that the above described project, which I plan to undertake, complies fully with the requirements of said policy. I am prepared to furnish, either in writing or orally, justification for any procedures if requested to do so. I also agree to furnish details of any change in plans or procedures made during the course of the investigation that is relevant to the protection of human participants involved in the project. Signed statements of consent from participants will be kept in my files and copies of all materials given to participants will be sent to the Institutional Review Board.

Below is a summary of the provisions that have been made for protection of participants to be used in this work. (If the space provided below for your reply is not adequate, please continue your explanation on a second page.)

1. PROTECTION OF THE RIGHTS AND WELFARE OF HUMAN PARTICIPANTS: (e.g., exposure to stress, physical, psychological or interpersonal hazard including possibility of pain, injury, disease, discomfort, embarrassment or anxiety; supervision of research personnel; fees; obligations; etc.)

2. METHODS USED TO OBTAIN INFORMED CONSENT: (e.g., how explained; precautions regarding anonymity, confidentiality, deception, obtaining of signatures, cooperation of parents or guardians of minors, legally incompetents, etc.?) PLEASE ATTACH SAMPLE OF CONSENT FORM TO BE USED.

3. RELATIVE WEIGHTS OF RISKS VERSUS BENEFITS:

Your approval is requested for this project.

_____
Signature of Principal Investigator

_____
Department

Chapter Highlights

- The major ethical question about carrying out a piece of research is whether the benefits of conducting the study outweigh the risks to persons participating in it.

- *Informed consent* involves making sure that potential subjects understand the general nature of the research project and pointing out aspects of the study that may influence them to decline to participate.

- Mentally competent adults (or the guardians of children or persons who may not be mentally competent) should sign a written consent form before participating in a study.

- *Concealment* occurs when a researcher tells subjects the truth, but not the whole truth about a study.

- *Deception* occurs when a researcher purposely provides subjects false information.

- Some researchers consider the use of deception as inherently unethical.

- At the conclusion of a study that has employed deception, researchers often use the process of (a) *dehoaxing* to make sure that subjects know they have been deceived and to avoid permanent damage or (b) *desensitization* to help subjects overcome negative feelings about behaviors they may have displayed while participating in a study.

- Although the use of volunteers as subjects may make it impossible to generalize a study's findings, the failure to do so raises serious ethical questions.

- Educators should not use their position of authority to coerce students to participate in a study.

- Participants in a study must be protected not only from physical danger but from mental stress as well.

- At the conclusion of a study, the researcher should make sure that participants, particularly children, do not leave with any misconceptions about what took place.

- Participants should be kept anonymous when possible, and information obtained during a study should be kept confidential.

- Gender and race bias can occur at any point in the research process, from conceptualizing the research topic to reporting the results of a study.

- Except under certain conditions described in the *Code of Federal Regulations,* all research proposals involving human subjects must be reviewed by an Institutional Review Board whose job is to make sure that subjects' rights are protected.

- Researchers have an ethical and legal responsibility to avoid plagiarism by crediting others by means of appropriate reference citations.

1. Define the term *informed consent*. What function does informed consent serve?

2. Compare *concealment* and *deception.*

3. List three reasons why researchers might consider using deception in carrying out a study.

4. What steps may researchers take to make the use of deception more justifiable ethically?

5. How do the processes of *dehoaxing* and *desensitization* differ?

6. What kinds of problems might arise as a result of using only volunteers as subjects in a study?

7. Describe the ethical issues confronting educators who carry out a study using their own students as subjects.

8. What kinds of mental stress may subjects experience as a result of participating in an educational research project?

9. What are some ways researchers may study the effects of stressful variables without placing subjects in stressful situations?

10. What steps should a researcher take after completing a study?

11. Why is it important to keep information gathered from subjects confidential?

12. In conducting research whose subjects include members of minorities, why is it important to report information about variables that may be highly correlated with group membership?

13. What measures can a researcher take to control for possible gender and race bias associated with conducting interviews?

14. What is the primary function of laws pertaining to research using humans as subjects?

15. Give an example of a research proposal that legally should be reviewed by an Institutional Review Board.

16. Under what conditions is it necessary for an Institutional Review Board to review a research proposal in which data are to be collected by means of interviews?

17. Give an example of plagiarism.

Chapter 6

Sampling: Choosing Participants for a Study

Pulling names out of a hat is probably the clearest example of random sampling.

Chapter Objectives

After completing this chapter, you should be able to:

- explain in what ways sampling units may vary
- name at least two ways of increasing response rate
- define *simple random sampling, stratified sampling, cluster sampling,* and *systematic sampling*
- use a table of random numbers to select a sample
- explain ways in which sampling procedures in ethnographic studies may differ from those used in quantitative studies

Most research questions pertain to populations. Studies carried out to answer these questions, however, are usually conducted with samples, not populations. Although the definition of

88

the population in a study is crucial, surprisingly it is often not reported in the literature. This chapter will focus on various ways of selecting samples so that it is reasonable to generalize a study's findings to the population from which the sample was selected.

Often the sampling unit is an individual person, but not necessarily. A researcher studying disruptive behavior in a classroom, for example, might decide to sample units of time. The researcher might select a sample of different times on different days of the week to observe the classroom because the amount of disruptive behavior might vary, depending on the time the observation is made.

A sampling unit may also consist of groups instead of individual persons. For example, a researcher may select a sample of first grade classrooms rather than a sample of individual first graders. Regardless of whether the sampling unit consists of nonhuman objects or events or individuals or groups of people, however, the same principles of sampling apply.

The first (and sometimes the only) question students usually raise about sampling is how large the sample must be. Unfortunately, there is no simple answer, because the question itself is not clear. To know how large a sample has to be, one first has to ask, "How large must a sample be to accomplish what purpose?" There are two reasons why researchers are concerned about sample size. The first has to do with how large a sample must be to be an accurate representation of the population from which it was drawn. The second question has to do with how large a sample has to be to achieve statistically significant results.

Both reasons for concern about the size of a sample are important. The answer to the question of how large a sample must be to be an accurate representation of the population is not simply a matter of deciding on some number of subjects. It is a question that perhaps more seriously involves deciding what procedures to use in selecting the subjects. The question of how large a sample should be for statistical analysis, on the other hand, is generally a matter of deciding to select some predetermined number of subjects to participate in the study. For more detailed information on sampling, see Jaeger (1984).

Samples as Representations of Populations

To gain some perspective on the issues involved in sampling, let us look at a hypothetical case. Suppose that the state department of education decides it is time to gather information about teacher practices in dealing with mainstreamed special education students. Because mainstreaming is relatively new, state authorities believe it is appropriate to determine how teachers go about instructing disabled students who are integrated into classes comprised mainly of nondisabled students. Perhaps the study is being conducted with the idea of producing guidelines to help regular education teachers throughout the state deal more effectively with disabled students, and the first step in establishing these guidelines is to ascertain what is currently taking place.

It would obviously be far too expensive and cumbersome for representatives from the state department of education to contact personally all the regular classroom teachers in the state who have had special education students mainstreamed into their classes. Consequently, it might be decided to conduct the study by mailing questionnaires to teachers throughout the state. When the completed questionnaires have been returned, the responses would be analyzed and an official report of the findings prepared.

There are many problems associated with questionnaires, and particularly with those that are mailed. However, for the moment let us focus only on problems that may arise because of sampling. Assuming that the questionnaire has been constructed well and that teachers have answered each question honestly and thoroughly, how much confidence can we have in the information the teachers have provided? Can we use that information to construct guidelines? It depends.

Response Rate

Let us assume that 3,000 teachers complete the questionnaire and return it. If there are in fact a total of 3,000 regular education teachers in the state who have special education students in their classes, the responses of 3,000 teachers means that 100% of the teachers surveyed have responded. We would be justified then in having considerable confidence in the information the teachers have provided. Suppose, however, that there are 30,000 such teachers in the state, all of whom have received the questionnaire. If 3,000 teachers return the questionnaire, it means that only 10% have responded. More importantly, 90% of the teachers surveyed have not responded. A sample size of 3,000 may appear large, but whether the 3,000 people in the sample adequately represent the population from which the sample was drawn is another story.

Can a sample that represents only 10% of the population be large enough to be an accurate representation of that population? It may surprise you to learn that a sample representing such a small percentage of the population might be quite sufficient. Think, for example, of the polls taken during election time. Pollsters obtain information from samples representing far less than 10% of the population of voters and yet are still able to predict the winners with considerable accuracy.

Sampling Bias. The question of whether the sample of 3,000 teachers constitutes a sufficiently large percentage to be an accurate representation of the population is not what we should be asking. A better question is what population the 3,000 teachers represent. Do the 3,000 teachers adequately represent the population of teachers who were surveyed? The answer is unequivocally *no!* The 3,000 teachers represent a sample of only those teachers who are willing to sit down and complete the questionnaire and mail it back. The 3,000 teachers do not represent the 27,000 teachers who did not complete it. In other words, the 3,000 teachers constitute a *biased sample* of the entire population.

Teachers who are willing to complete the questionnaire may be very different from teachers who are unwilling to complete it. We already know that the two groups differ with respect to their compliance with instructions from the state department of education, at least in terms of completing the questionnaire. It may be that the two groups differ as well in terms of the practices they follow in providing instruction to disabled students mainstreamed into their classrooms.

Consequently, the findings from the 3,000 teachers who responded can be justifiably generalized only to a population comprised of teachers who are willing to complete the questionnaire. The purpose of carrying out the survey, however, was to gather information that can be applied to all teachers in the state. If the sample of respondents is not an accurate representation of the population of all regular education teachers who have mainstreamed special education students in their classes, the survey has failed to achieve its goal.

Most educational research is carried out with subjects who have volunteered to participate in a study, such as the 3,000 teachers described previously. Rosenthal and Rosnow

(1975) have identified a number of characteristics that differentiate persons who volunteer to participate in a study and those who do not.

Volunteers, for example, tend to be more intelligent and better educated than nonvolunteers. Aside from the fact that volunteers represent a biased sample because they have different characteristics than other members of the population, the use of volunteers may sometimes lead to findings that are biased in predictable ways.

Suppose a school district decides to survey members of the community to find out the level of support for refurbishing a school's science laboratories with costly modern equipment. It is likely that people who voluntarily respond to the survey place more value on education than people who do not respond and consequently would probably tend to favor spending to modernize laboratory facilities.

Increasing Response Rate. The best way to overcome volunteer bias is to increase the response rate. Perhaps the survey of teachers described previously would have been more likely to succeed if different procedures for selecting the sample had been used. For example, one might have randomly selected the names of 500 regular teachers with mainstreamed classes, a number far less than 3,000. The point is that the 500 names have been randomly selected. Suppose again that only 10% of the 500 teachers fill out the questionnaire and return it. The researcher could then take steps to follow up on the 450 teachers who failed to respond. Perhaps some of the nonrespondents have misplaced the questionnaire or simply forgotten about it. Another mailing to the 450 teachers might be all that is necessary to get some of them to respond.

There will undoubtedly still be teachers in the sample who do not respond, but additional follow-up measures could be taken. Perhaps the researcher could place a phone call to the teachers who have not yet responded. Perhaps several phone calls would be necessary. Perhaps a phone call to the principals of the teachers' schools would do the trick, particularly if the researcher stresses to the principal how important it is to obtain as high a response rate as possible.

The researcher would hardly be completely successful in obtaining responses from all 500 teachers. A response rate of 85% or 90% of a relatively small number of randomly selected teachers, however, is more likely to yield reliable results than a biased sample of 3,000 teachers. Although the size of a sample is important in determining whether a sample accurately represents a population, it does not necessarily follow that larger samples are always better than smaller samples.

It is possible that respondents who answer after being followed up bear more resemblance to nonrespondents than to those who responded without any follow-up. Consequently, it is useful to compare statistically the responses of those who initially responded with the responses of those who responded after being followed up to see if there are significant differences.

Methods for Selecting a Sample

The single most important criterion for judging the adequacy of a sample of any size is the extent to which the sample is an unbiased representation of the population from which it was drawn. The best way to increase the chances of achieving an unbiased sample is to make sure that the sample is randomly drawn. When we say that a sample is a **random sample,** we mean that each member of the population had an equal chance of being selected as part of it.

Random Sampling

For example, if we had been able to put into a hat the names of the 30,000 regular education teachers in the state who have mainstreamed special education students in their classes and randomly pull out 500 names, we would have obtained a random sample. There is no guarantee that pulling names out of a hat will yield a sample that accurately represents the population, but the chances of such a result are increased. In part, how accurately a randomly drawn sample represents the population depends on the size of the sample that is drawn. We are surely likely to have a highly accurate representation if we pull 29,999 names out of a hat that contains 30,000 names. On the other hand, if we pull 5 names from a hat containing 30,000 names, it is unlikely that the sample will adequately represent the population even though the pull is completely random.

There are procedures for estimating how large a sample must be to represent a population within a specified margin of error. In practice, however, most researchers rely on their own intuitive judgments when deciding how large a sample should be drawn. To some extent, researchers' judgments about sample size are determined by statistical considerations, which will be discussed a bit further on. Let us focus simply on the concept of random sampling for the moment and what that concept means. Pulling names out of a hat is probably the clearest example of random sampling.

It should be obvious, however, that you cannot put the names of 30,000 teachers into a hat unless you can identify each teacher by name. The notion of putting the names of every member of a population into a hat in order to draw a random sample clearly conveys the principle of random sampling, but such a procedure is seldom used, particularly if the size of the population is large.

Instead of putting names into a hat, a researcher would probably use a table of random numbers to select the sample. Using a table of random numbers to generate a sample is more convenient than putting names in a hat, but both procedures rely on the same principle underlying random sampling, which is that the sample is drawn in such a way that every member of the population has an equal chance of being selected as part of the sample.

To demonstrate how one uses a table of random numbers to select a sample of 500 teachers from a population of 30,000 teachers, a portion of a table of random numbers is reproduced in Figure 6.1. In addition to a table of random numbers, it is necessary to have a listing of the names of all 30,000 teachers, which probably could be fairly easily generated in the form of a computer printout. Each teacher would be assigned a consecutive number beginning with 00001 and ending with 30000.

To use a table of random numbers one enters the table at any arbitrary point. Suppose one entered the table using number 27993, which is the second number in column b. The teacher whose number is 27993 on the computer printout then becomes the first teacher selected for the sample. One then continues down column b to the next number, which is 71146. Because there are only 30,000 teachers on the list, there is no teacher with the number 71146, so one skips 71146 and moves on to the next number in column b, which is 10005. The teacher whose number is 10005 on the computer printout then becomes the second teacher selected for the sample. The process continues until the desired sample size of 500 has been reached. After reaching the bottom of column b one moves to the top of column c and continues the process.

Suppose we have a population of 3,000 rather than 30,000 persons from which we wish to select a random sample. The numbers assigned to members of our population would

Figure 6.1   Part of a Table of Random Numbers

(a)	(b)	(c)	(d)
61424	20419	86546	00517
90222	27993	04952	66762
50349	71146	97668	86523
85676	10005	08216	25906
02429	19761	15370	43882
90519	61988	40164	15815
20631	88967	19660	89624
89990	78733	16447	27932

therefore begin with 00001 and end with 03000. In using the numbers listed in Figure 6.1, we would have to skip all those greater than 03000 because no member of our population has a number that large. Of the 32 numbers listed in Figure 6.1, only two are smaller than 03000. To avoid having to skip so many numbers in the table, a researcher would probably ignore the first digit appearing in the list of random numbers. For example, the first number in column a would be read as 1424 instead of 61424 as it appears in the table. By ignoring the first digit of the numbers in the table, 12 rather than two of the numbers in the list coincide with numbers that have been assigned to members of our population. If the population had consisted of 300 rather than 3,000 people, a researcher would ignore the first two digits of numbers in the table so that 61424 would be read as 424.

In most studies, sampling is necessarily carried out by procedures other than random sampling. Suppose, for example, one wished to determine if there is a significant difference between the attention span of neurologically impaired students and emotionally disturbed students. How could one possibly identify all neurologically impaired students or all emotionally disturbed students? Probably the best one could do is to find a group of each who one feels intuitively are probably representative of the respective populations. Most published studies rely on samples drawn in such a manner. It is usually up to the reader of an article to decide if the subjects in the study represent a reasonably unbiased sample of the population to which the results of the study are to be generalized.

Random Sampling and Random Assignment. It is useful at this point to clarify the difference between **random sampling** and **random assignment.** In a study comparing instructional methods, the notion of random sampling may be used in a hypothetical sense, but the process of random assignment is used in a very real sense. The names of students participating in a study comparing the effects of Method A with the effects of Method B often really are put in a hat and a random pull is used to assign the students to one instructional group or the other. However, randomly assigning students to the two instructional groups has nothing to do with randomly selecting the sample of students who participate in the study from some larger population of students.

Stratified Sampling

Situations frequently occur in educational settings for which simple random sampling may not be appropriate. If the accessible populations to be studied vary drastically in size, it is probably best to use what is called **stratified sampling.** Suppose that a researcher wishes to carry out a study in a school system to see how some instructional procedure works as a function of whether students are monolingual or bilingual. Let us assume that in the school system 75% of the students are monolingual and speak standard English, 20% are bilingual Hispanic students, and 5% are bilingual Asian students.

If the researcher is interested in determining how effective the instructional procedure is throughout the school system, the students in the system should first be stratified into three groups corresponding to the students' native language. From each group, a number of students would be selected that reflects the proportion of the total population represented by that group. In other words, if a total sample size of 100 is to be used, 75 students would be randomly selected from the monolingual group, 20 students from the bilingual Hispanic group and 5 students from the bilingual Asian group. If the students were not first stratified by their native language and the procedure of simple random sampling used, the result might be a sample that does not reflect accurately the proportion of students in the population having different native languages.

Size of Subgroups. On the other hand, perhaps the researcher is concerned with the possibility that the instructional procedure may have different degrees of success with bilingual students, depending on their native languages. Consequently, the researcher would probably decide to examine possible differences among the three groups of students. If the procedure of stratified sampling were used, only five Asian students would participate in the study.

A sample of five Asian students is far too small. Possible differences between the Asian students' performance and the performance of other students would likely go undetected simply because the number of students is so small. To be sure of having a sufficient number of students in each of the three samples, the researcher could first stratify the entire student population of the school system into three subpopulations, one consisting of monolingual students, one of Hispanic students, and one of Asian students. From each of the three subpopulations, the researcher would randomly draw the number of students deemed necessary to carry out an appropriate statistical analysis of the data. In all likelihood the researcher would select the same number of students from each of the three groups even though it is not mandatory that all groups have the same number of people.

The exact number of students to be selected for a sample is determined in part by what kind of statistical analysis the researcher intends to apply. In the current example, the researcher would be comparing the scores of three groups. Probably each sample would contain approximately 25 or 30 students. Had this been a correlational study, the researcher probably would have attempted to obtain larger sample sizes, perhaps on the order of 100 students each. Figure 6.2 illustrates the two uses of stratified sampling.

Cluster Sampling

Even in situations where every member of a population can be identified, the sample selected for participation in a study still may not be chosen by simple random sampling. For example, suppose that the state department of education wants to find out if including a unit on drug

| Figure 6.2 | Illustrations of Two Uses of Stratified Sampling |

Population of 4,000 students includes:

3,000 monolingual English-speaking students (75%)

800 bilingual Hispanic students (20%)

200 bilingual Asian students (5%)

A sample of 300 students reflecting the proportions of the three subgroups in the population would include:

225 monolingual English-speaking students (75%)

60 bilingual Hispanic students (20%)

20 bilingual Asian students (5%)

A sample of 300 students with equal numbers in each subgroup for a group comparison study would include:

100 monolingual English-speaking students (33%)

100 bilingual Hispanic students (33%)

100 bilingual Asian students (33%)

abuse in the seventh-grade social studies curriculum will reduce the amount of drug abuse among teenagers in the state. Furthermore, suppose that it would be possible to obtain a list of the names of all seventh graders in the state. It would not be feasible to select students to participate in the study by randomly choosing individual names. One would likely wind up with a sample consisting of individual students who reside in all parts of the state and who could not possibly be grouped together for instruction on drug abuse.

To conduct a study such as the one described, one would probably use a procedure called **cluster sampling** to obtain subjects. Cluster sampling is a form of random sampling in which a series of random selections is made from units of progressively smaller size. For example, one might first make a list of all the counties in the state. From that list, a random selection of counties would be made. Those counties not selected would be eliminated from further consideration and not included in the study. A list might then be made of all the school districts for each selected county. From each of these lists, a sample of school districts would be randomly drawn. A list of schools with seventh-grade classes would be made for each selected school district. From these lists, a sample of schools would be randomly selected, and finally from the selected schools, a random selection of seventh-grade classes would be made. The students in these classes would be the subjects in the study. Figure 6.3 illustrates the use of cluster sampling.

Systematic Sampling

As described earlier, one may use a table of random numbers to select a sample if one has access to a list of the names of every member of a population. Using a table of random numbers is not the only way, however, to select a sample from a population list. Suppose, for example, one wished to conduct a study using high school seniors in a particular school district. Assuming one had access to a list of the names of all of the seniors, one could select a sample by using an alternative method called **systematic sampling.**

Figure 6.3

The Use of Cluster Sampling to Select a Sample of Seventh Grade
Classrooms Within a State

Population:	All seventh grade classrooms in a state
Cluster 1:	Randomly selected counties within the state
Cluster 2:	Randomly selected school districts within counties comprising Cluster 1
Cluster 3:	Randomly selected schools within school districts comprising Cluster 2
Final Sample:	Randomly selected seventh grade classrooms within schools comprising Cluster 3

Figure 6.4

The Use of Systematic Sampling to Select a Sample of 50 Seniors from
a Population of 200

List of 200 Seniors

Student 001	Student ——
Student 002	Student ——
*Student 003	Student 186
Student 004	*Student 187
Student 005	Student 188
Student 006	Student 189
*Student 007	Student 190
Student 008	*Student 191
Student 009	Student 192
Student 010	Student 193
*Student 011	Student 194
Student 012	*Student 195
Student 013	Student 196
Student 014	Student 197
*Student 015	Student 198
Student ——	*Student 199
Student ——	Student 200

*Students selected in the sample. Beginning
with student 003, select every fourth student.

Assume there is a list of 200 seniors' names and one wished to select a random sample
of size 50. Dividing the total number in the population (200) by the desired sample size (50),
gives the number 4. By randomly starting with a number from 1 to 4 (e.g., 3), one would be
able to select a sample of size 50 by selecting that senior (i.e., the third student on the list)
and thereafter every fourth student on the list (i.e., the seventh student, the eleventh student,

the fifteenth student, and so forth) until the final student (number 199) has been selected as part of the sample. Figure 6.4 illustrates systematic sampling.

Systematic sampling may also be used to select a random sample from an indeterminate population. For example, suppose a researcher wishes to distribute a questionnaire to a sample consisting of 20% (i.e., one fifth) of the parents attending a PTA meeting. By randomly choosing a number between 1 and 5 and distributing the questionnaire to that parent who shows up and to every subsequent fifth parent, the researcher would obtain a random sample. If, for example, the researcher randomly chose the number 3, then the questionnaire would be distributed to the third, eighth, thirteenth, eighteenth, and so forth parent who arrived at the meeting.

Sample Sizes in Students' Research Projects

Despite all the preceding discussion about sampling issues, no definitive answer has been given to the question of how large the samples in your study should be. As you have no doubt realized by now, there is no definitive answer. However, it is possible to give you a few guidelines as to what is realistic in terms of the size of the samples you will select for your own study.

As much as possible you should try to use the procedures of simple random sampling, cluster sampling, systematic sampling, or stratified sampling. Which of the four sampling procedures you use depends on what particular situation you are in and what kind of research question you decide to investigate. Most students wind up using what may best be described as samples of convenience. Finding subjects to participate in a study is often difficult, and students are often forced to use whatever subjects they have available.

There is nothing wrong with using samples of convenience as long as you are aware that that is what you are doing and as long as you keep in mind that the purpose of carrying out your study is primarily to enable you to learn about research rather than to generate new knowledge. Knowledge based on data gathered from samples of convenience is obviously highly questionable. Do the best you can in selecting samples. Try to use sound sampling procedures and obtain as many subjects as feasible. Remember that you are not going to learn very much more about the research process whether you use samples of 30 or 300.

If you intend to carry out a group comparison study, try to obtain at least 15 subjects in each group. If you are planning a correlational study, aim for at least 30 subjects. In terms of statistical analysis, the larger the samples, the more likely you are to obtain statistically significant results. However, you should be aware that the increased likelihood of obtaining significant findings by increasing your sample sizes operates in a decelerating manner. In other words, if you are working with very small samples, the increase of every additional subject greatly enhances the likelihood of your obtaining significant results. If your sample sizes are already fairly large, adding more subjects will only slightly increase your chances of obtaining significant results.

Students in special education, for example, often have access to populations of very limited size. Every effort should be made to increase the number of subjects by even one more person. However, regardless of how small your samples are, you can still carry out a study. Unfortunately, small sample sizes are likely to yield nonsignificant findings, and you are likely to be denied the excitement one experiences when one's hypothesis turns out to be confirmed. Nevertheless, you can still learn much about the research process.

Sampling in Ethnographic Studies

We have so far examined methods of selecting random samples used mainly by quantitative researchers, whose objective is almost always to generalize their findings to populations. The objective of generalizing findings to persons who have *not* participated in a study forces researchers to select samples that accurately represent populations. The issue of generalizing a study's findings may or may not be of interest to ethnographic researchers. If they wish to generalize the findings of a study, ethnographic researchers also use random sampling. Regardless of whether ethnographic researchers choose to use random sampling or not, however, they characteristically use other sampling techniques that are sometimes called **purposeful sampling** or **criterion-based selection** (LeCompte & Preissle, 1993). In applying such techniques, ethnographic researchers identify particular attributes they want participants in a study to have and then actively seek persons who have them. Sometimes ethnographic researchers choose as part of their sample people they believe are likely to be particularly good sources of information about a particular question.

For example, a researcher carrying out an ethnographic study in an educational setting may purposely seek out a teacher who has been employed at the research site for a long time in order to gather information about the historical development of the setting. As another example, a researcher may choose to interview one person rather than another because that person seems particularly insightful and articulate.

Whereas quantitative researchers select samples before beginning to collect data, ethnographic researchers do not necessarily do so. Ethnographic researchers may begin their study with a tentative idea of who will comprise their samples, but as the nature of the study evolves and different questions emerge, so does the nature of the selected samples. See LeCompte and Preissle (1993), especially chapter 3, for more detailed information about sampling procedures used in ethnographic research.

Chapter Highlights

- Sampling units may consist of individuals or groups of persons or things.
- Larger samples are not necessarily better than smaller samples in terms of representativeness of a population; more important is the procedure used to select the sample.
- A low response rate to a mailed questionnaire is likely to yield a biased sample.
- The term *random sample* applies to samples that have been selected in such a way that every member of the population had an equal chance of being included in the sample.
- Researchers sometimes use a table of random numbers to select a random sample.
- *Random assignment* is different from *random sampling;* random assignment refers to the process in which persons in an experiment are assigned to the groups to be investigated.
- *Stratified sampling* requires that a population be broken into subpopulations prior to selecting the sample.

- The size of stratified samples may be chosen either to reflect the proportional representation of subgroups in the population or to have equal numbers.
- The procedure of *cluster sampling* involves the random selection of sampling units of progressively smaller size.
- *Systematic sampling* is a procedure of obtaining a random sample from a list of the members of a population by selecting every nth name.
- Samples of convenience are not random samples; they are groups of persons the researcher happened to be able to select with ease.
- Ethnographic researchers often use *purposeful sampling* in order to obtain persons who are most likely to be able to provide information about a particular research question.

Review Exercises

1. Give two reasons why the size of a sample is important to researchers.
2. What is the major sampling problem associated with studies using mailed questionnaires?
3. Describe some of the problems with using samples comprised of volunteers and ways in which these problems can be overcome.
4. Give an example of how you would select a random sample of students at your college or university.
5. Explain the difference between random sampling and random assignment.
6. Describe a situation in which it would be appropriate to use cluster sampling.
7. Describe a situation in which it would be appropriate to use systematic sampling.
8. Give an example of a situation where it would be appropriate to use stratified sampling and explain how you would carry out the sampling process.
9. Give an example of a situation in which a researcher might want to use purposeful sampling.
10. Give an example of a sample of convenience.

Chapter 7

Evaluating, Locating, and Constructing Measuring Instruments

Measures that involve some form of observation or that involve interpretation on the part of the evaluator are usually checked for objectivity by comparing the ratings assigned by two or more raters.

Chapter Objectives

After completing this chapter, you should be able to:

- define the terms *validity* and *reliability* and explain how they are related to one another
- describe at least three ways of determining the reliability of a test
- describe three types of validity and explain how they are related to one another
- distinguish among *obtained scores, true scores,* and *error scores*
- explain what *standard error or measurement* means
- describe the characteristics of an *objective measure*
- describe the properties of standardized tests
- identify at least five sources of information about commercially available tests and measuring instruments
- construct your own questionnaires, attitudinal measures, checklists, and rating scales

The last chapter discussed the important issue of selecting people to participate in a study. Various ways of sampling were presented that permit the researcher to select a sample representative of the population to which the findings of a study are to be applied. It was noted that sample size, in and of itself, is not a sufficient criterion for determining the adequacy of a sample. The single most important characteristic that determines whether a sample is adequate or not is whether the process used to choose the sample ensures that the sample is an unbiased representation of the population.

Let us now look at another factor involved in the preparations for conducting a study: the instruments used to measure the variables being investigated. Problems associated with the measurement of variables apply to all empirical studies.

Measuring Instruments and Operational Definitions

As noted before, many operational definitions in educational research are expressed in the form of test scores. When a researcher is investigating the variable of reading comprehension, for example, reading comprehension is defined operationally as the score on some reading comprehension test. When a researcher is investigating the variable of self-concept, the variable may be defined operationally by a score on a self-concept questionnaire.

Since tests are so frequently used to define variables operationally, it is useful to have some way to decide whether a test has been constructed well or not. The quality of a test is usually judged by its validity and reliability, two properties that characterize all tests. A test is valid to the extent that its scores permit one to draw appropriate, meaningful, and useful inferences, and it is reliable to the extent that whatever it measures, it measures consistently. Of the two properties, validity is the more important. It is much more difficult, however, to determine a test's validity than its reliability. See Gronlund and Linn (1990) for a comprehensive discussion of reliability and validity.

Before discussing test validity and test reliability, we should examine how they are related to each other. The concepts are related in such a way that it is sometimes possible to know something about a test's reliability if one already knows how valid the test is. Even more important in a practical sense is that if one knows how reliable a test is, one can sometimes make a judgment about the test's validity. Making a judgment about a test's validity on the basis of its reliability is important from a practical point of view because it is so much easier to determine reliability than validity.

Reliability and Validity

Shortly, we will discuss how to determine a test's reliability and validity. Assuming that we know how these test properties can be determined, let us focus only on how the two properties are related.

Consider the possibility that we have a test that is known to be a valid measure of one's ability to read French. Having such a test permits us to conclude that people who score high on the test are more proficient in reading French than those who score low. If, however, we were to administer the French test to a group of students studying Greek, the scores would tell us nothing about students' proficiency in reading Greek.

The Meaning of Test Validity

A test is valid only for some purpose and with some group of people. It is meaningless to speak of a test's validity in any absolute sense of the term. A French test may be valid for measuring one's proficiency in reading French, but it is not a valid test for measuring proficiency in reading Greek. Similarly, a French test may be a valid measure of college students' ability to read French but not a valid measure of the ability to read French exhibited by a group of junior high school students who are studying French. Throughout the following discussion of the relationship between validity and reliability, the term **validity** will be used to mean that scores on a test permit appropriate inferences to be made about a specific group of people for specific purposes.

The Meaning of Test Reliability

What does it mean when we say a test is reliable? We are saying that the test provides a consistent measure. **Reliability** refers to consistency of measurement; the more reliable a test is, the more consistent the measure. To illustrate the notion of consistency of measurement, suppose we had a *perfectly* reliable test. If we administered the test to a group of people and then could erase their memories of taking the test, the same people would make the exact same score on the test if we administered it to them again under precisely the same conditions.

The Relationship Between Validity and Reliability

If we know a test is valid, can we say anything about its reliability? Yes, we can. If a test provides scores that permit us to draw appropriate inferences, it must be doing so consistently. Consequently, a valid test must be a reliable test. Suppose, on the other hand, we know that a test is *not* valid. Can we say anything about the reliability of the test? No, we cannot. The fact that the scores on a test do not permit us to draw appropriate inferences does not mean that the test is not measuring anything consistently. For example, a test of mathematics achievement containing many word problems may not be a valid measure of mathematics achievement; it may, however, be a reliable measure of reading comprehension. A test that is not valid may or may not be reliable.

Consider a different set of circumstances. Suppose we know that a test is reliable. Can we say anything about its validity? No, we cannot. All we know is that the test is measuring something consistently, but we have no way of knowing if the test scores permit us to draw

Figure 7.1

Figure 7.1   The Relationship Between Validity and Reliability

If a test is known to be: One can conclude:

(1) valid   – – – – – ➤ the test must be reliable

(2) not valid   – – – – ➤ nothing about the reliability of the test

(3) reliable   – – – – – ➤ nothing about the validity of the test

(4) not reliable   – – – ➤ the test cannot be valid

appropriate inferences or not. The fact that a test is reliable tells us nothing about the test's validity. A reliable test may or may not be valid. Now let us look at the final possible combination of validity and reliability. Suppose we know that a test is *not* reliable. Can we say anything about its validity? Yes, we can. If the test is not measuring anything consistently, we cannot possibly use the test scores to make appropriate inferences. If a test is not reliable, it is not valid. Figure 7.1 shows the relationship between validity and reliability.

The fact that the lack of reliability signals the lack of validity often turns out to be useful in a practical way. To determine whether a test is a good one, what we really need to know is whether it is valid or not. Frequently it is not possible to determine how valid a test is. However, usually we can determine how reliable a test is fairly easily. Although establishing that a test is reliable does not permit us to determine whether it is valid or not, establishing that a test is *not* reliable enables us to know at least that it is not valid. Sometimes it is extremely useful to know that a particular test is not valid.

Determining Reliability

Recall the hypothetical description of reliability given earlier in this chapter. We saw that a test would be completely reliable if a group of people took the same test twice and scored exactly the same both times, assuming that hypothetically the test takers' memories of taking the test could be completely erased between the two administrations of the test. Ignore for the moment the impossibility of erasing people's memories completely between the two test administrations. We will shortly discuss how researchers cope with this impossibility. Instead, notice that in this hypothetical situation one could list the names of the test takers in rank order according to the scores they received the first time they took the test and then again according to their scores the second time.

If the test were perfectly reliable, each person's score on the first test would be identical to his or her score on the second test, so the two lists would be comprised of the same rank orderings of names. The more unreliable a test, the more the rank order of the names would differ on the two lists. The more reliable a test, the more alike the rank order of names would be on the two lists. The statistic used to describe how similar the two lists are is called the reliability coefficient and is symbolized by r. Reliability coefficients cannot exceed 1.00; an r value of 1.00 indicates perfect reliability. As r approaches 0, the reliability of a test becomes lower and lower. Reliability is a special instance of correlation, a topic that is discussed in chapter 8.

Test-Retest Reliability

The problem with the hypothetical description of reliability, of course, is that one cannot completely erase people's memories between the time the test is first administered and when it is administered again. We deal with this impossibility in two ways. The first way is to administer a test once and let time elapse before administering the test the second time. The question is how much time should elapse between the two test administrations. One wants to specify a sufficiently long time lapse so that one can be reasonably sure that the test takers will have forgotten most of the items on the test. On the other hand, the interval should not be so long that the people themselves have changed.

Suppose a researcher wants to establish the reliability of a reading readiness test. If the researcher administers the test to a group of kindergartners and waits only 10 minutes before readministering the same test to the same students, it is likely that most students will re-member many of the test items. If the researcher waits five years before administering the test the second time, the students will have matured so much in the meantime that they really are not the same as they were when they first took the test.

There is no hard and fast rule about how much time should elapse between the two test administrations. How much time a researcher decides on depends on the nature of the test as well as on the nature of the test takers. It is not uncommon to find the length of time that has elapsed between two administrations of the same test to range from one or two weeks to one or two months.

The procedure of checking a test's reliability by administering the same test twice is called the **test-retest method.** The same people must take the test twice. Administering the test once to one group of people and again to another group of people does not give any information about the test's reliability. The test-retest method of checking reliability is a fairly common way to determine the reliability of a test. The biggest drawback of the method is that there is no way of being sure that the test takers have really forgotten the items on the test. As we will see, however, no method of determining the reliability of a test is completely free of problems.

Parallel Forms Reliability

A second way researchers overcome the impossibility of completely erasing test takers' memories between two administrations of the same test is to develop two forms of the same test. In other words, two tests are developed to measure the same variable, but the items on the two tests are different. The two tests developed to measure the same variable are usually called **parallel forms** or **equivalent forms.**

For example, a researcher who is interested in establishing the reliability of an arithmetic achievement test by means of parallel forms would develop two tests with similar, but dif-ferent, items. If one function of the test is to measure how well students can add two one-digit numbers, on one form of the test an item might require the student to add 7 and 4, while on the other form of the test the student might be required to add 5 and 8. Even though the two items are not identical, both items are basically measuring the same thing, which is the student's ability to add two one-digit numbers.

The advantage of using parallel forms rather than the test-retest method is that, with parallel forms, the problem of memory is completely eliminated because the two forms consist of different sets of items. The disadvantage of using parallel forms, however, is that precisely because the sets of items on the two forms are different, one cannot be completely sure that they are really measuring the same thing.

Split-Half Reliability

One problem associated with both parallel forms and the test-retest method is the need of having to get the same group of people together twice for the purpose of administering the tests. Often it is difficult to get a group of people together once for administering a test, and to get the same people together twice can be extremely difficult.

To determine the reliability of a test without having to arrange for testing the same group of people twice, researchers have developed a method known as the **split-half reliability** method. The split-half method is probably the most commonly used way of determining a test's reliability. It is used so frequently because it is so easy to do. The statistical calculations are exactly the same as those used with the test-retest method and with parallel forms, but the decided advantage is that the test needs to be administered only once. Furthermore, the split-half method also overcomes the problem of test takers remembering questions from one test to another.

The Relationship Between Split-Half and Parallel Forms Reliability. Conceptually, the split-half method is similar to the method of parallel forms. However, instead of administering two forms of the same test at different times, the researcher administers a single test at a single administration. To determine the test's reliability, however, the researcher conceptualizes the one test that has been administered as consisting of two halves, which may be regarded as two parallel forms of the same test. In other words, it is as though the researcher pretends that all the items from two parallel forms of a test have been combined and administered as a single test.

The people taking the test are, of course, taking only one test, but the researcher treats the scores as though they have come from two parallel forms. For example, if a test consists of 100 items, the researcher pretends that 50 items constitute one form of the test and the other 50 items constitute a parallel form of the same test. In order to determine the reliability of the test, the researcher compares the ranking of people in terms of their scores on the one set of 50 items with their ranking on the other set. To the extent that the rankings are the same on both sets of 50 items, the test is reliable.

By comparing two subtotal scores from the same test, the researcher is able to determine the reliability of the test without having to administer the test more than once. Hypothetically, a test consisting of 100 items can be split a number of ways into two subtests, each of which is comprised of 50 items. For example, the researcher could compare the scores on the first 50 items with the scores on the second 50 items. In other words, one subtotal could be calculated from the scores on items 1 through 50 and compared with the other subtotal calculated from the scores on items 51 through 100. The researcher could combine the scores on items 1 through 25 with the scores on items 76 through 100 to get one subtotal and compare that subtotal with the subtotal calculated from the scores on items 26 through 75. In both cases the researcher would be comparing the scores of one set of 50 items with the scores on a different set of 50 items.

Splitting Items into Halves. In determining the reliability of a test using the split-half method, researchers always split the items into two halves consisting, respectively, of the

odd-numbered and the even-numbered items. To obtain one subtotal score, the researcher adds up the scores on items 1, 3, 5, 7, and so forth until the scores on all odd-numbered items have been summed, and then the researcher adds up the scores on all the even-numbered items to obtain the second subtotal score.

The reason researchers split the items into those with odd numbers and those with even numbers is to counterbalance any effects that may be associated with the order in which items appear on a test. For example, it may be that the items on a test are arranged so that the further one proceeds in the test, the more difficult the items become. Obviously, if one took the score on the first half of the items, it is likely to be higher than the score on the second half of the items. If the items on a test are of uniform difficulty throughout the test, the beginning items might serve as a form of practice, and people's performance might get better and better as they continue. Again, splitting the items into the first and last halves would likely yield different subtotal scores. By splitting the items in an odd-even fashion, any effects associated with the placement of items on the test are likely to apply comparably to both groups of items. (Box 8.3 in chapter 8 shows how to calculate a split-half reliability coefficient.)

Reliability and Test Length. Before leaving the topic of split-half reliability, it is important to point out one fundamental feature concerning reliability that has not yet been mentioned. The reliability of a test is directly related to the length of the test. A test of 100 items will generally be more reliable than a test of 15 items simply because of the larger number of items.

If one thinks of each item on a test as a sample of the behavior that the test is measuring, it seems reasonable that the more samples of the behavior one obtains, the more consistent the measure of the behavior will be. Remember, we are talking about reliability, not validity. We are not saying that the longer a test is, the more likely it is that it will be measuring what it claims to be measuring. We are only saying that whatever the test is measuring generally will be measured more consistently as the number of test items is increased.

The relationship between the number of items on a test and the test's reliability has nothing to do with the procedure that one uses to determine reliability. The greater the number of test items, the more reliable the test is likely to be regardless of whether the reliability is being determined by means of the test-retest method, the parallel forms method, or the split-half reliability method.

Correcting for Test Length. However, when one uses the split-half reliability method, one is really treating a test as though it contains only half the number of items it actually contains. When a split-half reliability coefficient is calculated for a test consisting of 100 items, it is as though one is calculating a reliability coefficient for parallel forms of a test that consists only of 50 items. Consequently, a split-half reliability coefficient always underestimates the reliability of a test because it is based on a reduced number of items. There is a way, however, in which a split-half reliability coefficient can be increased to provide a more accurate estimate of the test's reliability. We will not discuss that way other than to mention that it is called the Spearman-Brown prophecy formula. The formula is used to correct a reliability coefficient for test length and is used only with split-half reliability coefficients.

Figure 7.2   Ways of Determining Reliability

Stability Over Time	Internal Consistency
Test-Retest	Split-Half
Parallel or Equivalent Forms	Kuder-Richardson Formula 20
	Kuder-Richardson Formula 21
	Cronbach's Alpha

The Kuder-Richardson Formulas and Cronbach's Alpha

Researchers sometimes determine the reliability of a test by using one of two statistical formulas called **Kuder-Richardson Formula Number 20** and **Kuder-Richardson Formula Number 21.** The statistical calculations involved with K-R 20 are so complicated that K-R 21 was developed to allow a reasonably close approximation of the reliability coefficient generated by K-R 20 without having to carry out so many calculations.

The effect of the Kuder-Richardson formulas is to produce a reliability coefficient that is approximately what one would obtain if one were to split test items into all possible halves, calculate a split-half reliability coefficient for each split, and take the average of all the split-half reliability coefficients.

The Kuder-Richardson formulas may be used only with measuring instruments whose items are scored either correct or incorrect. The items on some measuring instruments, however, may take on several scores, such as questionnaires that consist of statements to which respondents are instructed to indicate their extent of agreement or disagreement. The possible responses for each statement often consist of *strongly agree, agree, undecided, disagree,* and *strongly disagree.* Consequently, the score a respondent receives on each statement may take on one of five values, depending on which response was selected. **Cronbach's alpha,** which is conceptually related to the Kuder-Richardson formulas, may be used to determine the reliability of such instruments (Cronbach, 1951).

The two most common ways used by students to determine the reliability of measuring instruments they themselves have designed are Formula 21 and the split-half reliability co-efficient. The test-retest method and parallel forms are almost never used by students.

A reliability coefficient is interpreted exactly the same way no matter what procedure was used to calculate it. The closer the reliability coefficient is to +1.00, the more reliable the test. The closer the reliability coefficient is to 0, the less reliable the test. Figure 7.2 lists various ways of determining reliability.

Interrater Reliability

The discussion of reliability so far has been based on the tacit assumption that the test whose reliability is to be determined is a paper and pencil test consisting of a number of discrete items. However, the kinds of measures used in educational research are not always paper and pencil tests and do not always consist of items that can be scored separately.

For example, tests of students' writing ability are usually in the form of essays. Essays may be a form of paper and pencil test, but they do not consist of separate items that can be objectively scored as correct or incorrect. It is becoming a common practice for essays to be graded holistically, a process that involves assigning grades to various aspects of an essay and typically involves using more than one rater to grade each essay.

Consider also the case of a researcher who is carrying out a study concerning students' disruptive behavior. Usually, disruptive behavior is measured by direct observation rather than by a paper and pencil test. Again, typically more than one person observes and rates the behavior.

Observer Agreement. The notion of reliability applies to all measures, not just to paper and pencil tests consisting of a series of individual items. Measures that involve some form of observation or that involve interpretation on the part of the evaluator are usually checked for objectivity by comparing the ratings assigned by two or more raters. This measure of consistency is called interobserver agreement or **interrater reliability** (Hartman, 1977) and is conceptually no different from the ways of determining reliability that have been presented in the previous sections of this chapter.

Suppose a researcher decides to investigate students' performance in art by having them draw pictures. It is likely that the researcher would have persons who are trained in art rate the artistic qualities of the pictures. To determine the reliability of the ratings, the ratings of one rater would be compared with those of another. In other words, students would be ranked according to artistic qualities of their pictures as rated by one rater and then ranked again according to the ratings by the other rater. As in all other methods used to determine reliability, the more similar the rankings on the two lists, the more reliable are the ratings.

In a way, the rating assigned by a rater is analogous to the score that a student achieves on a test. The use of two raters to rate a student's drawing is conceptually identical to the notion of parallel forms of a test, except that in this case each rater functions as a kind of parallel form. If a researcher decided to determine the reliability of ratings by having only one rater rate each student's picture twice and then compared the two sets of ratings, the process is conceptually identical to that of using the test-retest method with a paper and pencil test.

Percentage of Agreement. There is one way in which the ratings of more than one rater can be used to express the degree of consistency in measurement that is conceptually different from the basic notion of comparing the rank orders of names on two lists compiled by different raters. Sometimes consistency of measurement is expressed in the form of percentage of agreement.

Suppose a researcher decides to have two raters observe students' disruptive behavior and count the number of disruptive outbursts that occur during a given time unit. To obtain some measure of the consistency with which the two observers rated the students' disruptive behavior, the rater might simply compare the number of disruptive outbursts counted by the two raters for each time unit and report the percentage of agreement. In other words, the researcher would report the percentage of time the raters were in perfect agreement, the percentage of time the raters disagreed by a count of one, the percentage of time the raters disagreed by a count of two, and so forth. Often such comparisons are presented in the form of a table, and the reader can rapidly get some sense of how consistent the raters were. In the case where percentage of agreement is used to indicate reliability, however, no reliability coefficient is reported.

Reliability of Different Kinds of Tests

As noted previously, as r (the reliability coefficient) approaches $+1.00$, the test is more and more reliable and as r approaches zero, the test is less and less reliable. We have not yet, however, addressed the question of how reliable a test should be. What constitutes reasonable reliability depends on the kind of test. Some forms of human behavior are much more easily measured than others, so the degree of consistency one can expect from a measuring instrument depends on the kind of behavior the instrument has been designed to measure.

Academic achievement is relatively easy to measure, so reasonable reliability for achievement tests is generally set fairly high. Reliability coefficients of $+.90$ and higher are not uncommon. Reliability coefficients of achievement tests that fall below $+.80$ probably indicate that the test falls short of being well constructed, given the kind of behavior being measured.

Aptitude tests attempt to predict a person's performance some time in the future, and it is more difficult to predict future behavior than to measure current behavior. Consequently, aptitude tests with reliability coefficients of $+.80$ and higher represent a level of consistency of measurement that is realistic in terms of predicting future behavior.

People's attitudes and opinions are even more difficult to measure, mainly because it is difficult to define what constitutes a particular attitude or opinion. For example, when one includes an item concerning subjects' attitudes toward doing math homework using an instrument designed to measure attitude toward math, it is not clear to what extent a response is affected by the subject's attitude toward doing homework rather than by the subject's attitude toward math. Furthermore, attitudes may represent fairly unstable characteristics that vary markedly within an individual at any given time. Consequently, acceptable reliability coefficients for attitudinal measures may be as low as $+.70$.

Consistent measures of personality are probably the most difficult of all to obtain, again because it is often difficult to specify in the form of test items the various dimensions of behavior that collectively define a particular kind of personality. It is not uncommon for reliability coefficients of widely used personality measures to fall within the range of $+.60$ to $+.70$.

The Nature of Test Scores

No test score ever represents a completely accurate measure. Test scores always contain an error component. Consider the case of a person who on two different occasions takes the same test. Even if the test is known to be quite valid and reliable, it is unlikely that the person's score would be identical on both occasions. The more reliable the test, the less the difference between the two scores is likely to be, but nevertheless the scores are unlikely to be identical because of various sources of error. A student who scored 78 on the first administration of the test would likely score slightly higher or lower on the second administration. Similarly, because of the error component of test scores, it would be incorrect to conclude that there are true differences between the performance of one student who scores 78 on a test and another who scores 79.

Sources of Inconsistencies in Test Scores. Kubiszyn and Borich (1987) list the following four major sources of error that lead to inconsistencies in test scores:

1. the test taker, who may be tired, sick, upset by personal problems, and so forth
2. the test itself, which may contain poorly worded items or trick questions or may be written at a reading level that is too difficult for persons taking the test
3. the conditions under which the test is administered, which may vary in terms of physical comfort (e.g., temperature, humidity, or noise), instructions and explanations (some test administrators provide more information than others, e.g., providing hints or spelling words) or test administrator attitudes, that is, the way in which administrators monitor the test
4. test scoring, that is, errors that occur when scoring by hand or by machine, such as when a machine interprets a stray pencil mark as an error

Standard Error of Measurement

A person's test score is often referred to as the **obtained score** and is represented by the following equation:

$$\text{obtained score} = \text{``true score''} + \text{``error score''}$$

The **true score** is the score a person theoretically would obtain if the test were completely accurate. The **error score** represents that part of the obtained score due to inconsistencies associated with the test. The only score we are sure about is the obtained score. Although it is not possible to calculate the precise values of the true score and the error score, we can calculate a statistic called the **standard error of measurement** (s_m), which provides a measure of the range of scores within which a test taker's true score likely lies. The more reliable the test, the smaller the s_m.

Objective Measures

An **objective measure** is one on which a person's score would be the same no matter who scored the test, as long as the scorer is competent. Multiple-choice and true-false tests are good examples of objective measures. Essays are a good example of measures that lack objectivity. The score a person receives on an essay would probably vary, depending on who the scorer is. In general, objective measures are more reliable than nonobjective ones.

Determining Validity

In 1985, the American Psychological Association, the American Educational Research Association, and the National Council on Measurement in Education jointly published *Standards for Educational and Psychological Testing,* which changed the then prevailing thinking about validity in two important ways. First, the definition of validity was changed. Historically, most researchers had defined validity in terms of the extent to which a test actually measured what it claimed to measure. Validity is now defined in terms of ''the appropriateness, meaningfulness, and usefulness of the specific inferences made from test scores . . . The inferences regarding specific uses of a test are validated, not the test itself'' (p. 9).

Second, it had been thought that there were three different types of validity (content, criterion-related, and construct validity), each of which was used to validate different kinds of tests (e.g., achievement, aptitude, or personality tests). These types of validity are described in detail later; the important thing at the moment is to understand that the thinking about how these types of validity are related has changed.

Construct Validity

Previously, it was believed that "construct validity is evaluated by investigating what qualities a test measures, that is, by determining the degree to which certain explanatory concepts or constructs account for performance on the test" (Messick, 1992, p. 1489). Now, however, it is believed that "**construct validity** [boldface added] is based on an integration of any evidence that bears on the interpretation or meaning of the test scores—including content- and criterion-related evidence, which are thus subsumed as aspects of construct validity" (Messick, 1992, p. 1491).

The names we assign to various traits or characteristics that people have, such as *authoritarianism, anxiety, introversion,* and so forth, are often called **hypothetical constructs.** Such constructs are not observable in and of themselves, but rather are terms researchers devise to refer to regular patterns in an individual's behavior. When we say that someone is authoritarian, for example, we use the term *authoritarian* as a shorthand way of referring to a set of behaviors that differentiate authoritarian people from nonauthoritarian people.

Personality tests are the most common example of tests that measure hypothetical constructs. The process of construct validation is used to determine the validity of such tests. The discussion of construct validation that follows is based largely on information appearing in Wolf (1982, pp. 1994–1995).

Hypothetical constructs are derived from theories concerning (a) the nature of the construct; (b) characteristics of persons who manifest the construct; and (c) factors that are likely to affect the construct. To validate a test that purports to measure a particular construct, it is frequently necessary to conduct a series of studies based on the three aspects of the theory underlying the construct.

Suppose one wished to validate a test that claims to measure anxiety. One might administer to a group of people the anxiety test, a test of neuroticism, and a mechanical aptitude test. If the anxiety test is valid, one would expect people's scores on the anxiety test to correlate positively with their scores on the neuroticism test, because, theoretically, anxiety and neuroticism are related. Correspondingly, one would expect to find no significant correlation between people's scores on the anxiety test and their scores on the mechanical aptitude test because there is no theoretical basis underlying such a relationship.

One could also carry out a study in which groups of people who theoretically should differ with respect to anxiety are given the anxiety test and compare the groups' performance. Since neurotics are known to exhibit more anxiety than nonneurotics, one might give the anxiety test to these two types of people. The finding that the neurotic group scored higher on the test than the nonneurotic group constitutes additional evidence that the anxiety test is measuring what it claims to be measuring.

Also, one might expect students to exhibit more anxiety before taking a final exam than at times when they are not taking an exam. If a group of students who take the anxiety test immediately prior to taking a final exam obtain higher anxiety scores than a group of students not taking a final exam, one would have further evidence that the anxiety test is a valid measure of anxiety.

Construct validation of a test requires the integration of evidence from all three kinds of studies. One needs evidence that scores on the test (a) correlate positively with related constructs and do not correlate with unrelated constructs; (b) differentiate between groups of people who theoretically should exhibit different levels of the construct; and (c) change in the correct direction as a function of factors that theoretically should affect the construct.

Content Validity

"**Content validity** [boldface added] is evaluated by showing how well the content of the test samples the class of situations or subject matter about which conclusions are to be drawn" (Messick, 1992, p. 1489). For example, a researcher who wants to develop a test to measure fifth-graders' achievement in social studies must first determine what constitutes the content of fifth-grade social studies. A researcher who is developing a test that can be used throughout the country must first determine what kinds of things are taught in fifth-grade social studies classes across the nation. If a test is being developed for use within a particular school system, the researcher must first determine what kinds of things are taught in fifth-grade social studies classes throughout that system.

It may be helpful to think of the content of an academic subject area as a population consisting of particular kinds of knowledge and skills. An achievement test may then be thought of as a collection of items dealing with only a sample of the entire population of knowledge and skills. Developers of a valid achievement test must select a sample of test items that accurately represent the population of knowledge and skills from which the items are drawn.

Determining Academic Content

There are no precise guidelines to follow in establishing the content of a particular academic subject. It is up to the test developer to decide what the content of an academic subject consists of by gathering adequate information. Assume, for example, that a test developer wants to produce a valid test of fifth-graders' social studies achievement to be used in elementary schools nationwide. It is likely the test developer would first try to find out what textbooks are most commonly used in fifth-grade social studies. An examination of the contents of these textbooks would give the test developer some idea of what is being taught around the country. He or she would probably also want to consult curriculum guides used by various school districts and perhaps talk with persons teaching fifth-grade social studies.

Each of these sources of information would give some idea of the kinds of knowledge and skills that comprise fifth-grade social studies. The test developer might discover, for example, that fifth-grade social studies consists of various historical aspects of colonial North America; various geographical factors, such as the topography of the United States; and perhaps certain skills, such as the ability to read different kinds of maps. After listing the various topics and skills covered by fifth-grade social studies textbooks and curriculum guides, he or she would then determine what proportion of the total content of fifth-grade social studies deals with each specific topic and skill.

Suppose the researcher determines that of the total content of fifth-grade social studies, approximately 20% deals with colonial North America, 10% deals with the topography of the United States, 5% with map-reading skills, and so forth. The test developer would continue the process until 100% of the content had been divided proportionally among the various topics that are covered. The purpose of dividing the content proportionally among the various topics is to help in constructing a valid achievement test.

Proportional Numbers of Items

To increase the likelihood that the items on the test will be an accurate representation of the entire content of fifth-grade social studies, the test developer would make sure that 20% of the test items deal with the colonial period of North American history, 10% deal with the topography of the United States, and 5% deal with map-reading skills. By making the proportion of the total number of test items correspond to the proportion of the total content dealing with each topic, the test developer is apt to construct a valid test in the sense that the test items cover a representative sample of the total content.

The notion of content validity can and should be applied by teachers to the tests they make up for students in their classrooms. Such tests are essentially achievement tests, and the principles of content validity apply. A test lacks content validity if topics on the test were not taught by the teacher or if topics taught by the teacher are not on the test.

Criterion-Related Validity

"**Criterion-related validity** [boldface added] is evaluated by comparing the test scores with one or more external variables (called criteria) considered to provide a direct measure of the characteristic or behavior in question" (Messick, 1992, p. 1489). There are two forms of criterion-related validity: predictive and concurrent validity. "**Predictive validity** [boldface added] indicates the extent to which an individual's future level on the criterion is predicted from prior test performance," whereas "**concurrent validity** [boldface added] indicates the extent to which the test scores estimate an individual's present standing on the criterion" (Messick, 1992, p. 1489).

For example, an aptitude test that claims to measure students' ability to succeed in algebra is valid to the extent that students who score well on the test also do well in algebra, and students who do poorly on the test also do poorly in algebra. To determine the validity of an algebra aptitude test by means of predictive validity, one would administer the test and then wait until the students who took the test have completed a course in algebra. The validity of the test would be indicated by the extent to which the order of names ranked according to aptitude test scores corresponds to the order of names ranked according to algebra grades. To determine the validity of the same test by means of concurrent validity, one would take a group of students who have just completed an algebra course and administer the aptitude test to them. Again, the validity of the test would be indicated by the extent to which the order of names ranked according to algebra grades corresponds to the order of names ranked according to aptitude test scores.

Concurrent validity is sometimes used rather than predictive validity because it is usually more expedient to administer the aptitude test and the criterion measure at the same time.

Regardless of whether predictive or concurrent validity is used, a correlation coefficient is calculated to determine the extent to which the order of names ranked according to aptitude test score corresponds to the order of names ranked according to algebra grade. This coefficient is called the validity coefficient, and once more, the closer the coefficient is to $+1.00$, the more valid the test is.

LB3051 . A693

Selecting Measuring Instruments

Now that we have finished our discussion of the various kinds of test reliability and validity, let us consider the practical issue of how to find an appropriate existing test or design your own. A particularly useful source for information about characteristics of a good test is *Standards for Educational and Psychological Testing*, a joint publication of the American Psychological Association, the American Educational Research Association, and the National Council on Measurement in Education (1985). One of the best ways to decide how to measure a variable is to examine how other researchers have measured it. As you look through the professional literature dealing with your research topic, it is important not only to pay attention to the findings of a study, but also to take note of the kinds of tests and measuring instruments that were used to operationally define the variables in the study.

Types of Measuring Instruments

You will soon discover that researchers rely on a wide assortment of measuring instruments. They may use highly objective measures such as various kinds of standardized tests to obtain the data in their studies or they may use more subjective measures, such as interviews or the ratings of observers. The first rule of thumb is to try to select as objective a measure as possible. An objective test is one that can be scored in such a way that the person taking the test would receive the same score no matter who the scorer is. Multiple-choice tests are a prime example of an objective test. If you select an objective measure, you will have far less difficulty when it comes time to analyze your data because a person's score on such a test will be clear.

Standardized Tests. Many tests produced by commercial test developers are *standardized*, which means that the test has been designed so that the procedures for administering the test, the materials used in the test, and the way in which the test is scored are constant. A test manual accompanying the test gives precise instructions concerning how the examiner should administer and score the test. If the examiner follows these instructions, people who take the test at different times and in different places are all exposed to exactly the same conditions.

The Scholastic Assessment Test (SAT) and the Graduate Record Examination (GRE) are examples of standardized tests. Examiners administering these tests read aloud word by word the directions appearing in the test manual. They also allow people precisely the amount of time stated in the manual for completing the test, often using stopwatches to ensure that the time is exact. The test manual contains important information about the test's reliability and validity, as well as about the distribution of scores attained by people in a normative sample. The normative sample is a representative sample of persons for whom the test has been designed. Test developers use the scores of people in the normative sample to establish the test's norms. For example, the average score of a normative sample of fifth graders taking a reading comprehension test becomes the grade equivalent reading score of 5.0.

One of the most important characteristics of a standardized test is the objectivity of the test scores. A person's score on a standardized test is objective in the sense that the person's score would be the same no matter when or where the person took the test.

Scoring. If you select a subjective measure, it will be necessary to devise some sort of codification system to apply to the subjects' responses for scoring purposes before you can analyze the data. Suppose you are interested in a research question in which you want to see if there are differences among various groups of teachers in the disciplinary methods they use in their classrooms. One way to obtain information about this issue is simply to ask teachers to describe in their own words the kinds of disciplinary measures they use. However, when subjects are asked to give open-ended responses, the researcher has the problem of deciding if responses that may be worded differently really mean the same thing and how many different kinds of responses have actually been given by the group of subjects.

On the other hand, if you provide the subjects with a list of various kinds of disciplinary measures and a set of codes by which to record the frequency with which each disciplinary measure is used, it is quite easy to score subjects' responses. For example, you might decide to ask teachers to indicate how often they use each disciplinary measure by placing a check mark in one of several columns labeled "Never," "At least once a year," "At least once a month," "At least once a week," and "At least once a day."

It is usually clear in a research article whether the researcher has used a commercially available test or a test specifically designed for the study. If the researcher has developed the test, you can write directly to the researcher and request information about how to get a copy of the test. Most research journals list the address of the researcher. One problem with writing directly to researchers, however, is that they may have changed their institutional affiliation, particularly if the article you have read is fairly old. If the test used by the researcher is commercially available, the name of the publisher is given in the article, and you can write directly to the test publisher to obtain a copy. Of course, if the test has been published, you will be charged a fee for a copy.

Commercially Available Tests

There is an incredibly large number of tests available from test publishing firms that cover everything from spelling tests to self-concept measures. Most standardized tests are commercially available, but not all commercially available tests are standardized. Some publishers restrict the use of some psychological tests to persons who have had appropriate training in the administration and interpretation of such tests. Generally, publishers make such tests available to members of the American Educational Research Association or the American Psychological Association, or to persons with advanced academic degrees in psychology or related areas. If you wish to obtain a test that has restricted distribution, usually all you have to do is have the professor who is teaching your research course sign a statement that he or she will supervise your use of the testing instrument.

The definitive source of information about commercially available tests is a series of reference books originally edited by Oscar K. Buros called *Tests in Print* and *Mental Measurements Yearbook.* The works, which are invaluable tools for educators and psychologists, are periodically updated and new volumes are added to the series.

Tests in Print. *Tests in Print* (Mitchell, 1983), lists every test that is currently in print, along with the name and address of the publisher. There is also a useful index by topic that lists all published tests dealing with any given topic.

Mental Measurements Yearbooks. The second book is really a series of books that have been revised periodically over the years, beginning in 1938. These books are called the *Mental Measurements Yearbooks* (Kramer & Conoley, 1992). Information about any published test consists of the publisher's name and address, the cost of the test, a description of the test booklets and test items, validity and reliability information, the length of time it takes to administer the test, the kinds of people for whom the test is appropriate, whether the test can be administered to groups of people or must be given individually, and so forth. Most importantly, for each test there are one or more critical evaluations written by experts in the field. These evaluations point out the strengths and weaknesses of a test and tend to be more objective than information provided by the test publisher. There is also for each test a list of published research studies in which the test has been used.

In addition to the two major books described previously, there are individual volumes devoted to personality tests, intelligence tests, reading tests, and achievement tests in various academic subject areas. The series of *Mental Measurements Yearbooks* and related volumes are the undisputed definitive source of information about commercially available tests.

Tests and Test Critiques. Two other references give detailed information about tests. The first, *Tests: A Comprehensive Reference for Assessments in Psychology, Education and Business* (Sweetland & Keyser, 1986), gives concise descriptions of thousands of tests, including the test title, author, population for which the test is intended, whether the test is examiner- or self-administered, the test's major features, timing, scoring, cost, and publisher. The second, *Test Critiques* (Keyser & Sweetland, 1987), consists of six volumes of technical information about tests, such as reliability, validity, and normative development. The editors of the two references have designed them to be used together.

Tests in Education. *Tests in Education* (Levy & Goldstein, 1984) contains critical reviews of tests of early development, language, mathematics, composite attainments, general abilities, personality and counseling, and other topics. Each test review includes test content, purpose of the test, item preparation, administration, standardization, scoring, reliability, validity, interpretation, test use, general evaluations, and a list of references.

The ETS Test Collection Catalogs. The Educational Testing Service (ETS) has compiled a collection of over 16,000 tests and other measurement devices and has produced a four-volume index to the collection. Each volume consists of a main entry section, a subject index, an author index, and a title index. The subject index uses descriptors from the ERIC *Thesaurus.* There is information on approximately 14,000 achievement tests (volume 1); 1,400 vocational tests (volume 2); 1,700 tests for special populations (volume 3); and 1,300 tests of cognitive abilities, aptitude, and intelligence (volume 4).

The format of the ETS *Test Catalogs* is basically the same as that used in the *Current Index to Journals in Education (CIJE)* described in chapter 3. You locate the name of a test by entering the subject index. Each test has a unique accession number you use to locate information about the test appearing in the main entry section. This information includes the title of the test, where it can be obtained, the age and/or grade level of the target audience, the number of items the test contains, the number of minutes it takes to administer the test, and an abstract describing the nature of the test.

RIE Publication Type 160. As noted in chapter 3, one of the sections of *Resources in Education (RIE),* the index to ERIC documents on microfiche, is the Publication Type Index. Each educational document is assigned one or more three-digit publication type numbers and the Publication Type Index consists of a numerical listing by type of publication. Publication Type 160 is assigned to documents containing actual copies of tests, questionnaires, and other measuring instruments. Consequently, by looking up ''Pub Type 160'' one can locate a list of measuring instruments included in various educational documents.

It is possible to carry out a computer search of *RIE* by publication type. If you carry out such a search and include the descriptor for your research topic, you will be able to locate instantly any document containing a copy of a measuring instrument dealing with your topic. For example, if you are contemplating a study concerning students' self-concepts, you may search *RIE* by publication type and the descriptor ''SELF-CONCEPT'' and locate all documents that include copies of self-concept measures. See chapter 17 for information about computer searches.

Scales for the Measurement of Attitudes. One source of information on attitudinal inventories is a book written in 1967 by Marvin Shaw and Jack Wright called *Scales for the Measurement of Attitudes.* This book contains a collection of attitudinal measures developed by researchers and used for research purposes. The book contains actual copies of numerous attitudinal inventories as well as reliability and validity information for each inventory when such information is available. Even if one is unable to locate an existing attitudinal inventory on one's particular topic of interest, the book can be useful in providing examples of attitudinal scales that can serve as models for devising one's own measure.

Measures of Personality and Social Psychological Attitudes. *Measures of Personality and Social Psychological Attitudes* (Robinson, Shaver, & Wrightsman, 1991) contains information on over 140 measures, including the variables measured by the instrument, a description of the instrument and of the sample used in developing it, reliability and validity information, and where to locate the instrument. The editors have included actual copies of the measure when possible; otherwise, sample items are given.

Books consisting of measures of classroom instruction (Borich & Madden, 1977) and methods for evaluating behavior in early childhood education (Goodwin & Driscol, 1980) are sometimes of help to students interested in these topics.

Constructing Your Own Measuring Instrument

Sometimes a student finds there is no readily available instrument that seems appropriate for measuring the variables the student is interested in investigating. It is often possible in such situations for students to construct their own instruments. It does not necessarily follow that a measuring instrument designed by a student is bound to be worse than instruments that are commercially available. There are a number of disadvantages associated with having to develop an instrument of one's own, particularly in terms of the time and effort involved and the lack of reliability and validity information, but there can be some advantages as well. One of the advantages is that a self-designed instrument can be tailored to the specific research question.

Even in cases where excellent published tests are easily available, it may nevertheless be desirable for a student to consider using a self-made test. One of the most common situations in which a self-made test may be more appropriate than a published test is when a researcher is investigating students' academic achievement as a function of some kind of instructional intervention. For example, suppose a student has designed a study to determine which of several methods is better to use for teaching reading. There are numerous excellent reading achievement tests on the market, but these tests are likely to measure reading achievement in a way that is not directly related to a student's study.

Published reading achievement tests are usually designed to measure a variety of reading skills that often need considerable time for development. Very often the kind of research projects carried out by students must be completed in a relatively brief period and deal with only one kind of reading skill. Good commercially available reading achievement tests are fine to use for measuring reading achievement after a reasonably long period of instruction. Often, however, such tests do not focus specifically enough on the particular skill a student might be interested in. It is probably better to use a self-made instrument that can be targeted directly on the reading skill in question.

Commercially available achievement tests generally are designed to measure achievement rather broadly, while methods studies tend to investigate rather narrowly defined aspects of achievement. Using a standardized test to measure students' achievement as a function of instructional method is much like trying to detect differences in the individual weights of a litter of puppies on a bathroom scale. There may be differences, but a more finely calibrated scale is needed to detect them. See Gronlund (1982) for more information on constructing achievement tests.

Questionnaires

There are two basic principles to follow in designing questionnaires: (a) make the items as relevant as possible; and (b) word questions in a way that they are likely to be interpreted the same way by every respondent. The longer the questionnaire, the less likely it is that many people will take the time to complete it. Before constructing a questionnaire, it is best to have a clear idea of how the data are to be analyzed. Include only questions that yield information pertinent to the data analysis.

Open-ended questions that permit people to answer in their own words are likely to be interpreted differently by different people. It is best to follow each question with a set of possible responses so that people need only place an X next to the response of their choice. It is also best to include among the possible responses a category called *other,* so that people have the opportunity to give a response that was unanticipated by the researcher.

One Question per Item. Make sure that each item asks only one question. It is better to have several items, each of which asks one question, than one item that asks several questions. For example, it is better to use items 1 and 2 rather than item 3.

Item 1. Did you find learning how to use the computer interesting?
Item 2. Did you find learning how to use the computer easy?
Item 3. Did you find learning how to use the computer easy and interesting?

Item 3 cannot be answered accurately by persons who found learning how to use the computer interesting but difficult, or by persons who found it easy but uninteresting. Items 1 and 2, however, permit such people to respond accurately.

Eliminating Ambiguous Wording. Responses that call for people to indicate how frequently they do something are particularly prone to ambiguous wording. Consider the following item:

How often do you check your child's homework?
Rarely—Sometimes—Often

It is likely that different people will interpret the same response choice differently. The term *rarely* might be interpreted by one person as "less than once a month" and by another person as "less than twice a week." One way to eliminate the ambiguity of responses is to express the choices in terms of actual units of time. Instead of using a term such as *rarely,* for example, use a term such as *less than twice a month.*

Another way is to include a unit of time in the question itself. You might change the wording of the previous item to "How many days last week did you check your child's homework?" An additional advantage of including the unit of time in the question is that all respondents have exactly the same time frame in mind when responding to the item. Furthermore, if the time frame is kept relatively recent, people do not have to rely heavily on memory and the responses are likely to be more accurate.

Notice the ambiguity of the phrase *check your child's homework.* Some parents might interpret the term *check* to mean "make sure the child has spent time working on homework." Others might interpret it to mean "go over the child's work thoroughly." In short, it is desirable to use terms that are as precise as possible. Try to define ambiguous terms operationally so that respondents have a clearer understanding of the behaviors you are studying. One helpful way to spot ambiguous wording is to use the questionnaire in a pilot study with a few people similar to those who will participate in the final study. The responses of just a few people are often sufficient to indicate that some items have not been written clearly and need to be rewritten. See Berdie and Anderson (1974) for more detailed information concerning questionnaires, and see Henerson, Morris, and Fitz-Gibbon (1987) for instructions on developing your own attitudinal measures.

Attitudinal Scales

As an educator, you have probably had experience in designing achievement tests for classroom use. There are other kinds of measuring instruments sometimes used in research, however, that may be less familiar to you. One common kind of instrument has to do with measuring people's opinions or attitudes. There are numerous ways to measure attitudes. Probably, however, researchers most frequently use Likert scales.

Directions: Circle the response that best indicates the extent to which you agree or disagree with each
statement below, where

SA = Strongly Agree
A = Agree
U = Undecided
D = Disagree
SD = Strongly Disagree

1. Math is my favorite class...............	SA	A	U	D	SD
2. Learning math is a waste of time......	SA	A	U	D	SD

Likert Scales. **Likert scales** are not a particular set of attitudinal scales but rather a technique by which attitudinal scales are constructed. You have probably already had the experience of completing a measuring instrument comprised of Likert scale items. Such instruments consist of a series of statements, each of which is followed by a range of responses going, for example, from "strongly agree" to "strongly disagree." Subjects select for each item the response that best reflects their feelings. Figure 7.3 contains examples of Likert scale items.

The subject's response to each item is scored, and the scores for all items are summed to get a total score that represents the subject's attitude. An example of an item on a Likert scale measuring attitude toward math is "Math is my favorite class." The statement is positively worded, so agreement with the statement indicates a positive attitude toward math. A response of "Strongly Agree" would receive a score of +2, a response of "Agree" a +1, "Undecided" a 0, "Disagree" a −1, and "Strongly Disagree" a −2.

Another example of an item on the same attitudinal measure is "Learning math is a waste of time." This item is worded in such a way that agreement with the statement indicates a negative attitude toward math. Consequently, the scoring system for responses to the item is reversed. "Strongly Agree" receives a score of −2 rather than +2, "Agree" a −1, "Undecided" a 0, "Disagree" a +1, and "Strongly Disagree" a +2. Some people prefer to use ratings that range from 1 to 5 rather than from −2 to +2 to avoid negative numbers. Either set of ratings is acceptable.

The use of ratings ranging from 1 to 5 rather than from −2 to +2 does not affect the results of a study based on data collected with a set of Likert scales. Suppose one were using 20 items similar to those in Figure 7.3 to determine if there is a significant difference between females' and males' attitudes toward mathematics. If one used ratings ranging from 1 to 5, the lowest score a student could receive would be 20 (i.e., the student received a rating of 1 on each of the 20 items). The highest possible score would be 100 (i.e., 20 × 5).

Figure 7.4

Example of Likert Scale Items Measuring Conceptually
Unrelated Attitudes

1.	Most teachers in my school treat students courteously.	SA	A	U	D	SD
2.	The longer teachers have been teaching, the less they enjoy teaching.	SA	A	U	D	SD

If one used ratings ranging from -2 to $+2$, the lowest score a student could receive would be -40 (i.e., the student received a rating of -2 on each of the 20 items). The highest possible score would be $+40$ (i.e., $20 \times +2$). The important point is that regardless of which set of ratings is used, the difference between the lowest and highest possible scores remains 80.

Approximately half of the items on an instrument using Likert scales are worded so that *agreement* indicates a positive attitude and half are worded so that *disagreement* indicates a positive attitude. The scoring scheme for the two different types of items is reversed (i.e., "strongly agree" is scored $+5$ if agreement indicates a positive attitude, but $+1$ if disagreement indicates a positive attitude). The scores for all items are summed to get a total score. Consequently, the higher the total score, the more positive the subject's attitude.

Having the wording of half of the items opposite to the wording of the other half counterbalances any kind of response bias a subject might have. It is well known that some people have a tendency to agree with any item. Such people are called yea-sayers. Other people tend to disagree with any item and are called nay-sayers. By wording half the items positively and the other half negatively, the responses of a yea-sayer would cancel each other so that the person's total score would be approximately 0 (if you were using a scale of -2 to $+2$). The responses of a nay-sayer would also, of course, cancel each other and yield the same score of 0.

The placement of positively and negatively worded items on the instrument should be done by random assignment. It is not desirable to have all the odd-numbered items worded one way and the even-numbered items worded the other way.

Summing Across Likert Scale Items. Before adding up a person's ratings for each item to determine the person's total score on an attitudinal scale, it is important to make sure that the individual items deal with conceptually related material, such as the items in Figure 7.3. Sometimes researchers use a set of Likert scale items to measure attitudes, but the items deal with material that is conceptually unrelated, such as the items in Figure 7.4.

Conceptually it makes no sense to sum the ratings assigned to the items in Figure 7.4 because the items are measuring attitudes toward different things. If one wanted, for example, to compare females' and males' ratings on the items in Figure 7.4, it would only make sense to compare the responses to each item separately, not to sum ratings across items. In other words, do females and males rate item 1 significantly differently, and do they rate item 2 significantly differently?

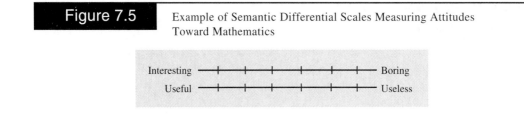

Figure 7.5   Example of Semantic Differential Scales Measuring Attitudes Toward Mathematics

Semantic Differential Scales. Another way of measuring attitudes is **semantic differential scales** (Osgood, Suci, & Tannenbaum, 1957). Such scales consist of two bipolar adjectives (i.e, adjectives that are antonyms), separated by a line divided into seven parts. The person completing the scale is instructed to place an X in the interval corresponding to his or her attitude toward some topic. Figure 7.5 shows examples of semantic differential scales measuring attitude toward mathematics.

The respondent receives a score for each scale, ranging from 6 (if the interval next to the positive adjective is checked) to 0 (if the interval next to the negative adjective is checked). The scores for each scale are then summed to yield a total attitude score.

Checklists and Rating Scales. Researchers who carry out observational studies often rely on checklists or rating scales to obtain data. A checklist is merely a listing of the kinds of behavior the researcher is interested in studying. Researchers may themselves observe and record subjects' behavior on the **checklist** or have someone familiar with the subject, such as a teacher, use a checklist to record students' behavior. Depending on the behavior, one may either note the presence or absence of a behavior or record its frequency.

For example, a preschool teacher may place a check next to an item such as ''Can tie shoe laces'' to indicate whether a child can or cannot perform the behavior. A researcher interested in studying students' disruptive behavior in a classroom might place a check next to an item such as ''Calls out without raising hand'' each time a student engages in the behavior.

One source for locating checklists is *Measures for Psychological Assessment: A Guide to 3,000 Original Sources and Their Application* (Chun, Cobb, & French, 1974). It is not uncommon, however, for students to develop their own checklists. In designing your own checklist, it is important that you define the behaviors to be checked operationally and make sure they are truly observable.

While checklists provide information about the presence or frequency of various kinds of behavior, **rating scales** attempt to provide information about qualitative aspects of behavior. For example, one may be interested in qualitative differences in how attentive students are in class. Some rating scales consist of frequency measures, as shown in Figure 7.6.

A major problem with such rating scales is that except for *always* and *never,* the frequency measures often mean different things to different raters. To some people *seldom* may mean the student fails to pay attention once or twice a day; to others it may mean once or twice a week. It is useful to provide a common frame of reference for the frequency measures, as shown in Figure 7.7.

Notice that in Figure 7.7 that there are 5 rating points marked on the horizontal line, but only the 2 marks at the end and the mark in the middle are given verbal descriptions. One

Figure 7.6	Example of a Rating Scale with Measures of Frequency

Place an X in the column that best describes the student's behavior.	Always	Frequently	Occasionally	Seldom	Never
Pays attention in class.					
Hands in homework assignments on time.					
Participates in class discussions.					

Figure 7.7	Example of a Rating Scale with a Common Frame of Reference

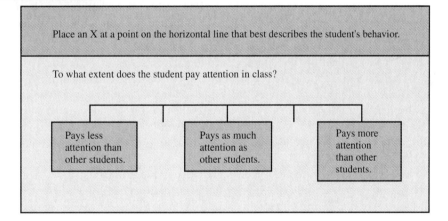

Place an X at a point on the horizontal line that best describes the student's behavior.

To what extent does the student pay attention in class?

Pays less attention than other students. — Pays as much attention as other students. — Pays more attention than other students.

may provide verbal descriptions for each mark, but it is usually unnecessary. The number of possible ratings for a given item on a rating scale usually ranges from 3 to 7. Generally it is not possible to make meaningful ratings along a continuum consisting of more than 7 units.

Some rating scales consist of a numerical rating scale, where the lowest number indicates the absence of or the presence of a mild form of the behavior being rated and the highest number indicates the presence of an extreme form of the behavior. For example, aggressive acts exhibited by emotionally disturbed students may be rated on a scale ranging from 1 to 5, where 1 represents a mildly aggressive act and 5 an extremely aggressive one. Such rating scales often involve subjective interpretations on the part of the rater, sometimes making it difficult to obtain ratings that are reliable (i.e., that exhibit consistency from rater to rater). More detailed information about checklists and ratings scales may be found in Gronlund and Linn (1990).

A Final Word of Caution About Self-Made Measuring Instruments

No matter how well designed a study is, the final outcome can be no better than the measures used to collect the data. It is important to try to use measures that are as valid and reliable as possible, which is the principal reason why many researchers often rely on measuring instruments that are already available, such as many standardized tests. The fact that a test has already been developed and is available to the researcher is no guarantee that it has good psychometric properties or that it is an appropriate measure of what the researcher wishes to measure. Any available test that is worth considering as a measure in your study should have information concerning the test's validity and reliability, which usually appears in the manual accompanying the test. If such information is not provided, don't assume that the test is a good measure.

If you decide it is best to develop your own test or measuring instrument for your research project, you should make every attempt to ensure that your instrument is valid. Although it is virtually impossible to guarantee that a test will be valid, and there is no way to check on its validity until after it has actually been administered, there are some precautions to take. You should at least try to administer the test or measuring instrument to a small group of people who will not participate in your study, but who are similar to those who will participate. A preliminary check of an instrument, even if conducted on a few people, can reveal ambiguities and weaknesses that were not apparent.

Similarly, if you intend to have observers rate various kinds of behavior, before you begin the collection of data you should carry out a few training sessions with the observers under the actual conditions in which they will be observing. The observers can discuss with you and with each other the ratings they made during the training sessions, and discrepancies of ratings can often be resolved by developing clearer definitions of the behaviors to be rated. Such a procedure is likely to increase the accuracy of ratings made by the observers during the actual study.

The more valid your instrument or test, the more reliable it is likely to be. Although it may not be possible to determine the validity of your instrument rigorously, you can and should always determine the instrument's reliability after it has been used to collect data.

Chapter Highlights

- Many operational definitions in educational research are test scores.
- *Validity* refers to the appropriateness of inferences made from test scores.
- *Reliability* refers to the degree of consistency of measurement.
- A reliable test may or may not be valid; an unreliable test cannot be valid.
- Reliability may be determined by examining the (a) stability of test scores over time, using the test-retest method or parallel forms; or (b) internal consistency of the test,

using the split-half method, the Kuder-Richardson Formulas No. 20 or No. 21 or Cronbach's alpha.

- The reliability coefficient is symbolized by r; the closer r is to $+1.00$, the more reliable the test.
- Increasing the number of items on a test leads to an increase in the test's reliability.
- The reliability of observational measures is determined by the extent of observer agreement.
- Acceptable levels of reliability (shown in parentheses) depend on the type of test: academic achievement (.80), aptitude (.80), attitudinal inventories (.70), personality (.60).
- A test score may be thought of as having two components: a "true score" and an "error score."
- Sources of errors leading to inconsistent scores include the test taker, the test, the conditions under which the test is administered, and test scoring.
- The *standard error of measurement* (s_m) provides a measure of the range within which a test taker's true score likely lies.
- An *objective measure* is one on which a person's score would be the same no matter who scored the test, as long as the scorer is competent.
- *Construct validity* is determined by integrating evidence that scores on the test (a) correlate positively with related constructs but not with unrelated ones, (b) differentiate between people who hypothetically should and should not exhibit different levels of the construct, and (c) change in an appropriate direction when exposed to factors that theoretically should bring about such a change.
- *Content validity* is determined by examining how well the items on a test reflect the instructional objectives of a unit of instruction.
- *Criterion-related validity* is determined by comparing predicted performance on the basis of test results with actual performance.
- A *standardized* test is designed so that the procedures for administering the test, the materials used in the test, and the way in which the test is scored are constant.
- All standardized tests are objective measures, but not all objective measures are standardized.
- Open-ended responses are particularly difficult to interpret.
- Each item on a questionnaire should ask no more than a single question.
- Likert scale items are statements followed by a range of choices going, for example, from "strongly agree" to "strongly disagree."
- When Likert scale items are used, half should be worded so that a response of agreement indicates a positive attitude and half worded so that a response of agreement indicates a negative attitude.
- Semantic differential scales consist of pairs of bipolar adjectives.
- Checklists are used to record the presence or frequency of some type of behavior; rating scales are used to provide qualitative information about the behavior.

1. Define the terms *reliability* and *validity.*

2. What conclusion can be reached regarding a test's validity if it is highly reliable? If it is unreliable?

3. Describe the following kinds of reliability: test-retest, parallel forms, and split-half.

4. Why is it necessary to correct a split-half reliability coefficient for test length?

5. Describe the circumstances under which it is necessary to use Cronbach's alpha rather than one of the Kuder-Richardson formulas.

6. Give an example of when and how one would use interrater agreement.

7. What determines whether the reliability coefficient of a test is adequate?

8. Define the terms *obtained score, true score,* and *error score.*

9. Name four sources that lead to inconsistencies in test scores.

10. Explain what *standard error of measurement* means.

11. Give an example of an *objective measure.*

12. Explain how construct, content, and criterion-related validity are related.

13. Describe how you would use content validity in constructing an examination to be given to a group of students you are teaching.

14. What distinguishes a standardized test from other kinds of commercially available tests?

15. What kinds of information should appear in the test manual that should accompany any reputable test?

16. Select a commercially available test that is frequently administered in your school. Using the *Mental Measurement Yearbooks,* write a brief evaluation of the test, including information on its reliability and validity.

17. Describe the ETS *Test Catalogs.*

18. How can you locate copies of tests appearing on ERIC microfiche?

19. Name a reference source that contains actual copies of attitudinal measures.

20. Discuss the advantages and disadvantages of constructing your own measuring instrument rather than using a commercially available one.

21. Construct an instrument consisting of six Likert scale items to measure students' attitudes toward the research course you are taking.

22. Construct a six-item semantic differential scale that could be used to measure students' attitudes towards the research course you are taking.

23. Describe the difference between checklists and rating scales.

Section IV

Understanding Statistics

O ne of the characteristics of quantitative studies is that the findings are typically reported in statistical terms, which often baffle students who are new to research. The purpose of this section is to enable you to grasp conceptually the rationale underlying the use of statistics and the role statistics plays in analyzing research data. The emphasis is *not* on how to calculate statistics, but rather on understanding the results of statistical calculations that appear in the published literature.

The first chapter in this section deals with descriptive statistics, which describes how variables are distributed among groups of people. Many variables of interest to educators are believed to be distributed normally among populations, so this chapter also includes information concerning the properties of normal curves. The second chapter deals with inferential statistics, which is the tool researchers use to determine how likely it is that the results of studies carried out with samples of people are generalizable to the populations from which the samples have been drawn.

Chapter 8
Descriptive Statistics and the Normal Curve

One easy mnemonic for helping you to remember the definition of median *is to think of the median on a highway, the strip of land running down the middle of a highway that divides the highway in half.*

Chapter Objectives

After completing this chapter, you should be able to:

- explain how descriptive and inferential statistics differ
- list four scales of measurement and give an example of each
- define *raw scores, percentiles, stanines,* and *Normal Curve Equivalent (NCE)* scores
- explain how *mean, median,* and *mode* differ
- explain in your own words what a *standard deviation* is and how it relates to the *variance*
- explain in your own words what *correlation coefficients* are and how to interpret them
- describe the properties of the normal curve
- define *z* scores

It is common for students initially to encounter difficulty in understanding the quantitative research literature, because, generally, most students have had little previous experience reading published studies. Many students are used to reading journal articles that are basically opinion papers or descriptions of various aspects of education, such as teaching techniques, curriculum planning, or the use of newly developed technology. Such articles, while useful in their own right, typically have little to do with quantitative research.

Quantitative research articles contain descriptions of how the authors collected data from persons participating in a study and what conclusions the authors have reached after analyzing the data. Usually, the data collected in a study consist of measures of some form of human behavior that the researchers have obtained, either by administering a paper and pencil test to a group of subjects or by directly observing how the subjects behaved under various conditions.

The difficulty students have understanding quantitative studies usually arises because researchers often report findings and describe the data analysis in terms of descriptive and inferential statistics. Such reporting may be almost totally incomprehensible for the reader who is unfamiliar with statistics. Fortunately, however, one can learn to interpret statistics and understand what the results of an inferential test of statistical significance mean without ever having to carry out a statistical analysis.

Statistical Treatment of Data

The field of statistics is often broken down into two major areas: descriptive statistics and inferential statistics. The functions of the two areas differ. In general, the function of **descriptive statistics** is to describe quantitatively how a particular characteristic is distributed among a group of people. Researchers use descriptive statistics when reporting the findings of a study. For example, when a researcher reports that, in a study comparing the relative effectiveness of two different methods of teaching reading to fourth graders, the average score of students taught by Method A was 74.32 and the average score of students taught by Method B was 86.75, the researcher has used descriptive statistics. The concept of *average* is a descriptive statistic.

Inferential statistics, on the other hand, is used to determine how likely it is that characteristics exhibited by a sample of people are an accurate description of those characteristics exhibited by the population of people from which the sample was drawn. In the previous example, the researcher reported that the average scores for two *samples* of fourth graders were 74.32 and 86.75. Inferential statistics is used to determine how likely it is that the average score of all fourth graders (i.e., the *population* of fourth graders) taught by Method A is 74.32 and the average score of all fourth graders taught by Method B is 86.75. Inferential statistics is used when researchers apply statistical tests of significance to their data to determine how likely it is that the results of their study are applicable to members of the populations who did not participate in the study. (More will be presented later about the concept of statistical significance.)

Scales of Measurement

Not all statistical procedures are equally powerful. In other words, some procedures are more likely than others to detect true differences among groups' averages in a group comparison study or to detect true relationships among variables in a correlational study. In general, a researcher wishes to use the most powerful statistical technique available, but whether it is appropriate to use a particular technique depends in part on assumptions one makes about the nature of the data to be analyzed. For example, more powerful statistical procedures often require one to assume that the data to be analyzed are normally distributed. If such an assumption does not seem justified, weaker statistical procedures must be used. (More will be presented shortly about normal distributions.)

Normality of distribution is only one consideration before deciding what statistical procedure to use. A factor that one must always consider before deciding to use one statistical procedure or another is how the data have been measured. Different kinds of data are measured by different scales that have different properties, some of which are more desirable than others because they permit one to use the most powerful statistical procedures available (Nunnally, 1967). Usually, the more powerful the statistical procedure, the more assumptions one must be able to make about the data. The fewer the assumptions one can make, the weaker the statistical procedures at one's disposal.

There are four **scales of measurement,** which from least to most desirable are: nominal, ordinal, interval, and ratio. Figure 8.1 lists the scales in hierarchical fashion and describes the properties of each. Sometimes, but not always, the researcher has a choice of measuring a variable with a nominal scale, an ordinal scale, an interval scale, or a ratio scale. These scales form a hierarchy in terms of desirability for research purposes. Each type of scale has its own set of statistical procedures that are used for analyzing data, and the power of the procedure increases as the desirability of the scale increases.

However, you should not conclude that you should never use nominal scales. Sometimes the variables we are interested in can be measured only by means of nominal scales, and their use is surely appropriate. The use of nominal scales means only that the researcher may find it harder to detect true differences between groups or true relationships among variables than if the variables could be measured with ratio, interval, or ordinal scales.

Nominal Scales

Nominal scales permit one to assign a name to each value of a variable whose values differ qualitatively, but not quantitatively. For example, gender is a variable whose values differ qualitatively. People are either female or male, and there is no way to assign numbers to these values in any meaningful fashion. Often, nominal scales are used when the variable refers to a group of people. Examples of nominal scales are academic major or athletic team. One can classify students as English majors, education majors, psychology majors, computer science majors, and so forth, but one cannot say that English majors rank higher or lower than education majors. Similarly, one can classify athletes as swimmers, basketball players, gymnasts, and so forth, but one cannot say that the difference between swimmers and basketball players is some given number of points. It is simply not possible to conceptualize academic major or athletic team in quantitative terms.

Ordinal Scales

An **ordinal scale** permits us to rank people on some variable but does not permit us to know by how much people differ on the variable. Ordinal scales have *unequal* units of measurement.

Figure 8.1   Hierarchy of Measurement Scales and Their Properties

Scale	Properties	Examples
Nominal	Qualitative units of measurement	Gender, Type of School
Ordinal	Unequal quantitative units of measurement	Percentiles, Grade Equivalents, Rankings
Interval	Equal quantitative units of measurement with no true zero point	Raw Scores, Fahrenheit Temperature
Ratio	Equal quantitative units of measurement with a true zero point	Length, Weight

Suppose a researcher decides to operationally define the variable of creative behavior by having teachers rank the students in their classes in terms of the amount of creative behavior the teachers believe each student exhibits. We know that the student who is ranked first exhibits more creative behavior, as far as the teacher is concerned, than the student who is ranked second, the second student exhibits more creative behavior than the student who is ranked third, and so on down the list. However, we do not know whether the difference in the amount of creative behavior exhibited by the first and second student is the same as the difference between the second and third student.

The teacher, for all we know, may have had great difficulty deciding how to rank the first two students because the amount of creative behavior they exhibit is so similar. On the other hand, the teacher may have had no difficulty ranking the third student because the amount of creative behavior exhibited by that student is considerably less than that exhibited by the first two students.

The same differences in students' rankings do not have the same meaning. Rankings permit us to order subjects from high to low on some variable, but we must not assume that the units of measurement used to rank the subjects are equal.

It is fairly easy to see that the rank ordering of students by a teacher constitutes an ordinal scale; sometimes, however, it is not so readily apparent. Two common kinds of test scores may appear to have equal units of measurement when in fact they do not: percentiles and grade equivalent scores. Both of these scores represent ordinal scales.

Percentiles. Perhaps we should clarify what a **percentile** is. When one says that a student has scored at the 90th percentile on a particular test, it means that 90% of the students in the norming sample scored at or below and 10% scored at or above where the student scored. If a student ranks at the 15th percentile, 15% of the students in the norming sample scored at or below and 85% scored at or above where the student scored.

We know that a student who scores at the 92nd percentile ranks higher than a student scoring at the 90th percentile and that a student scoring at the 50th percentile ranks higher than a student scoring at the 48th percentile. The difference between the 92nd and the 90th percentiles is two percentiles, which is the same as the difference between the 50th and the 48th percentiles. However, the difference of two percentiles does not mean the same thing in both of these cases.

The students who score at the 50th and 48th percentiles have scored near the middle of the norming group of students who have taken the test. Those at the 92nd and the 90th percentiles, however, have scored close to the top of the norming group. If we assume that the test scores are normally distributed, we know that most students score somewhere in the middle and that few students make either very high or very low scores.

A difference of one or two more correct items, for students scoring at percentile rankings in the middle of the range, might dramatically shift a student's percentile ranking upward because so many students have similar scores. A small increase in raw score might result in a large increase in the percentage of students scoring below that score. On the other hand, for students scoring at percentile rankings at the bottom or at the top end of the range, a student must answer many more items correctly in order for the percentile ranking to shift upward because not many students have very low or very high scores.

Percentiles divide a normal curve into 100 areas of equal size. The shape of the area, however, differs, depending on whether the percentile is in the center or at the tails of the normal distribution. The area between the 50th and the 51st percentile will be narrow, but tall. The area between the 98th and the 99th percentiles, on the other hand, will be wide but short. In other words, the difference of one percentile may represent a small or a large difference in the number of items correctly answered, depending on whether the percentile falls near the middle or at either end of the distribution.

Grade Equivalent Scores. **Grade equivalent scores** work in exactly the same way as percentiles. The same difference between grade equivalent scores means different things depending on whether the difference is in the middle or at the end of the range.

If the data collected in a study are either percentiles or grade equivalent scores, one is forced to use statistical procedures designed for use with ordinal scales. Such procedures are not as powerful as procedures designed for data collected by means of ratio or interval scales. If possible, one should always convert percentiles and grade equivalent scores back into raw scores to carry out a statistical analysis. The conversion to raw scores permits one to use the most powerful statistical procedures available because raw scores have equal units of measurement. (Raw scores are discussed later.)

Interval Scales

Many variables in education, such as academic achievement, attitudes, or self-concepts are measured by **interval scales,** which have *equal* units of measurement but no true values of zero. It is meaningless, for example, to say that a person completely lacks a self-concept. A person must have some degree of self-concept, whether it is positive or negative, but a person cannot have zero self-concept.

Vocabulary knowledge is another example of a variable that can be measured by an interval scale. The scores on a vocabulary test represent equal units of measurement because the same difference between two individuals' scores means the same thing no matter where on the scale the two individuals fall. Assume that several students are asked to define 100 words. If Student A defines 24 words correctly and Student B defines 29 words correctly, the difference between the students' scores is 5 points, which simply means that one student defined 5 more words correctly than the other student.

If Student C defines 92 words correctly and Student D defines 97 words correctly, the difference between the students' scores is also 5 points, which again means that one student has defined 5 more words correctly than the other. The fact that the difference between Student A's score and Student B's score means exactly the same thing as the difference between Student C's score and Student D's score indicates that the vocabulary test is a measuring instrument with equal units of measurement.

A student may score zero on a vocabulary test, but the score does not mean the student has no vocabulary. It simply means the student did not know any of the words on that particular vocabulary test.

Raw Scores. A person's **raw score** on a measuring instrument is determined by assigning a score to each item and summing the scores for all items. If a student takes a science test consisting of 25 items and gets 23 items correct, the raw score is 23. Teachers often mark tests on the basis of 100% and might assign the grade of 92% to the student who completed 23 items correctly. The student's raw score, however, is 23, not 92.

Most achievement tests and many other measuring instruments yield raw scores and may be regarded as instruments with interval scales. For example, an attitudinal inventory consisting of statements with which one agrees or disagrees yields a raw score. The difference between the attitudes of two students who score 72 and 75, respectively, on a math attitudinal inventory is exactly the same as the difference between the attitudes of two students who score 89 and 92. Ratings on a behavior checklist also yield scores that have equal units of measurement. The difference, for example, between two students who have engaged, respectively, in 7 and 9 disruptive acts means the same thing as the difference between two students who have engaged in 21 and 23 disruptive acts. In both cases the difference between the pairs of students is two disruptive acts.

Stanines. Sometimes scores on tests are reported in terms of **stanines,** which is an abbreviation of the term *standard nine.* Stanines divide a set of scores into nine equal units of measurement, ranging from 1 to 9, with 5 as the average. Stanines represent ranges of raw scores, so that students who achieve the same stanine score on a test do not necessarily have exactly the same raw score. Some educators prefer stanines to other kinds of scores because the band of raw scores comprising a stanine takes into account the lack of precision with which most tests measure. Figure 8.2 shows the relationship between stanine score and percentile ranges.

Normal Curve Equivalent (NCE) Scores. Many standardized tests report results in terms of **Normal Curve Equivalent (NCE)** scores. Whereas stanines divide a set of scores in nine equal units of measurement, NCE scores divide a set of scores into 100 equal units of measurement. Perhaps people sometimes confuse NCE scores with percentiles because both sets of scores range from 1 to 99. NCE scores are equal units of measurement; percentiles are not. The use of NCE scores makes it possible to carry out various statistical analyses

Figure 8.2

The Relationship Between Stanine Scores and Percentile Ranges

Stanine Score	Percentile Range
1	1st–4th
2	4th–11th
3	11th–23rd
4	23rd–40th
5	40th–60th
6	60th–77th
7	77th–89th
8	89th–95th
9	95th–99th

Figure 8.3

Percentiles and Their Corresponding NCE Scores

Percentile	99	90	80	70	60	50	40	30	20	10	1
NCE Score	99	77	67	61	55	50	45	39	33	23	1

that cannot be carried out with percentiles, and it is probably for this reason that NCE scores have become increasingly popular. Figure 8.3 shows the relationship between every tenth percentile and its corresponding NCE score.

Ratio Scales

The most desirable form of measurement is called a **ratio scale.** Such scales have the important property of equal units of measurement. For example, the difference between a person who weighs 110 pounds and one who weighs 120 pounds is 10 pounds. Similarly, the difference between a person who weighs 210 pounds and one who weighs 220 pounds is also 10 pounds. "Pound" is the unit of measurement in the example, and its definition remains the same whether it is applied to large or small weights.

Furthermore, it is accurate to say that a person who weighs 220 pounds is twice as heavy as a person who weighs 110 pounds. A unique feature of ratio scales is that they apply to variables that have a true value of zero (i.e., zero pounds represents the absence of weight). On the other hand, it is incorrect to say that a temperature of 50° F is twice as hot as 25° F, because 0° F designates a particular degree of coldness, not the absence of temperature.

Averages, or Measures of Central Tendency

It has already been noted that the concept **average** is a descriptive statistic. Actually, in descriptive statistics there are three kinds of averages used: the *mean,* the *median,* and the *mode.* Sometimes instead of *average,* the term *measure of central tendency* is used. The mean, median, and mode are all measures of central tendency.

The Mean

The **mean** is the most frequently used measure of central tendency in research. The mean is the arithmetic average of a set of scores. When a teacher reports that the students in her class had an average spelling test score of 73, for example, she really is reporting the mean score. To obtain the mean score, add up all the scores and divide by the number of scores. In other words, a teacher would add up the spelling test scores of all the students in the class and divide the total by the number of students to obtain the class mean.

The Median and Mode

Use of the median and mode as averages in research is much less frequent than use of the mean. The **median** is that score above which and below which half of the scores fall. (One easy mnemonic for helping you to remember the definition of *median* is to think of the median on a highway, the strip of land running down the middle of a highway that divides the highway in half. Similarly, the median in statistics is that score that separates the upper half of a set of scores from the bottom half.)

The **mode** is the score in a set of scores that occurs most frequently. Table 8.1 shows test scores of three groups of students, with five students in each group. The mean score for all three groups is 75 (375 ÷ 5 = 75). Note, however, that although Groups A and C have 75 as a median score, Group B's median score is 76. Also note that all three groups have different modes. Group A's mode is 75, Group B's is 72, and Group C's is 99. Notice how information conveyed about averages can vary dramatically, depending on which average one chooses to report.

Variability

To describe more precisely how the test scores in Table 8.1 are distributed within the three groups, one needs to report not only the groups' average scores, but also how much variability there is within each group's set of scores (i.e., how similar the scores within a set are to one another). The more similar the scores, the less the variability. Conversely, the more dissimilar the scores, the greater the variability.

In Table 8.1, it is clear that the distribution of scores within each group is not the same. The amount of variability of the scores differs from group to group. For example, there is no variability at all in the set of scores of students in Group A. All students achieved exactly the same score. In Group B, however, there is some variability among the distribution of scores. In Group C there is even more variability. In other words, the scores in Group A are more similar (actually, identical) than the scores in Group B, and the scores in Group B are more similar than those in Group C.

Measures of Variability

Students usually find nothing peculiar in expressing an average in terms of some number. The concept of *average* is familiar to most of us, and we are used to thinking of averages in quantitative terms. You may be surprised, however, to learn that there are also different ways of expressing variability in numerical or quantitative terms. Unfortunately, because we are

Table 8.1	Distribution of Test Scores and Average Scores for 3 Groups of 5 Students		
	Group A	Group B	Group C
	75	78	99
	75	77	99
	75	76	75
	75	72	56
	75	72	46
Sum	375	375	375
Mean	75	75	75
Median	75	76	75
Mode	75	72	99

not used to thinking of variability in quantitative terms, students sometimes find it difficult to grasp conceptually the meaning of measures of variability.

The Range

One way of expressing variability that probably is familiar to you is the **range.** The range of a set of scores is defined by the lowest and highest score in the set. For example, in Table 8.1, Group C has a range that goes from 46 to 99. Group B has a range that goes from 72 to 78. Group A has a range that goes from 75 to 75 (i.e., there is no range). The range is a rather crude measure of variability in that it only takes into account the lowest and highest scores in a set. It provides no information about the intermediate scores. For example, consider the following sets of scores:

(A) *25, 50, 50, 50, 100*
(B) *25, 42, 77, 86, 100*

The range in both sets A and B is identical: 25 to 100. However, the distributions of the scores in the two sets are considerably different. Use of the range as a measure of variability does not reveal how similar or dissimilar scores are that lie between the two end points. The range is used relatively infrequently in descriptive statistics because of the limited amount of information it provides concerning variability.

Variability About the Mean

Of more interest in descriptive statistics are measures of variability that describe how a set of scores is distributed about the mean score. Such measures take into account the variability of all scores in a set and distinguish between the amounts of variability exhibited by different groups' scores. In other words, these measures can inform us that in Table 8.1, the scores

Table 8.2		Differences Between Scores and Their Respective Means for Groups B and C		

Group B		Group C	
Scores	**Difference (Score − Mean)**	**Scores**	**Difference (Score − Mean)**
78	78 − 75 = +3	99	99 − 75 = +24
77	77 − 75 = +2	99	99 − 75 = +24
76	76 − 75 = +1	75	75 − 75 = 0
72	72 − 75 = −3	56	56 − 75 = −19
72	72 − 75 = −3	46	46 − 75 = −29
	Sum of Differences = 0		Sum of Differences = 0

of Group B are distributed relatively closely about Group B's mean, but that the scores of Group C are distributed relatively widely about Group C's mean.

Actually, one would like to know the average amount by which each score differs from the mean score. Surely the average amount by which each score in Group C differs from its mean is larger than the average amount by which each score in Group B differs from its mean. To make sure this statement is true, however, let us determine the average amount by which each score differs from its respective group mean.

The easiest way to check this is to subtract the group's mean from each score in the group as shown in Table 8.2. Add the differences in each group and divide by the number of differences to determine the average difference.

The Sum of Differences Equals Zero. Notice, however, what happens when one adds up the differences. For both groups, the sum of the differences turns out to be zero. If we divide zero by five (the number of differences in each group), we get zero. In other words, it appears that the average amount by which each score in the two groups differs from its group mean is zero. Clearly, something is wrong! One can see from the distribution of scores in Table 8.1 that only the scores in Group A have an average difference of zero from the mean. The average amount by which each score in Groups B and C differs from its respective mean is *not* zero. In fact, the average amount by which scores in Groups B and C differ from their respective means is not even identical—on the average, scores in Group C clearly differ more from Group C's mean than scores in Group B differ from Group B's mean.

What is the problem? The problem is that it makes no difference what set of numbers one takes, if one subtracts the mean of the set from each number in the set and adds up the differences, the sum is always zero. In fact, one can define the mean as that number, which when subtracted from all numbers in a set, yields a set of differences that adds up to zero.

It is at this point that many students begin to have difficulty with statistics. Students often are not told that subtracting the mean from each score in a set and adding up the differences *always* yields zero. By knowing this fact, it should be easier for you to grasp

Table 8.3		Squares of Difference Scores of Groups B and C	

Group B		Group C	
Difference (Score − Mean)	Difference^2 (Score − Mean)^2	Difference (Score − Mean)	Difference^2 (Score − Mean)^2
+3	+9	+24	+576
+2	+4	+24	+576
+1	+1	0	0
−3	+9	−19	+361
−3	+9	−29	+841
	Sum of Squares = 32		Sum of Squares = 2,354

conceptually why the computation of variability is not as straightforward as it would appear to be. In Table 8.2 the differences between scores and their respective means add up to zero because the negative differences cancel out the positive differences. The sum inevitably must be zero. For example, the positive differences in Group B are +3, +2, and +1, which add up to +6. The negative differences are −3 and −3, which add up to −6. Adding +6 to −6 yields a total of 0. Similarly, in Group C, the positive differences add up to +48 (+24 plus +24) and the negative differences add up to −48 (−19 plus −29).

Sum of Squares and Variance. One way to get out of this dilemma is to get rid of the negative differences. There are a number of ways to eliminate negative differences, but statisticians do so by squaring the difference scores. (Multiplying one negative number by another negative number yields a positive number.) Let us take the difference scores as shown in Table 8.2 for Groups B and C and square them. The results are shown in Table 8.3.

The resulting **sum of squares** for Group B is 32 and for Group C, 2,354. Dividing the sum of squares by the number of scores yields the **variance.** In this case, the variance for Group B is 32 ÷ 5 = 6.40, and the variance for Group C is 2,354 ÷ 5 = 470.80. The variance shows how much the average *squared* difference between each score and the mean score is.

Standard Deviation. However, one doesn't want to know how much the average *squared* difference is. Taking the square root of the variance gives the **standard deviation,** which is the most common measure of variability used in statistics. Technically, the standard deviation is the square root of the average squared difference between each score and the mean score. From a practical point of view, it is useful to think of the standard deviation as a close approximation of the average amount by which each score differs from the group's mean.

The variance of Group B's scores is 6.40. Consequently, Group B's standard deviation is 2.53 (the square root of 6.40). The variance of Group C's scores is 470.80. Group C's standard deviation is therefore 21.70 (the square root of 470.80). In other words, the average amount by which each score in Group B differs from Group B's mean is approximately 2.53, and the average amount by which each score in Group C differs from Group C's mean is approximately 21.70. The larger the standard deviation (*SD*), the greater the amount of variability. The *SD* of 21.70 for Group C indicates that the scores in Group C exhibit more variability than the scores in Group B, which have a *SD* of only 2.53.

The most important thing to understand about the concept of standard deviation is that a *SD* approximates the average amount by which each score in a group differs from the group's mean score. Because the sum of the differences between each score and the mean always equals zero, to calculate a *SD,* it is first necessary to square the differences to eliminate the negative differences and then take the square root to undo the squaring process.

Using descriptive statistics to describe how test scores are distributed among Groups B and C, one would report that Group B has a mean (*M*) = 75.00 and a *SD* = 2.53. Group C has a *M* = 75.00 and a *SD* = 21.70. This information indicates that although both groups have identical means, the scores in Group C exhibit more variability than those in Group B. Box 8.1 shows how to calculate the mean and standard deviation.

Averages and Variability

Descriptive statistics deals with expressing the average score and the variability of a set of scores for a group of people. Both the average, which is usually called the mean, and the variability, which is usually called the standard deviation, are expressed in numerical form. The fact that the mean and the standard deviation are expressed numerically enables us to understand easily the way in which a particular variable can be distributed differently among various groups. Groups may differ in terms of their means, their standard deviations, or both. For example, groups may have the same means but different standard deviations, as in the three groups of test scores shown in Table 8.1. All three groups have a mean of 75. However, Group A's *SD* is 0, Group B's is 2.53, and Group C's is 21.70.

Similarly, two groups may have different means but the same standard deviation. Suppose that one group of students has a mean reading grade level of 7.1 and another a mean of 4.2. It is possible that both groups could have a *SD* of 1.3. In such a case it simply means that one group on the average reads at a higher level than the other group, but the amount of variability in the reading levels of students within each group is the same.

Finally, two groups may have both different means and different standard deviations. Consider the following example: One group of students achieves a mean score of 72 points on a spelling test and another group achieves a mean of 80. It is clear that the group with a mean of 80 performed better than the other group. Suppose it turns out that on the same test one group has a *SD* of 3 and the other a *SD* of 10. It should be clear that there is more variability in the scores of the group with the *SD* of 10 than in the group with the *SD* of 3. In this example it has not been stated which group has which mean or which *SD*. The group with the lower mean might have either a lower or a higher *SD* than the group with the higher mean. There is no consistent relationship between the magnitude of a mean and the magnitude of a *SD*.

The Relationship Between Two Variables

The discussion so far has focused on using descriptive statistics to report how a single variable is distributed among a group of people. It is also common, however, for researchers to report the extent to which the distribution of two variables within the same group of

Box 8.1 Calculating the Mean and Standard Deviation

Mean $= \Sigma X \div n$

Standard Deviation $= \sqrt{\dfrac{\Sigma X^2 - \dfrac{(\Sigma X)^2}{n}}{n - 1}}$

$\qquad\qquad$ where $\Sigma X =$ the sum of the scores
$\qquad\qquad\qquad\quad n =$ the number of scores
$\qquad\qquad\qquad\ \Sigma X^2 =$ the sum of the squared scores
$\qquad\qquad\ \ (\Sigma X)^2 =$ the sum of the scores squared

It is best to set up a table with three columns. In column 1 list all of the subjects' names or code numbers. In column 2 list each subject's score. In column 3 list the square of each subject's score. Then add up the numbers in columns 2 and 3 and enter their respective totals.

(1)	(2)	(3)
1	20	400
2	12	144
3	10	100
4	9	81
5	4	16
Sum	55	741

Step 1. Divide the sum of column 2 by the number of subjects.
$\qquad$ $55 \div 5 = 11.00$
$\qquad$ The answer in Step 1 is the mean.
Step 2. Take the sum of column 2 times itself.
$\qquad$ $55 \times 55 = 3025$
Step 3. Divide the answer in Step 2 by the number of subjects.
$\qquad$ $3025 \div 5 = 605$
Step 4. Take the sum of column 3 and subtract the answer in Step 3.
$\qquad$ $741 - 605 = 136$
Step 5. Take the number of subjects and subtract 1.
$\qquad$ $5 - 1 = 4$
Step 6. Divide the answer in Step 4 by the answer in Step 5.
$\qquad$ $136 \div 4 = 34$
Step 7. Take the square root of the answer in Step 6.
$\qquad$ $\sqrt{34} = 5.83$
$\qquad$ The answer in Step 7 is the standard deviation.

Figure 8.4

Rank Order of Students as a Function of Performance on Math and
Science Tests (Perfect Positive Correlation)

Science Test	Math Test
1. Maria	1. Maria
2. Rob	2. Rob
3. Susan	3. Susan
4. Jose	4. Jose
5. Tyrone	5. Tyrone
6. Anita	6. Anita
7. Greg	7. Greg
8. Henry	8. Henry
9. Kim	9. Kim
10. Cindy	10. Cindy

people are correlated. For example, one might be interested in determining how seventh-grade students' performance in mathematics is correlated with their performance in science. In order to make this determination, one would carry out a correlational study by selecting a group of seventh graders and giving them a math test and a science test. Given the nature of the variables, one would probably expect students who score high on the math test also to score high on the science test and, conversely, students who score low on one test to score low on the other.

Perfect Correlation

To get a feeling for what a correlational study is like, imagine that the study described previously has been carried out and a perfect positive correlation is found. This means that the student who scored highest on the math test is the same one who scored highest on the science test. The student who scored second highest on the science test is the same one who scored second highest on the math test, and so on down to the student who scored lowest on the math test and lowest on the science test. In other words, if we used the math test scores and listed each student's name in rank order from the student who scored highest to the one who scored lowest and then made another list of rankings using the science test scores, the names on the two lists would appear in identical order, which is just another way of showing that the two variables are perfectly correlated. (See Figure 8.4.)

Figure 8.5 is a pictorial representation of the information provided in Figure 8.4. Such a representation is called a *scattergram*. Each dot in Figure 8.5 represents one student and the location of the dot is determined jointly by the student's rank on the math test and on the science test. When scores on two variables are perfectly positively correlated, the dots fall directly on a diagonal line sloping from the upper right-hand part of the diagram to the lower left-hand part.

When variables are perfectly correlated, we are able to make perfect predictions about a student's performance on one variable if we know how the student performed on the other variable. If we know that a student ranked fourth in the class on the math test,

Figure 8.5

Scattergram of Seventh Graders' Performance on Math and Science Tests (Perfect Positive Correlation)

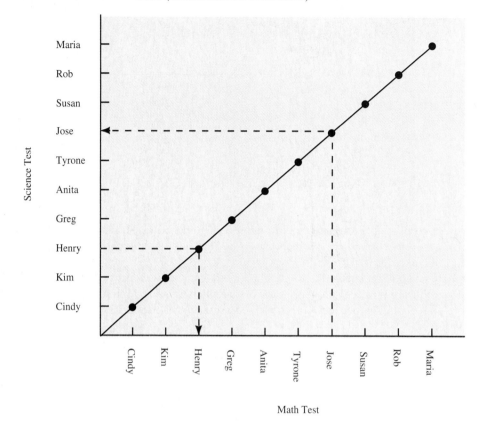

we know that the student also ranked fourth in the class on the science test. Similarly, if we know that a student ranked eighth on the science test, we know the same student ranked eighth on the math test.

In Figure 8.5 Jose scored fourth highest on the math test. By locating Jose's position on the horizontal axis, which represents math test performance, and extending a vertical (dotted) line up to the diagonal and then making a 90-degree turn to the left, one can locate Jose's exact position on the vertical axis, which represents science test performance. Similarly, by locating Henry's position on the vertical axis and extending a horizontal (dotted) line to the diagonal and then making a 90-degree turn downward, one can determine that Henry scored eighth highest on the math test as well as on the science test.

Less than Perfect Correlation

In the hypothetical correlational study described previously, it was assumed for instructional purposes that there was a perfect positive correlation between the two variables. In the real world it is virtually impossible to find a perfect correlation between two variables, at least not with the kinds of variables typically measured in educational research. A more realistic

Figure 8.6

Scattergram of Seventh Graders' Performance on Math and Science Tests (Less than Perfect Correlation)

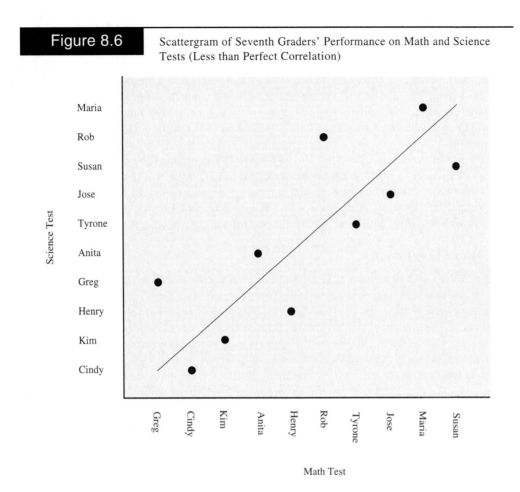

outcome of the study would be two lists of students' names in which the order of the names would be similar, but not identical. Some students would rank relatively higher on one test than on the other.

Figure 8.6 depicts the outcome of seventh graders' scores on a math test and a science test that are positively, but not perfectly correlated. The dots representing each student do *not* fall on a straight line. Nevertheless, it is clear that in general, there is a tendency for students who performed well on one test to perform well on the other and, conversely, for those who scored poorly on one test to score poorly on the other. When the dots in a scattergram do not automatically fall on a straight line, it is possible to draw a *line of best fit* through the dots. The line of best fit is that line that comes as close to all dots as possible. The diagonal line in Figure 8.6 is the line of best fit. For any given scattergram there is only one line of best fit, and the location of that line is determined by applying an algebraic formula.

The degree of similarity of the order of the students' names could vary markedly, depending on the nature of the variables being measured. The order of names on the two lists might appear very similar if the two variables seem to have something in common, as math and science performance might. If the two variables have little in common, then one would expect the order of names on the two lists to bear little resemblance to each other. To take a ludicrous example, suppose one carried out a correlational study to determine the extent to which the number of freckles on students' faces was correlated with the students' performance on a spelling test. The two variables would be the number of freckles and the scores on the spelling test. It is unlikely that these two variables have very much in common, so one would expect the order of names on the freckle list to be quite different from that on the spelling test list.

The point of noting that the degree of similarity in the order of the two lists of names can vary over a wide range is to draw your attention to the notion that it would be useful to have some way of designating how similar the rank orderings of names on two given lists actually are. By designating the degree of similarity between two lists, one could tell whether two variables are highly correlated, moderately correlated, or not correlated at all.

Correlation Coefficients

As you probably already have surmised, researchers do have a way of designating the degree of similarity of the orderings of names ranked on two variables. The designation is called a **correlation coefficient,** which is a statistical measure of the degree of relationship between two variables. The statistical symbol used for the correlation coefficient is r. Whenever you encounter the symbol r you can be sure that the researcher is concerned with the question of the extent to which two variables are correlated. Later you will learn how one determines the correlation coefficient for any given set of rankings. Now you need only understand generally that there is a statistic called the correlation coefficient that is symbolized by the letter r and that reflects the degree of relationship between two variables.

It may also be useful to know that correlation coefficients can range from $+1.00$ to -1.00. A correlation coefficient of $+1.00$ indicates that the names ranked on two variables appear in exactly the same order. A correlation coefficient of -1.00 indicates that the names ranked on two variables appear in exactly the reverse order.

The closer a correlation coefficient is to $+1.00$, the more nearly alike the rank orderings are. For example, an r of $+.87$ would indicate that the two variables are highly correlated but the correlation is not perfect. In other words, the order of names ranked on each of two variables is almost identical, but the relative position of the names is somewhat different on the two lists. Similarly, the closer the correlation coefficient is to -1.00, the more nearly the rank orderings are the reverse of each other. Box 8.2 shows how to calculate a correlation coefficient. Box 8.3 shows how to calculate a split-half reliability coefficient, which is a special instance of correlation. (Split-half reliability is discussed in chapter 7.)

Negative Correlation

Sometimes it is more reasonable to expect two variables to be negatively rather than positively correlated. Suppose that one is interested in studying the relationship between the number of years golfers have been playing golf and golfers' scores. Golf is different from most games in that the person with the lowest score is the winner. One would expect that the longer a person has been playing golf, the more proficient the person would be and the lower the score. If we ranked golfers from the golfer who has played the most to the one

Box 8.2 Calculating the Pearson Product Moment Correlation Coefficient (r)

$$r = \frac{N\Sigma AB - (\Sigma A)(\Sigma B)}{\sqrt{[N\Sigma A^2 - (\Sigma A)^2][N\Sigma B^2 - (\Sigma B)^2]}}$$

where N = number of pairs of scores

A = scores on the A variable

B = scores on the B variable

ΣA = sum of scores on the A variable

ΣB = sum of scores on the B variable

ΣA^2 = sum of squared scores on the A variable

ΣB^2 = sum of squared scores on the B variable

ΣAB = sum of the products of paired scores

ΣA^2 is not the same as $(\Sigma A)^2$. Square the scores for ΣA^2 and then sum. First sum the scores for $(\Sigma A)^2$ and then square.

Let us consider the following case for illustration. Suppose a researcher has administered a self-concept questionnaire and a reading achievement test to a group of six students. The researcher is interested in determining to what extent the students' scores on the two variables are related. In the example following, let us call the reading achievement test score variable "A" and the self-concept score variable "B." The scores in the example will be kept small to keep the calculations relatively simple, but the process described can be used regardless of the magnitude of actual scores.

First, set up a table with six columns. In column 1 list all of the subjects' names or code numbers. In column 2 list each subject's score on variable A. In column 3 list each subject's score on variable B. In column 4 list the square of each subject's score on variable A. In column 5 list the square of each subject's score on variable B. In column 6 list the product of each subject's scores on variables A and B, which is obtained by multiplying the subject's score in column 2 times the subject's score in column 3. Then add up the numbers in each column.

(1)	(2)	(3)	(4)	(5)	(6)
1	10	9	100	81	90
2	8	8	64	64	64
3	7	10	49	100	70
4	7	6	49	36	42
5	5	6	25	36	30
6	4	3	16	9	12
Sum	41	42	303	326	308

Step 1. Multiply the number of subjects times the sum of column 6.

$6 \times 308 = 1,848$

Step 2. Multiply the sum of column 2 times the sum of column 3.

$41 \times 42 = 1,722$

Box 8.2 continued

Step 3. Take the answer in Step 1 and subtract the answer in Step 2.

$1,848 - 1,722 = 126$

Step 4. Multiply the number of subjects times the sum of column 4.

$6 \times 303 = 1,818$

Step 5. Multiply the sum of column 2 times itself.

$41 \times 41 = 1,681$

Step 6. Take the answer in Step 4 and subtract the answer in Step 5.

$1,818 - 1,681 = 137$

Step 7. Take the square root of the answer in Step 6.

$\sqrt{137} = 11.70$

Step 8. Multiply the number of subjects times the sum of column 5.

$6 \times 326 = 1,956$

Step 9. Multiply the sum of column 3 times itself.

$42 \times 42 = 1,764$

Step 10. Take the answer in Step 8 and subtract the answer in Step 9.

$1,956 - 1,764 = 192$

Step 11. Take the square root of the answer in Step 10.

$\sqrt{192} = 13.86$

Step 12. Multiply the answer in Step 7 times the answer in Step 11.

$11.70 \times 13.86 = 162.16$

Step 13. Divide the answer in Step 3 by the answer in Step 12.

$126 \div 162.16 = .78$

The answer in Step 13 is the value of r and must fall between -1.00 and $+1.00$. If not, you have made a computational error.

Step 14. Using the number of subjects, enter the table of r values in appendix D.

In our example the number of subjects is 6. The corresponding r values in the table are .73 and .88. Since our calculated coefficient is .78, it is statistically significant at the .05 level. If the obtained value had been greater than .88, it would have been significant at the .01 level.

An r value may be either positive or negative, depending on whether the relationship between variables is positive or negative. Ignore the sign of the r value when consulting the table.

who has played the least and then ranked the same golfers from the one with the highest score (i.e., the worst score) to the one with the lowest score, we would expect the names on the two lists to appear more or less in reverse order.

Whether we expect two variables to be positively or negatively correlated often depends on how we decide to define them. For example, one would expect a correlation between reading grade level and the ability to spell correctly. In general, one would anticipate that students who are better readers are also better spellers. If we correlated reading grade level with the number of words spelled correctly on a spelling test, we would expect the correlation coefficient to be positive. However, if we correlated reading grade level with the number of errors students made on a spelling test, we would expect the correlation coefficient to be negative. Whether we define spelling ability in terms of the number of words spelled correctly

Box 8.3 Calculating the Split-Half Reliability Coefficient (r) and Correcting for Test Length

The split-half reliability coefficient is calculated exactly as is the Pearson r. Consequently, the computational procedures in Box 8.2 should be used. The only difference is that the numbers in columns 2 and 3 would represent the subtotal scores for odd-numbered and even-numbered items on a test rather than the scores on two variables. In other words, Subject 1 would have scored a total of 19 points on the test, receiving 10 points on the odd-numbered items and 9 points on the even-numbered items; Subject 2 would have scored a total of 16 points on the test, receiving 8 points on the odd-numbered items and 8 points on the even-numbered items; and so forth.

The split-half reliability coefficient underestimates the reliability of a test because it treats the test as though it is comprised of half the number of items that the test really has. Therefore, the reliability coefficient must be corrected for test length by applying the Spearman-Brown prophecy formula:

Step 1. Calculate a Pearson r between the odd-numbered and even-numbered subtotals following the steps in Box 8.2. Using the data in Box 8.2, $r = .78$

Step 2. Double the r value.
$2 \times .78 = 1.56$

Step 3. Add 1 to the r value.
$1 + .78 = 1.78$

Step 4. Take the answer in Step 2 and divide it by the answer in Step 3.
$1.56 \div 1.78 = .88$
The answer in Step 4 is the split-half reliability corrected for test length.

The issue of whether the reliability coefficient is statistically significant is irrelevant, so one does not check the reliability coefficient against the values listed in the table in appendix D. Instead, one decides if the coefficient represents an adequate level of reliability in terms of what kind of behavior the test is designed to measure. This decision is basically a matter of subjective interpretation.

or in terms of the number of words spelled incorrectly is an arbitrary decision. Nothing about the expected relationship between the two variables is changed except that in one case we predict there will be a positive correlation and in the other case a negative correlation.

Figure 8.7 shows a scattergram of students' reading grade level and the number of errors made on a spelling test, which are negatively correlated, that is, students with higher reading levels make fewer spelling errors, while students with lower reading levels make more spelling errors. The line of best fit slopes from the upper left of the diagram to the lower right.

The correlation coefficients of $+1.00$ and -1.00 both indicate a perfect relationship. Both correlations permit one to predict a person's ranking on one variable if one knows the person's ranking on the other variable. With a correlation coefficient of $+1.00$, we know that the student who is highest on one variable is also highest on the other variable. With a correlation of -1.00, we know that the student who is highest on one variable is *lowest* on the other variable. However, in either case we can predict with complete accuracy the ranking on one variable if we already know the ranking on the other.

Figure 8.7	Scattergram Showing the Negative Relationship Between Reading Grade Level and Number of Spelling Errors

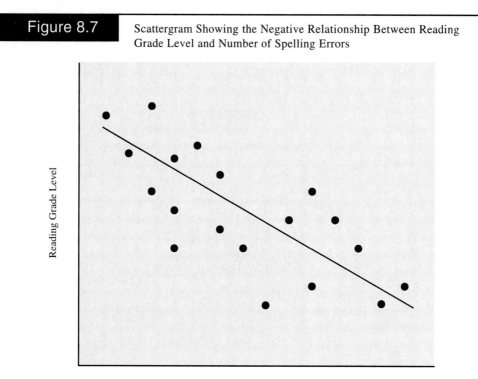

Reading Grade Level

Spelling Test Errors

Zero Correlation

A correlation coefficient of .00 means that the two variables are not correlated at all. Knowing where a student ranks on one variable does not enable us to predict with any accuracy where the student ranks on the other variable. One would expect, for example, the correlation coefficient between spelling test scores and the number of freckles on students' faces to be approximately .00, as shown in Figure 8.8.

The Problem of Restricted Range

The magnitude of the correlation coefficient can be affected by the range of the scores of the variables being correlated. If one (or both) of the variables being correlated has a restricted range, that is, all of the scores are similar to one another, the size of the correlation coefficient may be reduced dramatically. Given a restricted range, the slope of the line of best fit may approach zero. For example, if one were to examine the relationship between reading ability and reading comprehension among a group of gifted students, the correlation would very likely be quite low because all of the subjects in the study would probably have similar scores on both measures. On the other hand, if one conducted the same study among a group of average students, the correlation coefficient would probably turn out to be positive because the scores on both variables would cover a relatively wide range.

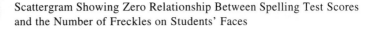

| Figure 8.8 | Scattergram Showing Zero Relationship Between Spelling Test Scores and the Number of Freckles on Students' Faces |

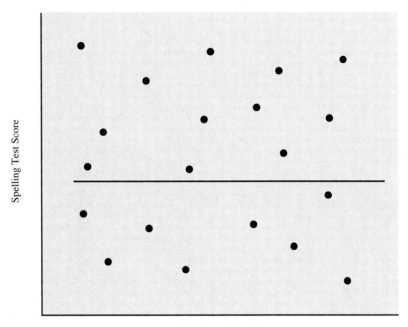

Measures of Relationship

To help you grasp more easily that the concept of correlation deals with the degree of relationship between two variables, the preceding examples were selected to show the degree of similarity in the rank order of people on two measures. However, some variables have values that are not amenable to ranking, such as gender, geographic location, or academic major. It is meaningless to rank order people by gender or locations by urban, suburban, or rural. Similarly, it makes no sense to rank order academic majors. Such variables are called **nominal** or **categorical variables** and have their own measures of relationship, which are described later.

Furthermore, in the examples given earlier, it was assumed that the nature of the relationship between the variables was *linear,* that is, the higher the person's score on one variable, the higher the person's score on the second variable. (In the case of negative correlation, the higher the score on one variable, the lower the score on the other variable.) Sometimes, however, one wishes to examine the degree of *curvilinear relationship* between two variables. For example, one might predict that people with little anxiety or lots of anxiety would tend to perform poorly on an academic achievement test, but that people with moderate amounts of anxiety would tend to perform well.

Figure 8.9 illustrates pictorially the nature of curvilinear relationship. As you might expect, the measure of the degree of curvilinear relationship differs from the measure of

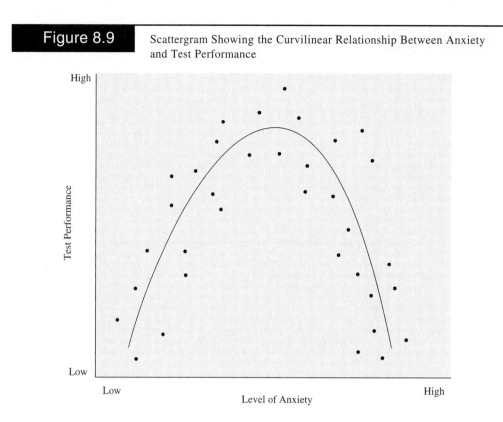

| Figure 8.9 | Scattergram Showing the Curvilinear Relationship Between Anxiety and Test Performance |

linear relationship. Figure 8.10 lists the most commonly occurring measures of relationship and the circumstances determining their use. See Borg and Gall (1989) for a comprehensive account of various correlation coefficients.

Interpreting Correlation Coefficients

Perhaps because correlation coefficients are expressed as decimals, students often incorrectly equate correlation coefficients with percentages. Correlation coefficients are not percentages. They are measures of the degree of relationship between variables, with the strongest degree of relationship expressed as +1.00 or −1.00 and the weakest degree by 0.

All correlation coefficients are interpreted the same way. The closer the measure is to +1.00 (or −1.00), the stronger the degree of relationship between the variables and the more likely the relationship is statistically significant. The larger the sample size, the smaller the correlation coefficient can be and still be statistically significant.

The Correlation Coefficient and Shared Variance

To interpret a correlation coefficient meaningfully, it is helpful to determine how much variability the two variables have in common, that is, how much variability in one variable is accounted for by the variability in the other variable. The measure of variability used is called the *variance* and the amount of shared variance between two variables is equal to r^2.

Figure 8.10

Figure 8.10   Commonly Used Measures of Correlation

Name of Measure	Statistical Symbol	Nature of Variables
Product-Moment	r	Both are continuous.
Rank Order (Rho)	ρ	Both are rankings.
Phi	ϕ	Both are nominal and each has two values.
Contingency	C	Both are nominal and each has more than two values.
Eta	η	Both are continuous (used to detect curvilinear relationships).

The larger the value of r, the greater the percentage of shared variance. Variables that have a correlation coefficient of .90 have 81% shared variance; variables that have a correlation of .80 have 64% shared variance, and so forth. The percentage of variance shared by variables that are negatively correlated is computed the same way. For example, variables with an r value of $-.90$ also have 81% shared variance.

To decide how meaningful a statistically significant correlation coefficient is, it is necessary to determine how much variance is shared by the two variables. If the sample size is large enough, an $r = .30$ would be statistically significant. However, the amount of variance shared between the two variables is only 9% (i.e., $.30 \times .30 = .09 = 9\%$). Whether 9% shared variance is meaningful or not, depends on the nature of the variables being investigated.

The Normal Distribution

You have no doubt encountered the concept of a **normal distribution** somewhere in the course of your studies. However, to refresh your memory, let us take a look at an example of a normal distribution. Not all characteristics, or variables, are distributed normally, but many are. IQ scores are an example of a characteristic that is normally distributed. When we say that IQ scores are normally distributed, all we mean is that very few people have very low or very high IQ scores and most people have IQ scores somewhere in the middle. If we made a graph showing the number of people at each IQ score, it would look like a bell, which is why a normal distribution is often called the bell-shaped curve.

If we administered the Stanford-Binet IQ test to a large group of people, we would find that the mean IQ score is 100. Since Stanford-Binet IQ scores are normally distributed, we would find that there are very few with IQ scores at the genius level, very few with IQ scores at the level of mental retardation, and many with IQ scores close to 100.

Why the Normal Distribution Is of Interest to Educators

There are two fundamental reasons why educators are interested in the normal distribution. The first is that, while not all characteristics are distributed normally, an extremely large number of characteristics of interest to educators are known to be or are believed to be distributed normally. Characteristics such as scores on achievement tests, aptitude tests, personality tests, and attitudinal inventories are all assumed to be normally distributed.

The second reason is that the normal distribution has certain useful properties. We know, for example, that the mean score is that which coincides with the peak of the curve. We also know that the normal distribution is symmetric about the mean. If we were to start at the peak of a bell-shaped curve and draw a line straight down through the middle of the curve, we would find that the one half of the curve is the mirror image of the other half. In other words, we know that 50% of the population have scored at the mean or higher, and 50% have scored at the mean or lower. On the Stanford-Binet IQ test, 50% of the population have an IQ of 100 or higher and 50% have an IQ of 100 or lower.

Construction of the Normal Curve

The normal curve and its properties are so fundamental to understanding statistical analyses of quantitative research data that it is important for you to grasp thoroughly how a normal curve emerges from a collection of data. First, however, it should be pointed out that a normal curve will not emerge from data unless the data are in fact normally distributed. Because IQ scores *are* normally distributed, let us use them as an example of how a normal curve is constructed.

Suppose I wish to describe statistically how Stanford-Binet IQ scores are distributed among some large group—let's say 20,000 people. I would first administer the Stanford-Binet to all 20,000 people and then calculate the mean and standard deviation. I would proceed in exactly the same way I calculated the means and *SD*s for the test scores described in Tables 8.1 through 8.3 except, of course, I would have a much larger number of scores to use in my calculations. Let us assume that my calculations result in a mean IQ score of 100 and a *SD* of 16. (Such an assumption is reasonable because it is well known that the Stanford-Binet is constructed so that the scores for large groups of people who have taken it have a mean of 100 and a *SD* of 16.)

Frequency Distributions. Suppose that in addition to describing the distribution of IQ scores statistically, I also wish to show pictorially how the 20,000 IQ scores are distributed. One way to do this is to construct a **frequency distribution.** Figure 8.11 shows a frequency distribution of the IQ scores of 10 people. In other words, I have taken the first 10 IQ scores of the 20,000 and plotted them on a graph, where the horizontal axis represents the range of IQ scores and the vertical axis represents the number of people (or frequency). Each box in Figure 8.11 represents the score of one person.

Figure 8.11   Frequency Distribution of IQ Scores of 10 People

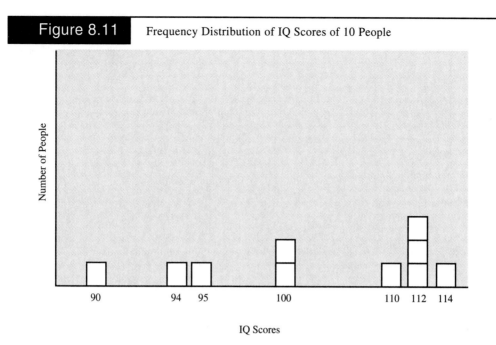

I locate each person's IQ score on the horizontal axis and place a box above it. There are 10 boxes, each corresponding to one of the 10 people whose IQ scores I have plotted. The number of boxes above an IQ score indicates how many people have achieved that particular IQ score. Figure 8.11 shows that the IQ scores of 90, 94, 95, 110, and 114 were each achieved by one person. Two people achieved IQ scores of 100, and three people achieved IQ scores of 112.

Histograms or Bar Graphs. If I continued to plot the remaining 19,990 IQ scores, Figure 8.11 would ultimately look like Figure 8.12. In Figure 8.12 the lines separating the boxes that represented individual people in Figure 8.11 have been erased. It is important to understand, however, that each column in Figure 8.12 actually has been created by placing one box on top of the other. The height of each column indicates how many people achieved each IQ score. Figure 8.12 is a type of frequency distribution called a **bar graph** or **histogram.**

The Bell-Shaped Curve. If I modify Figure 8.12 by connecting the midpoints at the top of each column and then erase the lines separating the columns, I now have the figure shown in Figure 8.13. This figure is a normal, or bell-shaped curve. The important thing to understand is that each of the 20,000 IQ scores falls somewhere beneath the curve. Remember, the area underneath the curve actually consists of 20,000 boxes that have been stacked on top of each other and placed above their respective IQ scores. All normal curves are constructed by following the steps outlined in Figures 8.11 through 8.13.

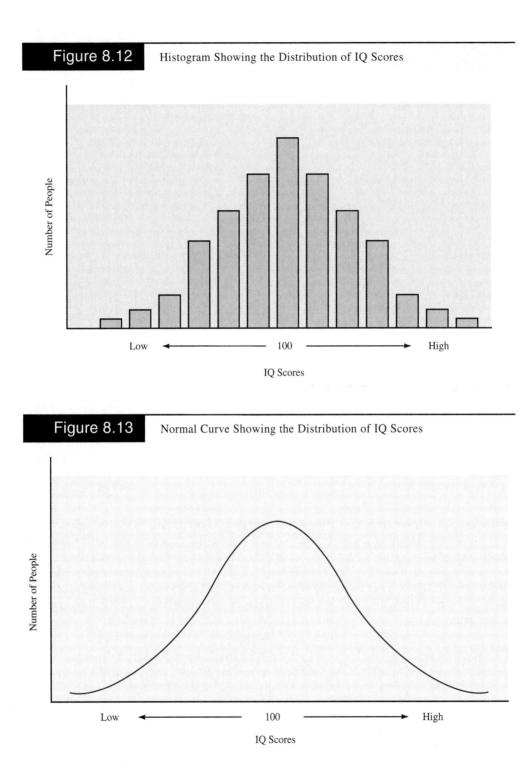

Figure 8.12   Histogram Showing the Distribution of IQ Scores

Number of People

Low ◄────────── 100 ──────────► High

IQ Scores

Figure 8.13   Normal Curve Showing the Distribution of IQ Scores

Number of People

Low ◄────────── 100 ──────────► High

IQ Scores

Figure 8.14

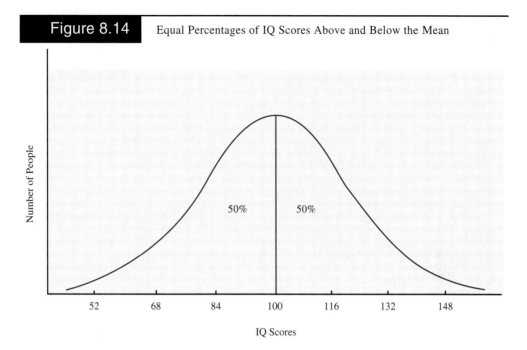

Figure 8.14 Equal Percentages of IQ Scores Above and Below the Mean

Number of People

50%   50%

52   68   84   100   116   132   148

IQ Scores

Properties of the Normal Curve

There is an infinite number of normal curves, all of which have the same bell-like shape. The particular normal curve one is dealing with is defined by the mean and the standard deviation. No matter which normal curve one is concerned with, however, they all share some known properties. One of the properties of all normal curves is that the mean score falls at a point on the horizontal axis directly beneath the peak of the curve. Notice in Figure 8.14 that the mean IQ score of 100 falls at the point under the peak of the curve, indicating that the most frequently occurring IQ score is 100. All normal curves are symmetric about the midpoint. In other words, half the people score at the mean or above and half score at the mean or below. Notice in Figure 8.14 that 50% of IQ scores are 100 or higher and 50% are 100 or lower.

The Mean Plus and Minus One Standard Deviation. By far the most important property of normal distributions is the constant relationship between the mean, the standard deviation, and the percentage of the population scoring within a range defined by the mean and the standard deviation. Just as we know that 50% of the population fall at the mean or above, it is also known that approximately 34% of the population fall between the mean and the mean plus one *SD*, as shown in Figure 8.15. You do not have to be concerned about why we know that approximately 34% of the population fall between the mean and the mean plus one *SD*. Just accept this fact as given. It is simply another known property of normal curves.

Knowing that IQ scores are normally distributed, that the mean is 100 and the *SD* is 16, we immediately know that 34% of the population have IQ scores ranging from 100 (the mean) to 116 (the mean plus one *SD*). Furthermore, because normal distributions are symmetric about the mean, we also know that approximately 34% of the population have IQ

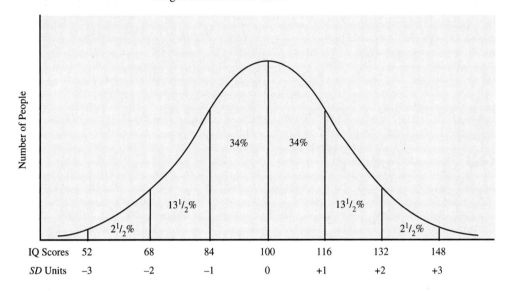

Figure 8.15 Approximate Percentages of People with IQ Scores Falling Within Ranges Defined in *SD* Units

scores ranging from 84 (the mean minus one *SD*) to 100 (the mean). In other words, the middle 68% of the population have IQ scores ranging from 84 to 116.

It doesn't make any difference what the mean and *SD* are of scores that are normally distributed; approximately 34% of the population always fall within the mean and one *SD* above the mean, and 34% within the mean and one *SD* below the mean. For example, suppose we have a set of achievement test scores that are normally distributed with a mean of 75 and a *SD* of 10. We know that approximately 34% of the students scored between 75 and 85 and approximately 34% scored between 65 and 75. Of course, we also know that 68%, or approximately two thirds, of the students scored between 65 and 85.

If we have another set of scores, again with a mean of 75, but with a *SD* of 6, we know that approximately 68% of the students made scores somewhere between 69 and 81. The mean score plus and minus one *SD* defines the range of scores obtained by 68% of the students.

The Mean Plus and Minus Two and Three Standard Deviations. In Figure 8.15 approximately 13½% of the population have IQ scores between 68 and 84 and another 13½% have IQ scores between 116 and 132. In other words, the middle 95% of the population (13½% + 34% + 34% + 13½% = 95%) have IQ scores ranging from 68 (the mean minus two *SD*s) to 132 (the mean plus two *SD*s). Furthermore, it can be seen that approximately 2½% of the population have IQ scores ranging between 132 and 148, and correspondingly, approximately another 2½% have IQ scores ranging between 52 and 68. In other words, for all practical purposes, 100% of the population have IQ scores ranging from 52 (the mean minus three *SD*s) to 148 (the mean plus three *SD*s).

Similarly, if we had a normally distributed set of scores with a mean of 75 and a *SD* of 6, we would know that the middle 95% of the population scored somewhere between 63 and

87. We multiplied the *SD* of 6 by 2 and got 12. Then we took the mean of 75 and added and subtracted 12, giving us the scores of 63 and 87, which are the end points of the range. And, of course, by adding and subtracting 18 points (three *SD*s) to the mean, we would know that virtually all people scored between 57 and 93.

To summarize briefly, consider the following hypothetical case. You have just administered a commercially available achievement test to the students in a class, and the test manual reports that the mean score of the test is 65 and the *SD* is 10. You now know that of all the students who took the test, 68% scored between 55 and 75, 95% scored between 45 and 85, and virtually all students scored between 35 and 95. It is now possible for you to look at your students' scores and determine how well they performed in comparison with other students.

Standard Scores (z Scores)

You learned previously that there is an infinite number of normal curves, each uniquely defined by its mean and *SD*. In the preceding discussion of the properties of normal distributions, several normally distributed sets of scores were used as illustrations. It is possible to express scores in terms of *SD* units. For example, an IQ score of 116 could be expressed as +1 in *SD* units, because 116 is one *SD* greater than the mean. An achievement test score of 75 could also be expressed as +1 in *SD* units, because 75 is one *SD* greater than the mean on the test in the previous example. Similarly, an IQ score of 68 could be expressed as −2 *SD* units, because 68 is two *SD*s less than the mean, or an achievement test score of 45 could be expressed as −2 *SD* units, because 45 is two *SD*s less than the mean.

Scores expressed in terms of *SD* units are called **standard scores** or **z scores.** One converts a score into a *z* score by subtracting the mean and dividing the result by the *SD:*

$$(\text{Score} - \text{Mean})/SD = z \text{ score}$$

For example, an IQ score of 132 has a *z* score value of +2.00:

$$(132 - 100)/16 = 32/16 = +2.00$$

An IQ score of 92 has a *z* score value of −0.50:

$$(92 - 100)/16 = -8/16 = -0.50.$$

When any set of scores is expressed in *z* scores, the resulting distribution has a mean of zero and a *SD* of one. When one refers to *the* normal curve, one is referring to a distribution expressed in *z* scores. Converting raw scores into *z* scores does not automatically result in a normally distributed set of scores. A set of *z* scores will be normally distributed only if the raw scores themselves follow a normal distribution.

Converting raw scores into *z* scores has the additional advantage of permitting one to make meaningful comparisons of a student's performance on various measures. Suppose, for example, one wanted to compare a student's performance on a math test with the student's performance on a vocabulary test. Assume the student achieved a score of 70 on both tests. It is incorrect to conclude on the basis of the two scores that the student performs equally well in math and vocabulary. Converting both of the student's scores into *z* scores, however, makes it possible to compare the performance on both tests.

Suppose the average score on the math test was 65 and the *SD* was 10. The student's *z* score on the math test is +.50 ([70 − 65]/10 = .50). Suppose the average score on the

Figure 8.16   Percentiles and Their Corresponding z Scores

Percentile	99	90	80	70	60	50	40	30	20	10	1
z score	+2.33	+1.28	+0.84	+0.52	+0.25	0.00	−0.25	−0.52	−0.84	−1.28	−2.33

vocabulary test was also 65 but the standard deviation was 5. The student's z score on the vocabulary test is $+1.00$ ([70 − 65]/5 = 1.00). A z score of 1.00 is greater than one of .50, so it is reasonable to conclude that the student performed better on the vocabulary test than on the math test. Figure 8.16 shows the relationship between every tenth percentile and its corresponding z score.

Chapter Highlights

- *Descriptive statistics* describe quantitatively how a particular characteristic is distributed among some group.
- *Inferential statistics* permit one to generalize findings based on a sample to the population from which the sample was selected.
- *Nominal* scales are used to measure variables whose values differ qualitatively, but not quantitatively.
- *Ordinal* scales provide a quantitative ranking, but the units of measurement are unequal; percentiles and grade equivalent scores are examples of ordinal scales.
- *Interval* and *ratio* scales provide quantitative measures with equal units of measurement; ratio scales have a meaningful zero point, but interval scales do not.
- A *raw score* is the number of items a person answers correctly on a test.
- *Stanines* divide a set of scores into nine equal units of measurement.
- *Normal Curve Equivalent (NCE)* scores divide a set of scores into 100 equal units of measurement.
- The *mean* is the arithmetic average of a set of scores; the *median* is the score above and below which half the scores in a set fall; the *mode* is the most frequently occurring score.
- The *range* is defined by the lowest and highest scores in a set.
- The *standard deviation* is a close approximation of the average amount by which each score in a group differs from the mean.
- *Correlation coefficients* indicate the degree of relationship between two variables, where $+1.00$ indicates a perfect positive relationship and -1.00 a perfect negative relationship.
- A restricted range of scores for one or both variables being correlated will result in a reduced correlation coefficient.

- The product-moment correlation coefficient (r) is used to describe the degree of linear relationship between two continuous variables.
- The rank order correlation coefficient (rho or ρ) is used to describe the degree of linear relationship between two variables that are rankings.
- Eta (η) is the correlation coefficient used to describe the degree of curvilinear relationship between two continuous variables.
- r^2 yields the percentage of variance two variables have in common.
- The *normal distribution* is symmetric about the midpoint; 68% of the area below the normal curve falls within the range defined by the mean and plus and minus one standard deviation; 95% falls within the range defined by the mean and plus and minus two standard deviations; and virtually 100% falls within the range defined by the mean and plus and minus three standard deviations.

Review Exercises

1. Describe the difference between descriptive and inferential statistics.
2. List the four kinds of scales of measurement from the most to the least desirable.
3. Define the term *raw score*.
4. Name two types of test scores frequently used in education that are examples of an ordinal scale.
5. Explain what a stanine is. What is the stanine of a student who scored in the 62nd percentile on a test?
6. What scale of measurement does each term below represent?
   a. The score on an inventory measuring teacher burnout
   b. The number of days a student attended school during the academic year
   c. A student's career goal
   d. An undergraduate's academic major
   e. The grade a student gets on an essay examination
7. Name three measures of central tendency. Which is the most commonly used?
8. Why is the range a relatively poor measure of variability?
9. What is the result if one subtracts the mean score from each score in a set and adds up the differences?
10. Explain what the term *sum of squares* means.
11. Describe the relationship between *sum of squares, variance,* and *standard deviation.*
12. How is the standard deviation related to the amount of variability exhibited by a set of scores?
13. Make a scattergram showing a moderate negative relationship between the number of days absent during the school year and grade point average for 30 students. Draw the approximate line of best fit by visually inspecting the data.
14. What is the range within which a correlation coefficient must fall?
15. Suppose English classes in a high school are comprised of students who have been

homogeneously grouped according to reading level. Why would one expect to find a low correlation between reading level and another variable, such as scores on a vocabulary test, among students in any given class?

16. Describe what it means when two variables are found to have a curvilinear relationship.

17. A correlational study of the relationship between attitudes toward reading and reading comprehension yielded an r of .79. Approximately what percentage of the variance in the two sets of scores is shared? What would the approximate percentage of shared variance be if two variables had an r of $-.79$?

18. Give two reasons why the normal curve is of interest to educators.

19. There is an infinite number of normal curves. To know which particular normal curve one is dealing with, what two pieces of information must one have?

20. What percentage of the population falls between the mean plus and minus one *SD?* Between the mean plus and minus two *SDs?* Between the mean plus and minus three *SDs?*

21. Given a set of normally distributed scores with a mean of 80 and a *SD* of 10, approximately what percentage of the population scored between 60 and 70? Express the following scores in standard deviation units: 70, 90, and 95.

22. What term is used to refer to scores that are expressed in standard deviation units?

Chapter 9

Inferential Statistics
and Statistical Significance

You are already thinking probabilistically if you understand that, in flipping a coin, the chances of getting a head or a tail are equal because the coin has two sides.

Chapter Objectives

After completing this chapter, you should be able to:

- explain the function of *inferential statistics* and the rationale underlying their use
- explain the concept of *degrees of freedom* and the rationale underlying their use
- explain what the *null hypothesis* is and describe its function
- define the terms *statistical significance* and *nonsignificance*
- describe when a researcher would use the following to analyze data:
  a. chi-square
  b. *t* test for independent means
  c. *t* test for nonindependent means
  d. analysis of variance (ANOVA)
  e. analysis of covariance (ANCOVA)
- explain the function of the following statistical techniques: multivariate analysis of variance, discriminant analysis, and meta-analysis
- distinguish between Type I and Type II errors
- explain the difference between statistical and practical significance

The previous chapter described the two major descriptive statistical concepts: average and variability. It also described the nature of normal distributions and, most importantly, how the percentage of the area under the normal curve falling between the mean plus and minus 1, 2, and 3 standard deviations remains constant.

Descriptive statistics permits researchers to describe quantitatively how variables are distributed among a group of people. Often, however, researchers wish to determine how likely it is that the findings of a study apply to populations larger than the groups of people who actually participated in the study, that is, to generalize the findings of a study within a given margin of error.

Inferential statistics is the term applied to the statistical techniques researchers use to generalize the findings of a study. Using inferential statistics permits researchers to use data collected from samples to make inferences about the nature of the populations from which the samples were drawn. Inferential statistics lies at the heart of quantitative analysis. Because it relies so heavily on the concepts of mean and *SD,* it was necessary first to introduce you to descriptive statistics before moving on to inferential statistics.

Answering Research Questions

Suppose we were interested in the research question of whether boys and girls differ in reading achievement. To answer the question we probably would administer a reading test to some boys and some girls and see which group had the higher average. Suppose we were trying to find out if the self-concepts of physically disabled students, emotionally disturbed students, and learning disabled students are different. We would administer some self-concept measure, probably in the form of a questionnaire, to students in the three groups. After adminstering the self-concept questionnaire, we could determine if the average self-concept scores of the three groups differ.

In the examples, we were interested in one case in seeing if the reading performance of boys and girls is different and in the other, if the self-concepts of three kinds of exceptional students differ. In some sense, though, the studies proposed to answer these research questions really would not give us answers to our questions. Perhaps on the surface the studies seem like a reasonable approach to the research questions, but think carefully about the actual questions.

The former study would permit us to find out if a group of boys performs differently from a group of girls on a reading test. However, we did not ask if a *particular* group of boys performs differently from a *particular* group of girls on that test. What we asked was if boys differ from girls with respect to reading performance, that is, if boys in general perform differently in reading than girls in general. Similarly, the implicit question concerning self-concepts of disabled students was whether *in general* students with the three kinds of disabilities have different self-concepts, not whether the *specific* students in our study have different self-concepts.

Populations and Samples

It is most important to understand that a researcher is almost always asking a question about some group of people in general, but a study can be carried out only with a specific group of people. In other words, in the former example, the research question has to do with differences in reading performance of the population of boys and girls, but the study is carried out on a sample of boys and girls.

Logically, the way to find out if two populations differ with respect to some variable is to get a measure of the variable from every member of the populations under investigation. That would be fine *if* one could do it in a practical way. However, it is obvious that one could not possibly obtain reading scores for all boys or all girls. One also could not obtain self-concept measures from all disabled students, either. It might seem silly that researchers always ask questions about more people than they can actually measure, but that in fact is what researchers do, at least researchers in the field of education. The idea is not as silly as it might appear.

Consider the case of a former student who was teaching a foreign language in high school. The student had experimented with a number of teaching techniques and had decided to carry out a research project to try to find out which of two methods worked better. Specifically, he wanted to know if his students learned more if he wrote new foreign vocabulary words on the board and had students copy them or if he did not write the words on the board at all. He instructed one group of students using the board and another without using the board for a number of weeks. At the end of the period of instruction he gave both groups a vocabulary test to see which group scored higher.

One could argue rather persuasively that the research question did not ask whether students in general learn foreign vocabulary words better with or without using the board. The teacher was only asking if the students he teaches learn better one way or another. After all, the teacher need only be interested in the students he teaches, not in all students or even in all students who study foreign languages. However, the students who participated in the study represented only a portion of all the students the teacher was currently teaching or would teach in the future. It is not very enlightening to find out if one teaching technique is better than another for students in a particular class. One has no way of knowing if the same technique will prove better with the next class of students. It is more useful to think of the students who participated in the study as a sample from the population of all students the teacher will teach and to conceptualize the research problem in terms of the population rather than in terms of the sample.

Using Samples to Make Inferences About Populations

One of the major problems confronting all researchers is how to reach a conclusion about some group of people in general if one can study only a specific group of people. The problem of generalizing findings from the group of people who participated in a study to similar groups that did not participate applies to correlational studies as well as to group comparison studies. In a correlational study, for example, one can determine the relationship between math and science performance only among a particular group of students, but the real research issue is what that relationship is among all students. Similarly, in a group comparison study one can determine, for example, that Method A works better than Method B in teaching a particular group of first graders how to read. The real research issue, though, is whether Method A is better for all first graders.

Let us return to the case of the foreign language teacher. Basically the teacher is trying to determine which of two teaching methods will permit his students in general to learn more foreign vocabulary words. The teacher is concerned about increasing the vocabulary of all the students he teaches, not just the students who participated in his study. The problem confronting him is how to make a correct judgment about teaching all of his students on the basis of evidence he has gathered from a single class of students.

There are a number of ways the teacher might proceed. He could simply conclude that, since one method worked better than the other for the one group of students who participated in his study, the same method ought to work better for other groups of students. In other words, he could generalize the findings of his study. How reasonable is it to conclude that because one group of students reacted in a particular way to a teaching technique all groups will react in the same way? As any teacher knows, it is common to find that a particular lesson may be successful with one group of students yet fail miserably with another group.

Replicating Studies. Instead of relying on the results of a single study, perhaps the teacher should repeat the study a few times to make sure that the one method is really better than the other. Certainly we would have more confidence in using a method with all students if the method had proved to be better for several groups of students rather than for a single group. The question, however, arises as to how many times the teacher should repeat the study: Twice? Three times? Ten times? At what point can the teacher stop repeating the study and confidently conclude that the method should be used with all students? Probably each of us would have a different idea about the minimum number of replications necessary to reach a sound conclusion. There is really no satisfactory answer to the question of how many replications are needed.

We have been assuming, so far, that every time the teacher replicates his study, the results are the same. That is, for every group of students, one method is constantly superior to the other. What happens, however, if the results are not always the same? Suppose that sometimes one method turns out to be better, sometimes the other method turns out to be better, and perhaps sometimes neither method turns out to be better than the other. In that case perhaps we should simply choose whichever method turns out to be superior in most of the studies. In what percentage of the studies would one method have to be superior to the other before the teacher could be reasonably confident about which method is really better? Again, each of us would probably have a different notion, and again there is no clear basis on which to answer the question.

Inconsistent Results. The problem of making an accurate judgment about which method to use could be even more complicated. Let us call one method "Method A" and the other "Method B" for convenience. Let us assume that the teacher has decided to carry out the study five times before deciding which method he should use with all of his students. Let us further assume that Method A is superior three times and Method B twice. To simplify matters, let us also assume that in each of the five studies the average vocabulary test score for students taught by Method A was 78. Students taught by Method B had average scores in each of the five studies of, respectively, 68, 68, 68, 94, and 96. Three times the students in Group A outscored the students in Group B by an average of ten points. Twice the students in Group B outscored the students in Group A, once by sixteen and once by eighteen points. Should the teacher conclude that Method A is better than Method B, or that Method B is better than Method A, or that there is no difference between the two methods, or that he should carry out the study five more times? It is difficult to know what conclusion the teacher should reach.

Aside from the fact that replicating a study requires the researcher to make a number of arbitrary, subjective judgments about matters such as how many replications should be done and how to interpret the combined results of the studies, replicating a study demands lots of time and effort. The suggestion to replicate a study was made earlier in an attempt to help the teacher in our example make an accurate decision concerning all his students on the basis of information obtainable from only some of them. After examining some of the issues involved with the process of replication, we should realize that replicating a study is no guarantee that it will be any easier for the teacher to make a decision or that the decision will be any more accurate. All replicating a study guarantees is that the teacher will have to expend considerable time and effort doing it.

Statistical Analysis and Generalization

The problem confronting the teacher confronts all researchers: How can one generalize a set of findings obtained from a sample of people to the entire population of people from which the sample was drawn? The answer is to use inferential statistical analysis. The use of inferential statistics permits a researcher to carry out a study only once and yet still be able to generalize the findings of the study to an entire population. Statistical techniques do not guarantee that the correct generalization will be made. They do, however, permit one to state how likely it is that the generalization is correct or, perhaps more importantly, how likely it is that it is incorrect.

In addition, one can determine in advance what probability of making an erroneous generalization is tolerable in any given set of circumstances. For example, one could decide that the results of a single study should not be generalized unless one is at least 95% sure that the generalization is correct. On the other hand, one could decide that it is reasonable under the circumstances to run a 20% risk of making an erroneous generalization.

Establishing the Probability of Incorrect Generalization. The probability that one is willing to operate within, in terms of making an incorrect generalization (which is called the **alpha level**), is strictly a matter of individual judgment. All kinds of factors may influence the judgment that is ultimately made. Suppose a school district wants to decide whether it is worth investing one hundred thousand dollars in new equipment and materials to implement a new method of teaching reading to all students in the district. Before investing so much money it would be wise to find out if the new method is really better, so a study would be carried out with a sample group of students. It would probably be decided that so much money should not be invested unless it could be demonstrated that the new method is very likely superior. On the other hand, if changing teaching methods involved little or no additional cost, one might implement a new method without demanding a high degree of likelihood that the new method is really better.

When deciding whether or not to generalize the findings from a study to an entire population, all researchers must decide what probability of generalizing incorrectly is justifiable. Virtually all researchers work with a maximum 5% chance of error in generalization. In other words, one must be at least 95% sure that the generalization of a study's finding is correct before any generalization is made. Suppose a researcher carries out a study to determine if Method A works better than Method B. If it turns out that students participating in the study learn better when Method A is used than when Method B is used, the researcher would still not conclude that Method A would be better for all students unless there is at least a 95% chance that this conclusion is correct.

Statistical Significance. You may be wondering how one knows whether the probability of making a correct generalization is at least 95%. The level of probability is established by statistical procedures that will be described shortly. Perhaps you have heard or read somewhere that the results of a study were statistically significant. The term *statistically significant* is used merely as a way of indicating that chances are at least 95 out of 100 that the findings obtained from the sample of people who participated in the study are the same as the findings would be if one were actually able to carry out the study with the entire population. Statistically significant also, of course, means that the chances are 5 out of 100 that the findings based on the sample are not the same as those one would obtain if the entire population were investigated.

Statistical Significance and Probability

Usually the point of doing research is to see if the results can be applied to a larger population with little likelihood of making an incorrect generalization. In other words, the researcher hopes to conclude that the results are statistically significant. To determine whether the results of a study are significant or not is the essential reason for carrying out a statistical analysis. The notion of statistical significance is so central to the entire research process that a thorough understanding of the notion is crucial to understand the statistical jargon appearing in published research.

It is useful to understand that statistical procedures are based on notions of probability and that to understand the results of statistical analyses it is necessary to think in probabilistic terms—which is not as difficult as it may sound. You are already thinking probabilistically if you understand that, in flipping a coin, the chances of getting a head or a tail are equal because the coin has two sides. Similarly, you are thinking in probabilistic terms if you understand that if a coin is flipped ten times in a row, it is most likely that five heads and five tails will result and least likely that ten heads or ten tails will result, although both outcomes are possible.

Factors Affecting the Accuracy of Inferences

Pretend that each of 20,000 IQ scores is written on a separate slip of paper and placed in a huge urn. Let us define these 20,000 scores as a population of scores that we know has a mean of 100 and a *SD* of 16. Suppose we ask a group of friends who do not know the mean of the 20,000 scores to try to estimate the population mean by randomly selecting a sample of scores.

Sample Size. Suppose we instruct each friend to select a sample of 10 scores and record the sample's mean. After each friend has completed this task, the 10 scores are placed back in the urn to make sure that the population mean remains at 100 and the population size remains at 20,000. It should be intuitively obvious that there is no guarantee that each sample of 10 scores will have a mean equal to the population mean of 100. Furthermore, it should be equally obvious that the means of the samples drawn by different friends will not necessarily be identical to one another.

Now suppose we again ask our friends to try to estimate the population mean but allow them to select samples consisting of 19,999 scores. In other words, the size of the *sample* is only one less than the size of the *population*. Again it should be intuitively obvious that the means of the samples drawn by various friends will be almost identical to each other and also almost identical to the population mean of 100. The point is that the accuracy with which one can estimate the mean of a population by knowing the mean of a sample drawn from the population varies as a function of the size of the sample. The larger the sample, the more accurate the estimate will be. Conversely, the smaller the sample, the less accurate the estimate will be.

Variability of Scores. Suppose we have another set of 20,000 scores, which represents a population of achievement test scores. Suppose we also know that the 20,000 scores have a mean of 75 and a *SD* of 2. After placing the scores in an urn, we ask our friends once more to try to estimate the population mean by randomly selecting a sample of scores. Regardless of whether our friends draw large or small samples, the means of the samples drawn by the various friends will probably be close to one another and close to the population mean of 75 because there is relatively little variability among the scores in the population, that is, the *SD* is only 2.

Now suppose we have yet another urn with 20,000 scores, which, like the scores in the previous example, also have a mean of 75 but which, unlike the scores in the previous example, have a *SD* of 20, not 2. Once again we ask our friends to estimate the population mean by randomly selecting a sample of scores.

If they select small samples, the sample means are likely to vary greatly because there is a lot of variability among the scores in the population, that is, the *SD* is 20. Given the large amount of variability among scores in the population, our friends would have to select relatively large samples to arrive at estimates close to one another and close to the population mean.

Figure 9.1

Distributions of Sample Means as a Function of Sample Size and
Population Variability

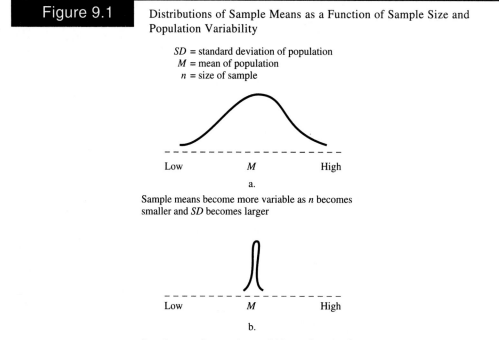

SD = standard deviation of population
M = mean of population
n = size of sample

Low   *M*   High

a.

Sample means become more variable as *n* becomes
smaller and *SD* becomes larger

Low   *M*   High

b.

Sample means become less variable as *n* becomes larger
and *SD* becomes smaller

The important point is that the accuracy with which one can estimate the mean of a
population by knowing the mean of a sample drawn from the population varies as a function
of variability of the scores in the population. The smaller the variability, the more accurate
the estimate will be. Conversely, the larger the variability, the less accurate the estimate will
be. Figure 9.1 shows the distributions of sample means as a function of sample size and
population variability.

Degrees of Freedom

When carrying out research using samples, it is necessary to *estimate* the variability of the
scores within the populations based on the variability of the scores found in the samples. It
is a well-known statistical fact that the variability found within samples underestimates the
actual variability within populations. This underestimate results because extreme scores occurring in a population are less likely to occur in the sample than scores closer to the average.
Furthermore, the smaller the sample, the larger the underestimate. To compensate for this
underestimate, researchers calculate the average amount of variability in a sample by dividing the total variability by one less than the size of the sample.

Such a procedure improves the chances of estimating the variability within the population more accurately because the resulting estimate is larger. In other words, dividing a
number by 7, for example, yields a larger answer than dividing the same number by 8. Notice
that the increase that results from dividing by a number one less than the sample size becomes

trivial when sample sizes are large. For example, dividing by 999 yields practically the same result as dividing by 1,000. However, with small samples, the resulting difference can be appreciable.

The term used to indicate that the sample size has been reduced by 1 is **degrees of freedom (df).** For example, if the number (n) of scores in a sample is 10, the $df = 9$. The main thing to note about df is that the df are always slightly smaller than n. Suppose one carried out a statistical test to determine if the means of two groups are significantly different. If one group consists of 15 scores and the other group consists of 18 scores, the combined sizes of the samples is $n = 33$. Correspondingly, the total $df = 31$, that is, $(15 - 1) + (18 - 1) = 31$.

The concept of df is often explained as follows. One calculates the mean of a sample to obtain an estimate of the mean of the population from which the sample has been drawn. Once the mean is calculated, the number of scores that may vary and still yield the same mean is one less than the number of scores. For example, if we have a sample consisting of 20 scores and calculate the mean, once the first 19 scores have been established, the 20th score is automatically determined—there is only one 20th score that will result in the same mean. In other words, 19 scores are free to vary, but the 20th score is not. Consequently, the df associated with 20 scores ($n = 20$) are 19.

Just as the df associated with scores within a group are equal to the number of scores minus one, there are also df associated with scores between groups. The between-group df equal the number of groups minus one. If one carries out a statistical test to determine the statistical significance of the difference between two groups, the between-group $df = 1$ (i.e., $2 - 1 = 1$). If one carries out a statistical test to determine if the means of three groups are significantly different, the between-group df are 2 (i.e., $3 - 1 = 2$).

Confidence Intervals

It was noted earlier that the accuracy of estimating the mean of a population from the mean of a sample drawn from the population depends on two things: the size of the sample and the amount of variability found in the population. It should also be pointed out that if we recorded the means of a large number of samples of a given size drawn from the same population, we would find that the sample means form a normal distribution.

As a result of knowing that the distribution of sample means is normal and being able to estimate the mean and variability of the population, researchers are able to determine what percentage of samples drawn from the same population are likely to have means that fall within a given range.

It is not unusual for researchers to state inferences about populations in terms of confidence intervals rather than in terms of a specific value. For example, a researcher might infer on the basis of information from a sample of IQ scores that the chances are 95 in 100 that the mean IQ score of the population lies between 96 and 104, or that the chances are 90 in 100 that the mean of a population of achievement test scores lies between 67 and 72.

A **confidence interval** consists of a range of numbers and a statement of how likely it is that the true population value falls within that range. Once again it is important to understand that although researchers often use confidence intervals when estimating population means on the basis of data from samples, means are not the only measure to which confidence intervals are applied.

Using Inferential Statistics in Actual Studies

In group comparison studies, researchers use data from samples to estimate how likely it is that populations have different means. Similarly, in correlational studies, researchers use data from samples to estimate how likely it is that two or more variables in a population are systematically related.

To help you understand better how inferential statistics is used in actual studies, consider the following: You have two urns, each of which contains 20,000 scores. Furthermore, the means of the scores in both urns are identical. If you were to draw a random sample from each urn, there is no guarantee that the two sample means would be identical, even though the populations from which they were drawn have identical means.

By knowing the size of the samples you draw and the *SD* of the scores in both urns, however, it is possible to establish a confidence interval within which you would expect the difference between the means of any two samples to fall 95% of the time. The size of the confidence interval would vary as a function of the sample size and the *SD* of the scores. The larger the sample size and the smaller the *SD,* the narrower the confidence interval would be.

The only difference between the example and an actual study is that you knew in advance that both urns (i.e., populations) had identical means, but a researcher does not. In fact that is precisely what the researcher wishes to find out.

Researchers analyze the findings of their study to test the **null hypothesis,** which is a statement that the average scores of the two *populations* involved in the study are identical. To grasp the logic underlying the null hypothesis, it is important to understand that just because two populations have identical averages, there is no guarantee that samples drawn from those populations will also have identical averages. The purpose of the null hypothesis is to permit researchers to determine the probability of obtaining differences of various magnitudes between *sample* averages if the samples were selected from populations with identical averages. By comparing the difference between the two sample averages obtained in their study with the range of possible differences that would be expected under the null hypothesis, researchers can state how likely it is that their findings apply to entire populations.

If the obtained difference between the two sample averages lies outside the range of possible differences expected under the null hypothesis, one concludes that it is highly likely that the averages of the two populations are truly different. In other words, one rejects the null hypothesis and concludes that it is highly likely that the findings of the study apply to the entire population. Findings of a study that permit a researcher to reject the null hypothesis are referred to as being **statistically significant.** Any statistically significant finding indicates that a null hypothesis has been rejected.

The null hypothesis is used in correlational studies as well as in group comparison studies. For example, if one were to examine the nature of the relationship between self-concept and grade point averages among a sample of junior high school students, the null hypothesis would be that there is no significant relationship between the two variables in the population of junior high school students. The researcher establishes a confidence interval within which one would expect the degree of relationship to fall by chance. If the degree of relationship found in the researcher's sample falls within the confidence interval, the researcher concludes that there is no relationship among the variables in the population and accepts the null hypothesis. On the other hand, if the obtained degree of relationship falls outside the confidence interval, the researcher concludes that the variables are systematically related in the population and rejects the null hypothesis.

Statistical Significance and Nonsignificance

If a finding of a study is statistically significant, one is at least 95% confident that the finding, which is based on an analysis of a sample, is the same finding one would obtain if the study had been carried out with the entire population. A researcher who reports that there is a significant relationship between variables in a correlational study, for example, is claiming that the chances are at least 95 in 100 that the same relationship would be found if the entire population, instead of a sample, had been used to study the variables. If the researcher is less than 95% confident, the relationship is reported as nonsignificant.

Similarly, a researcher carrying out a group comparison study would report the difference between group means as significantly different only if the chances are at least 95 in 100 that the same difference would be found if the populations, rather than samples, had been used in the study. If the chances are less than 95 in 100, the difference between group means is reported as nonsignificant.

Statistical Tests of Significance

There are numerous statistical tests that determine if the results of a study are statistically significant. As pointed out earlier, the particular statistical test one uses is determined by a number of factors, including the research design and the kinds of scales used to measure the variables.

All statistical tests of significance are based on probability theory and consequently yield conclusions about the statistical significance or nonsignificance of findings within a given margin of error. Furthermore, for each test of statistical significance there is a statistic that is symbolized by an English or Greek letter, such as t, F, or X^2, to name a few of the most commonly used statistics.

The result of a statistical test of significance is shown as the statistical symbol = some number. For example, the results may appear as F = some number or t = some number. The magnitude of the number that the statistic equals determines whether the finding is statistically significant or not. Generally, the larger the number, the greater the likelihood that the results of the study will be significant.

Probability and Levels of Significance

For every statistical test of significance, there is a minimum value that the computed statistic must exceed for the result to be regarded as statistically significant. The minimum value needed to claim a statistically significant finding varies as a function of the size of the samples used in the study. The larger the sample sizes, the smaller the minimum value the computed statistic must exceed for the findings to be statistically significant. As a result, it is easier to achieve statistical significance with large samples than with small ones.

Statistical significance indicates that the researcher is at least 95% confident that the results of the study would be the same if populations, rather than samples, had been studied.

Correspondingly, statistical significance indicates that there is a 5% chance that the researcher has reached an incorrect conclusion. In the research literature, the **level of statistical significance** is indicated by p, which represents the probability that the finding of the study is *incorrect*. In other words, "$p < .05$" (which is read as "probability less than .05") means that chances are 95 in 100 that the finding based on samples would be the same if the populations had been used.

The minimum value a computed statistic must exceed for the findings of a particular study to be statistically significant appears in a table of significant statistical values. All tables of significant statistical values work the same way. One must select the table of significant values for the statistic one is calculating and enter the table using the degrees of freedom to locate the minimum statistical value necessary for the findings to be considered statistically significant.

Let us use as an example a study in which we wish to determine if the difference between the means of two groups is statistically significant. The appropriate statistic for comparing two group means is t. Consequently, we must use the table of t values in appendix F. Suppose we have a nondirectional hypothesis, that is, we are predicting that the two group means will differ significantly, but we are not specifying which group will have the higher mean. Assume that one group consists of 15 subjects and the other group 13, which means that the total df are 26 (i.e., $(15 - 1 = 14)$ plus $(13 - 1 = 12) = 26$).

Entering the t table with $df = 26$, we see that the *minimum* t value we must obtain for a nondirectional hypothesis to be statistically significant is 2.06. In other words, if our obtained t value is 2.06 or higher, the results are statistically significant at the .05 level, that is, $p < .05$. (Note the .05 at the top of the column in which the t value of 2.06 appears.)

Notice in the table in the column to the right of the t value of 2.06 there appears a t value of 2.78. If our *obtained t* value turns out to be 2.78 or higher, the results are statistically significant at the .01 level, that is, $p < .01$. (Note the .01 at the top of the column in which the t value of 2.78 appears.)

If our hypothesis had been directional instead of nondirectional, we would have used the t values appearing in the two columns under the term *Directional Hypothesis*. Regardless of whether the hypothesis is directional or nondirectional, notice that as the df increases, that is, as the number of subjects increases, the minimal value of t necessary for the results to be statistically significant gets smaller. In other words, the larger the samples, the closer together the sample means may be and still be significantly different. Consequently, it is easier to obtain statistically significant results with large samples than with small ones.

In the previous example, where we had 26 df, we would expect our obtained t value to fall between 2.06 (where the mean of A is larger than the mean of B) to -2.06 (where the mean of B is larger than the mean of A) 95% of the time if the null hypothesis is correct. If the obtained t value is larger than 2.06 or smaller than -2.06, we reject the null hypothesis because we would expect such a value to occur less than 5% of the time by chance.

As the computed value of a statistic gets larger, the probability of its occurring by chance gets smaller. For example, a t value may be so large that the likelihood that it occurred by chance is less than 1 in 100 (i.e., $p < .01$) or less than 5 in a 1,000 (i.e., $p < .005$). The smaller the p value, the more confident the researcher is that the means of the two populations are really different.

In reporting significant findings, researchers typically indicate both the level of significance, or p value, and the df associated with the samples. For example, the results of a study that found that students taught by Method A performed significantly better than students taught by Method B would appear in a published report more or less as follows: ''The results of the study showed that students in Group A scored significantly higher than students in Group B, $t(28) = 2.87$, $p < .01$.'' Such a statement should be interpreted as meaning that the obtained t value is 2.87, the df are 28 (i.e., 30 students participated in the study), and the level of significance is less than .01.

Similarly, the results of a study that found significant differences in the performance of three groups of students taught by Methods A, B, and C would be reported more or less as follows: ''The results of the study showed that there were significant differences in the performance of the students in the three groups, $F(2, 27) = 5.62$, $p < .01$.'' Such a statement should be interpreted as meaning that the obtained F value is 5.62, the **between-groups** df are 2 (i.e., there were 3 groups), the **within-groups** df are 27 (i.e., 30 students participated in the study), and the level of significance is less than .01.

When t is the statistic used to determine the significance of the difference between group means, only the within-groups df are reported. There is no need to report the between-groups df because there are always two groups and the between-groups df always equal one.

On the other hand, when the F statistic is used, the between-groups df are not constant. On the contrary, they vary as a function of the number of groups. Consequently, when the F statistic is used, both the between-groups and the within-groups df are reported. For example, if one carried out a statistical test to determine if the means of three groups, each consisting of 100 scores, are significantly different, the df are reported as ''2, 297,'' where ''2'' equals the number of groups minus one ($3 - 1 = 2$) and ''297'' equals the total number of scores minus the number of groups ($300 - 3 = 297$). Similarly, if one were doing a test of statistical significance for the means of four groups, each group consisting of 50 scores, the df would be reported as ''3, 196,'' where ''3'' equals the number of groups minus one ($4 - 1 = 3$) and ''196'' equals the total number of scores minus the number of groups ($200 - 4 = 196$). In the case of df, like those in the previous examples, ''2, 297'' does *not* mean ''two thousand two hundred ninety-seven,'' nor does ''3, 196'' mean ''three thousand one hundred ninety-six.''

It is necessary to use tables of significant values if one carries out a statistical analysis by hand, but not if one uses a computerized statistical program. Most computerized statistical programs automatically compute not only the value of a statistic but also the exact probability of obtaining that value by chance. Suppose, for example, one carried out a t test on data gathered from two groups of 63 subjects. The results might be reported as ''$t(61) = 2.07$, $p < .05$'' or as ''$t(61) = 2.07$, $p = .04$,'' depending on whether the probability of obtaining a t value of 2.07 was calculated exactly (i.e., $p = .04$) or not (i.e., $p < .05$). Both forms of reporting the results, however, indicate that the obtained t value is statistically significant. (Illustrations of statistics computed by a computerized statistical program appear in chapter 17.)

Chi-Square (X^2)

When researchers are interested in seeing if two or more groups differ with respect to a nominal variable, they frequently use **chi-square** (symbolized as X^2) to determine if the difference is statistically significant. For example, a researcher might be interested in determining if there are proportionally more girls or boys among learning disabled, emotionally disturbed, and physically disabled students. Analyzing the data by means of X^2 permits the researcher to determine whether the relationship between gender and kind of disability is statistically significant. Box 9.1 shows how to calculate X^2.

The t Test for Independent (or Uncorrelated) Means

If the data have equal units of measurement and have been collected in an ex post facto study or in an experiment using simple random assignment, the appropriate test of statistical significance depends on the number of groups. If there are two groups, a *t* **test for independent means** should be used. If there are three or more groups, an analysis of variance (ANOVA) should be used. The statistic associated with an ANOVA is *F*.

It is also appropriate to use an ANOVA with two groups, but it is *not* appropriate to use several *t* tests for more than two groups. Suppose you carried out a group comparison consisting of five groups. It might seem reasonable to analyze the data by carrying out a *t* test for all possible pairs of groups, that is, Group 1 versus Group 2, Group 1 versus Group 3, . . . Group 4 versus Group 5. In other words, you would be carrying out a total of 10 separate *t* tests.

By carrying out multiple *t* tests, however, you would be increasing the likelihood of finding significant differences purely on the basis of chance (e.g., if one carried out 100 *t* tests comparing the means of groups that really do not differ, one would expect 5 *t* tests to yield significant differences on the basis of chance alone). It is for this reason that one should use ANOVA when comparing the means of three or more groups. The use of ANOVA reduces the likelihood that significant differences found between group means are due to chance. Box 9.2 shows how to calculate a *t* test for independent (or uncorrelated) means.

The t Test for Nonindependent (or Correlated) Means

If the data to be analyzed have equal units of measurement and have been collected by an experiment in which subjects were assigned to groups by means of matched pairs (see chapter 14), the *t* **test for nonindependent means** is the appropriate test of statistical significance. The *t* test for nonindependent means is also appropriate for analyzing two sets of data from the same group of people, as for example, when one wishes to see if students' academic performance is significantly better at the end of the school year than it was at the beginning. Box 9.3 shows how to calculate a *t* test for nonindependent (or correlated) means.

One-Way ANOVA

An analysis of variance used to see if there is a significant difference among two or more group means with respect to a single variable is called a **one-way ANOVA.** For example, one would use a one-way ANOVA to see if there is a significant difference among the mean self-concept scores of three groups of disabled students: physically disabled, emotionally disturbed, and learning disabled. Such an ANOVA is called a one-way ANOVA because only one variable is being examined. See Figure 9.2a.

Box 9.1 Calculating Chi-Square (X^2)

$$X^2 = \Sigma \frac{(O-E)^2}{E}$$

where O = observed number of cases in a category

E = expected number of cases in a category if the null hypothesis is correct

Σ = Sum up

Suppose you are interested in determining whether there is a relationship between a student's gender and kind of disability. Let us assume you are interested in finding out if there are proportionally more girls or boys among learning disabled (LD), emotionally disturbed (ED), and physically disabled (PD) students. The two variables are the gender of the student and the kind of disability. The gender of the student may take on one of two values, and the disability may take on one of three values. Neither variable is quantifiable.

Assume that you drew a random sample of 100 special education students. You would first classify each student according to gender and kind of disability as shown in Table 1. Next you would determine how many students of each gender you would expect to find with each disability if boys and girls are proportionally represented in each category.

Table 1		Actual Distribution of Students by Gender and Disability		
	LD	ED	PD	Total
Girls	12	5	9	26
Boys	20	37	17	74
Total	32	42	26	100

Note that 26% of the entire sample are girls and 74% are boys. Consequently, we would expect 26% of the students with each disability to be girls and 74% to be boys. For example, there are 32 LD students. If boys and girls are proportionally represented in the LD category, you would expect 26% of the 32 LD students, or 8.32, to be girls and 74%, or 23.68, to be boys. Taking 26% and 74% of the total number of students with each disability, construct a table of the expected distribution of students by gender and disability (as shown in Table 2).

The larger the discrepancy between the *actual* number of students and the *expected* number of students in each category, the more likely it is that boys and girls are not distributed proportionally. The larger the discrepancy, the larger the chi-square value will be and the more likely it is that the null hypothesis will be rejected.

Table 2		Expected Distribution of Students by Gender and Disability		
	LD	ED	PD	Total
Girls	8.32	10.92	6.76	26
Boys	23.68	31.08	19.24	74
Total	32	42	26	100

Box 9.1 continued

Step 1. List each number appearing in the categories in Table 1 and subtract the corresponding number appearing in Table 2.

$$12 - 8.32 = 3.68$$
$$5 - 10.92 = -5.92$$
$$9 - 6.76 = 2.24$$
$$20 - 23.68 = -3.68$$
$$37 - 31.08 = 5.92$$
$$17 - 19.24 = -2.24$$

Step 2. Take each of the six answers in Step 1 times itself and divide the product by the number you subtracted in Step 1.

$$3.68 \times 3.68 = 13.54$$
$$13.54 \div 8.32 = 1.63 \text{ (answer)}$$

$$-5.92 \times -5.92 = 35.05$$
$$35.05 \div 10.92 = 3.21 \text{ (answer)}$$

$$2.24 \times 2.24 = 5.02$$
$$5.02 \div 6.76 = .74 \text{ (answer)}$$

$$-3.68 \times -3.68 = 13.54$$
$$13.54 \div 23.68 = .57 \text{ (answer)}$$

$$5.92 \times 5.92 = 35.05$$
$$35.05 \div 31.08 = 1.13 \text{ (answer)}$$

$$-2.24 \times -2.24 = 5.02$$
$$5.02 \div 19.24 = .26 \text{ (answer)}$$

Step 3. Add up all the answers in Step 2.

$$1.63 + 3.21 + .74 + .57 + 1.13 + .26 = 7.54$$

The answer in Step 3 is the value of chi-square.

To determine if the chi-square value is statistically significant, it is first necessary to determine how many df there are. The df are determined by taking the number of rows minus 1 times the number of columns minus 1. In this case there are 2 rows (boys and girls) and 3 columns (type of disability). Consequently, the df are $(2 - 1) \times (3 - 1) = 2$. Using $df = 2$, enter the table of chi-square values listed in appendix E. The obtained X^2 value of 7.54 falls between the values in the table associated with $df = 2$ (i.e., 5.99 and 9.21) and is therefore significant at the .05 level (i.e., $p < .05$).

Box 9.2 Calculating the t Test for Independent (or Uncorrelated) Means

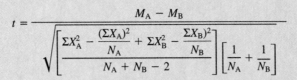

$$t = \frac{M_A - M_B}{\sqrt{\left[\dfrac{\Sigma X_A^2 - \dfrac{(\Sigma X_A)^2}{N_A} + \Sigma X_B^2 - \dfrac{(\Sigma X_B)^2}{N_B}}{N_A + N_B - 2}\right]\left[\dfrac{1}{N_A} + \dfrac{1}{N_B}\right]}}$$

The subscripts A and B indicate to which group the various values belong. For example, M_A = mean of group A, M_B = mean of group B.

Σ = Summation (Sum Up)
X = The score of one person
X^2 = The squared score of one person
ΣX^2 = Square each score and sum the squares
$\Sigma(X)^2$ = Sum the scores and square the sum
N = The number of scores

Let us assume we have a group of 10 students, half of whom are to receive reading instruction by Method A and half by Method B. At the end of a given period of instruction, students in both groups will be given a reading comprehension test.

For computational purposes, it is useful to arrange the data in six columns as shown in the following example. In column 1 list the names or code numbers of the students in Group A. In column 2 list the reading comprehension test score for each student in Group A. In column 3 list the squares of the scores appearing in column 2.

In column 4 list the names or code numbers of the students in Group B. In column 5 list the reading comprehension test score for each student in Group B. In column 6 list the squares of the scores appearing in column 5.

Enter the sums for columns 2, 3, 5, and 6.

(1)	(2)	(3)	(4)	(5)	(6)
A–1	90	8,100	B–1	73	5,329
A–2	87	7,569	B–2	76	5,776
A–3	85	7,225	B–3	80	6,400
A–4	80	6,400	B–4	70	4,900
A–5	78	6,084	B–5	65	4,225
Σ(Sum)	420	35,378	Σ(Sum)	364	26,630

Step 1. Add the sum of column 3 and the sum of column 6.
35,378 + 26,630 = 62,008
Step 2. Take the sum of column 2 times itself.
420 × 420 = 176,400
Step 3. Divide the answer in Step 2 by the number of subjects in Group A.
176,400 ÷ 5 = 35,280
Step 4. Take the sum of column 5 times itself.
364 × 364 = 132,496
Step 5. Divide the answer in Step 4 by the number of subjects in Group B.
132,496 ÷ 5 = 26,499.20

Box 9.2 continued

Step 6. Add the answer in Step 3 and the answer in Step 5.
35,280 + 26,499.20 = 61,779.20
Step 7. Take the answer in Step 1 and subtract the answer in Step 6.
62,008 − 61,779.20 = 228.80
Step 8. Add the number of subjects in Group A and the number of subjects in Group B.
5 + 5 = 10
Step 9. Take the answer in Step 8 and subtract 2.
10 − 2 = 8
Step 10. Divide the answer in Step 7 by the answer in Step 9.
228.80 ÷ 8 = 28.60
Step 11. Divide 1 by the number of subjects in Group A.
1 ÷ 5 = .20
Step 12. Divide 1 by the number of subjects in Group B.
1 ÷ 5 = .20
Step 13. Add the answer in Step 11 and the answer in Step 12.
.20 + .20 = .40
Step 14. Take the square root of the answer in Step 13.
$\sqrt{.40} = .63$
Step 15. Take the square root of the answer in Step 10.
$\sqrt{28.60} = 5.35$
Step 16. Multiply the answer in Step 14 times the answer in Step 15.
.63 × 5.35 = 3.37
Step 17. Take the sum of column 2 and divide by the number of subjects in Group A. This is the mean score for Group A.
420 ÷ 5 = 84
Step 18. Take the sum of column 5 and divide by the number of subjects in Group B. This is the mean score for Group B.
364 ÷ 5 = 72.80
Step 19. Take the answer in Step 17 and subtract the answer in Step 18.
84 − 72.80 = 11.20
Step 20. Divide the answer in Step 19 by the answer in Step 16.
11.20 ÷ 3.37 = 3.32
The answer in Step 20 is the value of *t*.

To determine if the *t* value is statistically significant, it is first necessary to determine how many *df* there are. The *df* are determined by taking the number of subjects in both groups minus 2. In this example there are a total of 10 subjects in both groups. Consequently, the *df* = 10 − 2 = 8. Using *df* = 8, enter the table of *t* values listed in appendix F.

The *t* values for *df* = 8 are 2.31 and 3.36 for a nondirectional hypothesis and 1.86 and 2.90 for a directional hypothesis. Since the obtained *t* value of 3.31 is greater than 2.31 but less than 3.36, we would conclude that if our hypothesis was nondirectional, the difference between the two sample means is significant at the .05 level ($p < .05$). However, the obtained *t* value is greater than both of the *t* values listed for a directional hypothesis. Consequently, if our hypothesis was directional, the difference between the two sample means is significant at the .01 level ($p < .01$).

A *t* value may be either positive or negative. Positive and negative *t* values are interpreted the same way. Ignore the sign of the *t* value when consulting the table. A negative *t* value simply means that the mean score in column B is higher than the mean score in column A. A positive *t* value means the mean score in column A is higher than the mean score in column B.

Box 9.3 Calculating the t Test for Nonindependent (or Correlated) Means

$$t = \frac{\bar{D}}{\sqrt{\dfrac{\Sigma D^2 - \dfrac{(\Sigma D)^2}{N}}{N(N-1)}}}$$

where $\bar{D}$ = The mean difference between the two sets of scores
Σ = Summation (Sum Up)
D = The difference between the scores of one person (or matched pair)
D^2 = The squared difference between the scores of one person (or matched pair)
ΣD^2 = Square each difference and sum the squares
$(\Sigma D)^2$ = Sum the differences and square the sum
N = The number of differences

Let us assume that we have given 10 students a pretest on reading comprehension. Using the pretest scores, we have formed two groups by the method of matched pairs. (Matched pairs is discussed in chapter 14). One group is instructed by Method A and the other by Method B. At the end of the period of instruction, we once again administer the reading comprehension test as a posttest. We now want to see if the means of the groups on the posttest are significantly different. Only the posttest scores are used in the t test.

It is useful to arrange the data in five columns as shown in the following example. In column 1 list the code number of each matched pair. In column 2 list the score made by the subject in that pair who has been instructed by Method A. In column 3 list the score made by the subject in that pair who has been instructed by Method B. In column 4 list the difference between each pair of scores by subtracting the score in column 3 from the score in column 2. In column 5 list the squares of the values appearing in column 4. Enter the sums for columns 4 and 5.

(1)	(2)	(3)	(4)	(5)
1	85	73	12	144
2	82	76	6	36
3	78	80	−2	4
4	75	70	5	25
5	72	65	7	49
Sum			28	258

Step 1. Divide the sum in column 4 by the number of pairs.
$28 \div 5 = 5.60$
Step 2. Take the sum in column 4 times itself.
$28 \times 28 = 784$
Step 3. Divide the answer in Step 2 by the number of pairs.
$784 \div 5 = 156.80$
Step 4. Take the sum in column 5 and subtract the answer in Step 3.
$258 - 156.80 = 101.20$

Box 9.3 continued

Step 5. Subtract 1 from the number of pairs.
$$5 - 1 = 4$$
Step 6. Multiply the answer in Step 5 times the number of pairs.
$$4 \times 5 = 20$$
Step 7. Divide the answer in Step 4 by the answer in Step 6.
$$101.20 \div 20 = 5.06$$
Step 8. Take the square root of the answer in Step 7.
$$\sqrt{5.06} = 2.25$$
Step 9. Divide the answer in Step 1 by the answer in Step 8.
$$5.60 \div 2.25 = 2.49$$

The answer in Step 9 is the value of *t*.

To determine if the *t* value is statistically significant, it is first necessary to determine how many *df* there are. The *df* are determined by taking the number of pairs of subjects minus 1. In this example there are 5 pairs of subjects. Consequently, the $df = 5 - 1 = 4$.

The *t* values for $df = 4$ are 2.78 and 4.60 for a nondirectional hypothesis and 2.13 and 3.75 for a directional hypothesis.

If we had predicted in our example that the means of the two groups' scores would be significantly different, but we did not specify which set of scores would be higher, we would have a nondirectional hypothesis. Since the obtained *t* value of 2.49 is not higher than 2.78 or 4.60, we would conclude that there is no significant difference between the two sets of scores.

If we had predicted that the mean of Group A would be significantly higher than the mean of Group B, we would have a directional hypothesis. Since the obtained *t* value of 2.49 is higher than 2.13, we would conclude that the difference between the two means is significant at the .05 level ($p < .05$). Since the obtained *t* value is less than 3.75, we could *not* claim significance at the .01 level.

A *t* value may be either positive or negative. Positive and negative *t* values are interpreted the same way. Ignore the sign of the *t* value when consulting the table. A negative *t* value simply means that the mean score in column 3 is higher than the mean score in column 2. A positive *t* value means the mean score in column 2 is higher than the mean score in column 3.

Higher Order ANOVAs

One of the most useful features of an ANOVA is that it permits the researcher to examine differences among the same groups of subjects with respect to more than one variable, as well as with respect to the interaction of the variables. Suppose one is interested in determining not only if there are significant differences among the self-concept scores of physically disabled, emotionally disturbed, and learning disabled students, but also whether there are differences as a function of the gender of the student. Such an ANOVA is called a *two-way* ANOVA because two variables are being examined.

It is also sometimes called a 2×3 ANOVA. The number of digits (two) indicates how many variables are being examined (i.e., kind of disability and gender) and the magnitude of each digit indicates how many values each variable can assume. The variable gender can assume one of two values and the variable kind of disability can assume one of three. The total number of groups is six (i.e., 2×3). See Figure 9.2b.

Figure 9.2 Examples of One-Way and Higher Order ANOVAs

	Physically Disabled	Emotionally Disturbed	Learning Disabled

a. One-way ANOVA

	Physically Disabled	Emotionally Disturbed	Learning Disabled
Female			
Male			

b. Two-way ANOVA (2×3).

	Physically Disabled		Emotionally Disturbed		Learning Disabled	
	Female	Male	Female	Male	Female	Male
Mainstreamed						
Nonmainstreamed						

c. Three-way ANOVA ($2 \times 3 \times 2$).

If one wanted to examine self-concept as a function of kind of disability, gender, and class placement, one would have a *three-way* ANOVA because three variables are being examined simultaneously. For example, suppose one wanted to examine self-concept as a function of gender (male or female), kind of disability (physically disabled, emotionally disturbed, or learning disabled) and class placement (mainstreamed or nonmainstreamed). Such an ANOVA is a $2 \times 3 \times 2$ ANOVA. The number of digits indicates that there are three variables being examined simultaneously, and the magnitude of the digits indicates that two variables (gender and class placement) may each take on one of two values, and another variable (type of disability) may take on one of three values. The total number of groups is 12 ($2 \times 3 \times 2$). See Figure 9.2c.

The number of variables and the number of values each variable can assume are theoretically infinite, although it is rare to find ANOVAs that examine more than four or five variables simultaneously. Nevertheless, it would be possible to have, for example, a $3 \times 5 \times 2 \times 7 \times 4 \times 8$ ANOVA, which is a *six-way* ANOVA. There are six variables being examined simultaneously and the number of values each variable can assume are 3, 5, 2, 7, 4, and 8 respectively. Such a study would have 6,720 groups!

Main Effects and Interactions

The use of higher order analyses of variance is efficient because it permits the researcher to examine in a single study how a dependent variable is affected by each factor separately, as well as by the combination of factors. For example, suppose one were interested in studying the effects of mainstreaming on the self-concepts of learning disabled and emotionally disturbed students. Using a two-way ANOVA, it is possible to examine separately the effect of class placement on self-concept and the relationship of kind of exceptionality with self-concept, as well as the effect of mainstreaming on self-concept for each type of exceptionality. The relationships of the dependent variable to each separate factor are called **main effects.** The relationships of the dependent variable to different combinations of values of the factors are called **interactions.**

A statistically significant main effect indicates that the mean values of the dependent variable (e.g., the mean scores on the self-concept measure) achieved by groups associated with different values of one factor (e.g., learning disabled or emotionally disturbed), are significantly different, regardless of which value of the other factor the group has been assigned (e.g., mainstreamed or nonmainstreamed). A statistically significant interaction indicates that the relationship of the dependent variable to the factors differs, depending on the factor (e.g., mainstreaming affects learning disabled students differently than it affects emotionally disturbed students). Whether main effects are statistically significant or not has nothing to do with whether the interactions are statistically significant, and vice versa.

Figure 9.3 shows four (of numerous) possible outcomes of the study. These outcomes are fictitious and are used only to illustrate significant and nonsignificant main effects and interactions. In Figure 9.3a, the main effect of exceptionality is statistically significant, (learning disabled students have significantly higher self-concepts than emotionally disturbed students). Neither the main effect of class placement nor the interaction of the two variables is significant. Figure 9.3b shows a statistically significant main effect for class placement (nonmainstreamed students have significantly higher self-concepts than mainstreamed students), but neither the main effect of exceptionality nor the interaction of the two variables is significant.

Figure 9.3c shows a statistically significant interaction (among learning disabled students, those who are mainstreamed have significantly higher self-concepts than those who are not, but among emotionally disturbed students, those who are not mainstreamed have significantly higher self-concepts than those who are), but neither main effect is significant. Figure 9.3d shows a statistically significant main effect both for class placement (nonmainstreamed students have significantly higher self-concepts than mainstreamed students) and exceptionality (learning disabled students have significantly higher self-concepts than emotionally disturbed students), as well as a statistically significant interaction (among learning disabled students, those who are not mainstreamed have significantly higher self-concepts than those who are, but among emotionally disturbed students, there is no significant difference between the self-concepts of those who are or are not mainstreamed).

Post Hoc Tests of Statistical Significance If an ANOVA is carried out and yields a nonsignificant F value, no further statistical computations are necessary. A nonsignificant F indicates that the means of the three or more groups are not significantly different. If, however, the computed F value is significant, additional statistical analysis is necessary. A significant F value only indicates that at least one of the group's means is significantly different

Figure 9.3

Possible Outcomes of a Study Comparing the Self-Concepts of
Learning Disabled (LD) and Emotionally Disturbed (ED) Students Who
Have Been Mainstreamed (MS) or Not (NMS)

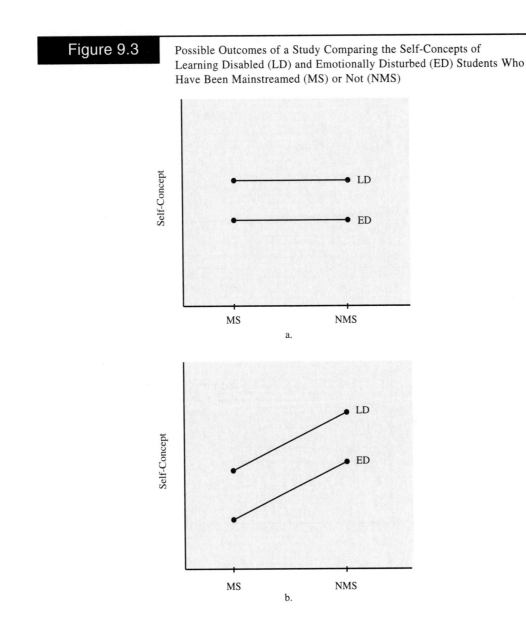

from at least one of the other group's means. Since there are at least three groups, it is impossible to determine which means are statistically different from each other simply by visually comparing their relative magnitudes.

For example, in the simplest case, where there are three group means, it may be that one mean is significantly different from the other two, but those two are not significantly different. It may also be that all three means are significantly different from each other. As the number of groups becomes larger, the number of possible outcomes increases.

To determine precisely which group means are significantly different from which other group means, it is necessary to carry out a **post hoc test of statistical significance.** There are

Figure 9.3   continued

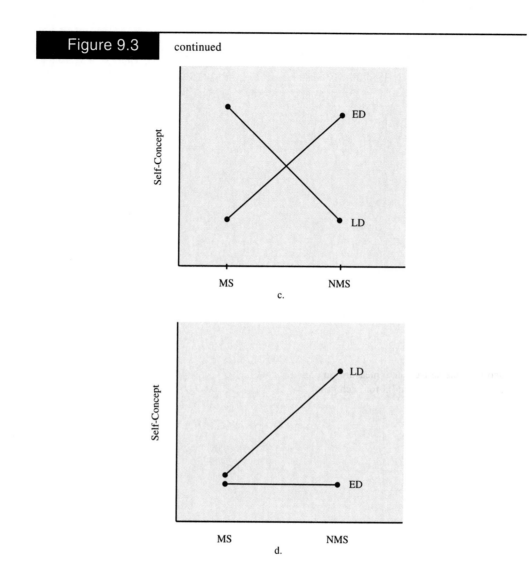

several commonly used post hoc tests, such as the Newman-Keuls, Tukey, Duncan's Multiple Range, and Scheffe, all of which function more or less in the same way. Box 9.4 shows how to calculate a 2 × 2 analysis of variance and the Scheffe test.

The Analysis of Covariance (ANCOVA)

The **analysis of covariance (ANCOVA)** is a statistical procedure researchers use to overcome the possibility that the simple random assignment of intact groups in a quasi-experiment may yield noncomparable groups. Unfortunately, the term *analysis of covariance* sounds a lot like the term *analysis of variance*. Both are statistical procedures used to analyze data, and in a way the procedures are similar, which probably accounts for the similarity of the terms. These two statistical procedures, however, are used for quite different purposes.

Box 9.4 Calculating a 2 × 2 Analysis of Variance and the Scheffe Test

Suppose one is interested in determining whether there are differences in the self-concepts of emotionally disturbed boys and girls who are and are not mainstreamed. The two variables are gender of student and class placement. Each variable has two values. A student's gender is either male or female. Class placement is either a mainstreamed or a nonmainstreamed class. Consequently, there are four possible groups to which a student may belong. Let us designate the four groups as follows.

	Mainstreamed	*Nonmainstreamed*
Boys	Group A	Group B
Girls	Group C	Group D

Suppose that 20 emotionally disturbed students have been randomly assigned in such a way that there are five boys and five girls in a mainstreamed class and five boys and five girls in a nonmainstreamed class. Assume that after a period of time each student is given a self-concept measure. A researcher wants to know if there are significant differences between the scores of boys and girls, between mainstreamed and nonmainstreamed students, and if there is a significant interaction between the student's gender and class placement. A significant interaction would mean that boys and girls react differently to mainstreaming in terms of their self-concepts.

It is helpful to arrange the data as shown in the following table. For each group there are three columns. In column 1 list each subject's name or code number. In column 2 list each subject's score on the self-concept measure. In column 3 list the square of the score appearing in column 2. Sum up columns 2 and 3 for each group.

Group A			Group B		
(1)	(2)	(3)	(1)	(2)	(3)
A–1	11	121	B–1	6	36
A–2	10	100	B–2	5	25
A–3	9	81	B–3	5	25
A–4	9	81	B–4	4	16
A–5	8	64	B–5	3	9
Sum	47	447	Sum	23	111

Group C			Group D		
(1)	(2)	(3)	(1)	(2)	(3)
C–6	6	36	D–1	12	144
C–2	6	36	D–2	11	121
C–3	4	16	D–3	11	121
C–4	3	9	D–4	9	81
C–5	3	9	D–5	8	64
Sum	22	106	Sum	51	531

Box 9.4 continued

Step 1. Take the sums of column 2 in all groups and add them together.
47 + 23 + 22 + 51 = 143

Step 2. Take the sums of column 3 in all groups and add them together.
447 + 111 + 106 + 531 = 1,195

Step 3. Take the answer in Step 1 times itself.
143 × 143 = 20,449

Step 4. Divide the answer in Step 3 by the total number of subjects in all groups.
20,449 ÷ 20 = 1,022.45

Step 5. Take the answer in Step 2 and subtract the answer in Step 4.
1,195 − 1,022.45 = 172.55

Step 6. Add the sum of column 2 in Group A and the sum of column 2 in Group C.
47 + 22 = 69

Step 7. Take the answer in Step 6 times itself.
69 × 69 = 4,761

Step 8. Take the answer in Step 7 and divide by the total number of subjects in Groups A and C.
4,761 ÷ 10 = 476.10

Step 9. Repeat Steps 6 through 8 using the data from Groups B and D (instead of Groups A and C).
23 + 51 = 74 (Step 6)
74 × 74 = 5,476 (Step 7)
5,476 ÷ 10 = 547.60 (Step 8)
Answer in Step 9 = 547.60

Step 10. Add the answer in Step 8 and the answer in Step 9.
476.10 + 547.60 = 1,023.70

Step 11. Take the answer in Step 10 and subtract the answer in Step 4.
1,023.70 − 1,022.45 = 1.25

Step 12. Repeat Steps 6 through 8 using the data in Groups A and B (instead of Groups A and C).
47 + 23 = 70 (Step 6)
70 × 70 = 4,900 (Step 7)
4,900 ÷ 10 = 490 (Step 8)
Answer in Step 12 = 490

Step 13. Repeat Steps 6 through 8 using the data in Groups C and D (instead of Groups A and C).
22 + 51 = 73 (Step 6)
73 × 73 = 5,329 (Step 7)
5,329 ÷ 10 = 532.90 (Step 8)
Answer in Step 13 = 532.90

Step 14. Add the answer in Step 12 and the answer in Step 13.
490 + 532.90 = 1,022.90

Step 15. Take the answer in Step 14 and subtract the answer in Step 4.
1,022.90 − 1,022.45 = .45

Step 16. Take the sum of column 2 in Group A times itself and divide the product by the number of subjects in Group A.
47 × 47 = 2,209
2,209 ÷ 5 = 441.80 (Answer)

Box 9.4 continued

Step 17. Repeat Step 16 for each of the other Groups.

        (B) $23 \times 23 = 529$

            $529 \div 5 = 105.80$ (Answer)

        (C) $22 \times 22 = 484$

            $484 \div 5 = 96.80$ (Answer)

        (D) $51 \times 51 = 2{,}601$

            $2{,}601 \div 5 = 520.20$ (Answer)

Step 18. Add the answer in Step 16 and all three answers in Step 17.

        $441.80 + 105.80 + 96.80 + 520.20 = 1{,}164.60$

Step 19. Take the answer in Step 18 and subtract the answer in Step 4.

        $1{,}164.60 - 1{,}022.45 = 142.15$

Step 20. Add the answer in Step 11 and the answer in Step 15.

        $1.25 + .45 = 1.70$

Step 21. Take the answer in Step 19 and subtract the answer in Step 20.

        $142.15 - 1.70 = 140.45$

Step 22. Take the answer in Step 5 and subtract the answer in Step 19.

        $172.55 - 142.15 = 30.40$

Step 23. Take the total number of subjects in all groups and subtract the number of groups.

        $20 - 4 = 16$

Step 24. Divide the answer in Step 22 by the answer in Step 23.

        $30.40 \div 16 = 1.90$

Step 25. Divide the answer in Step 11 by the answer in Step 24.

        $1.25 \div 1.90 = .66$

        This is the F value to use in comparing the difference between column means. It will tell whether the combined means of Groups A and C (the mainstreamed students) is significantly different from the combined means of Groups B and D (the nonmainstreamed students).

Step 26. Divide the answer in Step 15 by the answer in Step 24.

        $.45 \div 1.90 = .24$

        This is the F value to use in comparing the difference between the row means. It will tell whether the combined means of Groups A and B (boys) is significantly different from the combined means of Groups C and D (girls).

Step 27. Divide the answer in Step 21 by the answer in Step 24.

        $140.45 \div 1.90 = 73.92$

        This is the F value to use in determining whether there is a significant interaction between gender of student and class placement. It will tell whether the means of Groups A, B, C, and D are significantly different. A significant F value means that one or more of the means differ significantly from the others, but it will not tell you which means differ significantly.

To determine if any of the obtained F values is statistically significant, it is first necessary to determine the between-groups df for each variable, the within-groups df and the df for the interaction. The between-groups df is equal to the number of groups minus 1. There are two groups based on gender, so the df for gender is $2 - 1 = 1$. Similarly, there are two groups based on class placement, so the df for class placement is also $2 - 1 = 1$.

Box 9.4 continued

The within-groups *df* is equal to the total number of subjects minus the total number of groups. There is a total of 20 subjects and 4 groups, so the within-groups *df* is $20 - 4 = 16$. The between-groups *df* for the interaction is equal to the product of the *df*s for each variable in the interaction. In our example, the *df* for the interaction is $1 \times 1 = 1$ (i.e., the *df* for gender $\times$ the *df* for class placement).

Compare the *F* values from Steps 25, 26, and 27 with the *F* values in appendix G that correspond to between-groups *df* = 1 and within-groups *df* = 16 (i.e., 4.49 and 8.53). The obtained *F* value in Step 25 is only .66, which falls far short of 4.49. Consequently, one would conclude that there is no significant difference between the mean scores of students who are mainstreamed and those who are not.

The obtained value of *F* in Step 26 is only .24, which also falls far short of 4.49. One would conclude that there is no significant difference between the mean scores of boys and girls.

The obtained value of *F* in Step 27 is 73.92, which greatly exceeds 8.53. Consequently, one would conclude that the interaction between gender of student and class placement is significant at the .01 level. We now know that at least one of the four groups has a mean score that is significantly different from the others, and our next task is to determine which means are significantly different from which other means.

Had the *F* value been nonsignificant, we would end the analysis at this point. However, we have a significant *F,* so we proceed further.

When there is a significant *F* value for the interaction between variables, a simple inspection of the means is not sufficient to determine which means are significantly different, because there are four means. It may be that one of the four means differs significantly from the other three or that all four means differ significantly from each other or that two means, which themselves are not significantly different, nevertheless are significantly different from the other two means, which may or may not be significantly different from each other.

Numerous statistical techniques are available for determining which means are significantly different after one has obtained a significant *F* value. All of these techniques yield approximately the same results. The most commonly used techniques are Scheffe, Tukey, Duncan's Multiple Range, and the Newman-Keuls' Multiple Range tests. The following illustration shows how to apply the Scheffe test to the data.

Step 29. Multiply the answer in Step 24 by 2.
  $1.90 \times 2 = 3.80$
Step 30. Divide the answer in Step 29 by the number of subjects in each group.
  $3.80 \div 5 = .76$
Step 31. Find the square root of the answer in Step 30.
  $\sqrt{.76} = .87$
Step 32. Take the number of groups and subtract 1.
  $4 - 1 = 3$
Step 33. Multiply the answer in Step 32 times the *F* value in appendix G corresponding to the .05 level of significance.
  $3 \times 4.49 = 13.47$
Step 34. Take the square root of the answer in Step 33.
  $\sqrt{13.47} = 3.67$

Step 35. Multiply the answer in Step 34 times the answer in Step 31.

$3.67 \times .87 = 3.19$

The answer in Step 35 is the amount by which means must differ in order to be significantly different.

Step 36. To determine the means of each group divide the sums in column 2 for each group in the table by the number of subjects in each group.

Mean of Group A = $47 \div 5 = 9.40$

Mean of Group B = $23 \div 5 = 4.60$

Mean of Group C = $22 \div 5 = 4.40$

Mean of Group D = $51 \div 5 = 10.20$

Only those means that differ by at least 3.19 points are significantly different from one another. The means of Groups A and D (which are not significantly different) are significantly higher than the means of Groups B and C (which also are not significantly different). In other words, $(\overline{A} = \overline{D}) > (\overline{B} = \overline{C})$; that is, mainstreamed boys and nonmainstreamed girls have significantly higher self-concepts than do nonmainstreamed boys and mainstreamed girls.

Researchers use the analysis of covariance in situations where they wish to statistically control for any differences groups of subjects may exhibit prior to a study on a dependent variable or on some variable related to a dependent variable.

There are numerous situations in which it is appropriate to use an analysis of covariance. In educational research, however, one of the most common situations is a quasi-experimental design in which two (or more) intact groups are to be compared on some measure, as in the following example. Suppose a researcher is interested in seeing if students learn to read better by Method A than by Method B, but the study must be done with intact classes. The researcher would flip a coin to decide which class will be taught by Method A and which will be taught by Method B.

Since the researcher is interested in finding out if students perform better on a reading test as a function of the reading method to which they have been exposed, it is important that any initial differences between the two groups' reading ability be taken into account. The researcher would first administer a reading test to both groups to obtain a measure of the students' initial reading ability. This test is designated the pretest. The researcher could then analyze the pretest scores by means of a t test for independent means. If the pretest means are not significantly different, the researcher would analyze the posttest data by carrying out another t test for independent means.

On the other hand, if the pretest means are significantly different, the researcher would analyze the posttest data by carrying out an analysis of covariance. The analysis of covariance is a way of taking pretest scores that are different and adjusting them statistically so that they can be treated as being identical. Another way of conceptualizing the analysis of covariance is to think in terms of weighting each subject's posttest score in terms of the pretest score.

Adjustment of Scores. For example, assume that two subjects achieved the same posttest score of 70. The two scores of 70 really mean different things if one subject had a pretest score of 45 and the other a score of 72. In the one case, the subject improved quite a bit and in the other case the subject actually performed slightly worse on the posttest than on the pretest. The analysis of covariance permits the researcher to treat the identical posttest scores of 70 differently, depending on the subject's pretest score.

Conceptually, the analysis of covariance is analogous to computing change scores by subtracting pretest scores from posttest scores. The change scores for those who received the same posttest score of 70 would be $+25$ and -2, respectively. Change scores are really another way of weighting posttest scores in terms of subjects' pretest scores. However, as noted earlier, there are a number of technical problems that arise when change scores are used. The analysis of covariance adjusts a subject's posttest score in a much more complicated way than by simply subtracting the pretest score. Because of the other technical factors that the analysis of covariance takes into account, there are far fewer technical problems with scores adjusted by means of the analysis of covariance than there are with change scores.

You need not know what the technical difficulties are that make it unwise to use change scores. You only need to know that noncomparable groups may be justifiably treated as comparable by applying the analysis of covariance and that you should avoid using change scores.

Type I and Type II Errors

When a statistical test of significance is carried out, the researcher concludes that the null hypothesis should be rejected if the computed value of the statistic is sufficiently large. In other words, the researcher concludes that the chances are at least 95 in 100 that the findings based on the study of samples are not due to chance. On the other hand, if a statistical test of significance is carried out and the computed value of the statistic is not sufficiently large, the researcher does *not* reject the null hypothesis and concludes that the results are attributable to chance. In either case, the researcher can only conclude within a given probability of error that the decision to reject or not to reject the null hypothesis is a correct decision.

The important point is that whatever the researcher's decision, there is always a possibility that the decision is incorrect. There are two kinds of incorrect decisions. On the one hand, the researcher can erroneously conclude that the null hypothesis should be rejected, when in fact it should not be. Such an error is called a **Type I error.** The likelihood of making a Type I error corresponds to the p value selected by the researcher. On the other hand, the researcher can incorrectly conclude that the null hypothesis should not be rejected, when in fact it should be. Such an error is called a **Type II error.**

One may reduce the possibility of making a Type I error by increasing the level of significance that is acceptable, that is, by setting the alpha level at less than the conventional level of .05. However, in so doing, the possibility of making a Type II error is increased. One may also reduce the possibility of making a Type II error (for example, by increasing the sample sizes), but then the possibility of making a Type I error is increased.

The relative importance of making either a Type I error or a Type II error depends on the nature of the research question. For example, if a study is carried out to determine if using a new set of curriculum materials leads to significantly better academic achievement than the currently used materials and the new materials are relatively inexpensive, making a Type I error is not terribly serious. In other words, one would conclude incorrectly that the new materials are better than the current materials. The expense involved in obtaining the new materials is not great and the new materials are probably not any worse than the current materials.

On the other hand, if the new materials are expensive and perhaps involve extensive in-service training of teachers who are to use the new materials, a Type I error is much more important. It would be wasteful to spend a great deal of money, time, and energy to implement an instructional program based on the new materials, when in fact the new materials are no better than the ones currently in use.

Statistical and Practical Significance

It is important to understand that even though the results of a study turn out to be statistically significant, the findings may not necessarily have any practical significance whatsoever. For example, if one uses very large samples, often a relatively tiny difference between the two sample means will be statistically significant. However, the tiny difference may have no practical meaning.

Suppose, for example, a textbook publisher brings out a new high school biology text. To try to demonstrate its superiority, the publishing firm may carry out a study comparing the biology achievement test scores of students who have used the firm's text with the scores of students who have used a competitor's biology text. Furthermore, in attempting to sell the new book to high schools that are currently using the other text, the sales representatives of the publisher may correctly and honestly report that the results of the study show that the mean achievement score of students using the new text was significantly higher than the mean scores of students using the competing text.

However, the study may have been carried out with hundreds, or perhaps thousands, of students, so that even a slightly higher mean could be statistically significant. Perhaps students using the new book had a mean score of 76.21 and students using the competing text had a mean score of 74.89. Such a difference, while statistically significant, is not nearly large enough in a practical sense to justify switching to the new biology text, particularly if the switch involves spending much money.

In the final analysis, practical significance, is a value judgment. A given finding may or may not be regarded as having practical significance, depending on the context in which the finding is to be used. For example, a school superintendent who is facing criticism by members of the school board because of low student reading achievement levels may decide to adopt a new reading program even though the reading gains associated with it are minimal. If there is no urgent pressure to raise reading achievement levels, however, the same superintendent might decide the gains in reading achievement attributed to the program do not justify purchasing it.

The findings of group comparisons are sometimes reported in terms of **Effect Size (ES).** The *ES* expresses the difference between the experimental group's mean and the control group's mean in standard deviation units. The control group's mean is always set at 0, so that an *ES* of +1.00 indicates the mean score of the experimental group was 1 *SD* higher than the mean score of the control group. An *ES* of −1.00 indicates that the mean of the experimental group was 1 *SD* lower than the mean of the control group. Some researchers regard an *ES* of .33 or more as representing a meaningful difference. In other words, if experimental groups on the average have a mean that is at least one third of a *SD* higher than that of the control groups, the difference is considered meaningful.

Complex Statistical Analyses

The statistical tests described so far cover practically every kind of study students are likely to carry out and most of the statistical procedures students are apt to use. There are, however, other kinds of studies in the professional literature that we have not yet covered. Such studies are almost never undertaken by students who are just being introduced to research. Nevertheless, it is likely that you will encounter studies using the following procedures as you review the literature on a topic. The purpose of this section is to provide you with a capsule description of these procedures so that you will have some understanding of their intent.

Multivariate Analysis of Variance

Multivariate analysis of variance, which is sometimes abbreviated as **MANOVA,** is similar to the analysis of variance. The difference is that the analysis of variance (sometimes called univariate analysis of variance) is used to determine whether two or more groups differ with respect to a single dependent variable, while multivariate analysis of variance is used to determine whether two or more groups differ with respect to the combination of several different dependent variables. For example, if one were interested in determining if boys and girls differ with respect to reading comprehension scores, spelling scores, and arithmetic test scores, all considered at the same time, one would carry out a multivariate analysis of variance.

Discriminant Analysis

In a way, **discriminant analysis** is the opposite of multivariate analysis of variance. Instead of determining if two groups differ with respect to several different dependent variables taken into account simultaneously, one examines the differences in subjects' scores on several variables and determines if these differences separate the subjects into their respective groups. In other words, in multivariate analysis of variance, one starts with two groups of subjects and then sees if the two groups differ with respect to several variables simultaneously. In discriminant analysis, one starts with subjects' scores on several variables and then sees to what extent the difference between subjects' patterns of scores separates subjects into two discrete groups.

Meta-Analysis

Meta-analysis is a statistical technique that provides a quantitative means of synthesizing the findings of numerous studies dealing with the same topic so that one may determine the general, overall finding. For example, there are numerous studies dealing with the question of small versus large group instruction and reading comprehension. The findings of the studies may not all be the same. Meta-analysis permits one to examine the findings from all the studies and determine what the combined evidence suggests about the effect of instructional group size on reading comprehension.

Prior to the introduction of meta-analysis, reviews of the literature on a particular topic usually consisted of a verbal description of the findings of various studies and an attempt by the reviewer to synthesize the findings. The synthesis was based on a reviewer's subjective interpretation and evaluation of the literature. The appeal of meta-analysis is that it provides an objective synthesis and permits the overall finding to be expressed in quantitative terms.

There are two kinds of meta-analyses: one that synthesizes the findings of correlational studies and one that synthesizes the findings of group comparisons. Meta-analyses of correlational studies report the average correlation coefficient reported in the various studies being analyzed; meta-analyses of group comparisons report the average *Effect Size* of all studies being analyzed.

Chapter Highlights

- Although research questions usually pertain to populations, research studies are almost always carried out with samples.

- Inferential statistics permit researchers to generalize findings based on a sample to the population from which the sample was selected.

- Generalizations are made in probabilistic terms; the probability of making an incorrect generalization is called the *alpha level* and is designated as ''$p<$'' or ''$p=$.''

- Conventionally, the alpha level set by educational researchers is .05.

- When we say that findings are *statistically significant,* we mean that the probability that the findings are due to chance is less than 5%.

- The accuracy of inferences about a population based on sample data improves as (a) the sample size increases and (b) the variability of the scores in the population decreases.

- *Degrees of freedom* are closely related to the number of groups and the number of subjects in a study and are used to give a more accurate estimate of the population's variance.

- In a group comparison study, the *null hypothesis* states that there is no difference between the population means; in a correlational study, it states that there is no relationship between the variables within the population under investigation.

- Researchers test the null hypothesis by using data from samples to establish *confidence intervals* that consist of a range of numbers and a statement of how likely it is that some population value lies within that range.

- If a researcher is less than 95% confident that the results of a study are not due to chance, the results are reported as nonsignificant.

- Two of the most important factors determining what statistical tests are used to analyze data are: (a) the kind of research design used in a study and (b) the scale of measurement used to measure the variables in the study.

- Chi-square (X^2) is a statistic used to determine if groups differ with respect to a nominal variable.

- The *t* test for independent (or uncorrelated) means is used to determine if the means of two groups differ significantly when the groups contain different members; the *t* test for nonindependent (or correlated) means is used if the groups contain the same members or if the groups have been formed by matched pairs.

- The analysis of variance (ANOVA) is used to determine if the means of two or more groups differ significantly.
- A one-way ANOVA examines differences among group means with respect to a single variable.
- Higher order ANOVAs examine differences among group means with respect to more than one variable separately (the *main effects*) and in combination (the *interactions*).
- An ANOVA is a preliminary statistical test. A significant finding must be further examined by any one of several post hoc tests of statistical significance in order to determine which group means are significantly different from which other group means.
- The analysis of covariance (ANCOVA) is a procedure used to control statistically for any initial differences groups may exhibit on a dependent variable; it is most frequently used in analyzing data from quasi-experiments.
- A *Type I error* occurs when one incorrectly rejects the null hypothesis; a *Type II error* occurs when one incorrectly accepts the null hypothesis.
- Statistical significance is based on the probability of an outcome; practical significance is based on a person's subjective judgment.
- *Effect Size* is the difference between the means of the experimental and control groups expressed in standard deviation units, where the control group's mean is set at 0.
- *Multivariate analysis of variance* (MANOVA) is a statistical procedure used to determine if there are significant differences among groups with respect to a combination of several dependent variables.
- *Discriminant analysis* is a statistical procedure used to analyze the patterns of subjects' performance on several dependent variables to classify subjects into various groups.
- Meta-analysis is a statistical technique that provides a quantitative means of synthesizing the findings of several studies dealing with the same topic.

Review Exercises

1. What makes it possible for researchers to make inferences about populations on the basis of data obtained from samples?
2. What does it mean when the results of a study are said to be statistically significant?
3. Name two factors that affect the size of the difference between the means of two samples drawn from populations with identical means.
4. What conclusion should a researcher reach if the difference found between two sample means is likely to occur by chance less than 10% of the time if the populations from which the samples were drawn have identical means?
5. What does the term *degrees of freedom* mean? How many degrees of freedom are associated with two samples, each of which contains 10 people?

6. Give an example of a null hypothesis in a group comparison study.

7. Give an example of a null hypothesis in a correlational study.

8. What statistical test would be used to determine if there is a significant relationship between students' gender and placement in special education classes?

9. Give an example of a study in which it would be appropriate to use a t test for independent means and an example in which a t test for nonindependent means should be used.

10. Explain what "$p <$" means.

11. Give an example of a study that would be analyzed by a one-way ANOVA and a study analyzed by a three-way ANOVA.

12. In the example you used in Exercise 11, identify the main effects and the interactions.

13. Under what circumstances is it necessary to carry out a post hoc test of statistical significance?

14. Why is it important to carry out an analysis of covariance on posttest scores in a quasi-experiment when there are significant differences in the groups' pretest scores?

15. Explain the difference between Type I and Type II errors.

16. Why is it important to distinguish between statistical significance and practical significance?

17. Describe how MANOVA is related to ANOVA.

18. Describe how MANOVA and discriminant analysis differ.

19. What is the major function of a meta-analysis?

20. What statistic is computed when a meta-analysis of correlational studies is carried out?

21. For what kind of meta-analysis is ES computed?

22. How would you interpret an ES value of 1.30?

Section V

Research Methods

*T*his section discusses the major qualitative and quantitative methods used in carrying out educational research. Although researchers may combine aspects of both qualitative and quantitative methods within a single study, the orientation of most studies is either primarily qualitative or quantitative. Qualitative studies present findings in the form of a narrative that describes and discusses whatever phenomena the researcher has studied. If qualitative studies include statistical information, it is usually in the form of descriptive statistics; qualitative studies rarely use inferential statistics. Quantitative studies, on the other hand, are characterized by their reliance on both descriptive and inferential statistical procedures for analyzing data and generalizing findings.

Chapter 10 deals with research methods educational historians use. Historical research concerning educational issues has been conducted for a long time. In contrast, educational researchers did not begin to use ethnographic methods, which are covered in chapter 11, until the 1960s. Despite the relative recency of their emergence, ethnographic methods now constitute a major form of educational research.

Chapter 12 focuses on survey research and includes information concerning surveys and observational studies. In the next chapter you will learn how researchers use correlational methods to study relationships among variables. Chapter 14 explains how researchers use ex post facto methods, experiments, and quasi-experiments to explore the possibility that variables are causally related. Various ways of forming groups are presented, and factors affecting the validity of a study are discussed. The final chapter in this section deals with single-subject designs, a particularly important topic for researchers working in areas such as counseling or special education.

Chapter 10
Historical Research

Primary *sources are original documents and* secondary *sources are materials written by someone about the original document.*

Chapter Objectives

After completing this chapter, you should be able to:

- describe at least two ways in which historical research differs from other kinds of research
- distinguish between *primary* and *secondary* sources
- define *external* and *internal criticism*
- list and describe four points to consider in evaluating historical research
- define the term *revisionist history*

As a discipline, education has not produced its own set of research methodologies. On the contrary, educational researchers have relied heavily on research techniques used in other disciplines. It is only the educational nature of the research question that distinguishes educational research from that in other fields. For a long time, educational researchers have used the research techniques used by historians to investigate historical aspects of education. This chapter presents an overview of the nature of historical methods.

Historians face many of the same problems encountered by all researchers. For example, historians must decide what research question they are going to ask and devise a research plan for obtaining data relevant to the question. They must also identify and define the variables to be investigated. They must be concerned about the validity of their findings.

However, historians encounter other problems unique to their discipline. The most obvious difference between historical and other kinds of research is the nature of the data investigated. In most studies, the data analyzed typically come from groups of people, that is, the participants who take part in the study. In historical research, however, the major sources of data are various kinds of written documents, such as diaries, letters, newspaper articles, minutes of meetings, and so forth or other kinds of records of past events, such as photographs, films, audio- and videotapes, or testimony from eyewitnesses to an event.

Another, perhaps less obvious, difference is that historians cannot control the variables they elect to study. Although the ultimate goal of historical research is to determine causal relationships among variables, historians cannot manipulate variables to determine whether a causal relationship exists or not.

Historical Data

All researchers to some extent function as historians as they review the literature on their topic of investigation. Reviewing the literature is the process of determining the "history" of the researcher's topic by locating what is already known about the topic, for example, how the variables have been operationally defined by other researchers, which research strategies used in the past have been productive and which have not, and, of course, the findings obtained in previous studies.

The sources of such information are relatively straightforward. They are journal articles that may be located fairly easily by consulting indexes such as the *Current Index to Journals in Education* (*CIJE*) or *Psychological Abstracts,* or educational documents that may be found by consulting *Resources in Education* (*RIE*). (See chapter 3 for more detailed information concerning reviewing the literature.)

The sources of information for historians are many and varied, depending on the nature of the topic being investigated. Consequently, there is no specific set of reference tools historians use to uncover the information they need. They may need to use, for example, sources as varied as special libraries and catalogs, historical bibliographies, manuals, guides, almanacs, yearbooks, handbooks of statistical data, journal and newspaper articles, biographical materials, legal reference works, encyclopedias, and assorted government publications. See Poulton and Howland (1986) for a helpful overview of tools available for conducting historical research.

Primary and Secondary Sources

As noted in chapter 3, *primary* sources are original documents and *secondary* sources are materials written by someone about the original document. For example, a speech given by a school superintendent is a primary source, while a newspaper article written by a reporter about the superintendent's speech is a secondary source. Historians always try to use primary sources whenever possible to reduce the likelihood of incorporating inaccuracies or biases that may be introduced by the author of a secondary source. However, there are often problems associated with locating primary sources.

First, a primary source may have been lost, or in the case of paper documents, it may have simply disintegrated with the passage of time. The older the document, the less likely it is to have survived. Furthermore, active measures may even have been taken to destroy original documents, as happened in the Watergate affair. Second, sometimes primary sources are housed in special libraries, repositories, or archives that may be geographically far removed from where the researcher is working. Also, even if the researcher is able to travel to the repository, not all repositories grant access to their material to anyone who wants it. Consequently, if historians cannot get access to primary sources, they have little alternative but to rely on secondary sources. Useful sources for references on the history of American education are Balay and Sheehy (1992), Cordasco and Brinkman (1975), Freidel and Showman (1974), Sheehy (1986), and Woodbury (1982).

Selection and Refinement of Historical Research Topics

There are several common approaches historians use in carrying out their research. One might, for example, decide to describe the historical role a particular educator has played in the field or trace the origins and evolution of a particular educational movement. It is also not unusual for educational historians to focus on the historical development of some controversial educational idea that has currently emerged as an important issue. Topical issues, such as merit pay for teachers, the current reform movement to change the process by which prospective teachers may enter the field, or the creation of a national certification board for the teaching profession, are typical of the kinds of recent developments that historians might want to put in historical perspective.

It is common for historians initially to have only a general idea of the possible historical issues associated with a particular topic. As the research progresses, however, entirely different issues may emerge as potential explanations of the historical development of the topic. In contrast to other kinds of research, where the variables to be investigated are clearly defined before the research process begins, refinement of the variables to be investigated in historical research sometimes occurs after the research has begun.

External and Internal Criticism

The historian must critically evaluate the validity of the sources of information uncovered during the research process. **External criticism** is used to establish that the information is authentic. **Internal criticism** is used to determine how reliable or credible the information is.

It is necessary to establish who produced the information and under what circumstances. The information must be checked against other sources to determine how plausible it is. Historians reach their conclusions on the basis of the preponderance of the evidence.

When historical documents are used, it is possible to verify the date of the document by various means, such as carbon dating or comparing the quality of the paper and the ink with those of other documents from the same period. One may also ask if the date of a document places it in proper chronological sequence of other known events. Is the signature of an author genuine or a forgery? What possible motive might there have been for deliberately falsifying information? Are there possible biases the author may have had that may have influenced the way in which information has been recorded?

Critically Reviewing Historical Research

Carl F. Kaestle (1988), a noted educational historian at the University of Wisconsin at Madison, has identified four fundamental problems that one should be alerted to in evaluating historical research.

Confusion of Correlation and Causation

There is sometimes a tendency for historians to conclude incorrectly that because two phenomena have occurred simultaneously, one phenomenon is the cause of the other. The problem of confusing correlation with causation also occurs in other kinds of research, but it is even more of a problem in historical research. It is important for the historical researcher to rule out other possible causes.

For example, it may be true that the number of students who drop out of high school has increased as the number of hours students spend watching television has increased. However, one cannot conclude on the basis of such information that watching television causes students to drop out. Other factors, such as the increase in the total number of students entering high school or increased accessibility to high school for students with poorer academic preparation must also be taken into account.

Definition of Key Terms

Just as other researchers must define variables operationally, historians must define key terms in their research accurately and precisely. Even terms that on the surface appear to be relatively simple may turn out to be troublesome. For example, when a historian uses the term *student,* does the term include special education students as well as regular educational students? Does it include students at private schools and parochial schools as well as those at public schools? More complex terms, such as the *open classroom movement* lead to further definitional problems (Crowl, 1975). A major goal for historians is to eliminate vagueness in the definition of terms.

Another potential definitional problem is **presentism,** which is the error of interpreting terms used in the past as though they had the same meaning as they have today, or defining a historical phenomenon in terms that did not exist at the time. In interpreting historical data, the historian must try to use the frame of reference existing at that time and not to operate within today's frame of reference. A classic example cited by Kaestle is the term ''public school,'' which historically meant what we would call a ''private school'' today.

Prescriptive and Factual Evidence

Sometimes historical documents reflect what authorities felt should be done but do not shed any light on why they felt so. For example, the fact that there is considerable documentation of the establishment of "normal schools" for training teachers, in and of itself, does not permit one to conclude why such schools were founded. Did state legislatures act on the assumption that school teachers did not need training at the university level or were normal schools created to improve the quality of education teachers were then receiving?

Intent and Consequence

The fact that a particular historical phenomenon led to certain consequences is no guarantee that persons responsible for the phenomenon intended such consequences to occur. For example, standardized college admissions tests have sometimes been criticized as being biased in terms of gender and race. If the criticism is valid, a likely consequence is that women and members of ethnic minorities have been unfairly denied entrance to schools using the tests. One cannot, however, conclude that it was necessarily the intention of college administrators who introduced such tests to reduce the number of women and ethnic minority students admitted to their institutions. To come to such a conclusion it is necessary to uncover evidence that directly confirms such an intent at the time the tests were introduced.

Revisionist History

Historical research that uses different (and sometimes radical) assumptions to provide new interpretations of topics previously investigated by other historians is called *revisionist history*. The description of revisionist history that follows relies heavily on the work of Kaestle (1988).

Prior to the early 1960s, the history of American education was carried out for the most part within a traditional framework that made two basic assumptions: (a) the history of education was synonymous with the history of public schooling; and (b) the development of public schools throughout the United States was a positive achievement. The revisionist history of American education emerged largely as a challenge to these two assumptions.

As a result, the historical analysis of American education has broadened to include instructional agencies other than public schools, such as churches, the family, and workplace, particularly during the colonial period, when formal schooling played a relatively minor role in the instruction of children. See, for example, Bailyn (1960) or Cremin (1980).

Historians must now define carefully what they mean by the term *education,* for it no longer is necessarily equivalent to *public schooling.* Furthermore, emphasis has shifted from studying primarily figures who played prominent historical roles in the development of public schools to studying the educational history of ordinary citizens.

The challenge to the assumption that public schools were developed as a democratic means of affording American citizens the opportunity to learn and acquire knowledge has led to what is sometimes called *radical revisionism.* The work of radical revisionists often focuses on negative aspects of the schools, emphasizing such topics as the school's exploitative role in a capitalistic society and the threat to individual expression by forcing school children to embrace the cultural and social values espoused by the powerful and the elite.

An Example of Historical Research, with Comments

Trends in Elementary Writing Instruction, 1900–1959

Barbara von Bracht Donsky

a Historically, writing held a prestigious, although largely unexamined place within the elementary school curriculum. School books dating from the sixteenth century on indicated an awareness of the mechanics of the art of writing—requisite tools, correct techniques for sharpening quills, improved formulas for ink, appropriate size and slant for cursive strokes, and even the precise degree of angle permissible between quill and cheek—but showed little recognition of its communicative aspect. For the most part, writing, over and above what we would now refer to as penmanship, was an integral part of the study of grammar, calling for the written application of previously memorized language rules: not only as it was necessary to dot the *i* and cross the *t*, but also to punctuate, capitalize, and spell correctly. By the middle of the nineteenth century, a major shift in educational thinking occurred, allowing a subject defined as "composition" to emerge from these rather mechanistic, obscure beginnings and to become, by the end of the century, a focal point of the English curriculum.

b Deriving from the pronouncements of national committees in the 1890s, interest in written composition peaked as the study of English became, according to Baker and Thorndike (1912), the cornerstone of the elementary school curriculum and the main channel of culture and knowledge. Although composition instruction at the secondary level had been well researched by Bernhardt (1963), Judy (1967), Flanigan (1969), Botts (1970), Whitman (1973), Fay (1979), and others, instruction at the elementary level had not: the emergence, crystallization, and development of so central a portion *c* of the curriculum remained unclear. To remedy the situation somewhat, a survey of representative elementary school English textbooks published between 1900 and 1959 was undertaken with the express hope of placing the subject into historical perspective so that insights into the dynamics of educational change might be gleaned. The results and parameters of that study are as follows.

Design of the Study

In order to elicit trends in composition instruction for the period 1900 to 1959, the following steps were taken:

d 1. The sixty-year investigative period was apportioned into three roughly equal periods—1900 to 1917, 1918 to 1935, and 1936 to 1959. The starting point, 1900, in addition to marking the turn of a new century, saw the establishment of uniform college entrance requirements throughout the northeastern and mid-Atlantic states which had the effect of molding, "top-down," the curricula of both the elementary and secondary schools. The two other chronological demarcations, 1917–1918, and 1935–1936, were watershed periods witnessing the publication of landmark reports by nationally recognized educational authorities: the *Reorganization of English in Secondary Schools* by James Hosic was issued in 1917, and the *Experience Curriculum in English,* sponsored by the National Council of Teachers of English and prepared by a committee chaired by Wilbur Hatfield, was issued in 1935. The concluding year, 1959, represented approximately that point in time at which intellectual processes were conditioned more thoroughly by video than by print—a point of major cultural revolution, every bit as far-reaching as had been the invention of movable print in the mid-1400s.

2. A total of nine representative English language textbook series, intended for use in the elementary school, were selected as the data base, with three series chosen for each of the three chronological periods. Criteria for determining "representativeness" of the genre were as follows: (a) the series' prime purpose was the dissemination of English language instruction in the elementary school; (b) the textbooks demonstrated a certain robustness, having either been published by recognized authorities, or reprinted numerous times, thereby assuring their longevity; and (c) they were published by firms with nationwide distribution capabilities. The textbooks, publishers, and dates of publication were as follows: *Modern English Lessons,* Newson and Company, 1902; *Everyday English,* Macmillan, 1912; *McFadden Language Series,* Rand McNally, 1915; *New Essentials of English,* American Book, 1921; *Modern English,* Macmillan, 1932; *American Language Series,* Rand McNally, 1932; *Today's English,* Merrill, 1936; *Adventures in English,* Allyn and Bacon, 1952; and the *Good English* series, published by Laidlaw in 1952. *e*

3. A categorical framework was formulated, allowing for the allocation of tasks found within each volume into one of twelve categories, each depicting a separate facet of English language instruction: (1) modeling or patterning exercises; (2) oral language exercises linked to writing; (3) oral language exercises without immediate application to writing; (4) word development; (5) sentence development; (6) paragraph construction; (7) letter writing; (8) prose; (9) variegated forms—dramatic skits, poems, riddles, and so forth; (10) grammar and mechanics; (11) tangentially related skills—notetaking, outlining, proof-reading; and (12) residuals—a category of last resort for material such as arts and crafts, field trips, reviews and tests, deemed unclassifiable along the preceding lines. *f*

4. By apportioning the investigative period into three discrete intervals, it was possible to test: (1) whether significant changes occurred over time for any of the twelve instructional categories and (2) whether such differences could be described by either linear or quadratic trends. The level of probability was established *a priori* at the level $p < .10$; that is, significant differences were those whose likelihood of occurrence by chance was less than one in ten; statistically significant results were considered to have reflected real changes in the instructional aims and goals of textbooks examined. *g*

Findings

Trend analysis was performed for each of the twelve categories to test whether changes had occurred in the amount of time allocated each aspect of language instruction between 1900 and 1959. Ascending linear trends in the data reflected increased amounts of time allocated to oral language activities unrelated to writing (#3) and related skills (#11). Descending linear trends reflected lessened amounts of instructional time allocated to such components as modeling (#1), oral language exercises used as prewriting strategies (#2), word development (#4), letter writing (#7), and prose (#8). Quadratic trends, reflecting an increase in one period, followed by a decrease in the next, were registered for variegated forms (#9), that is, for creative writing, other than prose, and for residuals (#12). No significant changes were recorded for sentence construction (#5), paragraph development (#6), or grammar (#10), all of which remained relatively unchanged throughout the sixty-year interval.

Generally speaking, the majority of categories reflecting declining trends pertained to the written word; oral language exercises, though not necessarily those linked to writing, were increasingly favored; those nineteenth-century die-hards, grammar and sentence construction, plodded unerringly along, oblivious to changing times and changing educational currents.

Discussion

Textbooks provided handy barometers for measuring educational trends. Influenced by domestic events and international calamities, by immigration, industrialization, instructional theories, and evolving psychological insights, textbooks revealed the extraordinary adaptiveness of the nation's schools as they struggled to keep abreast of changing times, as well as changing concepts of composition instruction.

h   During the first decade of the century, textbook authors, adhering to nineteenth-century norms, strove to effect a literary atmosphere, in hopes of fostering an appreciation by students of "noble" literature and eminent thought. A wide array of literary selections for edification and emulation were interwoven among grammar drills and spelling exercises, and scores of "memory gems," fragments of prose and poetry, were sprinkled liberally throughout textbooks intended to strengthen memory, provide a commonality of experience, and, lastly, to fortify the spirit. Due to the numbers of immigrants arriving daily at the port of New York, and the increasing numbers of children attending school for whom English was not their native language, the period after the turn of the century was one of rapid expansion and upheaval for the public school systems. With immigration peaking in 1907, upon the admission of well over one million persons in that single year, the schools, faced with the monumental task of educating and Americanizing the "huddled masses," stripped the curricula of all literary trappings. Drastic measures were called for; all nonessentials were scrapped in an attempt to find time to teach those skills most in keeping with living, working, and fully participating in a democratic society; by the 1910s, the tenor of textbooks changed radically, with the aesthetic yielding to the pragmatic, and the long-esteemed goal of developing literary taste giving way to the more practical consideration of which language skills would hold students in best stead in the world of

i commerce. Oral language exercises became increasingly emphasized as teachers, fearful that the English language was on the verge of total corruption, mounted "crusades" enlisting children in the battle against slang or jargon, particularly as presented by those worst offenders of good speech—the comic book and the radio.

By the 1920s, a number of new directions emerged: according to Ball (1920), one result of the earlier emphasis on oral language was a tendency for many teachers to teach without benefit of text, plunging many classrooms into a "semi-grammarless" age. Authors, reflecting the cultural interest in science, emphasized the research-oriented premises of their language series; interest in diagnostic testing and measurement, spawned by the Stanford-Binet measures of intelligence, led to an increased differentiation of textbooks and a need for supplementary and compensatory materials.

By the 1930s, teachers' manuals and students' workbooks were published in tandem with textbooks; lessons were interdisciplinary, with a mixture of language instruction and lessons drawn from the natural and social sciences; a unit format, clustering language projects and activities into chapters, replaced the erstwhile lesson-by-lesson structure; and indications of activity-centered, project-oriented curricula were much in evidence in elementary school textbooks. Moreover, the traditional pattern of formal language instruction being offered for grades three through eight, was altered with the inclusion of textbooks for grades one and two. Oral rehearsal, as a prewriting strategy, was abandoned; oral and written language appeared farther apart than at any previous time; a general decline in written work

i paralleled the growth of the project-oriented curriculum. Social revision of composition involving peer teaching was much in favor: students, not teachers, were responsible for holding conferences with the writer and for questioning, evaluating, and judging the work. Undoubtedly, peer teaching was facilitated by group norms extolling cooperation over competition and the general well-being of the class above that of any individual.

Textbooks throughout both the 1920s and 1930s reflected the advent of a dazzling technology: page after page bore witness to the innovative genius of America, as the telegram, telephone, automobile, and "kodak" transformed the nation and its textbooks. Not so apparent were the effects of the Great Depression: while references to "bad times" never surfaced in children's textbooks, their presence was obliquely felt by the increasing importance attributed to business and to the readying of students for the workplace.

Stemming from interest in the experience-based curriculum, a continued reshuffling of educational priorities throughout the 1940s and 1950s was apparent; academics were downplayed, as were those venerable learning techniques of memorization and rote learning; concern for personal and social growth surfaced.

Teachers were cautioned about the natural timidity of young children, advised as to the development of comfortable classroom environments, and warned of the dangers of mandating creative writing; they were challenged to adopt less autocratic teaching methods, and a modern, democratic version of the dictatorial teacher of yore came into being.

By the 1950s, the precipitous fall from favor suffered by literary selections in language textbooks was nearly complete, with literature and language instruction effectively separated. With the study of literary classics no longer apparent in language textbooks, phonograph recordings added another dimension, as the voices of Maurice Evans as Hamlet, Raymond Massey as Abe Lincoln, and Otis and Cornelia Otis Skinner in scenes from Shakespeare filled the nation's classrooms. Recommended reading lists from the period, while attesting to the demise of the classics, now contained the names of writers who, in due time, were destined to become the classics in the field of children's literature: Jean de Brunhoff, A. A. Milne, Dr. Seuss, Margaret Wise Brown, and Robert McCloskey were but a few whose names surfaced as part of increased attention given younger learners, continued differentiation of reading matter, and a most hospitable technology.

Throughout the 1950s, textbooks reflected this technology, recording the growing significance of such diverse fields as aviation, ocean transport, broadcasting, motion pictures, and the nascent television industry. But, up until this point in time, no one technological achievement so enormously shaped the nature and emphasis of the curriculum as did the telephone. The immediacy of the instrument, permitting individuals world-wide to speak with one another as easily as over a backyard fence significantly reshaped communication patterns along the lines of oral cultures. Beginning in the 1930s, as the telephone connected more and more homes nationwide, textbook instructions formerly geared towards letter writing were superseded by those geared towards accomplishing the same things—introduction, brief message, and closing—but over the telephone.

Ease and speed of communication were accelerating; fed by a stream of inventions that began with the telegraph in 1835 and followed by the telephone in 1876, the radio in 1895, the television in 1920, and the first computer in 1930. Interestingly enough, there appeared to be a culturally-determined, built-in fifty-year gap between the inception of the technological product and its accession by substantial numbers of American households; thus, it was not until the 1930s that the telephone became established in the textbooks as a force with which to be dealt.

Considering the entire period, 1900 to 1959, educational practices and ideas were shaped not only by technology, but also by the social, economic, and cultural context of each period. As the functions of schools expanded to meet the needs of an increasingly diversified and complex society, courses of study grew apace and textbooks became increasingly differentiated. English language instruction, socially conditioned and culturally determined, malleable and reactive to the core, adapted to changing times and educational predilections.

Classroom Implications

Accepting the premise that most classroom teachers rely heavily upon textbooks for curriculum planning (Duffy 1982), the textbook then can become the singularly most important determinant of what is or is not taught in the classroom. Allowing that it accurately reflects vacillating educational currents and cultural phenomena, and allowing, too, that school systems, in general, appear to play mostly a reactive rather than an active role in sound change, the question originally raised by Postman (1979) regarding the information biases of the culture warrants further exploration. What in the preceding section was referred to as a fifty-year gap between the introduction of an idea and its widespread dissemination throughout society, a gap which in a real sense operated as a protective buffer offering a measure of stability, eroded with the new information technology. Today, teaching machines and computer-aided instruction and interactive materials, closed circuit television, broadcast lectures, video cassette teaching packages, films, tapes, slides, and computer graphics face obsolescence after but a few years on the market. Whether teachers will come to feel comfortable with the new technology remains an important consideration: should they continue to rely upon the textbook for curriculum structure, the question becomes one of whether textbooks should continue to mirror the culture, or should they be restrained and directed towards balancing the one-on-one nature of so much of the electronic software to effect a sense of shared experience and community. This question goes to the heart of the matter and is of vital concern to schools and publishers of educational materials.

On another front, the role of the teacher needs redefinition: ever since the 1930s, much ado has been made about the need for democratic classrooms, but little concern has been voiced over the need for democratic school administrations. Sundry articles recount the symptoms of "burnout," recording the frustrations, sense of powerlessness, and near-feelings of despair brought on, in large measure, by the absence of a spirit of fraternity, of mutual purpose and collegiality among educators at all levels: colleges accuse the secondary schools of inadequate preparation of students for upper level; secondary schools point the finger at elementary schools and they, in turn, blame parents who blame television. And so it goes. Moreover, removing teachers from the decision-making stages of curriculum planning has the undesirable effect of removing from them the responsibility for the success of those programs and thereby reducing their accountability; on the other hand, to expect teachers to be accountable for programs they have not participated in selecting is calling for robot-like behavior—the very antithesis of creative response so long requested of teachers.

Conclusions

Just as all research includes a full measure of evanescent leads and abrupt dead ends, so too it has moments of serendipity: in the course of this investigation, the latter appeared whenever the seeds of ideas circulating currently in professional journals were found embedded in the pages of textbooks published over fifty years ago. Although it is impossible to discuss herein all such linkages, a few should suffice to illustrate the point.

Much ado has been made of "process" versus "product" in recent years, yet the controversy appears more a chimera of the 1980s, a period enamored of electromagnetic transfers of energy. For in truth, good teachers have always been interested in process, that is, in the growth of the writer/ reader-speaker/listener, otherwise known as student; they attended to the product insofar as it provided a measure of anticipated growth. But the idea of "process" is one far more attuned to information technology in which the gerund is king: word processing, text processing, teleprocessing, central processing, conferencing, indexing, on-line searching are but a few of the buzzwords that best convey the simultaneous and ongoing nature of the technological revolution, just as "process" better describes the ongoing development of the writer than does "product."

But concepts regarding the symbiotic relationship between reading and writing, the possibility of teaching reading through writing, and the importance of revision, originated not with Graves (1983), but with Baker and Thorndike (1912), nearly seventy years ago. Writing as a process, one involving prewriting activities such as the maintenance of a personal log or journal, was likewise, central to the textbook series by Burleson, Burleson, and Cash (1952), which included caveats to the effect that writing was an ongoing process, one that might necessitate a given piece being completed over a period of weeks. And interest in the use of artistic activities to increase language output, an idea currently circulating in professional journals, flourished in textbooks of the 1930s, and could even be traced to Buehler's *Modern English Lessons* (1902). The benefits of peer teaching and of group conferencing, currently in vogue, were readily apparent to Pearson and Kirchwey (1921) and Hosic and Hooper (1932). Social revision, children talking to other children regarding the merits and shortcomings of compositions, was the norm for all texts published during the 1930s.

With respect to teachers, the idea of teacher as reader/writer/researcher (Brause and Mayher, 1983) actually surfaced with McFadden (1915), who conducted the research upon which the bellweather *McFadden Language Series* was predicated. Ideas for stimulating teacher creativity and for de-emphasizing the role of the textbook as the primary determinant of curriculum was reflected in the *Good English* series by Shane, Ferris, and Keener (1952).

Over the sixty-year interval that was the investigative province of this study, certain ideas appeared to bud, bloom, and wither on the vine, only to be reborn like the phoenix at a future date. And perhaps that is as it should be for, if all language is socially determined and the forms of expression culturally conditioned, then it is not surprising that ideas appearing in textbooks appear to go in cycles, reflecting the swing of the educational pendulum. Notwithstanding, the question of what the appropriate role for the textbook should be in an electronic age remains unanswered. Perhaps as the body of research on the nature of the verbal and nonverbal composing processes evolves, the answer of how the textbook can best meet the needs of both students and society will be forthcoming.

References

Baker, F., and Thorndike, A. *Everyday English.* 2 vols. New York: Macmillan, 1912.

Ball, A. *A Child's Own English Book.* Philadelphia: J. B. Lippincott, 1920, p. 5.

Bernhardt, N. ''Trends in the Teaching of English Composition in the Secondary Schools of the United States: 1900–1960.'' Doctoral dissertation, University of North Carolina at Chapel Hill, 1963.

Botts, R. ''Influences on the Teaching of English, 1917–1935: An Illusion of Progress.'' Doctoral dissertation, Northwestern University, 1970.

———. ''Writing and Rhetoric in American Secondary Schools, 1918–1935.'' *English Journal,* 68 (April 1979), 54–59.

Buehler, H. *Modern English Lessons.* New York: Newson and Company, 1902.

Burleson, D., Burleson, C., and Cash, L. *Adventures in English.* 6 vols. Boston: Allyn and Bacon, 1952.

Brause, R., and Mayher, J. ''Learning through Teaching: The Classroom Teacher as Researcher,'' *Language Arts* 60 (1983): 758–65.

Duffy, G. ''Response to Borko, Shavelson, and Stern: There's More to Instructional Decision-Making in Reading than the 'Empty Classroom.' '' *Reading Research Quarterly,* 17 (1982), 295–300.

Fay, R. ''The Reorganization Movement in Secondary English Teaching.'' *English Journal,* 68 (April 1979), 46–53.

Ferris, F., and Keener, E. *Learning Essential English.* Chicago: Laidlaw, n.d.

Flanigan, M. ''An Extension of the Tradition of English in the Secondary Schools, 1887–1917.'' Doctoral dissertation, Northwestern University, 1969.

Goodrich, B. *The Language Program in Grades One and Two.* New York: Charles E. Merrill, 1936.

Graves, D. *Writing: Teachers and Children at Work.* Exeter, N.H.: Heinemann, 1983.

Hatfield, W. Wilbur, and others. *An Experience Curriculum in English.* National Council of Teachers of English Monograph No. 4. New York: D. Appleton-Century, 1935.

Hosic, J. *Reorganization of English in Secondary Schools.* U.S. Bureau of Education Bulletin No. 2. GPS, 1917.

Hosic, J., and Hooper, C. *American Language Series.* 6 vols. New York: Rand McNally, 1932.

Judy, S. "The Teaching of English Composition in American Schools, 1850–1893." Doctoral dissertation, Northwestern University, 1967.

———. "Composition and Rhetoric in American Secondary Schools, 1840–1900." *English Journal,* 68 (April 1979), 34–39.

McFadden, E. *McFadden-Language Series.* 3 vols. Chicago: Rand McNally, 1915.

Pearson, H., and Kirchwey, M. *New Essentials of English.* 3 vols. New York: American Book Company, 1921.

Postman, N. *Teaching As a Conserving Activity.* New York: Delacorte Press, 1979.

Shane, H., Ferris, F., and Keener, E. *Good English.* 6 vols. Chicago: Laidlaw, 1952.

Traube, M., Goodrich, B., and Springsteed, C. *Today's English.* 6 vols. New York: Charles E. Merrill, 1935–36.

Whitman, R. "The Development of the Curriculum in Secondary English to 1960." Doctoral dissertation, University of Illinois at Urbana-Champaign, 1973.

Barbara von Bracht Donsky is an educational therapist in Oyster Bay Cove, New York.

Comments

a   The author's initial paragraph suffers from a lack of documented evidence for a number of allegations she makes. What evidence is there that historically, writing held a prestigious place? By whom? In what cultures? Does it make sense to look from a historical perspective at writing as a part of the elementary school curriculum? At what point in history did the concept of an "elementary school curriculum" emerge? It would help if references were given for some of the sixteenth century school books. In what countries were these books used? What evidence is there that writing was "an integral part of the study of grammar"? The author cites no evidence documenting that "a subject defined as 'composition'" emerged by the end of the nineteenth century as a focal point of the English curriculum.

b   The author gives no references to the pronouncements of national committees in the 1890s, making it impossible for an interested reader to confirm the author's claim.

c   Presumably, the author is referring to English textbooks used in North American schools.

d   Although the author justifies dividing the 60-year period into three segments, one might argue that the decision is nevertheless arbitrary. Why three periods instead of four, five or some other number? What does the author mean by writing that "intellectual processes were conditioned more thoroughly by video than by print" and on what basis is 1959 identified as the approximate date at which this took place?

e   The author lists criteria for selecting the nine textbook series, but the reader is not told from how many possible series the selection was made. In other words, the selected textbook series represent a sample, but we do not know what constitutes the population from which the sample was selected. Is it possible that a larger sample may have yielded more accurate information?

f   On what basis were the 12 categorical frameworks determined? How did the author determine which series contained which categories? How reliable were such determinations?

g   Here is an example of the use of quantitative analysis. The author claims to have examined changes in the "amount of time allocated" each of the 12 instructional categories during the 60-year period. "Amount of time" is the variable under investigation, but the author does not explain how this variable was measured. Furthermore, no information is given concerning the relative amount of time spent on each of the 12 instructional categories. Without such knowledge, it is difficult to interpret changes in the amount of time that occurred in any particular category. For example, even though there may have been a statistically significant increase in oral language exercises, the increase may have no practical meaning if (despite the significant increase) only a small proportion of total time was devoted to oral language exercises.

h   The author bases her characterization of textbooks during the first decade of the century on a single textbook series.

Chapter Highlights

- The goal of historical research is to establish causal relationships among variables, but historians cannot manipulate variables to determine whether a causal relationship exists or not.

- Historians try to use primary rather than secondary sources in order to reduce the chances of introducing bias.

- Primary sources, particularly old ones, may no longer exist or historians may be denied access to primary sources. Consequently, secondary sources must be used instead.

- *External criticism* is the process of determining if a particular document is authentic.

- *Internal criticism* is the process of determining if the information contained in a document is credible.

- In evaluating historical research, one should be aware of four possible sources of error:

  (1) the fact that phenomena occur simultaneously does not mean that one phenomenon is necessarily the cause of the other;

  (2) *presentism,* which is the error of interpreting terms used in the past as though they had the same meaning they do today;

  (3) historical documents may reflect what authorities believed should be done but not explain why they felt so; and

  (4) the fact that a historical phenomenon led to a particular consequence is no guarantee that the consequence was intended.

- Revisionist history of American education challenges the former assumptions that the history of education is synonymous with the history of public schools and that the development of public schools in the United States was a positive achievement.

Review Exercises

1. In what ways are the problems faced by historical researchers similar to those faced by researchers who conduct quantitative studies?

2. What problems do historical researchers encounter that are unique to their discipline?

3. What aspect of quantitative research is similar to historical research?

4. Name some of the sources of information historians use in conducting their research.

5. What are some of the problems historians encounter in trying to locate and use various sources of information?

6. Describe how defining variables in historical research differs from defining variables in quantitative research.

7. Describe the difference between external and internal criticism and give an example of each.

8. List four basic errors of which consumers of historical research should be aware.

9. Describe what is meant by *revisionist history*.

Chapter 11
Ethnographic Research

The product of ethnographic research is described as "a portrait of some group of people."

Chapter Objectives

After completing this chapter, you should be able to:

- define *ethnography*
- describe the characteristics of *ethnographic research* or *naturalistic inquiry*
- explain why qualitative methods have gained acceptance within the educational research community
- define *fieldwork*
- distinguish between *participant observers* and *privileged observers*

- describe the characteristics of fieldnotes and memos
- describe the concepts of *theoretical sensitivity* and *grounded theory*
- explain how researchers use *coding categories* in analyzing qualitative data
- describe factors affecting one's evaluation of a qualitative study

The previous chapter focused on historical methods, a form of inquiry that has a long tradition in educational research. This chapter focuses on ethnographic methods, a relatively recent addition to the strategies used by educational researchers that has rapidly achieved wide acceptance and popularity. The terminology used by ethnographic researchers can be confusing. Different researchers sometimes use the same term to refer to different phenomena and other times use different terms to refer to the same phenomenon. The term *ethnographic methods,* as used in this chapter, refers to methods used in carrying out "investigations described variously as ethnography, qualitative research, case study research, field research, or anthropological research" (LeCompte & Preissle, 1993, p. 2; Smith, 1979).

The editors of the *Handbook of Qualitative Research* report that they "discovered that the very term *qualitative research* means different things to many different people" (Denzin & Lincoln, 1994, p. xi). For example, some researchers use the terms *qualitative research* and *ethnographic research* synonymously to include a range of qualitative strategies; other researchers, however, use the term *ethnographic research* to refer to a particular type of qualitative research that most anthropologists use in describing various cultures (Bogdan & Biklen, 1992, p. 3). Erickson (1986) also notes that approaches to research "are alternatively called ethnographic, qualitative, participant observational, case study, symbolic interactionist, phenomenological, constructivist, or interpretive. These approaches are all slightly different, but each bears strong family resemblance to the others" (p. 119).

Another source of possible confusion is the term *qualitative method,* which is almost universally used even though the term *qualitative technique* is frequently more accurate, for as Erickson (1986) notes, "a research *technique* does not constitute a research *method*" (p. 120). To clarify the distinction between the terms, Erickson considers the situation in which researchers collect data by observing the behavior of persons who are participating in a study. He points out that what distinguishes an observational method that employs qualitative techniques from one that does not is the intent of the researcher to define the meanings of actions from the actors' point of view (p. 119). Researchers whose intent is to describe the actions of actors without attending to the meanings the actions have for the actors themselves are using the method of observation, but the technique is *not* qualitative.

Characteristics of Ethnographic Methods

The research carried out by anthropologists is usually called **ethnographic research** or **naturalistic inquiry.** Ethnography means "literally, a picture of the 'way of life' of some identifiable group of people" (Wolcott, 1988, p. 188), and the product of ethnographic research is described as "a portrait of some group of people" (LeCompte & Preissle, 1993, p. 141). Ethnographers acquire their skills through long apprenticeships during which they work under the guidance of experienced researchers in field settings. One of the most fundamental and difficult ethnographic skills to acquire is **theoretical sensitivity,** which is "the attribute of having insight, the ability to give meaning to data, the capacity to understand, and capability to separate the pertinent from that which isn't" (Strauss & Corbin, 1990, p. 42).

| Figure 11.1 | Features of Qualitative Research Identified by Bogdan and Biklen |

1. Qualitative research has the natural setting as the direct source of data and the researcher is the key instrument.
2. Qualitative research is descriptive. The data collected are in the form of words or pictures rather than numbers.
3. Qualitative researchers are concerned with process rather than simply with outcomes or products.
4. Qualitative researchers tend to analyze their data inductively.
5. "Meaning" is of essential concern to the qualitative approach. Researchers who use this approach are interested in the ways different people make sense out of their lives.

Source: Bogdan, R. C., & Biklen, S. K. (1992). *Qualitative research in education* (2nd ed.) pp. 29–32. Boston: Allyn & Bacon.

The purpose of ethnographic research is to determine how members of a culture function and interact within a natural setting. Ethnographic researchers do not enter a natural setting with the idea of manipulating variables to try to find out how various phenomena are causally related. On the contrary, ethnographers try to identify variables or constructs that occur naturally in the environment and to explain how these constructs are interrelated in ways that account for how the culture functions. For a comprehensive account of qualitative research, see Denzin and Lincoln (1994).

Although anthropologists may be best known for studying exotic cultures, such as Margaret Mead's well-known studies of Samoa and New Guinea, the culture under investigation may be as commonplace as a classroom. Ethnographic methods have attracted the interest of educational researchers because one may conceptualize various educational settings, such as classrooms or schools, as cultures because these settings contain a group of people who play various roles and behave in ways governed by habits and customs that are unique to that group. See LeCompte, Millroy, and Preissle (1992) for a comprehensive account of qualitative research in education.

Erickson (1986) states that "there is much disagreement among [qualitative] researchers about the proper conduct of their work and its theoretical foundations" (p. 120). Similarly, Denzin and Lincoln (1994) note "that the 'field' of qualitative research is far from a unified set of principles" (p. ix). Nevertheless, Bogdan and Biklen (1992) have identified five features they believe characterize qualitative research (pp. 29–32). They quickly caution, however, that not all qualitative studies exhibit all features to the same degree and that some studies barely exhibit any features. Figure 11.1 lists the five features identified by Bogdan and Biklen.

One of the most distinguishing characteristics of qualitative research is the flexibility researchers exercise in carrying out a study. Researchers have a great deal of flexibility in selecting and modifying the research question they are investigating even after the investigation is underway. Similarly, qualitative researchers may choose from a variety of methods to collect data and change the methods they use to adapt to new questions that arise.

Ethnography is a qualitative form of observational research that differs in several important ways from quantitative forms of observational research. In quantitative observational studies, researchers specify the variables they are going to investigate before beginning their study. The results of such studies often consist of frequency counts of specified events. A quantitative observational study of disruptive behavior in the classroom, for example, might yield findings consisting of the number of times students called out without raising their hands, got out of their seats, talked with other students, and so forth. (See chapter 12 for more information on quantitative observational research.) Ethnographers, however, begin their observations with what Stake (1988, p. 225) has called **foreshadowed problems,** which are nothing more than general notions of what is to be investigated. The actual problems selected for investigation emerge only as the study takes place and the researcher begins to understand which aspects of the culture under investigation are important.

The results of ethnographic studies are presented in the form of a written account that includes a description of what the researcher has observed and the researcher's analysis and interpretation of the observations. Whereas the objective of quantitative studies is often to provide an empirical test of some theory, the objective of ethnographic studies is to generate theories based on empirical data. Ethnographers attempt to devise theories on the basis of data they collect to account for what they have observed.

Qualitative Educational Research

Prior to the 1960s, educational researchers relied solely on quantitative methods to conduct their investigations because it was widely believed that quantitative methods permitted researchers to carry out their work in an objective manner. Educational researchers, who saw objectivity as a hallmark of the scientific method, generally agreed that qualitative methods lacked objectivity and consequently failed to qualify as science. The prevailing attitude among educational researchers was that the results of qualitative research depended too heavily on the researcher's subjective interpretation to be considered scientific.

Eventually, the notion that quantitative methods guaranteed objectivity was challenged. It was argued that all research, including quantitative studies, lacked objectivity. For example, the way in which a quantitative researcher decides to define a variable operationally reflects a subjective judgment. Indeed the very questions chosen for examination reflect the researcher's subjective opinions about what phenomena are important enough to study. This section presents an overview of qualitative educational research and draws heavily on the work of Bogdan and Biklen (1992) and LeCompte and Preissle (1993).

Among educational researchers, the terms *qualitative, naturalistic,* and *ethnographic research* are used more or less synonymously. The term *qualitative research,* however, did not come into use until the 1960s even though anthropologists and sociologists had been carrying out such research for a long time. Although qualitative researchers disagree among themselves both with respect to the theoretical foundations underlying their work and how one should go about conducting qualitative studies (Erickson, 1986), most would probably characterize their work as being ''rich in description of people, places, and conversations, and not easily handled by statistical procedures'' (Bogdan & Biklen, 1992, p. 2).

Educational researchers (as opposed to researchers from the fields of anthropology or sociology) first began to use ethnographic methods in the 1960s for several reasons. At that time there was considerable student unrest at many of the country's leading colleges and universities, which drew the focus of the public on problems confronting education. The civil rights movement also drew attention to the failure of the educational system to attend to the concerns of minority students. A number of educational researchers turned to ethnographic methods in order to be able to examine educational problems from the perspective of minorities because a fundamental goal of ethnographic research has always been to describe phenomena from subjects' points of view.

During the 1970s, interest in qualitative educational research continued to grow as funding became available to permit researchers to incorporate ethnographic methods in their evaluation studies of educational innovations. Two other factors have probably also contributed to the increase in educational researchers' interest in ethnographic methods: (a) by the 1980s and 1990s, advances in computer technology made it easier to sort and analyze the enormous amount of data typically gathered during ethnographic studies (see chapter 17); and (b) the rising influence of feminists, many of whom have found ethnographic methods ideally suited for examining educational issues from the perspectives of women and girls.

Common Questions About Qualitative Research

Bogdan and Biklen (1992, pp. 42–49) attempt to answer a number of questions commonly asked by persons who are encountering qualitative research for the first time. Some of these questions (and answers) follow.

Question: Can qualitative and quantitative research approaches be used together?

Answer: There are studies that have components of both approaches (e.g., qualitative studies that include descriptive statistics), but generally a study is basically one type or the other.

Question: Is qualitative research really scientific?

Answer: Yes, if one defines scientific research as "rigorous and systematic empirical inquiry that is data-based"; no, if one defines scientific research as only research "that is deductive and hypothesis-testing" (p. 43).

Question: Are qualitative findings generalizable?

Answer: Qualitative researchers are often less concerned about whether their findings are generalizable to similar settings and similar subjects than they are in identifying different kinds of settings and subjects to which their findings might apply.

Question: What about the researcher's opinions, prejudices, and other biases and their effect on the data?

Answer: Qualitative researchers try to guard against their biases by acknowledging them and taking them into account.

Question: Will two researchers independently studying the same setting or subjects come up with the same findings?

Answer: In general, qualitative researchers are not interested in this question because different researchers using the same setting and subjects will probably ask different questions, collect different data, and come up with different conclusions.

Fieldwork

Ethnographers use the term **fieldwork** to refer to the time they spend observing and inter-acting with members of the group they are studying. As the term implies, fieldwork takes place in the natural setting of the group. The field is the arena inhabited (permanently or temporarily) by the participants in the study; it literally defines the geographic boundaries within which the researcher will carry out his or her investigation.

Ethnographers rely on two primary means of collecting research data: *participant observation* and *interviewing*. Although interviewing is a technique commonly used by researchers carrying out widely different kinds of studies, participant observation is a technique unique to researchers using ethnographic methods. We will discuss participant observation in this chapter and postpone our discussion of interviewing until the following chapter on descriptive methods.

Participant Observation

As a participant observer, the researcher tries to become a part of the group he or she is investigating by spending a great deal of time with members of the group (sometimes actually living with them) and by participating in the activities in which group members engage. While participating in group activities, the researcher simultaneously observes what is taking place in the group, hence the term **participant observation.** Researchers typically write detailed accounts of what they have seen and heard during each observation period. These detailed accounts are called *fieldnotes* and constitute the data the researchers ultimately will analyze.

It is useful to think of participant observation as a continuum in which the degree of involvement varies from observation only, where the researcher does not actively participate at all, to *going native* (Gold, 1958), where the researcher becomes so much a part of the group that he or she loses the necessary distance to observe dispassionately and objectively, thereby sabotaging the initial intention to carry out a piece of research (Bogdan & Biklen, 1992, p. 88). It is also useful to think of participant observation in terms of the length of time of involvement. Traditionally, ethnographers studying exotic societies would spend at least a year living with the people they were studying.

The extent to which educational researchers using ethnographic methods become involved with the groups they are studying rarely approaches the intensity traditionally exhibited by other ethnographers. It is understandable that it might be difficult for ethnographers investigating classrooms to become active participants. For one thing, ethnographers are adults, whereas the students are likely to be children, and it is unlikely that many children would interact with an adult the way they interact with their peers. Wolcott (1988) has noted that ethnographers who receive permission to observe and record the events occurring in a classroom are best classified not as participant observers, but rather as **privileged observers.** Rist (1980) coined the term ''blitzkrieg ethnography'' to underscore the tendency for some educational researchers employing ethnographic methods to spend insufficient time with the groups they are investigating.

Although ethnographers originally devised the method of participant observation to gather data about social or cultural groups, educational evaluators have used the method since the 1970s to determine the effectiveness of newly implemented educational programs. Participant observation has also been used in conjunction with data gathered by means of

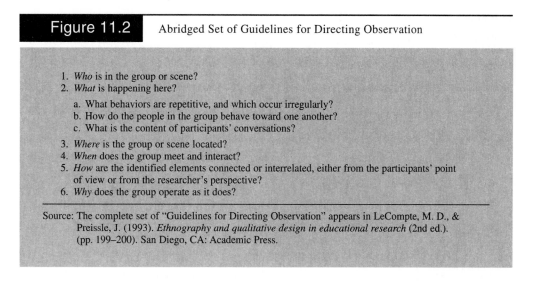

Figure 11.2   Abridged Set of Guidelines for Directing Observation

1. *Who* is in the group or scene?
2. *What* is happening here?
   a. What behaviors are repetitive, and which occur irregularly?
   b. How do the people in the group behave toward one another?
   c. What is the content of participants' conversations?
3. *Where* is the group or scene located?
4. *When* does the group meet and interact?
5. *How* are the identified elements connected or interrelated, either from the participants' point of view or from the researcher's perspective?
6. *Why* does the group operate as it does?

Source: The complete set of "Guidelines for Directing Observation" appears in LeCompte, M. D., & Preissle, J. (1993). *Ethnography and qualitative design in educational research* (2nd ed.). (pp. 199–200). San Diego, CA: Academic Press.

standardized tests and questionnaires to achieve a more comprehensive understanding of program implementation (LeCompte & Preissle, 1993, p. 198).

Acknowledging that it is impossible for a participant observer to record everything that takes place during an observational period, LeCompte and Preissle offer a set of guidelines for directing observation. See Figure 11.2 for an abridged version of these guidelines. Additional examples of observational questions for educational settings may be found in Bogdan and Biklen (1992, pp. 232–243). There are no strict rules regarding the length of a single observational period. It is suggested, however, that researchers keep the period short enough to be able to remember what took place during it and to have sufficient time immediately after the period to write up fieldnotes (Bogdan & Biklen, 1992, p. 95).

Fieldnotes and Memos

Fieldnotes are the researcher's written chronological account of what occurred during each observation session. Although different researchers use different formats in writing fieldnotes, most fieldnotes consist of two parts: (a) an objective part that contains a comprehensive and detailed description of what has taken place and (b) a subjective part that contains the researcher's reflections about what occurred during that particular observation session as well as a list of questions, hunches, or ideas the researcher may have concerning the study as a whole. **Memos** are relatively lengthy reflective pieces that researchers write at various times during their investigations to focus on the study as a whole, not on any particular observation session.

Researchers usually do not write fieldnotes during the observation session itself, but rather immediately after the session has concluded. On the other hand, it is not unusual for researchers to make brief notes during the observation session to help them recall accurately what took place. It is important to write fieldnotes that are as accurate and comprehensive as possible, for the fieldnotes constitute the data the researcher will ultimately analyze. Figure 11.3 provides an outline of the components of the descriptive and reflective parts of fieldnotes.

Figure 11.3   The Descriptive and Reflective Components of Fieldnotes

Descriptive Part

    a. Portrayal of the subjects: their physical appearance, dress, mannerisms, and style of talking and acting.

    b. Reconstruction of dialogue: conversations between subjects and between subjects and the researcher; contains direct quotes when possible, particularly when language unique to the setting is used.

    c. Description of physical setting: sketches of furniture arrangements; descriptions of things on blackboards, walls, and bulletin boards.

    d. Accounts of particular events: who was involved and in what manner.

    e. Depiction of activities: detailed descriptions of behavior in the order in which it occurred.

    f. Observer's behavior: records of the researcher's dress, action, and conversations and any kinds of behavior or assumptions that might affect how data are gathered and analyzed.

Reflective Part

    a. Reflections on analysis: speculations about what themes are emerging, what patterns are developing, how various pieces of the data may be connected, and any new ideas that may occur to the researcher.

    b. Reflections on method: describes procedures used and decisions made about the design of the study; comments on rapport with particular subjects, including problems or dilemmas and possible ways of solving them; what has been accomplished so far and what is still left to be done.

    c. Reflections on ethical dilemmas and conflicts: any ethical concerns dealing with the researcher's own values and responsibilities to subjects or to the research profession.

    d. Reflections of the observer's frame of mind: assumptions the researcher has about the subjects and setting, including opinions, beliefs, attitudes and prejudices; encounters during data collection that cause assumptions to be revised.

    e. Points of clarification: clarifications of information that is potentially misleading and correction of errors made in writing previous fieldnotes.

Source: Bogdan, R. C., & Biklen, S. K. (1992). *Qualitative research in education* (2nd ed.) (pp. 120–123). Boston: Allyn & Bacon.

Grounded Theory

It is common for ethnographers to make memos and draw diagrams concerning possible interpretations of their fieldnotes to serve as guidelines for future observations. The researcher then uses future observations to confirm or disconfirm possible explanations that seem to have emerged from previous fieldnotes. Throughout the study, the ethnographer constantly shifts back and forth from observing and notetaking to analyzing the observations. Ethnographers are constantly proposing a theoretical notion and checking to see if the notion is verified. The results of this interplay lead to what is sometimes called **grounded theory,** that is, a theory whose components and their relationships to one another are embedded in reality.

In addition to recording fieldnotes based on observations, ethnographers may also carry out interviews, administer questionnaires, and use written records, such as papers written by students or reports written by teachers or administrators. Previous attempts to analyze field notes may reveal parts of the theory that need more documentation and lead the researcher to seek out specific kinds of information. Researchers try to obtain information from multiple sources to cross-check and validate the information they gather.

Figure 11.4   Examples of Coding Categories Used to Organize Fieldnotes

Setting/Context Codes: General information about the setting, topic, or subjects. Examples: "Descriptions of Elementary School," "Midcity High School."

Definition of the Situation Codes: Data showing how subjects define the setting or topic. Examples: "Feminist Awareness," "Image of Present Self," "Influences on Interpreting Past."

Process Codes: Sequences of events or changes over time. Examples: "Moving to New Jersey," "Mrs. Nelson," "Elementary School after Mrs. Nelson."

Activity Codes: Regularly occurring kinds of behavior. Examples: "Joking," "Showing Films," "Special Education Case Conference."

Event Codes: Particular happenings that occur infrequently or only once. Examples: "A Teacher Strike," "The Riot," "A School Pageant."

Strategy Codes: Techniques people consciously use to accomplish various things. Example: "Techniques to Control Class."

Relationship and Social Structure Codes: Regular patterns of behavior among unofficial groups. Example: "Student Friendships."

Source: Bogdan, R. C., & Biklen, S. K. (1992). *Qualitative research in education* (2nd ed.) (pp. 167–171). Boston: Allyn & Bacon.

Analyzing and Interpreting Qualitative Data

A critical aspect of ethnographic research is interpreting the data. Some ethnographers believe that the goal of ethnographic research is to present as accurate an account as possible of what informants have said and what has been observed (see, for example, Wolcott, 1990, p. 130).

As noted in chapter 1, the data in a qualitative study consist of the researcher's fieldnotes and memos as well as any other materials that may have been collected, such as photographs, documents or other artifacts. The processes of data collection and data analysis are not as separate in qualitative research as they are in quantitative research. Qualitative researchers begin to analyze their data as soon as the data collection process begins. In fact, qualitative researchers rely on their ongoing data analyses to shape the direction the study takes. After the researcher has finished collecting data, a more formal analysis takes place.

LeCompte and Preissle (1993, pp. 235–236) point out the importance of beginning the formal data analysis by returning to the original research question, even though in the course of the study the original question has probably changed considerably. Returning to the original question helps the researcher to interpret the study's findings by explaining why decisions were made to modify the data collection process. The researcher then scans all of the data to develop **coding categories** to cover each topic or recurring theme. The number and kind of coding categories researchers use vary according to the nature of the investigation. Bogdan and Biklen (1992, pp. 176–177) suggest that researchers develop codes at differing levels of specificity and that the number of codes total between 30 and 50. Researchers often assign one or more codes to each paragraph. Figure 11.4 lists some typical coding categories used by qualitative researchers.

After having coded all the data, researchers then place all of the paragraphs having the same coding category together, either manually or by means of one of several computer programs (see chapter 17 for information about sorting qualitative data by computer). Having simultaneous access to all paragraphs dealing with the same topic makes it easier for the researcher to write the final report. There is no standard format in which qualitative reports are written, but they all attempt to inform the reader about what the researcher did and to present evidence documenting whatever interpretations the researcher has made. Many ethnographic researchers try to include numerous quotes from their fieldnotes so that the reader can vicariously experience being in the research setting and better understand how conclusions based on the study have been reached. Researchers also always use fictitious names of persons and places to protect the privacy of persons who have participated in a study.

Evaluating Qualitative Studies

How does one go about assessing how well a completed piece of research has been executed? There is, of course, no simple answer to this question; the answer depends among other things on the kind of study that is being evaluated. The criteria for evaluating quantitative studies are generally agreed on by researchers who undertake quantitative investigations. (See chapter 16 for information on evaluating quantitative research.) However, as LeCompte and Preissle (1993) point out:

> Assessing qualitative studies is difficult because of the inherent diversity of the designs. Research endeavors like ethnographies, characterized by phenomenological perspectives, naturalistic factors, multimodal strategies, eclectic approaches to theory, and participation of the researcher as instrument, resist simplistic recipes for evaluation. (p. 354)

Furthermore, they ''argue that no single approach to evaluation is adequate for assessing qualitative design . . . the best we can achieve are standards necessary and sufficient, applied case by case'' (LeCompte & Preissle, 1993, p. 321). Consequently, the criteria used to judge the quality of a piece of qualitative research vary, depending on who the evaluator is and what the purposes of the evaluation are.

An Example of Ethnographic Research, with Comments

a   The New Dependencies of Women*

Lynn Woodhouse**

The changing roles of women can be observed in many of the dynamics of our culture. These changing roles reflect a changing dependency of women. The potential impacts of changing roles and changing dependencies on women, children, and families are examined in this research at a day-care setting.
b   Ethnographic methodologies utilized include: participant observation and interviews with mothers, staff, children, and administrators. The analysis is used to create a description of this culture and to create a series of suggestions for supports for women and families that will enhance the environment of child care and facilitate interactive child development.

*Presented at the American Anthropological Association Convention, Chicago, IL, November, 1987.
**Lynn Woodhouse is an Associate Professor of Health at East Stroudsburg University, East Stroudsburg, PA 18301.
Key Words: day care, early childhood, ethnography, health, women.

"I'm having a nervous breakdown" bellows from a mother as she rushes into the classroom of the   *c*
day care center. "Hurry up, we're late. I love you, but we have to leave" (Woodhouse, 1987).

As mothers re-enter the world of 4-year-old day care to retrieve their children, fresh from the demands and seduction of career (Swanson-Kauffman, 1987), they are re-entering the world of traditional role prescriptions. This is a world they are changing; and as they change this world they are perhaps grieving its loss (Marris, 1974). But, this is a world they have, by choice or need, to some extent left behind. Unfortunately, change has not brought with it the resources or solutions for the experiences or problems created by the change. Thus, existing in their altered environment can be a challenge for mothers and their children.

The ability of people to exist in their environment was traditionally complemented by the efficacy of solutions provided by the culture. The repertoire of life skills a person developed was (and still is) dependent on the adequacy of the preparatory institutions (the institutions that function to socialize) to which a person was exposed (Mechanic, 1974). Change, in the past, was slower; so the repertoire of life skills provided adequate solutions to many expected and less varied problems in life (as long as the individual didn't venture out of prescribed roles). But the culture of individuals, and the culture supported by the socializing institutions, are undergoing rapid change. Consequently, the skills and attitudes learned in the culture may not meet the demands of the lives of some individuals.

Transitions of Women   *d*

The traditional woman, living in the traditional family of a generation or more ago, blended with her family's needs; her goals reflected their needs (McLaughlin et al., 1986). Her self-esteem was primarily derived from the maintenance of the constellation of relationships in her life (Sassen, 1980), which included her children and family. She was connected to people on many levels, and the quality of the connections, which included the happiness and future success of the people she was connected to, determined her success. She was the keeper of love. As caring relationships were central to her life (Woods, 1987), she remained relegated to the world of depleted power without personal and financial problem-solving resources. She was depended upon for nurturance, but dependent for survival needs. In her nurturing role she was supported by the culture, the skills she needed were provided by the culture, and her dependency was enhanced by the culture. She had the requisite skills and attitudes to solve the problems of her life. Though much of the psychology of women remains the same, it is becoming richer albeit more complex. New variables and choices are affecting all women, and these new variables and choices are making them more exposed to problems requiring varied skills and attitudes they may not have acquired in their nurturing roles.

Today more women are "primary individuals" with actions driven by a different environment and set of objectives (McLaughlin et al., 1986). The cultural push for independence, individualism (Hsu, 1975; Reynolds, 1984), and separation (Gilligan, 1982), so prevalent in our media, relays a consistent message that everyone can succeed, that everyone can become primary. Yet, many women, socialized for attachment and connectedness, who begin to follow this path, find that the new road to being a primary individual (McLaughlin et al., 1986) can be bumpy and long and saturated with conflict and contradiction on a personal, interpersonal, and institutional level; at least Dorothy had a yellow brick road.

Culture and Potential   *e*

Dependency on the knowledge and beliefs of the culture, which are designed to reify the culture, may limit the ability of women and girls to function adaptively in their rapidly changing world (Mead, 1970). Culture can actually limit the beliefs, range of communication patterns, values, and behaviors of the individual (LeVine, 1982). Consequently, culture can cause disharmony in the individual as the messages learned can be antagonistic to the needs of the individual.

In addition, the culture may limit the ability of individuals to shed standardized performance, break rules for behavior, and defy norms of conduct (LeVine, 1982). As women break out of traditional roles to become primary individuals and attempt to change the level of their dependencies, a tangled web of dependencies and outside supports emerges. During this transition, women frequently turn to institutions of the culture for support. These institutions, like day care, are constructed to maintain the culture and cannot provide support for change. Consequently, women, as individuals, are pushed and pulled, torn between dependence and independence, attachment and separation. The road to independence clearly produces conflict and contradictions for women, especially women who are trying to become primary individuals while they continue to fulfill traditional nurturing roles. It is important to understand the impact of conflicting and contradicting variables on women, some of which are very subtle. Such information can be used to create resources that will effectively support the period of transition.

The Institution of Day Care

An institution in a culture functions for the survival of the group in relation to the external environment (LeVine, 1982). However, in this capacity, institutions are structured to reinforce the culture through the system of rewards and punishments and the specific opportunities they offer (Coleman, 1987; LeVine, 1982).

The values, beliefs, and norms of the culture can be found in the institutions. Sometimes they are obvious, sometimes they are subtle; but either way they are present in the system of rewards and punishments and availability of opportunities (Coleman, 1987). It is clear that during change, when the culture pushes to maintain itself, the institution of day care will reflect this pressure.

The institution of day care primarily supports women and young families whose emerging roles and needs are perhaps most contrary to the maintenance of the culture. Over 60% of the mothers of preschool children work (U.S. Department of Labor, 1985). Consequently, the institution of day care provides a unique vantage point for the study of women and girls as they interact in the pushes and pulls of the culture. Examining the culture of day care means being sensitive to the multiple levels of interactions including: how the mothers interact with the institution of day care, how the transitions of the culture impact the children's interaction with their mothers and their interactions with others in the day-care setting, and how the culture of day care impacts the women and girls.

Setting, Subjects, and Methods of Study

f   To start looking at the culture in this transition period, a setting was chosen that reflected the push for independence by women—a day-care facility serving young professionals. It is located in a large eastern city that pulsates with power and importance. The day-care facility is in a country setting, about 20 minutes from the center of the city, a location which makes it attractive to the busy commuter.

In this day-care setting I became involved in the culture of the children in the 4-year-old class. There were 12 children, half boys and half girls. During the 10 months of this ethnographic research,
g I was an observer 6 to 8 hours per week, collecting field notes at all times. I interviewed staff directors,
h counselors, and mothers, both formally and informally, audiotaping interviews when possible. My efforts were assisted by mothers and staff through the keeping of activity and health records of the children.

i   Analysis of the data was conducted throughout the study by examining the categories or units of analysis as they developed (Goetz & LeCompte, 1984). Lofland and Lofland (1984) present units of analysis for examining social settings which include: meanings (philosophies, rules, norms); events; interactions between people; roles (social types of persons); and relationships (how people interact with regularity). These units served as the organizing structure for the data analysis. The results of this analysis will follow a discussion of the subjects.

The culture of four girls was studied very closely, as they were the only four children who *j* remained clients of the center throughout the 10 months of intensive data collection and whose mother or father brought them to and from school. Two of these girls were from single-parent homes (mother-headed), and two were from two-parent homes. One of the children was adopted from another country.

Three of the children were only children during most of the study. One of the married mothers had a son a year older than the daughter in this study. He also attended this center. However, one single mother, the mother of the adopted daughter, adopted another foreign child more than halfway through data collection. This mother said that she didn't believe in putting off what you want and she *k* wanted children. The adoption process was a tremendous strain on the mother and daughter. This mother, an executive, pressed forward very hard, reportedly refusing to follow the norms, always seeking new challenges, reporting tremendous stress, but apparently oblivious to the impact it was having on her daughter. Her daughter had been in day care since she arrived. Though she spoke English like a native, she didn't seem to grasp the nuances of the language she was supposed to be preparing to learn to read. This child was talented in many ways, she loved people, was a budding gymnast, and could make everyone smile. Though she was reported by the staff to show the signs of a stressful life since she had been a client at the center, the wear and tear of the year slowly intensified her distant and withdrawn behaviors and her illness levels. According to the staff, she received very little social-emotional support at home.

The other single mother, a quieter yet more driven woman, laughed when questioned about her stress level. Her behaviors indicated a constant push for change. Though she had a graduate degree, she was working on another one. She was getting married again, moving for the third time in a year, and making choices that were causing several other important changes. She too seemed oblivious to the tremendous synergistic impact the pace of her life and the resistant culture was having on her daughter. There was little social-emotional support for mother or child. Her daughter was very bright and had a knack for the ''readiness'' workshops; cognitive skills developed easily. Yet she had a deep darkness that crept closer to her surface as the months wore on and the stress she lived with escalated. This was evidenced in emotional and physical signs like withdrawn behavior and crying.

The two children of two-parent homes were quite different. The one child was constantly busy, talking, refusing to sleep, running everywhere, unable to pay attention in learning situations. She was uninterested in cognitive activities. This child's behavior worsened during the year. The mother of this child reported that the most distressing part of her day was picking up the children at the center because she sensed no time between work and home. She was able to schedule a day off each week which she didn't think her children knew about because she took them to day care anyway (however, from their comments, they did seem to know). She was a very traditional woman, describing her household as one with the discipline handled by the father and the cooking and cleaning handled by the mother. She told me that her daughter was her voice, that they were connected and very dependent. This child received some social-emotional support, but she had many emotional, social, and physical signs of stress.

The other child of a two-parent home seemed quite well adjusted during the year. Her behavior did not worsen, it became better. Early in the year her mother reported the child tried to gain control *k* of her. The mother described the situation as being connected to her extended work hours. The mother was a teacher, and the first month of school was very busy for her, so she had to work late. Her daughter punished her for the stress, she believed, and tried to punish her for working longer hours and having less energy for her. This family was unique for this setting as they stressed the cognitive as well as the social-emotional aspects of their child. In addition, they were able to care for the child's physical needs including staying home with her when she was sick. Probably because of a combination of more flexibility of time, two supportive parents, and social-emotional support to complement the cognitive support, this child grew more mature and seemed much more stable than the other three as the year progressed. Though she had her share of illnesses, her behavior did not indicate chronic stress.

Characteristics of the Culture

From the units of analysis used as an organizing structure (meanings, events, interactions between people, roles, and relationships), themes or characteristics of the culture surrounding these 4-year-old girls emerged. The results indicated strong potential impacts on mothers and children. The culture that surrounded these 4-year-olds in day care was one of rapid change, high expectations, and minimal support (Woodhouse, 1987). This culture reflected the larger culture as many of these themes are correlated with economic success in the adult world. Several themes of the culture which point to these definitions developed from the data analysis and are reviewed in the following paragraphs.

The atmosphere of this setting presented a theme of subtle competition. Constant activity and a rigid schedule required the children to be ready for change at all times. Being ready for dealing with multiple variables is a sign of success in the adult world.

Success in the cognitive skill area was clearly of paramount importance in this setting. Everything revolved around preparing the children for kindergarten. The ''workshops'' to give the skills necessary for kindergarten were groups of children (usually five) with one teacher concentrating on some theme of learning letters or numbers. These groups were ability grouped, keeping the smarter children together. Even the names of the groups, ''brites'' for the smart children, reflected their superiority. They were first to go outside, to lunch, to the bathroom, and so forth. The other children noticed this as they asked why it happened.

The competition for cognitive ''readiness'' was pervasive. Without asking one was always told who was ready, who was borderline, and who was never going to be ready. Counselors, staff, and mothers discussed who was ready and in what areas children were or were not ready. Rarely did any social-emotional variables enter the discussion. When there is so much emphasis on cognitive preparation there is a de-emphasis on social or emotional needs. Teachers kept records on anything that related to cognitive preparation. Records were kept on social skills, but the outcomes of these records were not discussed with much importance. Academic success in school is correlated with economic success in the adult world.

Play (a way to work out roles, understand life conflicts, and manage stress) was secondary. It had to seep into the cracks of the rushed schedule. In addition, play had to be halted when it was time for any other activity.

Friend groups for the girls were discouraged. The two girls of single mothers in this study became very close. This closeness was obviously comforting to them. The mother of the more academically oriented girl came in one day and yelled at the other child because she was getting her daughter in trouble. Although this was not the case, the mother demanded they be separated. In other instances children who were close were separated at naps or at meals. At playtime the children would immediately seek each other out. When conflict evolved between friends, the staff consistently encouraged the children to find another friend. Clearly, there was little attempt to develop conflict resolution skills and little importance placed on friends.

Traditional sex roles were emphasized in this setting. All the caretakers were females, which reinforced the nurturing role stereotype (Bronfenbrenner, 1979). These caretakers were also helpless, having no power over their jobs and getting very low pay, which further emphasized traditional sex roles. Decisions about jobs, from the lack of substitute teachers to in-service training, were made by the administrator with little input from the child-care staff. Once the administrator arbitrarily decided the staff didn't need a week of their vacation, so she cancelled it without consulting anyone; such an action only added to the powerless feeling relayed by the staff. (This job was described as a job you took only after you exhausted all other possibilities.) Traditional sex roles were also emphasized at the center in the differential treatment of boys and girls. Traditional patterns were followed, with boys being encouraged to be more active.

The culture was a culture of the negative. Single mothers reported a lack of buffer between their child and their own anger. One mother reported this was one of her major concerns but the problem continued. Another mother reported that she gets mad at her daughter for things her daughter can't help, then realizes after it is too late that "the poor little kid couldn't help that." Anger seemed to be a product of multiple role conflicts experienced by these mothers. The theme of anger in parents, both the reasons for it and the impacts, needs to be expanded in research.

Coercive control was rewarded in the setting, as children, mothers, and administrators who used defiant and manipulative tactics frequently got their way, only adding to the negative emphasis of the culture. Another negative emphasis was the search for negative behaviors in the children. The staff reported that mothers usually asked about negative behaviors in their children. The teachers were then forced to emphasize the negative, making them less conscious of the positive behaviors of the children. This doesn't give much material to support the developing self-concept of children.

The culture was a rushed culture. Every second of the children's lives was regulated. All day long you heard "hurry up" or "only two minutes left." Such an emphasis on a rigid schedule made completing anything difficult. When the children were picked up, they were rushed by an exhausted parent. There was little chance for these children to feel in control. One child started running and hiding to force her mother inside to look at her pictures. Another would be perfectlyhappy, but begin crying when her mother appeared so as to delay the transition. Another child became bossy and mean to her mother. Another child became limp when her mother arrived, already defeated, having no control left at all. Transitions were very important. If these children stayed past four o'clock, they were ready to leave; sometimes they waited for almost two hours for their mothers, and their mothers didn't even stay long enough to look at a picture. It was a devaluing experience.

The culture was a culture of stressful life events. The mothers, especially the single mothers, reported excessive amounts of stress which came from role conflicts. They described their situations as incredibly stressed; they laughed at the situation and described it as unbelievable, yet they reported they are looking for new challenges.

The life events of the four girls were examined month by month and compared with illness data. The frequency and intensity of illness paralleled the increase in life events. One little girl moved twice, took a 6000-mile journey in 10 days, had her mother remarry (gaining a stepfather and grandmother), testified as a victim at a child molestation trial (related to another day-care center), existed as her mother went to graduate school 2 nights a week and one day a weekend, and was preparing to move across the country, during the 10 months of this data collection phase of this research. Throughout this time she had multiple illnesses and stress-related disorders including flu, ear infections, psoriasis, and conjunctivitis.

The culture was a culture with an emphasis on illness, yet illness affects people differently. Frequently, the children (except for one child) had to endure their illnesses without being able to retreat to a comforting environment to get well; they came to day care sick and frequently stayed at day care sick. The problem was worse for children of single mothers. One mother actually admitted that she gave her child a fever reducer in the morning before she took her to day care as she had to go to work. Though the center had a health policy, it was usually ignored, especially for the children of single mothers. Multiple cases of conjunctivitis, strep throat, ear infections, flu, diarrhea, and stress-related problems (like psoriasis) were ignored by the staff. In a chicken pox epidemic every child in the 4-year-old section broke out with chicken pox at school and had to be sent home. Many came back with active pox and were sent home again. Well children were exposed to illness when sick children attended school. Teachers got sick. When anyone was sick the environment changed. This impacted everyone. Many times a staff member would say "it's no fun to have to be at school sick" to a crying, sick child. But no one forced the issue, except when they knew a parent would be available or if there was a high fever. (I contracted conjunctivitis six times during my observations of the children—it was not fun and I didn't go to school sick.)

Discussion

As mothers push for independence and butt up against a nonsupportive culture, their own and their children's potential for holistic growth in social, emotional, and physical areas appears to be suffering. As women's roles are changing, their children's roles may be disappearing (Kagan, 1984). Preschool was a place for nurturing, a supportive extension of a nurturing family (Clarke-Stewart, 1982). Now there are limits to the nurturing of the family (related to the stress and role conflict of the mother) and an emphasis on cognitive rather than social or emotional pursuits in the day-care setting. Though day care isn't necessarily preschool, many day-care settings are following a theme of preparing children for school. (Elkind, 1987, has reported extensively on the negative effects of an excessive emphasis on cognitive skills for young children.)

m   From the results of this study, it can be concluded that these children are supposed to learn to "fit" their environment, to fall into a mold that will enhance future competitive success. A few years ago advice published for parents about day care suggested they shop around until they find a setting that "fits" their child (Clarke-Stewart, 1982). Since there is such a shortage of day care, this is impossible.

But there is more than just a failure to fit. These children are being pushed into a mold to become "ideal" individuals. It is almost as if acting like children gets in the way. We may be witnessing a shortening of the length of childhood. Childhood is defined by the culture; the length of childhood meets the needs of the culture (Aries, 1962). Perhaps this shortening of childhood is the cultural response to the pushes and pulls on women—a response that needs to be carefully structured to avoid hurting children.

Impacts on the Children in the Setting

This research clearly indicates that the emphasis on becoming an "ideal" or "primary" individual is pervasive in this setting. Children are socialized to be able to: function in competition, not be too interdependent (while the girls are getting a conflicting message about traditional roles), be able to work while ill, be fluent in coercive control, be able to rush through life, be superior cognitive problem solvers, and endure ever escalating life events. This push may be one message of the culture (the message for securing future economic success), but acting on the message is supported for men or boys, not the women or girls in this setting.

Only one of the four girls "fits" in this setting. That one is able to accomplish what the setting demands without showing signs of stress or deterioration. She fits because her parents take responsibility for the interactive effects of her social, emotional, cognitive, and physical health and development as noted earlier.

The raw material for social health and development of the girls (the ability to function in the roles of their lives) is limited for those girls not as well supported at home. Interpersonal skills are downplayed, attachment is devalued, yet stereotypical sex roles are emphasized. The process of developing socially is ignored. Roles are confused. They witness role conflict everywhere. The emphasis on self-sufficiency, gaining fluency in the individualistic culture, conflicts with the message of support from the culture for behaving in a traditional sex-roled manner. Social supports, and the skills needed to develop and use social support, are discouraged. Mothers and teachers are isolated and dependent. In this environment conflict resolution and friendship are discouraged and devalued, yet dependency (for girls) is rewarded, again, the contradiction which breeds role conflict.

In this setting, the need to emphasize emotional health (personal control, healthy self-concept, and coping skills) is disregarded. With the emphasis on the cognitive, there are few chances to develop a multifaceted self-concept, especially if you are not one of the advanced children. Children's needs are overlooked. Most are not sent home when sick; many are ignored when they cry, even if they cry for their mothers for hours or days at a time. Rapid-fire anger is present in the single mothers, with no buffers for the effects on the children. If children learn to react to conflict with anger they have little chance to develop healthy self-esteem (Kagan, 1984).

The culture is one of chronic stress (Thoresen & Eagleton, 1983), requiring all individuals to adapt to ever escalating demands. At home the children have little control of events, and at school they have little time to relax. The intensities can be felt in the cries and seen in the withdrawn faces and repeated illnesses of those most affected by it. Since health and wellness are products of the social, emotional, and physical forces, this is clearly an antiwellness culture (Woodhouse, 1987).

Women and Families

Working women are "adjunct" in our society (Hobfall, 1986). It causes more stress to take ground, to become primary individuals, than to maintain ground in our culture because there is not support for those who defy the norms, rules, values, or codes of behavior (Hobfall, 1986). Consequently, there are multiple role conflicts and few opportunities for the development of self-esteem in this setting.

Families can be a buffer from stress for women and children, and a good place to learn effective coping strategies (Pearlin & Turner, 1987), if they are families with characteristics supported by the rules of the culture. When families abandon these rules, whether for need or desire, the cultural supports disappear, and there is no place for comfort, no place to learn coping and problem solving, no reward for life choices. In these situations, families can become a place where role conflicts abound. Consequently, mothers, especially single mothers, can become very dependent on day care for support during role conflicts. In some ways they get aid (their sick children aren't sent home as often). But, as they push to abandon the rules of the culture and follow the messages of individualism and independence (the messages of economic success), they grow more dependent on the institution of day care (to take over the nurturing and connectedness functions). The conflict develops because day care, as an institution of the culture, functions to maintain the culture by encouraging separateness and devaluing social-emotional areas. In addition, when out of their primary nurturing role, many women find they do not have the beliefs, types of communication patterns, and necessary behaviors to succeed. The children grow to need the center for emotional and social development they cannot get at home, yet these areas are devalued and not facilitated at the center.

A time bomb appears to be ticking for these families. Women may be working toward independence, yet they seem to be devoid of self-power and the strength derived from connectedness—a contradiction for the very meaning of their lives. The stress of such a situation is only likely to intensify as families and mothers with young children become more and more dependent for the support necessary to perform nurturing child care (Halpern, 1987).

Defining the New Dependencies of Women

The new dependencies of women can be defined as the gap between what the culture provides and what the individual needs. The culture provides specific skills, beliefs, values, services, individual resources, and some level of what Coleman (1987) calls the "social capital" (attention, personal interest, intensity of involvement, persistence, continuity over time, and a degree of intimacy which cumulatively lead to a conception of self). However, the social capital provided in an institution of the culture may not come in ways that are useful to the individual. The individual needs a specific spectrum of resources, beliefs, values, and social capital which may not be complemented by the culture.

For many women, the needed resources and what the culture provides do not match; there is a gap. The resources, supports, and philosophies in this gap are traditionally supplied by the family or extended support network via the mother, but now the mother is in the midst of role conflict. Not all her goals match the needs of her family, and her resources may not meet the needs of her family. To meet these needs she becomes dependent on the institutions. The institutions, like day care and schools, put an emphasis on the rules of the culture, offering opportunities, demands, and rewards (Coleman, 1987) which are designed by the culture to reify the culture, so nothing fills the gap. As the gap widens, the women and children may become increasingly vulnerable, relying for support on institutions that enhance the conflict and intensify the contradictions rather than providing the critical support and resources necessary for the complex needs of social, emotional, and physical health and development. If the mother is lacking financial resources, as many mothers are, this process is intensified.

∩ Filling the Gap

Klausner (1971) says that to understand an individual's ability to exist in their environment the demands, constraints, and resources of the individual and the environment must be studied. The results of this effort indicate that women and children, existing in our changing culture, need some specific philosophical support and physical resources. It is clear that the social capital and resources must come from the environment (Coleman, 1987). A natural source for this social capital would be day care. The following paragraphs begin the process of helping educators, counselors, day-care administrators, and policymakers, who serve young families and children, structure some supports.

Children in all settings need positive female role models—mothers and teachers with power and control over their environment. This could be partially accomplished in many child-care settings through higher pay for staff, more interactive management styles, and enough substitute teachers. The children need healthy schedules; employers, day care, schools, and parents must work together to create an environment in which children have adequate supervised time for play, rest, eating, social and emotional development, and support for the pace of their cognitive development. They need successes in their lives to develop and maintain a healthy self-concept.

Positive environments are required to facilitate the interactive developmental needs of all children, not environments that make them rush to get "ready." They need to develop social, emotional, and physical health in addition to cognitive skills. Mothers of sick children need sick child care to be readily available. Counselors working in these settings or dealing with mothers should be alert to the warning signals of stress in children and mothers so they can intervene before the contradictions and role conflicts become downward spirals of constant failure. In all these areas of child care specific policy which would help day care be a supportive extension of the supportive family is needed. Day care should have a profamily policy, one that supports the needs of the clients as defined by them, not as defined by the culture. Dispelling the perception that day care is a temporary solution to a temporary need (Schiller, 1980) is an essential first step to creating a sound societal approach to day care.

Women and mothers need support, attention to their successes as people, a chance to find the resources necessary to balance the pushes of the culture with the pulls of the role conflicts. These resources are financial and personal. Rather than being blamed because of change, which takes the focus away from the system, they should be supported by a system which is sensitive to their needs (Margolis, 1982). They need to be promoted from their "adjunct" status (Hobfall, 1986). Day-care centers can help construct an environment which can eliminate some of the conflicts which keep women adjunct, this would in turn help them enhance their own self-esteem while they provide the resources necessary for the development of healthy self-esteem in their children. Though families previously got these resources from family and social networks (Halpern, 1987), now they must come from the system, in the form of changes in policy that lend support for family needs and facilitate the development of more effective social networks.

Day-care policy could help meet these needs through providing training for staff and parents about the potential levels of impact of culture on the people who interact within the setting. In addition, training staff and parents about the interactive effects of child development, the impacts of stress, and the causes and consequences of role conflicts would help create a more supportive climate in which personal needs could be defined and met. Interdependence needs to be enhanced rather than devalued.

Child care settings can supply social capital if it is policy to do so. Children need the chance to be children, to be nurtured, and to develop at their own pace. Blaming or punishing mothers for their needs or problems must be avoided. Mothers require the resources to nurture. However, without employers with employee-sensitive policies like flex-time and supported on-site day care, many of the role conflicts will persist.

References

Aries, P. (1962). *Centuries of childhood: A social history of family life.* New York: Vintage Books.

Bronfenbrenner, U. (1979). *The ecology of human development.* Cambridge, MA: Harvard University Press.

Clarke-Stewart, A. (1982). *Daycare.* Cambridge, MA: Harvard University Press.

Coleman, J. (1987). Families and schools. *Educational Researcher,* **16**(6), 32–38.

Elkind, D. (1987, March). Superbaby syndrome can lead to elementary school burnout. *Young Children,* p. 14.

Gilligan, C. (1982). *In a different voice.* Cambridge, MA: Harvard University Press.

Goetz, J., & LeCompte, M. (1984). *Ethnography and qualitative design in educational research.* New York: Academic Press.

Halpern, R. (1987, September). Major social and demographic trends affecting young families: Implications for early childhood care and education. *Young Children,* pp. 34–43.

Hobfall, S. (1986). *Stress, social support, and women.* Washington, DC: Hemisphere.

Hsu, P. (1975). American care value and national character. In J. P. Spradley & M. A. Rynkiewich (Eds.), *The nacireina: Readings on American culture* (pp. 378–394). Boston: Little Brown.

Kagan, J. (1984). *The nature of the child.* New York: Basic Books.

Klausner, S. (1971). *On man and his environment.* San Francisco: Jossey-Bass.

LeVine, R. (1982). *Culture, behavior and personality* (2nd ed.). New York: Aldine.

Lofland, J., & Lofland, L. (1984). *Analyzing social settings: A guide to qualitative observation and analysis* (2nd ed.). Belmont, CA: Wadsworth.

Margolis, M. (1982). Blaming the victim: Ideology and sexual discrimination in the contemporary United States. In C. Kottak (Ed.), *Researching American culture* (pp. 212–227). Ann Arbor: University of Michigan Press.

Marris, P. (1974). *Loss and change.* New York: Pantheon Books.

McLaughlin, S., Billy, J., Johnson, T., Melber, B., Winges, L., & Zimmerle, D. (1986). *The Cosmopolitan report on the changing life course of American woman.* Seattle, WA: The Hearst Corporation.

Mead, M. (1970). *Culture and commitment.* Garden City, NJ: Doubleday.

Mechanic, D. (1974). Social structure and personal adaptation: Some neglected dimensions. In G. V. Coelhs, D. A. Hawburg, & J. E. Adams (Eds.), *Coping and adaptability* (pp. 32–44). New York: Basic Books.

Pearlin, L., & Turner, H. (1987). The family as a context of the stress process. In S. Kasl & C. Cooper (Eds.), *Stress and health: Issues in research methodology* (pp. 143–165). New York: John Wiley and Sons.

Reynolds, A. (1984, November). *Educational philosophy and the process of socialization.* Paper presented at American Anthropological Association, Denver, CO.

Sassen, G. (1980). Success anxiety in women: A constructivist interpretation of its source and its significance. *Harvard Education Review,* **50**, 13–24.

Schiller, J. (1980). *Child-care alternatives and emotional well-being.* (Praeger Special Studies.) New York: Praeger Scientific.

Swanson-Kauffman, K. (1987). *Women's work, families, and health: The balancing act.* Washington, DC: Hemisphere.

Thoresen, C., & Eagleton, J. (1983). Chronic stress in children and adolescents. *Theory into Practice,* **22**(1), 48–56.

U.S. Department of Labor (1985). Labor force activity of mothers of young children continues at record pace. *Bureau of Labor Statistics News* (USDL No. 85–381:1–8). Washington, DC: U.S. Government Printing Office.

Woodhouse, L. (1987). *The culture of the four-year-old in day care: Impacts on social, emotional, and physical health.* Unpublished dissertation, University of Cincinnati, College of Education.

Woods, N. (1987). Women's lives: Pressure and pleasure, conflict, and support. In K. Swanson-Kauffman (Ed.), *Women's work, families, and health: The balancing act* (pp. 9–20). Washington, DC: Hemisphere.

Comments

a This study is an example of the use of ethnographic methods to investigate a topic of particular interest to feminists.

b Two of the most commonly used techniques for gathering data in ethnographic studies.

c Here are quotes from participants that vividly convey the sense of urgency and commotion that characterize the day-care setting. It would help the reader to form a portrait of the culture being studied if the author had included more direct quotes from participants. Throughout the study the author relies more on analysis than description.

d The author uses parts of the existing professional literature to situate her study in the larger context of transitions of women.

e The author provides a theoretical framework within which she is going to examine the setting of day care.

f The author describes the day-care facility, taking care to keep it anonymous by not even naming the city in which it was located. It is not clear on what basis the author concluded that the setting "reflected the push for independence by women."

g Despite the author's earlier claim that she was a participant observer (see Comment b), it appears that in fact she was probably a privileged observer.

h The author describes methods of data collection used in addition to observation.

i The author notes that she used a set of coding categories that had already been established for examining social settings. Ethnographers, however, often develop their own set of codes that are unique to their study.

j The author notes that she limited her study to four girls who were in attendance during the entire investigation and whose mother or father brought them to and from school. The author does not discuss how this decision may have limited the outcome of her study. In fact, the author does not seem to address any possible sources of bias or confounding that may have entered into her analysis and interpretation of her data.

k It would help the reader to form a portrait of the culture being studied if the author had included more direct quotes from participants.

l Throughout this section the author could have presented specific instances as evidence to document her various characterizations of the day-care setting. The author refers the reader to her doctoral dissertation (i.e., Woodhouse, 1987) instead of providing first-hand evidence in the article itself. The reader has access to too little evidence to decide if the author's interpretations seem reasonable or not.

m To what extent were the mothers in this study actually successful in locating a day-care facility they felt met their child's needs? The author provides no information about how the choice to send a child to this facility was made. Was it by default, as the author suggests by citing the shortage of day care or were other factors operating?

n To what extent is it reasonable for the author to make such sweeping suggestions for change on the basis of a study that focused on the impact of a single day-care facility on only four girls and their mothers?

- The research carried out by anthropologists is usually called *ethnographic research* or *naturalistic inquiry.*

- *Ethnography* literally means "a picture of a way of life of some identifiable group of people."

- *Theoretical sensitivity* refers to the researcher's ability to use insight in giving meaning to data.

- Characteristics of qualitative research:

  (1) takes place in a natural setting and uses the researcher as the key instrument;

  (2) deals with descriptive data in the form of words and pictures rather than numbers;

  (3) focuses on process, not merely product;

  (4) relies on inductive rather than deductive data analysis; and

  (5) focuses on how different people make sense of their lives.

- *Foreshadowed problems* are researchers' general ideas of what problems they will investigate prior to undertaking a qualitative study.

- Educational researchers began to use qualitative methods in the 1960s largely as a result of the national attention given to educational problems and the civil rights movement.

- Feminist educational researchers have found ethnographic methods particularly well suited for examining educational issues from the perspectives of women and girls.

- Although studies may include both qualitative and quantitative methods, in general, a study is basically one type or the other.

- Whether qualitative research is regarded as scientific or not depends on one's definition of science.

- Many qualitative researchers are not interested in whether their findings can be generalized to similar subjects in similar settings.

- It is unlikely that two researchers independently studying the same setting or subjects will come up with the same findings because different researchers using the same setting and subjects will probably ask different questions, collect different data, and come up with different conclusions.

- *Fieldwork* is the term researchers use to refer to the time they spend observing and interacting with members of the group they are studying.

- The two primary means of collecting ethnographic data are *participant observation* and *interviewing.*

- Qualitative researchers compile *fieldnotes,* which are detailed accounts of what took place during an observation period; fieldnotes constitute the data researchers ultimately will analyze.

- In classroom settings ethnographic researchers more often engage in *privileged observation,* in which they have received permission to observe, rather than in *participant observation,* in which they actively participate as well as observe.

- Fieldnotes usually consist of an objective part that contains a description of what has taken place during an observation session and a subjective part that contains the researcher's reflections about what occurred during that particular session.

- *Memos* are reflective pieces that focus on the study as a whole, not on any particular observation session.

- In qualitative research, data analysis takes place at the same time data are being collected.

- Each paragraph appearing in fieldnotes is assigned one or more *coding categories* to cover each topic or recurring theme.

- Researchers use the coding categories to establish a framework for writing their final reports.

- There is no standard set of criteria that all researchers agree should be applied to evaluating the quality of an ethnographic study.

Review Exercises

1. What are some of the terms that are used more or less synonymously with "qualitative research"?

2. What is meant by the term *theoretical sensitivity* and how do qualitative researchers become theoretically sensitive?

3. What is the fundamental intent of ethnographic research?

4. Explain why educational researchers became interested in the use of ethnographic methods.

5. List five major characteristics that are associated with qualitative research.

6. Give an example of a *foreshadowed problem.*

7. Describe how theory is used differently in qualitative and quantitative research.

8. How has the feminist movement influenced the use of ethnographic methods in educational research?

9. Explain how quantitative and qualitative researchers handle the question of generalizing the results of a study.

10. Name and describe the primary methods researchers use to collect data while carrying out fieldwork.

11. Describe what is meant by *participant observation* and explain why it is often not used in educational research settings.

12. How does *privileged observation* differ from *participant observation?*

13. What are some criticisms of the way in which ethnographic methods are applied in educational settings?

14. Prepare a sample fieldnote that contains an objective and a subjective part.

15. Describe what *memos* are and explain how researchers use them.

16. Explain what *grounded theory* means.

17. How does data analysis in qualitative and quantitative studies differ?
18. Describe how *coding categories* are used and give at least two examples at differing levels of specificity. How many categories are considered too few? Too many?
19. Explain why it is difficult to evaluate qualitative studies.

Chapter 12

Survey Research

In education, one of the most common forms of behavior that is best measured by direct observation is behavior in a classroom setting.

Chapter Objectives

After completing this chapter, you should be able to:

- name three techniques researchers use to collect survey data
- describe factors that determine whether researchers use surveys or direct observation
- describe the advantages and disadvantages of telephone and face-to-face interviews
- explain what an *interview protocol* is and how to use one
- explain how *depth interviews* differ from other kinds of interviews
- describe the nature and function of *focus groups*
- distinguish between cross-sectional and longitudinal surveys
- describe the process of *time sampling*
- describe the process of *content analysis*

As noted in the previous chapter, qualitative research is a form of research that attempts to provide a narrative description of some phenomenon. All qualitative research is descriptive. Some forms of quantitative research are also descriptive. The goal of quantitative descriptive research, however, is to provide a numerical or statistical description of how one or more variables are distributed among members of a population.

For example, a quantitative researcher might be interested in determining how the variable of gender is distributed among students in special education classes in a particular school district. The population consists of all students in all special education classes in the school district, and the researcher is interested in determining the percentages of boys and girls. It is the expression of the findings in numerical form that makes this descriptive study quantitative.

Basically, there are two ways to determine how a variable is distributed. One may either directly observe how a variable is distributed or one may carry out a survey by asking people questions about the variable. Three basic techniques are used to collect survey data: mail surveys, telephone interviews, and face-to-face interviews. Often, the nature of the variable determines whether a researcher uses direct observation or one of the survey techniques.

If one is interested in a variable such as ''disruptive behavior in the classroom,'' one would probably use direct observation to determine what kinds of disruptive behaviors occur and how frequently. On the other hand, if one were interested in the variable ''attitudes toward bilingual education,'' one would undoubtedly have to use a survey, because attitudes cannot be reliably observed.

Surveys

Surveys are typically used to determine not only the distribution of variables that are impossible or difficult to observe, but also when the population under consideration is relatively large. Survey data may be collected by means of questionnaires or by interviews. If the sample size is relatively large and the number of variables relatively small, questionnaires are usually used.

On the other hand, if the sample size is relatively small and the number of variables to be studied is relatively large or if the variables are complex, data are more likely to be collected by means of interviews. Information concerning interviews follows. Information concerning questionnaires appears in chapter 15, which describes the selection and construction of measuring instruments. For more detailed information on surveys, see Fink (1995) or Jaeger (1988).

Interviews

Data in a descriptive study may be collected by interviews, either by speaking with respondents face to face or by telephone. Face-to-face interviews are more difficult and costly to carry out than telephone interviews. It is also easier to reach a broader sample by telephone. For example, it would be possible to conduct telephone interviews, but not face-to-face interviews, with a sample from a large geographic area. On the other hand, conducting a telephone interview would automatically eliminate from the sample (perhaps fatally compromising it) persons who do not have a telephone.

Interviewer Training. Whichever method is used, it is important for interviewers to receive training in conducting the interview. Effective interviewing requires more skill than you may realize. Interviewers need to understand fully what variables are being investigated and how to elicit as accurate and complete information as possible from the people they are interviewing. Effective interviewers establish rapport with respondents by creating a non-threatening atmosphere and explaining clearly to respondents what the purpose of the interview is. They also assure respondents that responses will be kept confidential and reported only as part of the entire group of responses.

It is a good idea to have interviewers practice conducting the interview before they are asked to collect data for a study. It is particularly effective to tape practice interview sessions, using audio- or videotapes for telephone and face-to-face interviews, respectively. Tapes of practice interviews permit interviewers to receive corrective feedback that may lead to improved techniques.

The Structure of Interviews. Interviews vary in terms of how structured they are. An interviewer carrying out a completely structured interview asks each respondent exactly the same questions in exactly the same order. In contrast, the interviewer conducting an unstructured interview asks each respondent a set of different questions, where subsequent questions depend on the respondent's previous answers. Many interviews carried out in educational research are semistructured, in which some of the questions the interviewer asks each respondent are identical, but some are different. In a semistructured interview the interviewer may ask some respondents additional questions in an effort to probe for more information concerning the respondent's answer to an earlier question.

The Interview Protocol. It is best if interviewers follow an *interview protocol,* which consists of a written set of questions that are to be asked in a set order, and, if the interview is semistructured, a list of probing questions to ask and the conditions under which to ask them. The protocol may also contain a list of questions that respondents are likely to ask the interviewer and a set of instructions to the interviewer about how to answer certain questions and what kinds of questions not to answer.

Protocols often provide interviewers with information about how to record respondents' answers, and, if the information being gathered is not especially complex, may even include a form on which to note answers. It is best if the amount of writing the interviewer must do to record responses is held to a minimum because notetaking may inhibit or distract the respondent.

It is desirable for the interviewer to use a tape recorder during an interview, even though its use may initially inhibit respondents from answering honestly to sensitive questions. If the interviewer successfully establishes rapport, however, this difficulty can be overcome. Taped interviews have a decided advantage in that they may be listened to repeatedly and interpreted by other trained interviewers, increasing the likelihood of gathering accurate information.

It is best to use as few questions in an interview as possible and to restrict them to those that yield information pertinent to the data analysis. Using questions that have a set of responses from which the respondent can choose, rather than open-ended questions, makes the analysis of the data more reliable and easier. See Mishler (1986), and Frey and Oishi (1995) for more information on interviewing.

Depth Interviewing. Depth interviewing is a form of interviewing frequently used by ethnographers as a way of collecting information from subjects' points of view. Interviewers ask open-ended questions that encourage respondents to express their feelings, attitudes, and perceptions. For example, as part of an ethnographic study of beginning teachers, an interviewer might ask teachers how they feel about the undergraduate training in education they received. This kind of open-ended question permits persons being interviewed to respond in any way they choose. Contrast this with the situation where people are asked to respond to the same question by selecting one of the following responses: (a) very satisfied, (b) somewhat satisfied, (c) not too satisfied, or (d) not at all satisfied. One of the characteristics of depth interviewing is that the persons being interviewed respond in their own words. Furthermore, the interviewer may follow up on a person's response by asking for clarification or elaboration. See Patton (1987, pp. 108–143) for more information on depth interviewing.

Focus Groups. A focus group is a form of group interview that originated in the field of market research and is now frequently used to collect qualitative data in evaluation research. Focus groups usually consist of people who are similar to one another in some way related to the research question. For example, in a study dealing with students' adjustment to college life, a focus group might be formed that consists of newly arrived college freshmen. In a study dealing with issues of bilingual education, a focus group might be formed that consists of parents of children whose native language is not English.

Although the size of focus groups varies from 4 to 12, the usual range is from 7 to 10 (Krueger, 1988, p. 27). The task of the members of the group is to focus collectively on questions posed by an interviewer. Focus groups typically meet from about one-half to two hours. It is important to understand that a focus group differs from a group discussion. In a focus group, the interviewer asks a predetermined set of open-ended questions in a predetermined sequence that should appear logical to members of the group.

All members of the group hear everyone's responses and may make additional comments to their initial responses as a result of hearing what others have to say. It is unimportant whether the members of the group agree with one another or not. The purpose of the focus group is to have people ''consider their own views in the context of the views of others'' (Patton, 1987, p. 135). It is best if members of a focus group do not know one another. If members do know one another and interact with one another on a regular basis, their responses may not be completely candid. It is also best if the interviewer is not familiar with members of the group for the same reason. See Krueger (1988) for more detailed information concerning focus groups.

Kinds of Surveys

Regardless of whether one decides to use questionnaires or interviews in carrying out a survey, there are two basic kinds of surveys. **Cross-sectional** surveys examine the distribution of a variable at a given point in time. **Longitudinal** surveys permit researchers to trace possible changes in the distribution of a variable over time.

Cross-Sectional Surveys. Suppose one is interested in determining how much knowledge of world geography students in the third, fifth, seventh, ninth, and twelfth grades have. To determine how this knowledge is distributed among students in the above grade levels in 1996, one would conduct a cross-sectional survey by administering a questionnaire or a test to a sample of students in each grade level simultaneously.

Longitudinal Surveys. On the other hand, if one were interested in determining how the variable ''knowledge of world geography'' may have changed its distribution over time, one would carry out a longitudinal survey by administering a test or questionnaire, let us say, once in 1976, again in 1986, and finally in 1996. Such information permits one to trace any changes in the distribution of the variable over a 20-year period.

Longitudinal surveys may involve gathering information from different people or from the same people in each grade level on each subsequent survey. In other words, in the current example, the fifth graders surveyed in 1976 are not the same fifth graders who were surveyed in 1996. It is also possible, however, to conduct a longitudinal survey using the same people over a period of time. It would be possible to survey the knowledge of world geography a group of students exhibit when they are in the third grade, again when they are in the fifth grade, and so forth until they are in the twelfth grade. A classic study of this type was carried out by Lewis Terman (1925) who studied various characteristics of people with exceptionally high IQs from the time they were in elementary school until they had achieved adulthood.

Observational Studies

There are numerous forms of behavior that can best be measured by direct observation rather than by paper-and-pencil tests or by questionnaires. In education, one of the most common forms of behavior that is best measured by direct observation is behavior in a classroom setting. For example, if one is interested in studying ways in which teachers interact with students in the classroom, one is likely to obtain more accurate information by actually observing how teachers interact than by asking teachers to describe how they interact. Self-reports at best contain information about how teachers *believe* they interact with students (or perhaps how they believe they *should* interact), which may or may not reflect accurately their actual behavior. Similarly, if one is concerned with studying students' disruptive behavior in the classroom, it is probably more accurate to rely on direct observation than on reports from teachers or the students themselves.

As with any measure of behavior, the accuracy of direct observation is a function of validity and reliability. A special problem associated with the validity of direct observation is defining the behavior to be observed. The issue of validity is typically handled by training the people who are to do the observing. Often examples of behavior that are to be measured (as well as examples of behavior that are *not* to be measured) are provided during training sessions. Observers are frequently given practice at recording behavior before the actual data-collection process begins. The issue of reliability is typically handled by having at least two observers so that the researcher can check the extent to which the observers agree with one another. The second observer might be another teacher, a paraprofessional, or perhaps an older student.

Problems in Direct Observation

The larger the number of subjects to be observed, the more problematic direct observation becomes. In general it is probably not a good idea to try to observe all subjects at the same time, but rather to focus on one at a time and systematically observe one after another until the entire sample has been observed.

Time Sampling. Suppose, for example, one decides to investigate ways of reducing disruptive behavior of students. One must define disruptive behavior operationally by describing each overt act that will be considered disruptive. Sometimes it is difficult to decide how to distinguish between the frequency of various disruptive acts and the duration of the acts. If out-of-seat behavior is one of the acts defined as disruptive, how does one differentiate between a student who is briefly out of his or her seat five times and another student who gets out of the seat only once, but remains out for five minutes? One way might be to time each instance of out-of-seat behavior, but such a procedure makes it difficult to follow a systematic plan of observation. An effective way to resolve this measurement dilemma is to use **time sampling.**

Time sampling involves recording exactly what behavior is going on at a given instant and then moving on to observe the next subject. It is the frequency of the behavior that is measured, but if recording intervals are relatively brief, duration of behavior will also be taken into account.

It is especially helpful when using time sampling to have a checklist of behaviors to be observed. If the number of behaviors to be observed is small, one can list them across the top of a sheet of paper as column headings. The names of the students in the class could be arranged randomly down the left-hand margin. If there are many different kinds of behavior to be observed, one may have to list them all on a sheet of paper and use a separate sheet for each subject.

The frequency of disruptive behavior may vary depending on the time of day. Students may tend to be more disruptive at the beginning and the close of the school day or just before lunch or recess. Time sampling can take this kind of variation into account. One could decide, for example, that at a given time and once every half-hour thereafter each student will be observed at 10-second intervals. In other words, at the first time of observation the behavior of the first student on the list is recorded on the chart by checking the appropriate column. After recording that student's behavior at that instant, the observer waits 10 seconds and then observes and records the instant behavior of the second student on the list, and so on until each student's behavior has been recorded. No further recordings are made until a half-hour later, at which time the entire recording procedure is repeated. Information about checklists and rating scales appears in chapter 7.

Content Analysis

Content analysis differs from other forms of descriptive research in that instead of using people as subjects in a study, various forms of communication, such as books, films, and speeches are used. As the term implies, the purpose of content analysis is to analyze the content of some piece of communication. For example, one might analyze the content of fourth-grade arithmetic books to compare the percentages of word problems dealing with stereotypic activities associated with boys (e.g., problems involving scores in sporting events) or girls (e.g., problems involving measurements used in cooking).

Typically, content analysis involves counting the frequency with which various values of a variable occur. One of the difficulties in content analysis is defining what to count in such a way that the count can be made reliably. For example, in analyzing the content of a report issued by an educational commission, one could count fairly reliably the number of passages dealing with race relations because the variable may be defined objectively. On the other hand, it might be difficult to count reliably the number of passages that use inflammatory language because the variable is open to various subjective definitions.

Sampling: The Critical Issue in Survey Research

A prime example of survey research is the census carried out every 10 years by the federal government. The intent of a census is to obtain various kinds of information from every person in a population. It is rare, however, that survey research is carried out with entire populations because of financial considerations and practical problems of contacting every person. Consequently, as with most quantitative research, survey research is carried out with samples. The intent, however, is to generalize the findings (within a given margin of error) to the populations from which the samples have been drawn.

Sampling is an important issue in all kinds of empirical research, but it is especially critical in surveys. In an experiment with seventh graders to determine if Method A is superior to Method B in teaching geography, it makes relatively little difference if the sample of seventh graders participating in the study is a bit more or less academically competent than the entire population of seventh graders, because the focus of the study is on which teaching method produces better results.

On the other hand, if the purpose of the study is to describe how much knowledge seventh graders have of geography, it would be misleading to generalize the findings to the population of seventh graders if the knowledge of students participating in the study were not typical of the knowledge of seventh graders in general. One of the difficulties students face in carrying out survey research is the practical problem of selecting a representative sample of a population that is worth investigating.

Students wishing to carry out a survey often find that because of sampling problems, they are forced to define the population to be studied so narrowly that the research question becomes trivial. For example, it seems reasonable to carry out a survey that describes the kinds of materials high school teachers read during their leisure time if one can draw a representative sample of high school teachers in general. It seems far less interesting, however, to define the population as teachers in a particular high school and carry out a survey to determine the kinds of reading materials they read during their leisure time.

Reporting Findings of Survey Research

It should come as no surprise to learn that descriptive statistics are used to report the findings of surveys. Which statistics are used, however, depends on the nature of the data being described. If the data are in numerical form, such as age, years of teaching experience, or grade point average, findings are usually expressed in terms of a numerical average and a description of the amount of variability the data exhibit.

On the other hand, data that cannot be expressed in numerical form, such as gender or academic major, are usually reported in terms of number (often symbolized by n) and percentages. Often data pertaining to more than one variable are reported simultaneously in cross-tabulation tables, such as the one shown in Table 12.1

It is also common for data like those appearing in Table 12.1 to be presented in pictorial form, such as a bar graph or histogram. Table 12.2 shows the same distribution of undergraduates by gender and academic major in the form of a histogram or bar graph.

Table 12.1	Number and Percent of Undergraduates by Gender and Academic Major

Academic Major

Gender	Education		Business		Liberal Arts		Total
	n	$\%$	n	$\%$	n	$\%$	n
Male	24	12	78	39	98	49	200
Female	68	34	58	29	74	37	200
Total	92	23	136	34	172	43	400

Table 12.2	Histogram Showing the Distribution of Undergraduates by Gender and Academic Major

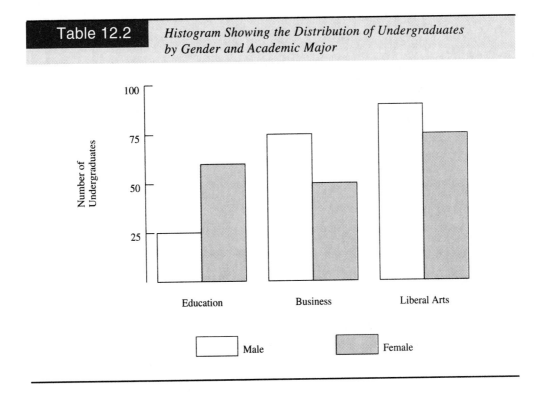

An Example of Survey Research, with Comments

High School Seniors React To Their Teachers And Their Schools

David L. Clark

For the most part, seniors like school, give their own schools high ratings, and view their teachers as knowledgeable and competent. Mr. Clark finds strong foundations on which reform can be built.

a High school seniors in the United States do not express alarm over the schools they attend or the teachers with whom they work. By and large, they like school, give their schools high ratings, and view their teachers as both knowledgeable and competent.

b A surprising number of U.S. high school seniors report that they would like to become teachers. They worry about such matters as substance abuse, disciplinary infractions in school, and the way their schools handle discipline. They want to be more involved in discussing school problems and establishing and enforcing rules of conduct. Some of their observations confirm the results of various polls of adults; e.g., ''disruptive student behavior is a major school problem.'' But others are not at all like adult views; e.g., ''teachers' knowledge of subject matter is no problem'' in classroom instruction.

c In the spring of 1986 Phi Delta Kappa and the Center for Survey Research at Indiana University surveyed 1,712 high school seniors in 421 high schools across the country.[1] The data and discussion that follow are based on that survey.[2]

Teachers

Grading teachers. If you are looking for a problem that students see in U.S. high schools, don't look at their teachers. Asked to assign grades to their teachers, 26% of high school seniors gave their teachers an A and 48% gave them a B. Only one in 20 assigned a grade of D or F.

Clark, David L. High school seniors react to their teachers and their schools. *Phi Delta Kappan,* March, 1987, 503–509. Reprinted with permission.

d 1. The study was designed and executed by Stanley Elam, editor emeritus of the *Phi Delta Kappan,* and Jon Masland, co-director of the Center for Survey Research (CSR). Elam had initial help from N. L. Gage, Jack Frymier, Jerome Kopp, and Larry Barber. Terry F. White succeeded Masland as CSR co-director during the period of the study. She conducted the data analysis and prepared the technical report on the study.

2. The sampling design for the study guaranteed diversity but not representativeness. The primary sampling unit was the school, and participation by the school was voluntary. The voluntary participation rate of the national sample of schools was 56%. The school response rate from among the volunteers was 75%. The response rate of students was 70% (1,712 of 2,442). Nonrespondents were not followed up. The end result was predictable. In comparison to National Opinion Research Center (NORC) data on national occupational groups in 1983–84–85, the student self-report on father's occupation in this study overrepresented professional occupations (i.e., 21.7% in this study; 16.5% in the NORC study). The clerical and skilled trades and service occupations are underrepresented in this study by about 5%. Blacks are underrepresented—9.6% of the respondents were black. Poor children are underrepresented.

To compensate for the sampling bias, each item response was examined for differences by race, gender, school grades, and socioeconomic status. Where such differences existed, they are noted. However, even this correction does not eliminate the problem. High school students in trouble, personally or academically, would almost certainly be represented less frequently in the respondent group, and the more extreme responses of this subgroup may not be represented at all. On individual items, this poll inevitably represents young persons predisposed to give a positive response. Readers should keep in mind that this is a skewed sample of survivors (i.e., seniors) of the high school experience. The average or modal response to each question probably represents best the attitudes of those high school students bound for college or for a technical school. More successful students are overrepresented; less successful students are underrepresented.

There are systematic differences in student grading of teachers by type of school[3] and by the socioeconomic status of the student.[4] Students in private schools rate their teachers more highly than students attending public schools. Forty-one percent of private school students assigned their teachers an A, while only 24% of public school students did so. Thirty percent of those in the highest socio-economic group gave their teachers an A, while only 23% of those in the lowest socioeconomic group did so.

Becoming a teacher. If students are favorably disposed toward their teachers, why don't more of them want to become teachers? In fact, many of them do. Twenty-two percent of the seniors surveyed said that they would like to become teachers. This is in contrast to the 6.2% of entering college freshmen who declared an interest in teaching.[5] Twenty-two percent is almost exactly the percentage of the college graduating class that the Carnegie Forum on Education and the Economy has stated will be required to meet the need for teachers for the early 1990s. Of course, saying that they would "like to become" teachers is different from declaring an interest in education as an undergraduate major.

The positive news, however, is the remarkably large group of high school seniors that is favorably disposed toward teaching. Those who responded positively said that they did so because they liked helping or working with others (32.5%). Those who responded negatively commented on teachers' low salaries (28%) and the problems and frustrations faced by teachers (24%). Only 3% cited the lack of status and recognition accorded to teachers as a reason why they would not like to become teachers. This often-cited disincentive to pursue a career in teaching apparently goes unrecognized until later in the process of career choice.

An interest in teaching is more frequent among seniors in public schools (23%) than among their counterparts in private schools (17%), and more frequent among young women (27%) than young men (17%). The poll found no significant difference by socioeconomic status or race. There is a positive relationship between grades and desire to become a teacher. Table 1 shows (1) that the pool of inter-ested young women has not dried up; (2) that high school students from minority groups are still interested in teaching; and (3) that high school students who would like to become teachers are not the academically least able students.

Teacher characteristics. What characteristics do students feel are important in teachers? The *e* students surveyed said that to "help students in class" teachers need to be understanding, knowl-edgeable, and fair. Asked how many of their teachers exhibited such characteristics, the students rated their teachers highest in knowledgeability and lower on fairness and understanding. Table 2 shows that students hold the following provocative perceptions of teachers:

- Teachers are more demanding and strict than they need to be.
- Teachers are rated low on both being interesting and being creative. A majority of respondents found few or none of their teachers exhibiting such characteristics. The students felt that being interesting is more important for teachers than being creative.
- Students do not give teachers low ratings on their knowledge of content or on their level of competence, though such characteristics are being called into question by current reform studies. *b*

3. One hundred fifty-seven of the 1,712 respondents (9.2%) attended private schools.

4. The students were divided into four groups according to socioeconomic status (measured by father's occupation, home ownership, and level of father's education). These data were all obtained directly from the respondents, not from their parents. The categories ranged from highest (professionals and managers who own their own homes and have education beyond high school) to lowest (laborers with less than a high school education or unemployed). Roughly 40% of the study population fell into groups 1 and 3 (highest and lower-middle), and 10% each fell into groups 2 and 4 (upper-middle and lowest). One hundred cases were not classifiable because of incomplete data. *d*

5. Carnegie Task Force on Teaching as a Profession, *A Nation Prepared: Teachers for the 21st Century* (New York: Carnegie Forum on Education and the Economy, 1986), p. 31.

Table 1

Percent of High School Seniors Who Would Like to Become Teachers

Student Category	Yes %	No %
Public school students	23.0	77.0
Nonpublic school students	17.1	82.9
Male	17.0	83.0
Female	27.2	72.8
Black	26.4	73.6
Hispanic	30.8	69.2
White	21.8	78.2
Average grade of student		
$\quad$ A/A$^-$	22.6	77.4
$\quad$ B$^+$/B/B$^-$	24.1	75.9
$\quad$ C$^+$/C	20.6	79.4
$\quad$ C$^-$/D	15.3	84.7
Vocational plans		
$\quad$ Four-year college	25.6	74.4
$\quad$ Graduate school	26.7	73.3

Table 2

Characteristics of Teachers

Characteristic	Rank	Needed % Saying Very Important	Rank	Demonstrated % Noting Most or All
Understanding	1	82	6	66
Knowledgeable	2	81	1	87
Fair	3	78	4	71
Interesting	4	72	9	41
Organized	5	67	5	69
Competent	6	62	3	75
Friendly	7	60	2	80
Creative	8	44	10	33
Demanding	9	22	7	62
Strict	10	10	8	44

Figures add to more than 100% because of multiple answers.

Reactions to some teacher characteristics varied substantially by the socioeconomic status of the students. Students from a low socioeconomic background felt that, in order to be helpful to students, teachers needed to be friendlier, more understanding, and stricter. They placed correspondingly less

Table 3		*Teachers' Perceived Favoritism*			

	Students Responding "Frequently" (%)			
Item	A/A⁻	B⁺/B/B⁻	C⁺/C	C⁻/D

Item	A/A⁻	B⁺/B/B⁻	C⁺/C	C⁻/D
Teachers seem to teach mainly for the benefit of top students.	7.4	11.2	13.7	21.7
Teachers do not appear to care whether all students learn the subject or not.	6.7	10.7	14.6	21.7

emphasis on teachers' being interesting, fair, knowledgeable, and competent. In practice, seniors from low socioeconomic backgrounds found teachers to be less friendly, less knowledgeable, and less competent than did students from upper socioeconomic groups. These data are consistent with the higher grades awarded to teachers by students in the upper socioeconomic groups.

Teacher behaviors. The students were presented with eight teaching behaviors that are sometimes *b* said to create problems. They were asked to indicate whether such problems occurred in their school. The major concern of students was easy to identify. Eighty-one percent of the students said that sometimes (48%) or frequently (33%), "Teachers give special attention to favorite students." No other item commanded a response rate above 18.5% in the category "frequently."

Other items that more than half of the students cited as more than rare occurrences were: "Teachers waste too much time on things that are not important" (frequently, 13.5%; sometimes, 40.5%); "Teachers show bias in assigning grades" (frequently, 11.5%; sometimes, 44.8%); "Teachers give homework that is too long or difficult to complete on time" (frequently, 11.7%; sometimes, 44.7%); "Teachers seem to teach mainly for the benefit of top students" (frequently, 11.6%; sometimes, 38.9%); "Teachers do not use effective teaching methods" (frequently, 8.2%; sometimes, 46.7%).

Even taking into account the ease with which a respondent could check "sometimes" (almost everything happens sometimes), less than half of the students checked the following problems as occurring in their schools: "Teachers do not appear to care whether students learn the subject or not." "Teachers do not know the subject well enough to teach it effectively." Despite persistent criticisms of the subject-matter background of teachers, 72% of these high school seniors said that lack of knowledge of the subject being taught never or rarely interfered with effective teaching in their schools.

There were a few significant differences in reactions to teacher behaviors by subgroups of respondents. Students in private schools viewed their teachers more favorably, as might have been anticipated from the higher grades they assigned to teachers. A substantially larger proportion of public school students indicated concern that their teachers (1) taught mainly for the benefit of top students; (2) wasted time; and (3) did not appear to care whether or not students learned the subject. Gender had no statistically significant effect on student responses to teacher behaviors. Non-white students were concerned about teachers teaching mainly for the benefit of top students. In two categories, the average grade of the students reflected special student concerns. The lower the average grade, the more likely that the student felt that teachers are uninterested in whether students learn and that they concentrate on the top students.

Table 3 illustrates the nagging problem of alienation among students who have not performed well in school but have nonetheless remained in school through the senior year. Many of their peers, who would have shared their concern on these issues, have already dropped out at earlier grades.

Table 4

Table 4 — *How High School Seniors Rate Schools*

Grade	Your Own School			Public Schools in Community			Public Schools in Nation		
	All %	Public %	Non-Public %	All %	Public %	Non-Public %	All %	Public %	Non-Public %
A	24.1	22.2	42.6	8.2	8.7	3.3	5.7	6.3	0.7
B	48.1	48.5	43.9	44.3	45.9	28.9	35.3	36.2	26.3
C	23.8	25.0	11.6	38.8	39.0	37.5	48.8	48.2	53.9
D	3.4	3.5	1.9	7.6	5.8	25.7	9.5	8.8	17.1
F	0.7	0.8	0.0	1.0	0.7	4.6	0.7	0.5	2.0

Schools

Grading schools. High school seniors believe that the public schools in the U.S. are in trouble. Only about one in 20 (5.7%) would give them a grade of A. Less than 1% of nonpublic school students would assign the public schools an A. Nearly 20% of nonpublic school seniors and 10% of public school seniors would give public schools grades of D or F. The median grade that the students would award to the public schools is C.

On the other hand, most students give the school they attend a good grade (see Table 4). Fewer than one in 20 rate their school below average. One-quarter of all students think that their school deserves an A. Three-quarters would grade their own school A or B.

When it comes to assessing schools, lack of familiarity breeds contempt. As Table 4 shows, high school seniors believe that the trouble with public education is elsewhere. High school seniors think that the quality of their own schools is high, but they doubt the quality of public secondary schools in general. Ratings of schools decline precipitously when students are asked to rate schools in the community as a whole rather than the school they attend, and the ratings continue to decline when students are asked to render an opinion about the nation's schools. (This same phenomenon has appeared in ratings of schools by parents in Gallup Polls of the Public's Attitudes Toward the Public Schools.)

A disturbing feature in these data is the reaction of seniors in nonpublic schools. They hold quite strong negative feelings about public schools and react even less favorably to public schools about which one would assume they know something (i.e., schools in their own communities) than toward schools in the nation as a whole.

Students with higher average grades rated their schools distinctly higher than did students with lower grade-point averages. For example, A students were 2½ times more likely to give their schools an A than were C students. Seniors in academic tracks rated their schools higher than did seniors in vocational or technical tracks. Students in the highest socioeconomic category were more likely to give their schools an A (28%) than were students in the lowest socioeconomic category (21%), and those in the highest socioeconomic category were also less likely (3.3% to 5.3%) to give their schools a grade of D or F. As was the case with their ratings of teachers, students who need more support from school may also have more difficulty obtaining it, since they are less well disposed toward the institution. However, even among students in the lowest socioeconomic category and among students with the lowest grades in their coursework, 60% to 65% gave their own schools an A or a B.

Table 5		How High School Seniors Feel About Their School			

	I do not like my school at all.			I like my school very much.	
	0	1	2	3	4
	%	%	%	%	%
All students	1.8	7.3	27.1	44.9	18.9
Public school students	1.9	7.7	26.2	46.0	18.2
Nonpublic school students	0.6	3.2	25.8	44.5	25.8
Average grade of students					
A/A⁻	1.4	3.9	18.1	47.2	29.4
B⁺/B/B⁻	1.5	6.9	24.7	48.7	18.1
C⁺/C	2.2	9.4	33.3	39.8	15.2
C⁻/D	6.7	5.0	36.7	38.3	13.3

Liking school. High school seniors like school. Table 5 displays their responses to the question, "How do you feel about the school where you are now enrolled?"

Two-thirds of the students chose a positive response; 9.1% responded negatively. Students attending nonpublic schools were again more favorably inclined toward their schools. The most striking finding from this question becomes apparent when we look at the distribution of responses from students with different average grades. Students with higher average grades are much more inclined to like school. This self-rating of performance is not simply a surrogate measure of socioeconomic status. In this population of respondents, socioeconomic status was not correlated with liking school at a statistically significant level.

Although the overall picture is positive—that is, most students like their schools—significant numbers of seniors do not like school. Moreover, liking school is strongly related to success in school even among high school seniors, a group that does not include those young people who have already dropped out. The subculture of failure in the schools is a continuing problem for students and school personnel alike.

Policies, Practices, Problems

School policies and practices. High school seniors disagree with school authorities about the way in which they are involved in solving school problems, especially discipline problems (see Table 6). A majority of the students said (1) that they are not provided with enough opportunities to discuss school problems; and (2) that they are not given enough responsibility for judging the behavior of fellow students and assessing penalties for misconduct.

High school seniors were split almost 50/50 on the question of whether students are given enough responsibility in establishing rules of conduct. Student reaction to these practices is especially important because the most irritating problem noted by students from a set of often-cited school problems was, "Some students' behavior is so disruptive that many who want to learn cannot." When students were presented with an opportunity to provide free responses to a list of problems, they mentioned discipline problems most frequently. Students are concerned about discipline and student behavior, and they think they can help do something about it. The majority of high school seniors do not feel that their problem-solving abilities are being tapped.

b   Many practices cited by others as problems for teachers or students were viewed as relatively unimportant by these respondents (see Tables 6 and 7). Three-fourths of the high school seniors surveyed indicated that classes are rarely interrupted by announcements over the public address system. The majority indicated that classes are not too large for teachers to handle them effectively, and they did not feel that the presence of slow students interferes with overall class progress. The students also reported that their schools place sufficient emphases on such traditional subjects as English, history, math, and science.

Seniors attending public schools equivocated on the questions of whether the schools place sufficient emphasis on developing students' ability to think or on character and citizenship education. About one-third viewed these areas as problems; an almost equal number discounted them; the remainder neither agreed nor disagreed. Students in non-public schools were satisfied with the emphases on both counts. Seniors in both public and nonpublic schools reported that students are required to work hard enough in their classes and that the homework assigned is sufficient. A substantial majority felt that the school provides enough help with academic problems, but the respondents split evenly on the question of the adequacy of the help that schools provide with personal problems. Responses were similarly divided on the matter of whether cooperation between school authorities and parents is sufficient.

This picture of American high schools is different from the one that is often presented in the media. The respondents in this survey were undoubtedly better-than-average students; hence they might be expected to be critical of slovenliness in school practice. But they viewed their schools as:

- work-oriented in the classroom,
- requiring sufficient out-of-class homework assignments,
- emphasizing traditional academic subjects,
- including character and citizenship education, and
- providing adequate academic counseling.

High schools range from the chaotic to the scholarly; they should not all be swept up in generalizations about either extreme. But at the very least, in considering high school reform, one should listen to the voices of those most immediately involved.

Two statistically significant differences in responses to items in this category emerged when the socioeconomic status of the students was taken into account. Students in schools from areas with low socioeconomic status agreed more frequently that there is not enough cooperation between school authorities and parents at their school, and they were more likely to feel that their school does not provide enough help to students with academic problems.

School problem inventory. The seniors were asked to list any problem in their high school that they believed to be serious. High school seniors bring a sense of immediacy to their views of school problems. Although they are not unconcerned about academic problems, the behavioral problems that they face every day trouble them more. Table 8 summarizes their responses.

Discipline dominated the responses. Almost half of the seniors (43.5%) mentioned student behavior violations. But nearly as many (35.2%) noted that efforts to deal with these problems had become a problem in their own right. Under the heading of efforts to handle discipline, 17.2% of the students reported that their schools have too many rules (the second most frequently mentioned individual item). However, an almost equal percentage (18.1%) said that the problem is too few rules, rules that are inconsistent, or a particular obnoxious rule.

The second most frequently cited category of school problems was substance abuse, mentioned by 37.2% of the respondents. The single problem cited most frequently came under this heading: drug abuse, mentioned by 19.2% of the respondents; in addition, 10% of the seniors surveyed mentioned alcohol abuse.

Item	Strongly Disagree %	Disagree %	Neither %	Agree %	Strongly Agree %
My school provides enough opportunities for student discussion of school problems.	21.1	35.3	14.7	24.6	4.3
Students in my school are given enough responsibility for judging the behavior of fellow students and assessing penalties for misconduct.	14.4	36.9	23.6	22.7	2.3
Students in my school are given enough responsibility in establishing rules of conduct.	10.0	28.9	19.4	38.2	3.5
My school does not place enough emphasis on such traditional academic subjects as English, history, math, and science.	30.3	49.1	12.4	6.1	2.0
My school does not place enough emphasis on developing students' ability to think.	11.2	34.1	21.5	24.4	8.9
My school does not place enough emphasis on training in character and citizenship.	8.1	25.3	30.5	28.7	7.4
Students in my school are not required to work hard enough in their classes.	11.4	44.7	21.7	19.1	3.2
Teachers in my school assign too little homework.	20.2	46.8	24.1	7.7	1.1
My school provides enough help to students with academic problems.	6.2	15.6	20.9	45.9	11.4
My school provides enough help to students with personal problems.	13.5	23.2	23.9	32.1	7.4
There is not enough cooperation between school authorities and parents of students at my school.	7.3	26.6	33.6	22.8	9.8

Table 6 *Reactions of High School Seniors to School Policies and Practices*

Table 7 · Reactions of High School Seniors to Selected Conditions in Their School

Item	Never %	Rarely %	Sometimes %	Frequently %
Classes are too large for teachers to handle them effectively.	15.0	38.1	37.1	9.9
Classes are interrupted by frequent public address announcements.	18.7	54.7	18.7	7.8
The presence of many slow students keeps classes from progressing satisfactorily.	16.9	49.1	29.6	4.4

Table 8 · Serious School Problems Identified by High School Seniors

Rank	Problem	% Reporting
1	Discipline	43.5
2	Substance abuse (drugs, alcohol, tobacco)	37.2
3	Efforts to handle discipline	35.2
4	Facilities	15.2
5	Relationships with teachers	13.4
6	Curricular problems	12.8

Figures add to more than 100% because of multiple answers.

One thing is certain. The school environment of most high school students is directly affected by problems of student behavior and substance abuse. Students are deeply concerned about these problems, and they are unpersuaded that current solutions are ameliorating the situation.

But the dominance of the drug and discipline issues should not be allowed to obscure other problems mentioned by the students.

- Racial problems were mentioned by 8% of the respondents.
- Despite the good grades given to teachers, 13% of the respondents noted serious teacher/pupil problems, such as unfair or uncaring teachers.
- A relatively large number of respondents mentioned crowded or inadequate facilities.
- The most frequently mentioned curricular problem was a too-narrow set of course offerings or the absence of a desired course of study.

In this survey, high school seniors offered some good news about the American high school. They rated their teachers highly. They had an interest in becoming teachers. They liked school and rated their own schools above average. They were disturbed about behavior and drug problems, but they thought they could help in solving these problems.

How do these responses fit into the picture of the troubled American high school presented by such critics as Theodore Sizer and Patrick Welsh? First, the respondents in this survey were survivors of the system. The students for whom the high school fails most dramatically do not stay around long enough to become seniors. Second, in this survey both the schools and the respondents themselves were volunteers. As I noted earlier, the respondents are not representative of all groups of high school seniors in the U.S. schools and students in trouble were underrepresented in this sample.

Finally, this was an opinion poll, and modal responses are always overemphasized. While most of these seniors rated their teachers A or B, 5% of them rated their teachers as failures, i.e., D or F. Consistently, students with lower self-reported average grades and students with fewer out-of-school learning resources (i.e., lower socioeconomic status) noted greater dissatisfaction with teachers, schools, policies, and practices.

Current in-depth case studies have dramatically portrayed some of the gravest shortcomings of *b* the American high school. There is solace to be taken from the fact that last year's high school graduates had some positive responses to their schools and teachers. This fact denies neither the problems of the high school as an organization nor the self-evident fact that it fails to reach far too many students. However, organizational reform needs to be rooted in an organization's positive achievements. The American high school has some strong foundations on which reform can be built. At least, its clients think so.

DAVID L. CLARK (Indiana University Chapter) is the Parrish Professor of Education in the Curry School of Education at the University of Virginia, Charlottesville. A copy of the full 96-page research report on which this article is based can be obtained by writing Stanley Elam, Poll Coordinator, Phi Delta Kappa, P.O. Box 789, Bloomington, IN 47402. The cost is $15, including postage. Make checks payable to Phi Delta Kappa.

Comments

a *The introductory part of this report fails to present the rationale underlying the decision to conduct the study and to provide a review of the literature dealing with the topic under investigation.*

b *It would be useful if bibliographic information were given so that the interested reader could examine the original sources.*

c *One wonders why the average number of students per high school who participated in the study is only slightly more than 4 (i.e., 1,712 ÷ 421 = 4.16).*

d *Notice how much attention is paid to the sampling procedures used in the study. (Contrast this with how little information is given about sampling procedures in the other articles reproduced in this text.) These footnotes are loaded with important information. We are told that the sampling design guaranteed diversity but not representativeness, but we are not told what the sampling procedures were nor why a representative sample was not sought. Using the percentages given here, the original sample must have consisted of 1,002 schools. Of these, 561 schools (i.e., 56%) volunteered to participate, and of these, 421 (i.e., 75%) actually responded. We do not know how the original sample of the approximately 1,000 schools was selected. Note that students whose fathers had professional occupations were overrepresented and those whose fathers had nonprofessional occupations were underrepresented. Note too that black students and poor students were underrepresented in the sample. Measures are described that were taken to compensate for the sampling bias, but it is acknowledged that they did not eliminate the problem. We are given the percentage of students who attended private schools, but we are not told what percentage of schools were private. (Could it be that the overwhelming majority of private school students came from a small number of schools? We do not know.) We also are told that responses to each item were examined for differences by gender, but we do not know how many students were girls and how many were boys. In short, it is difficult to know what population this sample of students represents.*

e *This passage typifies a general problem throughout the report. No information is given about how the questionnaire was constructed. How were items selected? Is the questionnaire valid and reliable?*

- The goal of survey research is to provide a numerical description of how one or more variables are distributed among a population.

- Survey research is carried out either by direct observation, by questionnaires, or by interviews.

- Conducting interviews by telephone automatically eliminates from the sample people who do not have telephones.

- Interviewers need to be trained to conduct interviews and should have the opportunity to practice before starting to collect data.

- In structured interviews the interviewer asks each respondent exactly the same questions in exactly the same order.

- In semistructured interviews the interviewer asks each respondent some identical questions but also some different questions, depending on how the respondent responds to earlier questions.

- An interview protocol provides the interviewer with a set of guidelines for conducting the interview.

- It is best to tape record interviews so that the accuracy of information can be checked.

- Depth interviewing is characterized by open-ended questions that qualitative researchers use in order to collect information from subjects' points of view.

- Focus groups usually consist of 7 to 10 people who are similar to one another in some way related to the research question.

- Members of a focus group discuss collectively predetermined questions that the interviewer presents in a predetermined order.

- Members of focus groups are encouraged to present their own views, not necessarily to reach consensus.

- Cross-sectional surveys are carried out with different groups of people at the same time.

- Longitudinal surveys are carried out either with the same or different groups of people at different points in time.

- At least two observers should be used in observational studies so that reliability can be checked.

- Time sampling is used in observational studies to record exactly what behavior is going on at fixed time intervals.

- Content analysis involves determining the frequency with which some variable appears in various kinds of communications.

- Sampling is important in all research, but it is particularly critical in surveys.

- The findings of surveys are presented in numerical form, such as percentages, averages, and measures of variability.

1. What is the basic purpose of survey research?

2. Name two ways in which data in surveys are often collected. What frequently determines which way is used?

3. Under what circumstances is a survey likely to be carried out by means of interviews rather than by questionnaires?

4. Design an interview protocol to determine students' opinions about various aspects of the degree program they are in and conduct an interview with at least one student. Note any problems that occur during the interview.

5. Describe how depth interviews differ from structured interviews.

6. Describe the nature of focus groups and how they are used.

7. Describe the difference between cross-sectional and longitudinal surveys.

8. How are the issues of validity and reliability dealt with in studies involving direct observation?

9. Describe how you would use time sampling to measure on-task behavior of students in a classroom.

10. Give an example of a study that would involve content analysis.

Chapter 13
Correlational Research

If one were examining the relationship between how long golfers have been playing golf and their average score, one would probably predict that the two variables are negatively correlated. In other words, the longer golfers have been playing, the lower their average golf score would be.

Chapter Objectives

After completing this chapter, you should be able to:

- explain why researchers carry out correlational studies
- describe the relationship between correlation and causality
- explain what is meant by *multiple* and *partial correlation*
- describe the concepts of *simple* and *multiple regression* and explain how they are related to correlation

The last chapter dealt with survey research, in which the researcher is interested in describing how one or more variables are distributed within a population. It was noted that most descriptive research is carried out with samples, but the findings are generalized to populations within a given margin of error. Results of survey studies are usually reported in terms of the average value of a variable and a measure of variability.

The objective of descriptive studies is to answer the research question of how one or more variables are distributed among a population. Descriptive studies characteristically are not designed to test a hypothesis. Many quantitative studies, however, *are* designed to test one or more hypotheses, and it is to these kinds of studies we now turn.

In the preceding chapters it was pointed out that hypotheses are statements that predict the nature of the relationship between two or more variables. Hypotheses may be stated in either directional or nondirectional form, depending on the kind of evidence available in the existing research literature. Null hypotheses predict no relationship between variables and are used only to enable one to analyze research data by means of statistical procedures and to conclude whether the results of a study are statistically significant or not. It is also necessary for the variables in a hypothesis to be defined operationally so the reader can know what the researcher means by a particular variable in terms of how the variable has been measured. The same variable may be given different operational definitions by different researchers.

The Objective of Correlational Methods

Correlational methods are used to determine the extent to which two or more variables are related among a single group of people. For example, one would carry out a correlational study to determine to what extent students' performance on a reading comprehension test is related to their performance on a vocabulary test. It is likely in this case that the researcher would predict that students' reading comprehension and vocabulary scores would be positively correlated. In other words, one would expect that students who score high in reading comprehension would also score high on a vocabulary test, and conversely, students who score low in reading comprehension would score low on a vocabulary test. If one were examining the relationship between how long golfers have been playing golf and their average scores, one would probably predict that the two variables are negatively correlated. In other words, the longer golfers have been playing, the lower their average golf scores would be.

The most frequently used measure of correlation is the **Pearson Product-Moment correlation coefficient,** which is symbolized by r. The value of r may range from $+1.00$ (perfect positive correlation) to -1.00 (perfect negative correlation). An r value of zero indicates the lack of a relationship between variables.

Correlation and Causality

Even when the correlation coefficient between two variables is close to perfect, one cannot draw any conclusion about a causal relationship between the variables. For example, if there is a high positive correlation between students' attitudes toward school and their academic performance, one cannot conclude that students perform well academically because they like school. One could just as easily argue that students like school because they perform well academically. To infer a causal relationship between variables, it is necessary not only to show that there is a statistically significant relationship between them, but also that the causal variable occurred prior to the other variable and that there are no other factors that could account for the cause.

Suppose I have taught algebra to high school students for a number of years and I have noticed that there seems to be a positive relationship between students' self-confidence and their performance in algebra. The better performers in algebra appear to me to be those students who exhibit more self-confidence. Suppose also that my review of the related research literature basically confirms my hunch. Other studies have found for the most part that students with more self-confidence tend to perform better academically than students with less self-confidence.

I decide therefore to hypothesize that there will be a significant positive correlation between students' self-confidence and their scores on an algebra test. Consequently, I administer a questionnaire that measures self-confidence and give an algebra test to a group of students. To emphasize the point in question, let us further assume that the results of my study indicate there is a perfect positive relationship between the two variables.

It occurs to me that since self-confidence is perfectly correlated with algebra performance, it might be wise to try to increase the self-confidence of the students in my classes to enable them to perform better in algebra. The decision to try this is based on the assumption that it is the degree of self-confidence that causes students to perform well or poorly in algebra. However, such an assumption is obviously unwarranted. It may be that because students do well in algebra they exhibit lots of self-confidence rather than vice versa.

The Noncausal Nature of Correlation

In a correlational study it is possible to conclude only to what extent two variables may be related. It is not possible to conclude that there is a causal relationship between the variables. We have no evidence from a correlational study to conclude that changing one variable will lead to changes in the other variable. It may be that changes in variable A will cause changes in variable B or that changes in variable B will cause changes in variable A. We do not know which variable is the cause and which is the effect. It may be that there is no cause and effect relationship between variables A and B at all. It may be that changes in both variables are caused by some other variable or variables we are not even aware of.

For example, it may be that students who do well in algebra have parents who take an active interest in their children's education and insist that their children complete homework assignments correctly, and that students who perform poorly in algebra have parents who do not care whether their children complete homework assignments or not. Students who have a history of successfully completing homework assignments may tend to develop a sense of self-confidence, and they are also likely to perform better academically. Therefore, it may be the kind of parents a student has that is the cause of both how much self-confidence the student has and how well the student performs in algebra.

It should be clear that a correlational study cannot determine if one variable is the cause of another. In a correlational study it may be intuitively appealing to conclude that one variable is the cause of the other. Logically, though, there is no evidence to reach such a conclusion. Only experimental studies permit one to draw inferences about causality, a topic that is discussed in detail in chapter 14.

One advantage of correlational studies is the ease with which they can be carried out. One need only obtain measures on two or more variables from a single group of people. In educational research, information about one or both variables may even already be available, for example, students' grade point averages or scores on various standardized tests. Researchers sometimes first conduct a correlational study to see if two variables are significantly correlated prior to carrying out an experiment, which typically involves much more time and effort. If the correlational study reveals that two variables are significantly related to one another, the researcher might then invest the additional time and effort to carry out an experiment to see if there is a causal relationship between the variables. On the other hand, if the results of the correlational study reveal no significant relationship between two variables, it would be inappropriate to carry out an experiment.

Correlation is a necessary but not a sufficient condition for determining causality. If, for example, a correlational study showed that students' self-concepts and their performance in algebra were not significantly correlated, it would be pointless to carry out an experiment to determine if increasing students' self-concepts would cause students to perform better in algebra. Of course, even if the correlational study revealed a significant positive relationship between students' self-concepts and their algebra performance, there is no guarantee that an experiment would demonstrate that increasing students' self-concepts would result in better performance in algebra.

Hypotheses in Correlational Studies

There is a direct connection between the kind of study that is being carried out and how a hypothesis is stated. In correlational studies, the researcher is predicting that within a single group of people two variables will be significantly related to one another. In group comparison studies, the researcher is predicting that the average scores of two or more groups of people will differ with respect to a single variable. Whether a hypothesis is stated in directional or nondirectional form, however, does not depend on whether the study is correlational or a group comparison.

Directionality and the Related Literature

For example, in a correlational study one might predict that among special education students there is a significant relationship between students' self-concepts and the length of time they have spent in mainstreamed classrooms. This hypothesis is stated in nondirectional form. The researcher is predicting only that a significant relationship will be found between length of time in mainstreamed classes and self-concept. It may be that the longer students are mainstreamed, the more positive their self-concepts will be, or the longer students are mainstreamed, the less positive their self-concepts will be.

The researcher could, of course, state the hypothesis in directional form. He or she might predict that there will be a significant positive relationship between the length of time spent in mainstreamed classrooms and students' self-concepts. In other words, the longer students spend in mainstreamed classrooms, the more positive their self-concepts will be. The researcher might predict that there will be a significant negative relationship between the length of time spent in mainstreamed classrooms and students' self-concepts. This hypothesis is the reverse of the previous one because the researcher is predicting that the longer students spend in mainstreamed classrooms, the less positive their self-concepts will be. It is the researcher's evaluation of the existing related research literature that determines whether the hypothesis will be stated in nondirectional form or in the directional form of a positive or negative relationship.

Multiple and Partial Correlation

Correlation may be further subdivided into multiple or partial correlation. Multiple correlational studies are identical to the kind of correlational studies previously described, with one exception. **Multiple correlation** permits a researcher to establish the degree of relationship between one variable and several variables instead of the degree of relationship between only two variables. The multiple correlation statistic is R and is interpreted the same as r. The closer R is to $+1.00$, the stronger the degree of relationship. R differs from r in that it may vary only from 0 to $+1.00$, rather than from -1.00 to $+1.00$.

In some sense partial correlation is the opposite of multiple correlation. **Partial correlation** permits a researcher to determine the degree of relationship between two variables when their relationship to other variables has been removed. For example, suppose one has administered a math achievement test, a math aptitude test, and a self-concept questionnaire to a group of students. It is possible through regular correlational techniques to determine the correlation coefficient between any two of the three scores. Partial correlation, however, enables one to remove, or *partial out,* the relationship between one variable and the other two. One could use partial correlation, for example, to determine the degree of relationship between self-concept and math achievement after removing the effects of math aptitude.

An Example of Correlational Research, with Comments

Relationship of Computer Science Aptitude with Selected Achievement Measures among Junior High Students

Linda Coates
St. Margaret Mary School, Omaha, Nebraska

Larry Stephens
University of Nebraska at Omaha

Computer science aptitude was measured for 69 students at the junior high level by the Konvalina, Stephens and Wileman Computer Science Aptitude Test (KSW). These aptitude scores were correlated with the following: (a) the composite score of the Survey of Basic Skills Test (published by Science Research Associates), (b) the mathematics subtest result of the composite Basic Skills Test score, (c) the first and second semester mathematics achievement scores for students in a mathematics course which utilized computer assisted instruction, and (d) programming achievement scores for students in the same courses. The relationship between computer science aptitude and all five achievement measures was strong for both seventh and eighth graders with the eighth graders demonstrating a stronger relationship than the seventh graders for all five measures. The r-squared values ranged from 40–50% for eighth graders and from 15–35% for seventh graders. In addition, computer science aptitude was compared for males and females and no significant difference was found.

Coates, L., & Stephens, L. (1990). Relationship of computer science aptitude with selected achievement measures among junior high students. *Journal of Research and Development in Education, 23*(3), 162–164. Reprinted with permission.

Recent surveys indicate that over 60% of teachers in the United States are using computers for instruction (Riccobono, 1984). The use of computer-based instruction (CBI) ranges from drill-and-practice programs for reading readiness in kindergarten to graduate degrees in some disciplines. Following this trend, the number of research studies investigating computer science aptitude has been increasing.

The purpose of this study was to examine the relationship between computer science aptitude and achievement at the junior high level. Specifically, the objectives were: (a) to determine the correlation between computer science aptitude and general achievement, mathematical achievement, and achievement in courses using CAI, and (b) to investigate for differences in aptitude based on sex.

Research at the college level has shown that mathematical achievement, competency, and background are related to computer science aptitude and achievement (Alspaugh, 1972; Konvalina, Wileman, & Stephens, 1983; Peterson & Howe, 1979; Wileman, Konvalina, & Stephens, 1981). With   *a* the appearance in recent years of magnet schools at both the junior and senior high level, where computer science is stressed in all subjects, there is a need to investigate the same relationships with younger students. Recently Hearne, Poplin, and Lasley (1987), using junior high subjects, found a significant correlation between mathematical achievement on the SAT math subscales and computer aptitude, as measured by the Computer Aptitude, Literacy and Interest Profile (CALIP). Further, in keeping with earlier findings among college students (Stephens, Wileman, & Konvalina, 1981), this research also found no difference in aptitude due to the sex of subjects.

Method

The subjects for this study were seventh- and-eighth-grade upper-middle class students from a private   *a*
metropolitan junior high school. Ages ranged from 11 to 14 years. Of the 69 students, 35 were male   *b*
and 34 were female. Students in the eighth grade had had programming experience in the seventh grade, and all students had had some type of CAI prior to seventh grade.

The Konvalina, Stephens, and Wileman Computer Science Placement Test (KSW) was used as the   *c*
computer science aptitude measure in the correlation research. The validity and reliability of the KSW   *d*
as a predictor of achievement in computer science classes has been demonstrated in several studies (Konvalina, Wileman, & Stephens, 1983; Stephens, Wileman, Konvalina, & Teodoro, 1985; Wileman, et al., 1981). In Wileman et al. (1981), the instrument was reported to have a Kuder-Richardson #20 measure of reliability equal to 0.76 and an overall correlation of 0.46 with a final exam. Point biserial correlation coefficients were computed for all 25 questions and average values were reported for the five component parts of the test; these ranged from 0.25 to 0.60. Similar reliability and validity mea-   *e*
sures have been obtained in further studies of the instrument as well as in the current study. The test consists of 25 questions with 5 items covering each of the following subjects: number and letter sequences, logical reasoning, operation of a hypothetical calculator, algorithmic execution, and algebraic word problems.

The following is a description of the achievement variables used and the coding for each:

1. SRAC—The Science Research Associates Survey of Basic Skills Test composite score, based on three subtest results: reading, mathematics, and language.
2. SRAM—The mathematics subtest result of the composite SRAC score.
3. MATH1—The students' first semester math grade. For both seventh and eighth grade, this score   *f*
   was the average of three subtotals: chapter tests, quizzes, and graded assignments. All students had the same instructor and grading method. The math curriculum for both grade levels involves programming in BASIC and LOGO. Drill-and-practice software programs and tutorials, such as *Math Blaster* (Davidson & Eckert, 1983) and *Introductory Algebra* (Joesten, 1982), were also included in the course work.

Table 1	Correlation of Computer Science Aptitude (KSW) Scores With Achievement Variables by Groups				
	SRAC	SRAM	MATH1	MATH2	PROG
WHOLE (*n* = 69)	.62**	.59**	.50**	.51**	.52**
8ALL (*n* = 34)	.71**	.67**	.68**	.63**	.63**
7ALL (*n* = 35)	.59**	.52**	.39**	.39**	.45**

* $p < .05$
** $p < .01$

Table 2	Comparisons of the KSW Score for Sex			
	Sex	Mean	*t*-Value	2-Tail Probability
KSW	M	8.83	−1.59	.116
	F	10.29		

* $p < .05$
** $p < .01$
(*n* male = 35)
(*n* female = 34)

f   4. MATH2—The second semester math grade, obtained in the same manner as MATH1.
g   5. PROG—The final first semester exam score for the programming work done in BASIC.

The students in the study were arranged into three groups and coded as follows: WHOLE—entire population, 8ALL—eighth-grade students, and 7ALL—seventh-grade students. To measure the relationship between the KSW computer science aptitude scores and the achievement factors for each group, the Pearson correlation coefficient was calculated by means of SPPSX (Nie, Hul, Jenkins, Steinbrenner, & Bent, 1983). The 2-sample t-test was used to test for differences in computer science aptitude for males and females.

Results

Table 1 shows a high positive correlation between KSW performance and each of the achievement factors for all groups. The *r*-squared values ranged from 40–50% for eighth graders and from 15–35% for seventh graders, indicating a strong relationship. The SRA composite and math subtest scores generally showed the strongest relationships to computer science aptitude in all three groups. For all variables, the eighth grade evidenced a higher correlation between aptitude and achievement than did the seventh grade.

Table 2 shows the results for the t-test for KSW scores and sex of subject. The findings indicate no difference in computer science aptitude test scores for males and females.

Discussion

The findings in this research show a strong relationship between computer science aptitude and general achievement (as measured by the SRA Composite score) and mathematical achievement (as measured by the SRA math subtest and achievement scores made in a mathematics course) among junior high students.

With the appearance in recent years of magnet schools at both junior and senior high levels, where computer science is stressed in all subjects, there will be a continuing need for accurate methods of placing students on the basis of computer science aptitude. The KSW test can be useful in assuring *i* proper placement.

As this study supports prior research indicating no difference in computer science aptitude based on sex, even in younger students, it is suggested that success for women in computer science depends *j* on the development of a positive attitude and an interest in the area. Instructors at the junior high level and below can assist in this process by developing computer-assisted instruction that appeals to all students and by encouraging any student indicating interest or ability in the subject.

References

Alspaugh, C. (1972). Identification of some components of computer programming aptitude. *Journal for Research in Mathematics Education, 18,* 89–94.

Davidson, J., & Eckert, R., Jr. (1983). Math blaster [Computer program]. Torrance, CA: Davidson and Associates.

Hearne, J. D., Poplin, M. S., & Lasley, J. (1987). Predicting mathematics achievement from measures of computer aptitude in junior high students. *Educational Research Quarterly, 10,* 18–24.

Joesten, V. (1982). Introductory algebra [Computer program]. Eugene: Avant-Garde.

Konvalina, J., Wileman, S. A., & Stephens, L. J. (1983). Math proficiency: A key to success for computer science students. *Communications of the ACM, 26,* 377–380.

Nie, N. H., Hul, C. H., Jenkins, J. G., Steinbrenner, I., & Bent, K. H. (1983). *Statistical package for the social sciences.* New York: McGraw-Hill.

Peterson, C. G., & Howe, T. G. (1979). Predicting academic success in introduction to computers. *Association for Educational Data Systems Journal, 12,* 182–191.

Riccobono, J. A. (1984). *Availability, use, and support of instructional media 1982–83.* Washington, DC: National Center for Educational Statistics.

Stephens, L. J., Wileman, S., & Konvalina, J. (1981). Group differences in computer science aptitude. *Association for Educational Data Systems Journal, 11,* 84–95.

Stephens, L. J., Wileman, S., Konvalina, J., & Teodoro, E. V. (1985). Procedures for improving student placement in computer science. *Journal of Computers in Mathematics and Science Teaching, 4,* 46–49.

Wileman, S., Konvalina, J., & Stephens, L. J. (1981). Factors influencing success in beginning computer science courses. *Journal of Educational Research, 74,* 223–226.

Comments

a *The authors' rationale for conducting their study is the need to investigate the relationships between computer science aptitude and other variables among younger students because of "the appearance in recent years of magnet schools at both the junior and senior high level, where computer science is stressed in all subjects." They select as a sample a group of "seventh- and eighth-grade upper-middle class students from a private metropolitan junior high school." One wonders how reasonable it would be to generalize findings from such a sample to the population of students who may wish to attend magnet schools that stress computer science.*

b *The authors give the number of boys and girls for both grade levels combined, but not separately for each grade level. Was the gender distribution comparable at both grade levels? The authors do not describe the amount or kind of programming experience or the nature of the CAI. Since both seventh and eighth graders in the study had already had some kind of programming or CAI experience, the findings of the study can logically be generalized only to other seventh and eighth graders who have had similar experience, not to seventh and eighth graders in general.*

c *The authors give no explanation as to why the KSW test was used instead of the Computer Aptitude, Literacy and Interest Profile (CALIP) that was used by Hearne, Poplin, and Lasley (1987). It is possible that the CALIP was not available at the time the authors conducted their study.*

d *It is not unusual for researchers who have developed measuring instruments to carry out their own reliability and validity studies. It appears that the KSW test has previously been used in three studies whose coauthors were also the developers of the test. (A coauthor of the current study is also one of the test developers.) The authors report that validity and reliability of the KSW was established in three studies, but give reliability and validity coefficients based on a single study. Presumably the "overall correlation of 0.46 with a final exam" is a validity coefficient. The authors, however, do not report what material the final exam tested.*

e *No references to the "further studies" are given.*

f *Although course grades are sometimes used as operational definitions of achievement, it is impossible to determine how valid and reliable the grades are unless they are based solely on the results of objective tests. It is not clear why the authors used two semester grades in math rather than combining the grades into a single full-year math grade.*

g *It would have been useful if the authors had at least reported the reliability of the programming exam that was given at the end of the first semester. One also wonders why a similar exam was not given at the end of the second semester after the students had had a full academic year's experience with programming.*

h *It would have been interesting if the authors had reported correlation coefficients between the students' SRA composite scores and their grades in math and programming as well as the correlation coefficients between students' SRA math composite scores and their grades in math and programming.*

i *Since the authors are interested in achieving proper placement of students, one wonders why they did not investigate the possibility that KSW scores used in conjunction with other scores, such as the SRA composite or math scores might yield more accurate predictions than the use of KSW scores alone.*

j *Wouldn't this also apply to men?*

Simple and Multiple Regression

A concept closely related to correlation is **regression.** If two variables are correlated, one can use values of one variable to predict values of the other variable, and the stronger the degree of relationship between the two variables, the smaller the margin of error associated with the predicted value. If variable A and variable B have an *r* of $+1.00$ or -1.00, it is possible to use a person's value on variable A to predict perfectly that person's value on variable B. As the size of *r* gets closer to 0, the range within which the predicted value falls becomes larger, that is, the margin of error in prediction becomes greater.

Usually, however, researchers do not use correlation as a means of predicting the value of one variable from the value of another variable. The reason is quite simple. Although two variables may be correlated, in practice one wishes only to predict values of one variable from values of the other and not vice versa.

For example, if college grade point averages and scores on a college admission test are positively correlated, one typically wishes to predict a student's college grade point average from the student's admission test score. It would make little sense to predict the student's admission test score from the student's college grade point average.

Figure 13.1   Regression Lines of X on Y and Y on X

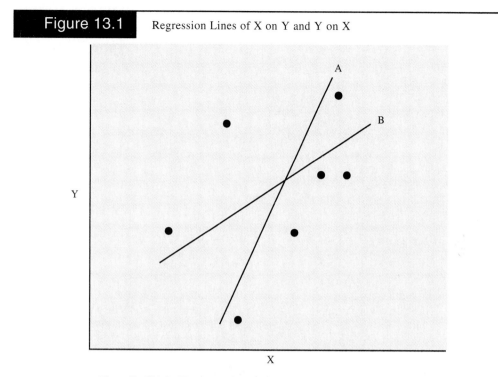

To predict X from Y, one uses the *regression line of X on Y* (line A) because the summed *horizontal* distance from each point is minimal.

To predict Y from X, one uses the *regression line of Y on X* (line B) because the summed *vertical* distance from each point is minimal.

Consequently, researchers use regression, not correlation, when they wish to predict values of one variable from values of another variable. To make the prediction it is necessary to set up an equation for a straight line, which is called a *regression line*. Except for the special case when variables are perfectly correlated, the regression line for predicting values of variable X from given values of variable Y is not the same as the regression line for predicting values of variable Y from given values of X. (See Figure 13.1.)

When researchers write about regression coefficients, they are referring to the slopes of regression lines. In studies having more than two variables, there are multiple regression equations that have coefficients for each variable. Sometimes researchers carry out the regression in such a way that the variable accounting for the most variance in a set of scores is identified and the amount noted, then the variable accounting for the second largest amount of variance is identified, and so on. This process continues until all the variables have been examined and one has a list of variables ranging from the variable that accounts for most of the variance down to the one that accounts for the least.

The statistic F is used to test the statistical significance of a regression coefficient. A significant F value indicates that the slope of the regression line differs significantly from zero. In other words, there is a statistically significant relationship between the variables. See Pedhazur (1982) for a thorough description and explanation of regression.

An Example of Regression Analysis, with Comments

Predicting Performance on the National Teacher Examinations Core Battery

Paul J. Egan
Victor A. Ferre
Peru State College

ABSTRACT   This study examined factors that predict performance on the National Teacher Examinations (NTE) Core Battery. We found strong relationships between a student's undergraduate grade point average (GPA), American College Test (ACT) subtests, and the NTE Core Battery tests. We developed and used regression equations to predict NTE Core Battery test scores for a cross-validation group of students whose scores were not used in developing the original equations. Predictions ranged in accuracy from $r = .73$ for professional knowledge to $r = .92$ for general knowledge. Results are discussed in terms of comparing current predictors of success on the NTE Core Battery with past predictors of success on the NTE Common Examinations and the implications for teacher educators.

With the growing movement toward competency testing prior to certification (Sandefur, 1984; State Education Statistics, 1987), faculty members in teacher education programs need reliable information that can provide an accurate assessment of a student's potential for success, that is, the ability to complete the educational requirements of a teacher education program and pass a competency examination. This need for reliable information is most important when a student applies for admission to a teacher education program because early identification of deficiencies would allow ample time for remediation (AACTE, 1983).

Previous research on predicting success in teacher education programs typically measured success using the National Teacher Examinations (Quirk, Witten, & Weinberg, 1973; Ayers & Rohr, 1974; Ayers & Qualls, 1979; Tarver & Carr, 1983). By 1983–84, however, the Educational Testing Service replaced the NTE Common Examinations with the NTE Core Battery. The Common Examinations consisted of one 195-min. test yielding four area scores: professional education; written English expression; social studies, literature, and fine arts; science and mathematics, plus one weighted score, the Weighted Common Examinations Total (WCET). The Common Examinations emphasized basic academic preparation in liberal arts and education. The Core Battery consists of three 120-min. tests yielding scores in communication skills, general knowledge, and professional education. The Core Battery, while still measuring basic academic knowledge, emphasizes problem solving and decision making. These substantive changes in the NTE suggest a need to reexamine previously established relationships between selected predictors and success, as measured by the NTE Core Battery.

a   Success on the Core Battery, however, like its predecessor the Common Examinations, continues to be more a matter of academic ability than actual teaching ability (Lovelace & Martin, 1984). Unfortunately, this fact is the norm for teacher competency tests in general. As Pugach and Raths (1983) state in their examination of the teacher testing issue, ''There is scant evidence to support the contention that performance on a teacher competency test is correlated with effective teaching.'' The lack of empirical evidence has not stopped legislative bodies in 35 states from requiring successful

Egan, P. J., & Ferre, V. A. (1989). Predicting performance on the National Teacher Examinations Core Battery. *Journal of Educational Research, 82*(4), 227–230. Reprinted with permission of the Helen Dwight Reid Educational Foundation. Published by Heldref Publications, 4000 Albemarle St., N.W., Washington, D.C. 20016. Copyright © 1989.

performance on some type of teacher competency test (17 specify the NTE) so that graduates of teacher education programs may apply for certification by the state department of education (State Education Statistics, 1987). Clearly, use of the NTE Core Battery test scores as criteria for certification is not the most desirable situation, but it is one that has been legally mandated. Because of this situation, the teacher education faculty would benefit most if they were able to accurately predict performance on this important exit-level test.

With this caveat in mind, the purpose of this study was to (a) examine the relationship between   *b* previously identified predictors of success and the NTE Core Battery; (b) develop prediction equations based on this relationship; and (c) use these equations to predict NTE Core Battery test scores.

Method

Subjects

Peru State College is a small, rural, midwestern institution offering undergraduate programs with a special emphasis on teacher education, as well as masters'-level programs in education. The sample   *c* was composed of those graduates ($N = 94$) who completed the baccalaureate degree in education between May 1984 and 1986 and who had taken both the ACT in high school and the NTE as college seniors, approximately 60% of the graduates during this period. A group of 73 elementary and sec-   *d* ondary education students (25 men and 48 women) who completed the teacher education program from 1983–84 through the fall of 1985–86 served as a reference group. Another group of 21 elementary and secondary education students (12 men and 9 women) who completed the teacher education program during the spring of 1985–86 served as the cross-validation group.

Material

We obtained the following information from each student's cumulative record folder during the first semester of their sophomore year when they applied for admission to teacher education: overall grade point average (GPA) at the time of application (5.25 minimum on a 9-point scale used by the college, about a C+ on a 4-point scale), American College Test (ACT) subtest scores (English, mathematics, social science, natural science, and composite) required for admission to the college, and NTE Core Battery test scores taken by most education majors during their last semester.

Design and Procedure

We calculated means and standard deviations on all variables for both groups and developed correlations for GPA, ACT subtest scores, and NTE Core Battery test scores. We also performed a stepwise regression analysis for each NTE Core Battery test, using GPA and ACT subtests as predictors. Then we developed equations and correlated predicted scores with obtained scores from the cross-validation group to test the accuracy of the equations.

Results

We divided the results of the study into three parts: (1) an examination of the distributions and correlations among the variables for both groups; (2) regression analyses and development of prediction equations; and (3) a prediction of NTE Core Battery test scores using the equations developed above.

Means and standard deviations of all variables for both groups are shown in Table 1. The results   *e* suggest that both groups are approximately equal because they achieved a GPA of slightly higher than a B and scored around the 50th percentile on both ACT subtests and NTE Core Battery tests.

Correlations computed for GPA, ACT subtest scores, and NTE Core Battery test scores showed a significant correlation for each pair of variables at the .01 level for the reference group (see Table 2). Results in Table 3 indicate a similar pattern for the cross-validation group at the .05 level, with one exception: the correlation between GPA and ACT math subtest score was not significant.

Table 1		Means and Standard Deviations for GPA, ACT, and NTE		

| | Reference group[a] | | Cross-validation group[b] | |
Variable	M	SD	M	SD
GPA	7.24	.89	6.81	.99
ACT English	18.66	4.82	15.91	5.69
ACT mathematics	17.89	6.77	15.76	7.11
ACT social studies	17.73	6.96	18.38	6.20
ACT natural science	21.19	5.70	19.24	5.12
ACT composite	18.97	5.10	17.29	4.95
NTE communication skills	657.71	11.51	654.24	11.86
NTE general knowledge	657.41	10.31	654.48	13.67
NTE professional knowledge	654.96	10.95	650.81	13.37

[a]n = 73. [b]n = 21.

Table 2		Intercorrelation Matrix—Reference Group		

| | | ACT | | | | | NTE | | |
	GPA	Eng	Math	Soc s	Nat sci	Comp	CS	GK	PK
GPA	1.00	.54	.46	.44	.57	.58	.59	.54	.64
ACT English			.55	.73	.67	.84	.84	.71	.75
ACT mathematics				.48	.58	.78	.57	.61	.50
ACT social studies					.77	.88	.72	.70	.65
ACT natural science						.89	.72	.75	.68
ACT composite							.82	.82	.73
NTE communication skills								.78	.79
NTE general knowledge									.68
NTE professional knowledge									1.00

Note. n = 73.

Regression analyses, using the reference group, indicated that ACT English and ACT composite scores were the best predictors of NTE communication skills scores (F = 105.2, df = 2, 70; p < .001), accounting for 75% of the variance (R = .87). The ACT composite subtest score was the best predictor of NTE general knowledge scores (F = 140.2, df = 1, 71; p < .001), accounting for 66% of the variance R = .81). The ACT English subtest score and GPA were the best predictors of NTE professional knowledge scores (F = 61.8, df = 2, 70; p < .001), accounting for 64% of the variance (R = .79).

The resulting equations were as follows:

1. Communication skills = 618.1558 + 1.2 (ACT English) + .9049 (ACT composite).
2. General knowledge = 626.1789 + 1.6462 (ACT composite).
3. Professional knowledge = 601.1751 + 1.2901 (ACT English) + 4.1067 (GPA).

Using the cross-validation group, we tested the predictive ability of these equations. Predicted and obtained NTE Core Battery test scores were correlated and found to be strongly related: communication

Table 3					Intercorrelation Matrix—Cross-Validation Group					

			ACT					NTE		
	GPA	Eng	Math	Soc s	Nat sci	Comp		CS	GK	PK
GPA	1.00	.39	.08[a]	.48	.44	.39		.55	.48	.68
ACT English			.67	.64	.61	.87		.84	.78	.59
ACT mathematics				.51	.45	.80		.54	.63	.44
ACT social studies					.69	.84		.77	.83	.73
ACT natural science						.80		.70	.86	.66
ACT composite								.83	.92	.71
NTE communication skills									.85	.86
NTE general knowledge										.83
NTE professional knowledge										1.00

Note. $n = 21$.
[a]Not significant at the .05 level.

skills, $r = .86$; general knowledge, $r = .92$; and professional knowledge, $r = .73$. In the case of general knowledge, the correlation is higher than normally would be expected. This result is unusual, but it does occur.

Discussion

We found significant relationships between undergraduate GPA, ACT subtests, and the NTE Core Battery tests. This finding is important for three reasons. First, although substantive changes have occurred in the NTE, a comparison of results for the new NTE Core Battery to published results for the old NTE Common Examinations suggests that both undergraduate GPA and ACT subtest scores continue to be significant predictors of success on both examinations. Quirk, Witten, and Weinberg (1973), in their review of the literature on concurrent and predictive validity of the NTE Common Examinations, reported 16 correlations between the NTE Weighted Common Examinations Total and undergraduate GPA, ranging from .23 to .74, with a median of .55.

Similar findings for ACT subtest scores and the WCET were reported by Ayers and Rohr (1974) and Ayers and Qualls (1979), who stated that the best predictors of WCET scores were ACT composite scores. Tarver and Carr (1983) examined not only the relationship between WCET and ACT Composite (.79) but also the various other subscores on the ACT and NTE Common Examinations that ranged from .63 between ACT mathematics and NTE science and mathematics to .69 between ACT English and NTE written English expression. A considerable overlap clearly exists between GPA and ACT with the NTE, whether it is the new Core Battery or old Common Examinations.

Second, based on the strong relationship between undergraduate GPA and ACT subtests with the NTE Core Battery tests, we developed regression equations that proved successful in predicting student achievement on the Core Battery. Because the NTE is currently being used or is under consideration by many states as a requirement for teacher certification, this use should aid students in making career decisions and also benefit college program planners. Early, accurate prediction of Core Battery test scores will promote realistic advising of students and better utilization of departmental time and money.

Third, other researchers (Lovelace & Martin, 1984) also have noted a strong relationship between the ACT and NTE Core Battery. The researchers have suggested that rather than overtesting education majors, the NTE should provide an exemption for those who score high enough on the ACT. This idea is interesting, particularly in light of the development of a new screening test for teacher education majors, the Pre-Professional Skills Test (PPST), that is supposed to be given prior to admission to teacher education and provide information about basic proficiencies in math, writing, and reading. Initial research on the PPST by Stoker and Tarrab (1985) and Aksamit, Mitchell, and Pozehl (1987) suggested much overlap between the PPST and ACT. This overlap led both sets of authors to question the necessity of another test for teacher education majors, although Aksamit, Mitchell, and Pozehl (1987) further suggested that the PPST may be used to test students who scored low on the ACT to determine if their deficiencies had been overcome.

In conclusion, undergraduate GPA and ACT subtest scores continue to correlate as well with the new NTE Core Battery as they did with the old NTE Common Examinations. These high correlations allow accurate prediction of NTE Core Battery test scores with material available at the time of admission to teacher education. This ability means that one can identify deficiencies early when they can be corrected and also leads to the possibility of exempting some students from taking the NTE at the end of their training.

References

Aksamit, D. L., Mitchell, J. V., Jr., & Pozehl, B. J. (1987, April). *Relationship between PPST and ACT scores and their implications for the basic skills testing of prospective teachers.* Paper presented at the 71st Annual Meeting of the American Educational Research Association, Washington, DC.

American Association of Colleges of Teacher Education. (1983). *Educating a profession: Competency assessment.* Washington, DC: American Association of Colleges of Teacher Education.

Ayers, J. B., & Qualls, G. S. (1979). Concurrent and predictive validity of the National Teacher Examinations. *Journal of Educational Research, 73,* 86–92.

Ayers, J. B., & Rohr, M. E. (1974). Relationship of selected variables to success in a teacher preparation program. *Educational and Psychological Measurement, 34,* 933–937.

Lovelace, T., & Martin, C. E. (1984). *The revised National Teacher Examinations as a predictor of teacher's performance in public school classrooms.* Lafayette, LA: University of Southwestern Louisiana. (ERIC Document Reproduction Service No. ED 251 416)

Pugach, M., & Raths, J. (1983). Testing teachers: Analysis and recommendations. *Journal of Teacher Education, 34*(1), 37–43.

Quirk, T. J., Witten, B. J., & Weinberg, S. F. (1973). Review of studies of the concurrent and predictive validity of the National Teacher Examinations. *Review of Educational Research, 43,* 89–113.

Sandefur, J. T. (1984). Competency assessment of teachers: The 1984 report. *Journal of Human Behavior and Learning, 1*(3/4), 3–12.

State education statistics: Student performance, resource inputs, reforms, and population characteristics, 1982 and 1986. (1987, February). *Education Week,* pp. 20–21.

Stoker, W. M., & Tarrab, M. (1985, Spring). The relationship between preprofessional skills tests and American College Tests. *Teacher Education and Practice,* 43–45.

Tarver, L. K., & Carr, D. B. (1983, April). *Teacher proficiency and performance in Louisiana.* Paper presented at the 67th Annual Meeting of the American Educational Research Association, Montreal, Quebec. (ERIC Document Reproduction Service No. ED 228 305)

Address correspondence to Victor A. Ferre, Peru State College, Peru, NB 68421.

a Why do the authors include in their introduction references indicating the lack of relationship between scores on teacher competency tests and actual teaching performance? Although this may be true, it seems tangential to the purpose of the current study.

b The authors state in the introduction that the purpose of their study was to "examine the relationship between previously identified predictors of success and the NTE Core Battery," but they cite no references until the discussion section.

c The authors note that the sample used in the study represents only 60% of the population from which it was drawn. To what extent might this sample be biased?

d It is not clear why the authors took the 94 students in the sample and split them into two groups based on the year of graduation. As a result, the size of one sample is almost 3.5 times as large as the other.

e The authors note that the two groups were "approximately equal because they achieved a GPA of slightly higher than a B and scored around the 50th percentile on both ACT subtests and NTE Core Battery tests." A t test reveals, however, that the reference group's ACT English score is significantly higher than the cross-validation score ($t(92) = 2.21$, $p < .05$). The difference is particularly noteworthy because the ACT English score is a variable in two of the three equations used to predict scores on the NTE subtests.

Chapter Highlights

- Correlational methods are used to determine the extent to which two or more variables are related.

- The most commonly used measure of correlation is r, the Pearson Product-Moment correlation coefficient.

- Values of r fall between $+1.00$ (perfect positive correlation) and -1.00 (perfect negative correlation).

- A significant correlation between variables does not necessarily mean the variables are causally related.

- If variables A and B are significantly correlated, changes in variable A may cause changes in variable B; changes in variable B may cause changes in variable A; or changes in a third variable (variable C) may cause changes in both variables A and B.

- Correlational studies are sometimes carried out to establish whether two variables are significantly correlated prior to conducting an experiment to determine if the variables are causally related.

- Correlation is a necessary but not a sufficient condition for determining causality.

- Hypotheses in correlational studies (as hypotheses in group comparison studies) are stated in directional or nondirectional form as a function of what the existing literature shows about the variables under investigation.

- The multiple correlation coefficient is symbolized by R and indicates the strength of relationship between one variable and several others.

- Partial correlation is used to establish the degree of relationship between two variables after the effects of their relationship to other variables have been removed.

- Simple regression is used to predict values of one variable on the basis of values of another variable.
- Multiple regression is used to predict values of one variable on the basis of values of two or more other variables.

Review Exercises

1. Give an example of a research question that could be answered by using correlational methods.
2. Why might a researcher carry out a correlational study before conducting an experiment?
3. Give an example of a nondirectional hypothesis for a correlational study. Give examples of (a) a directional hypothesis predicting a positive relationship between two variables; and (b) a directional hypothesis predicting a negative relationship between two variables.
4. Contrast multiple and partial correlation.
5. Why is it logically impossible to draw a causal inference between variables that are significantly correlated?
6. Describe how regression and correlation are related concepts.

*C*hapter *14*

Group Comparison Research

Researchers often use the process of matched pairs when working with small groups to make sure that the two groups are initially comparable on the dependent variable.

Chapter Objectives

After completing this chapter, you should be able to:

- identify instances of three kinds of group comparisons: ex post facto, experiments, and quasi-experiments
- explain how ex post facto, experimental, and quasi-experimental procedures differ in design and in the kinds of information they provide
- differentiate between threats to internal and external validity
- describe eight threats to internal validity
- explain why it is necessary in an experiment to have at least one control or comparison group
- describe three experimental designs that are internally valid
- describe two threats to external validity

- explain the function of random assignment in experiments
- describe how to use the method of matched pairs and the circumstances under which it should be used
- describe how random assignment is used in quasi-experiments
- describe a problem associated with the use of pretests
- distinguish between the Hawthorne and John Henry effects
- describe the difference between parametric and nonparametric statistics and the conditions under which each should be used

While correlational research is characterized by one group of subjects and two or more variables, **group comparison research** is characterized by two or more groups and one variable. Correlational research may be conceptualized as investigations that determine the extent to which two or more variables are related to one another. In correlational research the information collected about the two (or more) variables under investigation comes from the *same* group of people. In correlational research the group of people usually represents a sample, not a variable.

It is helpful to conceptualize the research question in group comparison research as finding out if two (or more) groups of people exhibit significantly different average values with respect to a single variable. For example, do students taught by Method A have a significantly different average score on a spelling test than do students taught by Method B? Do mainstreamed special education students have a significantly different average score on a self-concept questionnaire than do nonmainstreamed special education students?

In group comparison research, the groups themselves represent different values of some variable. In the first example, the two groups differed in terms of the method of instruction they received, that is, one group received Method A and the other, Method B. "Method of instruction," is the variable, and the two kinds of instruction are the values the variable can assume. Similarly, in the second example, the two groups differed with respect to class placement, that is, one group was mainstreamed and the other was not. "Class placement" is the variable, and mainstreamed or not mainstreamed are the values that the variable can assume.

Both studies are examples of group comparisons because each group exhibited a different value of one variable. The research question is whether these groups also exhibit a significant difference in their average values on another variable. In correlational research, there is only one group, and no comparison of average values is made.

Types of Group Comparisons

There are three different types of research designs for group comparison studies, called ex post facto (or causal comparative) designs, experiments, and quasi-experiments. There is only one factor that distinguishes the three designs from one another, but that factor is crucial: how the groups are formed. The way in which groups in a group comparison are formed determines whether one can draw a cause-and-effect inference or not and what kinds of statistical analyses of the data are appropriate.

Briefly, in an **ex post facto** (Latin for *after the fact*) design, the groups to be compared are already formed in terms of the values of a variable to be studied, that is, the researcher does *not* form the groups. For example, if a researcher is comparing boys and girls with respect to some variable, the group of boys and the group of girls are already formed. In an experiment or a quasi-experiment, however, the groups are not already formed. It is the researcher who forms the groups.

In an experiment, the researcher randomly assigns people *on an individual basis* to groups, each of which exhibits a different value of a variable to be studied. In a quasi-experiment, the researcher randomly assigns *intact groups* to different values of a variable to be studied. Suppose a researcher wishes to compare the relative effectiveness of two different methods of instruction. In an experiment, the researcher would randomly assign students on an individual basis to be taught by Method A or by Method B. In a quasi-experiment, the researcher would randomly assign students in an intact classroom to be taught by Method A and those in another intact classroom to be taught by Method B.

It is possible for more than one research design to occur within the same study if the study addresses more than one research question. For example, a researcher could design an experiment to determine the relative effectiveness of two methods of instruction by randomly assigning students to be taught by one method or the other. It would also be possible within the same study, however, for the researcher to compare the performance of boys with that of girls. The important point is that an experiment has been used to examine academic performance as a function of instructional method, but an ex post facto design has been used to examine academic performance as a function of students' gender, because the groups are already formed by gender. The researcher cannot randomly assign students to be one gender or the other. It is essential to determine what kind of design has been used to investigate a research question because it is the research design that determines the kinds of conclusions one may draw from the research findings.

Independent and Dependent Variables

Much research in education deals with the relationship of *independent* and *dependent* variables. An **independent variable** is the variable the researcher uses to form the groups to be studied in an experiment or a quasi-experiment. It is the variable whose values the experimenter manipulates. For example, if a researcher is interested in determining the relationship between various methods of reading instruction and students' reading comprehension, "method of reading instruction" is the independent variable because it is the researcher who decides what values "methods of reading instruction" will be given in the study. Furthermore, the students participating in the study will be grouped according to the method of instruction they are to receive.

A researcher may decide to compare the "whole word approach" with the "phonics approach," or perhaps to compare the results of teaching reading by the "whole word approach" with an approach using the Initial Teaching Alphabet. On the other hand, the researcher might decide that it is more informative to compare all three methods of reading instruction simultaneously. In other words, it is the researcher who determines how many values and which specific values will define the independent variable.

At the completion of an experiment, the researcher wishes to determine if the groups exhibit different values associated with a particular variable. This variable is the **dependent variable.** In the previous example, "reading comprehension" is the dependent variable whose values are represented by reading comprehension scores. The researcher wants to determine how reading comprehension *depends* on the method of instruction used. In an experiment or quasi-experiment, a researcher purposely forms groups that differ with respect to the independent variable to determine how such differences may cause the groups to exhibit different values with respect to a dependent variable.

The terms *independent* and *dependent variables* are also used in ex post facto studies. The independent variable in an ex post facto study is the variable whose values distinguish the groups being studied before the researcher begins to collect data. The dependent variable is the variable the researcher measures. Suppose, for example, the researcher wants to see if principals and teachers exhibit different levels of burnout. The independent variable is "educational role," that is, principal and teacher. The dependent variable is "degree of burnout," which might be represented by a score on a questionnaire measuring burnout.

In correlational studies, the independent and dependent variables are sometimes called, respectively, *predictor* and *criterion variable*. In a correlational study examining the relationship between students' performance on a college entrance examination and their college grade point average, the predictor variable is "performance on the entrance examination" and the criterion variable is "grade point average."

Confounding Variables

In designing an experiment, the researcher attempts to form groups that differ systematically only with respect to the independent variable. Suppose in a study of methods of teaching reading, the researcher assigns two values to the variable "method of reading instruction": the "whole word approach" and the "phonics approach." Students participating in the study would be randomly assigned to one of the two groups. The use of random assignment increases the likelihood that the two groups of students will differ systematically only with respect to the method of reading instruction to which they are exposed.

Suppose, however, that the researcher carries out a study comparing two different reading methods, but assigns girls to be taught by one method and boys by the other. The two groups would then differ systematically on two variables, "method of reading instruction" and "gender." In this case, gender is a *confounding variable*. The researcher is interested in determining the effects of methods of reading instruction, not the effects of gender.

Any variable on which groups in an experiment systematically differ, other than the variable whose effect the researcher is interested in determining, is a confounding variable. It is confounding because, if at the end of the experiment the two groups exhibit a difference in performance on a reading comprehension test (i.e., the dependent variable), the researcher does not know if the difference is caused by the method of instruction or students' gender. Most confounding variables in experiments are less obvious than the variable of gender in the example. However, the important thing to note is that confounding variables should be avoided because they make the results of an experiment uninterpretable.

Ex Post Facto (or Causal Comparative) Designs

The following research studies represent examples of ex post facto designs: (a) a comparison of regular and special education teachers' attitudes toward mainstreaming; (b) a comparison of gifted and nongifted students' perception of morality; (c) a comparison of parochial school and public school students' beliefs about the appropriateness of various kinds of disciplinary procedures used by teachers.

In these examples, the people participating in each study are already grouped in terms of a variable of interest to the researcher before the study begins. The researcher did not assign teachers to be regular or special education teachers or assign students to be gifted or nongifted or to attend parochial or public school.

Ex Post Facto Designs and Causality

Ex post facto designs are frequently used to identify *possible* causal relationships between variables. One must be cautious, however, about inferring *actual* causal relationships between variables studied by means of an ex post facto design.

Consider the following ex post facto study. A researcher is interested in finding out if children who have attended nursery school perform better in reading in the first grade than those who have not attended nursery school. The researcher divides a group of first graders into two groups comprised, respectively, of those who have attended nursery school and those who have not, and administers a reading test to both groups. Suppose it turns out that the mean reading score of the children who have had nursery school experience is significantly higher than that of the others.

Obviously, the researcher has found the answer to the research question. Children in the study who had attended nursery school did perform significantly better than the children who had not attended nursery school. It should be equally obvious that the researcher cannot conclude that attending nursery school *caused* children to perform better in reading when they reached first grade. The researcher knows that the two groups of children differ with respect to whether they have had nursery school experience or not. However, the researcher has no way of knowing to what extent the two groups of children differ with respect to other variables that may account for their difference in reading performance.

It may be that in comparison with the children who have not attended nursery school, children who have gone to nursery school come from families with larger incomes and have parents who are better educated. It is possible that the difference in the two groups' reading performance could be accounted for by differences in the children's home environments that are associated with different socioeconomic levels. Families with larger incomes are likely to have more books in their homes, and parents who are better educated are more likely to read to their children and encourage their children to learn how to read. It is possible that the child's experiences at home rather than at the nursery school have caused the group of nursery school children to read better than the other group.

On the other hand, suppose the researcher had found no significant difference between the average reading scores of children who had and those who had not attended nursery school. Can the researcher conclude that attending nursery school has no effect on how well children will read when they are in the first grade? Again, because the researcher has no way of knowing in what ways the two groups of children may differ other than in terms of nursery school attendance, no conclusion can be drawn concerning the lack of a causal relationship between nursery school experience and first-grade reading performance.

It is possible, for example, that the children who had attended nursery school tended to come from single-parent homes of lower socioeconomic level where, in order to hold a full-time job, parents were forced to send their children to nursery school. Perhaps the children who had not attended nursery school came from homes where one parent did not work full time and could afford to stay home and look after the children. It may be that nursery school experience did have an effect on the children's reading performance, for without the experience they may have scored significantly lower than the other children.

The main point here is that, in an ex post facto study, one can draw no logical conclusion about whether there is or is not a causal relationship between two variables. One cannot be sure that the two groups do not differ with respect to variables other than the variable of interest.

An Example of Ex Post Facto (or Causal Comparative) Research, with Comments

Summer Birth Date Children: Kindergarten Entrance Age and Academic Achievement

Sandra L. Crosser
Ohio Northern University

ABSTRACT   Academic achievement indices taken at fifth or sixth grade for summer birth date children who entered kindergarten at age 5 were compared with the academic achievement indices of summer birth date children who entered kindergarten at age 6. Scores on standardized achievement tests were analyzed for 45 pairs of subjects who were matched for ability and gender. All statistically significant differences favored those summer birth date children who entered kindergarten at age 6.
a Dependent t tests indicated a statistically significant difference ($p < .05$) in composite test battery scores favoring both older males and older females. Older males scored significantly higher than younger males did in total reading subscores ($p < .01$). Results of the study indicated a general academic advantage at fifth or sixth grade for summer birth date children who postponed kindergarten entrance 1 year. A particular advantage in reading at fifth or sixth grade was indicated for summer birth date males who postponed kindergarten entrance 1 year.

At some time around a child's fifth birthday, parents and educators in our country generally expect that the process of formal education will begin. Barring complications, the child moves uniformly through the grades with classmates who are approximately the same age. Bracey (1989), however, reported a trend, particularly among affluent parents, to postpone enrolling their children in kindergarten if those children would otherwise be among the youngest in the class. The following year, the children who were held back would be among the oldest entrants. The term "graying of the kindergarten" has been popularized to reflect the resulting change in the age composition of kindergarten classes (Bracey, 1989, p. 732).

Recent literature reflects specific interest in holding back one group of children in particular (Elkind, 1987; Karweit, 1988; Lofthouse, 1987; Uphoff & Gilmore, 1986). That group of children includes those born during the months of June, July, August, and September. The group, labeled "summer children," has been the subject of studies researching possible birth date effects. Assuming a September 30 cutoff date, the youngest child in a kindergarten entrance class could have been born September 30, and the oldest child could have been born May 31 of the previous year. In that situation, there would be an age range of nearly 16 months, rather than the 12-month range typically expected with any set cutoff date. The additional 4-month difference in ages represents a significant portion of the young child's developmental life. Because of the range in ages between the youngest and oldest groups, one should ask whether each group would be academically advantaged or disadvantaged.

A review of the literature revealed that those who studied entrance age of summer birth date children commonly cited a score of research reports. Those frequently referenced studies were evaluated on the basis of their research design characteristics to determine whether they might inform decision making about kindergarten entrance age for summer birth date children (see Table 1). The criteria used in that evaluation were as follows:

1. Inferential statistics should be reported. Tests of statistical significance should be set at least at the .05 alpha level.
2. Academic achievement should be based on objective measures such as standardized achievement test scores. Subjective measures, such as letter grades, number of retentions, and parent or teacher ranking, should not be acceptable measures because of possible complications in situational variables.
3. The sample size of comparison groups should be large enough to reasonably support conclusions.
4. Comparison groups should be limited to children continuously enrolled in the same school district in a regular classroom setting. Retained children and special education children should not be included.
5. There should be controls for ability and gender.

Three studies met all of the evaluative criteria—Green and Simmons (1962), Reinherz and Kinard (1986), and Sweetland and DeSimone (1987). The work of Baer (1958) met all of the criteria except control for gender. None of the studies that met the evaluative criteria investigated achievement of summer birth date subjects in particular. Those studies were, however, the only ones that did control for intelligence, a control that is absolutely vital for any comparisons of achievement. Research designs that did not provide controls for intelligence offered little insight into the question of optimum entrance age for summer birth date children because subjects of unlike ability might have been compared. Therefore, I reviewed only the four studies that met the control for the intelligence criterion.

A causal-comparative design was used by Baer (1958) to compare achievement of students representing the youngest 2 months and the oldest 2 months of an entrance class. The youngest group was admitted on the basis of tested IQ, as measured by the Revised Stanford Binet, Form L. The oldest group was selected on the basis of matched IQ, as measured by the same instrument. The mean IQ for both groups was between 111 and 112.

Baer (1958) reviewed the students' cumulative records after they had completed 11 years of school. Unspecified scores from unspecified achievement tests were used to compare elementary school achievement of the two groups. The older group scored significantly higher at the .01 level on reading at Grades 3, 6, and 8; on mathematics at Grades 4, 6, and 8; and on social studies at Grade 5. No significant differences were found for spelling at Grade 5, for language at Grade 8, or for science at Grade 7.

Table 1 — Research Design Characteristics of Studies Commonly Cited in Summer Birth Date School Entrance Age Literature

	Date	Summer birth date research	Statistical analysis	Objective measures	Sufficient sample size	Subjects continuously enrolled	Regular classroom subjects	Control for IQ	Control for gender
Baer	1958	—	X	X	X	X	X	X	—
Bigelow	1934	—	—	X	X	X	X	—	—
Dickinson & Larson	1963	—	X	X	X	—	X	—	X
Dietz & Wilson	1985	—	X	X	X	?	X	—	X
Gilmore	1984	X	—	X	—	?	?	—	—
Green & Simmons	1962	—	X	X	X	X	X	X	X
Hall	1963	—	—	X	X	?	X	—	—
Hamalainen	1952	—	—	—	X	—	X	—	—
Hobson	1948	—	—	X	X	—	X	—	—
Huff	1984	X	—	X	X	X	?	—	—
Reinherz & Kinard	1986	—	X	X	X	X	X	X	X
King	1955	—	X	X	X	X	X	—	—
Knight & Manuel	1930	—	X	—	X	X	X	—	—
Langer, Kalk, & Searls	1984	—	X	X	X	—	X	—	X
May & Welch	1986	—	X	X	X	X	X	—	X
Miller	1957	—	—	X	—	—	X	—	—
Miller & Norris	1967	—	X	X	—	X	X	—	X
Partington	1937	—	—	—	X	—	X	—	—
Sweetland & DeSimone	1987	—	X	X	X	X	X	X	X
Uphoff	1986	X	—	X	—	?	X	—	—

Note. X (yes); — (no); ? (unreported).

Although the older group outperformed the younger group on some measures, Baer stated that "most of the underage children made average school progress. As a group, they made average marks in subjects, average scores on achievement tests. . . ." (Baer, 1958, p. 19). Because of the nature of the IQ scores, achievement for both groups could have been expected to have been somewhat above average.

If Baer's (1958) findings were assumed to be correct for children who represented the youngest 2 months and oldest 2 months of an entrance age group, and if summer birth date children were represented by the younger group, then his results would suggest that summer birth date children might benefit in some respects by postponing kindergarten entrance. However, such a generalization would be highly suspect because Baer's youngest group was actually composed of underaged early kindergarten entrants with November and December birth dates.

Green and Simmons (1962) indicated findings similar to prior research by Baer (1958) in which the younger entrants demonstrated average achievement even though they were outperformed by the older entrants. Green and Simmons compared the achievement of children who entered first grade before they attained the age of 6 years (younger group) with those who were 6 years or older upon entering first grade (older group). As with Baer's work, application of the findings of Green and Simmons to summer birth date children would not be appropriate because the younger group was composed of underaged early entrants.

Reinherz and Kinard (1986) tested 467 fourth graders who had been continuously enrolled in the same school district since kindergarten. Given a December 31 cutoff date, all the subjects were divided into birth date groups of 2 months each over the calendar year. Rather than being the youngest group, some of the children with summer birth dates were actually among the oldest subjects in the Kinard and Reinherz work. In order to accurately interpret findings for understanding the summer birth date population, the Kinard and Reinherz oldest group would have to have been the youngest group compared in a 1-year age range. One should exercise caution in translating the researchers' conclusions to other age-comparison groups.

Achievement, as measured on the Comprehensive Test of Basic Skills at the sixth-grade level, was analyzed by Sweetland and DeSimone (1987) in relation to subjects' birth quartiles over a 1-year span. Statistically significant differences ($p < .05$ or less) were found only for the subjects born in the fourth quartile. Youngest subjects achieved less well only in relation to their older classmates, not in relation to national norming groups. Because the significant differences in achievement appeared only in children with October, November, and December birth dates, findings could not be generalized to the summer birth date population.

Nevertheless, the results raise an interesting question. Would those children born in the summer reflect the relative achievement of Sweetland and DeSimone's (1987) fourth birth quartile if they had been the youngest group? In other words, if the oldest children had been represented by the October through December born, would the summer birth date children have achieved significantly lower than that oldest group? The summer birth date population was represented by the third birth quartile. Therefore, Sweetland and DeSimone's findings suggest no significant difference in achievement of summer birth date children who entered kindergarten at age 5, compared with peers born in the first and second birth quartiles.

The existing knowledge base for making decisions about optimum entrance age for summer birth date children is weak, at best. After 50 years of seeking answers, the question of optimum age for school entrance remains, in most respects, unanswered. Nevertheless, the question has gained importance for both parents and educators. The question has become particularly urgent because of the tendency for some educators to advise parents to hold back those children with summer birth dates (Elkind, 1987). Parents have been advised to give their children an additional year to mature before beginning kindergarten, particularly if the children are male (Uphoff, Gilmore, & Huber, 1987). That advice has been cited as the course of wisdom, generalized to a sizable segment of the school entrance population, but has been based, in large part, on hopes and fears rather than a strong, empirically rigorous knowledge base.

Given the limited research base, a study that compared the academic achievement indices of summer birth date children who entered kindergarten at age 5 with the academic achievement indices of summer birth date children of similar abilities who entered kindergarten at age 6 would be valuable. A knowledge base anchored in such research would assist in guiding informed decision making. Such a study was implemented in 1989; it was based on the hypothesis that academic achievement indices taken at fifth or sixth grade for summer birth date children who entered kindergarten at age 5 will not differ significantly from the academic achievement indices of summer birth date children who entered kindergarten at age 6.

Method

Subjects

Subjects were drawn from seven public school districts in northwestern Ohio. Six districts were local and constituted one larger county school system. The seventh jurisdiction was classified as a city school district.

All the subjects were in seventh, eighth, or ninth grade during the 1988–89 school year. Official school records were used to identify all the pupils with birth dates between June 1 and September 30.
b The subject pool was composed of summer birth date (June 1 through September 30) pupils who had not been retained in any grade and who had been in continuous enrollment in regular classrooms since kindergarten. There were 122 males and 131 females. Of the total 253 potential subjects, 190 enrolled in kindergarten at age 5 and 63 enrolled at age 6.

c　　Based on official school records, the 63 subjects who enrolled in kindergarten at age 6 were matched for gender and intelligence with subjects who enrolled in kindergarten at age 5. Scores on standardized ability tests administered during the intermediate grades provided the vehicles for matching same-gender subjects for intelligence. Two school districts had administered the Test of Cognitive Skills (CTB/McGraw-Hill, Level g, 1982). Five districts had administered the Cognitive Abilities Test (Riverside Publishing Company, Level c, 1982). Pairing of subjects was restricted to potential matches who had taken the same standardized ability test.

Subjects were then matched by randomly drawing from a pool of all same-gender subjects scoring within one standard error of measurement (SEM) on identical tests of intellectual ability. Limiting the range of possible matches to 1 SEM resulted in a 68% confidence interval, or two chances out of three that the true score resides within ± 1 SEM of the obtained score (Borg & Gall, 1983).

d　　The matching process resulted in 45 pairs of subjects identified by ability and gender. There were 29 male pairs and 16 female pairs. Although 63 pupils had enrolled in kindergarten at age 6, there were 18 potential subjects who were lost to analysis because they could not be matched for intelligence within ± 1 SEM.

Design

The causal-comparative design of the study employed a records search for achievement and ability scores of subjects. The nature of the design dictated that the testing instruments that had been selected for use by each school district at some point in the past would necessarily provide the data for the study.

I hypothesized that academic achievement indices taken at fifth or sixth grade for summer birth date children who entered kindergarten at age 5 would not differ significantly from the academic achievement indices of summer birth date children who entered kindergarten at age 6. An alpha level of .05 was set.

Procedures

Achievement and ability test scores that had been administered by regular classroom teachers in the fifth or sixth grade were collected from official school records. In addition to birth date and kindergarten entrance date information, scores for measures of intelligence and national percentile ranks for measures of total reading, total mathematics, and composite scores were recorded for each subject. In an effort to reduce the likelihood of possibly complicating variables, those pupils who had been retained or who had not been continuously enrolled in regular classrooms were excluded from the study.

The use of percentile ranks to compare scores has been criticized because percentile ranks do not represent an equal-interval scale (Green & Simmons, 1962; Hinkle, Wiersma, & Jurs, 1982; Lyman, 1978). Moreover, percentile ranks have been determined to be inappropriate for both statistical computations (Borg & Gall, 1983) and comparisons between test batteries (Hinkle et al.). Because the present study required statistical comparisons of scores between test batteries, I used a normalized standard score, the normal curve equivalent (NCE) score, for data analysis. A percentile to NCE conversion table was used to convert national percentile ranks on the achievement measures to NCE scores for statistical computations.

Instrumentation

Two nationally standardized tests of ability and three nationally standardized tests of achievement had been administered to the subjects by the participating school districts. The resulting problem of comparability of test scores was resolved, as previously described, by use of the NCE scores.

All the tests had been administered to groups of subjects by regular school faculty. Also, all tests had been machine scored. Data were collected from the pupil profile printouts affixed to individual official school records. Because assessing the content validity of the three achievement tests administered to the subjects was beyond the scope of the present study, I assumed that district personnel had selected each particular test with the question of content validity in mind.

The Cognitive Abilities Test (CAT), Level c, Form 3 (Riverside Publishing Company, 1982) was the ability measure used for fifth-grade pupils in five of the participating school districts. National percentile ranks for verbal, quantitative, and nonverbal subtests were available in records data. Same-form retest reliability with a 6-month interim between tests resulted in reliabilities ranging between .76 and .94, and the Kuder-Richardson 20 reliabilities were high, ranging from .89 to .96 (Ansorge, 1985). Construct validity was based on correlations between the CAT and Stanford-Binet, which resulted in respectable correlations of .65 to .75 (Ansorge). Standardization and norming procedures were rigorous (Ansorge).

The remaining two districts that participated in the present study had administered the Test of Cognitive Skills (TCS), Level g, Forms u and v (CTB/McGraw-Hill, 1982). The TCS is an ability measure co-normed with the Comprehensive Tests of Basic Skills (CTBS) (CTB/McGraw-Hill); it correlates between .60 and .82 with the composite CTBS score (Shepard, 1985). Two of the school districts participating in the present study had administered the TCS in conjunction with the CTBS either at Grade 5 or at Grade 6. The combined TCS and CTBS standard error of estimate was 31.42 at Grade 5 and 27.33 on Grade 6 in scaled score units, as indicated in the preliminary technical report. The standard error of measurement for the TCS is ± 5 (J. Reginal, personal communication, June 6, 1989).

The Iowa Test of Basic Skills (ITBS), Level 12, Form 8 (Riverside Publishing Company, 1977), was administered as the achievement measure in four of the participating districts. The Kuder-Richardson

20 reliability for the composite score is .98 (Airasian, 1985). Subtest K-R 20 reliabilities are high, ranging from approximately .85 to .90 (Airasian). The ITBS correlates between .60 and .80 with the CAT (Airasian), which was administered in conjunction with the ITBS in four of the school districts included in the present study.

The STS Educational Development Series (STS-EDS), Level 15, Form A (Scholastic Testing Service, Inc., 1967) was administered as an achievement measure at Grade 5 in one participating district. Mehrens (1978) reported respectable concurrent validity in the test because the STS-EDS correlates at approximately .90 with the Iowa Test of Basic Skills as well as with composite scores of other major achievement tests.

The Comprehensive Tests of Basic Skills (CTBS), Level g, Forms u and v, third edition (CTB/McGraw-Hill, 1981) was administered by two of the school districts participating in the present study. Shepard (1985) defended the adequacy of CTBS reliability on the basis of inference from standard errors and intercorrelations. Norming and standardization procedures were upheld as "extensive" (Shepard, 1985, p. 388).

Results

Forty-five subjects who entered kindergarten at age 6 were matched on the basis of intelligence quotients with same-gender subjects who entered kindergarten at age 5. Pairs of subjects were matched for intelligence within ± 1 SEM on standardized ability tests administered at Grades 5 or 6 (see Tables 2 and 3). Of the resulting 45 pairs of subjects, 29 pairs were male and 16 pairs were female. As indicated in Table 4, there was little difference in mean intelligence scores for all groups. Matched pairs resulted in comparable groups.

e   Achievement scores were analyzed separately by gender for reading, mathematics, and the composite test battery. A dependent t test was used to analyze the data. As illustrated in Table 5, there was a significant difference ($p < .05$) in achievement at the intermediate grade level, as measured by composite test battery scores when children of similar intellectual ability (± 1 SEM) were compared. The older summer birth date male entrants exhibited a statistically significant ($p < .05$) advantage over younger summer birth date males. The older summer birth date females exhibited a statistically significant advantage over the younger summer birth date females ($p < .05$).

Reading subscore analysis revealed larger mean score same-gender differences for males than for females (see Table 6). Males who entered kindergarten at age 6 scored significantly higher on reading in fifth or sixth grade ($p < .01$) than did males who entered kindergarten at age 5. Six-year-old female entrants scored higher in reading in fifth or sixth grade than did their 5-year-old counterparts ($p < .10$), but not at the .05 alpha level set for the study.

Mean NCE scores for mathematics achievement at the intermediate level were not significantly different at the .05 alpha level for younger and older summer birth date subjects (see Table 7). However, mathematics scores for males did demonstrate a difference at the .10 alpha level, $t(28) = 1.767$, $p < .10$.

Comparisons of all 6-year-old entrants with all 5-year-old entrants without regard for gender revealed a significant difference on the reading subtest scores, $t(44) = 3.55$, $p < .001$. When similar comparisons were made for total groups mathematics subscores, significance did not reach the .05 alpha level; a lower level of significance, however, was indicated, $t(44) = 1.68$, $p < .10$. Similar results were indicated for composite test battery scores, $t(44) = 1.866$, $p < .10$. The composite test battery scores included subscores from other areas in addition to the total reading and total mathematics subscores. However, only total reading and total mathematics subscores were singled out for separate analysis. The results did not support the hypothesis: Academic achievement indices taken at fifth or sixth grade for summer birth date children who entered kindergarten at age 5 will not differ significantly from the academic achievement indices of summer birth date children who entered kindergarten at age 6.

Table 2	*Male Subject Pairs Matched for Intelligence*	
	Intelligence quotients by age at kindergarten entrance	
Matched pairs	5 years	6 years
1	110	110
2	112	113
3	114	116
4	115	117
5	114	118
6	120	120
7	122	121
8	128	128
9	82	80
10	89	87
11	82	81
12	92	87
13	90	89
14	93	90
15	97	94
16	98	96
17	100	97
18	100	97
19	102	99
20	105	102
21	101	102
22	103	103
23	104	103
24	104	104
25	105	105
26	103	106
27	105	106
28	106	110
29	110	110

Discussion

Given similar levels of intelligence, males with summer birth dates tended to be advantaged academically by postponing kindergarten entrance one year. That advantage was greatest in the area of reading. Summer birth date females who postponed kindergarten entrance 1 year were not significantly advantaged in reading or mathematics, but were generally at an advantage, as indicated by composite battery scores on standardized tests.

Academic achievement is only one of the variables to be considered when making entry-age decisions for individual children. Social, emotional, and physical implications deserve careful consideration as well. The child's total adjustment to school must be the overriding consideration in any particular decision situation. If, however, a group of children may be at an academic advantage

Table 3 — Female Subject Pairs Matched for Intelligence

Matched pairs	Intelligence quotients by age at kindergarten entrance	
	5 years	6 years
1	85	81
2	88	84
3	88	84
4	90	90
5	89	92
6	102	101
7	104	102
8	99	103
9	101	106
10	102	106
11	109	106
12	107	109
13	122	119
14	120	121
15	126	121
16	122	127

Table 4 — Measures of Central Tendency for Matched Pairs Groups

Entrance age	Intelligence quotients			
	n	M	Mdn	SD
Males				
Age 5	29	103.66	104	11.02
Age 6	29	103.14	103	12.26
Females				
Age 5	16	103.38	102	14.24
Age 6	16	103.25	105	13.54

or disadvantage simply by enrolling in school at a particular age, then that knowledge would be a potentially important bit of information to know.

The existing knowledge base for decision making about school entrance age for summer birth date children is not particularly strong. Sources have been quoted and misquoted without thorough examination of the nature of the subjects or the nature and rigor of the research. Experts have offered advice to parents of summer birth date children based on less-than-rigorous research, studies of underaged gifted children, or even studies of learning disabled subjects. There is a need to focus on a stronger knowledge base on which to build entrance-age recommendations.

Table 5	Composite Achievement Test Means Taken at Fifth or Sixth Grade, Compared by Kindergarten Entrance Age				

Kindergarten entrance age	n	M NCE[a]	SD	Dependent t ratio	p
Males	58			2.16	<.05
Age 5	29	48.586	15.754		
Age 6	29	54.828	21.114		
Females	32			2.19	<.05
Age 5	16	55.250	15.661		
Age 6	16	56.125	20.020		

[a]NCE = normal curve equivalent scores.

Table 6	Reading Achievement Subscore Means Taken at Fifth or Sixth Grade, Compared by Kindergarten Entrance Age				

Kindergarten entrance age	n	M NCE[a]	SD	Dependent t ratio	p
Males	58			2.799	< .01
Age 5	29	49.034	18.490		
Age 6	29	58.170	19.968		
Females	32			1.878	> .05 but < .10
Age 5	16	49.438	21.003		
Age 6	16	57.375	20.073		

[a]NCE = normal curve equivalent scores.

Table 7	Mathematics Achievement Subscore Means Taken at Fifth or Sixth Grade, Compared by Kindergarten Entrance Age				

Kindergarten entrance age	n	M NCE[a]	SD	Dependent t ratio	p
Males	58			1.77	> .05 but < .10
Age 5	29	47.345	15.472		
Age 6	29	53.345	22.259		
Females	32			.329	> .05
Age 5	16	54.375	17.308		
Age 6	16	55.625	18.333		

[a]NCE = normal curve equivalent scores.

Recommendations for Future Research

I conclude this article with four recommendations for additional research. First, the present study was limited to a sample of school children in northwestern Ohio. Researchers should involve a wider range of children to better inform decision making. Second, assess pupil attitudes toward postponement, as sampled at various points in the child's school career, to lend insight that would inform practice. Third, clarify the influence of socioeconomic status on academic achievement of summer birth date children who enter kindergarten at age 5, compared with those who enter at age 6. And fourth, explore the relationship between type of educational program or curriculum and achievement of summer birth date entrants.

References

Airasian, P. W. (1985). Review of Iowa Test of Basic Skills, forms 7 and 8. In J. V. Mitchell, Jr. (Ed.), *The ninth mental measurements yearbook.* Lincoln, NE: University of Nebraska Press.

Ansorge, C. J. (1985). Review of cognitive abilities test, form 3. In J. V. Mitchell, Jr. (Ed.), *The ninth mental measurements yearbook.* Lincoln, NE: University of Nebraska Press.

Baer, C. J. (1958). The school progress and adjustment of underage and overage students. *Journal of Educational Psychology, 48,* 17–19.

Bigelow, E. B. (1934). School progress of under-age children. *The Elementary School Journal, 25,* 186–190.

Borg, W. R., & Gall, M. D. (1983). *Educational research.* White Plains, NY: Longman.

Bracey, G. W. (1989). Age and achievement. *Phi Delta Kappan, 70,* 732.

Dickinson, D. J., & Larson, D. J. (1963). The effects of chronological age in months on school achievement. *The Journal of Educational Research, 56,* 492–493.

Dietz, C., & Wilson, B. J. (1985). Beginning school age and academic achievement. *Psychology in the Schools, 22,* 93–94.

Elkind, D. (1987). *Miseducation.* New York: Alfred A. Knopf.

Gilmore, J. E. (1984, May). How summer children benefit from a delayed start in school. Paper presented at the 1984 annual conference of the Ohio School Psychologists Association, Cincinnati, OH.

Green, D. R., & Simmons, S. V. (1962). Chronological age and school entrance. *The Elementary School Journal, 63,* 41–47.

Hall, R. V. (1963). Does entrance age affect achievement? *The Elementary School Journal, 63,* 391–395.

Hamalainen, A. (1952). Kindergarten—primary entrance age in relation to later school adjustment. *The Elementary School Journal, 52,* 406–411.

Hinkle, D. E., Wiersma, W., & Jurs, S. G. (1982). *Basic Behavioral Statistics.* Boston: Houghton Mifflin.

Hobson, J. R. (1948). Mental age as a workable criterion for school admission. *The Elementary School Journal, 48,* 312–321.

Huff, S. (1984). The pre-kindergarten assessment: A predictor for success of early and late starters. A research project at Wright State University, Dayton, OH.

Karweit, N. (1988). Effective preprimary programs and practices. *Principal, 67,* 18–21.

King, I. B. (1955). Effect of age of entrance into grade 1 upon achievement in elementary school. *The Elementary School Journal, 55,* 331–337.

Knight, J., & Manuel, H. T. (1930). Age of school entrance and subsequent school record. *School and Society, 32,* 24–26.

Langer, P., Kalk, J. M., & Searls, D. (1984). Age of admission and trends in achievement: A comparison of Blacks and Caucasians. *American Educational Research Journal, 21,* 61–78.

Lofthouse, R. (1987). A national cutoff date for entering kindergarten. *Education Digest, 53,* 44–45.

Lyman, H. B. (1978). *Test scores and what they mean.* Englewood Cliffs, NJ: Prentice-Hall.

May, D. C., & Welch, E. (1986). Screening for school readiness: The influence of birthdate and sex. *Psychology in the Schools, 23,* 100–101.

Mehrens, W. A. (1978). STS educational development series. In O. K. Buros (Ed.), *The eighth mental measurements yearbook.* Highland Park, NJ: Gryphon Press.

Miller, V. V. (1957). Academic achievement and social adjustment of children young for their grade placement. *The Elementary School Journal, 57,* 257–263.

Miller, W. D., & Norris, R. C. (1967). Entrance age and school success. *Journal of School Psychology, 6,* 47–59.

Partington, H. M. (1937). The relation between first-grade entrance age and success in the first six grades. *Elementary School Principals, 16,* 298–302.

Reinherz, H., & Kinard, E. M. (1986). Birthdate effects on school performance and adjustment: A longitudinal study. *Journal of Educational Research, 79,* 366–371.

Shepard, L. A. (1985). Review of the Comprehensive Test of Basic Skills, forms u and v. In J. V. Mitchell, Jr. (Ed.), *The ninth mental measurements yearbook.* Lincoln, NE: University of Nebraska Press.

Sweetland, J. D., & DeSimone, P. A. (1987). Age of entry, sex, and academic achievement in elementary school children. *Psychology in the Schools, 24,* 406–412.

Uphoff, J. K., & Gilmore, J. (1986). Pupil age at school entrance—how many are ready for success? *Young Children, 41,* 11–16.

Uphoff, J. K., Gilmore, J. E., & Huber, R. (1986). *Summer children ready or not for school.* Middletown, OH: J. & J. Publishing.

Address correspondence to Sandra L. Crosser, Department of Education, The Getty College of Arts and Sciences, Ohio Northern University, Ada, OH 45810.

Comments

a *Usually this test is called a t test for nonindependent means or a t test for correlated means.*

b *The author eliminated from the study children who had been retained or who had not been continuously enrolled in regular classrooms. To what extent does this limit the generalizability of the study's findings?*

c *The author matched younger and older children on IQ and gender. What is the rationale for matching children on these two characteristics rather than some other characteristics? If the author is going to use matching to control for variables, one wonders why, for example, she did not match children on socioeconomic level, especially since Bracey (1989) reports that there is a tendency for affluent parents "to postpone enrolling their children in kindergarten if those children would otherwise be among the youngest in the class." One of the problems associated with matching subjects on one or more variables is the possibility that the two groups will then differ systematically on one or more unmatched variables. It would have been better if the author had not matched the groups on any variable but instead had selected subjects from the two groups randomly. The data could then have been analyzed by an ANCOVA.*

The use of randomization is the best tool researchers have available to reduce the possibility that groups do not differ with respect to variables other than the variable of interest. Using matched pairs in this ex post facto study is not the same as using matched pairs in an experiment because the author could not randomly assign children to groups after they had been matched on IQ and gender. The author could not, for example, take two girls who have identical IQs and then randomly assign one girl to be "younger" and the other to be "older." As a result, the two groups studied may have differed systematically on one or more variables other than the age at which they entered kindergarten.

Another problem with matching is that it rules out the variable used for matching as a possible cause for differences between groups. Suppose, for example, children in one group have higher IQs than children in the other group. By matching children from both groups on IQ, the researcher has eliminated the possibility of detecting achievement differences associated with differences in IQ.

d *The author was able to match only 45 pairs of children, which means she studied a total of 90 children from a population of 253. One wonders to what extent the 90 matched children differed from the 163 children who could not be matched. To what extent do the 90 children represent a biased sample of the population?*

e *The author restricted data analysis to a comparison of achievement scores between younger and older children of the same gender. If the author had used random sampling techniques and analyzed the data by an ANCOVA, she could have compared scores between boys and girls and examined possible interaction effects of gender and age. The data shown in Table 5 and Table 7, for example, suggest that except for younger boys, the performance of the other three groups was comparable.*

Internal and External Validity of Experiments and Quasi-Experiments

Before discussing the nature of experiments and quasi-experiments, let us focus on factors affecting their validity. The validity of an experiment or a quasi-experiment depends on two factors: (a) the extent to which changes in the dependent variable are attributable solely to the independent variable (i.e., not to confounding variables); and (b) the extent to which it is reasonable to generalize the findings of the study. When a study has been conducted so that sources of confounding have been controlled, it is said to have **internal validity.** When a study has been conducted so that it is reasonable to generalize the findings to other groups, it is said to have **external validity.**

Threats to Internal Validity

A study may lack internal validity if changes in the dependent variable are due to factors other than changes in the independent variable. Campbell and Stanley (1963) have identified the following eight threats to internal validity:

1. *History.* Any changes in the environment in addition to the experimenter's intervention that may have occurred during the period between the pre- and posttest; the longer the period between the pre- and posttest, the greater the potential threat.
2. *Maturation.* Any biological or psychological changes that subjects may undergo as a function of the time lapse between the pre- and the posttest; subjects may become older, hungrier, more tired, more bored, and so forth. It is primarily because of the threats of *history* and *maturation* that it is necessary to have at least two groups participating in an experiment or quasi-experiment: an experimental group that receives the experimental treatment, and a control group that does not. Changes in history or maturation would occur in both groups, so any differences between the experimental and control groups must be attributable to the experimental treatment rather than to history or maturation.
3. *Pretesting.* The effects of taking a test upon the scores of a second testing.
4. *Measuring instruments.* Changes that might occur in the measuring instrument (either tests or observers) between the pre- and posttest. For example, with the passage of time, essay graders might alter their grading standards or observers may become tired or bored.

5. *Statistical regression.* The well-known tendency for subjects who score extremely high or extremely low on a pretest to score closer to the mean on a posttest. In studies carried out with groups of people who have been selected because they scored extremely well or extremely poorly on a pretest, it is difficult to know if changes in their posttest scores are due to the experimental treatment or to statistical regression. For example, if students with especially low self-concepts are selected as subjects in an experiment to test the effects of a new program designed to foster positive self-concepts, the students are likely to score higher the second time their self-concepts are measured, regardless of whether they participated in the program or not.

6. *Differential selection of subjects.* Biases introduced because members in the experimental and control groups exhibit differences on the dependent variable prior to the start of the experiment.

   This situation is most likely to occur in quasi-experiments. For this reason it is necessary to administer a pretest so that any initial differences between the groups can be adjusted statistically.

7. *Experimental mortality.* The differential loss of subjects from the experimental and control groups.

   For example, more low-scoring subjects in one group than the other may drop out of the experiment. Consequently improvements in posttest scores may be accounted for by the absence of poorer performers rather than by the experimental treatment.

8. *Selection-maturation interaction.* Groups that perform comparably on a pretest might exhibit characteristics having nothing to do with the experimental treatment that nevertheless lead to better performance on the posttest. For example, volunteers and nonvolunteers may perform comparably on a pretest, but because volunteers may be more motivated than nonvolunteers, their performance on the posttest may be higher simply as a result of their level of motivation. Statistical procedures are not effective in adjusting for these kinds of differences.

In their classic work, *Experimental and Quasi-experimental Designs for Research,* Campbell and Stanley (1963) identified various research designs and discussed them in terms of threats to internal and external validity. The following is a discussion of some undesirable and desirable designs most frequently used by students who are first learning about educational research. To make it easier to compare the strengths and weaknesses of the various designs, let us apply each design to the same research question. Let us assume that a college English instructor wants to find out if having students write their weekly compositions on a word processor will cause students to have positive attitudes toward writing.

Pre-Experimental Designs

Design 1. One-Shot Case Study.

Treatment   Observation
   X   O

In the one-shot case study, the instructor would have one class of students write their compositions on a word processor (X) and then fill out a questionnaire designed to measure their attitudes toward writing (O).

The one-shot case study design does not permit the instructor to conclude anything about the effects of X on O. The biggest problem is the lack of a control group that did not receive X. The students' scores on the attitudinal questionnaire may have nothing to do with the fact that they learned how to use a word processor.

Design 2. One-Group Pretest-Posttest Design.

Pretest	Treatment	Posttest
O_1	X	O_2

The one-group pretest-posttest design differs from the one-shot case study in that the questionnaire is administered twice: once as a pretest (O_1) before students start writing with the word processor (X) and again as a posttest (O_2) after students have used the word processor. One could argue that Design 2 is superior to Design 1 because the instructor can compare students' pre- and posttest attitudes to see if there has been an improvement. Even if students' attitudes have improved, however, one still does not know if using the word processor has caused the change. Other factors that occurred between (O_1) and (O_2) may account for the change. Suppose, for example, that between (O_1) and (O_2) a noted writer gave a guest lecture at the college and many of the students in the writing course attended. Perhaps the lecturer so inspired students that their attitudes toward writing became dramatically more positive. The positive change in students' attitudes resulted not from using the word processor but rather from attending an inspirational lecture.

Design 3. Static Group Comparison.

	Treatment	Posttest
Experimental Group	X	O
Control Group		O

In using the static group comparison design, the instructor would have one class of students use the word processor (X) and another class not use it. (The line in the diagram indicates that two intact classes were used.) Students in both classes would fill out the attitudinal questionnaire (O). Although Design 3 is superior to Designs 1 or 2, it still fails to provide the instructor with valid evidence concerning the effect of X on O. The major difficulty is that the instructor does not know if students in both groups had comparable attitudes toward writing before the one group began to use the word processor. If students in the experimental group for whatever reasons had a more positive attitude toward writing than students in the control group, the groups' scores would reflect initial differences in attitude and have nothing to do with use of the word processor. A major problem with this design is that students are not randomly assigned on an individual basis to the experimental and control groups.

True Experimental Designs

We now turn to several designs that overcome all of the threats to internal validity.

Design 4. Pretest-Posttest Control Group Design.

	Random Assignment	Pretest	Treatment	Posttest
Experimental Group	R	O_1	X	O_2
Control Group	R	O_1		O_2

In the pretest-posttest control group design, students are randomly assigned on an individual basis (R) to one of the two groups. Students in both groups fill out the questionnaire twice: once as a pretest (O_1) before students in the experimental group start writing with the word processor (X) and again as a posttest (O_2) after students in the experimental group have used the word processor. Students in the control group do not use a word processor. This design makes it possible for the instructor to compare the two groups' initial attitudes (O_1) and to take into account any initial differences by analyzing the posttest attitude scores (O_2) by means of an analysis of covariance. Any significant difference in the groups' O_2 scores must be attributable to use of the word processor because that is the only factor to which the experimental group has been exposed and the control group has not been.

Design 5. Posttest-Only Control Group Design.

	Random Assignment	Treatment	Posttest
Experimental Group	R	X	O
Control Group	R		O

The posttest-only control group controls for the effects of pretesting and the interaction of pretesting and treatment, although the effects are not measured. In most situations, however, these effects are of no concern. Design 5 circumvents problems associated with pretesting by simply not administering a pretest. Design 5 is a particularly powerful design for situations in which genuine random assignment can take place.

Design 6. Solomon Four-Group Design.

	Random Assignment	Pretest	Treatment	Posttest
Experimental Group	R	O_1	X	O_2
Control Group	R	O_1		O_2
Experimental Group	R		X	O_2
Control Group	R			O_2

The **Solomon four-group design** is a combination of Designs 4 and 5 and consequently yields the same information as both of them. In addition to controlling for the effects of pretesting and the interaction between pretesting and treatment, Design 6 measures these effects.

Quasi-Experimental Designs

There are several quasi-experimental designs that successfully deal with threats to internal validity. The following is a description of the nonequivalent control group design, which is the most commonly used quasi-experimental design by students in educational research courses.

Design 7. Nonequivalent Control Group Design.

	Pretest	Treatment	Posttest
Experimental Group	O_1	X	O_2
Control Group	O_1		O_2

The nonequivalent control group design is identical to Design 4, except for one major difference: instead of randomly assigning students on an individual basis to the experimental and control groups, intact classes are randomly assigned. (The line in the diagram indicates that two intact classes were used.) Students in both groups fill out the questionnaire twice: once as a pretest (O_1) before students in the experimental group start writing with the word processor (X) and again as a posttest (O_2) after students in the experimental group have used the word processor. Students in the control group do not use a word processor. This design makes it possible for the instructor to compare the two groups' initial attitudes (O_1) and to take into account any initial differences by analyzing the posttest attitude scores (O_2) by means of an analysis of covariance interaction between O_1 and X.

The relationship between the 7 designs and controls for threats to internal validity appear in Figure 14.1.

Threats to External Validity

Factors that affect the external validity of a study, that is, the extent to which the findings of a study may be generalized to persons other than those who participated in the study, fall into two categories: population validity and ecological validity (Bracht & Glass, 1968). **Population validity** concerns the use of appropriate sampling techniques, so that persons participating in the study are an accurate representation of the population to which the findings of the study are to be applied. The results of a study can be applied only to the population that the sample represents, which may or may not be the population a researcher claims the sample represents. For example, the results of a study using mailed questionnaires can be applied only to the population of persons who return the questionnaire, not to the entire population who were sent the questionnaire.

Ecological validity refers to the extent to which the findings of a study can be generalized to other settings because the findings are attributable to the independent variable, rather than to aspects of the experimental situation itself. The Hawthorne and John Henry effects, which are discussed later, are examples of threats to ecological validity because the performance of subjects is affected by the group they have been assigned to, not by the independent variable. Another example of a threat to ecological validity is the Experimenter effect, (Rosenthal, 1966) in which the experimenter inadvertently provides cues to subjects that affect subjects' performance.

The most effective way to control the Experimenter effect is to use the doublemasked technique that is sometimes used in medical research. For example, in testing the effectiveness of a new drug, half the people in the study are given the drug and the other half are given a placebo (a tablet that looks like the drug but has no medicinal value). Neither the subjects participating in the study *nor* the doctors carrying out the study know which subjects are receiving the drug and which are receiving the placebo. It is fairly unusual, however, to use the doublemasked technique in educational research.

Figure 14.1

The Relationship Between Design and Controls for Threats to Internal Validity

DESIGN	History	Maturation	Testing	Instrumentation	Regression	Selection	Mortality	Interaction of Selection and Maturation
1. One-Shot Case Study X O	No	No	N/A	N/A	N/A	No	No	N/A
2. One-Group Pretest-Posttest Design O_1 X O_2	No	No	No	No	?	Yes	Yes	No
3. Static Group Comparison X O ———— O	Yes	?	Yes	Yes	Yes	No	No	No
4. Pretest-Posttest Control Group Design R O_1 X O_2 R O_1 O_2	Yes	Yes	Yes	Yes	Yes	Yes	Yes	Yes
5. Posttest-Only Control Group Design R X O R O	Yes	Yes	Yes	Yes	Yes	Yes	Yes	Yes
6. Solomon Four-Group Design R O_1 X O_2 R O_1 O_2 R X O_2 R O_2	Yes	Yes	Yes	Yes	Yes	Yes	Yes	Yes
7. Nonequivalent Control Group Design O_1 X O_2 ———— O_1 O_2	Yes	Yes	Yes	Yes	?	Yes	Yes	No

Experiments

It seems clear that it is more informative to know if there is a causal relationship between two variables than just to know to what extent the variables are related. So far, however, we have not identified a research strategy that permits us to draw a cause-and-effect inference from the data we are able to collect. In the example of the ex post facto study given previously, the fundamental reason why we could not infer a cause-and-effect relationship between nursery school attendance and reading performance was that we could not be sure that the two groups did not differ on some variable other than nursery school attendance, which might have been the true cause of differences in reading performance.

If we were somehow able to know that two groups do not differ on any variable other than the one we are interested in, we could then conclude whether that variable has an effect on some other variable. For example, if we could be positive that attending nursery school was the only difference between the group of children who attended and the group that did not, and if the nursery school group scored significantly higher on the reading test, we could then be sure that it was the nursery school experience that caused the one group to perform better than the other group.

Unfortunately, there is no way by which we can be absolutely sure that two groups do not differ on some variable other than the one we are interested in. However, there is a way that we can increase the likelihood that two groups do not differ on any variable other than the one of interest, at least for some variables. That way is called **random assignment.**

The problem of how to assign subjects to groups does not occur in ex post facto designs because the groups are already formed. In experiments, however, it is the researcher who assigns subjects to groups, and the way in which subjects are assigned to various groups is of utmost concern. The procedures used to form groups of subjects in an experiment play a crucial role in determining whether the study will really be addressing the research question or not. An experiment is the most rigorous kind of research design for determining whether there is a causal relationship between variables. Precisely because subjects are randomly assigned to groups, the researcher can determine if changes in the independent variable are the cause of changes that may occur in the dependent variable.

The Function of Random Assignment

For example, to conclude that Method A is better than Method B in teaching reading, we must assume that the only thing that differentiates the group of students taught by Method A from the students taught by Method B is the method of instruction. As noted previously, there is no way to be absolutely sure that the method of instruction is the only thing on which the two groups differ. It is more reasonable to assume that the two groups differ only in terms of method of instruction if the students have been randomly assigned to Group A or B.

If we put in a hat the names of all students who are going to participate in the study and then randomly draw one name at a time, assigning the first student to be instructed by Method A, the second student to be instructed by Method B, the third student to A, the fourth student to B, and so on, the groups have been established by random assignment. By randomly assigning students to the two instructional methods, we increase the probability that the method of instruction is the only variable on which the two groups systematically differ.

Random assignment makes it likely, but not certain, that roughly the same number of boys would end up in Group A as in Group B, approximately the same number of girls would end up in both groups, the socioeconomic level of the two groups would not differ appreciably, the number of students coming from single-parent families would be about the same in both groups, and so forth. In short, random assignment increases the chances that the two groups would not exhibit very much difference on any variable except the independent variable, which is the one the researcher manipulates.

In this example the independent variable is the method of instruction. The researcher manipulates this variable by randomly assigning students to one method or the other. The dependent variable comprises the scores on the reading test that both groups of students will take after a specified period of instruction. The researcher wants to determine to what extent reading scores depend on the method of instruction used to teach reading. The research question is whether a change in the independent variable causes a change in the dependent variable.

Random Assignment and Confounding Variables. The major function of random assignment is to reduce the likelihood that groups will differ systematically on variables other than those of interest to the researcher. Such variables are called **confounding variables.** Researchers sometimes claim that their study has investigated one research question, when in fact the study has been carried out in such a way that it really has addressed a different question.

Statistically significant findings of a study shed no light on whether the study actually provides evidence about the research question the researcher thinks was being asked. To dramatize the idea that a study may not be addressing the question the researcher claims to be addressing, let us take a look at an example of a study that is so obviously bad that no researcher would ever consider doing it.

Suppose a researcher is trying to find out if Method A is a better way of teaching reading than Method B. The researcher teaches a group of seventh graders by Method A and a group of fourth graders by Method B. The researcher gives the same reading comprehension test to both groups of students after a given period of instruction and not surprisingly finds that the students taught by Method A performed significantly better than those taught by Method B. There is no doubt that the findings of the study are statistically significant. However, it would be ridiculous to conclude that the results of the study show that Method A is superior to Method B. The research question addressed in the study was not whether Method A is superior to Method B, which is the question the researcher claims to have been asking, but rather whether seventh graders taught by Method A perform better than fourth graders taught by Method B.

The findings of the study do not tell us if Method A is superior to Method B. For that matter, the results of the study do not tell us whether seventh graders are better readers than fourth graders, although such a conclusion seems intuitively appealing. It may indeed be true that seventh graders read better, but the study provides no evidence that this is so. If we wanted empirical evidence about whether seventh graders read better than fourth graders, we would have to carry out a study in which both groups of students were taught by the same method. In the design of the current study the variables of grade level and method of instruction are confounded. Both groups exhibit different values of both variables.

Random Assignment and Causality

Random assignment to groups is critical because it is the only method available to us to increase the likelihood that the groups of subjects in a study are comparable in every way except with respect to the independent variable. Random assignment permits us to rule out the possibility that variables other than the one the researcher has manipulated have caused the performance of two groups to be different.

It might occur to you that no two groups of subjects can ever be exactly alike, and that is undoubtedly true. However, the process of random assignment permits us to establish groups that are as alike as possible. It might also occur to you that if one wants to see, for example, whether a particular method of instruction is a good way to teach reading, one could first administer a reading test to a group of students, then begin teaching reading to the students by means of the method one is interested in, and finally readminister the same reading test. (See Design 2 on page 290.) If students' performance on the second test is significantly better than on the first test, one would know that it was the new method that caused the students' reading performance to increase.

The previous procedure might seem particularly appealing because there can be no question as to whether the scores from the two tests came from comparable groups of students; they came from exactly the same students. The problem with such a procedure is that even if the scores on the second test are much higher than those on the first test, one still has no way of knowing if the new method caused the difference in the two sets of scores. All kinds of things may have occurred between the first time the test was administered and the second time that could account for the increase in scores.

Suppose the study had been carried out with second graders who were tested in September and then retested in June. The very fact that the students are nine months older might account for the improvement in reading scores. Suppose that in September a new school librarian was hired who uses a great deal of creativity and imagination in setting up the library in such a way that students love going there and spend lots of time doing all sorts of reading. It may be the increase in the time students spend reading, for which the librarian is responsible, that accounts for dramatic gains in reading scores. The teacher's new method of teaching reading may have nothing to do with performance gains.

There are countless things that can intervene between the pretest and the posttest that might account for any difference in the two sets of scores. The only way to counteract the possible effects of other factors is to establish two groups, one of which receives instruction by the new method and one of which receives instruction by some other method. In this way, for example, any effect on reading scores that may occur because the students are nine months older would appear in both groups. We would know if the students who are taught by the new method score higher than the students taught by some other method, the difference is not due to the fact that the students are older, because both groups of students are nine months older. Similarly, if a new librarian had been hired, both groups would have been equally affected, and we would know that any difference between the groups' scores could not have been caused by something the librarian had done.

Experimental and Control (or Comparison) Groups. In an experiment there must be at least two groups that are comparable except with respect to the independent variable.

Often the groups in an experiment are referred to, respectively, as the **experimental group** and the **control (or comparison) group.** If, for example, a researcher wants to determine whether students who work with materials in a mathematics laboratory perform significantly better than students who receive only textbook instruction, the laboratory group would typically be called the experimental group and the textbook group would be called the control group.

Sometimes, however, each group serves as a control group for the other group. For example, suppose a researcher wants to test the relative effectiveness of two new methods of instruction. If the researcher does not indicate which method should be better but predicts only that there will be a significant difference in performance between students taught by the two methods, Group A serves as a control for Group B, and Group B simultaneously serves as a control for Group A. If the researcher, however, had predicted that students taught by Method A would perform significantly better than students taught by Method B, Group A is typically referred to as the experimental group and Group B as the control group. The major point is that an experiment must consist of at least two groups of subjects who have been randomly assigned to the groups.

Problems with Random Assignment

There are two problems with the process of random assignment. The first problem is that some variables are simply not amenable to random assignment. In the nursery school example given earlier, it would not be feasible to randomly assign children to attend nursery school or not to attend nursery school. How do you think parents would react if a researcher told them that, to find out if nursery school attendance improves the reading of first graders, half of the parents' children would be forced to attend nursery school and the other half would not be allowed to attend?

Suppose a researcher is interested in finding out if intelligence causes people to have more positive self-concepts. It is simply impossible for a researcher to randomly assign people to different levels of intelligence and then see if their self-concepts differ. Intelligence is not a variable like method of instruction, where people can be assigned to one type or the other. People come to the researcher with their levels of intelligence already established.

There are numerous variables that are of interest to educational researchers to which groups of people cannot be randomly assigned, either because of logical or practical reasons. Researchers cannot hope to find out the cause-and-effect relationships of such variables. The most one can do is to ascertain to what extent the variables are related by carrying out an ex post facto study.

The second problem with random assignment is that it works best when the number of people participating in a study is relatively large. Suppose we know that girls tend to read better than boys. Consequently, we would not want all girls to be taught by Method A and all boys to be taught by Method B. If such were the case and the results of the study showed that students taught by Method A performed significantly better than students taught by Method B, we would not know if the outcome demonstrates that Method A is better than Method B or merely reflects the fact that girls read better than boys. In this example, the gender of the student is a confounding variable. We are interested in examining possible differences in the effects of two instructional methods, but the groups differ with respect to gender as well as method of instruction.

If 1,000 students participated in a study—500 boys and 500 girls—it is likely that by randomly pulling students' names out of a hat, each instructional group would end up with approximately 250 students of each gender. As a result, the study's findings would not be confounded by the variable of gender. However, if we had only eight students participating in the study, four of whom were boys and four of whom were girls, it is certainly conceivable that randomly drawing the names of the students could result in the assignment of all four girls to one method and all four boys to the other, thus ensuring confounded results.

The fact that random assignment may not work so well with small groups is not particularly serious because randomly pulling names from a hat is not the only way by which to carry out the process of random assignment. One obvious way out of the dilemma is to use two hats, one containing girls' names and the other containing boys' names, and randomly assigning students to the two instructional methods by pulling names from both hats. Such a procedure would guarantee that half of the students of each gender would be taught by each method.

However, gender is only one of many potential confounding variables, most of which we may be totally unaware of. When there are few people participating in a study, the possibility of confounding looms large. Fortunately, there are various methods available for handling the random assignment of small groups. They will be presented later.

Random Assignment and Sample Size

The process of random assignment has previously been illustrated with the example of placing names in a hat and assigning people to groups by randomly drawing the names. It has also been pointed out that this kind of simple random assignment works best when the samples are relatively large. If, for example, one is carrying out a study comparing two groups and each group contains at least 15 subjects, the process of simple random assignment is likely to yield two reasonably comparable groups. On the other hand, simple random assignment may not yield reasonably comparable groups if the number of subjects in each group is much less than 15.

Assignment by Matched Pairs

Simple random assignment is not the only randomization procedure available. There are other ways researchers use to assign subjects to groups that reduce the likelihood of obtaining noncomparable groups when the number of subjects is small. One commonly used procedure is called **matched pairs.**

To understand the rationale underlying the process of matched pairs, it is helpful to remember that a researcher is interested in determining at the conclusion of the experiment if the various groups of subjects differ with respect to the dependent variable. If the groups do in fact differ, the researcher wants to be able to conclude that it is the independent variable that has caused the difference. Consequently, it is most important in assigning subjects to groups that the groups be comparable with respect to the dependent variable before the experiment starts. In other words, if a researcher wants to compare two methods of reading instruction, while it would be nice if the two groups of subjects were comparable on all variables except the kind of reading instruction they receive, it is especially important that the two groups be comparable in terms of initial reading performance.

Reading performance is the dependent variable that the researcher is interested in. At the end of the experiment the researcher will examine the difference in the reading scores of the two groups, so it is particularly desirable for the two groups to have had comparable reading scores prior to receiving instruction by either method. If large groups of subjects are used in a study, simple random assignment is likely to yield groups that are comparable on all variables, including initial level of reading performance.

The Use of Matched Pairs with Small Samples. When working with small groups, researchers often use the process of matched pairs to make sure that the two groups are initially comparable on the dependent variable. For example, if a researcher is comparing two methods of teaching reading and has access only to a small number of subjects, before the researcher starts the experiment the students in the study would be given a reading test. In fact, the students would probably be given the same test that they will be given at the end of the experiment. In other words, the same reading test may be given once as a **pretest** and again as a **posttest.**

The purpose of giving the reading test as a pretest is to enable the researcher to determine the level of reading performance currently exhibited by the students. Once the students' current level of performance is known, one can form two groups of students with comparable reading levels. To select two such groups, the process of matched pairs is used.

The first thing one does in using matched pairs is to rank the subjects in terms of their pretest scores. A list of subjects' names is prepared, beginning with the name of the subject who has the highest pretest score at the top all the way down to the name of the subject who has the lowest score. The researcher then takes the names of the subjects with the two highest scores and randomly assigns one of the subjects to Group A and the other subject to Group B. These two subjects constitute the first pair who have been matched on their pretest scores. Next the researcher takes the names of the subjects who ranked third and fourth on the pretest and randomly assigns one of them to Group A and the other to Group B. These subjects constitute the second matched pair. The researcher continues matching pairs of subjects on the basis of their pretest scores and randomly assigning each member of the pair to one of the two groups until all subjects have been assigned. (See Figure 14.2.)

Establishing Comparable Groups. It should be obvious that this kind of matching procedure is likely to yield two groups of subjects of equal size who have approximately the same average on the pretest and the same amount of variability in their scores. It is relatively unimportant if the two groups of subjects do not turn out to be comparable with respect to variables other than their initial level of reading performance. If it turns out, for example, that the students assigned to Group A have blue eyes and the students assigned to Group B have brown eyes, it only means that the variable of eye color is not correlated with reading level. There is no reason to be concerned about group differences on variables unrelated to reading performance. The important thing to understand is that if the two

Figure 14.2

The Use of Matched Pairs to Assign Students to Two Different Instructional Methods

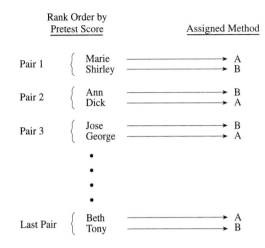

groups start at approximately the same reading level, any difference in their reading performance at the end of the experiment is most likely to have been caused by the method of reading instruction used.

The Function of Pretest and Posttest Scores. At the end of the experiment the researcher will have pretest and posttest scores for both groups of subjects. To analyze the data from the study, the researcher needs only to determine if the average posttest scores of the two groups are significantly different. The pretest is used solely for establishing comparable groups by means of matched pairs. Once the groups have been formed, the pretest scores are of no further interest. The function of the posttest is to enable one to find out if one method of reading instruction is superior to the other. The functions of the pretest and the posttest are different. The pretest is used to establish comparable groups, and the posttest is used to determine if the independent variable has caused changes in the dependent variable.

Students who use the process of matched pairs in their own research projects sometimes feel that, to determine if one group improved significantly more than the other group, it is necessary to examine the difference between the posttest scores and the pretest scores for each group. Such a procedure is unnecessary. If the two groups differ with respect to their posttest scores, we know that the group with the higher score improved more than the other group because both groups began at the same level of reading performance. Subtracting pretest scores from posttest scores is not only unnecessary, it is undesirable for a number of technical reasons. You do not have to worry about what these technical reasons are. Just remember that the use of "change scores" (i.e., the scores that result from subtracting the pretest scores from the posttest scores) should be avoided.

An Example of an Experiment, with Comments

Effects of Computer-Assisted Telecommunications on School Attendance   *a*

Carroll M. Helm
Walters State Community College

Charles W. Burkett
East Tennessee State University

ABSTRACT   The purpose of this study was to determine if selected students whose homes were called, using a computer-assisted telecommunications device, on days when they were not in school would show an expected difference in school attendance, compared with selected students whose homes were not called. We also compared students in the control group with students in experimental groups by race, sex, and socioeconomic level. The results of the year-long study revealed that students whose homes were called on days when they were absent, using the computer-assisted telecommunication device, showed higher subsequent attendance rates than did students whose homes were not called.

The purpose of this study was to determine if selected students who were absent from school and who received calls to their homes from the principal, via a computer message device, would have a better school attendance record than would students whose homes were not called.

We expected that students who were absent on a particular day, and whose homes were called by a programmed computer device, would have better attendance records than would students whose homes were not called. It was also anticipated that there would be improved school attendance by students of differing sexes, races, and socioeconomic levels whose homes were called when they were absent from school when compared with the attendance of those whose homes were not called. Finally, we expected that no difference in attendance among the three schools would result when we compared the experimental groups with the control groups.

This study is important for at least two reasons. First, school absence is one of the first indications that a student will eventually drop out of school if no action is taken. Second, in most states, school funding is received from the state based on average daily attendance; therefore, poor school attendance decreases school revenue.

The subject of parent notification of student absenteeism and its effect on subsequent attendance patterns has not received much attention in the literature to date. Although Butler (1925) authored one   *b* of the first truancy-related studies in the United States, little research has been done since that time. One of the first studies relating to school-parent involvement and its effect on attendance was completed by Copeland, Brown, Axelrod, and Hall (1972). By telephoning the parents of absent students, school officials achieved a significant increase in attendance.

Other studies (Fiordaliso, Largeness, Filipczak, & Friedman, 1977; Sheats & Dunkleberger, 1979)   *c* concluded that a well-formulated plan of school-initiated contacts to parents of chronically absent students offers the school a means of achieving a significant reduction in absenteeism. Bittle (1976) completed two studies that initially used a recorded message by school officials to keep parents informed of their child's academic performance and attendance record. Bittle concluded that telephone communication between parents and school administrators was an effective way of reducing student absenteeism but that individual telephone contacts could be a time-consuming process.

d   The first study to use a computer dialing device to monitor school attendance was conducted by McDonald (1986). McDonald found that a strong and positive relationship existed between the variables of parent notification and improved school attendance. He also found that students of families receiving computer calls showed a higher rate of attendance than students receiving personal calls or

e no calls. Poor school attendance has been referred to as a "red flag" or indicator that students are undergoing a crisis (Sargent, 1985). If a computer-assisted telecommunications device could increase average daily attendance and if the device could save valuable administrative time, then administrators would have a tool for helping students and the schools.

Method

We selected participants for the study from two high schools and one middle school in Hamblen County, Tennessee. Fifty students were selected from each school to serve in the control group. We chose these 150 students at the beginning of the school year by using a simple random sample technique. No calls were made to the homes of the students who were absent in the control group. A second sample for the experimental group was drawn. We followed the same procedure for selecting the sample for this group as for the control group and selected 150 students, 50 from each school. Each of these students was called at the end of the days that they were absent from school, using the automatic dialing device.

Procedures

We sent a letter to all of the participants' parents explaining that the schools were testing the effects of a computer dialing device and that their cooperation was needed. Parents who wished not to be called with the device were given that option. We tested the computer devices and then put them into operation in the first month of the school year. Secretaries or student workers keyed in the names of the students who were absent on a particular day. The device self-activated at 6:00 P.M. each school day and continued dialing until the home of each student, whose name was on the absentee list, was reached. When the telephone was answered at the home of the absent child, a prerecorded message from the principal was heard by whoever answered the telephone.

       A typical message might say:

This is Sam Horne, principal of Powell Valley High School. Our records indicate that your child missed school today. If we are in error, or if you have any questions or comments about this absence, please call Mr. Bewley from 9:00 A.M. until 11:00 A.M. tomorrow. Thank you.

       The computer dialing device generated a daily list of who was called and of who was reached or not reached by the computer dialing device.

       Data collection took place after the eighth month of the school year (May, 1987). A computer-generated record of each student's attendance was taken from the Tennessee Register Program (a computer attendance software package developed for the schools by the state of Tennessee). The two data screens contained all the information necessary to make the analysis. A report was generated from the computer telecommunications program that summarized the daily activity by the automatic

f calling device. We used this information to determine what percentage of student homes called were actually reached by the computer dialing device. Then we gathered and analyzed the attendance data on the control and experimental groups and compared the attendance records.

Table 1		Comparison of Attendance of Students Whose Homes Were Called With the Computer Device and Students Whose Homes Were Not Called		
Group	N	Mean days absent	SD	Difference
Called	147	6.55	3.38	3.38
Not called	127	11.18	11.69	

Note. t = 3.0009. *df* = 272. *p* < .05. Required *t* value = 1.645.

Data Analysis

We postulated the hypotheses and statistically tested the null form of each. The *t* test for independent samples was used to determine expected differences in hypothesis 1. We also used four factorial ANOVAs to determine the interaction among the mediating variables of sex, race, socioeconomic level, and schools in hypotheses 2, 3, 4 and 5. In all cases involving comparison, the minimum acceptable level for determining statistical significance was .05. The hypotheses and the results of the tests follow.

Results

Hypothesis 1 stated:

There are no differences in attendance between students whose homes are called with the computer device and students whose homes are not called.

The data testing hypothesis 1 are presented in Table 1.

Those students who were called by the calling device had better attendance records than did those who were not called. The findings in Table 1 show, without exception, that the attendance of students whose homes were called each day was greatly improved. Therefore, the expectations associated with hypothesis 1 were supported by these findings.

Hypothesis 2 stated:

Students whose homes are called on days that they are absent from school show better attendance records than do students who are not called, when the students are sorted and compared by sex.

The comparisons displayed in Table 2 show that the calls to the homes made a difference in attendance records. The sex of the students who were called or not called made no difference. The main effect that we tested was whether there would be a difference between the attendance of students who were absent on a particular day and whose homes were called on that day and that of students who were not called. The ANOVA test for differences between and within students who were not called showed that when the sex of students was taken into account the main effect (whether the students were called or not called) was the only significant effect.

Hypothesis 3 stated:

Students whose homes are called on the days they are absent do not have a better attendance record than do those not called when the students are sorted and compared by the socioeconomic level of their families.

The data testing hypothesis 3 are presented in Table 3. The socioeconomic levels of the students had no bearing on attendance. Students whose homes were called had better attendance regardless of their socioeconomic levels. The ANOVA showed that there were no significant interactions between or within students' attendance based on the socioeconomic levels. This proved true when we compared the attendance records of students from low-socioeconomic levels who were called versus students

Table 2

Table 2	Comparison of Attendance by Sex of Students Whose Homes Were Called With the Computer and Students Not Called

Source of variation	SS	df	MS	F	Significance of F
Treatment	567.93	1	567.93	8.14	0.0049
Sex	180.47	1	180.47	2.59	0.1048
Interaction	31.74	1	31.74	< 1.00	0.5077
Residual	18690.32	268	69.74		
Total	20281.64	271	71.84		

Table 3	Comparison of Attendance of Students Whose Homes Were Called With the Computer and Students Whose Homes Were Not Called, by Socioeconomic Level

Source of variation	SS	df	MS	F	Significance of F
Treatment	718.51	1	718.51	8.10	0.0050
Socioeconomic	182.49	1	182.49	2.06	0.1489
Interaction	181.06	1	181.46	2.04	0.1505
Residual	23962.50	270	88.75		
Total	25045.02	273	91.7		

from low-socioeconomic levels who were not called; students from high-socioeconomic levels who were called versus students from high-socioeconomic levels who were not called; students from high-socioeconomic levels who were called versus students of low-socioeconomic levels who were not called, and vice versa. The only significant effect occurred between students who were called and those not called.

Hypothesis 4 stated:

Students whose homes are called on days that they are absent do not have a greater attendance record than do those not called, when the students are sorted and compared by race.

The data for testing hypothesis 4 are presented in Table 4. Students whose homes were called had better attendance irrespective of their race. We compared student attendance records between White students called and White students not called, Black students called and Black students not called; White students called and Black students not called, and Black students called and White students not called. The ANOVA test showed that no significant interactions existed between or within students's attendance based on race.

Hypothesis 5 stated:

There is no difference in attendance among the three schools for students whose homes were called with the computer dialing device and students whose homes were not called.

Table 4

Comparison of Attendance of Students Whose Homes Were Called With the Computer Device and Students Whose Homes Were Not Called, by Race

Source of variation	SS	df	MS	F	Significance of F
Treatment	841.51	1	841.51	10.02	0.0021
Race	402.70	1	402.70	4.79	0.0276
Interaction	000.00	0	000.00	< 1.00	0.0000
Residual	22848.00	272	84.00		
Total	24092.82	274	87.93		

i

Table 5

Comparison of Attendance of Students Whose Homes Were Called With the Computer and Students Not Called, by School

Source of variation	SS	df	MS	F	Significance of F
Treatment	725.44	1	725.44	8.93	0.0034
Schools	425.92	2	212.96	2.62	0.0726
Interaction	247.00	2	123.50	1.52	0.2189
Residual	21853.56	269	81.24		
Total	23251.64	274	84.86		

The data testing hypothesis 5 are presented in Table 5.

No significant difference in attendance was found among the three schools for students whose homes were called with the computer dialing device or for students whose homes were not called. The comparisons displayed in Table 5 show that the calls to the homes made a difference in the attendance record but not in the school the student attended. The main effect (whether students were called or not called) was the only effect that was significantly different from chance findings. This finding indicated that students were similarly affected by the computer device at each school.

Discussion

The results of the present study indicated that students whose homes were called with a computer dialing device had a better overall attendance record than students who were not called. In every instance when students whose homes were called with the computer dialing device were compared with students whose homes were not called, we found a significant difference.

The computer dialing device evidently had the same effect on students in the three schools used in the study. This finding indicates that similar results could be obtained in areas similar to the one in which we conducted this study.

j

Brimm, Forgerty, and Sadler (1978) reported that principals cited student absenteeism as one of their primary concerns, along with a feeling that too much administrative time is allocated to attendance-related tasks (Brimm, et al.). The results of the present study suggest that both concerns could be alleviated in part by using a computer dialing device to combat the attendance problem. A computer dialing device not only saves valuable administrative time but also is proven to be an effective tool in increasing school attendance. Most school systems are funded based on a formula that takes into account the average daily attendance (ADA). By increasing the ADA, therefore, a school system could receive larger amounts of ADA funds. In addition to increased funding, principals would not have to use their valuable time making telephone calls to the homes of truants. Last, but not least, students ought to benefit from being in school regularly; but that is another study.

k

References

I

Bittle, R. (1975). Parent-teacher communication through recorded telephone messages. *Journal of Educational Research, 69,* 87–95.

Brimm, J., Forgerty, J., & Sadler, K. (1978). *Student absenteeism: A survey report.* National Association of Secondary School Principals, 65.

Butler, C. (1925). *School achievement and attendance.* School Review, 450–452.

Copeland, R., Brown, R., Axelrod, S., & Hall, V. (1972). Effects of a school principal praising parents for student attendance. *Educational Technology,* pp. 57–59.

Fiordaliso, R., Largeness, A., Filipczak, J., & Friedman, R. (1977). Effects of feedback on absenteeism in the junior high school. *Journal of Educational Research, 70,* 188–192.

McDonald, M. (1986). *A comparison of the effect of using computer calls and personal calls for improving pupil attendance in public schools.* Doctoral dissertation, University of Tennessee.

Sargent, E. (1985, April). On the road to the street. *The Washington Post,* pp. D1, D5.

Sheats, D., & Dunkleberger, G. (1979). A determination of the principal's effect in school initiated home contacts concerning attendance of elementary school students. *Journal of Educational Research, 72,* 310–312.

Address correspondence to Carroll M. Helm, Director, Walters State Community College, Greenvile Center, Route 3, Box 49, Greenville, TN 37743.

Comments

a   The title is somewhat vague in that it is not clear what the function was of telecommunications. A more informative title might be "Increasing attendance by placing computerized phone calls to homes of absent students."

b   Why is a reference made to the 1925 study by Butler? No information about the study is given that relates it to the current investigation.

c   Although the authors include references to some literature supporting their prediction that students whose homes were called would have better attendance records than students whose homes were not called, they present no rationale for hypothesizing differences in attendance records as a function of gender, race, or socioeconomic level. The authors' literature review deals with studies in which the parents of chronically absent students were contacted, but the subjects in their own study apparently were not chronically absent. Also, it is not clear if parents actually received the phone message because it was heard by whoever first answered the phone.

d   The authors note that McDonald (1986) found that students whose families received computer calls had better attendance records than students whose families received personal calls, but no explanation is given for this finding. (Is it possible that the principal's voice was used on the computer call and that someone with less authority than the principal made the personal calls?) The finding deserves more attention because it is especially relevant to the current study, which argues that the use of computer calls can save administrative time.

e   The authors claim that "school absence is one of the first indications that a student will eventually drop out of school if no action is taken," which may be correct, but they offer no evidence that this is so. They only point out that Sargent (1985) has noted that poor attendance is an "indicator that students are undergoing a crisis."

f   The authors claim they determined "what percentage of student homes called were actually reached by the computer dialing device," but the reader is never given the percentage.

Quasi-Experiments

All the procedures described so far for assigning subjects to groups are based on the assumption that it is possible to assign individual subjects to the various groups. However, much educational research is carried out in institutional settings, where frequently it is not feasible for the researcher to assign subjects individually. Often administrative procedures at the institution make it virtually impossible for a researcher to regroup people on an individual basis without disrupting institutional routine.

Consider again the case of a researcher who wishes to compare the relative effectiveness of two methods of reading instruction. It is likely that such a study would be carried out in a school, where students in one class would be taught by Method A and students in another class would be taught by Method B. It is also likely that the researcher would be forced to work with intact groups. The students who will be taught by Method A have already been assigned to one classroom and the students by Method B to another classroom.

Ideally, the researcher would like to be able to put the names of all the students from both classrooms in a hat and randomly assign half the students to Group A and the other half to Group B. The problem with that, however, is that the students assigned to each method would come from both classrooms. It would probably be disruptive for the students to have to be regrouped during part of the day in order to take part in the study. Consequently, the researcher may have to design the study so that it is not necessary for some of the students to change classrooms.

Random Assignment of Intact Groups

The only form of random assignment available to the researcher is to flip a coin to decide which classroom will be instructed by Method A and which by Method B. Studies in which a researcher can only randomly assign groups of subjects rather than individual subjects are called **quasi-experiments.**

Because the researcher cannot assign individual students to the two groups, there is no way of knowing if the two groups are initially comparable with respect to current reading level. Even in schools where it is claimed that students in classrooms are heterogeneously grouped, the students in the two classrooms still may not be comparable in terms of reading performance. There are often many factors that account for the assignment of some students to one classroom rather than another. For example, it may be known that certain teachers are particularly adept at dealing with certain kinds of disruptive students, and an effort is consequently made to assign those students to the teachers who are most likely to be effective with them. It may also be that disruptive students tend to be poorer readers than nondisruptive students.

Also the process of assigning students to classes by computer that is sometimes used in secondary schools can result in groups of students who differ markedly from class to class. For example, the class schedules of foreign language students might cause these students to be assigned to different English classes than nonlanguage students. The former may exhibit numerous characteristics that are different from the latter, and these differences may influence the outcome of a research study comparing the two groups.

If, for example, two such English classes were used in a study comparing different ways of teaching English, one might expect the foreign language students already to be better performers in English than those not studying a foreign language. Consequently, the study would yield inaccurate information about the relative effectiveness of teaching methods because the different methods would be confounded with different levels of English performance. Without evidence about subjects' performance in English prior to the start of the experiment, the researcher is likely to make an erroneous conclusion concerning the relative effectiveness of the different methods of instruction.

Usually researchers who are forced to use a quasi-experimental design administer a pretest before the study begins. This is to determine if the intact groups that are to be assigned to different values of the independent variable (e.g., ''method of instruction'') already differ with respect to the dependent variable (e.g., ''reading comprehension'') or some variable related to the dependent variable (e.g., ''vocabulary scores'').

At the conclusion of the study, students would take a reading comprehension posttest. It is not necessary for the pretest and the posttest to be exactly the same test, but that is often the case. The pretest scores could be examined to see if the average scores of the two groups differ. If they do, students' posttest scores can be adjusted to take initial differences into account.

Problems Associated with Pretests

The only procedure for assigning subjects to groups that does not involve the use of a pretest is simple random assignment, which is used in experiments when large numbers of subjects are available. One might be tempted to wonder why pretests are not administered to groups just because the groups have been formed by simple random assignment. One might even be tempted to conclude that, if pretests were given, one could check to see if the process of simple random assignment really did yield groups that are comparable with respect to the dependent variable.

Sometimes researchers do administer pretests to groups that have been formed by simple random assignment. However, when this is done, the researcher often includes more than one control group in order to determine whether the pretest itself had any effect on posttest scores.

The biggest problem with administering pretests is the possibility that a subject's performance on the posttest will be affected simply because the subject has already been administered the pretest. Subjects who have taken a pretest are different from those who have not. If subjects are able to remember some of the items from the pretest, their performance on the posttest may improve because of their memories rather than because of any experimental treatment. Perhaps subjects who have taken the pretest will react differently to the experimental procedures used in the study than those who have not taken it.

Suppose, for example, that students have been placed by simple random assignment into two groups to determine the effect of using a film to teach a science lesson. Let us assume that one group is to be shown a film demonstrating some scientific procedure and the other group is to be given a lecture on the same scientific procedure. Suppose too that both groups have been given a pretest consisting of questions dealing with the scientific procedure to which they are shortly going to be exposed. The very fact that the students have been administered the pretest might cause them to attend more carefully to certain parts of the procedure than others, because they have just tried to answer questions pertaining to those parts of the procedure.

Measuring Changes in Attitudes

Possible effects of pretesting are particularly troublesome in studies examining ways to change people's attitudes. Perhaps a researcher is interested in finding out whether a workshop for teachers in which various kinds of problems encountered by disabled students are discussed will cause teachers to have more positive attitudes toward disabled students. If prior to the workshop teachers fill out a questionnaire concerning their attitudes toward disabled students, teachers may be sensitized to the kinds of things taking place in the workshop, and the effects of the workshop may be more dramatic than if the teachers had not first been exposed to the questionnaire.

In determining if taking an attitude pretest has any effect on posttest attitude scores, it would be necessary for the researcher to use the Solomon Four-Group design in randomly assigning subjects to the following four groups:

Group A	Pretest	Workshop	Posttest
Group B	Pretest	—	Posttest
Group C	—	Workshop	Posttest
Group D	—	—	Posttest

By comparing the mean posttest scores of Groups B and D, the researcher would be able to determine if the pretest itself is affecting posttest scores. A comparison of the posttest scores of Groups C and D would reveal effects associated only with the workshop. The combined effects of the pretest and the workshop would be determined by comparing the mean posttest scores of Groups A and D.

The Hawthorne Effect

A researcher's major concern in carrying out an experiment or quasi-experiment is to follow procedures that make it possible to conclude that any change in a dependent variable is due to the independent variable and not to some other variable or set of variables. The bulk of this chapter has dealt with procedures for randomly assigning subjects to groups in an experiment because random assignment is the only method available to researchers to try to eliminate sources of confounding arising from groups of subjects who are not comparable. However, as we have seen in the section dealing with the problems of pretests, there are sources of confounding that have to do with aspects of an experiment other than the assignment of subjects to various groups.

Of the many possible sources of confounding, we will focus for the moment on the one known as the **Hawthorne effect.** The Hawthorne effect is of particular concern in studies comparing various methods of instruction, and the research literature in education contains many such studies.

The Hawthorne effect derives its name from the name of a Western Electric plant, where in the 1920s a study was carried out to determine what kinds of changes in working conditions would increase productivity. The productivity of workers assigned to the experimental group was compared to that of workers in the control group. The control group workers continued to work under normal conditions, but the working conditions of the workers in the experimental group were changed from time to time to see how the change affected worker output. The results of the study showed that the productivity of the workers in the experimental group was always superior to that of the workers in the control group regardless of how the working conditions were altered.

For example, if the level of illumination was increased, the experimental workers' productivity increased. Surprisingly, if the level of illumination was decreased, the experimental workers' productivity continued to increase. What seemed to account for the experimental group's superiority was the fact that they belonged to the experimental group and knew they were taking part in an experiment. Because the working conditions of the control group were not altered, workers in this group were not aware that they too were part of the experiment.

Typically, when some new instructional technique is being investigated, all kinds of things happen to the students in the experimental group that normally do not occur, and the students may realize that they are receiving special treatment. The students may perform differently as a result of this realization rather than as a result of the new method of instruction.

The John Henry Effect

In opposition to the Hawthorne effect is the **John Henry effect,** in which subjects in the control group realize they are not receiving special treatment and consequently exert extra effort to perform better than subjects in the experimental group. The name of the effect comes from John Henry, a legendary black laborer in a North American ballad who died trying to outperform a steam hammer with his sledge hammer.

Controlling the Hawthorne and John Henry Effects

To try to control the Hawthorne and John Henry effects, researchers frequently involve subjects in the control group in such a way that these subjects too believe they are receiving special treatment. As a result, members of the experimental and control groups are unaware of the groups to which they belong. For example, if a researcher has chosen an experimental group of students to solve math problems with computers to see if math performance is increased, the researcher might have the control group work with computers for some other purpose, such as learning spelling words. By having both groups work with the computer, the novelty of using the computer should affect both groups in the same way. Any increase in math performance by the experimental group may be regarded as due to the use of the computer for solving math problems and not merely to the novelty of using a computer.

An Example of a Quasi-Experiment, with Comments

The Effects of Peer Evaluation on Attitude Toward Writing and Writing Fluency of Ninth Grade Students   *a*

Joyce Katstra
Stanley, Kansas

Nona Tollefson
Edwyna Gilbert
University of Kansas

ABSTRACT   The researchers hypothesized that peer evaluation as part of the writing process would lead to improved attitude toward writing and increased fluency in a sample of ninth grade students. Seven intact classrooms taught by three different teachers were randomly assigned to experimental and comparison groups so that each teacher had one class in each condition. Both experimental and comparison groups wrote a first draft of a paper. The experimental group received peer evaluation training and rewrote their papers based on assistance from their peer evaluation group. The control group rewrote their papers receiving assistance from the teacher only when they requested help. The subjects responded to two attitude instruments as pretest and posttest measures. A significant increase   *b* in positive attitudes toward writing was observed for the experimental group. Girls in both the experimental and comparison groups showed more positive attitudes toward writing than did boys at both pre- and posttesting. Writing fluency was measured by a count of words on pre- and post-treatment drafts. There was a decrease in word count from the first to the last draft for the experimental group.

Most students entering high school dislike writing. Although research indicates that "90% of all children come to school believing that they can write" (Calkins, 1983, p. 11), children apparently learn through years of public schooling that most of the time their written efforts are returned to them with many red markings. According to Elizabeth Haynes (1978), students from the early grades through high school write compositions "with the a priori knowledge that the correction of errors will follow" (p. 82). The childhood enthusiasm for writing is replaced by worry over form, margins, and making the story sound right. This kind of "word by word writing (worrying over mechanics, spelling, and form) probably destroys fluency" (Calkins, 1983, p. 33). As this destruction continues through each grade, the student eventually enters high school convinced that he or she cannot write and that he or she has nothing worthwhile to say.

Kirby and Liner (1981) suggest that educators can encourage written fluency by studying the way young children acquire oral language. The acquisition process for written expression and oral expression involves the same kind of synthesis. Young children enjoy producing oral language, and they experience many successes in the acquisition. Through the child's formative years, parents offer positive reinforcement, and the success rate for acquisition of oral language speaks for itself. The success rate for written expression, however, is not nearly so impressive. In fact, most students, although fluent talkers (Zoellner, 1969), have had so many discouraging experiences with writing by the time they reach high school that they have difficulty with written expression.

What seems to be most important in developing and maintaining fluency is the establishment of a climate of trust between student writer and evaluator. As teachers respond positively, "students who are scared of writing begin to increase the length of their efforts, and those puny six-to-ten lines of timid prose become longer and more forceful" (Beaven, 1977, p. 139). Honest, positive comments motivate students to write more.

Attitudes formed within a positive climate of trust and reinforcement are ones that encourage writing fluency. These attitudes can be enhanced through the use of peer groups. King (1979) concluded that "allowing time for peer interaction and formulation of ideas may result in better attitudes toward writing" (p. 18).

The peer group is a powerful motivator in a teenager's life. It is one that can be used positively to influence attitudes toward writing. As a student learns how to function within the peer evaluation group, she or he develops a sense of self. The student becomes accepted as an important part of the

c group as she or he helps others with their writing. Beaven (1977) suggests that "as the dynamics of the small group continue to work, peers develop a sense of trust, group inclusion, support and acceptance" (p. 152). This translates into a positive attitude toward the task at hand, writing. The peer evaluation group fulfills that need for affiliation and achievement that McClelland, Atkinson, Clark, and Lowell (1953) have identified as necessary for achievement motivation.

Research supports the observation that young people's judgments are influenced more by their peers than by their teachers (Campbell, 1964). Pierson (1967), in a study of 153 ninth graders, comments that "participants reported that the atmosphere of peer method classes was characterized by an *esprit de corps,* an enthusiasm, an independence of thought, and an amount of noise that were not evident in the conventional classes" (p. 85). It is this *esprit de corps* and enthusiasm that, in part, makes the peer group such an invaluable tool in the writing process. Alvina T. Burrows (1959) observed that "in classes in which stories are joyously shared, the pupils write more and better" (p. 21). Calkins (1983) found that the peer conference or evaluation was an ongoing process that began informally with the topic choice and continued through the writing process to a more formal extended

d evaluation when the draft was completed. Peer evaluations increase fluency and improve the writer's attitude toward writing. The most important others in a teenager's life are his or her peers. The peer evaluation group, therefore, provides powerful motivation.

The purpose of this study was to determine whether peer evaluation could improve attitudes

e toward writing and increase the writing fluency of ninth grade students. It was hypothesized that there would be a significant difference between ninth grade students who peer evaluate and students who do not peer evaluate on a measure of attitude toward writing and a measure of writing fluency.

Method

Subjects

The sample consisted of seven intact high school classes taught by three teachers (two female and one *f* male). The high school was located in a rapidly growing, white, suburban, upper-middle class neighborhood and enrolled approximately 1,450 students. A decision was made to include all ninth grade students (89 boys, 88 girls) enrolled in the English classes taught by the three teachers even though one teacher taught three classes of ninth grade students and the other teachers taught two sections of the ninth grade English class. Random assignment of classes to treatment was used to assign one class for each teacher to the comparison condition. The comparison group included 39 boys and 30 girls. Four classes, including 50 boys and 58 girls, were randomly assigned to the treatment condition. Each teacher had at least one class assigned to the treatment condition and one class assigned to the comparison condition.

Procedure

Prior to the study, a climate of trust was encouraged in each of the seven classes through journal *g* writing and personal writing that was shared between student and teacher and among students. A unit entitled "Understanding People Who Are Different from Us" furthered this sensitization. The unit included visiting with profoundly deaf students, reading *The Miracle Worker,* watching the film *Welcome Home, Jellybean,* and conducting a library search for information about famous people who had overcome disabilities.

Day 1. Two attitude instruments were administered to students in both groups. The teachers then read a model written assignment. Following this activity, students participated in a brainstorming activity on the topic for their personal narratives, "How I Overcame a Disability/Problem."

Day 2. After discussion of the criteria for the writing assignment, experimental and comparison groups responded in writing to a memory chain activity related to the writing topic. Students then wrote the first draft of a personal narrative. The number of words in the first draft was counted and recorded as the pretest measure of writing fluency.

Days 3–6. The treatment was introduced on day 3 and was conducted over a 4-day period. The *h* experimental group received instruction in peer evaluation of content and mechanics. The teacher *i* modeled what should happen in the peer evaluation groups, giving students confidence for the task. The students then participated in the peer evaluation writing activities.

For each day the experimental group was involved with peer evaluation, the comparison group worked on the second draft. Students received help from the teacher based on specific student questions. The second drafts of both experimental and control groups were collected on day 6. The students *j* counted the number of words on the second draft and this became the posttest measure of writing fluency. Teachers administered the attitude instruments as posttests.

Instruments

Two attitude scales and a measure of writing fluency were used. The first attitude scale (Attitude I), *k* a 15-item questionnaire, was constructed specifically for this study, because review of existing instruments that assessed attitudes toward writing revealed no instruments that measured attitudes toward peer evaluation as a process. It included 12 positive and 3 negative statements about writing. Students *l* responded to the statements on a four-point Likert scale. Response options ranged from strongly agree to strongly disagree. The questionnaire assessed general attitudes toward writing and, more specifically, students' attitudes toward the peer evaluation process. Examples of the general attitude items are: I find writing is a pleasant task. I become frightened when I have to write. I enjoy writing letters. Examples of items assessing attitude toward the peer evaluation process are: I like to read my writing to small groups of my classmates. I like to read classmates' papers and offer advice. *m*

Content validity was established for this scale by the process of expert judgment. Three persons, an English teacher, a chairperson of an English department, and a director of curriculum, all of whom had participated in the National Writing Project, reviewed the items for relevance. They also classified the items as assessing either general attitudes toward writing or specific attitudes toward peer evaluation. All items included in the final form of the scale were judged to be content valid. Further validity evidence was obtained by administering the scale to four classes of sophomore English and assessing the social desirability of the items. All items included on the final scale had item means in the mid-range of the scale and standard deviations of about 1.0.

The Emig-King Writing Attitude Scale for Students (WASS) (Emig & King, 1979) was also administered. This 40-item questionnaire is divided into three clusters: preference for writing, perception of writing, and process of writing. Students respond to a five-point Likert scale ranging from almost always to almost never. The WASS was developed for use in the New Jersey Writing Project and data are available from 25 teachers and 1,600 students who participated in the initial study. It has internal consistency reliability coefficients (coefficients alpha) in the .60 to .72 range (Emig & King). The WASS was selected as a second attitude measure because it had been designed specifically for use with junior and senior high school students.

Writing fluency was measured by a count of words on pre- and posttreatment drafts of the writing task. Although number of words does not necessarily equal quality of writing, it does represent an accomplishment for students who have not been fluent writers. Fluency is a first step in improving the quality of writing, and for this reason, it was selected as an outcome measure. As the objective of the peer evaluation treatment was to change attitudes and to increase fluency, a measure of quality of writing was not used as an outcome measure.

Data Analysis

Data were analyzed using analysis of covariance (ANCOVA) procedures. Separate analyses were conducted for each dependent variable. The design was a $3 \times 2 \times 2$ factorial design with three covariates. Independent variables were (a) teachers, three levels, (b) sex of student, two levels, and (c) treatment condition, two levels (experimental and comparison). Covariates were scores on standardized vocabulary and reading comprehension tests and the pretest measure for the dependent variable used in data analysis. All main effects and interactions were tested, and alpha was set at .05.

Results

The $3 \times 2 \times 2$ ANCOVA for the Attitude I scale showed a significant three-way interaction., $F(2, 155) = 3.25$, $p < .05$, a significant two-way interaction, teacher by sex, $F(5, 1550) = 4.84$, $p < .05$, and significant main effects for sex, $F(1, 155) = 24.54$, $p < .05$ and group, $F(1, 155) = 6.80$, $p < .05$. Two covariates were also significant: Vocabulary, $F(1, 155) = 5.07$, $p < .05$ and Pre-Attitude I, $F(1, 155) = 318.29$, $p < .05$. Table 1 reports posttest means and standard deviations for this attitude scale.

The three-way interaction between teacher, sex, and group indicated that boys and girls in the experimental groups of Teacher 1 and Teacher 3 had significantly higher mean scores on Attitude I than did boys and girls in the comparison groups taught by these teachers. The opposite pattern was observed for Teacher 2, where boy and girl students in the comparison groups had higher mean scores than boy and girl students in the experimental groups. The two-way interaction between teacher and sex showed girls had significantly higher mean attitude scores than boys for all three teachers. Figure 1 depicts this significant two-way interaction. Overall, the experimental groups had a significantly higher mean posttest attitude score ($M = 38.45$) than the comparison groups ($M = 36.47$), and girls had a significantly higher mean score than boys.

Table 1 — Posttest Means and Standard Deviations for Attitude I Scores

Instructor		Experimental		Control	
		M	*SD*	*M*	*SD*
Teacher 1	Boys	40.22	6.22	33.50	9.85
	Girls	40.00	5.37	38.75	4.56
Teacher 2	Boys	34.73	5.69	35.47	6.07
	Girls	40.83	5.75	41.86	6.84
Teacher 3	Boys	34.42	5.00	31.93	6.87
	Girls	41.48	4.85	39.50	6.00

Figure 1 — Post Attitude I Means for Teachers/Sex Interaction

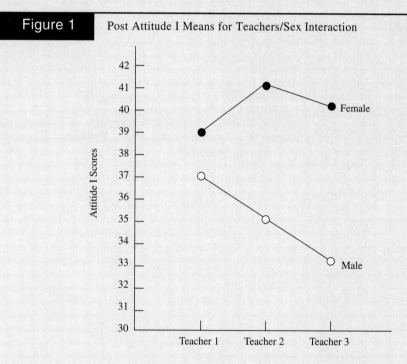

The analysis for Attitude II (WASS) also showed a significant three-way interaction between teacher, sex, and group, $F(2, 169) = 4.94$, $p < .05$. The pretest attitude measure was the only significant covariate in this analysis, $F(1, 155) = 273.27$, $p < .05$. Table 2 reports the posttest means and standard deviations for the WASS. Data in Table 2 show that boys taught by Teacher 1 had a higher mean attitude score than girls taught by this teacher. The opposite pattern (higher posttest mean attitude scores for girls than for boys) was evident for Teachers 2 and 3.

𝒳

Table 2		Experimental		Control	

Posttest Means and Standard Deviations for Attitude II Scores

		Experimental		Control	
Instructor		M	SD	M	SD
Teacher 1	Boys	117.78	11.89	109.50	22.19
	Girls	111.41	15.35	107.88	9.89
Teacher 2	Boys	112.00	8.51	107.41	14.08
	Girls	106.33	11.12	127.43	13.30
Teacher 3	Boys	109.08	6.71	106.36	10.69
	Girls	111.93	13.23	112.00	11.62

Figure 2 Post Writing Fluency (Word Count) Means by Teacher for the Experimental and Control Groups

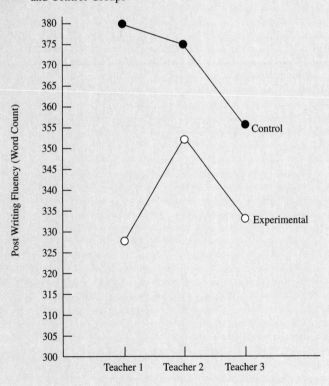

Writing fluency was analyzed by a $3 \times 2 \times 2$ ANCOVA using a count of words on the posttest as the dependent variable. There were no significant main effects or interactions at the prespecified alpha level of .05. The posttest count of words was consistently, though not significantly, lower for the experimental group than for the comparison group. Figure 2 depicts the posttest fluency score by teacher for the experimental and comparison groups.

bb1

Conclusions and Implications

The results of this study support the hypothesis that peer evaluation may be instrumental in improving attitudes toward writing. The experimental groups showed significantly more positive attitudes toward writing than did the comparison groups. Peer evaluation may be a place to begin rebuilding fragile attitudes toward writing.

Inspection of individual items on the Attitude 1 scale indicates that peer evaluation assisted in reducing the fear of writing. Students who peer evaluated reported more frequently than did students in the comparison groups that they liked to share their writing, that they liked to read classmates' papers and to offer advice, that they intended to rewrite, and that they thought their writing was improving. These findings suggest that writing teachers might use peer evaluation groups to develop positive attitudes toward writing.

The success of the peer evaluation procedures in changing attitudes was probably a function of three factors: (a) the time and effort devoted to establishing a climate of trust in the classroom, (b) the ground rules for student interaction, and (c) the composition of the group. The need to spend time developing trust and respect for others is paramount. The treatment that appeared to be short actually took several weeks to implement. The peer evaluation activities took place in an atmosphere that afforded respect. Ground rules specified that positive comments would be offered initially, suggestions for improvements would follow, and ''put-downs'' would not occur. Finally, the peer evaluation groups were constituted of students with heterogeneous writing abilities. This heterogeneity permitted all group members to profit from suggestions of knowledgeable peers.

The second major finding of this study was that girls had significantly more positive attitudes toward writing than did boys and that sex of student and sex of teacher interacted. Boy students taught by the male teacher had more positive attitudes toward writing than girl students taught by the male teacher. The opposite finding was observed for girl students taught by female teachers.

y

The strong sex effect in this study, although not hypothesized, merits further discussion. The data show that girl students as a group come into the writing classroom with more positive attitudes toward writing than do boys. These perhaps are attitudes unknowingly reinforced by female teachers. Girls in the experimental and comparison groups taught by the two female teachers in this study showed significantly more positive attitudes toward writing than did the boys in these classrooms. However, attitude scores of the boys in the experimental group taught by Teacher 1, a male, were almost the same as the attitude scores of the girls. These data seem to suggest that we as educators need to be aware of the conscious and unconscious signals that we may be giving students in the classroom. We need to be aware that boys come into the writing classroom with less positive attitudes (substantiated by pretest means), and perhaps they need extra encouragement as they approach the writing process. Students need to have strong male models in the English classroom who are sensitive about literature and who are excited about writing.

z

aa

Statistical results of this study do not support the hypothesis that peer evaluation will increase writing fluency. The decrease in word count on second drafts written by students in the experimental group suggests, however, that peer evaluation may lead to a tightening of writing. This is a step beyond fluency and a goal for all writers. Further research using both attitude measures and measures of writing quality is needed to determine whether peer evaluation procedures do improve the quality of writing.

bb2

Several factors need to be considered in interpreting the results of this study. The study employed a quasi-experimental design and used analysis of covariance to equalize pretest differences in *cc* experimental and control groups. Pretest attitudes were significantly related to posttest attitudes for both attitude measures; future researchers may want to introduce pretest attitude as an independent variable and test whether peer evaluation produces a differential effect for different levels of entry attitude toward writing.

This study was conducted in an affluent school district populated by students with well above average achievement scores. The results are probably best generalized to a similar school population.

This study found significant differences in posttest attitudes after a relatively short treatment. Future studies conducted over longer time periods would provide information about whether continued use of peer evaluation in a writing program would lead to greater changes in attitudes. It is hypothesized that continued success with peer evaluation would decrease fear of writing and would eventually make writing, if not a pleasant task, at least one that would not be avoided.

The peer evaluation procedures described in this study provide a way to improve attitudes toward writing and perhaps, if used early enough, to prevent negative attitudes from forming. Further research testing the appropriateness of this teaching/learning process with both junior high and senior high students would be worthwhile.

References

Beaven, M. H. (1977). Individualized goal setting, self evaluation, and peer evaluation. In C. R. Cooper & L. Odell (Eds.), *Evaluating writing* (pp. 135–153). Champaign, IL: National Council of Teachers of English.

Burrows, A. T. (1959). *Teaching composition.* Washington, DC: Department of Classroom Teachers, American Educational Research Association of the National Education Association.

Calkins, L. M. (1983). *Lessons from a child.* London: Exeter Heinemann Educational Books.

Campbell, J. (1964). Peer relations in childhood. In M. L. Hoffman & L. W. Hoffman (Eds.), *Review of child development research.* New York: Russel Sage Foundation.

Emig, J., & King, B. (1979). *Emig-King attitude scale for students.* New Brunswick, NJ: Rutgers University/Douglass College. (ERIC Document Reproduction Service No. ED 236 630)

Haynes, E. (1978). Using research in preparing to teach writing. *English Journal, 67,* 82–88.

King, B. (1979), *Measuring attitudes toward writing: The King construct scale.* Presented at the College Conference on Composition and Communication, Minneapolis, MN. (ERIC Document Reproduction Service No. ED 172 258)

Kirby, D., & Liner, T. (1981). *Inside out.* Montclair, NJ: Boyton Cook, Inc.

McClelland, D. C., Atkinson, J. W., Clark, R. A., & Lowell, E. L. (1953). *The achievement motive.* New York: Appleton-Century-Crofts.

Pierson, H. (1967). Peer and teacher correction: A comparison of the effects of two methods of teaching composition in grade nine English classes (Doctoral dissertation, New York University, 1967). *Dissertation Abstracts International, 28,* 4A.

Zoellner, R. (1969). Talk-write: A behavioral pedagogy for composition. *College English, 30,* 267–320.

Address correspondence to Nona Tollefson, University of Kansas, 2 Bailey, Lawrence, KS 66045.

Comments

a *The use of the term "writing fluency" is not an accurate description of the variable measured. It would have been more helpful to call the variable something else, for example, "number of written words."*

b *This implies that there were significant increases from pre- to posttest measures of attitudes, but the authors do not include pretest means or give the results of a statistical test of significance they presumably used.*

c *The authors offer no documented evidence that "this translates into a positive attitude toward the task at hand, writing." Small group dynamics may be beneficial in many ways, but there is no guarantee that one of the results is a* positive attitude toward the task the group is working on. There are many tasks that would probably continue to evoke negative attitudes from members of the group. Consider the numerous unpleasant tasks small groups of military recruits must perform during basic training, or worse yet, on the battlefield.

d There is no documentation for this assertion. If this assertion is already known to be true, one wonders why the researchers are carrying out their study because that seems to be exactly what they wish to find out.

e Given the nature of the introduction, one would expect the authors to state their hypotheses in directional, not nondirectional form.

f No further information is given about the teachers, such as how much teaching experience they had. It would seem important to point out other distinguishing characteristics of the teachers, especially because the findings of the study reveal significant interactions between teacher and sex of student and between teacher and treatment.

g What evidence is there that such a climate was in fact established or if it was equally well established in all seven classes?

h What did students in the experimental group actually do during the process of peer evaluation? How large were the groups? Was there more than one group in each class? Did all students participate actively? How long did peer evaluation take place each day?

i What evidence is there that the modeling procedure actually gave students confidence?

j The authors do not report if any students were absent during the study. Were the data from all students used regardless of how often they may have been absent?

k The authors developed the Attitude I scale because there were no "existing instruments . . . that measured attitudes toward peer evaluation as a process." The Attitude I scale, however, measured two things: "general attitudes toward writing" and "students' attitudes toward the peer evaluation process." Furthermore, the authors do not report how many of the 15 items measured "general attitudes toward writing" and how many measured "attitudes toward peer evaluation." No reliability information is given for the Attitude I scale.

l Why was the number of positively worded statements so much larger than the number of negatively worded statements?

m This sample item is poorly constructed because it measures two things: "liking to read classmates' papers" and "liking to offer advice." An item should only measure one thing.

n It is not clear what constitutes "content valid." Does it mean that all three judges had to agree that an item was valid before it was included or perhaps that two of three judges had to agree? The use of the term "final form" implies that there were preliminary forms of the Attitude I scale. It would be informative to know how many items from the preliminary version(s) were eliminated in developing the final form. It is not clear how the authors went about having four sophomore English classes rate the social desirability of each item on the Attitude I scale. Furthermore, the authors provide no information concerning the validity or reliability of the sophomores' responses.

o The authors provide no evidence that the Attitude I scale and the WASS were measuring different things. It would have been helpful if the authors had reported correlation coefficients between students' scores on both measures.

p The authors' rationale for not using a measure of quality of writing does not seem very compelling.

q Nothing in the review of literature addresses sex differences associated with students' attitudes toward writing or writing fluency, yet sex of student is included as a variable when the data are analyzed.

r It is unclear why the authors chose as covariates students' scores on a standardized vocabulary and reading comprehension tests in addition to the pretest measures of the dependent variables.

s This must be a printing error.

t The authors do not discuss the finding that the groups differed significantly on the vocabulary covariate or on the pretest measure of the Attitude I scale. Which group scored higher? Furthermore, if the F value of 318.29 for the pre-Attitude I scores is not a printing error, one can only wonder what accounts for such a large value.

u The authors' interpretation of the three-way interaction between teacher, sex of student, and group for Attitude I scores fails to show what role sex of student played in the interaction. It appears that the authors interpreted the three-way interaction as though it were a two-way interaction between teacher and group.

v *The authors seem to interpret the two-way interaction between teacher and sex of student for Attitude I scores as though it were a significant main effect for sex of student.*

w *On the Attitude I scale, the experimental group's mean is 1.98 points higher than the comparison group's mean. One wonders if a difference of about 2 points has much practical significance.*

x *The reported F value of 273.27 is extremely large. Is this another printing error? It is difficult to account for such a large difference, especially since the authors report that classes were randomly assigned to groups. The df of 169 must be a printing error. The authors' interpretation of the three-way interaction between teacher, sex of students, and group for WASS scores fails to show what role group played in the interaction. It appears that the authors interpreted the three-way interaction as though it were a two-way interaction between teacher and sex of student.*

y *This conclusion contradicts the authors' previously reported finding on the Attitude I scale: "The two-way interaction between teacher and sex showed girls had significantly higher mean attitude scores than boys for all three teachers." Furthermore, Table 2 shows that for Teacher 2 (a female) girls scored higher only in the control (i.e., comparison) group, not in the experimental group.*

z *The authors do not report the mean pretest scores or if the girls' more positive attitudes are significantly so.*

aa *This assertion appears true only for the Attitude I scale. The data in Table 2 show that the assertion is not true for the Attitude II (WASS) scale. Girls in the experimental group taught by Teacher 2 (a female) scored lower than boys, and the scores for boys and girls in the experimental group taught by Teacher 1 (a male) were less similar than the scores of boys and girls for the two female teachers.*

bb1 *Although the authors report that there was no significant difference in the number of words the experimental and comparison groups wrote on the posttest, they conclude that:*

bb2 *"peer evaluation may lead to a tightening of writing."*

cc *What data substantiate this claim?*

Statistical Analyses of Group Comparisons

The appropriate test of statistical significance to use to analyze data collected in an ex post facto study or an experiment is determined by several things: the number of groups in the study; the scale of measurement used to measure the variable to be analyzed; normality of distribution; and, in the case of experiments, whether the groups were formed by simple random assignment or by matched pairs. The most powerful and most frequently used tests are called *parametric* tests of statistical significance. Such tests may be used only when the data to be analyzed have equal units of measurement, such as raw scores on a test and are normally distributed.

If the data to be analyzed do not have equal units of measurement or if there is a marked departure from normality of distribution, *nonparametric* tests of statistical significance should be used (Siegel, 1956). When possible, it is desirable to use parametric rather than nonparametric tests because differences between groups are more likely to be detected.

Chapter Highlights

- There are three types of group comparisons which differ in terms of how the groups are formed.

- In an *ex post facto* design, the groups are already formed in terms of a variable of interest to the researcher; the researcher does *not* form the groups.

- It is incorrect to draw a causal inference from the findings obtained through the use of an ex post facto design.

- An experiment is said to have *internal validity* to the extent that changes in the dependent variable are caused by the independent variable and *not* to confounding variables.

- Threats to internal validity include:
  History: changes in the environment that may have occurred during the period between the pre- and posttest
  Maturation: biological or psychological changes that subjects may undergo during the period between the pre- and posttest
  Pretesting: the effects of taking a test upon the scores of a second testing
  Measuring instruments: changes that may occur in measuring instruments (or observers) between the pre- and posttest
  Statistical regression: the tendency of subjects who score extremely high or low on a pretest to score closer to the mean on a posttest
  Differential selection of subjects: biases that result because subjects in the experimental and control groups differ with respect to the dependent variable prior to the start of the experiment
  Experimental mortality: differential loss of subjects from the experimental and control groups during the course of the experiment
  Selection-maturation interaction: Groups that perform comparably on a pretest might exhibit characteristics unrelated to the experimental treatment that lead to better performance on the posttest.

- Pre-experimental designs that are not internally valid are:
  one-shot case study
  one-group pretest-posttest design
  static group comparison

- True experimental designs that are internally valid are:
  pretest-posttest control group design
  posttest-only control group design
  Solomon four-group design

- The nonequivalent control group design is a commonly used quasi-experimental design that is internally valid.

- External validity refers to the extent that the findings of an experiment are generalizable to other persons (population validity) or to other settings (ecological validity).

- The random assignment of subjects on an individual basis to the experimental and control groups makes it possible to draw cause-and-effect inferences from findings obtained by means of experiments.

- Assignment by matched pairs is used in experiments when samples are small; one member of each pair of subjects matched on pretest scores is randomly assigned to the experimental and the other member to the control group.

- In quasi-experiments, existing intact groups are randomly assigned to the experimental or control group.

- A major problem with the use of pretests is the possibility that having taken the pretest will affect subjects' performance on the posttest.
- The Hawthorne effect refers to increased performance by subjects because they are members of the experimental group.
- The John Henry effect refers to increased performance by subjects because they are members of the control group.
- Parametric statistical tests are more powerful than nonparametric tests but should be used only when the data to be analyzed have equal units of measurement and are normally distributed.

Review Exercises

1. Explain how experiments, quasi-experiments, and ex post facto studies differ. Give an example of each.
2. What kind of group comparison makes it possible for the researcher to determine if there is a causal relationship between variables?
3. How do researchers increase the likelihood that members of the experimental and control groups do not differ systematically on variables other than those being investigated?
4. Describe two ways to form an experimental and a control group.
5. Give an example of an experiment, noting the independent and dependent variables.
6. What function does the control group serve in an experiment?
7. Give an example of an experiment in which matched pairs would be used. In such an experiment, what is the function of the pretest? Of the posttest?
8. How does a quasi-experiment differ from an experiment?
9. Describe some of the problems resulting from the use of pretests.
10. Compare the Hawthorne and John Henry effects and explain how to control for both of them.
11. Describe the difference between internal and external validity.
12. Explain what the term *statistical regression* means.
13. Design a study that would permit a researcher to determine whether students using cooperative learning techniques have a more positive attitude toward learning than students not using such techniques.
14. List the factors that determine which test of statistical significance should be used to analyze data from a group comparison.
15. Describe the difference between parametric and nonparametric statistical tests.

Chapter 15

Single-Subject Research

The goal of single-subject research is to determine if altering the subject's environment causes the subject's behavior to change.

Chapter Objectives

After completing this chapter, you should be able to:

- define the term *time series design*
- explain how single-subject research differs from case studies
- define the terms *baseline* and *treatment conditions* and differentiate between them
- describe a *reversal* and *double reversal* design and explain under what circumstances each should be used
- explain how *multiple baselines* are used
- explain under what circumstances replication of a single-subject study is desirable

The fundamental objective of any group comparison is to determine if two or more groups exhibit statistically significant differences with respect to a variable. There are, however, situations in which it is appropriate to investigate possible changes in behavior of a single person over time. Such situations occur fairly frequently in special education, for example, where individualized instruction is emphasized, or in counseling, where counselors work with individual students. Single-subject research designs are particularly well suited for examining the effects of behavior modification techniques that special educators often use to try to alter the behavior of a single student.

Characteristics of Single-Subject Studies

Single-subject research involves multiple measurements of the behavior of a single individual at different points in time prior to, during, and following the use of some intervention designed to change the individual's behavior. Studies in which data are collected from the same individual (or a single group) at different points in time typically use one of several techniques often called **time series designs.** The objective of single-subject research is to determine if the intervention has significantly changed the behavior of the subject. The major difficulty with single-subject research is how to be certain that changes in behavior following intervention have been caused by the intervention and not by something else. Various ways of controlling possible sources of confounding are discussed in the following sections. See Cook and Campbell (1979) or Hersen and Barlow (1976) for comprehensive accounts of time series designs in single-subject research.

Single-subject research differs from case studies. Case studies typically involve the observation of a single individual in a naturalistic setting that permits the researcher to describe the results of the study in a qualitative way. No attempt is made in case studies to control any aspects of the environment in which the individual is being observed.

Single-subject research, on the other hand, involves the systematic collection of data over time (often in the form of observations) from an individual under environmental conditions that have purposely been altered in specific ways. The goal of single-subject research is to determine if altering the subject's environment causes the subject's behavior to change. Single-subject research is often used in situations where it is difficult to carry out a group comparison. For example, it would probably be exceedingly difficult to establish an experimental design comparing the behavior of groups of autistic children, although it would be feasible to carry out research with a single autistic child.

The use of time series designs need not be restricted to the study of a single individual. It is possible to use time series research designs to study changes in the behavior of a single group rather than a single individual. For example, changes in the average behavior of all students in a classroom may be studied over time as a function of systematic intervention.

Multiple Measurements over Time

One of the ways researchers using single-subject designs increase the likelihood of determining whether changes in the subject's behavior are a result of the intervention, rather than of some other unrelated factor that has simultaneously taken place, is to measure the subject's behavior at numerous points in time. The use of multiple measurements over time highlights a fundamental distinction between single-subject research and experimental group comparisons. An experiment always includes a control group that has not been exposed to the intervention. Single-subject research has no such control.

It is possible in an experiment comparing the behavior of *groups* of subjects to conclude that there is a causal relationship between variables by measuring subjects' behavior only once before the intervention (e.g., a pretest) and again only once after the intervention (e.g., a posttest). It is, however, necessary to make multiple measurements when a single subject is the object of study. In an experiment, causal relationships between variables can be determined with so few measurements because there is a control group. The lack of a control group makes it necessary to carry out multiple measurements in single-subject research.

To help clarify the need for multiple measurements in single-subject research, look at Figure 15.1, which illustrates three possible outcomes of a single-subject study. The three outcomes are decidedly different. However, if the subject's behavior had been measured only once prior to and once following the intervention (i.e., M-4 and M-5 respectively), in each case one would probably conclude that the change in the subject's behavior was in fact caused by the intervention.

By examining all eight measurements in each graph, however, it becomes clear that the change in behavior following the intervention was caused by the intervention only in Graph A. The shape of Graph B indicates that the behavior under investigation is fairly unstable and that the difference between the behaviors occurring at M-4 and M-5 is a typical fluctuation that has nothing to do with the intervention. Similarly, in Graph C it is clear that the frequency of the behavior under investigation was progressively increasing over time and that the increase measured between M-4 and M-5 is unrelated to the intervention.

Baseline and Treatment Conditions

Time series designs usually involve measuring the behavior to be studied several times, as it is occurring under normal circumstances, to determine how frequently the behavior typically occurs. These measurements constitute the **baseline condition** and serve as a bench mark against which to compare measurements made after the intervention. To establish a stable baseline, some researchers suggest that measurements continue during the baseline condition until the range in variation over a period of 10 consecutive observations is less than 5% of the mean. For example, if one is studying disruptive behavior and the mean number of occurrences is 20, one would continue to measure until the mean number of occurrences on 10 consecutive measurements ranged between 19 and 21 (i.e., 20 plus and minus 5% of 20).

To obtain a stable baseline, it may be necessary to increase the unit of time during which observations are made, particularly if the behavior being studied exhibits very much variability. Suppose a student engages in a great deal of disruptive behavior at some points during the day and relatively little at other points. In such a case, it may be impossible to establish a stable baseline if one uses the number of disruptions per hour as the baseline measurement. On the other hand, if the baseline measurement is changed to the number of disruptions per day, a more stable measurement can be obtained.

The unit of time used for each measurement during the baseline condition depends on the variability of the behavior being studied. Behaviors that are relatively stable may be measured in shorter time units, while more variable behaviors should be measured in longer time units.

Figure 15.1

Possible Outcomes of a Single-Subject Study with Intervention
Between Measurements 4 and 5

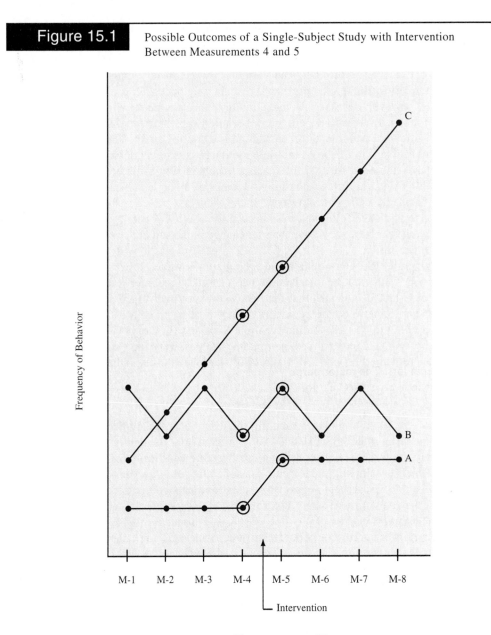

Measurements over Time

After a stable baseline has been established, intervention is applied and the **treatment condition** of the study begins. Measuring the behavior continues during the treatment condition. It is usually best to make the same number of measurements during the treatment condition as during the baseline condition. The time unit used during the treatment and baseline conditions should also be the same. Similarly, the same kind of measurement should be used during both conditions to avoid confounding. For example, if one set of observers was used during the baseline condition and another set during the treatment condition, one would not be sure if changes in behavior during the treatment condition were because of the intervention or of changes in the way observers recorded data.

Reversals and Double Reversals

There are two kinds of time series designs frequently used in single-subject research: reversals and double reversals. A **reversal** is sometimes referred to as an A-B-A design, where A represents measurements made during the baseline condition (i.e., when there is no intervention) and B represents measurements during the treatment condition. A **double reversal** is sometimes referred to as an A-B-A-B design, which differs from a reversal design only in that after the reversal has been completed, an additional set of measurements is made during a second treatment condition.

Figure 15.2 shows examples of an A-B-A and an A-B-A-B design used to study the effects on frequency of a student's participation in class discussion as a function of teacher praise. During the baseline conditions (A), the student's participation is not followed by teacher praise. During the treatment conditions (B), the teacher praises the student for participating in the class discussion. The decision to use a double reversal rather than a reversal design is often made on the basis of whether it would be ethically more appropriate to end the study during a treatment condition than during a baseline condition.

Time series designs may be used to determine the effect of the intervention both on increasing the frequency of desirable behaviors as well as on decreasing the frequency of undesirable behaviors. The major purpose of time series designs is to permit the researcher to determine whether a causal relationship exists between the intervention and the behavior being studied.

Multiple Baselines

Sometimes occasions arise where it is either undesirable or impossible to return to the baseline condition after the intervention has taken place. For example, it may be that the intervention causes a permanent change in behavior that continues even after the treatment condition has been concluded. In such a case it is difficult to know whether the intervention or some other factor caused the change in behavior because termination of the treatment condition does not result in a return to the frequency of behavior exhibited during the baseline condition.

One way to determine whether the intervention has a causal effect is to measure its effect on more than one behavior of the person being studied by introducing the intervention for the several behaviors in a staggered fashion. Such a procedure is called a **multiple-baseline** design. Suppose, for example, a teacher wants to see if the use of token reinforcers can improve a student's academic behavior. The teacher might decide to try to improve the following behaviors: on-task behavior during reading instruction; participation in class discussions; and number of completed homework assignments.

After a stable baseline has been obtained for all three target behaviors, the treatment condition is introduced only for on-task behavior during reading instruction. The baseline condition continues for the other two target behaviors. Later, while the treatment condition for on-task reading behavior continues, the treatment condition is introduced for participation in class discussions. The baseline continues only for the third target behavior. Finally, the treatment condition is introduced for handing in completed homework assignments, so that

Figure 15.2

Examples of Reversal and Double-Reversal Designs in Single-Subject Research

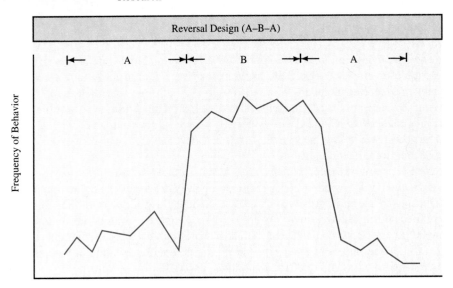

Reversal Design (A–B–A)

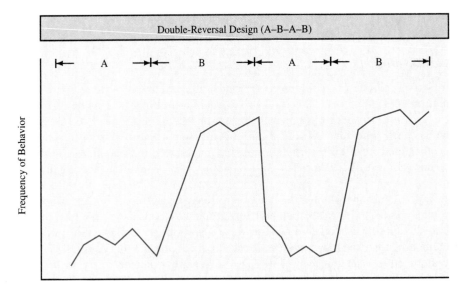

Double-Reversal Design (A–B–A–B)

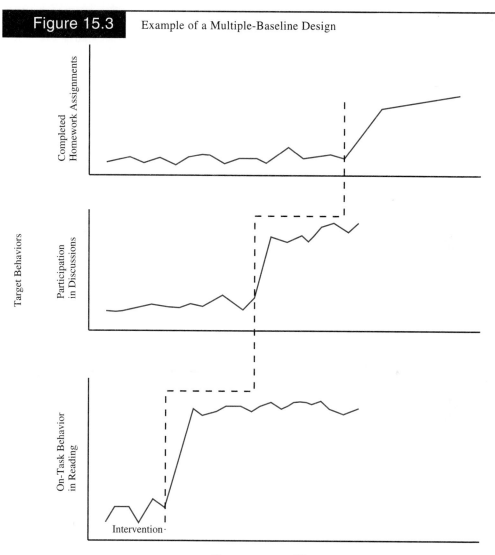

Figure 15.3   Example of a Multiple-Baseline Design

Target Behaviors

Completed Homework Assignments

Participation in Discussions

On-Task Behavior in Reading

Intervention

Measurements over Time

ultimately the treatment condition takes place for all three target behaviors simultaneously. (See Figure 15.3.)

If the treatment is causing the student's academic behavior to improve, the improvements in each target behavior should occur only *after* the intervention has been introduced. In other words, increases should first occur in on-task reading behavior, then in participation in class discussions, and finally in the number of completed homework assignments, as shown in Figure 15.3. If some factor other than the intervention had caused improvement in the target behaviors, one would detect the increase in participating in class discussions and in the number of completed homework assignments *before* the treatment condition had been introduced.

Replication

A multiple-baseline design is a replication of the intervention with the same individual under differing conditions (e.g., the different target behaviors shown in Figure 15.3). The double-reversal design is a replication of the intervention with the same individual under the same conditions. Even if one has no desire to generalize the findings of a study beyond the single subject who participated in it, replication is extremely useful in determining if the intervention has a causal effect.

If, on the other hand, one wishes to generalize the findings to persons who have not been studied, replication is essential. In such a case, the study should be replicated under the same conditions as those in the original study, but with a different individual.

An Example of Single-Subject Research, with Comments

A Self-Instructional Social Skills Training Program for Mentally Retarded Persons

Johnny L. Matson and Joyce Adkins

a   Abstract: A multiple baseline was employed across two mentally retarded institutionalized adults to test a self-instructional method of training social skills. Training consisted of having subjects listen to audiotapes in a small classroom. Following this, they reviewed material on appropriate social behavior covered on the audiotapes with a therapist, including rehearsal between the therapist and subject on appropriateness of responses. The treatment was found to be effective and saved staff time as compared to the standard method of social skills training.

Despite the importance of remediating social skills deficits among mentally retarded persons (Charles & McGrath, 1962; Gibson & Fields, 1970; Schalack & Harper, 1978), only recently have attempts been made to develop treatment procedures. A treatment package that has proven effective involves the use of instructions, performance feedback, modeling, role-rehearsal and social reinforcement. The procedure was modeled after procedures successfully used to treat assertion problems experienced by college students (McFall & Marston, 1970), and social skill deficits of chronic schizophrenics (Hersen & Bellack, 1976). The technology developed has proven useful for treating a wide range of social deficits of mentally retarded persons including eye contact, physical aggression, appropriate assertiveness (Matson & Stephens, 1978; Matson & Zeiss, 1979), and decreasing inappropriate verbal statements (Matson, 1979).

Despite the effectiveness of the treatment procedure it has, with only a few exceptions been employed on an individual basis with two therapists present. Additionally, training has usually been of 30 minutes duration and has been given on a daily basis. Although this manner of training may prove effective, the time commitment on the part of the therapist makes widespread implementation questionable. This is because a practical outcome for mental health systems would be fewer psychological services than can be provided using current social skill training methods.

Matson, J. L., & Adkins, J. (1980). A self-instructional social skills training program for mentally retarded persons. *Mental Retardation, 18*(5), 245–248. Used by permission of American Association on Mental Retardation, 1719 Kalomara Rd., NW, Washington, DC 20009.

The purpose of the present study was to test a self-instructional method of social skills training with mentally retarded persons based on the same training procedures as those described in earlier studies. The purpose was to provide a more time and cost efficient yet effective treatment procedure for remediating social skills deficits.

Method

Subjects

Persons selected for the study were Jane, a female, age 24, and George, a 29 year old male. Both were in the moderate range of mental retardation using American Association on Mental Deficiency (AAMD) criteria (Grossman, 1977). Subjects had been institutionalized continuously for more than 10 years and lacked rudimentary social skills such as how to carry on a conversation. Jane had had a history of extreme physical aggression while George had, on occasion, refused to participate in training activities but rarely *acted out.*

Target Behaviors

Behaviors selected for treatment were conversational skills on which subjects were particularly deficient. Target behaviors were designated as appropriate social interactions and inappropriate social interactions. Definitions of these target behaviors were as follows:

Appropriate Social Interactions. The subject initiates positive statements with others. Categories of appropriate social interactions included initiating conversations (makes a statement to another person that leads to a socially appropriate interchange), complimenting others (makes positive statement about someone), making appropriate requests (asking for a service or an item without offending others), or responds appropriately to requests (acknowledges and agrees to comply to reasonable requests made by others or acknowledges but declines to comply with unreasonable requests made by others).

Inappropriate Social Interactions. This target behavior was defined as any socially incorrect verbal statement (e.g., cursing, making unreasonable requests) or failure to respond verbally when socially appropriate (e.g., subject is greeted but fails to acknowledge the person greeting him). The same categories for appropriate social interactions were used; however, unlike the other target behavior, responses were scored whether or not the subject initiated the interaction.

Assessment

To assess the effectiveness of training in the natural environment, ratings were taken during leisure *h* time in the evening (7–8:30 P.M.). During observations, all subjects met in the recreation hall (10 × *b* 40 meters), which was furnished with a couch, chairs, tables, magazines, table games such as checkers and cards, pingpong equipment, a record player, and a television set for the residents use. Staff were present during the hours that the recreation hall was open. These hospital personnel served as instructors in the use of leisure equipment and as supervisors to ensure that leisure materials or residents were not injured.

Ratings were done by staff blind to the purposes of the study. Other precautions taken to ensure *c* that ratings were independent and reliable during the 30 minute observation periods included having both raters present for all observations, physically separating observers to afford independence of observations and refraining from labeling either rater as the calibrating reliability assessor.

Reliability was calculated based on percent agreement. Agreement between raters was scored *d* only if both judges agreed that the target behavior had or had not occurred. A disagreement was scored if only one judge acknowledged the occurrence of a target behavior. Reliability was calculated for sessions only where there was an occurrence of a target behavior. This procedure was utilized because percentage agreement is heavily dependent on rate/frequency of the behavior for the session in which it is calculated (Hartmann, 1977). Percentage agreement ranged from 50 to 100% with a mean reliability of 88%.

Procedure

e   A series of 10 scenes involving the appropriate use of the target skills in a leisure situation were used. These scenes were placed on an audiotape. Two audiotapes were employed, one had the answers to the scenes on it and a second presented the scenes with no feedback provided. Having two tapes was necessary because answers to the scenes were part of the social skills training package and therefore could not be used during the phases preceding it (baseline and attention). The presentation of a tape during baseline and attention phases was used so that more adequate comparisons between experi-

e   mental conditions could be made by eliminating the variable of presenting an audiotape. A typical scene consisted of the therapist presenting the situation: e.g., ''you can get along better with people if you say nice things. You might say something nice about their appearance.'' This statement was followed by a prompt, ''can you say something nice about someone,'' followed by 10 seconds of silence to allow the subject time to respond. For the tape with answers on it a response was then provided, ''if you said I like your hair, that would be something nice. Did you make a comment that would make the person feel good about their appearance?''

f   During baseline subjects were taken individually to the training room (4 × 3 meters) which was equipped with the audiotape player, a chair and table. Subjects were shown how to turn the tape player on and off. After playing the audiotape without the answers to the scenes they informed the therapist. The therapist then went to the treatment room with the subject and made sure all scenes had been played by turning the tape player on briefly. Scenes were then gone over with the subject by reading each situation to him/her and scoring the subject's response to the prompt. No other forms of training aimed at teaching specific verbal responses to target behaviors were employed.

g   The attention phase was identical to baseline except that the therapist attempted to provide as much social reinforcement as possible during those portions of the session when therapist and subject were together. Subjects were praised for attending sessions, operating the audiotape player correctly (the audiotape without answer was used), and answering the scene prompts provided by the therapist. As in baseline no other form of training aimed at teaching specific verbal responses to target behaviors was provided.

       Social skills training followed the procedures described in the attention phase except that the audiotape with answers on it was substituted for the audiotape with identical scenes but no answers. In addition, during the second phase of training, when the therapist reviewed scenes with the subject, the therapist provided instructions, performance feedback, modeling, and role-playing as needed to ensure that the subject could provide a correct response. All target behaviors were reviewed at least once for each scene, and social praise was provided for appropriate behavior. If an incorrect answer was made it was practiced until handled correctly or until the patient had practiced three times. For example, after a subject's initial response to a scene, the therapist might say, ''That was better, George; you did not say anything bad about how I look. However, instead of saying I have brown shoes, you might say, I like your brown shoes. Now you say I like your brown shoes and look at me while you do it.'' If the subject's second try was done appropriately, the next scene was presented without regard to the appropriateness of the subject's response.

Experimental Design and Setting

h   The experimental design consisted of a multiple baseline across subjects in an A (baseline), B (attention), C (social skills training) format. There were 30 observation sessions held in the leisure area of the training facility (in a separate area than where training occurred) to measure the effects of training

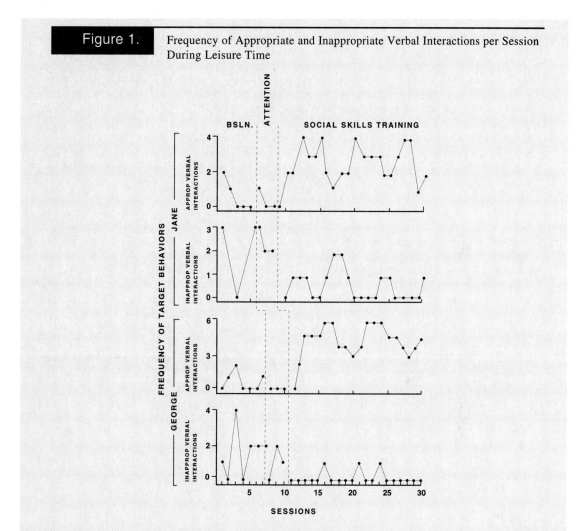

Figure 1. Frequency of Appropriate and Inappropriate Verbal Interactions per Session During Leisure Time

(held on Monday, Wednesday and Friday) **and 50 therapy sessions in the room with the audiotape recorder held each weekday.** The number of social skills training sessions were 23 for Jane and 30 for George and sessions were 20 to 60 minutes in length ($\overline{X}$ length = 28 minutes). **Variability in length of sessions was due to individual problems of each subject exhibited in daily sessions. An additional factor in the variability of session length was how readily subjects assimilated and overtly demonstrated training information. Baseline and attention training sessions were of 30 minutes duration in all cases.** *i*

h

Results and Discussion

Appropriate verbal interactions were at low levels during baseline and remained at low levels during the attention phase. Introduction of social skills training resulted in marked increases in appropriate verbal interactions although there was some variability in the responding as evidenced by scores on sessions 16, 17, 18, 24, 25, 29 and 30 for Jane, and sessions 20 and 27 for George. **Improvement in** *j* response levels proved to be better for George. This finding may be related to the fact that Jane had had a history of aggressive behavior for several years prior to initiation of treatment.

Response frequencies for inappropriate verbal interactions followed a similar pattern compared to appropriate verbal interactions in that little change occurred with the introduction of the attention condition. The marked improvement in the inappropriate behavior occurred during the social skills phase. As with appropriate verbal interactions, changes were not as positive for Jane. Another interesting finding was that the highest levels of inappropriate and appropriate responding for both target behaviors corresponded closely, particularly with Jane (e.g., sessions 17 and 18).

Results are made more striking because effects were measured in a *live environment*, the leisure hour, rather than using analogue responses to scenes. This has often been the mode of assessing effects of social skills training.

k   Additionally, the self-instructional training proved to be considerably more time efficient for therapists and required only a small amount of inexpensive equipment in comparison to the standard method of training social skills which involved two trainers (Hersen & Bellack, 1976; Matson & Zeiss, 1979). It was estimated that about 25% of the time was required with self-instruction compared to the standard social skills training system since only one therapist was present for about 50% of each training session (the other half of the session subjects listened to audiotapes). One question that could not be answered here that deserves further consideration is how much, if any, treatment effectiveness was lost by using the self-instructional method versus conventional social skills training procedures. Therefore, a comparison study of the self-instructional and more traditional methods of social skills treatment would be valuable. Additional variables such as cognitive ability, independent functioning, and related skills would also be valuable.

References

Charles, D. C. & McGrath, K. The relationship of peer and staff ratings to release from institutionalization. *American Journal of Mental Deficiency,* 1962, *67,* 414–417.

Gibson, D. & Fields, D. L. Habilitation forecast in mental retardation: The configured search strategy. *American Journal of Mental Deficiency,* 1970, *74,* 558–562.

Grossman, H. *Manual on terminology and classification in mental retardation* (2nd ed.). American Association on Mental Deficiency, Washington, D.C., 1977.

Hartmann, D. P. Considerations in the choice of interobserver reliability estimates. *Journal of Applied Behavior Analysis,* 1977, *10,* 103–116.

Hersen, M. & Bellack, A. S. A. A multiple-baseline analysis of social skills training in chronic schizophrenics. *Journal of Applied Behavior Analysis,* 1976, *9,* 239–245.

Matson, J. L. Decreasing inappropriate verbalizations of a moderately retarded adult by a staff assisted self-control program. *The Australian Journal of Mental Retardation,* 1979, *5,* 242–245.

Matson, J. L. & Stephens, R. M. Increasing appropriate behavior of explosive chronic psychiatric patients with a social skills training package. *Behavior Modification,* 1978, *2,* 61–65.

Matson, J. L. & Zeiss, R. A. The buddy system: A method of generalized reduction of inappropriate interpersonal behavior of retarded psychotic patients. *British Journal of Social and Clinical Psychology,* 1979, *18,* 401–405.

McFall, R. M. & Marston, A. R. An experimental investigation of behavior rehearsal in assertive training. *Journal of Abnormal Psychology,* 1970, *76,* 295–303.

Schalack, R. L. & Harpe, R. S. Placement from community-based mental retardation programs: How well do clients do? *American Journal of Mental Deficiency,* 1978, *83,* 240–247.

Authors: Johnny L. Matson, Ph.D., Department of Psychiatry, Western Psychiatric Institute and Clinic, University of Pittsburgh, School of Medicine, Pittsburgh, PA 15261: Joyce Adkins, Doctoral Student (Psychology) Peabody School of Education and Human Development, Vanderbilt University, Vanderbilt, TN 37203.

a The authors use the term "multiple baseline" differently from the way the term is usually used. A multiple baseline design usually involves obtaining baseline measurements on two or more different behaviors and staggering the times at which the intervention is used to alter the behaviors.

b The authors state "During observations, all subjects met in the recreation hall. . . ." Since there were only two subjects, one wonders why the word "all" is used.

c No information is given about the raters other than that they were staff members. Were the raters given any instructions? Were they given any training in rating procedures? How did they record their ratings, that is, did they make written notes or simply place a check mark under columns labeled "appropriate behavior" and "inappropriate behavior"?

d Was the percentage of rater agreement the same for both subjects? Was the percentage of rater agreement the same for both appropriate and inappropriate behaviors?

e It would be helpful to have more information about the "10 scenes involving the appropriate use of the target skills in a leisure situation." The authors describe only one "typical scene."

f The authors used the audiotape without answers during the baseline and attention phases in an attempt to eliminate any effects that might be caused simply by presenting an audiotape. It would have been better if they had used audiotapes that did not contain material used in the study. One does not know in what way subjects' behavior during the baseline (and attention) phases may have been affected by the material they heard on the tape.

g The authors could have explained more clearly why they used the attention phase. Presumably it was to control for possible effects social reinforcement from the therapist might have on subjects' behavior. One can determine how the training tapes affected subjects' behavior by comparing their behavior when they listened to training tapes and received praise from the therapist with their behavior when they only received praise by the therapist.

h The authors report that thirty 30-minute observation sessions were held in the leisure area sometime between 7 and 8:30 P.M. The authors also report that one subject had 23 and the other 30 training sessions. The authors do not report, however, how many training sessions occurred on the same days observations were made or when the training sessions took place. It is possible that a training session early in the day might be less effective than one immediately prior to the observation period.

i The authors report that the length of training sessions ranged from 20 to 60 minutes, with a mean of 28 minutes. The authors do not, however, report this information for each subject separately so one doesn't know how much training each subject actually received.

j The authors list the days on which subjects' appropriate behavior occurred less frequently. They do not report whether subjects had attended a training session on these days.

k It would have been useful if the observations had continued after the use of the training tapes had ceased so that one could determine if the frequency of appropriate and inappropriate behaviors remained constant or reverted to baseline frequencies.

Analyzing Data from Single-Subject Studies

Usually, data collected in a single-subject study are presented in the form of graphs, such as those in Figures 15.2 and 15.3. Whether such data should be analyzed by statistical tests of significance or merely by visual inspection of the graphed data is debatable (Kratochwill, 1978). Furthermore, even among researchers who believe that statistical analysis is justified, there is disagreement as to which statistical procedures are appropriate.

Sometimes, researchers using a double-reversal (A-B-A-B) design combine the data collected during the two baseline conditions (A) and compare the average score with that of the combined treatment conditions (B). A *t* test is used to see if the resulting two means are significantly different. On the other hand, some researchers regard the use of the *t* test with single-subject data as inappropriate because they believe such data do not satisfy the necessary assumptions underlying the use of a *t* test.

Instead they argue that the data should be analyzed using an analysis of variance (ANOVA) with repeated measures. In other words, the data from the two baseline (or from the two treatment) conditions are not combined; instead all four means are analyzed simultaneously using an analysis of variance (ANOVA). An ANOVA with repeated measures is used when the means to be compared have been collected from the *same* group of subjects.

Chapter Highlights

- In single-subject research, the subject may be a single individual or a single group.

- Time series designs involve making multiple measurements of the frequency of behavior of a single individual or a single group prior to, during, and following some intervention designed to change the individual's behavior.

- In single-subject studies, the researcher purposely alters the subject's environment to determine how the alteration affects the subject's behavior; in case studies, the researcher observes the subject in a naturalistic setting and makes no attempt to alter the setting.

- The lack of a control group in single-subject research makes it necessary to make multiple measurements of the subject's behavior in order to draw a cause-and-effect inference between the independent and dependent variables.

- The baseline condition refers to the period of time prior to the intervention during which the frequency of behavior under normal conditions is measured.

- The baseline condition continues until a stable measure of the behavior occurs, which is sometimes defined as 10 consecutive observation periods during which the frequency of behavior varies less than 5% of the mean frequency.

- Shorter time units are used to measure relatively stable behaviors; longer time units are used to measure behaviors that are more variable.

- The treatment condition refers to the period of time during the intervention during which the frequency of behavior is measured.

- The results of single-subject research are determined by comparing the frequency of behavior occurring after intervention with the frequency occurring prior to the intervention.

- An A-B-A design is called a reversal; the baseline condition (A) is followed by the treatment condition (B), which in turn is followed by the baseline condition (A).

- An A-B-A-B design is called a double reversal; double reversals are often used in situations where it would be unethical to end the study during a baseline condition (A).

- In a multiple-baseline design the intervention is applied to several different behaviors in staggered fashion; if the treatment has a causal effect, changes in each behavior should not occur until after the treatment has been administered.

- It is important to replicate single-subject studies if the researcher's intent is to generalize the findings to different subjects or different settings.
- Some researchers believe the results of single-subject studies should be presented in graphic form; others believe results should be analyzed statistically.

Review Exercises

1. What does the term *time series design* mean?
2. Describe the difference between single-subject research and case studies.
3. Why is it necessary to make multiple measurements in single-subject research?
4. Why is it unnecessary to make multiple measurements in group comparisons?
5. Give an example of a single-subject study using a reversal design, then double-reversal design. Indicate the baseline and treatment conditions in each.
6. Give an example in which it would be more appropriate to use a multiple-baseline design rather than a reversal or double reversal.
7. Name two tests of statistical significance sometimes used to analyze data from single-subject research.

Section VI

Guidelines for Writing and Evaluating Research

*T*his section presents information about how to write a research proposal and a final report in the style advocated in the fourth edition of the *Publication Manual of the American Psychological Association* (American Psychological Association, 1994). It also includes a checklist you can use to evaluate your own study or studies appearing in the professional research literature.

Chapter 16
Writing and Evaluating Research Reports

There is one general rule to follow in writing the Method section. The information should be presented in sufficient detail to permit the reader to replicate your study on the basis of your description, assuming the reader had access to the subjects and materials used in your study.

Chapter Objectives

After completing this chapter, you should be able to:

- describe differences and similarities between research proposals and final reports
- identify the sections of a final report and explain what kind of information appears in each section
- write a research proposal and a final report using the style presented in the fourth edition of the *Publication Manual of the American Psychological Association* (1994)
- evaluate published studies in terms of how well they meet the criteria of high-quality research

No matter what kind of research project you intend to carry out, it is necessary first to write a research proposal, which describes the research question you intend to investigate and how you plan to carry out your study. Once the study is completed, you should prepare a final written report. The sequence of events is first to write a proposal, then carry out the study and, finally, write a report describing the research question you investigated, how you investigated it, and what conclusions you have reached on the basis of your investigation. The same basic format is used in writing proposals and final reports for any quantitative research project, regardless of whether the study is descriptive, correlational, single-subject, or a group comparison.

There is no standard format for writing proposals and projects dealing with qualitative research, such as historical or ethnographic studies. Students interested in pursuing historical research will find helpful guidelines in Barzun and Graff (1977), Berlinger (1978), or Gottschalk (1969). Students interested in carrying out ethnographic research will find helpful information in Bogdan and Biklen (1992) or Pelto and Pelto (1978).

The remainder of this chapter describes the steps in writing a proposal and a final report for quantitative studies.

Proposals and Final Reports: Differences and Similarities

The contents of a proposal and a final report differ, but it is important to understand how they are conceptually related. What follows is a discussion of characteristics that proposals and final reports do and do not share.

Proposals

A research **proposal** is a detailed account of: (a) the research question you intend to pursue; (b) why it is of interest to pursue the question; and (c) how you intend to gather and analyze data so that you can answer the question. Proposals can serve various functions. Public and private educational funding agencies, for example, typically require researchers applying for money to carry out a project to submit a research proposal. The proposal plays a crucial role in an agency's decision to provide financial assistance to a researcher.

Graduate schools often require students to submit a research proposal as part of the requirements for completing a course in educational research or as a preliminary requirement before embarking on a thesis or a dissertation. Despite the various functions a proposal may serve, they all share one common property: proposals enable people to determine the quality of a study before it is actually carried out.

Final Reports

Final reports may take a variety of forms. The final report of a project funded by an educational agency may be a written document that the researcher sends to the funding agency. It may also take the form of an educational document included in the ERIC system. In addition, it may take the form (usually, greatly reduced in content) of an article in a professional journal.

The final reports of graduate students in doctoral programs typically take the form of theses or dissertations that are bound and placed in the library of the institution awarding the student the doctorate. In addition, condensed versions of doctoral dissertations may

Table 16.1	*Outlines of a Proposal and a Final Report*

Outline of a Proposal

1. Title page
2. Introduction, including a review of the literature and a statement of the hypotheses
3. Method section (written in the future tense)
4. Data analysis indicating what kinds of statistical analyses you intend to use with what data (This section corresponds to the results section of the final report.)
5. List of references

Outline of a Final Report

1. Title page
2. Abstract (a brief summary of the study)
3. Introduction, including a review of the literature and a statement of the hypotheses
4. Method section (written in the past tense)
5. Results
6. Discussion: you may combine the results and discussion sections into a single section labeled "Results and Discussion"
7. List of references
8. Appendices (optional: used for including copies of materials such as self-made measuring instruments)

---

appear as journal articles. The final reports of graduate students in master degree programs often are either a thesis, which is in many ways similar to a dissertation, or a research paper, which is in many ways similar to a journal article.

Outlines of a proposal and a final report are shown in Table 16.1. There is considerable overlap in the material in the two documents, but the final report contains more information than the proposal does. For example, the introduction section of the final report may contain a more extensive review of the literature than appears in the proposal. Of course, the results of the study and their implications appear only in the final report.

Much of the overlap occurs in the description of the method section. The method section of the proposal should be written in the future tense because nothing has yet been undertaken. On the other hand, the method section of the final report should be written in the past tense because the study has been completed. If the method described in the proposal turns out to be identical to the method you actually use in carrying out your study, it is necessary only to change the verb tense from the future to past when writing the final report. Even if you have changed the method from the time you wrote the proposal until the time the study is carried out, usually the changes are relatively minor.

The proposal serves as a blueprint of the study you have in mind, and the extent to which you are successful in devising a proposal you can actually follow to the letter, the easier it is to carry out the final project. On the other hand, the proposal is only a statement of what you intend to do, albeit a rather detailed statement. If unforeseen circumstances develop between the proposal stage and the final stage of your project, or if you uncover new research information that you feel you should take into account, feel free to deviate from the original proposal when you actually carry out the study.

Writing Style

Different journals adhere to different styles of writing, and it is up to the author who is submitting an article for possible publication to write it according to the style used by the journal. Various writing styles are described in manuals by Campbell, Ballou, and Slade (1990), Turabian (1973), and the Modern Language Association of America (Gibaldi & Achtert, 1988). The most common writing style used by journals in education is the style advocated by the American Psychological Association (1994).

You will be expected to write the research proposal and the report of your final project in accordance with the writing style used at your college or institution. Regardless of what writing style you are required to use, the content of research reports almost never varies. Many departments of education follow the writing style of the American Psychological Association. The following information, which describes the content of a research report, has been written according to the style of the American Psychological Association.

Sample copies of research proposals and final reports written in the writing style of the American Psychological Association appear in Appendices H and I, respectively. These may be used as models if you write your own proposal and final report according to the American Psychological Association style. If additional information is needed, consult the *Publication Manual* or the appropriate writing style manual used at your institution.

Because the final report includes all the material appearing in a proposal, the following discussion of writing style is in terms of a final report. Parts of the discussion apply to research proposals as well.

There are two components of writing style: how to divide a research report into various sections and how to cite references to the published works of others. Both these components are more or less standard for any educational research article.

Sections of a Final Report

The number of sections in a final report and the order in which they appear almost never vary. The emphasis in writing a research report should be on clear, concise communication rather than on the use of fancy literary devices. Almost all research reports contain exactly the same components, so it has become customary for all researchers to use basically the same format in reporting their studies. The sections described are presented in the order in which they appear in the final report, not necessarily in the order in which they are written.

Figures 16.1a through 16.1e show the major sections of a report. Each page is numbered, and the page number is placed one inch from the right-hand side of the page and one inch beneath the upper edge of the page. A short title, which is usually the first couple of words of the title, is placed on every page about five spaces before the page number.

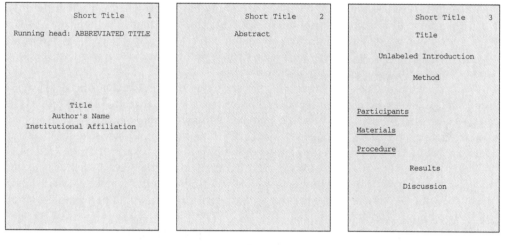

Figure 16.1 (a) The title page appears on a separate page; (b) The abstract appears on a separate page; (c) The body of the text begins on a new page and continues on additional pages until completed; (d) The list of references begins on a new page (# represents whatever the page number would be); (e) Each Appendix begins on a new page (# represents whatever the page number would be).

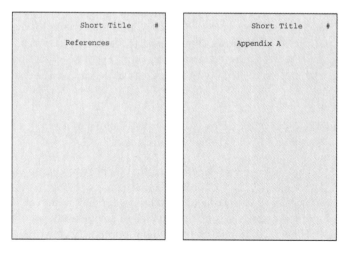

Title Page

The title page consists of the title of the project, the author's name and institutional affiliation, and a running head. The following is a description of each part of the title page.

The Title. The very first part of a research report is its title. Surprisingly, the title often turns out to be rather difficult to write. A title should contain no more than 12 to 15 words and should be written so that the variables the study has investigated appear in the title. Furthermore, the title should convey briefly what the study is about. The choice of correct terminology in a study's title is extremely important when an article is to be published because it is the words appearing in the title that determine what descriptor terms will be used to list the article in the various indexes.

Students tend to make two kinds of errors in giving their projects a title. Often many redundant and unimportant words are used. For example, consider the following title: ''The effects of the use of spaced and massed practice with the cloze procedure on the reading comprehension scores of fifth-grade boys and girls in an urban elementary school.'' The title could easily be shortened without losing important information: ''Massed and spaced practice with the cloze procedure and fifth graders' reading comprehension.'' The fact that the students attend a school in an urban area does not seem particularly important and should be included only if there is reason to believe that urban students would perform differently from other kinds of students.

The second error is to use the hypothesis as the title. In general, the title of a study is less detailed than the hypothesis.

Running Head. A running head is a shortened version of the title of your project that would appear at the top of each page if it were published in a journal. A good title permits one to write an informative running head easily. The head should contain no more than 50 characters, counting letters, punctuation, and spaces. Using the previous example, the running head might be: ''Cloze procedure and reading comprehension.''

The title of the project, your name and institution, and the running head all appear on the title page of your report. The title page is the first page of your final project. See Figure 16.1a.

Author's Name and Institutional Affiliation. This is the easiest section of a report to write. Simply list your name and the name of your college or university.

Abstract

An **abstract** of your project appears as the second numbered page in your final report, but it is the very last thing you should write. An abstract is a brief summary of your study, which can be written only after the study has been completed and the final report has been written.

The abstract appears by itself on page 2 and is simply labeled ''Abstract.'' See Figure 16.1b. It should be no longer than 120 words. The abstract is intended to give the reader a brief summary of your project. It may be the most difficult part of your final report to write because it should contain a number of specific bits of information that must be presented in very limited space.

An abstract should contain a statement of the problem, a description of the research procedures used, the number and kinds of subjects, the names or descriptions of the materials used, the results of the study, including the statistical levels of significance, and any implications of the study. No material should appear in the abstract that does not appear in the body of the final project.

Sometimes students write abstracts that are either far too lengthy or fail to include the specific information previously listed.

Introduction

The introduction, which is the first section of the body of the text of the final report, is *not* labeled. Simply begin the introduction on page 3 of the final report, immediately after the abstract.

The introduction serves several functions. First of all, it should answer the question of why the study is important. In other words, what is the point of the study? It is often helpful in describing the importance of your study to point out how your research question is related to broader educational issues. The introduction usually opens with a general statement of the research question and how the researcher intends to investigate the question. Within the first paragraph or so, the objective of the study should be clearly stated. The introduction ends with a clear statement of the hypotheses. Often the hypotheses are followed by operational definitions of the variables to be investigated.

The bulk of the introduction occurs between the initial clarification of the objective of the study and the final statement of the hypotheses. The intermediate part of the introduction consists of your review of the literature. (See chapter 3 for detailed information about reviewing the literature.)

It is inevitable that your introduction will not include references to all of the literature you have reviewed. It is important for you to cull from the literature you have reviewed only those references that are pertinent to your study. Some references may be pertinent because they permit you to establish the importance of your research question. Others may be important because they permit you to develop a documented rationale for whatever you are hypothesizing, which is the major function of the introduction.

Developing a Documented Rationale. The primary function of the introduction is to document your rationale for whatever you are hypothesizing. To develop your rationale in a logical sequence, you must synthesize the findings of other studies. It is often helpful to group together studies that are similar and to report significant overall findings in a general way, supporting your conclusions with evidence from individual studies. Link the findings of different studies together so that the reader can understand how a logical analysis of these findings would lead to your hypothesis. The major purpose of the review of the literature is to provide a basis for your prediction. Its purpose is not to convince the reader that you have read everything there is to read on your topic.

In effect, the review of the literature provides the reader with an opportunity to follow your line of thinking as you went about developing your hypotheses. Consequently, it is useful to stress the important aspects of previous studies that bear on your hypothesis. It is unnecessary and may even be distracting to report in detail everything in a previous investigation. Choose carefully the information you wish to include in your own report and eliminate information that fundamentally has nothing to do with your hypothesis.

Students often make two kinds of errors in their reviews of the literature. Many simply report the findings of one study after another in sequential order without ever showing how the findings are connected with one another or how they pertain to the student's own hypothesis. Others report on studies that are at best only marginally related to their own hypothesis. Often the studies reported are clearly related to the topic under investigation, but the relationship to the specific hypothesis is unclear. It is as though the student is writing all around the hypothesis without ever focusing squarely on the hypothesis itself.

Method

Immediately after you have stated your hypotheses in the introductory part of your report, you should start a section that is labeled "Method." See Figure 16.1c. There is one general rule to follow in writing this section. The information should be presented in sufficient detail to permit the reader to replicate your study on the basis of your description, assuming the reader had access to the subjects and materials used in your study. The method section typically consists of three subsections, each with its own label.

Participants. The first subsection in the method section deals with the participants (or subjects) in your study. Here you report how many subjects there were, how they were selected for participation, and important demographic characteristics such as gender, age, grade level, any kind of exceptionality, and the kinds of institutions from which the subjects were chosen.

If your study includes more than one group of subjects, you should report how many there were in each group. Report also how many subjects were originally scheduled to participate in your study who did not complete it. For example, if you have mailed questionnaires, report how many you mailed and how many were actually completed and returned.

Materials. The second subsection of the Method section is labeled "Materials." In this subsection you should list all the materials used in the study, including the names of all commercially available tests, a description of any self-made measuring instruments, and a list of any equipment used. If you have not already done so, you should provide operational definitions for the variables to be measured in your study. Validity and reliability information for all tests and measuring instruments should be given here. If you are using a self-made instrument, you should report what kind of reliability check was used.

Procedure. In the procedure subsection you should describe in sequence how you went about collecting the data. If your study has an experimental design, the first thing you should describe is the method you used to assign subjects to the various groups.

Describe in detail what was done to each group of subjects. Any instructions that may have been given to the subjects should be briefly reported. It is not necessary to report instructions accompanying standardized tests.

In an experimental study you should report how long the experiment lasted. If your study compares the effects of different treatments, such as teaching methods, given to the groups of subjects, you should indicate how many periods of treatment (instruction) there were and how long each period lasted.

Results

The results section is usually the shortest section of a final report. Because the results of a study are determined by applying some statistical analysis to the data, they can be reported briefly. Use tables or graphs only if they clarify complicated or confusing information. Report means and standard deviations for data having equal units of measurement (i.e., data that have been measured by an interval scale, such as raw scores). Also report which statistical tests you applied to which data.

If your findings are not statistically significant, it is necessary only to report the statistical procedure you have used. If your findings are statistically significant, however, report the computed value of each statistic, the degrees of freedom, and the level of statistical significance, as well as the name of the statistical test you used. Suppose, for example, you carried out a group comparison with two groups of 15 subjects each and found a significant t value of 3.24 using a nondirectional t test for independent means. You should report the finding as "$t(28) = 3.24, p < .01$." If you have used a computerized statistical program to analyze your data and are given the exact value of p, report the finding as "$t(28) = 3.24, p = .008$."

Discussion

It is often possible to combine the results and discussion sections into a single section if the results are brief and simple. However, sometimes it is clearer to present a separate section labeled "Discussion."

The first thing to point out in this section is which of your hypotheses have been confirmed and which have not. You should discuss how your results fit in with previous findings. To what extent do your findings agree or disagree with the existing literature? In this section you should present any practical or theoretical implications of your findings. You should also present any possible alternative explanations for your findings and point out any limitations your study might have.

You are free to speculate in the discussion section about your findings as long as you indicate that you are merely speculating. You may note weaknesses in your study, particularly those that did not occur to you until after the study was completed. You may also point out further areas of research suggested by your study.

References

The last section, labeled "References," appears at the top of a new sheet of paper. (See Figure 16.1d.) The reference section is a list of the works of others that you have cited in your own study. The references are listed alphabetically according to the last name of the first author of the work. If you have more than one work by the same author or authors, the works should be listed according to date of publication, with the earliest appearing first. If the same author or authors have published more than one work within the same year, distinguish the works by adding after the date the letters "a," "b," and so forth. You should list all the references you referred to in your study and only those. If you did not refer to a work, even though you may have read it, do not list it here.

Appendices

If you wish to include information in your report that has not been covered by one of the standard sections comprising a research study, it may be useful to add one or more appendices. Any appendices appear after the list of references. Material in appendices often includes such things as sample copies of researcher-made instruments, letters used to obtain parental consent, or infrequently used statistical calculations. Each appendix starts on a new page. If you have more than one appendix, identify each with a letter, beginning with A and continuing through the alphabet. (See Figure 16.1e.)

Citing References

Two ways of citing references are used. One cites references in the reference list at the end of the report; the other cites them as they appear in the text of the report. We will first turn to citing references in a reference list.

Citations in the Reference List

References in the reference list appear in alphabetical order according to the last name of the first author of the work. The format in which each work is cited depends on the kind of work being cited. Journal articles, books, and ERIC documents all have their own unique citation format. Detailed information for citing references appears in Figures 3.11–3.13 in chapter 3. All references, however, regardless of their citation format are given at the end of your report in a single alphabetized list. Citation information for references not shown in the examples in Chapter 3 may be found in the *Publication Manual* (American Psychological Association, 1994).

Citations in the Body of the Text

During the introduction section of your final report, you will refer to published studies to document the rationale underlying your hypothesis. You will also refer to published studies in the discussion section of your report as you explain how the findings of your study fit in with the existing literature. Every time you refer to a published work in the text of your own study you must cite the work. Some writing styles require footnotes to refer to others' works, but you need only give the authors' names and the year in which the work was published.

How you cite the authors' names and year of publication depends on whether the names are part of a sentence or not. Compare the following examples.

Example of Citation when Authors' Names Are Part of a Sentence.
Crowne and Marlowe (1964) developed the Social Desirability Scale, an instrument designed to measure the need for social approval.

The authors' names, Crowne and Marlowe, form a grammatical part of the sentence. Consequently, the year of publication is indicated in parentheses immediately after their names. The reader who wishes to obtain the complete bibliographic information of Crowne and Marlowe's work need only look in the list of references at the end of the study.

Examples of Citations when Authors' Names Are Not Part of a Sentence.
The Social Desirability Scale (Crowne & Marlowe, 1964) is an instrument designed to measure the need for social approval.

The authors' names do not form a grammatical part of the sentence and are consequently inserted with the year of publication in parentheses at some logical point in the sentence. If there is more than one author, use an ampersand, not the word *and*.

Sometimes several studies are cited simultaneously as in the following example:

It has been found that the grades teachers assign to students' essays are influenced by the quality of students' penmanship (Briggs, 1970, 1980; Huck & Bounds, 1972; Marshall & Powers, 1969; Soloff, 1973).

This form of citation is a convenient way to indicate that several studies have investigated the same issue.

When several works are referred to simultaneously, the references are placed inside the parentheses alphabetically according to the last name of the first author of the work. References are *not* listed chronologically by year of publication. If an author has published more than one work on the same topic, the author's name appears only once, and the years of the publications are listed in chronological order after the author's name. When referring to one of several works published by the same author or authors in the same year, include the letter ''a,'' ''b,'' and so forth corresponding to the letter used in the list of references so that the reader will know to which of the several works you are referring.

The use of authors' names and the year of publication within the body of the text of a report makes the report easier to read than if footnotes are used. The continuity of reading is not disrupted, and one knows immediately who the authors of a piece of work are and when the study was carried out.

Guidelines for Evaluating Published Research

As you go through the literature you have reviewed, it is necessary to evaluate the quality of the material you are reading. It is up to you to decide if the study has been conducted in accordance with accepted research practices. You should not necessarily believe everything you read. The fact that an article appears in print says nothing about the quality of the article. Articles vary considerably in terms of quality, and even high quality articles are apt to contain flaws.

It is best to approach articles you have located with a degree of skepticism, keeping in mind that it is up to the authors of the article to convince you that what they have written is credible. Obviously, you should not include in your introduction references to poorly conducted studies. The results of such studies are questionable and potentially misleading. Figure 16.2 contains a checklist guide for evaluating published research.

All of the articles reproduced in earlier chapters of this text originally appeared as journal articles, and they too vary in quality. The articles were selected in order to give you some concrete examples of the kinds of studies you are likely to encounter when conducting your own literature review, not necessarily to provide you with examples of ideal studies. See if you can detect flaws in some of the studies appearing in the text by applying the checklist appearing in Figure 16.2.

Characteristics of Quality Studies

The most notable characteristics of high quality studies are clear writing and logical reasoning. In good studies there is no doubt as to what research question or hypotheses the researcher is addressing. If you find yourself reading the introductory part of a study over and over again to try to determine what question or hypotheses the study addresses, it may

Figure 16.2	Checklist for Evaluating Research

All of the questions below will receive an answer of "yes" if the research is of high quality.

1. The introductory part of the study

   a. Has the author stated the nature of the research question or the research hypotheses unambiguously?
   b. Has the author explained why it is important to carry out the study?
   c. Has the author related the importance of carrying out the study to information already known about the research question?
   d. Has the author provided a logical, documented rationale for every hypothesis?
   e. Has the author developed each rationale in an unbiased manner?
   f. Can you identify clearly what variables are being investigated?
   g. Has the author provided appropriate operational definitions for all variables?

2. Participants

   a. Has the author explained how the participants in the study were selected?
   b. Has the author explained how many of the participants originally selected to participate in the study actually did?
   c. Has the author explained why participants originally selected may not have participated in the study?
   d. Has the author selected the sample of participants in such a way that they accurately represent the population to which the findings of the study are to be applied?
   e. Has the author stated the precise number of participants in the study?
   f. Has the author provided sufficient demographic information about the participants, such as age, sex, and other characteristics that might be relevant to the research question being investigated?

3. Materials

   a. Has the author provided a description of all materials that have been used in the study?
   b. Has the author given information concerning the validity and reliability of tests and measuring instruments used in the study?
   c. Do the tests and measuring instruments have adequate validity and reliability?

4. Procedure

   a. Is the procedure used to carry out the study described in sufficient detail that you could replicate the study if you had access to the same kinds of subjects and materials?
   b. Has the author used a research design appropriate for answering the research question?
   c. If the study is an experiment or a quasi-experiment, is it clear how subjects were assigned to experimental and control groups?
   d. Has the author designed the study in such a way to eliminate effects of possible confounding variables?

5. Results

   a. Has the author used appropriate statistical techniques to analyze the data?
   b. Has the author accounted for every hypothesis by indicating which have been confirmed and which have not?
   c. Has the author refrained from analyzing data in ways that pertain to hypotheses other than the ones the author originally established?

6. Discussion

   a. Has the author related the study's findings to the existing literature, indicating in what ways the findings agree or disagree with previous findings?
   b. Has the author pointed out possible limitations of the study?
   c. Has the author pointed out any practical or theoretical implications that the study's findings have?

Figure 16.2   continued

7. References

    a. Has the author included in the list of references all of the works cited in the study?
    b. Has the author included recent as well as older references?
    c. Has the author used mostly primary sources as references?

8. Quality of the journal in which the study appears

    a. Does the journal in which the study appears have an editorial board comprised of people who appear to be competent professionals?
    b. Does the journal in which the study appears follow a masked review policy?

be that the study is inferior. If the researcher is unable to specify in written form precisely the nature of the research question, one can only suspect that the question lacks conceptual clarity. If a research question is imprecisely conceptualized, it is pointless to investigate it.

High quality studies address important new questions that researchers formulate on the basis of what is already known about a topic. The research question and hypotheses stem from a logical, documented rationale that systematically links what is to be investigated with what is known.

Quality studies not only pose clear questions, they also provide appropriate operational definitions for all variables so that readers know exactly how the variables have been measured. Ask yourself if the operational definitions are good ones; are the measurements used valid and reliable? A study should report validity and reliability information for all measuring instruments so that the reader can determine the adequacy of the instruments. Are the definitions consistent with your own interpretation of the variables and interpretations that other researchers have used?

A good study includes sufficient information about the subjects who participated in it so that the reader can determine if the subjects accurately represent the population to which the findings of the study are to be generalized. It is important for researchers to describe exactly how subjects were selected and to inform readers not only of how many subjects participated, but also how many did not so that the reader can decide how likely it is that the sample is biased.

Has the researcher described the procedures in sufficient detail to permit you to replicate the study easily if you had access to the subjects and the instruments used in the study? If a researcher fails to describe procedures clearly and in detail, one wonders whether they were followed rigorously and competently.

Is the research design of the study appropriate to test the hypotheses? Has the researcher stated one kind of hypothesis and set up the study so that the hypothesis cannot be tested? For example, has the researcher stated a hypothesis of cause and effect but used an ex post facto or a correlational design instead of an experimental design, which such a hypothesis demands?

Do the findings of the study pertain to the hypotheses? Has the researcher reported results that are only peripherally related? Has the researcher accounted for every hypothesis by indicating which hypotheses have been confirmed and which have not?

Are the statistical procedures appropriate? For example, if the study compares the mean scores of three groups, has the researcher used an analysis of variance rather than a series of *t* tests? If the study is quasi-experimental, has the researcher used pretests and analyzed the data by an analysis of covariance?

Finally, one can often get some idea of the quality of an article by noting the quality of the journal in which it appears. Good journals have editorial boards and a policy of having a researcher's work evaluated by other professionals before the study is accepted for publication. If a journal has an editorial board, see if the editors are people you have heard of or are at least affiliated with institutions you believe are reputable.

Usually on the inside of the front or back cover of a journal, or in some conspicuous place, there is information for people who wish to submit articles for publication. Check the instructions to authors for the journal's review policy. It has become more and more common for good journals to follow a **masked** (or blind) **review** policy. In a masked review, authors are instructed to put their names on a separate sheet of paper and not on the pages of the study itself. When the study is sent out for other professionals to review, the reviewers have no idea who the author is, and the chances are better that a study will be accepted on its merits as a study, rather than just because the person who wrote it happens to be well known.

How Many Pages and How Many References?

Students invariably want to know how many pages they are expected to write and how many references they should use. There is no simple answer to either question, because the length of a report and the number of references depend completely on the nature of the study. Some studies can be reported briefly, while others require more space. Sometimes a student can build a cogent argument in the introductory section of the report with a few pertinent articles. Other times one must cite numerous references to develop a logical rationale.

It may be helpful, however, for you to know the length of papers that are generally submitted by students. Proposals tend to run from perhaps 5 to 8 pages. Final reports run from about 8 to 15 pages. Experimental studies generally require lengthier proposals because it is necessary to describe in detail the kinds of interventions the student is going to carry out with the experimental and control groups. Ex post facto and correlational studies tend to be rather short because no intervention is to take place.

The number of references varies dramatically, depending on the amount of literature available on a particular topic and whether the literature pertains directly to the student's hypothesis. Sometimes students submit as few as half a dozen to 8 or 10 references, and other times they include 20 or more.

A student carrying out a research project involving some Piagetian task, for example, is likely to be overwhelmed by the amount of existing literature and must try to weed out studies that do not bear directly on the hypothesis. On the other hand, a student carrying out a project on a topic that has only recently become popular, such as inclusion or portfolio assessment, may be forced to work with far fewer references because to date there has been relatively little research on the topic. Ultimately it is not the number of references that counts, but rather the logic of the argument the student uses in developing a documented rationale for the hypothesis.

- A research proposal serves as a blueprint for carrying out a study.
- A final report is a written account of why the study was carried out, how it was carried out and what the findings are.
- There is considerable overlap in the material contained in a proposal and a final report, but the final report contains more information.
- Research articles appearing in professional journals must be written according to one of several popular writing styles; the writing style advocated in the *Publication Manual of the American Psychological Association* is the most commonly used style in education journals.
- The format of final reports is more or less standard and contains the following parts:
  Title page
  Abstract
  Introduction (untitled)
  Method
     Participants
     Materials
     Procedure
  Results
  Discussion
  References
  Appendices (optional)
- The format for citing references differs, depending on the type of reference (e.g., book, journal article, educational document).
- Most researchers agree on the criteria for judging the quality of a quantitative study, which include among other things, clear writing, logical reasoning, and enough detail to permit the reader to replicate the study.
- The number of references cited in a study varies greatly, depending on the nature of the research question and the availability of literature pertaining to the question.

Review Exercises

1. List the guidelines for evaluating published research.
2. Submit a written introduction, including a review of the literature, concerning a research question of interest to you.
3. Submit a complete research proposal concerning a research question of interest to you.

Section VII

Technology and Educational Research

*T*his section focuses on the impact of modern technology on educational research. Examples are given of the uses of technology in diverse ways, such as searching the literature, conducting qualitative studies, and analyzing quantitative data.

*C*hapter *17*

The Cutting Edge: Using Technology in Educational Research

Let us begin our discussion of the expanding role of technology by focusing on some of the ways researchers use computers.

Chapter Objectives

After completing this chapter, you should be able to:

- carry out a computer search of the literature on a topic of interest
- describe how qualitative and quantitative researchers use computers to analyze data
- describe how researchers use audiotapes, videotapes, and microfilms

The previous chapter focused on how to develop a research proposal and write a final report. It also discussed ways of evaluating research that you may wish to conduct yourself or that appears in the form of journal articles in the professional literature. This chapter examines the expanding role that technology plays in virtually every aspect of educational research, from searching the literature to preparing final reports. Let us begin our discussion of the expanding role of technology by focusing on some of the ways researchers use computers.

Conducting a Computer Search of the Literature

Information was given in chapter 3 that explained how to carry out a manual search of the literature on a topic by using indexes such as the *Current Index to Journals in Education, Education Index, Resources in Education,* and *Psychological Abstracts.* The information in most printed indexes, however, is now also available on computer discs, making it possible to search the literature by means of computer.

Information contained on computer discs is frequently called a *data base.* For example, everything that appears in any printed issue of *CIJE* is also available on computer discs. The data base contained on such discs is *CIJE,* and contains all bibliographic information pertaining to an article, the article's EJ number, major and minor descriptors assigned to the article, and a summary of the article. It is important to understand that the data base does *not* include the article itself.

On-Line Computer Searches

It is common these days for college and university libraries to have facilities that permit students to search the data bases of various indexes by computer. Generally the library subscribes to an information service that connects by modem (i.e., by telephone line) terminal in the library to various data bases. There are several information services, the most common of which are probably DIALOG, BRS, and SDC/ORBIT. It is relatively unimportant which service your library subscribes to because all of the services operate in basically the same way.

Searching ERIC by Computer

The ERIC data base, which consists of all information appearing in both *CIJE* and *RIE,* is probably the data base most frequently used by researchers in education. The preliminary steps in a computer search of the ERIC data base are identical to those in a manual search. One must first manually locate descriptor terms relevant to one's research question in the ERIC *Thesaurus.* Having found the terms, one then uses the computer to search *CIJE* and *RIE.* The biggest advantage of carrying out a computer search is the speed with which the search can be conducted. What may take hours and hours to do manually can be accomplished in minutes by computer.

Librarians trained in computer searching techniques are often available to carry out computerized searches of the literature for students. The librarian must have a thorough understanding of what the student's research question is to carry out a successful search. At some libraries students are asked to fill out a computer search form, providing a description of their research question, a list of ERIC descriptors they believe to be relevant, and the bibliographic information on any relevant article or document they have already located. In addition, some libraries request that students have a personal interview with the librarian so that possible ambiguities concerning the research question can be resolved and perhaps more detailed information added.

Using information provided by the student, the librarian develops a search strategy by selecting and combining descriptor terms in various ways so that when they are entered into the computer, a list of articles and documents relevant to the student's research question should result. To a large extent the success of the search depends on the soundness of the search strategy. Developing a search strategy that is on target is sometimes as much of an art as an exercise in logical thinking, and it is sometimes necessary to use more than one strategy to complete a search successfully.

Having settled on a search strategy, the librarian then retrieves the information from the data base. Most of the cost of a computer search is determined by how much time is spent on-line. Consequently, one factor taken into account in developing a search strategy is the cost of on-line time.

Using Connectors in Search Strategies. Suppose you were interested in the question of how mainstreaming might be related to the reading performance of learning disabled and emotionally disturbed students. After consulting the ERIC *Thesaurus* you might decide that possible relevant descriptor terms are "READING ACHIEVEMENT," "READING ABILITY," "EMOTIONAL DISTURBANCES," "LEARNING DISABILITIES," and "MAINSTREAMING." One may enter these descriptors into the computer either singly or in combination by using connectors, that is, the words *and* or *or*. Within seconds the number of articles and educational documents listed in *CIJE* and *RIE* under the descriptors will appear on the computer screen.

The biggest advantage a computer search has over a manual search is that one may locate articles and documents by searching several descriptors simultaneously. (In a manual search, only one descriptor at a time may be searched.) It is important to understand, however, that the results of searching several descriptors simultaneously depend on how the connectors *and* and *or* are used.

In Figure 17.1 each circle represents all articles and documents listed under one descriptor. The area defined by the overlap of the circles indicates those articles and documents that have been listed under both descriptors. If one enters the descriptors "READING ACHIEVEMENT" *or* "READING ABILITY," the computer will list the number of items contained in both circles. If, however, one enters "READING ACHIEVEMENT" *and* "READING ABILITY," only the number of items within the shaded area representing the overlap of the two circles will be indicated.

One may search simultaneously as many descriptors as one wishes using both *and* and *or* as connectors. The use of parentheses determines which descriptors are grouped together. For example, the shaded areas in Figure 17.2 show which items would be counted. The top diagram would result from a search consisting of "MAINSTREAMING" *and* ("READING ACHIEVEMENT" *or* "READING ABILITY"). On the other hand, a search consisting of ("MAINSTREAMING" *and* "READING ACHIEVEMENT") *or* "READING ABILITY" would yield the bottom diagram.

Every *and* connector restricts the search and yields fewer items. If one uses too many *and* connectors, the resulting number of items may be zero or close to it. An article or a document must be listed under all descriptor terms that are connected by *and* in order for

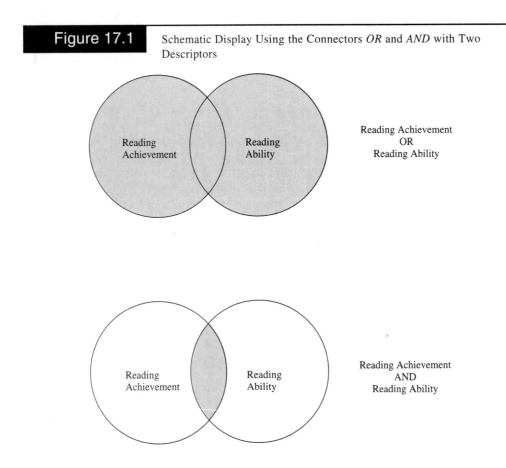

Figure 17.1   Schematic Display Using the Connectors *OR* and *AND* with Two Descriptors

the article or document to be listed. It is unlikely to find many articles or documents that are simultaneously listed under exactly the same set of several descriptors.

After seeing how many articles and documents are listed under various combinations of descriptors, one may instruct the computer to display on the screen all information contained in *CIJE* or *RIE* for each article or document. If one wishes, one may obtain a hard copy of the displayed information in one of two ways. One may instruct the computer to print the information immediately, or one may instruct the computer to have the information printed later and mailed.

The Cost of On-Line Computer Searches. The cost of a computer search is determined by the amount of time spent on-line (which represents the largest expense), the number of items located, and how one elects to receive a hard copy. (Instant printing is more expensive than having copies mailed.) There are numerous ways to control the total cost of a computer search. For example, one may restrict the number of articles and documents to be searched to a given time period (e.g., the last 5 years), or one may restrict the search to only journal articles, or one may have less than the complete information sent. (One actually only needs an article's EJ number or a document's ED number to look up the summaries in *CIJE* and *RIE*. Of course, having hard copies of the summaries printed is more convenient—but it is also more expensive.)

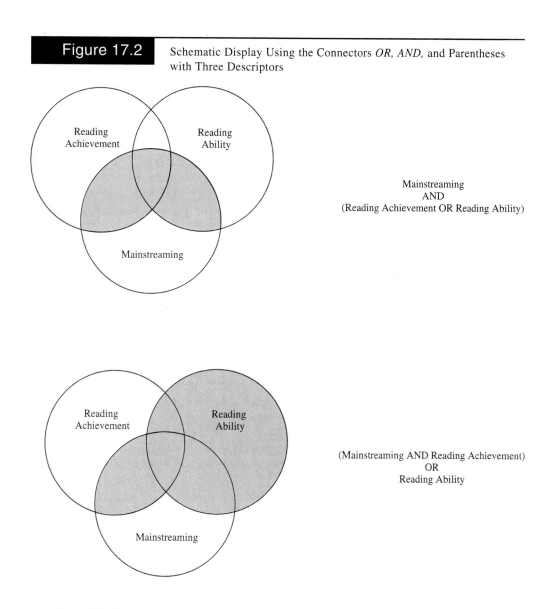

Figure 17.2   Schematic Display Using the Connectors *OR, AND,* and Parentheses with Three Descriptors

Mainstreaming
AND
(Reading Achievement OR Reading Ability)

(Mainstreaming AND Reading Achievement)
OR
Reading Ability

If possible, it is advisable to be present when the librarian actually conducts your computer search. The initial search strategy may yield information that is only marginally related to your research question. Remember, it is you, not the librarian, who should determine whether the documents retrieved in a search are pertinent to your research question or not. The librarian's function is only to conduct the computer search. It is up to you to let the librarian know if the items appearing on the screen are on target or not. If they are not, then the librarian might be able to try a different search strategy.

There may be several ways to modify a search. The librarian can explain to you the differences in the various modifications and usually give an estimate of how much each kind of modification may cost. You can then decide how much money you are willing to invest in a search, considering the amount and kind of information the search is likely to yield.

Compact Disc (CD ROM) Searches

On-line computer searches of the ERIC data base give access to all information that has been entered into the data base up until the moment the search is conducted. In addition, however, ERIC also has available data bases on two compact discs. One disc covers material entered into *CIJE* and *RIE* from the inception of ERIC through 1979. The second disc contains material from 1980 until the present. The type of disc on which the information is stored is called a **compact disc read only memory** or **CD ROM.**

It is becoming more and more common for libraries to purchase the ERIC CD ROMs. Every three months the disc with information from 1980 until the present is exchanged for an updated version. Although the amount of information on the disc is always somewhat less than the total amount of information in the ERIC system, by replacing the disc every three months, the gap is kept from becoming too large.

Most libraries that purchase the CD ROMs have computer terminals with CD ROM readers. The readers permit one to use the computer to gain access to the information on the CD ROM. Searching the literature by CD ROM is very similar to on-line computer searching. One enters descriptor terms from the ERIC *Thesaurus* into the computer to find out how many articles and documents are listed under the descriptors. It is also possible to instruct the computer to show on the terminal screen all the information pertaining to an article or document indexed in *CIJE* or *RIE*.

There are several important differences between on-line searching and using CD ROM. There is no charge for using a CD ROM because the library has already purchased the disc. The use of a CD ROM precludes going on-line and having to pay for the time spent on-line. Remember that on-line searching permits one to search the entire ERIC data base, while the CD ROM may lack information in the data base for up to the last three months. However, the fact that use of CD ROMs costs nothing compensates for the lack of complete information. Furthermore, if one wishes to search the data base lacking on the CD ROM, one can always have an on-line computer search done for only that short period, which is much cheaper than a full-blown search.

Another important difference between CD ROMs and on-line searching is that students themselves may use the CD ROMs. It is not necessary to have a librarian carry out the search as in on-line searching. When one uses the CD ROM, a list of commands appears in the form of a computer menu. Because one merely chooses from the options shown on the menu, students rarely have much difficulty mastering the menu commands.

One of the biggest advantages of searching by CD ROM is that one can keep trying various search strategies to retrieve pertinent information. The use of the CD ROM is free, so the amount of time one spends using it is unrelated to cost. (Trying various search strategies during an on-line search can become costly because of the fees associated with on-line searching.) Often the major time restriction is the fact that other students may be waiting to use the CD ROM facility.

Example of a Computer Search

Carrying out a computer search of the literature depends on the particular information service one is using, although the general procedures are similar. It is possible to search the literature on some CD ROMs using a ''menu-driven'' program. Such programs display on the computer screen step-by-step directions for carrying out the search and are relatively self-explanatory.

Other methods of searching the literature are also easy to use, but one must obtain instruction on how to use them. The following example was carried out using DIALOG, one of the most commonly used nonmenu-driven information systems. The search was done using an ERIC CD ROM, but exactly the same procedures would be used in an on-line search.

Suppose one were interested in locating literature dealing with the effects of assigning homework on reading achievement and mathematics achievement. Conceptually, one would want to locate literature that has been indexed under either "MATHEMATICS ACHIEVE-MENT" and "HOMEWORK," or under "READING ACHIEVEMENT" and "HOME-WORK." Schematically, one would search for ("MATHEMATICS ACHIEVEMENT" or "READING ACHIEVEMENT") and "HOMEWORK." There are several ways to locate such information without using ERIC descriptors, but one is more likely to locate relevant articles and documents by restricting the search strategy to the use of ERIC descriptors.

The initial prompt that appears when the computer is turned on is a question mark. One then types S (for select), space, and the descriptor, followed by /DE (which stands for descriptor), as shown:

```
?S MATHEMATICS ACHIEVEMENT/DE
```

One then presses the Enter key and the screen will display the following:

```
?S MATHEMATICS ACHIEVEMENT/DE
     S1   1,217 MATHEMATICS ACHIEVEMENT/DE
?
```

This indicates that there are 1,217 articles or documents indexed under the descriptor "MATHEMATICS ACHIEVEMENT." The ? indicates that the computer is ready for the next command. One then types S, space, and the next descriptor (i.e., "READING ACHIEVEMENT"), and presses Enter, and the screen will display the following additional information:

```
?S READING ACHIEVEMENT/DE
     S2   1,883 READING ACHIEVEMENT/DE
?
```

In addition to knowing how many articles or documents are listed under "MATHE-MATICS ACHIEVEMENT" (see S1 in the second example), you now know that there are 1,883 articles and documents indexed under the descriptor "READING ACHIEVEMENT" (see S2 in the third example). One continues as before, entering the next descriptor term, which in this example is "HOMEWORK." The screen will then display the following additional information:

```
?S HOMEWORK/DE
     S3   263 HOMEWORK/DE
?
```

Each step in the search is designated by S followed by the sequential number of the step. Step 1 (i.e., S1) was MATHEMATICS ACHIEVEMENT/DE, step 2 was READING

ACHIEVEMENT/DE, and step 3 was HOMEWORK/DE. If one wishes to continue the search by combining various steps, one need only type in S and the number of the step. For example, instead of typing S (MATHEMATICS ACHIEVEMENT/DE OR READING ACHIEVEMENT/DE) AND HOMEWORK/DE, one may simply type the following:

```
?S (S1 OR S2) AND S3
```

The screen will then display the following:

```
?S(S1 OR S2) AND S3
        1,217     S1
        1,883     S2
          263     S3
   S4     21      (S1 OR S2) AND S3
?
```

This indicates that there are 21 articles or documents that have been indexed under ''HOMEWORK'' and either ''MATHEMATICS ACHIEVEMENT'' or under ''HOMEWORK'' and ''READING ACHIEVEMENT.''

It is possible to enter more than one descriptor in one step. For example, one could have initially entered:

```
?S (MATHEMATICS ACHIEVEMENT/DE OR READING
    ACHIEVEMENT/DE) AND HOMEWORK/DE
```

and have achieved the same results as shown in S4. However, it frequently turns out to be less confusing to enter one descriptor for each step and then combine various S-numbers, so that you don't have to type the same descriptors over and over when combining them. This is particularly useful if you add new descriptors as you continue your search.

If you continue to search using various strategies, that is, by adding new descriptors and trying various combinations of them, it is easy to lose track of what steps you have tried. It is possible, however, at any time to review your search steps. When the ? prompt appears, you need only type in DS (which stands for Display Steps), and the sequential list of S-numbers will be listed on the screen. Using the DS command does not erase whatever information you have already retrieved. It is simply a convenient way for you to review what you have done.

Displaying and Printing Information. All the information appearing in *CIJE* or in *RIE* is in the data base. One may display information concerning any or all documents on the computer screen or print the information if the computer is connected to a printer by using the following sequence:

Command/Search Step Number/5/Document Numbers

Look at the following example:

```
?T 4/5/1-10
```

T is the command to display information on the screen. The 4 tells the computer you are referring to Step 4 in your search. The 5 is the code to display all information about the document. (Numbers other than 5 may be used to display only part of the information, such as the title of the document, but to avoid having to memorize a list of numbers, it is simpler always to use 5). The 1–10 indicates that you are interested only in the first 10 documents located in Step 4. If you were interested in all documents, you would type:

?T 4 / 5 / ALL

The information for the first document appears on the screen. If there is more information than can appear on a single screen, press the Page Down key to get to the next screen. To get to the second document, hold down the Control key and simultaneously press the Page Down key.

If your computer is connected to a printer, you may print the information rather than displaying it on the computer screen by typing PR (for Print) rather than T. In other words, if you typed the following:

?PR 4 / 5 / 1–3

information on the first three documents in Step 4 would be printed.

It is usually best to view all documents using the T command before printing any of them because probably only some of them will be of interest to you. While you are using the T command, it is possible to print information appearing on the screen by pressing the Print Screen key. The information currently appearing on the screen will be printed. Remember, however, that if the information pertaining to a document covers more than one screen, you must advance to each subsequent screen (by using the Page Down key) and press the Print Screen key for each screen.

If you wish to interrupt a search, simply type DS and press Enter. If you are finished searching or wish to begin a new search, type the term LOGOFF and press Enter. (More complete information on using DIALOG may be found in the Users Guide to DialogOnDisc prepared by DIALOG Information Services, Inc.)

Using Computers in Qualitative Research

Qualitative researchers often generate hundreds of pages of fieldnotes and memos, which constitute the bulk of the data in ethnographic studies. Computers and various computer programs have revolutionized the way in which ethnographers typically conduct their work. For example, the development of laptop computers has made it possible for ethnographers to write fieldnotes during observation periods.

By far the most important use of computers for qualitative researchers is to manage and analyze data. Researchers using computers usually create a separate file with a unique name for data collected during each observation unit. Computer software used by ethnographers ranges from ordinary word processing programs to programs specifically designed to analyze qualitative data. Many qualitative researchers use both a word processing program for entering and storing data and one of the various specialized programs for analyzing qualitative data, such as QUALPRO, ETHNOGRAPH (for IBM or IBM compatibles), or HYPERQUAL (for Macintosh).

Some researchers also use memory-resident note takers for writing memos. These note takers are small commercial programs that can be stored on a hard disk and loaded automatically whenever a computer session begins. These programs, which can be used simultaneously with a data analysis program, do not appear on the screen until they are called up from memory. They can be accessed at any time while using an analysis program simply by typing in a designated combination of key strokes. After having finished adding notes, the researcher can return to the regular screen by pressing an exit key. Memory-resident note takers make it possible for researchers to enter notes whenever an idea occurs to them without first having to save and retrieve the document they are working on. Also it is possible to retrieve a specific note from a large set of notes by searching for a single word contained in the note.

Ethnographic researchers divide their data into analysis units, which are text passages that can be understood even when taken out of context. It is not unusual for the boundaries of analysis units to overlap or to be nested within one another. Prior to the development of qualitative analysis programs, researchers had to make multiple printed copies of their data so they could literally cut out overlapping or nested analysis units. Qualitative computer programs, however, can handle overlapping and nested units with no difficulty.

The researcher assigns one or more category codes to each analysis unit. It is possible for a word processor program to retrieve all units with the same code. Word processing programs can usually be used with one file at a time. Text retriever programs are available, which can accept files created by word processors and locate all analysis units having the same code regardless of the file the unit is located in. In short, one of the advantages of using these computer programs is the enormous amount of time it saves in compiling and sorting data, thereby giving the researcher more time to spend analyzing and interpreting data.

In addition to the kinds of descriptive tasks computers are used for in qualitative research, there are also theory-building analysis programs. These programs permit researchers to search their data for various combinations of coding categories to see if previously undetected patterns occur or if new complex categories emerge. See LeCompte and Preissle (1993, pp. 279–314) for more detailed information on the use of computers in qualitative research.

Using Computers in Quantitative Research

Whereas the data in qualitative research take the form of words, data in quantitative research take the form of numbers. Consequently, it is probably not surprising to learn that the computer applications in quantitative research deal largely with the statistical analysis of data. Just as computers relieve qualitative researchers from the time-consuming chores of compiling and sorting data, computerized statistical programs relieve quantitative researchers from the time-consuming chore of carrying out mathematical computations.

One of the most commonly used statistical programs used by educational researchers is SPSS (Statistical Package for the Social Sciences). The following are illustrations of analyses carried out by SPSSPC, which is a version of SPSS for use with personal computers.

Procedures for Calculating the Pearson Product-Moment Correlation Coefficient (r) Using SPSSPC

Suppose a researcher has administered a self-concept questionnaire and a reading achievement test to a group of six students. The researcher is interested in determining to what extent the students' scores on the two variables are correlated. Following are the students' scores on both measures.

Student	Reading Achievement	Self-Concept
1	10	9
2	8	8
3	7	10
4	7	6
5	5	6
6	4	3

Let us arbitrarily call reading achievement variable 1 and self-concept variable 2. Using these scores, type the following:

```
data list /var1 1-2 var2 4-5.
begin data
10 09
08 08
07 10
07 06
05 06
04 03
end data.
correlation variables=var1 var2 /options 5 /statistics 1.
```

"var1 1–2" means that the numbers corresponding to variable 1 are typed in columns 1 and 2. Similarly, "var2 4–5" means that the numbers corresponding to variable 2 are typed in columns 4 and 5. (Column 3 has been skipped in order to make it easier to read the data on the screen.) Some scores have two digits and others have only one. It is necessary to place a 0 before a one-digit number, for example, for "9" type "09" to keep the columns lined up correctly. In other words, "var1 1–2" indicates that two columns have been allocated to the numbers corresponding to variable 1. (The number of columns allocated to a variable must equal the number of digits, e.g., if variable 1 had three-digit numbers, one would type "var1 1–3"; if variable 1 had four-digit numbers, one would type "var1 1–4," and so forth.)

After you have finished typing, move the cursor to the top of the screen, directly on "d" in the term "data list." Press the function key, F–10, and the screen will look like this:

```
Correlations:       VAR1              VAR2

VAR1               1.0000              .7769
                   (     6)           (     6)
                   P= .               P= .035


VAR2                .7769             1.0000
                   (     6)           (     6)
                   P= .035            P= .
```

(Coefficient / (Cases) / 1-tailed Significance)

''.'' is printed if a coefficient cannot be computed

The value of r is .7769. The significance level, p, is .035. Therefore, in the previous example, the correlation between students' reading achievement scores and self-concept scores is statistically significant.

Procedures for Calculating a Split-Half Reliability Coefficient Using SPSSPC

Suppose a researcher has administered a 20-item test and wants to calculate the test's reliability coefficient using the split-half method. The researcher first determines the subtotal score for all odd- and even-numbered items as shown below.

Student	Odd-Numbered Subtotal	Even-Numbered Subtotal
1	10	9
2	8	8
3	7	10
4	7	6
5	5	6
6	4	3

Let us arbitrarily call the odd-numbered subtotal variable 1 and the even-numbered subtotal variable 2. Using these scores, type the following:

```
data list /var1 1-2 var2 4-5.
begin data
10 09
08 08
07 10
07 06
05 06
04 03
end data.
reliability /variables=var1 var2
/scale (split) = all /model = split.
```

"var1 1–2" means that the numbers corresponding to variable 1 are typed in columns 1 and 2. Similarly, "var2 4–5" means that the numbers corresponding to variable 2 are typed in columns 4 and 5. (Column 3 has been skipped in order to make it easier to read the data on the screen.) Some scores have two digits and others have only one. It is necessary to place a 0 before a one-digit number, for example, for "9" type "09" to keep the columns lined up correctly. In other words, "var1 1–2" indicates that two columns have been allocated to the numbers corresponding to variable 1. (The number of columns allocated to a variable must equal the number of digits, e.g., if variable 1 had three-digit numbers, one would type "var1 1–3"; if variable 1 had four-digit numbers, one would type "var1 1–4," and so forth.)

After you have finished typing, move the cursor to the top of the screen, directly on "d" in the term "data list." Press the function key, F–10, and the screen will look like this:

RELIABILITY ANALYSIS-SCALE (SPLIT)

1.   VAR1
2.   VAR2

RELIABILITY COEFFICIENTS

N OF CASES =   6.0   N OF ITEMS = 2

CORRELATION BETWEEN FORMS =   .7769

EQUAL LENGTH SPEARMAN-BROWN =   .8744

GUTTMAN SPLIT-HALF =   .8675

UNEQUAL-LENGTH SPEARMAN-BROWN =   .8744

   1 ITEMS IN PART 1   1 ITEMS IN PART 2

ALPHA FOR PART 1 =   1.0000   ALPHA FOR PART 2 =   1.0000

The split-half reliability, corrected for test length, is .8744.

Procedures for Calculating t for Independent (or Uncorrelated) Means Using SPSSPC

Assume we have a group of 10 students, half of whom received reading instruction by Method A and half by Method B. At the end of a given period of instruction, students in both groups were given a reading comprehension test. Their test scores are shown below.

Student	Method A	Method B
1	90	73
2	87	76
3	85	80
4	80	70
5	78	65

Let us call students taught by Method A, Group 1 and those taught by Method B, Group 2. Using these scores, type the following:

```
data list /group 1 score 3-4.
begin data
1 90
1 87
1 85
1 80
1 78
2 73
2 76
2 80
```

```
2 70
2 65
end data.
t-test groups=group/variables=score.
```

The number of the group appears in column 1. The term "score 3–4" means that the score of each person (regardless of group) appears in columns 3 and 4. (Column 2 has been skipped in order to make it easier to read the data on the screen.) If scores had consisted of three rather than two digits, the term "score 3–4" would have to be changed to "score 3–5" in order to allow three columns for each score.

After you have finished typing, move the cursor to the top of the screen, directly on "d" in the term "data list." Press the function key, F–10, and the screen will look like this:

Independent samples of GROUP

Group 1:   GROUP EQ 1   Group 2:   GROUP EQ 2
t-test for: SCORE

	Number of Cases	Mean	Standard Deviation	Standard Error
Group 1	5	84.0000	4.950	2.214
Group 2	5	72.8000	5.718	2.557

F Value	2-Tail Prob.	Pooled Variance Estimate			Separate Variance Estimate		
		t Value	Degrees of Freedom	2-Tail Prob.	t Value	Degrees of Freedom	2-Tail Prob.
1.33	.786	3.31	8	.011	3.31	7.84	.011

The results show that $t = 3.31$ and $p = .011$.

Procedures for Calculating t for Nonindependent (or Correlated) Means Using SPSSPC

Assume we use the process of matched pairs to assign half of a group of 10 students to receive reading instruction by Method A and half by Method B. At the end of a given period of instruction, students in both groups were given a reading comprehension test. Their test scores are shown below.

Pair	Method A	Method B
1	90	73
2	87	76
3	85	80
4	80	70
5	78	65

Using these scores, type the following:

```
data list /score1 1-2 score2 4-5.
begin data
90 73
87 76
85 80
80 70
78 65
end data.
t-test pairs=score1 with score2.
```

The term "score1 1–2" means that the score of each student taught by Method A appears in columns 1 and 2. The term "score2 4–5" means the score of each paired student taught by Method B appears in columns 4 and 5. (Column 3 has been skipped in order to make it easier to read the data on the screen.) If scores had consisted of three rather than two digits, the term "score1 1–2" would have to be changed to "score1 1–3," and "score2 4–5" to "score2 4–6."

After you have finished typing, move the cursor to the top of the screen, directly on "d" in the term "data list." Press the function key, F–10, and the screen will look like this:

```
Paired samples t-test:SCORE1
                     SCORE2
```

Variable	Number of Cases	Mean	Standard Deviation	Standard Error
SCORE1	5	84.0000	4.950	2.214
SCORE2	5	72.8000	5.718	2.557

(Difference) Mean	Standard Deviation	Standard Error	Corr.	2-Tail Prob.	t Value	Degrees of Freedom	2-Tail Prob.
11.2000	4.382	1.960	.671	.215	5.72	4	.005

The results show that $t = 5.72$ and $p = .005$.

Procedures for Calculating a Two-Way Analysis of Variance and a Scheffé Test Using SPSSPC

Suppose one is interested in determining whether there are significant differences in the self-concepts of special education students as a function of gender and whether they are mainstreamed or not. Suppose too that 20 special education students have been randomly assigned in such a way that there are five boys and five girls in a mainstreamed class and five boys and five girls in a nonmainstreamed class. Assume that after a period of time each student is given a self-concept measure. Students' scores appear on the following page.

	Mainstreamed	Nonmainstreamed
Boys	(Group 1)	(Group 2)
	71	66
	70	65
	69	65
	69	64
	68	63
Girls	(Group 3)	(Group 4)
	66	72
	66	71
	64	71
	63	69
	63	68

Let us make gender variable 1, with values of "1" and "2" representing boys and girls, respectively. Let us make class placement variable 2, with values of "1" and "2" representing mainstreamed and nonmainstreamed, respectively. Using these scores, type the following:

```
data list /var1 1 var2 3 score 5-6.
begin data
1 1 71
1 1 70
1 1 69
1 1 69
1 1 68
1 2 66
1 2 65
1 2 65
1 2 64
1 2 63
2 1 66
2 1 66
2 1 64
2 1 63
2 1 63
2 2 72
2 2 71
2 2 71
2 2 69
2 2 68
```

```
end data.
anova variables=score by var1(1,2) var2(1,2).
means variables=score by var1 var2.
means variables=score by var1 by var2.
if (var1 eq 1 and var2 eq 1) c=1.
if (var1 eq 1 and var2 eq 2) c=2.
if (var1 eq 2 and var2 eq 1) c=3.
if (var1 eq 2 and var2 eq 2) c=4.
oneway variables=score by c(1,4) /ranges=scheffe.
```

The values for "var1" (gender) appear in column 1, the values for "var2" (class placement) appear in column 3, and students' self-concept scores appear in columns 5 and 6. (Columns 2 and 4 have been skipped in order to make it easier to read the data on the screen.) If scores had consisted of three rather than two digits, the term "score 5–6" would have to be changed to "score 5–7" in order to allow three columns for each score.

After you have finished typing, move the cursor to the top of the screen, directly on "d" in the term "data list." Press the function key, F–10, and the screen will look like the table below. The results show that neither main effect (i.e., gender or class placement) is significant, but the interaction is significant ($F = 73.921, p = .000$).

* * * A N A L Y S I S   O F   V A R I A N C E * * *
SCORE
BY VAR1
   VAR2

Source of Variation		Sum of Squares	DF	Mean Square	F	Signif of F
Main Effects		1.700	2	.850	.447	.647
VAR1		.450	1	.450	.237	.633
VAR2		1.250	1	1.250	.658	.429
2-way Interactions		140.450	1	140.450	73.921	.000
VAR1	VAR2	140.450	1	140.450	73.921	.000
Explained		142.150	3	47.383	24.939	.000
Residual		30.400	16	1.900		
Total		172.550	19	9.082		

Continue to press the Enter key, and the screen will look like the table below, which shows the following:

Group	Mean	Standard Deviation
(1) Mainstreamed Boys (1, 1)	69.4000	1.1402
(2) Nonmainstreamed Boys (1, 2)	64.6000	1.1402
(3) Mainstreamed Girls (2, 1)	64.4000	1.5166
(4) Nonmainstreamed Girls (2, 2)	70.2000	1.6432

```
Summaries of SCORE
By levels of  VAR1
              VAR2
Variable          Value Label          Mean          Std Dev          Cases

For Entire Population                   67.1500       3.0136           20

VAR1                   1                67.0000       2.7487           10
   VAR2                1                69.4000       1.1402            5
   VAR2                2                64.6000       1.1402            5

VAR1                   2                67.3000       3.4010           10
   VAR2                1                64.4000       1.5166            5
   VAR2                2                70.2000       1.6432            5

Total Cases = 20
```

Continue to press the Enter key, and the screen will look like the table below, which shows that the means of Groups 2 and 3 do not differ significantly, nor do the means of Groups 1 and 4. However, the means of Groups 1 and 4 are both significantly different from the means of Groups 2 and 3. In other words, mainstreamed boys and nonmainstreamed girls have significantly higher mean self-concept scores than nonmainstreamed boys and mainstreamed girls.

```
Homogeneous Subsets (Subsets of groups, whose highest and
                     lowest means do not differ by more than the
                     shortest significant range for a subset of
                     that size)

SUBSET 1

Group        Grp 3          Grp 2
Mean         64.4000        64.6000
----------------------------------------

SUBSET 2

Group        Grp 1          Grp 4
Mean         69.4000        70.2000
----------------------------------------
```

Other Uses of Technology

Researchers not only use computers for analyzing data, but also for preparing final reports. There are numerous word processing programs, such as WordPerfect, that permit researchers to write and edit final reports without having to retype the entire manuscript. There are also various graphics programs, such as Harvard Graphics, that make it easy for researchers to include in their final reports bar graphs, pie charts, and other graphic representations.

Researchers also use audio and video recording equipment to collect data consisting of interviews or observations so that there is a permanent record that can be reanalyzed as often as necessary. Historical researchers have also benefitted by having easier access to microfilms of various documents, such as the federal census data of the nineteenth century.

Chapter Highlights

- It is possible to carry out a literature search by means of computer, which permits one to conduct a search using several descriptors simultaneously.
- On-line computer searches of the literature are carried out by modems that are connected to various data bases.
- Computer searches of the literature are also carried out using compact discs, which are updated every few months.
- Qualitative researchers use various commercially available programs specifically designed to analyze ethnographic data.
- Quantitative researchers primarily use computers to carry out statistical analyses of data.
- Researchers frequently use word processing programs to write their final reports and graphics programs that make it easy to include various kinds of graphs in the final report.
- Audio- and videotaping permits researchers to have a permanent record of data consisting of interviews or observations.
- The use of microfilming has made historical documents more easily available to a larger number of historical researchers.

Review Exercises

1. What information is contained in the ERIC data base?
2. Show by means of a circle diagram which items would be retrieved using the following search strategy: (''PRESCHOOL or KINDERGARTEN'') and (''READINESS ACTIVITIES'' or ''READING READINESS'').
3. Describe the difference between an on-line search and a CD ROM search.
4. Describe some of the ways qualitative researchers use computer programs.
5. What is the major way in which quantitative researchers use computers for analyzing data?
6. Use a statistical program to which you have access to verify the analyses of any of the sets of data appearing in this chapter.
7. Describe ways in which researchers use audiotapes, videotapes, and microfilms.

Appendices

Appendix A

Ethical Standards of the American Educational Research Association

Foreword

Educational researchers come from many disciplines, embrace several competing theoretical frameworks, and use a variety of research methodologies. AERA recognizes that its members are already guided by codes in the various disciplines and, also, by organizations such as institutional review boards. AERA's code of ethics incorporates a set of standards designed specifically to guide the work of researchers in education. Education, by its very nature, is aimed at the improvement of individual lives and societies. Further, research in education is often directed at children and other vulnerable populations. A main objective of this code is to remind us, as educational researchers, that we should strive to protect these populations, and to maintain the integrity of our research, of our research community, and of all those with whom we have professional relations. We should pledge ourselves to do this by maintaining our own competence and that of people we induct into the field, by continually evaluating our research for its ethical and scientific adequacy, and by conducting our internal and external relations according to the highest ethical standards.

The standards that follow remind us that we are involved not only in research but in education. It is, therefore, essential that we continually reflect on our research to be sure that it is not only sound scientifically but that it makes a positive contribution to the educational enterprise.

I. Guiding Standards: Responsibilities to the Field

A. Preamble. To maintain the integrity of research, educational researchers should warrant their research conclusions adequately in a way consistent with the standards of their own theoretical and methodological perspectives. They should keep themselves well informed in both their own and competing paradigms where those are relevant to their research, and they should continually evaluate the criteria of adequacy by which research is judged.

B. Standards

1. Educational researchers should conduct their professional lives in such a way that they do not jeopardize future research, the public standing of the field, or the discipline's research results.
2. Educational researchers must not fabricate, falsify, or misrepresent authorship, evidence, data, findings, or conclusions.
3. Educational researchers must not knowingly or negligently use their professional roles for fraudulent purposes.

The Ethical Standards of the American Educational Research Association were developed and, in June 1992, adopted by AERA to be an educational document, to stimulate collegial debate, and to evoke voluntary compliance by moral persuasion. Accordingly, it is not the intention of the Association to monitor adherence to the Standards or to investigate allegations of violations to the Code.

4. Educational researchers should honestly and fully disclose their qualifications and limitations when providing professional opinions to the public, to government agencies, and others who may avail themselves of the expertise possessed by members of AERA.

5. Educational researchers should attempt to report their findings to all relevant stakeholders, and should refrain from keeping secret or selectively communicating their findings.

6. Educational researchers should report research conceptions, procedures, results, and analyses accurately and sufficiently in detail to allow knowledgeable, trained researchers to understand and interpret them.

7. Educational researchers' reports to the public should be written straight-forwardly to communicate the practical significance for policy, including limits in effectiveness and in generalizability to situations, problems, and contexts. In writing for or communicating with nonresearchers, educational researchers must take care not to misrepresent the practical or policy implications of their research or the research of others.

8. When educational researchers participate in actions related to hiring, retention, and advancement, they should not discriminate on the basis of gender, sexual orientation, physical disabilities, marital status, color, social class, religion, ethnic background, national origin, or other attributes not relevant to the evaluation of academic or research competence.

9. Educational researchers have a responsibility to make candid, forthright personnel recommendations and not to recommend those who are manifestly unfit.

10. Educational researchers should decline requests to review the work of others where strong conflicts of interest are involved, or when such requests cannot be conscientiously fulfilled on time. Materials sent for review should be read in their entirety and considered carefully, with evaluative comments justified with explicit reasons.

11. Educational researchers should avoid all forms of harassment, not merely those overt actions or threats that are due cause for legal action. They must not use their professional positions or rank to coerce personal or sexual favors or economic or professional advantages from students, research assistants, clerical staff, colleagues, or any others.

12. Educational researchers should not be penalized for reporting in good faith violations of these or other professional standards.

II. Guiding Standards: Research Populations, Educational Institutions, and the Public

A. Preamble. Educational researchers conduct research within a broad array of settings and institutions, including schools, colleges, universities, hospitals, and prisons. It is of paramount importance that educational researchers respect the rights, privacy, dignity, and sensitivities of their research populations and also the integrity of the institutions within which the research occurs. Educational researchers should be especially careful in working with children and other vulnerable populations. These standards are intended to reinforce and strengthen already existing standards enforced by institutional review boards and other professional associations.

B. Standards

1. Participants, or their guardians, in a research study have the right to be informed about the likely risks involved in the research and of potential consequences for participants, and to give their informed consent before

participating in research. Educational researchers should communicate the aims of the investigation as well as possible to informants and participants (and their guardians), and appropriate representatives of institutions, and keep them updated about any significant changes in the research program.

2. Honesty should characterize the relationship between researchers and participants and appropriate institutional representatives. Deception is discouraged; it should be used only when clearly necessary for scientific studies, and should then be minimized. After the study the researcher should explain to the participants and institutional representatives the reasons for the deception.

3. Educational researchers should be sensitive to any locally established institutional policies or guidelines for conducting research.

4. Participants have the right to withdraw from the study at any time, unless otherwise constrained by their official capacities or roles.

5. Educational researchers should exercise caution to ensure that there is no exploitation for personal gain of research populations or of institutional settings of research. Educational researchers should not use their influence over subordinates, students, or others to compel them to participate in research.

6. Researchers have a responsibility to be mindful of cultural, religious, gender, and other significant differences within the research population in the planning, conduct, and reporting of their research.

7. Researchers should carefully consider and minimize the use of research techniques that might have negative social consequences, for example, negative sociometrics with young children or experimental interventions

that might deprive students of important parts of the standard curriculum.

8. Educational researchers should be sensitive to the integrity of ongoing institutional activities and alert appropriate institutional representatives of possible disturbances in such activities which may result from the conduct of the research.

9. Educational researchers should communicate their findings and the practical significance of their research in clear, straightforward, and appropriate language to relevant research populations, institutional representatives, and other stakeholders.

10. Informants and participants have a right to remain anonymous. This right should be respected when no clear understanding to the contrary has been reached. Researchers are responsible for taking appropriate precautions to protect the confidentiality of both participants and data. Those being studied should be made aware of the capacities of the various data-gathering technologies to be used in the investigation so that they can make an informed decision about their participation. It should also be made clear to informants and participants that despite every effort made to preserve it, anonymity may be compromised. Secondary researchers should respect and maintain the anonymity established by primary researchers.

III. Guiding Standards: Intellectual Ownership

A. Preamble. Intellectual ownership is predominantly a function of creative contribution. Intellectual ownership is not predominantly a function of effort expended.

B. Standards

1. Authorship should be determined based on the following guidelines, which are

not intended to stifle collaboration, but rather to clarify the credit appropriately due for various contributions to research.

a) All those, regardless of status, who have made substantive creative contributions to the generation of an intellectual product are entitled to be listed as authors of that product.

b) First authorship and order of authorship should be the consequence of relative creative leadership and creative contribution. Examples of creative contributions are: writing first drafts or substantial portions; significant rewriting or substantive editing; and contributing generative ideas or basic conceptual schemes or analytic categories, collecting data which requires significant interpretation or judgment, and interpreting data.

c) Clerical or mechanical contributions to an intellectual product are not grounds for ascribing authorship. Examples of such technical contributions are: typing, routine data collection or analysis, routine editing, and participation in staff meetings.

d) Authorship and first authorship are not warranted by legal or contractual responsibility for or authority over the project or process that generates an intellectual product. It is improper to enter into contractual arrangements that preclude the proper assignment of authorship.

e) Anyone listed as author must have given his/her consent to be so listed.

f) The work of those who have contributed to the production of an intellectual product in ways short of these requirements for authorship should be appropriately acknowledged within the product.

g) Acknowledgment of other work significantly relied on in the development of an intellectual product is required. However, so long as such work is not plagiarized or otherwise inappropriately used, such reliance is not ground for authorship or ownership.

h) It is improper to use positions of authority to appropriate the work of others or claim credit for it.

i) Theses and dissertations are special cases in which authorship is not determined strictly by the criteria elaborated in these standards. Students' advisors, who might in other circumstances be deserving of authorship based on their collaborative contribution, should not be considered authors. Their creative contributions should, however, be fully and appropriately acknowledged.

j) Authors should disclose the publication history of articles they submit for publication; that is, if the present article is substantially similar in content and form to one previously published, that fact should be noted and the place of publication cited.

2. While under suitable circumstances, ideas and other intellectual products may be viewed as commodities, arrangements concerning the production or distribution of ideas or other intellectual products must be consistent with academic freedom and the appropriate availability of intellectual products to scholars, students, and the public. Moreover, when a conflict between the academic and scholarly purposes of intellectual production and profit from such production arise, preference should be given to the academic and scholarly purposes.

3. Ownership of intellectual products should be based upon the following guidelines:

a) Individuals are entitled to profit from the sale or disposition of those intellectual products they create. They may therefore enter into contracts or other arrangements for the publication or disposition of intellectual products, and profit financially from these arrangements.

b) Arrangements for the publication or disposition of intellectual products should be consistent with their appropriate public availability and with academic freedom. Such arrangements should emphasize the academic functions of publication over the maximization of profit.

c) Individuals or groups who fund or otherwise provide resources for the development of intellectual products are entitled to assert claims to a fair share of the royalties or other profits from the sale or disposition of those products. As such claims are likely to be contentious, funding institutions and authors should agree on policies for the disposition of profits at the outset of the research or development project.

d) Authors should not use positions of authority over other individuals to compel them to purchase an intellectual product from which the authors benefit. This standard is not meant to prohibit use of an author's own textbook in a class, but copies should be made available on library reserve so that students are not forced to purchase it.

IV. Guiding Standards: Editing, Reviewing, and Appraising Research

A. Preamble. Editors and reviewers have a responsibility to recognize a wide variety of theoretical and methodological perspectives and, at the same time, to ensure that manuscripts meet the highest standards as defined in the various perspectives.

B. Standards

1. AERA journals should handle refereed articles in a manner consistent with the following principles:

   a) Fairness requires a review process that evaluates submitted works solely on the basis of merit. Merit shall be understood to include both the competence with which the argument is conducted and the significance of the results achieved.

   b) Although each AERA journal may concentrate on a particular field or type of research, the set of journals as a whole should be open to all disciplines and perspectives currently represented in the membership and which support a tradition of responsible educational scholarship. This standard is not intended to exclude worthy innovations.

   c) Blind reviews, with multiple readers, should be used for each submission, except where explicitly waived. (See #3.)

   d) Judgments of the adequacy of an inquiry should be made by reviewers who are competent to read the work submitted to them. Editors should strive to select reviewers who are familiar with the research paradigm and who are not so unsympathetic as to preclude a disinterested judgment of the merit of the inquiry.

   e) Editors should insist that even unfavorable reviews be dispassionate and constructive. Authors have the right to know the grounds for rejection of their work.

2. AERA journals should have written, published policies for refereeing articles.

3. AERA journals should have a written, published policy stating when solicited and nonrefereed publications are permissible.

4. AERA journals should publish statements indicating any special emphases expected to characterize articles submitted for review.
5. In addition to enforcing standing strictures against sexist and racist language, editors should reject articles that contain *ad hominem* attacks on individuals or groups or insist that such language or attacks be removed prior to publication.
6. AERA journals and AERA members who serve as editors of journals should require authors to disclose the full publication history of material substantially similar in content and form to that submitted to their journals.

V. Guiding Standards: Sponsors, Policymakers, and Other Users of Research

A. Preamble. Researchers, research institutions, and sponsors of research jointly share responsibility for the ethical integrity of research, and should ensure that this integrity is not violated. While it is recognized that these parties may sometimes have conflicting legitimate aims, all those with responsibility for research should protect against compromising the standards of research, the community of researchers, the subjects of research, and the users of research. They should support the widest possible dissemination and publication of research results. AERA should promote, as nearly as it can, conditions conducive to the preservation of research integrity.

B. Standards
1. The data and results of a research study belong to the researchers who designed and conducted the study, unless specific contractual arrangements have been made with respect to either or both the data and results, except as noted in II B.4. (participants may withdraw at any stage).

2. Educational researchers are free to interpret and publish their findings without censorship or approval from individuals or organizations, including sponsors, funding agencies, participants, colleagues, supervisors, or administrators. This understanding should be conveyed to participants as part of the responsibility to secure informed consent.
3. Researchers conducting sponsored research retain the right to publish the findings under their own names.
4. Educational researchers should not agree to conduct research that conflicts with academic freedom, nor should they agree to undue or questionable influence by government or other funding agencies. Examples of such improper influence include endeavors to interfere with the conduct of research, the analysis of findings, or the reporting of interpretations. Researchers should report to AERA attempts by sponsors or funding agencies to use any questionable influence.
5. Educational researchers should fully disclose the aims and sponsorship of their research, except where such disclosure would violate the usual tenets of confidentiality and anonymity. Sponsors or funders have the right to have disclaimers included in research reports to differentiate their sponsorship from the conclusions of the research.
6. Educational researchers should not accept funds from sponsoring agencies that request multiple renderings of reports that would distort the results or mislead readers.
7. Educational researchers should fulfill their responsibilities to agencies funding research, which are entitled to an accounting of the use of their funds, and to a report of the procedures, findings, and implications of the funded research.

8. Educational researchers should make clear the bases and rationales, and the limits thereof, of their professionally rendered judgments in consultation with the public, government, or other institutions. When there are contrasting professional opinions to the one being offered, this should be made clear.

9. Educational researchers should disclose to appropriate parties all cases where they would stand to benefit financially from their research or cases where their affiliations might tend to bias their interpretation of their research or their professional judgments.

VI. Guiding Standards: Students and Student Researchers

A. Preamble. Educational researchers have a responsibility to ensure the competence of those inducted into the field and to provide appropriate help and professional advice to novice researchers.

B. Standards

1. In relations with students and student researchers, educational researchers should be candid, fair, nonexploitative, and committed to their welfare and progress. They should conscientiously supervise, encourage, and support students and student researchers in their academic endeavors, and should appropriately assist them in securing research support or professional employment.

2. Students and student researchers should be selected based upon their competence and potential contributions to the field.

Educational researchers should not discriminate among students and student researchers on the basis of gender, sexual orientation, marital status, color, social class, religion, ethnic background, national origin, or other irrelevant factors.

3. Educational researchers should inform students and student researchers concerning the ethical dimensions of research, encourage their practice of research consistent with ethical standards, and support their avoidance of questionable projects.

4. Educational researchers should realistically apprise students and student researchers with regard to career opportunities and implications associated with their participation in particular research projects or degree programs. Educational researchers should ensure that research assistantships be educative.

5. Educational researchers should be fair in the evaluation of research performance, and should communicate that evaluation fully and honestly to the student or student researcher. Researchers have an obligation to report honestly on the competence of assistants to other professionals who require such evaluations.

6. Educational researchers should not permit personal animosities or intellectual differences vis-à-vis colleagues to foreclose student and student researcher access to those colleagues, or to place the student or student researcher in an untenable position with those colleagues.

Appendix B

Sample Consent Forms

Example of a Research Participant Consent Form

Research Participant Consent Form

I ___(Printed Name of Participant)___ agree to participate in the research project, ___"Title of Project"___ , being carried out by ___Name(s) of researcher(s)___ . I have been informed by the researchers of the general nature of the project and of the following potential risks:

___(List any risks, or "none," if applicable)___
_____ .

I understand that I may withdraw from this project at any time, and that even if I do not withdraw, I have the right to withhold permission for the researcher(s) to use any data based on my participation.

I also understand that upon my request, the researcher(s) will provide me with a written summary of the project's findings.

___(Participant's signature)___   ___(Date)___

Example of a Parental Consent Form

Parental Research Consent Form

I ___(Printed Name of Parent or Guardian)___ agree to permit ___(Printed Name of Child)___ to participate in the research project, ___"Title of Project"___ , being carried out by ___Name(s) of researcher(s)___ . I have been informed by the researcher(s) of the general nature of the project and of any foreseeable potential risks. I understand the following:

1. My child may withdraw from this project at any time.
2. I may withdraw permission for my child to participate in the project at any time.
3. Even if my child completes the project, I have the right to withhold permission for the researcher(s) to use any data based on my child's participation.
4. Upon my request, the researcher(s) will provide me with a written summary of the project's findings.

___(Signature of Parent or Guardian)___   ___(Date)___
___(Relationship to Child)___

Appendix C

Flowchart for Determining When to Use Which Statistical Procedure for Analyzing Data

To select the correct statistical procedure to analyze data, you must take into account two factors: (a) the scale of measurement used to measure the data to be analyzed and (b) the kind of research design. This flowchart will help you decide which statistical procedure is appropriate to analyze data in your study.

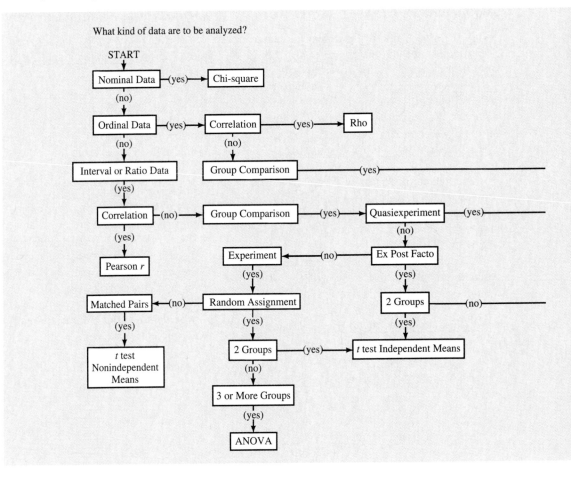

Enter the chart by asking yourself, "What kind of data are to be analyzed in my study?"

It is best to use one of many available computerized statistical programs for complex statistical analyses. Students who do not have access to a computerized statistical program, however, can find step-by-step procedures for calculating many complex statistics by hand in Bruning and Kintz (1987).

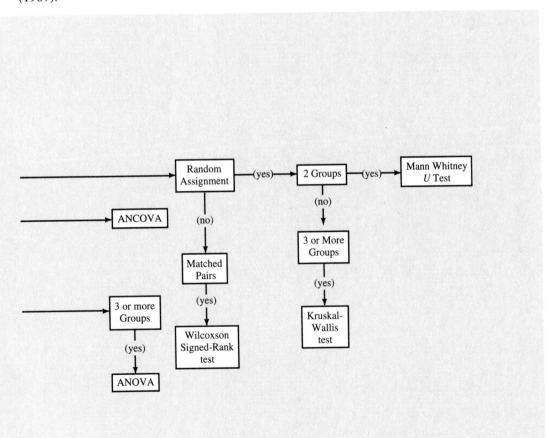

Appendix D

Table of Significant *r* Values

Number of Subjects	Significance Level	
	.05	.01
6	.73	.88
7	.67	.83
8	.62	.79
9	.58	.75
10	.55	.72
11	.52	.69
12	.50	.66
13	.48	.63
14	.46	.61
15	.44	.59
16	.43	.57
17	.41	.56
18	.40	.54
19	.39	.53
20	.38	.52
21	.37	.50
22	.36	.49
23	.35	.48
24	.34	.47
25	.34	.46
26	.33	.45
27	.32	.45
28	.32	.44
29	.31	.43
30	.31	.42
32	.30	.41
42	.26	.36
52	.23	.32

Source: This table is an adapted version of Table VII from Fisher & Yates: *Statistical Tables for Biological, Agricultural and Medical Research* published by Longman Group Ltd., London (previously published by Oliver and Boyd Ltd., Edinburgh) and is used by permission of the authors and publishers.

Appendix E

Table of Significant Chi-Square Values

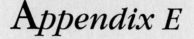

df	Significance Level	
	.05	.01
1	3.84	6.64
2	5.99	9.21
3	7.81	11.34
4	9.49	13.28
5	11.07	15.09
6	12.59	16.81
7	14.07	18.48
8	15.51	20.09
9	16.92	21.67
10	18.31	23.21

Reprinted with permission of University of Adelaide from STATISTICAL METHODS FOR RESEARCH WORKERS (14th Ed.) by R. A. Fisher. Copyright © 1970 by University of Adelaide.

Appendix F

Table of Significant *t* Values

| | Significance Level | | | |
| | Nondirectional Hypotheses | | Directional Hypotheses | |
df	.05	.01	.05	.01
3	3.18	5.84	2.35	4.54
4	2.78	4.60	2.13	3.75
5	2.57	4.03	2.02	3.37
6	2.45	3.71	1.94	3.14
7	2.37	3.50	1.90	3.00
8	2.31	3.36	1.86	2.90
9	2.26	3.25	1.83	2.82
10	2.23	3.17	1.81	2.76
11	2.20	3.11	1.80	2.72
12	2.18	3.06	1.78	2.68
13	2.16	3.01	1.77	2.65
14	2.15	2.98	1.76	2.62
15	2.13	2.95	1.75	2.60
16	2.12	2.92	1.75	2.58
17	2.11	2.90	1.74	2.57
18	2.10	2.88	1.73	2.55
20	2.09	2.85	1.73	2.53
22	2.07	2.82	1.72	2.51
24	2.06	2.80	1.71	2.49
26	2.06	2.78	1.71	2.48
28	2.05	2.76	1.70	2.47
40	2.02	2.70	1.68	2.42
60	2.00	2.66	1.67	2.39

Source: This table is an adapted version of Table II from Fisher & Yates: *Statistical Tables for Biological, Agricultural and Medical Research* published by Longman Group Ltd., London (previously published by Oliver and Boyd Ltd., Edinburgh) and is used by permission of the authors and publishers.

Appendix G

Table of Significant *F* Values

	p	Between-Groups				
		1	2	3	4	5
1	.05	161.45	199.50	215.71	224.58	230.16
	.01	4052	4999	5403	5625	5764
2	.05	18.51	19.00	19.16	19.25	19.30
	.01	98.49	99.00	99.17	99.25	99.30
3	.05	10.13	9.55	9.28	9.12	9.01
	.01	34.12	30.81	29.46	28.71	28.24
4	.05	7.71	6.94	6.59	6.39	6.26
	.01	21.20	18.00	16.69	15.98	15.52
5	.05	6.61	5.79	5.41	5.19	5.05
	.01	16.26	13.27	12.06	11.39	10.97
6	.05	5.99	5.14	4.76	4.53	4.39
	.01	13.74	10.92	9.78	9.15	8.75
7	.05	5.59	4.74	4.35	4.12	3.97
	.01	12.25	9.55	8.45	7.85	7.46
8	.05	5.32	4.46	4.07	3.84	3.69
	.01	11.26	8.65	7.59	7.01	6.63
9	.05	5.12	4.26	3.86	3.63	3.48
	.01	10.56	8.02	6.99	6.42	6.06
10	.05	4.96	4.10	3.71	3.48	3.33
	.01	10.04	7.56	6.55	5.99	5.64
11	.05	4.84	3.98	3.59	3.36	3.20
	.01	9.65	7.20	6.22	5.67	5.32

(Left axis label: Within-Groups)

This table is an adapted version of Table V of Fisher & Yates: *Statistical Tables for Biological, Agricultural and Medical Research* published by Longman Group Ltd., London (previously published by Oliver and Boyd Ltd., Edinburgh) and is used by permission of the authors and publishers.

Table of Significant *F* Values (continued)

	p	Between-Groups				
		1	2	3	4	5
12	.05	4.75	3.88	3.49	3.26	3.11
	.01	9.33	6.93	5.95	5.41	5.06
13	.05	4.67	3.80	3.41	3.18	3.02
	.01	9.07	6.70	5.74	5.20	4.86
14	.05	4.60	3.74	3.34	3.11	2.96
	.01	8.86	6.51	5.56	5.03	4.69
15	.05	4.54	3.68	3.29	3.06	2.90
	.01	8.68	6.36	5.42	4.89	4.56
16	.05	4.49	3.63	3.24	3.01	2.85
	.01	8.53	6.23	5.29	4.77	4.44
17	.05	4.45	3.59	3.20	2.96	2.81
	.01	8.40	6.11	5.18	4.67	4.34
18	.05	4.41	3.55	3.16	2.93	2.77
	.01	8.28	6.01	5.09	4.58	4.25
19	.05	4.38	3.52	3.13	2.90	2.74
	.01	8.18	5.93	5.01	4.50	4.17
20	.05	4.65	3.49	3.10	2.87	2.71
	.01	8.10	5.85	4.94	4.43	4.10
21	.05	4.32	3.47	3.07	2.84	2.68
	.01	8.02	5.78	4.87	4.37	4.04
22	.05	4.30	3.44	3.05	2.82	2.66
	.01	7.94	5.72	4.82	4.31	3.99
24	.05	4.26	3.40	3.01	2.78	2.62
	.01	7.82	5.61	4.72	4.22	3.90
26	.05	4.22	3.37	2.98	2.74	2.59
	.01	7.72	5.53	4.64	4.14	3.82
28	.05	4.20	3.34	2.95	2.71	2.56
	.01	7.64	5.45	4.57	4.07	3.75
30	.05	4.17	3.32	2.92	2.69	2.53
	.01	7.56	5.39	4.51	4.02	3.70
40	.05	4.08	3.23	2.84	2.61	2.45
	.01	7.31	5.18	4.31	3.83	3.51
60	.05	4.00	3.15	2.76	2.52	2.37
	.01	7.08	4.98	4.13	3.65	3.34
120	.05	3.92	3.07	2.68	2.45	2.29
	.01	6.85	4.79	3.95	3.48	3.17
∞	.05	3.84	2.99	2.60	2.37	2.21
	.01	6.64	4.60	3.78	3.32	3.02

Within-Groups

Appendix H
Sample Student Research Proposals

This appendix consists of two sample research proposals written by former students in my educational research course. The final reports based on these proposals appear in Appendix I. These proposals have been single-spaced to conserve space. Your proposal should be double-spaced.

School Attitudes of Ninth Graders Attending a Senior or
Junior High School
Denise Aubrey and Meg Lukawski

*The title should consist
of 10–12 words and
identify the variables
and populations under
investigation.*

In New York City a ninth grade student may attend
school either as a first year senior high school student or as
a last year junior high school student. Where the student
goes for ninth grade is largely a matter of zoning or may be
a matter of family choice. Currently a controversy exists as
to whether school districts should subdivide the intermediate
grades into middle schools consisting of grades six through
eight, or into junior high schools consisting of grades seven
through nine.

*The introductory section
of the proposal is **not**
labeled ''Introduction.''
The first two
paragraphs explain why
the authors feel it is
important to carry out
the proposed study.*

The debate over which grade level arrangement is most
appropriate for early adolescents has been growing over the
last twenty-five years. Many school districts are changing
from the conventional seventh through ninth grade
organization of the junior high school to the sixth through
eighth grade level arrangement of the middle school.

*The authors indicate
they have searched the
literature for empirical
evidence directly
related to their topic.*

The recent move toward middle schools is based on the
claims of middle school advocates that students will receive a
better education and develop more positive attitudes toward
school. The only empirical evidence found in the literature,
however, that supports this claim is a single study conducted
by Schoo in 1970. His findings revealed that middle school
students had a significantly more positive attitude toward
school than did junior high school students. On the other
hand, Wood (1973) found no significant difference between
the school attitudes of middle school students and those of
junior high school students. Therefore, before school districts
make a decision to restructure the entire educational system
to accommodate middle school advocates, it seems
imperative to obtain further empirical evidence concerning
the optimal grade level arrangement for early adolescents.

*Having found little
directly related
empirical evidence, the
authors cite literature
that is conceptually
related to their topic.
The authors have
synthesized the
literature by identifying
three different
approaches that others
have used in addressing
the problem under
investigation.*

In reviewing the literature on the rationale underlying
various grade level arrangements, it appears that there have
been three different approaches to the problem. The first
approach has determined those grade levels at which
students exhibit similar degrees of physical and emotional
maturation. The second approach has examined how the

number of grade levels in a particular school structure affects students' academic progress and social development in any given grade. And the last approach has analyzed student behavior and attitudes toward school as a function of various combinations of grade levels comprising a school.

A good example of the "similarity approach" is the work of Dacus (1963), who studied the social, emotional, and physical maturity of students in the fifth through tenth grades to determine the grade levels at which students possessed the most similar degree of maturation. He found sixth graders were most similar to seventh graders, and ninth graders were most similar to tenth graders. Based on these findings, Dacus recommended that middle schools should consist of the sixth, seventh, and eighth grades in order to take advantage of the similarities of students in these grades. This kind of argument has been used in support of the middle school by many school districts.

The authors describe a study exemplifying the first approach and contrast the studies by Dacus and by Blythe and Traeger.

One problem with this approach, however, is that it does not take into account the fact that there are enormous emotional, physical, and cognitive changes taking place in the early adolescent and that these changes occur at different rates for different individuals. According to Blythe and Traeger (1983), these changes are not correlated with age, and there can be huge differences in maturity among adolescents of the same age. Therefore, the minor similarities that may be found are insignificant when compared to the overwhelming differences that still remain. Another problem with the similarity approach is that it fails to consider the possible negative consequences of placing ninth graders in a senior high school setting.

The second approach to determine the optimal grade level organization is to see how the number of grade levels in a school building may affect students at a particular grade level. White (1967) demonstrated that a student's academic achievement is hindered when the majority of students in the school are in the grades above that student. He found a negative effect on the academic achievement and personal adjustment of seventh graders attending schools comprised of seventh, eighth, and ninth grades. This finding suggests that students in the lowest grade of a school comprised of three or more grade levels are at a disadvantage socially and academically.

The authors describe studies exemplifying the second and third approaches. The findings of the cited studies indicate that the younger students in a school are at a disadvantage academically and socially and have more negative attitudes toward school than do older students. These findings justify the authors' decision to hypothesize on page 4 that ninth graders in a junior high school will have significantly more positive attitudes toward school than ninth graders in a senior high school.

The third approach to solving the problem of effective grade level organization is to examine the consequences of varying grade level arrangements (Blythe, Simmons & Bush, 1978; Blythe, Smythe & Hill, 1984). A prime example of this approach is a study by Blythe, Hill and Smythe (1981). Their study found that seventh graders were negatively affected by the presence of ninth graders, but that there were even more detrimental consequences for ninth graders who have been moved into a school containing tenth graders. It was also found that ninth graders became much more precocious in the presence of tenth graders. The most significant finding, however, was that the school attitudes of ninth graders attending high school were significantly more negative than the attitudes of seventh and eighth graders attending junior high school.

Having given background literature concerning the problem to be investigated, the authors narrow their focus to a specific research question.

The debate about grade level organization is a complex one and leaves many questions still unanswered. For example, which school structure is better for early adolescents—middle school or junior high school? Which grades benefit most from each type of structure? Which structure is more beneficial to sixth graders? Although it is not possible to address all of these questions within the parameters of this study, we shall examine one aspect of the debate: the attitudes toward school exhibited by ninth graders attending a senior high school compared to those exhibited by ninth graders attending a junior high school.

It has been found among teachers and administrators that ninth graders are not wanted in junior high schools because of their negative effects on the younger students (Schoo, 1970; White, 1967). Nor are they wanted in senior high schools, because of the negative influence older students have on them (Blythe, Hill & Smythe, 1981). The obvious question is: Which school structure benefits the ninth grader more?

The authors explain how their proposed study is related to the earlier study by Blythe, Hill, and Smythe.

The objective of the present study is to determine whether the structure of the school ninth graders attend is related to their attitudes toward school. Whereas Blythe, Hill and Smythe (1981) compared the school attitudes of ninth graders attending senior high school to the attitudes of seventh and eighth graders in junior high school, in the present study the attitudes of ninth graders attending a senior high school will be compared to those of ninth graders attending a junior high school. Also, whereas the high school used in Blythe, Hill and Smythe's study consisted only of the ninth and tenth grades, the high school to be used in the present study consists of grades nine through twelve.

It is hypothesized that students attending ninth grade in a junior high school will have significantly more positive attitudes toward school than will students attending ninth grade in a senior high school.

The authors state a directional hypothesis in unambiguous terms.

Method

Participants

Approximately 60 ninth graders attending a public junior high school and 60 ninth graders attending a public senior high school will participate in the study. No students in special programs at either school will be used. Students who are repeating the ninth grade will be eliminated from the sample.

Materials

A questionnaire measuring students' attitudes toward school will be used. If no suitable questionnaire can be located, the researchers will develop their own questionnaire, which will include Likert-type statements concerning students' attitudes toward self, peers, and teachers. The questionnaire will include a biographical section asking students to indicate their age, gender, and whether they are repeating the ninth grade.

Procedure

The questionnaires will be distributed during homeroom period. Due to the short amount of time available for homeroom, the students will be asked to complete the questionnaires at home and to return them within the next few days to their homeroom teacher. Three randomly selected homerooms will be used in each school. After five days, the questionnaires will be collected and the responses from each homeroom will be divided according to the gender of the respondent. The responses of approximately 10 boys and 10 girls will be randomly selected from each homeroom, yielding a sample of 30 males and 30 females from each of the two schools.

The procedures for collecting data are described in sufficient detail to permit the reader to replicate the study.

Data Analysis

The authors note that it is necessary to determine the reliability of a self-made measuring instrument.

If the researchers develop their own questionnaire, the questionnaire's reliability will be determined by means of the split-half reliability coefficient.

Responses to the questionnaire will be weighted from 1 (strongly disagree) to 5 (strongly agree) for positively worded statements, with the weights reversed for negatively worded statements.

A t-test will be used because the means of two groups are to be compared.

A directional t-test for independent means will be carried out to determine if the mean attitudinal score of ninth graders attending the junior high school is significantly higher than that of ninth graders attending the senior high school.

References

Blythe, D. A., Hill, J. P., & Smythe, C. K. (1981). The influence of older adolescents: Do grade level arrangements make a difference in behaviors, attitudes, and experiences? Journal of Early Adolescence, 1, 85–100.

Blythe, D. A., Simmons, R. G., & Bush, D. (1978). The transition into early adolescence: A longitudinal comparison of youth in two educational contexts. Sociology of Education, 51, 149–160.

Blythe, D. A., Smythe, C. K., & Hill, J. P. (1984). Grade level arrangements—What are the differences? NAASP Bulletin, 68, 105–117.

Blythe, D. A., & Traeger, C. M. (1983). The self-concept and self-esteem of early adolescence. Theory into Practice, 22, 91–97.

Dacus, W. P. (1963). Study of the grade organizational structure of junior high school as measured by social maturity, emotional maturity, physical maturity, and opposite sex choices. Dissertation Abstracts International, 24, 1461A–1462A. (University Microfilms No. 63–06, 787)

Haertel, G. D., Walburg, H. J., & Haertel, E. H. (1981). Socio-psychological environments and learning: A quantitative synthesis. British Educational Journal, 7, 27–36.

Schoo, P. H. (1970). Students' self-concept, social behavior, and attitudes toward school in middle and junior high schools. Dissertation Abstracts International, 31, 6322A. (University Microfilms No. 71–15, 296)

White, W. D. (1967). Pupil progress and grade combinations. NAASP Bulletin, 51, 87–90.

Wood, F. H. (1973). A comparison of student attitudes in junior high and middle schools. The High School Journal, 57, 355–361.

The list of references begins on a new page. References are listed alphabetically by the first author's last name.

The title should consist of 10–12 words and identify the variables and populations under investigation.

Parental Attitudes toward Prekindergartners' Gender-stereotyped Toys
Margaret Hamilton and Gail Rossi

*The introductory section of the proposal is **not** labeled ''Introduction.'' The first sentence explains why the authors feel it is important to carry out the proposed study. The authors move directly into a description of the empirical research literature dealing with their topic.*

Toys are one of children's major sources of socialization, and according to Miller (1987), early play experiences of girls and boys may contribute to gender differences found in the social behavior of females and males. In studies dealing with children as young as ten months of age, researchers have found differences in the way parents respond to the play of boys and girls (Fagot, 1978; Roopnarine, 1986; Snow, Jacklin & Maccoby, 1983).

For example, Roopnarine found that by ten months of age, girls were already showing a preference for dolls and were more likely to offer the doll to parents than were boys. Doll play was encouraged by favorable parental responses made to pre-toddler and toddler age girls (Fagot, 1978; Roopnarine, 1986). Fagot also found that parents reacted significantly more favorably to the child when the child was engaged in a same-gender preferred behavior and more negatively in a cross-gender preferred behavior. Girls received more negative responses when engaged in active large motor activities and more positive responses when engaged in adult oriented dependent behavior.

O'Brien and Huston (1985) reported that parents choose same-gender typed toys and expect same-gender typed play from their children, and that by the age of three, children show patterns of or preferences for toys that are socially stereotyped for their gender (O'Brien & Huston, 1985; Robinson & Morris, 1986). It is possible that children's gender-stereotypic toy preferences may result from their parents' gender-stereotypical attitudes toward their children's play activities.

Based on their review of the literature, the authors state a directional hypothesis. The hypothesis is worded in an unambiguous manner and the variable is defined operationally.

It is hypothesized that parents of preschoolers will have significantly more favorable attitudes toward gender-stereotyped toys than toward nongender-stereotyped toys. Parental attitudes will be operationally defined by the scores received on a Toy Preference Questionnaire (TPQ), which will be formulated by the researchers.

Method

Participants

Parents of approximately 39 prekindergarten children from a private, nonsectarian nursery school will be asked to participate in the study.

Materials

In order to formulate the TPQ, a list will first be made of the toys found in the children's nursery school classroom. Five early childhood teachers will be asked to rate each of the toys appearing on the list as male-stereotypical, female-stereotypical, or neutral. No toy will be included on the TPQ, unless four of the five teachers agree on its gender-stereotypical rating.

The authors describe how they intend to construct their measuring instrument.

The items on the TPQ will consist of pairings of male- and female-stereotypical toys. It is expected that the TPQ will consist of 50 items. The TPQ will also contain a biographical questionnaire on which parents will be asked to indicate their gender and age, as well as the gender, age, and grade level of their children.

Procedure

The TPQ will be distributed to parents, who will be asked to complete and return it in an enclosed stamped, self-addressed envelope within 10 days. After seven days a reminder will be distributed to those who have not yet responded, asking them to do so within the next three days.

The procedures for collecting data are described in sufficient detail to permit the reader to replicate the study.

For each of the 50 pairs of toys appearing on the TPQ, parents will be asked to select the one with which they would prefer their child to play. The TPQ will be scored in such a way that each respondent will receive two scores: one indicating the number of gender-stereotyped toys, and another indicating the number of nongender-stereotyped toys that have been selected. Parents of boys will receive a gender-stereotyped score for each male-stereotypical toy selected, and conversely, parents of girls will receive a gender-stereotyped score for each female-stereotypical toy selected.

A t test for nonindependent means will be used because the two sets of scores to be compared come from the same group of parents.

Data Analysis

A t-test for nonindependent means will be used to see if the mean gender-stereotyped score is significantly higher than the mean nongender-stereotyped score. A split-half reliability coefficient will be calculated for the TPQ.

The authors note that it is necessary to determine the reliability of a self-made measuring instrument.

References

The list of references begins on a new page. References are listed alphabetically by the first author's last name.

Fagot, B. (1978). The influence of sex of child on parental reactions to toddler children. Child Development, 49, 459–465.

Miller, C. (1987). Qualitative differences among gender-stereotyped toys: Implications for cognitive and social development in girls and boys. Sex Roles, 16, 473–487.

O'Brien, M., & Huston, A. C. (1985). Development of sex typed play behaviors in toddlers. Developmental Psychology, 21, 866–871.

Robinson, C., & Morris, J. (1986). The gender-stereotyped nature of Christmas toys received by 36-, 48-, and 60-month old children: A comparison between nonrequested vs. requested toys. Sex Roles, 15, 21–32.

Roopnarine, J. (1986). Mothers' and fathers' behaviors toward the toy play of their infant sons and daughters. Sex Roles, 14, 59–68.

Snow, M., Jacklin, C., & Maccoby, E. (1983). Sex-of-child differences in father-child interaction at one year of age. Child Development, 54, 227–232.

Appendix I

Sample Student Final Reports

This appendix consists of two sample final reports written by former students in my educational research course. The proposals on which these reports are based appear in Appendix H. These final reports have been single-spaced to conserve space. Your final report should be double-spaced.

A short title, usually consisting of the first couple of major words of the actual title (i.e., ''School Attitudes''), appears at the upper right edge of each page. The short title may be used to identify which pages belong to a manuscript in the event that the pages are misplaced.

Running head: SCHOOL ATTITUDES OF NINTH GRADERS

The running head is an abbreviated version of the title that is printed on alternate pages in a journal if the manuscript is published as an article. (The authors' names are printed on the other pages.)
The title should consist of 10–12 words and identify the variables and populations under investigation.

School Attitudes of Ninth Graders Attending a Senior or
Junior High School
Denise Aubrey and Meg Lukawski
The College of Staten Island

Abstract

This study compared school attitudes of ninth graders attending a junior high school and ninth graders attending a senior high school. A researcher-constructed attitudinal questionnaire was administered to 3 ninth grade classes in a junior and 3 in a senior high school. From 60 respondents in each school, the questionnaires of 12 girls and 12 boys were randomly chosen for analysis. A two-way ANOVA (school × gender) showed that junior high ninth graders had significantly more positive attitudes than senior high ninth graders ($p < .01$), suggesting that attitudes are related to students' ages relative to other students in the school. Neither the main effect of gender nor the interaction between gender and school was significant. The questionnaire had a split-half reliability coefficient of .92.

The abstract appears on a separate page and should not exceed 120 words. It should state the problem, the types of subjects used, the procedures used to collect data, the measuring instruments, the findings (including statistical levels of significance), and the conclusions.

School Attitudes of Ninth Graders Attending a Senior or Junior High School

*The introductory section of the report is **not** labeled "Introduction." The first two paragraphs explain why the authors feel it is important to carry out the proposed study.*

In New York City a ninth grade student may attend school either as a first year senior high school student or as a last year junior high school student. Where the student goes for ninth grade is largely a matter of zoning or may be a matter of family choice. Currently a controversy exists as to whether school districts should subdivide the intermediate grades into middle schools consisting of grades six through eight, or into junior high schools consisting of grades seven through nine.

The debate over which grade level arrangement is most appropriate for early adolescents has been growing over the last twenty-five years. Many school districts are changing from the conventional seventh through ninth grade organization of the junior high school to the sixth through eighth grade level arrangement of the middle school.

The authors indicate they have searched the literature for empirical evidence directly related to their topic.

Having found little directly related empirical evidence, the authors cite literature that is conceptually related to their topic. The authors have synthesized the literature by identifying three different approaches that others have used in addressing the problem under investigation.

The recent move toward middle schools is based on the claims of middle school advocates that students will receive a better education and develop more positive attitudes toward school. The only empirical evidence found in the literature, however, that supports this claim is a single study conducted by Schoo in 1970. His findings revealed that middle school students had a significantly more positive attitude toward school than did junior high school students. On the other hand, Wood (1973) found no significant difference between the school attitudes of middle school students and those of junior high school students. Therefore, before school districts make a decision to restructure the entire educational system to accommodate middle school advocates, it seems imperative to obtain further empirical evidence concerning the optimal grade level arrangement for early adolescents.

In reviewing the literature on the rationale underlying various grade level arrangements, it appears that there have been three different approaches to the problem. The first approach has determined those grade levels at which students exhibit similar degrees of physical and emotional maturation. The second approach has examined how the number of grade levels in a particular school structure affects students' academic progress and social development in any given grade. And the last approach has analyzed student behavior and attitudes toward school as a function of various combinations of grade levels comprising a school.

A good example of the "similarity approach" is the work of Dacus (1963), who studied the social, emotional, and physical maturity of students in the fifth through tenth grades to determine the grade levels at which students possessed the most similar degree of maturation. He found sixth graders were most similar to seventh graders, and ninth graders were most similar to tenth graders. Based on these findings, Dacus recommended that middle schools should consist of the sixth, seventh, and eighth grades in order to take advantage of the similarities of students in these grades. This kind of argument has been used in support of the middle school by many school districts.

The authors describe a study exemplifying the first approach and contrast the studies by Dacus and by Blythe and Traeger.

One problem with this approach, however, is that it does not take into account the fact that there are enormous emotional, physical, and cognitive changes taking place in the early adolescent and that these changes occur at different rates for different individuals. According to Blythe and Traeger (1983), these changes are not correlated with age, and there can be huge differences in maturity among adolescents of the same age. Therefore, the minor similarities that may be found are insignificant when compared to the overwhelming differences that still remain. Another problem with the similarity approach is that it fails to consider the possible negative consequences of placing ninth graders in a senior high school setting.

The second approach to determine the optimal grade level organization is to see how the number of grade levels in a school building may affect students at a particular grade level. White (1967) demonstrated that a student's academic achievement is hindered when the majority of students in the school are in the grades above that student. He found a negative effect on the academic achievement and personal adjustment of seventh graders attending schools comprised of seventh, eighth, and ninth grades. This finding suggests that students in the lowest grade of a school comprised of three or more grade levels are at a disadvantage socially and academically.

The third approach to solving the problem of effective grade level organization is to examine the consequences of

The authors describe studies exemplifying the second and third approaches. The findings of the cited studies indicate that the younger students in a school are at a disadvantage academically and socially and have more negative attitudes toward school than do older students. These findings justify the authors' decision to hypothesize on page 6 that ninth graders in a junior high school will have significantly more positive attitudes toward school than ninth graders in a senior high school.

varying grade level arrangements (Blythe, Simmons & Bush, 1978; Blythe, Smythe & Hill, 1984). A prime example of this approach is a study by Blythe, Hill and Smythe (1981). Their study found that seventh graders were negatively affected by the presence of ninth graders, but that there were even more detrimental consequences for ninth graders who have been moved into a school containing tenth graders. It was also found that ninth graders became much more precocious in the presence of tenth graders. The most significant finding, however, was that the school attitudes of ninth graders attending high school were significantly more negative than the attitudes of seventh and eighth graders attending junior high school.

Having given background literature concerning the problem to be investigated, the authors narrow their focus to a specific research question.

The debate about grade level organization is a complex one and leaves many questions still unanswered. For example, which school structure is better for early adolescents—middle school or junior high school? Which grades benefit most from each type of structure? Which structure is more beneficial to sixth graders? Although it is not possible to address all of these questions within the parameters of this study, we shall examine one aspect of the debate: the attitudes toward school exhibited by ninth graders attending a senior high school compared to those exhibited by ninth graders attending a junior high school.

It has been found among teachers and administrators that ninth graders are not wanted in junior high schools because of their negative effects on the younger students (Schoo, 1970; White, 1967). Nor are they wanted in senior high schools, because of the negative influence older students have on them (Blythe, Hill & Smythe, 1981). The obvious question is: Which school structure benefits the ninth graders more?

The authors explain how their proposed study is related to the earlier study by Blythe, Hill, and Smythe.

The objective of the present study was to determine whether the structure of the school ninth graders attend is related to their attitudes toward school. Whereas Blythe, Hill and Smythe (1981) compared the school attitudes of ninth graders attending senior high school to the attitudes of seventh and eighth graders in junior high school, in the present study the attitudes of ninth graders attending a senior high school were compared to those of ninth graders attending a junior high school. Also, whereas the high school used in Blythe, Hill and Smythe's study consisted only of the ninth and tenth grades, the high school used in the present study consisted of grades nine through twelve.

It was hypothesized that students attending ninth grade in a junior high school would have significantly more positive attitudes toward school than would students attending ninth grade in a senior high school.

The authors state a directional hypothesis in unambiguous terms.

Method

Participants

Twenty-four ninth graders from a senior high school comprised of grades nine through twelve and 24 ninth graders from a junior high school comprised of grades seven through nine participated in the study. Each group consisted of 12 boys and 12 girls, whose ages ranged from 13 to 17 years, with a mean age of 14.72 years. All junior high school subjects had been in attendance since grade seven. The high school subjects had entered their school that year as freshmen. The socioeconomic status of the students in both schools would probably be considered lower middle.

The authors describe the number and kinds of subjects who participated in the study.

Materials

The questionnaire used in this study was developed by the researchers and consisted of 47 Likert scale items designed to assess the attitude of ninth graders toward their class and school environment. (A copy of the questionnaire appears in the appendix.) "School attitude" was operationally defined as the score the subjects received on the questionnaire.

The authors operationally define the variable.

Procedure

Within the senior high school, the questionnaire was distributed to all students present in three intact social studies classes. Within the junior high school, the questionnaire was distributed to all students present in three intact English classes. No modified, scholarship, or special education students were used for this study in either school.

Data collection took place on a single day in May. Therefore, the senior high school students had been in their school for approximately eight months, while the junior high school students were finishing their third year in the school. All students were given written as well as oral instructions to ensure proper understanding and completing of the questionnaire. It was made clear to the students that their responses would not be seen by their teachers.

The procedures for collecting data are described in sufficient detail to permit the reader to replicate the study.

Results

The authors report the reliability of their self-made measuring instrument.

The authors carry out an ANOVA because they are comparing the means of more than two groups (i.e., junior high boys, junior high girls, senior high boys and senior high girls). In their proposal the authors had intended to examine only differences associated with kind of school. In their final project, however, they decided to examine differences associated with students' gender as well as type of school. Consequently, the number of groups becomes four rather than two.

The authors report means and standard deviations.

A split-half reliability coefficient, corrected for test length, was computed for the questionnaire and found to be .92. Responses to statements on the questionnaire were scored in such a way that +94 represented the maximum positive and −94 represented the maximum negative school attitude score. Twelve boys and 12 girls were randomly selected from each school, and their scores were analyzed by a 2 × 2 analysis of variance (school × gender).

The junior high school ninth graders exhibited a significantly more positive attitude toward school than did the senior high school ninth graders, $F(1, 20) = 13.65$, $p < .01$. (Means and standard deviations are shown in Table 1.) There was no significant difference between boys' and girls' attitudes, nor was there a significant interaction between gender of student and type of school.

Discussion

A review of the literature revealed that the ninth grader is not wanted by either the senior or the junior high schools (Schoo, 1970; White, 1967). It occurred to the present researchers that because ninth graders are the ones caught in the middle of this controversy, they should be the ones called upon to try to solve the problem.

Based on an informal analysis of students' responses to specific statements, it appears that in comparison to ninth graders attending senior high school, junior high school ninth graders (a) have a more positive attitude toward their class and school environment, (b) perceive their teachers in a more positive light, (c) feel more comfortable and visible in their school, and (d) receive more encouragement to participate in school activities.

The authors show how their findings relate to the existing literature on the topic.

Similar results have been reported in the literature. For example, Reece (1975) found that in comparison with senior high school ninth graders, junior high school ninth graders believe their teachers are more interested in their welfare and more concerned about their problems. Reece also noted that many senior high school administrators adopt a "wait your turn" attitude toward ninth graders, resulting in less participation by ninth graders in school activities and fewer leadership opportunities for them. Furthermore, Blythe, Hill and Smythe (1981) found that senior high school ninth graders become more precocious in the presence of older students and that students in the lowest grade in a school comprised of three or more grade levels have more academic, personal, and social adjustment problems.

Haertel, Walburg, and Haertel (1981) have summarized the findings of numerous studies showing that students' attitudes toward school may be used as an accurate predictor of learning outcomes. The negative school attitudes of senior high school ninth graders will almost certainly affect students' scholastic performance adversely.

One wonders why there is a national trend to establish middle schools, which result in sending ninth graders to senior high school. What is this trend based on—emotions, politics, or hard evidence? Who benefits by sending ninth graders to high school? The results of the present study suggest that it is not the ninth graders who benefit.

A limitation of the present study is that the ninth graders who participated in it came from a single senior high school or a single junior high school. Consequently, one cannot rule out the possibility that the findings of this study are due to unique characteristics of the schools that were investigated rather than the grade level arrangement.

The authors note limitations of their study.

Further research is needed to establish what grade level structure is optimal for ninth graders. It would be useful to carry out additional investigations using a larger sample of senior and junior high schools.

The list of references begins on a new page. References are listed alphabetically by the first author's last name.

References

Blythe, D. A., Hill, J. P., & Smythe, C. K. (1981). The influence of older adolescents: Do grade level arrangements make a difference in behaviors, attitudes, and experiences? Journal of Early Adolescence, 1, 85–100.

Blythe, D. A., Simmons, R. G., & Bush, D. (1978). The transition into early adolescence: A longitudinal comparison of youth in two educational contexts. Sociology of Education, 51, 149–160.

Blythe, D. A., Smythe, C. K., & Hill, J. P. (1984). Grade level arrangements—What are the differences? NAASP Bulletin, 68, 105–117.

Blythe, D. A., & Traeger, C. M. (1983). The self-concept and self-esteem of early adolescence. Theory into Practice, 22, 91–97.

Dacus, W. P. (1963). Study of the grade organizational structure of junior high school as measured by social maturity, emotional maturity, physical maturity, and opposite sex choices. Dissertation Abstracts International, 24, 1461A–1462A. (University Microfilms No. 63–06, 787)

Haertel, G. D., Walburg, H. J., & Haertel, E. H. (1981). Socio-psychological environments and learning: A quantitative synthesis. British Educational Journal, 7, 27–36.

Reece, J. L. (1975). Ninth grade dilemma: Who wants them? Thresholds in Education Foundations, 1, 10–11.

Schoo, P. H. (1970). Students' self-concept, social behavior, and attitudes toward school in middle and junior high schools. Dissertation Abstracts International, 31, 6322A. (University Microfilms No. 71–15, 296)

White, W. D. (1967). Pupil progress and grade combinations. NAASP Bulletin, 51, 87–90.

Wood, F. H. (1973). A comparison of student attitudes in junior high and middle schools. The High School Journal, 57, 355–361.

Appendix

The authors include a copy of their questionnaire in the form of an appendix.

Directions:

1. Please fill out the biographical information section. Your name should <u>not</u> be written on the questionnaire.
2. There are 47 statements in this questionnaire. Please indicate your own personal opinion of each statement by placing a check mark under the column that best describes your opinion.
3. Please do not write what you <u>OUGHT</u> to believe or what other people want you to believe. Try to indicate what you really think about these statements.
4. Work fast. Do not think too long about any one statement. Write your first impulse.
5. Do not leave any statements unchecked.

* REMEMBER TO BE HONEST. YOUR NAME IS NOT ON YOUR PAPER *

THIS QUESTIONNAIRE HAS NO EFFECT ON YOUR GRADE THERE IS NO RIGHT OR WRONG ANSWER

<u>BIOGRAPHICAL INFORMATION</u>

1. Age _____
2. Gender _____
3. Write in the month and year you came to this school _____

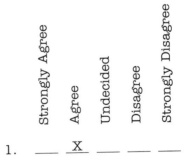

EXAMPLE:
1. I like ice cream.

Appendix (Continued)

	Strongly Agree	Agree	Undecided	Disagree	Strongly Disagree
1. Classrooms are dull places.	—	—	—	—	—
2. I enjoy going to class.	—	—	—	—	—
3. I would go to class even if I didn't have to.	—	—	—	—	—
4. When I am in class I think of what is going on tonight.	—	—	—	—	—
5. Classrooms are O.K. if you have friends there.	—	—	—	—	—
6. Rules make school seem like prison.	—	—	—	—	—
7. We should all follow the rules with courtesy.	—	—	—	—	—
8. Rules are consistently enforced.	—	—	—	—	—
9. Rules count equally for students at all levels.	—	—	—	—	—
10. Some rules were made to be broken.	—	—	—	—	—
11. Some rules are stupid and unreasonable.	—	—	—	—	—
12. Teachers like to teach ninth graders.	—	—	—	—	—
13. Sometimes teachers' rules are strict and stupid.	—	—	—	—	—
14. Teachers try hard to do a good job teaching.	—	—	—	—	—
15. Teachers care about their students.	—	—	—	—	—
16. I would feel comfortable going to one of my teachers if I had a problem.	—	—	—	—	—
17. Teachers often favor certain students.	—	—	—	—	—

Appendix (Continued)

	Strongly Agree	Agree	Undecided	Disagree	Strongly Disagree
18. Some teachers are lazy.	18. ___	___	___	___	___
19. Some teachers should be in the students' chair and the student should be teaching.	19. ___	___	___	___	___
20. I enjoy school.	20. ___	___	___	___	___
21. It is a privilege to attend this school.	21. ___	___	___	___	___
22. Ninth grade is interesting.	22. ___	___	___	___	___
23. Ninth grade is easy.	23. ___	___	___	___	___
24. This school is too noisy.	24. ___	___	___	___	___
25. The classrooms are neat, clean and organized.	25. ___	___	___	___	___
26. The cafeteria is a terrible place to have to eat.	26. ___	___	___	___	___
27. It's difficult to get to use the bathrooms in this school.	27. ___	___	___	___	___
28. The bathrooms rarely have soap, paper towels or toilet paper.	28. ___	___	___	___	___
29. There are better things to do than going to school.	29. ___	___	___	___	___
30. I like when schools are closed.	30. ___	___	___	___	___
31. I find it hard to concentrate due to other students' behavior.	31. ___	___	___	___	___
32. I study hard and do homework regularly.	32. ___	___	___	___	___
33. I like studying and doing homework.	33. ___	___	___	___	___

Appendix (Continued)

	Strongly Agree	Agree	Undecided	Disagree	Strongly Disagree
34. Studying and homework interfere with my other plans and activities.	—	—	—	—	—
35. It is easy to get from one class to the next.	—	—	—	—	—
36. It's wild in the halls between classes.	—	—	—	—	—
37. I benefit from doing homework.	—	—	—	—	—
38. Homework and studying are a bother.	—	—	—	—	—
39. I have been encouraged by people in my school to join activities.	—	—	—	—	—
40. I have had little opportunity to participate in activities.	—	—	—	—	—
41. Ninth graders have little control or input into the school.	—	—	—	—	—
42. Teachers and other staff let students from other grades get away with too much.	—	—	—	—	—
43. School is a safe place.	—	—	—	—	—
44. I have felt threatened in school.	—	—	—	—	—
45. I have felt afraid in school.	—	—	—	—	—
46. I feel like I belong in my school.	—	—	—	—	—
47. Many people in my school know who I am.	—	—	—	—	—

Table 1

Means and Standard Deviations of Ninth Graders'
Scores on the School Attitude Questionnaire as a
Function of Type of School and Gender of Student

	Mean	Standard Deviation
Junior High School		
Boys	+7.08	17.31
Girls	+4.08	18.31
Senior High School		
Boys	−18.91	21.87
Girls	−14.54	13.71

Running head: PARENTAL ATTITUDES TOWARD TOYS

A short title, usually consisting of the first couple of major words of the actual title (i.e., ''Parental Attitudes''), appears at the upper right edge of each page. The short title may be used to identify which pages belong to a manuscript in the event that the pages are misplaced.

The running head is an abbreviated version of the title that is printed on alternate pages in a journal if the manuscript is published as an article. (The authors' names are printed on the other pages.)
The title should consist of 10–12 words and identify the variables and populations under investigation.

Parental Attitudes toward Prekindergartners' Gender-
stereotyped Toys
Margaret Hamilton and Gail Rossi
The College of Staten Island

Abstract

This study examined parents' attitudes toward the toys their prekindergarten aged children use. A Toy Preference Questionnaire (TPQ), formulated by the researchers to determine parents' attitudes toward gender-stereotyped toys, was completed by 34 parents, 17 of whom had girls and 17 of whom had boys attending a private, nonsectarian prekindergarten school. It was found that parents had a significantly more positive attitude toward gender-stereotyped than toward nongender-stereotyped toys ($p < .01$), indicating that parental attitudes may foster gender role stereotyped behavior among prekindergarten children. The split-half reliability coefficient for the TPQ was .98.

The abstract appears on a separate page and should not exceed 120 words. It should state the problem, the types of subjects used, the procedures used to collect data, the measuring instruments, the findings (including statistical levels of significance), and the conclusions.

Parental Attitudes toward Prekindergartners' Gender-stereotyped Toys

*The introductory section of the report is **not** labeled "Introduction." The first sentence explains why the authors feel it is important to carry out the proposed study. The authors move directly into a description of the empirical research literature dealing with their topic.*

Toys are one of children's major sources of socialization, and according to Miller (1987), early play experiences of girls and boys may contribute to gender differences found in the social behavior of females and males. In studies dealing with children as young as ten months of age, researchers have found differences in the way parents respond to the play of boys and girls (Fagot, 1978; Roopnarine, 1986; Snow, Jacklin & Maccoby, 1983).

For example, Roopnarine found that by ten months of age, girls were already showing a preference for dolls and were more likely to offer the doll to parents than were boys. Doll play was encouraged by favorable parental responses made to pre-toddler and toddler age girls (Fagot, 1978; Roopnarine, 1986). Fagot also found that parents reacted significantly more favorably to the child when the child was engaged in a same-gender preferred behavior and more negatively in a cross-gender preferred behavior. Girls received more negative responses when engaged in active large motor activities and more positive responses when engaged in adult oriented dependent behavior.

O'Brien and Huston (1985) reported that parents choose same-gender typed toys and expect same-gender typed play from their children, and that by the age of three, children show patterns of or preferences for toys that are socially stereotyped for their gender (O'Brien & Huston, 1985; Robinson & Morris, 1986). It is possible that children's gender stereotypic toy preferences may result from their parents' gender stereotypic attitudes toward their children's play activities.

Based on their review of the literature, the authors state a directional hypothesis. The hypothesis is worded in an unambiguous manner and the variable is defined operationally.

It was hypothesized that parents of preschoolers would have significantly more favorable attitudes toward gender-stereotyped toys than toward nongender-stereotyped toys. Parental attitudes were operationally defined by the scores received on the Toy Preference Questionnaire (TPQ), which was formulated by the researchers.

Method

Participants

Parents of 40 prekindergarten children from a private, nonsectarian nursery school participated in the study. The parents were predominantly white with middle to upper middle class socioeconomic backgrounds. Of the 40 parents who were given the TPQ, 34 responded. Seventeen parents had girls and 17 had boys enrolled in the program.

The authors describe the number and types of subjects who participated in the study.

Materials

In order to formulate the TPQ, a list was made of the toys found in the nursery school classroom of the children whose parents participated in the study. Twelve early childhood teachers were asked to rate each of 38 toys appearing on the list as male-stereotypical, female-stereotypical, or neutral.

The authors describe how they constructed their measuring instrument.

It was decided to include on the TPQ only those toys that at least two-thirds of the teachers rated as gender-stereotypical. Eight female- and seven male-stereotypical toys met the criterion for inclusion on the TPQ. (See Appendix A.)

Each item on the TPQ consisted of the names of two toys. Of the 56 possible pairings of male and female gender-stereotypical toys, 35 were randomly selected for use on the TPQ. In order to make the comparison of male- and female-stereotypical toys less obvious, an additional 15 same-gender stereotypical pairings (seven female and eight male) were randomly selected and included, yielding a total of 50 items.

The TPQ also included a biographical questionnaire on which respondents were asked to indicate their gender and age, as well as the gender, age and number of children in the family, including the gender and birth order of their preschool child. (A copy of the TPQ appears in Appendix B.)

Procedure

The TPQ was distributed to 40 parents, who were asked to complete it anonymously and return it in an enclosed stamped, self-addressed envelope within 10 days. After seven days a reminder was distributed to all parents, asking those who had not yet responded to do so within the next three days.

The procedures for collecting data are described in sufficient detail to permit the reader to replicate the study.

For each of the 50 pairs of toys appearing on the TPQ, parents were asked to select the one with which they would prefer their child to play. The TPQ was scored in such a way that each respondent received two scores: one indicating the number of gender-stereotyped toys, and another indicating the number of nongender-stereotyped toys that had been selected. Only the responses to the 35 items in which a male-gender-stereotyped toy was paired with a female-gender-stereotyped toy were scored. Parents of boys received a gender-stereotyped score for each male-stereotypical toy selected, and conversely, parents of girls received a gender-stereotyped score for each female-stereotypical toy selected.

Results and Discussion

The authors report the results of the t test and list the means and standard deviations.

A $\underline{t}$-test for nonindependent means revealed that the mean gender-stereotyped score ($\underline{M}$ = 26.29, $\underline{SD}$ = 6.67) was significantly higher than the mean nongender-stereotyped score ($\underline{M}$ = 8.71, $\underline{SD}$ = 6.67, $\underline{t}$(33) = 7.69, $\underline{p}$ < .01). The split-half reliability of the TPQ, corrected for test length, was .98.

The authors show how their findings relate to the existing literature on the topic.

As predicted, parents had a significantly more positive attitude toward gender-stereotypical toys than toward nongender-stereotypical toys, which confirms the findings of previous studies, such as those by Miller (1987), O'Brien and Huston (1985), and Roopnarine (1986).

The authors report an unanticipated finding.

While scoring the questionnaires of boys' parents, the researchers noted a strong preference for certain female-stereotypical toys. Upon further investigation it was found that nine of the 35 items with cross-gender pairings had a female-stereotypical toy paired with either guns or soldiers. It is interesting to note that 76 of a total of 123 nongender-stereotyped points received by boys' parents were attributable to these nine items. It appears that parents of boys would rather have their sons play with female-stereotypical toys than with war-related toys.

The authors note limitations of their study and suggest future research questions.

It should be noted that 31 of the 34 respondents were mothers. Perhaps a future study might compare the attitudes of mothers with those of fathers toward children's toys. Other suggestions for future research include using as subjects a more diverse group of parents in terms of educational and socioeconomic background, as well as investigating parental attitudes as a function of their children's ages.

In conclusion, it seems apparent from the results of this study that parents prefer their children to play with gender-stereotypical toys. It seems important to conduct further investigations in order to determine the extent to which such attitudes are related to the development of children's gender identity.

References

The list of references
begins on a new page.
References are listed
alphabetically by the
first author's last name.

Fagot, B. (1978). The influence of sex of child on parental reactions to toddler children. Child Development, 49, 459–465.

Miller, C. (1987). Qualitative differences among gender-stereotyped toys: Implications for cognitive and social development in girls and boys. Sex Roles, 16, 473–487.

O'Brien, M., & Huston, A. C. (1985). Development of sex typed play behaviors in toddlers. Developmental Psychology, 21, 866–871.

Robinson, C., & Morris, J. (1986). The gender-stereotyped nature of Christmas toys received by 36-, 48-, and 60-month old children: A comparison between nonrequested vs. requested toys. Sex Roles, 15, 21–32.

Roopnarine, J. (1986). Mothers' and fathers' behaviors toward the toy play of their infant sons and daughters. Sex Roles, 14, 59–68.

Snow, M., Jacklin, C., & Maccoby, E. (1983). Sex-of-child differences in father-child interaction at one year of age. Child Development, 54, 227–232.

The authors include a copy of the questionnaire given to teachers in appendix A and a copy of the questionnaire given to parents in appendix B.

Appendix A[1]
Gender-stereotypical Toy Rating List

Below is a list of toys for prekindergartners. Please place an "M" next to those toys you feel are stereotypically male, an "F" next to those that are stereotypically female, and an "N" next to any toy you feel is not stereotypically gender-typed.

Thank you for your time and help.

1. Puzzles
2. Lotto matching games
*3. Stringing Beads (F-8)
4. Sensory alphabet sand letters
5. Number matching puzzle
6. Lacing
7. Matching shapes
*8. Construction toys (M-10)
*9. Soldiers (M-12)
10. Writing table
11. Science table
12. Books
13. Record & record player
14. Paint
15. Scissors
16. Rulers
17. Collage materials
18. Crayons
19. Markers
20. Pencils
*21. Male dress-up items (M-11)
*22. Female dress-up items (F-11)
*23. Dolls (F-12)
*24. Cradle (F-12)
*25. Store (F-10)
*26. Sink (F-8)

[1]Note: Items preceded by an asterisk are those rated as gender-stereotypical. The letter appearing in parentheses after the item indicates whether the toy was rated as male (M) or female (F), and the number indicates the number of raters agreeing with the rating. This information did not appear on the original list that was used in rating the toys.

Appendix A (Continued)

27. Grocery store
28. Food (including plastic vegetables, eggs, meat, etc.)
*29. Carriage (F-10)
*30. High chair (F-10)
31. Blocks
*32. Trucks (M-12)
*33. Planes (M-11)
*34. Trains and tracks (M-11)
35. People (block figures of families, community helpers)
36. Wooden traffic signals
*37. Guns (M-12)
38. Marbles

Appendix B
Toy Preference Questionnaire

Please fill in the following information:
Person filling out the questionnaire: mother _____father _____
Age of person filling out the questionnaire _____
Number of children in family _____
Gender of children _____
Age of children _____
Gender of preschooler _____
Rank in family of preschool age child _____

When responding to the following questionnaire, please answer with your preschool age child in mind. Please put a circle around the letter of the toy or activity you prefer your child to play with.

1. A. Stringing beads	B. Construction toys
2. A. Planes	B. Dolls
3. A. Stove	B. Cradle
4. A. Soldiers	B. Female dress-up toys
5. A. Planes	B. Trucks
6. A. Male dress-up toys	B. Female dress-up toys
7. A. Dolls	B. Trains and tracks
8. A. Cradle	B. Trucks
9. A. Planes	B. Stove
10. A. High chair	B. Train and tracks
11. A. Trucks	B. Soldiers
12. A. Guns	B. Sink
13. A. Carriage	B. Stringing beads
14. A. Planes	B. Carriage
15. A. Sink	B. Truck
16. A. Construction toys	B. Guns
17. A. Cradle	B. Planes
18. A. Dolls	B. Construction toys
19. A. Guns	B. Trucks
20. A. Planes	B. Female dress-up toys
21. A. Dolls	B. Male dress-up toys
22. A. Stove	B. High chair
23. A. Soldiers	B. Cradle
24. A. Construction toys	B. Female dress-up toys
25. A. Soldiers	B. Stringing beads
26. A. Stove	B. Sink

Appendix B (Continued)

27. A. Male dress-up toys   B. Cradle
28. A. Female dress-up toys   B. Train and tracks
29. A. Cradle   B. Dolls
30. A. Trucks   B. Carriage
31. A. Sink   B. Planes
32. A. Male dress-up toys   B. Construction toys
33. A. Guns   B. High chair
34. A. Sink   B. Train and tracks
35. A. Soldiers   B. Guns
36. A. Trucks   B. Stringing beads
37. A. Stove   B. Construction toys
38. A. Cradle   B. Dolls
39. A. Soldiers   B. High chair
40. A. Guns   B. Female dress-up toys
41. A. High chair   B. Trucks
42. A. Stove   B. Dolls
43. A. Carriage   B. Guns
44. A. Stove   B. Soldiers
45. A. Stringing beads   B. Planes
46. A. Construction toys   B. Sink
47. A. Male dress-up toys   B. Soldiers
48. A. Trains and tracks   B. Stringing beads
49. A. Carriage   B. Construction toys
50. A. Guns   B. Planes

Glossary

A

A-B-A design. *See* Reversal.

A-B-A-B design. *See* Double reversal.

Abstract. A summary of a study that contains a statement of the problem; a description of the research procedures used; the number and kinds of subjects; descriptions of the materials used; and the results, including the statistical levels of significance.

Alpha coefficient. *See* Cronbach's alpha.

Alpha level. The level of probability that one is willing to operate within in terms of incorrectly rejecting the null hypothesis. Same as level of statistical significance.

Analysis of covariance (ANCOVA). A statistical technique used to determine if posttest scores that have been weighted as a function of pretest scores exhibit a statistically significant difference.

Analysis of variance (ANOVA). A statistical technique used to determine if the means of two or more groups exhibit a statistically significant difference. Also used in regression analysis to determine if variables are significantly correlated.

Anonymity. The state of affairs when a researcher does not know who the participants in a study are.

Average. A measure of central tendency. *See* Mean, Median, and Mode.

B

Bar graph. A graph depicting a frequency distribution in terms of column heights.

Baseline condition. The period prior to intervention in single-subject research, during which the natural frequency of behavior is recorded. *See* Treatment condition.

Between-group sum of squares. The sum of the squared differences between group means and their grand mean.

Blind review. *See* Masked review.

C

Case study. The quantitative or qualitative study of a single individual or group in a naturalistic setting.

Categorical variable. *See* Nominal variable.

Causal comparative studies. *See* Ex post facto studies.

CD ROM. Compact Disc Read Only Memory. The type of disc on which information in the ERIC system is stored so that literature can be searched by computer.

Checklist. A list of predetermined behaviors whose frequency is to be recorded during an observational study. *See* Rating scales.

Chi-square (X^2). A statistic used to determine whether the relationships among nominal variables are significant.

Cluster sampling. A system of sampling in which the unit is not the individual subject but, instead, is a group of subjects, such as a classroom or an entire school. Often sampling occurs in stages in which successively smaller units are drawn, for example, first one might randomly select entire schools and then from the selected schools randomly select classrooms.

Coding categories. Terms used by ethnographic researchers to identify topics and recurring themes.

Comparison group. *See* Control group.

Concealment. Withholding information from participants in a study.

Concurrent validity. A method of determining the validity of a test by administering the test and simultaneously obtaining an independent measure of the behavior the test purports to measure.

Confidence interval. A range of numbers and a statement of how likely it is that the true population value falls within that range.

Confidentiality. The state of affairs when a researcher knows who the participants in a study are but will not divulge their names.

Confounding variable. A variable other than those the researcher is investigating that could account for the outcome of a study.

Construct. *See* Hypothetical construct.

Construct validity. A method of determining the validity of tests by administering the test to various groups of people who theoretically differ with respect to the construct being measured to determine if the test scores of the groups differ in the predicted direction.

Content analysis. The analysis of some form of communication by counting the various kinds of units comprising the communication.

Content validity. A method of validating academic achievement tests by having the proportion of test items regarding a particular subtopic correspond to the proportion of the total academic content represented by that subtopic.

Continuous variable. A quantitative variable that theoretically can assume an infinite number of values.

Control group. The group in an experiment that receives no intervention or treatment.

Correlation coefficient (r or ρ). A statistic used to express the degree of relationship between two variables that may

vary from $+1.00$ (perfect positive correlation) to -1.00 (perfect negative correlation).

Correlational studies. Studies carried out to see to what extent within a single group of people, two or more variables are related.

Covariate. A variable that varies systematically with a second variable, such as IQ and academic performance.

Criterion-based selection. *See* Purposeful sampling.

Criterion-related validity. A way of determining the validity of a test by comparing test scores with direct measures of the behavior or characteristic the test has been designed to measure.

Criterion variable. The variable that is predicted in a correlational study.

Cronbach's alpha. A measure of test reliability that may be used with tests such as Likert scales, whose items have answers that can be scored along a continuum, rather than simply as correct or incorrect.

Cross-sectional surveys. Surveys that are made of various segments of the population at a given point in time. *See* Longitudinal surveys.

D

Deception. Providing false information to participants in a study.

Degrees of freedom (*df*). Numbers slightly less than the number of subjects and the number of groups participating in a study, by which the total variability of a sample is divided to estimate the average amount of variability in the

population from which the sample was drawn.

Dehoaxing. The process by which the researcher makes sure after the completion of a study that participants fully understand that they have been deceived so that no permanent damage can be done to the participants.

Dependent variable. The variable measured at the conclusion of an experiment to see if the groups have significantly different values.

Descriptive statistics. Statistics that are used to describe how variables are distributed throughout a group of people, the two most common of which are the mean and the standard deviation.

Descriptors. Terms listed in the ERIC *Thesaurus* that are used in indexing articles and documents in *CIJE, RIE,* and *ECER*.

Desensitization. The process by which the researcher helps eliminate negative feelings participants may have as a result of how they behaved during a study.

Dichotomous variable. A variable that may assume one of only two values.

Directional hypotheses. Hypotheses in group comparison studies that predict not only that groups will differ with respect to a variable, but also which group will score higher. Also, hypotheses in correlational studies that predict whether the correlation coefficient will be positive or negative.

Discriminant analysis. A statistical procedure that examines differences in subjects' scores on several variables to determine if these differences separate the subjects into their respective groups.

Double reversal. A design used in single-subject research symbolized by A-B-A-B, where A represents the baseline condition and B the treatment condition. *See* Reversal.

E

Ecological validity. The extent to which the findings of an experiment may be generalized to other settings because the findings are attributable to the independent variable, rather than to the experimental situation itself.

Effect size. The average amount by which subjects in experimental groups differ from subjects in control groups expressed in standardized scores, that is, in terms of standard deviation units.

Empirical research. Research in which the researcher makes firsthand observations of phenomena being investigated.

Error score. That part of a person's test score due to inconsistencies associated with the test.

Ethnographic research. A form of qualitative observational research that uses a variety of qualitative methods, but relies heavily on the methods of participant observation and interviewing.

Experiment. A group comparison study in which subjects are randomly assigned on an individual basis to experimental and control groups.

Experimental group. The group in an experiment that receives the intervention or treatment.

Ex post facto studies. Group comparisons in which the groups being compared already differ with respect to one of the variables of interest to the researcher. Such studies are often used to identify *possible* causal relationships.

External criticism. The process of determining that the data in historical research are authentic.

External validity. The extent to which the findings of a study may be generalized to a larger population.

F

Factor analysis. A statistical technique by which numerous variables are correlated with one another, and factors, which consist of groups of variables that correlate highly with one another, are identified.

Factorial designs. Group comparison studies in which the groups being studied differ simultaneously on more than one variable.

Fieldnotes. An ethnographer's written chronological account of what occurred during each observation session.

Fieldwork. The time ethnographers spend observing and interacting with members of the group they are studying.

Foreshadowed problems. An ethnographer's initial general notion of what is to be investigated.

Frequency distribution. A tally of the number of persons exhibiting various values associated with a given variable.

G

Grade equivalent score. A score that represents the typical score achieved by someone at a particular grade level.

Grounded theory. A theory frequently devised by ethnographers to ensure that the components of the theory and their relationships are embedded in reality.

Group comparison research. Studies in which two or more groups are compared with respect to a single variable; the most common group comparison studies are experiments, quasi-experiments, and ex post facto studies.

H

Hawthorne effect. Increases in the performance of subjects in an experimental group attributable to the subjects' knowledge that they are participating in an experiment, rather than to the independent variable. Opposite of the John Henry effect.

Histogram. *See* Bar graph.

Hypothesis. A predictive statement about the nature of the relationship among variables.

Hypothetical construct. A term applied to terms we invent to refer to complex phenomena that consist of a constellation of unobservable characteristics. Examples of hypothetical constructs are self-concept, underachievement, anxiety, and creativity.

I

Independent variable. The variable in an experiment used by the researcher to assign members to experimental and control groups.

Inferential statistics. Statistical techniques based on

probability theory that permit researchers to generalize findings from samples to the populations from which the samples were drawn.

Informed consent. Obtaining participants' consent to take part in a study after informing them about the general nature of the research project and about aspects of the study that may influence them to decline to participate.

Interaction. The relationship of the dependent variable to different combinations of values of two or more factors under investigation.

Internal criticism. The process of determining that the data in historical research are credible.

Internal validity. The extent to which possible sources of confounding have been controlled in a group comparison study.

Interrater reliability. The extent to which the ratings of two or more raters are in agreement.

Interval scales. Scales that have equal units of measurement, such as raw scores.

Interviewing. The process of collecting data in a study by asking participants oral questions.

J

John Henry effect. Increases in the performance of subjects in a control group attributable to the fact that subjects know that they are in the control group and consequently exert extra effort to perform better than the experimental group. Opposite of the Hawthorne effect.

K

Kuder-Richardson formulas 20 and 21. Methods of determining the reliability of a test or measuring instrument.

L

Level of statistical significance. The probability of having incorrectly generalized the findings obtained from a sample to the population from which the sample was drawn. Its statistical symbol is ''p.'' *See* Alpha level.

Likert scales. Statements on an attitudinal inventory requiring respondents to select one of a range of choices, such as strongly agree, agree, undecided, disagree, strongly disagree.

Longitudinal surveys. Surveys that are conducted at several different points in time with the same group of people. *See* Cross-sectional surveys.

M

Main effect. The relationships of the dependent variable to each separate factor under investigation.

Masked review. Having the name of the author of a manuscript removed before submitting the manuscript to journal reviewers.

Matched pairs. A method of randomly assigning subjects to experimental and control groups on the basis of pretest scores.

Mean. The arithmetic average of a set of scores.

Median. The score in a set of scores above and below which half of the set falls.

Memos. Relatively lengthy reflective pieces that ethnographers write at various times during their

investigations to focus on the study as a whole.

Meta-analysis. A statistical technique used to analyze the combined findings of several different studies dealing with the same research question.

Mode. The most frequently occurring score in a set of scores.

Multiple baselines. The periods prior to intervention in single-subject research, during which the natural frequencies of several different behaviors are recorded.

Multiple correlation coefficient (R). A statistic used to express the degree of relationship among three or more variables that may vary from 0 (absence of correlation) to 1.00 (perfect correlation).

Multiple regression. A statistical procedure for predicting values of one variable on the basis of two or more other variables.

Multivariate Analysis of Variance (MANOVA). A statistical procedure used to determine if two or more groups differ with respect to the combination of several different dependent variables.

N

Naturalistic inquiry. *See* Ethnographic research.

Nominal scales. Scales of measurement that are qualitative, or categorical, in nature.

Nominal variable. A variable that may assume values that vary qualitatively.

Nondirectional hypotheses. Hypotheses in group comparison studies that predict that groups will differ with respect to a variable, but do not specify which group will score higher. Also, hypotheses in correlational studies that predict a relationship between variables without specifying whether the relationship will be positive or negative.

Nonparametric statistics. Statistical techniques that are appropriate for analyzing data representing nominal or ordinal scales or when data are not normally distributed.

Normal Curve Equivalent (NCE) score. A score derived by dividing a normal distribution of scores into 100 equal units of measurement.

Normal distribution. The bell-shaped curve that is symmetrical about the midpoint and covers an area defined by the mean plus and minus three standard deviation units.

Null hypothesis. In group comparison studies, the statement that the means of the populations under investigation are equal. In correlational studies, the statement that the variables being studied are not related to one another among the population under investigation. In both cases the function is to establish a band within which either sample means would be expected to fall, or within which the sample correlation coefficient would be expected to lie on the basis of chance.

O

Objective. A statement of what is to be investigated empirically in a study.

Objective measure. A measure on which a person's score would be the same no matter who scored the test, as long as the scorer is competent.

Obtained score. A person's score on a test that is represented by "true score" + "error score."

One-tailed *t* test. The statistical procedure used to analyze the difference between means in a group comparison study with two groups and a directional hypothesis.

One-way ANOVA. An analysis of variance used to see if there is a significant difference among two or more group means with respect to a single variable.

On-line computer searches. Computer searches of the literature in which the computer is connected to a data base by telephone.

Operational definitions. Definitions of variables in terms of how the variables are measured.

Ordinal scales. Scales of measurement that are rank orderings and have unequal units of measurement.

P

Parallel forms reliability. A measure of test reliability in which scores on two versions of the same test are correlated.

Partial correlation. The degree of relationship between two variables when their relationship with other variables has been removed.

Participant. Any person who participates in a research study.

Participant observation. A research technique ethnographers use in which the ethnographer participates as a member of the group under investigation and simultaneously observes what is taking place in the group.

Pearson *r*. *See* Correlation coefficient.

Percentile. That point beneath which a given percentage of people scored on a test.

Plagiarism. The act of using someone else's ideas or words without giving that person credit.

Population. The entire group of people to whom researchers wish to generalize the findings of a study, including persons who did not participate in the study.

Population validity. The extent to which the persons participating in a study accurately represent the population to which the study's findings are to be applied.

Post hoc tests of statistical significance. Statistical tests that are carried out after a significant *F* value has been obtained in group comparison studies of three or more groups to determine which group means are significantly different.

Posttest. A test given after intervention or treatment in a group comparison study.

Predictive validity. A method of determining the validity of a test by first administering the test and then, after a period of time has elapsed, correlating the test scores with an independent measure of the behavior the test purports to measure.

Presentism. The error of interpreting historical data within a contemporary framework.

Pretest. A test given prior to intervention or treatment in a group comparison study.

Primary source. A report written by the person who

actually carried out the investigation. *See* Secondary source.

Privileged observer. An observer who has been given permission by someone in authority to observe a group in a natural setting.

Product-moment correlation coefficient. *See* Correlation coefficient.

Proposal. A written plan describing how a research project would be carried out, including an introduction, a review of the literature, hypotheses, method, and form of data analysis to be used.

Purpose. A statement of why and for whom a study is being carried out.

Purposeful sampling. A sampling procedure in which ethnographic researchers identify particular attributes they want participants in a study to have and then actively seek persons who have them.

Q

Qualitative research. *See* Ethnographic research.

Quantitative research. Research whose findings are reported in numerical form as well as in terms of verbal description.

Quasi-experiment. A group comparison study in which intact groups are randomly assigned to experimental and control groups.

Questions. Asking how the variables to be investigated in a study might be related.

R

Random assignment. The process of assigning subjects to experimental and control groups in such a way that each

individual has the same chance of being assigned to either group.

Random sample. A sample selected so that each individual in the population has an equal chance of being selected.

Range. The lowest and highest scores in a set of scores.

Rank order correlation coefficient (ρ) **Rho.** The correlation coefficient used with ordinal data.

Rating scales. A form on which qualitative judgments of various types of behavior are made. *See* Checklist.

Ratio scales. Scales that have both equal units of measurement and a true zero point, such as weight or height.

Raw score. The number of items on a test that have been answered correctly.

Regression. A statistical procedure used to determine if two (simple regression) or more (multiple regression) variables are significantly correlated.

Reliability. The extent to which a test or measuring instrument measures something consistently. *See* Validity.

Research. The acquisition of knowledge through systematic investigation.

Research hypothesis. The predicted outcome of a quantitative study.

Reversal. A design used in single-subject research symbolized by A-B-A, where A represents the baseline condition and B the treatment condition. *See* Double reversal.

Reviewing the literature. The process of locating, evaluating, and synthesizing information dealing with a given research question.

Rho. *See* Rank order correlation coefficient.

S

Sample. A subset of a population.

Scales of measurement. *See* Interval scales, Nominal scales, Ordinal scales, and Ratio scales.

Scheffe test. A commonly used post hoc test of statistical significance.

Secondary source. A report written by someone other than the person who carried out the investigation. *See* Primary source.

Semantic differential scales. Attitudinal scales consisting of two bipolar adjectives separated by a line divided into seven parts.

Single-subject research. Research that is carried out with only one participant.

Solomon four-group design. A research design in which subjects are assigned to one of four groups: Group 1 receives the pretest, the intervention, and the posttest; Group 2 receives the pre- and posttest, but does not receive the intervention; Group 3 receives the intervention and the posttest but does not receive the pretest; Group 4 receives only the posttest.

Split-half reliability. A measure of test reliability in which the odd-numbered subtotal and even-numbered subtotal scores of a test are correlated.

Standard deviation. The approximate average amount by which each score in a set of scores differs from the mean.

Standard error of measurement. A measure of the range within which a test taker's true score likely lies.

Standard score. (*z* score.) A score expressed in standard deviation units.

Stanines. (Standard Nine.) The division of the horizontal axis of the normal curve into nine equal segments labeled 1 through 9.

Statistical significance. Said of results when the probability of their occurrence by chance is less than a given level (often .05).

Stratified sampling. The process of either selecting a sample in such a way that subgroups in the population are proportionately represented in the sample, or dividing the population into various subgroups and selecting samples of equal size from each subgroup.

Subject. *See* Participant.

Sum of squares. The sum of the squared differences between each score and the mean.

Survey research. Research that describes how different variables are distributed throughout a population.

Systematic sampling. A method of drawing a sample from an existing list of the members of a population by selecting every *n*th name.

T

Test-retest reliability. A measure of test reliability in which scores on the same test administered to the same people at two different times are correlated.

Theoretical sensitivity. ''The attribute of having insight, the ability to give meaning to data, the capacity to understand, and capability to separate the pertinent from that which isn't'' (Strauss & Corbin, 1990, p. 42).

Time sampling. A procedure used in observational studies in which each subject is systematically observed at a predetermined point in time.

Time series designs. The procedure used in single-subject research in which the subject's behavior is measured at several different points over time.

Topic. An area of interest distinct from other areas of interest.

Treatment condition. The period of intervention in single-subject research, during which the frequency of behavior is recorded. *See* Baseline condition.

True score. The score a person theoretically would obtain on a test if the test were completely accurate.

t test for independent (or uncorrelated) means. A statistical test used to determine if the means of two groups consisting of different people are significantly different.

t test for nonindependent (or correlated) means. A statistical test used to determine if the means of two groups consisting of the same people or matched pairs are significantly different.

Two-tailed *t* test. The statistical procedure used to analyze the difference between means in a group comparison study with two groups and a nondirectional hypothesis.

Type I error. Rejecting the null hypothesis when it should not be rejected.

Type II error. Not rejecting the null hypothesis when it should be rejected.

V

Validity. The extent to which test scores permit one to draw appropriate, meaningful, and useful inferences.

Value. Any one of a set of mutually exclusive characteristics that a variable may have.

Variable. An entity that may take on one of two or more mutually exclusive values.

Variance. The standard deviation squared.

W

Within-group sum of squares. The total squared differences between each score and the mean score of each group.

Z

z **score.** *See* Standard score.

References

Alkin, M. C. (Ed). (1992). *Encyclopedia of educational research* (6th ed.). New York: Macmillan.

American Educational Research Association. (1985). AERA guidelines for eliminating race and sex bias in educational research and evaluation. *Educational Researcher, 14*(6), 16–17.

American Educational Research Association. (1992). Ethical standards of the American Educational Research Association. *Educational Researcher, 21*(7), 23–26.

American Psychological Association. (1982). *Ethical principles in the conduct of research with human participants.* Washington, DC: Author.

American Psychological Association. (1992). Ethical principles of psychologists and code of conduct. *American Psychologist, 47,* 1597–1611.

American Psychological Association. (1994). *Publication manual of the American Psychological Association* (4th ed.). Washington, DC: Author.

American Psychological Association, American Educational Research Association, & National Council on Measurement in Education. (1985). *Standards for educational and psychological testing.* Washington, DC: American Psychological Association.

A new Assignment for student teachers. (1988, July/August). *The Harvard Educational Newsletter,* p. 3.

Bailyn, B. (1960). *Education in the forming of American society.* Chapel Hill, NC: University of North Carolina Press.

Balay, R., & Sheehy, E. P. (Eds.). (1992). *Guide to reference books (covering material from 1985–1990).* (Supplement to E. P. Sheehy, (Ed.). (1986). *Guide to reference books* (10th ed.). Chicago: American Library Association.)

Banks, J. A., & Magee Banks, C. A. (Eds.). (1994). *Handbook of research on multicultural education.* New York: Macmillan.

Barr, R., Kamil, M. L., Mosenthal, P., & Pearson, P. D. (Eds.). (1991). *Handbook of reading research.* White Plains, NY: Longman.

Barzun, J., & Graff, H. F. (1977). *The modern researcher* (3rd ed.). New York: Harcourt Brace Jovanovich.

Berdie, D., & Anderson, J. (1974). *Questionnaire design and use.* Metuchen, NJ: Scarecrow Press.

Berlinger, R. E. (1978). *Historical analysis: Contemporary approaches to Clio's craft.* New York: Wiley.

Bogdan, R. C., & Biklen, S. K. (1992). *Qualitative research in education* (2nd ed.). Boston: Allyn & Bacon.

Borg, W. R., & Gall, M. D. (1989). *Educational research* (5th ed.). New York: Longman.

Borich, G. D., & Madden, S. K. (1977). *Evaluating classroom instruction: A sourcebook of instruments.* Reading, MA: Addison Wesley.

Boyan, N. J. (Ed.). (1988). *Handbook of research on educational administration.* White Plains, NY: Longman.

Bracht, G. H., & Glass, G. V. (1968). The external validity of experiments. *American Educational Research Journal, 5,* 437–474.

Bruning, J. L., & Kintz, B. L. (1987). *Computational handbook of statistics* (3rd ed.). Glenview, IL: Scott Foresman.

Campbell, D. T., & Stanley, J. C. (1963). *Experimental and quasi-experimental designs for research.* Chicago: Rand McNally.

Campbell, W. G., Ballou, S. V., & Slade, C. (1990). *Form and style: Theses, reports, term papers* (7th ed.). Boston: Houghton Mifflin.

Carnegie Forum on Education and the Economy (1986). *A nation prepared: Teachers for the 21st century.* New York: Author.

Chun, K. T., Cobb, S., & French, J. R. P., Jr. (1974). *Measures for psychological assessment: A guide to 3,000 original sources and their applications.* Ann Arbor, MI: Institute for Social Research, University of Michigan.

Code of Federal Regulations, Paragraph 46.101(b)(1–5), 45 CFR 46.

Colwell, R. (Ed.). (1992). *Handbook of research on music teaching and learning.* New York: Macmillan.

Cook, T. D., & Campbell, D. T. (1979). *Quasi-experimentation.* Chicago: Rand McNally.

Cordasco, F., & Brinkman, W. W. (1975). *A bibliography of American educational history: An annotated and classified guide.* New York: AMS.

Cremin, L. A. (1980). *American education: The national experience: 1783–1876.* New York: Harper & Row.

Cronbach, L. J. (1951). Coefficient alpha and the internal structure of tests. *Psychometrika, 16,* 297–334.

Crowl, T. K. (1971). White teachers' evaluations of oral responses given by white and Negro ninth grade males (Doctoral dissertation, Columbia University, 1970). *Dissertation Abstracts International, 31,* 4540A.

Crowl, T. K. (1975). Examination and evaluation of the conceptual basis for the open classroom. *Education, 96,* 54–56.

Current Index to Journals in Education. (1969 to date). Phoenix: Oryx Press.

Denzin, N. K., & Lincoln, Y. S. (1994). Preface. In N. K. Denzin, & Y. W. Lincoln (Eds.). *Handbook of qualitative research.* Thousand Oaks, CA: Sage Publications.

Dissertation Abstracts International. (1938 to date). Ann Arbor, MI: University Microfilms International.

Duell, O. K. (1994). Extended wait time and university student achievement. *American Educational Research Journal, 31,* 397–414.

Educational Testing Service. (1986). *The ETS test collection catalog. Vol. 1: Achievement tests and measurement devices.* Phoenix: Oryx Press.

Educational Testing Service. (1986). *The ETS test collection catalog. Vol. 2: Vocational tests and measurement devices.* Phoenix: Oryx Press.

Educational Testing Service. (1986). *The ETS test collection catalog. Vol. 3: Tests for special populations.* Phoenix: Oryx Press.

Educational Testing Service. (1986). *The ETS test collection catalog. Vol. 4: Cognitive, aptitude and intelligence tests.* Phoenix: Oryx Press.

Eichelberger, R. T. (1989). *Disciplined inquiry.* New York: Longman.

Ennis, R. H. (1964). Operational definitions. *American Educational Research Journal, 1,* 183–201.

Erickson, F. (1986). Qualitative methods in research on teaching. In M. C. Wittrock (Ed.). *Handbook of research on teaching* (3rd ed.) (pp. 119–161). New York: Macmillan.

Exceptional child education resources. (1969 to date). Reston, VA: Council for Exceptional Children.

Faculty directory of higher education. (1988). Detroit: Gale Research.

Fink, A. (1995). *The survey handbook.* Thousand Oaks, CA: Sage Publications.

Flood, J., Jensen, J. M., Lapp, D., & Squire, J. R. (Eds.). (1991). *Handbook of research on teaching the English language arts.* New York: Macmillan.

Freidel, F., & Showman, R. K. (Eds.). (1974). *Harvard guide to American history* (revised ed.). Cambridge, MA: Belnap Press.

Frey, J. H., & Oishi, S. M. (1995). *How to conduct interviews by telephone and in person.* Thousand Oaks, CA: Sage Publications.

Gabel, D. (Ed.). (1994). *Handbook of research on science teaching and learning.* New York: Macmillan.

Gagne, E. D. (1985). *The cognitive psychology of school learning.* Boston: Little Brown.

Gibaldi, J., & Achtert, W. S. (1988). *MLA handbook for writers of research papers.* New York: Modern Language Association of America.

Gold, R. L. (1958). Roles in sociological field observations. *Social Forces, 36,* 217–223.

Goodwin, W. L., & Driscol, L. (1980). *Handbook for measurement and evaluation in early childhood education.* San Francisco: Jossey Bass.

Goswami, D., & Stillman, P. R. (Eds.). (1987). *Reclaiming the classroom: Teacher research as an agency for change.* Upper Montclair, NJ: Boynton Cook.

Gottschalk, L. (1969). *Understanding history: A primer of historical method.* New York: Knopf.

Gronlund, N. E. (1982). *Constructing achievement tests* (3rd ed.). Englewood Cliffs, NJ: Prentice Hall.

Gronlund, N., & Linn, R. (1990). *Measurement and evaluation in teaching* (6th ed.). New York: Macmillan.

Grouws, D. A. (Ed.). (1992). *Handbook of research on mathematics teaching and learning.* New York: Macmillan.

Hartman, D. P. (1977). Considerations in the choice of interobserver reliability methods. *Journal of Applied*

Behavior Analysis, 10, 103–116.

Henerson, M. E., Morris, L. L., & Fitz-Gibbon, C. T. (1987). *How to measure attitudes.* Newbury Park, CA: Sage Publications.

Hersen, M., & Barlow, D. H. (1976). *Single case experimental designs.* New York: Pergamon.

Holmes, D. S. (1976a). Debriefing after psychological experiments: I. Effectiveness of postdeception dehoaxing. *American Psychologist, 31,* 858–867.

Holmes, D. S. (1976b). Debriefing after psychological experiments: II. Effectiveness of postexperimental desensitizing. *American Psychologist, 31,* 868–875.

Houston, J. (Ed.). (1987). *Thesaurus of ERIC descriptors* (11th ed.). Phoenix: Oryx Press.

Houston, W. R. (Ed.). (1990). *Handbook of research on teacher education.* New York: Macmillan.

Howe, K. R., & Dougherty, K. C. (1993). Ethics, Institutional Review Boards, and the changing face of educational research. *Educational Researcher, 22*(9), 16–21.

Huff, D., & Geis, I. (1954). *How to lie with statistics.* New York: Norton.

Hymes, D. (1982). Ethnographic monitoring. In H. T. Treuba, G. P. Guthrie, & K. H. Au (Eds.). *Culture in the bilingual classroom.* Rowley, MA: Newbury House.

Jackson, P. W. (Ed.). (1992). *Handbook of research on curriculum.* New York: Macmillan.

Jaeger, R. M. (1984). *Sampling in education and the social sciences.* New York: Longman.

Jaeger, R. M. (1988). Survey methods in education. In R. M. Jaeger (Ed.). *Complementary*

methods for research in education (pp. 303–336). Washington, DC: American Educational Research Association.

Kaestle, C. F. (1988). Recent methodological developments in the history of American education. In R. M. Jaeger (Ed.). *Complementary methods for research in education* (pp. 61–73). Washington, DC: American Educational Research Association.

Kerlinger, F. N. (1979). *Behavioral research.* New York: Holt, Rinehart and Winston.

Keyser, D. J., & Sweetland, R. C. (Eds.). (1987). *Test critiques. Vols. I–VI.* Kansas City, MO: Test Corporation of America.

Kimmel, A. J. (1988). *Ethics and values in applied social research.* Beverly Hills, CA: Sage Publications.

Kramer, J. J., & Conoley, J. C. (1992). *The eleventh mental measurements yearbook.* Lincoln, NB: The Buros Institute of Mental Measurements. The University of Nebraska–Lincoln.

Kratochwill, R. R. (Ed.). (1978). *Single-subject research: Strategies for evaluating change.* New York: Academic Press.

Krueger, R. A. (1988). *Focus groups.* Newbury Park, CA: Sage Publications.

Kubiszyn, T., & Borich, G. (1987). *Educational testing and measurement* (2nd ed.) (pp. 313–315). Glenview, IL: Scott, Foresman and Company.

LeCompte, M. D., Millroy, W. L., & Preissle, J. (Eds.). (1992). *The handbook of qualitative research in education.* New York: Academic Press.

LeCompte, M. D., & Preissle, J. (1993). *Ethnography and qualitative design in educational research* (2nd ed.).

San Diego, CA: Academic Press.

Levy, P., & Goldstein, H. (Eds.). (1984). *Tests in education: A book of critical reviews.* London: Academic Press.

Majchrzak, A. (1984). *Methods for policy research.* Newbury Park, CA: Sage Publications.

Mann, T. (1987). *A guide to library research methods.* New York: Oxford.

Messick, S. (1989). Validity. In R. L. Linn (Ed.). *Educational measurement* (3rd ed.). New York: Macmillan (pp. 13–103).

Messick, S. (1992). Validity of test interpretation and use. In M. C. Alkin (Ed.). *Encyclopedia of educational research* (6th ed.) (pp. 1487–1495). New York: Macmillan.

Miller, G. A. (1956). The magical number seven plus or minus two: Some limits on our capacity for processing information. *Psychological Review, 63,* 81–97.

Mishler, E. G. (1986). *Research interviewing.* Cambridge, MA: Harvard University Press.

Mitchell, J. V., Jr. (Ed.). (1983). *Tests in print III.* Lincoln, NB: The Buros Institute of Mental Measurements, The University of Nebraska–Lincoln.

National faculty directory. (1994). Detroit: Gale Research.

Nunnally, J. C. (1967). *Psychometric theory.* New York: McGraw-Hill.

Osgood, C. E., Suci, G. J., & Tannenbaum, P. H. (1957). *The measurement of meaning.* Urbana, IL: University of Illinois Press.

Patton, M. Q. (1987). *How to use qualitative methods in evaluation.* Newbury Park, CA: Sage Publications.

Pedhazur, E. J. (1982). *Multiple regression in behavioral research* (2nd ed.). New York: Holt, Rinehart and Winston.

Pelto, P. J., & Pelto, G. H. (1978). *Anthropological research: The structure of inquiry* (2nd ed.). New York: Cambridge.

Poulton, H. J., & Howland, M. S. (1986). *The historian's handbook: A descriptive guide to reference works.* Norman, OK: University of Oklahoma Press.

Psychological Abstracts. (1927 to date). Washington, DC: American Psychological Association.

Reitzug, U. C. (1994). A case study of empowering principal behavior. *American Educational Research Journal, 31,* 283–307.

Resources in Education. (1966 to date). Washington, DC: National Institute of Education.

Review of Research in Education. (1973 to date). Washington, DC: American Educational Research Association (annual volumes).

Rist, R. C. (1980). Blitzkrieg ethnography: On the transformation of a method into a movement. *Educational Researcher, 9*(2), 8–10.

Robinson, J. P., Shaver, P. R., & Wrightsman, L. S. (Eds.). (1991). *Measures of personality and social psychological attitudes.* San Diego, CA: Academic Press.

Rosenthal, R. (1966). *Experimenter effects in behavioral research.* New York: Appleton-Century-Crofts.

Rosenthal, R., & Rosnow, R. L. (1975). *The volunteer subject.* New York: Wiley.

Scriven, M. (1988). Philosophical inquiry methods in education. In R. M. Jaeger (Ed.). *Complementary methods for research in education* (pp. 129–151). Washington, DC: American Educational Research Association.

Shaver, J. P. (Ed.). (1991). *Handbook of research on social studies teaching and learning.* New York: Macmillan.

Shaw, M. E., & Wright, J. M. (1967). *Scales for the measurement of attitudes.* New York: McGraw-Hill.

Sheehy, E. P. (Ed.). (1986). *Guide to reference books* (10th ed.). Chicago: American Library Association.

Short, P. M. (1992). What do we really mean by teacher empowerment? *Journal of School Leadership, 2,* 376–378.

Siegel, S. (1956). *Nonparametric statistics for the behavioral sciences.* New York: McGraw-Hill.

Singer, R. N. (Ed.). (1992). *Handbook of research on sport psychology.* New York: Macmillan.

Smith, L. M. (1979). An evolving logic of participant observation, educational ethnography, and other case studies. *Review of Research in Education, 6,* 316–377.

Social Sciences Citation Index. (1973 to date). Philadelphia: Institute for Scientific Information.

Spodek, B. (Ed.). (1993). *Handbook of research on the education of young children.* New York: Macmillan.

Stake, R. E. (1988). Case study methods in educational research: Seeking sweet water. In R. M. Jaeger (Ed.). *Complementary methods for research in education* (pp. 254–276). Washington, DC: American Educational Research Association.

Strauss, A., & Corbin, J. (1990). *Basics of qualitative research.* Newbury Park, CA: Sage Publications.

Sweetland, R. C., & Keyser, D. J. (Eds.). (1986). *Tests: A comprehensive reference for assessments in psychology, education, and business* (2nd ed.). Kansas City, MO: Test Corporation of America.

Terman, L. M. (Ed.). (1925). *Genetic studies of genius,* (Vol. 1), Stanford, CA: Stanford University Press.

Thesaurus of ERIC Descriptors. (12th ed.). (1990). Phoenix: Oryx Press.

Thesaurus of Psychological Index Terms (7th ed.). (1994). Washington, DC: American Psychological Association.

Turabian, K. (1973). *A manual for writers of term papers, theses and dissertations* (4th ed.). Chicago: University of Chicago Press.

U.S. Department of Education. (1987). *What works.* (2nd ed.). Washington, DC: U.S. Government Printing Office.

Wittrock, M. C. (Ed.). (1986). *Handbook of research on teaching* (3rd ed.). New York: Macmillan.

Wolcott, H. F. (1988). Ethnographic research in education. In R. M. Jaeger (Ed.). *Complementary methods for research in education* (pp. 187–210). Washington, DC: American Educational Research Association.

Wolcott, H. F. (1990). On seeking—and rejecting—validity in qualitative research. In E. W. Eisner, & A. Peshkin (Eds.). *Qualitative inquiry in education: The continuing debate.* (pp. 121–152). New York: Teachers College Press.

Wolf, R. M. (1982). Validity of tests. In H. E. Mitzel (Ed.). *Encyclopedia of educational research* (5th ed.) Vol. 4 (pp. 1991–1998). New York: Free Press.

Woodbury, M. (1982). *A guide to sources of educational information* (2nd ed.). Arlington, VA: Information Resources Press.

Name Index

Subject Index

D

Data analysis, determining statistical procedures for, 384–85
Deception, 78–79, 86
Definitions, operational, 66–68, 72
Degrees of freedom (*df*), 168–69, 193
Dehoaxing, 79, 86
Dependent variables, 273–74
Depth interviewing, 236–37, 252
Descriptive research, 15
Descriptive statistics, 129–60
Descriptors, ERIC, 40–44
  alphabetical listing of, 42
  major and minor, 45
  rotated display of, 41
Desensitization, 79, 86
Designs, research
  causal-comparative, 13, 16, 274–88
  correlational, 11, 16, 254–58
  ethnographic, 11, 16, 211–33
  experimental, 13, 16, 294–307
  ex post facto, 13, 16, 274–88
  group comparison, 12–14, 15, 271–322
  historical, 10, 16, 197–210
  quasi-experimental, 14, 16, 307–20
  single-subject, 323–37
  survey, 11, 16, 234–53
DIALOG, 356
Directional hypotheses, 70, 72, 73
Discriminant analysis, 192, 194
Discussion section of final report, 347
Dissertation Abstracts International, 54
Document resumes in *RIE,* 49
Double reversal, 327, 336
Duncan's multiple range test, 184

E

ECER (Exceptional Child Educational Resources), 50–51
Ecological validity, 292
EDRS (Educational Document Reproduction Service), 49
Educational Document Reproduction Service (EDRS), 49
Educational research, scope of, 5–8
Educational Resources Information Center. *See* ERIC
Educational Testing Service (ETS), 116–17
Education and schooling, 23
Education Index, 51, 61
Effect size, 191–92, 193, 194
Empirical research, definition of, 6–7, 15
Encyclopedia of Educational Research, 24–25
Equivalent forms reliability, 104–5
ERIC (Educational Resources Information Center), 38–51, 61
  clearinghouses, 39, 61
  descriptors, 40–44
  searching by computer, 356–60
Eta correlation coefficient, 159
Ethical Principles in the Conduct of Research with Human Participants, 76
Ethical Principles of Psychologists and Code of Conduct, 76
Ethical Standards of the American Educational Research Association, 76, 376–82
Ethics, 75–82

ETHNOGRAPH, 363
Ethnographic research, 11, 16, 211–33
  example of, 220–30
  sampling in, 98
Ethnography, 212, 231
ETS (Educational Testing Service), 116–17
Evaluating research reports, 349–52
Evaluation research, 8, 15
Evidence, prescriptive and factual, 201
Exceptional Child Educational Resources (ECER), 50–51
Experiment, 13, 16, 273, 294–300
  example of, 301–7
Experimental groups, 296–97
Ex post facto research, 13, 16, 274–76, 320, 321
  example of, 276–88
External criticism, 199, 209
External validity, threats to, 292

F

F, table of significant values, 389–90
Factorial designs, 180–84
Faculty Directory of Higher Education, 47
Family Educational Rights and Privacy Act, 82
Feminist educational researchers, 215, 231
Fieldnotes, 217, 218, 231–32
Fieldwork, 216, 231
Final reports
  examples of student, 401–25
  and proposals, 340–42
  sections of, 342–48, 353
Flowchart for determining when to use which statistical procedure for analyzing data, 384–85
Focus groups, 237, 252
Foreshadowed problems, 214, 231
Frequency distributions, 152–53, 154

G

GC (Group Code), 43
Gender bias, elimination of, 83, 86
Grade equivalent scores, 132, 158
Grounded theory, 218
Group Code (GC), 43
Group comparison research, 12–14, 15, 271–322
Guidelines for evaluating ethnographic research, 220
  historical research, 200–201
  quantitative research, 349–52

H

Handbook of Research on Teaching, 25
Handbooks of research, 25
Hawthorne effect, 309–11, 322
Histogram, 153, 154, 240, 241
Historical research, 10, 16, 197–210
  example of, 202–9
HYPERQUAL, 363
Hypotheses
  in correlational studies, 257
  directional, 70, 72
  nondirectional, 71–72
  null, 170, 193
  and related literature, 69–71, 73, 257, 269
  research, 63–73
  and variables, 68–69
Hypothetical constructs, 111–12

I

Independent variables, 273–74
Indexes and journal articles, 38
Inferential statistics, 129, 162, 165, 193
Informed consent, 77–78, 86
Institutional Review Boards, 82, 84, 86
  request for approval by, 85
Instruments. *See* Measuring instruments
Intent and consequence, 201